Mastering BEA WebLogic Server™

Best Practices for Building and Deploying J2EE™ Applications

Gregory Nyberg
Robert Patrick
Paul Bauerschmidt
Jeffrey McDaniel
Raja Mukherjee

Wiley Publishing, Inc.

Vice President and Executive Publisher: Bob Ipsen
Publisher: Joe Wikert
Executive Editor: Robert M. Elliott
Developmental Editor: Brian McDonald and Emilie Herman
Editorial Manager: Kathryn A. Malm
Senior Production Editor: Angela Smith
Text Design & Composition: Wiley Composition Services

This book is printed on acid-free paper. ∞

Published by Wiley Publishing, Inc., Indianapolis, Indiana

Published simultaneously in Canada

Library of Congress Cataloging-in-Publication Data:

ISBN: 0-471-28128-X

Printed in the United States of America

10 9 8 7 6 5 4 3

To Meredith –

For her patience, love, and support.

Greg

To Li Yan –

*For her love, encouragement, and patience
over the past five years.*

Robert

Contents

Acknowledgments

The authors would like to thank the many people who helped create this book:

- To our editor, Robert Elliott, thank you for your patience and support.
- To our development editors, Emilie Herman and Brian MacDonald, thank you for helping us craft a readable and well-organized book.
- To the many people who helped review the technical content and provided critical assistance along the way, our heartfelt thanks. Special recognition to key folks in BEA's Engineering organization who provided invaluable insight and suggestions: Rob Woollen, Seth White, Cedric Beust, Smitty (a.k.a. Michael Smith), Chris Fry, Greg Brail, Tom Barnes, Zach (a.k.a. Stephen Zachwieja), Mark Griffith, Andrew Sliwkowski, Craig Blitz, Neil Smithline, Peter Bower, Tony Vlatas, Viresh Garg, and many others. Thanks also to additional technical reviewers Mark Willis, Prasad Muppirala, Ben Johnson, Kelly Nawrocke, and Tim Dawson. This book would not be what it is without the help of all these fine people. Any errors or omissions should be attributed solely to the authors.

I would like to thank my wife, Meredith, for her support and encouragement over these many months. It's finally done! I'd also like to thank my co-author, Robert, for his steadfast dedication to accuracy and completeness; the book would be much less than it is without you. I'd also like to thank the guy who signs my paychecks, Chris Spurgat, for his support and flexibility when the book dominated my life. Finally, I'm very thankful for the grace and peace I've been given through a carpenter's son. All things are possible.

— Greg Nyberg

I would like to thank my wife for her incredible patience, support, and prodding throughout the entire process. I would also like to thank my boss, Scott Dietzen, for giving me encouragement as well as the time to finish the book. I'd like to give thanks to Paul Bauerschmidt, Jeff McDaniel, and Raja Mukherjee for their contributions to the book and their patience in helping me review their material. Finally, I would like to give special thanks to Greg Nyberg for his extreme patience with me through the writing process. Without you, this book would have never gotten finished!

— Robert Patrick

Introduction

The book you are holding is different from other books about WebLogic Server 8.1 and related technologies.

First, it is an advanced book designed to complement the BEA online documentation and other introductory books on J2EE and WebLogic Server technologies, providing intermediate- to advanced-level developers, architects, and administrators with in-depth coverage of key J2EE development and deployment topics. You won't find much introductory material in this book, and the book will not replicate basic references or information available through other sources. This book starts where other books and references stop.

Second, this is a book with an *opinion*. As the subtitle indicates, *Mastering BEA WebLogic Server* focuses on best practices for building and deploying J2EE applications in WebLogic Server 8.1. The authors want to share their real-world experience with the technology and help you understand not only how things *can* be done, but also how things *should* be done. Different design solutions, architectures, construction techniques, deployment options, and management techniques will be presented and explained—but we do not stop there. We go on and explain the benefits of a given alternative and when to use it.

Finally, the primary example application built and described in these pages is a realistic, complex application that highlights many of the features of J2EE technologies in general and WebLogic Server 8.1 in particular. The example application leverages key technologies such as JSP, Jakarta Struts, JMS, EJB, and Web Services to demonstrate their use, and the text walks you through each decision made during the development and deployment of the application to assist you in making similar decisions in your own efforts.

Organization of the Book

Mastering BEA WebLogic Server is organized around three key themes:

- Walking you through the design, construction, and deployment of a realistic example application
- Discussing advanced topics and best practices in areas such as administration, performance tuning, and configuration of WebLogic Server environments
- Providing you with best practices for developing and deploying your own WebLogic Server applications

The first 10 chapters focus on the first theme, and the next 4 target the second theme; best practices are a focus throughout the entire book. Here is a brief description of each chapter to help you understand the scope and organization of the book:

Chapter 1 reviews key Web application concepts and technologies and then discusses advanced topics such as response caching, custom tags, and servlet filtering.

Chapter 2 examines the presentation-tier requirements that drive Web application architectures, compares JSP-centric and servlet-centric architectures, and makes specific recommendations to help you choose an appropriate architecture for your WebLogic Server application.

Chapter 3 details the design of the presentation-tier layer of a fairly large and complex J2EE application. Topics include alternative page-assembly techniques, business-tier interfaces, and the requirements of the example application that lead to the chosen design.

Chapter 4 walks through the construction of the Struts- and JSP-based example Web application. Construction techniques unique to WebLogic Server are emphasized along with the components and techniques resulting from the choice of presentation approach, Web application architecture, and business-tier interaction techniques.

Chapter 5 discusses the steps required to package and deploy a WebLogic Server Web application with an emphasis on WebLogic-specific techniques and best practices.

Chapter 6 examines options and best practices related to the implementation of Enterprise JavaBeans (EJB) technology in WebLogic Server 8.1. After a brief review of EJB technology and the WebLogic Server EJB container, the chapter presents WebLogic-specific features and capabilities and explains how best to leverage them in your development efforts.

Chapter 7 walks through the design and construction of the business tier of the example application, highlighting key concepts and best practices. Candidate business-tier architectures are identified and examined in light of a representative set of business-tier requirements, construction options for EJB components are compared, and selected business-tier components in the example application are examined to highlight implementation details and best practices.

Chapter 8 discusses the steps required to package and deploy WebLogic Server EJB applications in a development environment. The basic structures of EJB and enterprise applications are reviewed, Ant-based build processes are presented, options for packaging applications are compared, and deployment techniques for WebLogic Server development environments are examined.

Chapter 9 presents information and best practices related to the WebLogic Server JMS implementation. Topics include JMS clustering, quotas, flow control, transactions, application design, asynchronous consumers, and foreign providers.

Chapter 10 covers important topics related to WebLogic Server Security, including details on the WebLogic Security Framework and available security providers. This chapter also presents techniques for configuring secure clients and servers, setting up secure server-to-server communication, and managing application security using WebLogic Security features.

Chapter 11 focuses on WebLogic Server administration and the architecture of the WebLogic Server product. This is not a users' guide to the administration console, but rather an in-depth look at the internal architecture of WebLogic Server, a discussion of important administrative concepts such as server health states and network channels, and a thorough treatment of the configuration, monitoring, and management of WebLogic Server and WebLogic Server-based applications.

Chapter 12 presents best practices for delivering and troubleshooting scalable high-performance systems. It includes a discussion of core principles and strategies for scalable J2EE systems, a collection of important design patterns and best practices that affect performance and scalability, and steps and techniques you can use to improve performance and solve scalability issues in your systems.

Chapter 13 rounds out the discussion of development-related best practices with recommendations in key areas related to the development environment. Topics include development-environment hardware and software, organizing your project directory structure, establishing a build process, choosing appropriate development tools, and creating a unit-testing infrastructure for your project.

Chapter 14 discusses strategies and best practices for deploying Weblogic Server applications in a production environment, focusing on production deployment strategies, global traffic-management solutions, and production-security best practices.

Chapter 15 reviews Web Services technology, describes WebLogic Server's Web Services support, and presents best practices related to Web Services. Example Web Services are created using WebLogic Server utilities, advanced Web Services features in WebLogic Server are discussed, and a Web Service is built to interface with the primary example program in the book.

Chapters 1 through 10 cover key development-related topics such as Web application design and development, EJB design and development, JMS, and security. Numerous best practices are presented in these chapters as topics and options are presented and explained. You should probably read these chapters in order as they also track the design and development of the example application and build on each other to some extent.

Chapters 11 through 15 cover best practices related to administration, deployment, performance tuning, environment configuration, and Web Services development. These chapters tend to be less dependent on earlier chapters and can be read independently if the topics are of interest.

Who Should Read This Book

Mastering BEA WebLogic Server is targeted at J2EE application developers and architects with an intermediate to advanced level of expertise. Although this book is targeted primarily at users of the BEA WebLogic Server product, many of the best practices and advanced topics will also be of value to users of other J2EE-compliant application servers.

Because this is an advanced book, beginning J2EE programmers should consider reading one or more introductory texts on J2EE technologies and WebLogic Server before reading this book. Good references include *Mastering Enterprise JavaBeans*, 2nd Edition, by Ed Roman, Scott Ambler, and Tyler Jewel (John Wiley & Sons, 2001), *Core Servlets and JavaServer Pages* by Marty Hall (Prentice Hall PTR, 2000), and *BEA WebLogic Server Bible, Second Edition*, by Joe Zuffoletto and Lou Miranda (John Wiley & Sons, 2003).

Tools You Will Need

The examples and best practices in this book are based on BEA's WebLogic Server 8.1 application server, available from the BEA dev2dev site at http://dev2dev.bea.com/subscriptions. Download and install this product if you plan to build and deploy any of the example applications. The WebLogic Server 8.1 installation includes the Java 2 SDK, the Ant build tool, and all libraries and utilities used in this book.

In addition to WebLogic Server 8.1, you will need a decent Java-aware editor or integrated development environment (IDE) to view the example code properly. See the IDE discussion in Chapter 13 for some help in selecting a product if you do not already own one.

Finally, the main example program in this book assumes that you have a copy of the Oracle RDBMS available. See the companion Web site for information on porting the example to a different database product.

Online Resources

The companion Web site for this book, http://www.wiley.com/compbooks/mastering weblogic, contains additional WebLogic Server resources and links, book errata, and all example code described in this book. The site also contains bonus material supplementing the discussion of Web application architectures in Chapter 2 with a detailed walkthrough of a complete example application built in both JSP-centric and servlet-centric architectures.

The authors also maintain an online discussion group for comments, questions, and bug reports related to this book and its example programs. The group is located at http://groups.yahoo.com/groups/mastering-weblogic.

About the Authors

Gregory Nyberg has over 16 years of experience in the design and development of object-oriented systems and specializes in large mission-critical systems using BEA WebLogic Server. Mr. Nyberg is the founder of and a frequent speaker at the Minneapolis BEA Users' Group, and he has spoken at the BEA eWorld conference and other national conferences numerous times. Mr. Nyberg recently wrote the book *WebLogic Server 6.1 Workbook for Enterprise JavaBeans 3rd Edition* (O'Reilly & Associates, 2002), a companion workbook for *Enterprise JavaBeans 3rd Edition* by Richard Monson-Haefel (O'Reilly & Associates, 2001). Mr. Nyberg has also written and delivered training classes in C++, Forte, Java, and J2EE technologies, and he currently works as an architect and consultant for clients employing WebLogic Server in mission-critical J2EE applications.

Robert Patrick is the Director of Technology, Office of the CTO, for BEA Systems, Inc. Mr. Patrick has over 10 years' experience in the design and development of distributed systems, and he specializes in designing and troubleshooting large, high-performance, mission-critical systems built with BEA WebLogic Server and BEA TUXEDO. Mr. Patrick has worked for BEA Systems for the past 5 years and spends most of his time advising Fortune 1000 companies how to best apply BEA technology to solve their business problems. He has written several papers and is a frequent speaker at the BEA eWorld Conference.

Paul Bauerschmidt has six years' experience in the design and development of Java systems, specializing in security frameworks. Prior to his current position at the Chicago Mercantile Exchange, Mr. Bauerschmidt spent four years in the WebLogic Security team at BEA Systems, Inc., where he helped plan, develop, and support all security features in WebLogic Server. Before that, Mr. Bauerschmidt worked on the Java port of Intel's implementation of the Common Data Security Architecture (CDSA). Mr. Bauerschmidt is also a frequent speaker at BEA eWorld and other security conferences.

Jeff McDaniel is currently the Senior Director of the Technical Solutions Group at BEA Systems, Inc. Mr. McDaniel specializes in the design and validation of distributed architectures utilizing Enterprise JavaBeans, CORBA, and BEA TUXEDO. While leading BEA's technical S.W.A.T. team, Mr. McDaniel worked with many of BEA's Fortune 100 customers, consulting in areas such as performance management and deployment best practices.

Raja Mukherjee has over 12 years of experience designing and deploying mission-critical systems for Fortune 1000 companies. As a Director of the Technical Solutions Group for BEA Systems, Inc., Mr. Mukherjee leads a team of architects specializing in troubleshooting, performance tuning, and benchmarking J2EE applications using the BEA WebLogic Platform. Prior to joining BEA, Mr. Mukherjee was Senior Technical Architect for a major consulting company, where he helped design high-availability infrastructures for Fortune 500 clients. He has extensive experience tuning C/C++ and database applications and has written many papers.

CHAPTER

1

Building Web Applications in WebLogic

Web applications are an important part of the Java 2 Enterprise Edition (J2EE) platform because the Web components are responsible for key client-facing presentation and business logic. A poorly designed Web application will ruin the best business-tier components and services. In this chapter, we will review key Web application concepts and technologies and their use in WebLogic Server, and we will provide a number of recommendations and best practices related to Web application design and construction in WebLogic Server.

This chapter also provides the foundation for the discussion of recommended Web application architectures in Chapter 2 and the construction and deployment of a complex, realistic Web application in Chapters 3, 4, and 5.

Java Servlets and JSP Key Concepts

In this section we will review some key concepts related to Java Servlets and JavaServer Pages. If you are unfamiliar with these technologies, or if you need additional background material, you should read one of the many fine books available on the subject. Suggestions include *Java Servlet Programming Bible* by Suresh Rajagopalan et. al. (John Wiley & Sons, 2002), *Java Servlet Programming* by Jason Hunter (O'Reilly & Associates, 2001), and *Core Servlets and JavaServer Pages* by Marty Hall (Prentice Hall PTR, 2000).

Characteristics of Servlets

Java servlets are fundamental J2EE platform components that provide a request/response interface for both Web requests and other requests such as XML messages or file transfer functions. In this section, we will review the characteristics of Java servlets as background for a comparison of servlets with JavaServer Pages (JSP) technology and the presentation of best practices later in the chapter.

Servlets Use the Request/Response Model

Java servlets are a request/response mechanism: a programming construct designed to respond to a particular request with a dynamic response generated by the servlet's specific Java implementation. Servlets may be used for many types of request/response scenarios, but they are most often employed in the creation of HyperText Transfer Protocol (HTTP) responses in a Web application. In this role, servlets replace other HTTP request/response mechanisms such as Common Gateway Interface (CGI) scripts.

The simple request/response model becomes a little more complex once you add chaining and filtering capabilities to the servlet specification. Servlets may now participate in the overall request/response scenario in additional ways, either by preprocessing the request and passing it on to another servlet to create the response or by postprocessing the response before returning it to the client. Later in this chapter, we'll discuss servlet filtering as a mechanism for adding auditing, logging, and debugging logic to your Web application.

Servlets Are Pure Java Classes

Simply stated, a Java servlet is a pure Java class that implements the `javax.servlet.Servlet` interface. The application server creates an instance of the servlet class and uses it to handle incoming requests. The `Servlet` interface defines the set of methods that should be implemented to allow the application server to manage the servlet life cycle (discussed later in this chapter) and pass requests to the servlet instance for processing. Servlets intended for use as HTTP request/response mechanisms normally extend the `javax.servlet.http.HttpServlet` class, although they may implement and use the `Servlet` interface methods if desired. The `HttpServlet` class implements the `Servlet` interface and implements the `init()`, `destroy()`, and `service()` methods in a default manner. For example, the `service()` method in `HttpServlet` interrogates the incoming `HttpServletRequest` object and forwards the request to a series of individual methods defined in the `HttpServlet` class based on the type of request. These methods include the following:

- `doGet()` for handling `GET`, conditional `GET`, and `HEAD` requests
- `doPost()` for `POST` requests
- `doPut()` for `PUT` requests
- `doDelete()` for `DELETE` requests
- `doOptions()` for `OPTIONS` requests
- `doTrace()` for `TRACE` requests

The doGet(), doPost(), doPut(), and doDelete() methods in HttpServlet return a BAD_REQUEST (400) error as their default response. Servlets that extend HttpServlet typically override and implement one or more of these methods to generate the desired response. The doOptions() and doTrace() methods are typically not overridden in the servlet. Their implementations in the HttpServlet class are designed to generate the proper response, and they are usually sufficient.

A minimal HTTP servlet capable of responding to a GET request requires nothing more than extending the HttpServlet class and implementing the doGet() method.

WebLogic Server provides a number of useful sample servlets showing the basic approach for creating HTTP servlets. These sample servlets are located in the samples/server/examples/src/examples/servlets subdirectory beneath the Web-Logic Server home directory, a directory we refer to as $WL_HOME throughout the rest of the book. We will examine some additional example servlets in detail during the course of this chapter. These example servlets are available on the companion Web site for this book at http://www.wiley.com/compbooks/masteringweblogic.

Creating the HTML output within the servlet's service() or do*XXX*() method is very tedious. This deficiency was addressed in the J2EE specification by introducing a scripting technology, JavaServer Pages (JSP), discussed later in this chapter.

Servlets Have a Life Cycle

A servlet is an instance of the servlet class and has a life cycle similar to that of any other Java object. When the servlet is first required to process a request, the application server loads the servlet class, creates an instance of the class, initializes the instance, calls the servlet's init() method, and calls the service() method to process the request. In normal servlet operation, this same instance of the servlet class will be used for all subsequent requests.

Servlets may be preloaded during WebLogic Server startup by including the <load-on-startup> element in the web.xml file for the Web application. You can also provide initialization parameters in this file using <init-param> elements. WebLogic Server will preload and call init() on the servlet during startup, passing the specified initialization parameters to the init() method in the ServletConfig object.

An existing servlet instance is destroyed when the application server shuts down or intends to reload the servlet class and create a new instance. The server calls the destroy() method on the servlet prior to removing the servlet instance and unloading the class. This allows the servlet to clean up any resources it may have opened during initialization or operation.

Servlets Allow Multiple Parallel Requests

Servlets are normally configured to allow multiple requests to be processed simultaneously by a single servlet instance. In other words, the servlet's methods must be thread-safe. You must take care to avoid using class- or instance-level variables unless access is made thread-safe through synchronization logic. Typically, all variables and objects required to process the request are created within the service() or do*XXX*() method itself, making them local to the specific thread and request being processed.

BEST PRACTICE Servlets that allow multiple parallel requests must be thread-safe. Do not share class- or instance-level variables unless synchronization logic provides thread safety.

Servlets may be configured to disallow multiple parallel requests by defining the servlet class as implementing the `SingleThreadModel` interface:

```
...
public class TrivialSingleThreadServlet
    extends HttpServlet implements SingleThreadModel
{
    public void init(ServletConfig config) throws ServletException
    {
        super.init(config);
        System.out.println("Here!");
    }
...
```

This simple change informs the application server that it may not process multiple requests through the same servlet instance simultaneously. The application server can honor this restriction in multiple ways: It may block and queue up requests for processing through a single instance, or it may create multiple servlet instances as needed to fulfill parallel requests. The servlet specification does not dictate how application servers should avoid parallel processing in the same instance.

WebLogic Server satisfies the single-threaded requirement by creating a small pool of servlet instances (the default pool size is five) that are used to process multiple requests. In older versions of WebLogic Server, multiple parallel requests in excess of the pool size would block waiting for the first available servlet instance. This behavior changed in WebLogic Server 7.0. The server now creates, initializes, and discards a new instance of the servlet for each request rather than blocking an execute thread under these conditions. Set the pool size properly to avoid this extra servlet creation and initialization overhead.

You can configure the size of the pool at the Web application level using the `single-threaded-servlet-pool-size` element in the `weblogic.xml` deployment descriptor. If you choose to employ single-threaded servlets in high-volume applications, consider increasing the pool size to a level comparable to the number of execute threads in the server to eliminate the potential overhead required to create extra servlet instances on the fly to process requests.

Although instance variables are safe to use in single-threaded servlets, class-level static variables are shared between these instances, so access to this type of static data must be thread-safe even when using the `SingleThreadModel` technique. Deploying and executing this `TrivialSingleThreadServlet` example verifies this pooling behavior in WebLogic Server. The first servlet request causes WebLogic Server to create five instances of the servlet, as evidenced by five separate invocations of the `init()` method and the subsequent writing of five "Here!" messages in the log.

BEST PRACTICE In general, you should avoid using single-threaded servlets. If you find that you need to use servlets that implement the SingleThreadModel, use the `single-threaded-servlet-pool-size` **element to set the pool size properly to avoid the overhead of creating and initializing extra servlet instances to handle peaks in the number of concurrent requests to the servlet.**

Servlets May Access Request Data

The `HttpServletRequest` parameter passed in to the `service()` or `do`*XXX*`()` method contains a wealth of information available to the servlet during the processing of the request. Useful data in the `HttpServletRequest` is summarized in Table 1.1.

This is not an exhaustive list of the methods available on the `HttpServletRequest` class or its superclass, `ServletRequest`. Refer to the servlet javadocs at http://java.sun.com/products/servlet/2.3/javadoc/index.html or a good reference book on servlets for a complete list including parameter types, return types, and other details.

Table 1.1 Information Available in the HttpServletRequest

TYPE OF INFORMATION	ACCESS METHODS
Parameters passed in the query string or through form input fields	`getParameterNames()`, `getParameter()`, `getParameterValues()`, `getQueryString()`
Server information	`getServerName()`, `getServerPort()`
Client characteristics	`getRemoteAddr()`, `getRemoteHost()`, `getAuthType()`, `getRemoteUser()`
Request information	`getContentType()`, `getContentLength()`, `getProtocol()`, `getScheme()`, `getRequestURI()`
HTTP headers	`getHeaderNames()`, `getHeader()`, `getIntHeader()`, `getDateHeader()`
Cookies sent by browser	`getCookies()`
Session information	`getSession()`, `getRequestedSessionId()`, `isRequestedSessionIdValid()`, ...

A useful servlet packaged with the WebLogic Server examples, `SnoopServlet`, illustrates the use of many of the methods available on the `HttpServletRequest` object. For example, this section of `SnoopServlet` illustrates how to retrieve and display the names and values of all parameters passed to the servlet:

```
...
Enumeration e = req.getParameterNames();
if (e.hasMoreElements()) {
    out.println("<h1>Servlet parameters (Single Value style):</h1>");
    out.println("<pre>");
    while (e.hasMoreElements()) {
        String name = (String)e.nextElement();
        out.println(" " + name + " = " + req.getParameter(name));
    }
    out.println("</pre>");
}
...
```

This servlet can be very useful for debugging HTML forms during development. Specify `SnoopServlet` as the action for an HTML form to view all of the parameters, cookies, and headers sent by the browser during submission of the form. Nothing is more frustrating than spending time debugging a servlet only to find that the HTML form had an improperly named input item.

BEST PRACTICE Use the `SnoopServlet` as an action target during development and debugging to inspect request information and verify HTML forms.

Note that `SnoopFilter`, a servlet filter discussed later in this chapter, provides a superior mechanism for viewing request information for some or all pages in the Web application.

Servlets Use Session Tracking

A servlet is a request/response mechanism that treats each incoming request as an independent processing event with no relationship to past or future requests. In other words, the processing is stateless. The HTTP protocol is also a stateless protocol: Each request from the Web browser is independent of previous or subsequent requests. Linking current requests to previous requests from the same client requires a mechanism for preserving context or state information from request to request. There are a number of HTML-based techniques for preserving context or state information:

- *Cookies* may be set in previous requests and passed back to the server on subsequent requests.
- *URL-rewriting* may be used to encode small amounts of context information on every hyperlink on the generated page.
- *Hidden form fields* containing context information may be included in forms.

These techniques all have limitations, and none provides the robust data types and flexibility needed to implement true state management. Fortunately, the session tracking capability defined in the J2EE servlet model provides an excellent solution.

Session tracking provides a flexible hash-table-like structure called an `HttpSession` that can be used to store any serializable Java object and make it available in subsequent requests. To identify the specific client making the request and look up its session information, session tracking uses a cookie or URL-encoded session ID passed to the server on subsequent requests. In WebLogic Server, this session ID has the name `JSESSIONID` by default and consists of a long hash identifying the client plus creation-time and cluster information. The format of the session ID is

```
JSESSIONID=SESSION_ID!PRIMARY_JVMID_HASH!SECONDARY_JVM_HASH!CREATION_TIME
```

WebLogic Server uses exclamation marks to separate portions of the session ID. The first portion is used by the session tracking implementation in WebLogic Server to look up the client's `HttpSession` object in the Web application context. Subsequent portions of the session ID are used to identify primary and secondary servers for this client in a WebLogic Server cluster and to track the creation time for this session. Chapter 11 will discuss WebLogic Server clustering in detail as part of the discussion of administration best practices.

Using session tracking in a servlet is as simple as calling the `getSession()` method to retrieve or create the `HttpSession` object for this client and then utilizing the `HttpSession` interface to get and set attributes in the session. For a good example, see the `SessionServlet` example provided in the WebLogic Server examples.

WebLogic Server supports several forms of session persistence, a mechanism for providing session failover. The two most commonly used forms are in-memory replication and JDBC persistence. When using these types of session persistence, be careful not to place very large objects in the `HttpSession`. WebLogic Server tracks changes to the session object through calls to the `setAttribute()` method. At the end of each request, the server will serialize each new or modified attribute, as determined by the arguments to any `setAttribute()` calls, and persist them accordingly.

Recognize that persisting a session attribute will result in WebLogic Server serializing the entire object graph, starting at the root object placed in the `HttpSession`. This can be a significant amount of data if the application stores large, coarse-grained objects in the session. Multiple fine-grained objects can provide superior performance, provided that your application code updates only a subset of the fine-grained objects (using `setAttribute`) in most cases. We will talk more about in-memory session replication and clustering in Chapter 11.

BEST PRACTICE Use session tracking to maintain state and contextual information between servlet requests. When using session persistence, avoid placing large objects in the session if your application tends to update only a small portion of these objects for any particular request. Instead, use multiple fine-grained objects to reduce the cost of session persistence.

To summarize, servlets are a reliable pure-Java mechanism for processing HTTP requests. It can be tedious to generate the HTML response through the simple `println()` methods available on the response `Writer` object, however. As we will discuss in Chapter 2, servlets are better suited for processing incoming requests and interacting with business objects and services than for the generation of HTTP responses.

If servlets are a tedious way to create HTML, what is available in the J2EE specification for efficiently creating HTML responses? JavaServer Pages technology, the subject of the next section of this chapter, is specifically design to be a powerful tool for creating HTML.

Characteristics of JavaServer Pages

JavaServer Pages (JSP) technology was introduced in the J2EE platform to provide an alternative to servlets for the generation of server-side HTML content. Although a detailed discussion of JSP technology is beyond the scope of this book, some key concepts and characteristics are worth a brief review.

JSP Is a Scripting Technology

Recall that one of the important characteristics of servlets is their pure Java nature. Servlets are Java classes that are written, compiled, and debugged much like any Java class. JavaServer Pages, on the other hand, are a script-based technology similar to Microsoft's Active Server Pages (ASP) technology or Allaire's Cold Fusion scripting language. Like these scripting languages, special tags and script elements are added to a file containing HTML to produce a combination of static and dynamic content. In the case of JSP, these added elements are Java code or special JSP tags that interact with Java beans and other J2EE components in the application.

JSP Pages Are Converted to Servlets

The key to understanding JSP pages is to recognize that the JSP file itself is simply the input for a multistep process yielding a servlet. In the key processing step, the JSP page is parsed by the application server and converted to the equivalent pure-Java servlet code. All text that is not part of JSP tags and scripting elements is assumed to be part of the HTTP response. This text is placed in `out.print()` calls within the generated servlet request-processing method. All Java scripting elements and tags become additional Java code in the servlet. The generated servlet is then compiled, loaded, and used to process the HTTP request in a manner identical to a normal servlet.

Figure 1.1 depicts this process for a trivial sample JSP page with a small amount of scripted Java code embedded on the page. The `sample.jsp` page is converted to the equivalent pure-Java servlet code, compiled into a servlet class, and used to respond to the original and subsequent HTTP requests.

The parsing, conversion, compiling, and classloading steps required to accomplish this transformation are handled by the application server. You don't have to perform any of these steps ahead of time or register the resulting servlet—all of this is done automatically by the server. Note that the processing and compiling can be done prior to deployment using utilities provided by WebLogic Server, a technique known as pre-compiling the JSP pages. We will discuss this technique in detail later in this chapter.

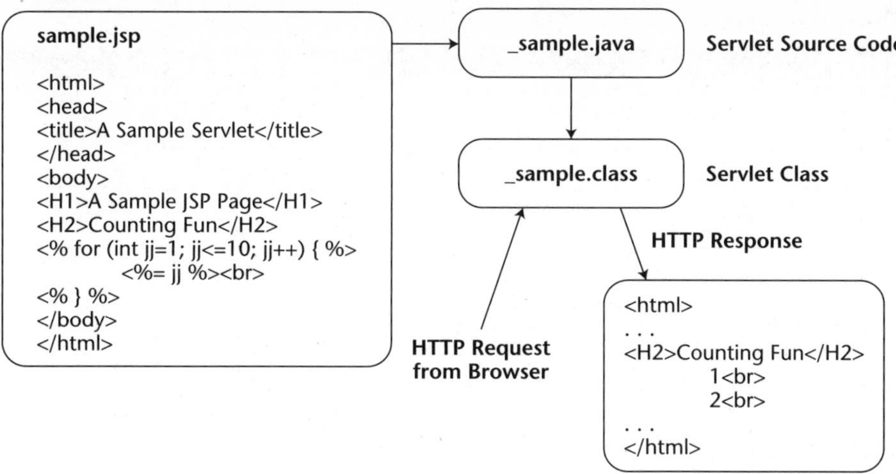

Figure 1.1 JSP page is converted to a servlet.

In WebLogic Server, the resulting servlet is a subclass of `weblogic.servlet.jsp.JspBase` by default. `JspBase` is a WebLogic-provided class that extends `HttpServlet` and forwards `service()` calls to a method called `_jspService()`. You may also create a custom base class for JSP-generated servlets to replace the default `JspBase` class, a technique discussed at end of this chapter.

Many Tags and Scripting Elements Are Available

JSP technology provides a rich set of scripting elements and tags for creating dynamic content. Table 1.2 lists some of the important elements available.

Table 1.2 JSP Syntax Elements

ELEMENT	SYNTAX	DESCRIPTION
Scriptlet	`<%` *scriptlet code* `%>`	Java code placed directly in `_jspservice()` method at this location.
Declaration	`<%!` *declaration* `%>`	Java code placed within the generated servlet class above the `_jspservice()` method definition. This usually defines class-level methods and variables.
Expression	`<%=` *expression* `%>`	Java expression evaluated at run time and placed in the HTML output.

(continued)

Table 1.2 *(continued)*

ELEMENT	SYNTAX	DESCRIPTION
page directive	`<%@ page` *attribute*`=` `"`*value*`" ... %>`	Controls many page-level attributes and behaviors. Important attributes include `import`, `buffer`, `errorPage`, and `extends`.
Include	`<%@ include` *file*`="`*filename*`" %>`	Inserts the contents of the specific file in the JSP page and parses/compiles it.
Taglib	`<%@ taglib uri= "..." prefix="..." %>`	Defines a tag library and sets the prefix for subsequent tags.
jsp:include	`<jsp:include page="..."/>`	Includes the response from a separate page in the output of this page.
jsp:forward	`<jsp:forward page="..."/>`	Abandons the current response and passes the request to a new page for processing.
jsp:useBean	`<jsp:useBean id="..." scope="..." class="..."/>`	Declares the existence of a bean with the given class, scope, and instance name.

Many more elements and tags are available. A detailed discussion of these elements is beyond the scope of this book. Consult one of the books listed at the beginning of this chapter for a complete list of JSP elements and tags, or browse Sun's JSP area at http://java.sun.com/products/jsp/ for more information.

All Servlet Capabilities Are Available

Because JSP pages are converted to servlets, all of the capabilities and techniques available in servlets are also available in JSP pages. The `HttpServletRequest` and `HttpServletResponse` parameters are available, along with a number of predefined variables available in the JSP page, as listed in Table 1.3.

Table 1.3 JSP Implicit Objects

OBJECT	TYPE	DESCRIPTION
request	`javax.servlet.http .HttpServletRequest`	Provides access to request information and attributes set at the request scope.
response	`javax.servlet.http .HttpServletResponse`	Reference to the response object being prepared for return to the client.

Table 1.3 *(continued)*

OBJECT	TYPE	DESCRIPTION
pageContext	`javax.servlet.jsp .PageContext`	Provides access to attributes set at the page scope.
session	`javax.servlet.http .HttpSession`	Session object for this client; provides access to attributes set at the session scope.
application	`javax.servlet .ServletContext`	Application context; provides access to attributes set at the application scope.
out	`javax.servlet.jsp .JspWriter`	PrintWriter object used to place text output in the HTTP response.
config	`javax.servlet .ServletConfig`	Reference to the servlet configuration object set during initialization; provides access to initialization parameters.

JSP scriptlet code may make use of all implicit objects because scriptlet code is placed in the generated `_jspService()` method after these objects are defined, as shown in this partial listing:

```
...
public void _jspService(javax.servlet.http.HttpServletRequest request,
                        javax.servlet.http.HttpServletResponse response)
        throws java.io.IOException, javax.servlet.ServletException
{
    // declare and set well-known variables:
    javax.servlet.ServletConfig config = getServletConfig();
    javax.servlet.ServletContext application =
       config.getServletContext();
    Object page = this;
    javax.servlet.jsp.JspWriter out;
    javax.servlet.jsp.PageContext pageContext =
       javax.servlet.jsp.JspFactory.getDefaultFactory().getPageContext(
           this, request, response, null, true, 8192, true);

    out = pageContext.getOut();

    javax.servlet.http.HttpSession session = request.getSession(true);
    ...
    // scriptlet code and generated out.print() statements go here
    ...
}
```

You should recognize that these implicit objects are available in scriptlet code but are *not* automatically available in methods defined using the `<%! ... %>` declaration scripting element or in methods in a custom base class used for the JSP page. It is common to pass the necessary implicit objects to these methods as parameters.

Session tracking is available by default in JSP pages, providing the `session` implicit object throughout the scriptlet code. If your application is not using session tracking, you should disable it to avoid unnecessary session persistence. Although there is no explicit way to disable session tracking for the entire Web application, servlets will not create sessions unless the servlet code calls the `getSession()` method. JSP pages may disable sessions using the `page` directive:

```
<%@ page session="false" %>
```

Even if your JSP does nothing with the session information, WebLogic Server must persist the last access time for the session at the end of the request processing. It is best to explicitly disable session tracking in JSP pages that do not use it.

BEST PRACTICE Disable session tracking in JSP pages that do not require this feature to avoid unnecessary session persistence.

Like servlets, JSP pages are normally multithreaded and may process multiple requests simultaneously. The same thread-safety restrictions that apply to servlets also apply to JSP pages unless the JSP is configured to be single threaded. In a JSP page a special `page` directive is used to configure this attribute:

```
<%@ page isThreadSafe="false" %>
```

If the `isThreadSafe` attribute is set to `false`, the resulting servlet will implement the `SingleThreadModel` interface, and WebLogic Server will create a pool of servlet instances and synchronize access to them in the same manner it uses for a pure-Java servlet that implements this interface.

BEST PRACTICE As with servlets, you should generally avoid declaring JSP pages to be single threaded. If you find yourself needing to do that, make sure that the pool size is large enough to avoid creating and initializing new instances on the fly to process concurrent requests.

JSP Response Is Buffered

As we said, servlets and JSP pages are request/response mechanisms: An HTTP request is made by the browser, and an HTML response is generated by the servlet or JSP page. In both cases, this response is normally *buffered*, or held in memory on the server temporarily, and sent back to the calling browser at the end of the processing.

By default, output created using the `print()` and `println()` methods on the implicit `JspWriter` object (`out`) are buffered, along with HTTP headers, cookies, and status codes set by the page. Buffering provides you with these important benefits:

- Buffered content may be discarded completely and replaced with new content. The `jsp:forward` element relies on this capability to discard the current response and forward the HTTP request to a new page for processing. Note that the `errorPage` directive uses `jsp:forward` to send the processing to the error page if an error is caught in the JSP page, so buffering is also required for proper error-page handling.
- Buffering allows the page to add or change HTTP headers, cookies, and status codes after the page has begun placing HTML content in the response. Without buffering, it would be impossible to add a cookie in the body of the JSP page or change the response to be a redirect (302) to a different page once `print()` or `println()` has been called because the headers and cookies have already been sent.

When the buffer fills, the response is committed, and the first chunk of information is sent to the browser. Once this commit occurs, the server will no longer honor `jsp:forward`, HTTP header changes (such as redirects), or additional cookies. The server will generate an `IllegalStateException` if any of these operations is attempted after the buffer fills and the response is committed.

The default size of the JSP output buffer is 8KB in WebLogic Server, which you can control using the `page` directive in each JSP page:

```
<%@ page buffer="32kb" %>
```

Output buffering may also be turned off using this directive by specifying "none" for a size, but this practice is not recommended.

Output buffers should be set to at least 32KB in most applications to avoid filling the buffer and committing the response before the page is complete. The minor additional memory requirement (32KB times the number of threads) is a small price to pay for correct error-page handling and the ability to add cookies and response headers at any point in large pages.

BEST PRACTICE **Always use output buffering in JSP pages. Increase the size of the buffer to at least 32KB to avoid redirect, cookie,** `jsp:forward`**, and error-page problems.**

JSP Pages Have Unique Capabilities

Unique capabilities are available in JSP pages that are not present in servlets. Two important JSP-only capabilities are custom tags and `jsp:useBean` elements.

Custom tags provide a mechanism to interact with a custom-developed Java class that encapsulates business logic, presentation logic, or both. Custom tag elements are placed in the JSP page by the developer and then parsed and preprocessed by the application server during the conversion from JSP to servlet. The tag elements are converted by the server to the Java code required to interact with the tag class and perform the desired function. Later in this chapter we will discuss custom tags in more detail and present best practices for their use in WebLogic Server.

The `jsp:useBean` element provides a mechanism to declare and establish the existence of a bean instance for use in scriptlet code or in conjunction with `jsp:getProperty` and `jsp:setProperty` tags. The `jsp:useBean` syntax allows the developer to specify the class of the bean, the name of the reference to the bean, the type of the reference, and the scope in which the bean should be created. We will discuss the strengths and weaknesses of the `jsp:useBean` element later in this chapter during the discussion of best practices.

To summarize, JavaServer Pages technology is a scripting language used to create HTML responses. JSP pages are converted to pure-Java servlets by the application server during processing, and they can perform nearly any task a pure-Java servlet can perform. JSP pages also have unique directives, features, and customization capabilities unavailable to servlets.

Why not use JSP for everything and forget servlets completely? Although it is possible to do so, servlets often provide a better mechanism for implementing presentation-tier business logic. Chapter 2 will address this issue in detail and provide guidance for the proper use of each technology.

Web Application Best Practices

Now that you have reviewed some of the key concepts related to Web applications in WebLogic Server, it's time to dig in and discuss best practices. So many options are available to designers and developers of J2EE Web applications that it would require an entire book to list and explain all of the Web application best practices we could conceivably discuss. In this section, we've attempted to discuss the best practices we feel are applicable to the widest variety of development efforts or are most likely to improve the quality or performance of your WebLogic Server Web applications.

The best practices contained in this chapter cover everything from recommended techniques for using custom tags to proper packaging of your Web application to caching page content for performance. They are presented in no particular order of importance, as the importance of a given best practice depends greatly on the particular application you are building.

Ensure Proper Error Handling

Unhandled exceptions that occur during the execution of a servlet or JSP-generated servlet cause the processing of that page to stop. Assuming the response has not been committed, the JSP output buffer will be cleared and a new response generated and returned to the client. By default, this error response contains very little useful information apart from the numeric error code.

What you need is a friendly, informative error page containing as much information as possible to help during debugging. Fortunately, there is a built-in mechanism for specifying a custom error page for use in handling server errors during processing.

First, you construct an error page JSP to present the error information to the user in a friendly fashion. At a minimum, it should display the exception information and a stack trace. To be more useful during debugging, it can display all request and HTTP header information present using the same methods employed by `SnoopServlet`, discussed earlier. Portions of an example error page are shown in Listing 1.1. The entire page is available on the companion Web site (http://www.wiley.com/compbooks/masteringweblogic).

```
<%@ page isErrorPage="true" %>
<html>
<head><title>Error During Processing</title></head>
<body>
<h2>An error has occurred during the processing of your request.</h2>
<hr>
<h3><%= exception %></h3>
<pre>
<%
    ByteArrayOutputStream ostr = new ByteArrayOutputStream();
    exception.printStackTrace(new PrintStream(ostr));
    out.print(ostr);
%>
</pre>
<hr>
<h3>Requested URL</h3>
<pre>
<%= HttpUtils.getRequestURL(request) %>
</pre>

<h3>Request Parameters</h3>
<pre>
<%
Enumeration enum = request.getParameterNames();
while(enum.hasMoreElements()){
    String key = (String)enum.nextElement();
    String[] paramValues = request.getParameterValues(key);
    for(int i = 0; i < paramValues.length; i++) {
        out.println(key + " : "  + paramValues[i]);
    }
}
%>
</pre>

<h3>Request Attributes</h3>
<pre>
```

Listing 1.1 ErrorPage.jsp. *(continued)*

```
...
</pre>

<h3>Request Information</h3>
<pre>
...
</pre>

<h3>Request Headers</h3>
<pre>
...
</pre>
```

Listing 1.1 *(continued)*

Second, place a `<%@ page errorPage="..." %>` directive on all JSP pages in the application specifying the location of this error JSP page. Listing 1.2 presents a simple example JSP page that declares the error page explicitly. Normally you would do this through a common include file shared by all pages rather than including the directive on every page.

```
<%@ page errorPage="ErrorPage.jsp" %>
<html>
<head></head>
<body>
<!-- Do something sure to cause problems -->
<% String s = null; %>
The string length is: <%= s.length() %><p>
</body>
</html>
```

Listing 1.2 ErrorCreator.jsp.

Accessing the `ErrorCreator.jsp` page from a browser now causes a useful error message to be displayed to the user. The page could conform to the look and feel of the site itself and could easily include links to retry the failed operation, send an email to someone, or go back to the previous page.

As an alternative to specifying the `errorPage` on each individual JSP page, a default error-handling page may be specified for the entire Web application using the `error-page` element in `web.xml`:

```
<error-page>
    <error-code>500</error-code>
    <location>/ErrorPage.jsp</location>
</error-page>
```

These two mechanisms for specifying the error page may look very similar but are, in fact, implemented quite differently by WebLogic Server. The `<%@ page errorPage="..." %>` directive modifies the generated servlet code by placing all JSP scriptlet code, output statements, and other servlet code in a large try/catch block. Specifying the error page in `web.xml` does not affect the generated servlet code in any way. Instead, uncaught exceptions that escape the `_jspService()` method in the original page are caught by the Web container and forwarded to the specified error page automatically.

Which technique is best? Unless the target error page must differ based on the page encountering the error, we recommend the `error-page` element in `web.xml` for the following reasons:

- A declarative and global technique has implicit benefits over per-page techniques. Individual pages that require different error pages can easily override the value in `web.xml` by including the `page` directive.
- The information describing the original page request is more complete if the `error-page` element is used rather than the `page` directive. Specifically, calling `request.getRequestURL()` in the error page returns the URL of the original page rather than the URL of the error page, and additional attributes are placed on the request that are not present if the `page` directive is employed. Note that WebLogic Server correctly includes the special `javax.servlet.error.request_uri` attribute in the request after forwarding to the error page using either the `error-page` element or the `page` directive, so there is always at least one consistent way to retrieve the original page name.

The examples available for this chapter include error-creation pages using both techniques for your examination. `ErrorCreator.jsp` uses the `page` directive, and `BadErrorCreator.jsp` simply creates an error without specifying an error page, thereby relying on the `error-page` element in `web.xml` to specify the correct error page. Accessing these two pages from your browser and observing the output will help you understand the differences in request information available depending on the technique used to declare the error page.

BEST PRACTICE **Create a friendly and useful error page, and make it the default error page for all server errors using the** `error-page` **element in** `web.xml`**. Override this default error page using the** `page` **directive in specific pages, if necessary.**

Use jsp:useBean to Reduce Scriptlet Code

The `jsp:useBean` element provides a powerful mechanism for declaring beans on a JSP page. Beans are given names by this element and may be declared in different scopes: page, request, session, and application. The scope determines the bean's availability in other servlets and page requests:

- *Page* scope places the bean reference in the `PageContext` and makes it available in subsequent scriptlet code, elements, and custom tags during this page processing only. This is the default scope if no `scope` attribute is present in the `jsp:useBean` element.
- *Request* scope places the bean reference in the `HttpServletRequest` using `setAttribute()`, making it available on this page and in any pages included during this processing cycle using `jsp:include` or `jsp:forward` elements.
- *Session* scope places the bean reference in the `HttpSession` object for this client, making it available on this page and in all subsequent requests by this particular client until removed from the session.
- *Application* scope places the bean in the `WebApplicationContext`, which makes it available to any page in this particular Web application until the application server is shut down or the Web application is redeployed.

In its simplest form, the `jsp:useBean` element can be considered a shorthand for scriptlet code that establishes a bean instance in the given scope. For example, consider the element shown here:

```
<jsp:useBean id="currentrez" class="examples.Reservation" />
```

This can be considered equivalent to the following scriptlet code:

```
<% examples.Reservation currentrez = new examples.Reservation(); %>
```

The true advantage of `jsp:useBean` is not apparent until you use a scope other than `page`. For example, the following element declaring the `Reservation` object to be in the `session` scope requires significant coding in the equivalent scriptlet. The `jsp:useBean` element is straightforward:

```
<jsp:useBean id="currentrez"
             class="examples.Reservation" scope="session" />
```

The corresponding scriptlet code is fairly complex:

```
<%
Object obj = session.getAttribute("currentrez");
if (obj == null) {
    obj = new examples.Reservation();
    session.setAttribute("currentrez", obj);
}
examples.Reservation currentrez = (examples.Reservation)obj;
%>
```

Clearly, there is an advantage to using the jsp:useBean element in this case. Note that the name of the bean, defined by the id attribute in jsp:useBean, will be used as the key in the getAttribute() call to find the bean in the HttpSession object. It is important that the name be unique enough to avoid naming conflicts with other items placed in the session.

BEST PRACTICE **Declare beans used in JSP pages using jsp:useBean, especially when the bean is in the request, session, or application scope. Use names descriptive enough to avoid naming conflicts with other beans defined at the same scope.**

Beans declared using jsp:useBean are available in subsequent scriptlet code and in special jsp:getProperty and jsp:setProperty elements used to access and modify bean attributes. These special elements can be used to eliminate some scriptlet code from your JSP pages. For example, the jsp:getProperty element eliminates the need for expression scriptlets when displaying data in beans, as shown in Listing 1.3.

```
<%@ page import="mastering.weblogic.ch01.example1.Person" %>

<jsp:useBean id="pp" class="mastering.weblogic.ch01.example1.Person"
             scope="request" />

<html>
<head><title>Show the Person Data</title></head>
<body>

Here is the Person from the request:<BR>
First Name: <jsp:getProperty name="pp" property="firstName"/><BR>
Last Name: <jsp:getProperty name="pp" property="lastName"/><BR>
Age: <jsp:getProperty name="pp" property="age"/><BR>

</body>
</html>
```

Listing 1.3 ShowPerson.jsp.

This represents a slight improvement in readability over the equivalent code using expression scriptlets, and it may prove easier to maintain for nonprogrammers working with the visual elements on JSP pages.

The jsp:setProperty element calls set methods on the related bean, passing in data supplied in the element or from the current HttpServletRequest object, depending on the attributes supplied in the element. For example, in the JSP action page shown in Listing 1.4, the jsp:setProperty elements interrogate the HTTP request and place data for lastName, firstName, and age in the corresponding bean attributes:

```
<%-- Create a "Person" object, load it with data from request params,
     and store it on http request --%>

<%@ page import="mastering.weblogic.ch01.example1.Person" %>
<jsp:useBean id="pp" class="mastering.weblogic.ch01.example1.Person"
             scope="request" />

<jsp:setProperty name="pp" property="lastName" />
<jsp:setProperty name="pp" property="firstName" />
<jsp:setProperty name="pp" property="age" />

<jsp:forward page="ShowPerson.jsp" />
```

Listing 1.4 EnterPerson_action.jsp.

The `jsp:useBean` element also includes an initialization feature allowing the execution of scriptlet code or custom tags if the declared bean was not found in the specified scope. The initialization code may also use `jsp:setProperty` elements to initialize the bean and may perform any operations normally allowed in JSP scriptlet code. This feature is useful when declaring a bean in the request or session scope that may already have been defined by an earlier page in the process. For example, the following element declares a bean at the session scope and initializes its attributes using the `jsp:setProperty` elements if it was not already present in the session:

```
<jsp:useBean id="pp" class=" mastering.weblogic.ch01.example1.Person"
             scope="session">
    <jsp:setProperty name="pp" property="lastName" value="Nyberg" />
    <jsp:setProperty name="pp" property="firstName" value="Greg" />
    <jsp:setProperty name="pp" property="age" value="39"/>
</jsp:useBean>
```

We will make limited use of the `jsp:useBean` element and related `jsp:getProperty` and `jsp:setProperty` elements during the construction of the sample Web application in Chapters 3 and 4.

Use Custom Tags for Selected Behaviors

Custom tags are a powerful mechanism for extending the basic JSP tag syntax to include custom-developed tags for interacting with Java components, modifying response content, and encapsulating page logic. As with `jsp:useBean` elements, using custom tags can reduce or eliminate the need for scriptlet code in the JSP page and improve maintainability. Custom tags are more powerful and flexible than `jsp:useBean` elements because they allow the manipulation of JSP content and provide a much richer interface.

The power of custom tags comes with a cost, of course: complexity. Unlike `jsp:useBean` elements, which are essentially a shortcut for common tasks typically done through scriptlet code, custom tags add an entirely new layer to the architectural picture and require a strictly defined set of classes and descriptor files to operate.

While a detailed description of the steps required to create custom tags is beyond the scope of this text, it is instructive to review the key concepts to frame the recommendations we will be making.

Custom Tag Key Concepts

Custom tags require a minimum of three components:

- The *Tag Handler Class* is a Java class implementing either the `javax.servlet.jsp.tagext.Tag` or `BodyTag` interfaces. The Tag Handler Class defines the behavior of the tag when invoked in the JSP page by providing set methods for attributes and implementations for key methods such as `doStartTag()` and `doEndTag()`.
- The *Tag Library Descriptor (TLD) File* contains XML elements that map the tag name to the Tag Handler Class and provide additional information about the tag. This file defines whether the tag contains and manipulates JSP body content, whether it uses a Tag Extra Information (TEI) class, and the name of the library containing this tag.
- *JSP Pages* contain `<%@ taglib ... %>` declarations for the tag library and individual tag elements in the page itself to invoke the methods contained in the Tag Handler Class.

Custom tags may also define a Tag Extra Information (TEI) class, extending `javax.servlet.jsp.tagext.TagExtraInfo`, that defines the tag interface in detail and provides the names and types of scriptlet variables introduced by the tag. During page generation, the JSP engine uses the TEI class to validate the tags embedded on the page and include the correct Java code in the servlet to introduce scriptlet variables defined by the custom tag.

Custom Tag Use Is Easy—Development Is Complex

It is important to keep the appropriate goal firmly in mind when evaluating a new technology or feature for potential use on your project. In the case of `jsp:useBean` elements or custom tags, the goal is normally to improve the readability and maintainability of the JSP pages. The assumption is that by reducing or eliminating scriptlet code the page will be easier to understand and maintain, which is true enough. But the JSP pages are only one part of the total system being developed. The beans and custom tags are part of the system as well, and any improvement in maintainability of the JSP pages must be weighed against the complexity and maintenance requirements of the beans and tags themselves.

Custom tag development, in particular, is complex. The complexity is not evident until the tasks being performed become more realistic, perhaps requiring TEI classes, body content manipulation, handling of nested tags, or other more advanced behaviors. Examine the source code for some tag libraries available in the open-source community (see the libraries in http://jakarta.apache.org/taglibs, for example) to get a sense of the requirements for a realistic, production-ready tag library. Is your development team ready to tackle this level of development? Are the people being earmarked for maintenance of the application capable of maintaining, extending, or debugging problems in the tag library? These are valid questions you should consider when making your decision to build a custom tag library.

Using custom tags, on the other hand, is relatively easy. It requires a simple declaration at the top of the JSP page and a few straightforward XML elements in the page to invoke the custom tag and produce the desired behavior. Although there may be cases when scriptlet code is still the appropriate solution, we recommend using custom tags for most development efforts.

In the end, the decision comes down to the benefits of using custom tags versus the effort to develop and maintain the custom tags. Clearly a tag that is developed once and used on many pages may pay for itself through the incremental benefits accrued across multiple uses. Taken to the limit, the most benefit will come from a tag used in many pages that is acquired rather than internally developed, eliminating all development and maintenance effort on the tag itself. This should be your goal: Use custom tags, but don't develop them.

BEST PRACTICE **Custom tags are easy to use but difficult to develop and maintain, so make every effort to locate and use existing tag libraries from reputable sources rather than developing your own custom tags.**

Many useful tag libraries are available from various vendors and open-source communities. Table 1.4 provides a short list to get you started in your search.

Table 1.4 Custom Tag Sources

LOCATION	DESCRIPTION
http://jakarta.apache.org/taglibs	This source has a large number of open-source tag libraries, providing everything from string manipulation to regular-expression handling to database access.
http://jakarta.apache.org/struts	Struts is a model-view-controller framework that includes a number of useful tag libraries.
http://www.servletsuite.com/jsp.htm	This commercial vendor, with more than 80 different tag libraries, offers free binary download and evaluation.
http://www.sourceforge.net/projects/jsptags	This source has open-source tag libraries created by members of the SourceForge community. Many different libraries and functions are included.
http://www.jsptags.com	This is a good reference site that lists many available tag libraries.

In addition, BEA packages a few custom tags in the WebLogic Server product, including a very useful caching tag we will examine in the next section.

We will be using selected custom tags from the Struts framework in the example application in Chapters 3 and 4 to display bean data and create HTML form elements with automatic handling of posted data during processing.

Cache Page Output to Improve Performance

Caching is a time-honored mechanism to improve performance. Database products use caching to improve throughput, application servers use caching to improve EJB performance, and many applications include caching in the business or services layer to avoid costly calculations or data access. All of these layers of caching are important, but in a Web application the surest way to improve performance is to cache the page output itself whenever possible because caching page output can completely eliminate calls to the business services and data-access routines.

Custom tags provide a powerful mechanism for caching page output because tags are allowed to access and modify the content placed in their body and skip the processing of that body content during subsequent invocations. In other words, a properly designed custom tag can "surround" a section of page output, allow the page to process normally the first time, store the generated HTML response, and use the stored response instead of processing the content for subsequent requests.

WebLogic Server includes a caching custom tag called `wl:cache` in the `weblogic-tags` tag library. This tag can cache page output based on any key value in the session, request, page, or application scope, can cache at any one of these scopes, and can be set to cache for a limited or indefinite time. Caching is performed using Java system memory for maximum performance, unlike some open-source page-caching tags that use disk storage.

Some simple examples will show you how the `wl:cache` custom tag works. The format for the `wl:cache` tag, when used to cache output, is this:

```
<wl:cache name="..." key="..." scope="..." timeout="..." size="...">
...
// Body content to be cached..
// Can be HTML, JSP scriptlets, directives, other tags, etc.
...
</wl:cache>
```

In the simplest form, with no key or scope information supplied in the attributes, the `wl:cache` tag caches the generated body content for the specified length of time for all clients (because `application` scope is default):

```
<wl:cache timeout="60s">
...
// Body content to be cached..
...
</wl:cache>
```

Listing 1.5 shows the `CacheTest1.jsp` example program that demonstrates the use of the caching tag in this simple manner. The content above the `wl:cache` tag is evaluated with every page invocation, but the content in the tag is evaluated the first time the page is accessed by any user and cached for 60 seconds.

```
<%@ taglib uri="weblogic-tags.tld" prefix="wl" %>
<HTML>
<BODY>
Current time is: <%= System.currentTimeMillis() %><br>
<wl:cache timeout="60s">
<% System.out.println("Inside cached body"); %>
Cached time is: <%= System.currentTimeMillis() %><br>
</wl:cache>
</BODY>
</HTML>
```

Listing 1.5 CacheTest1.jsp.

Accessing this JSP page repeatedly will produce browser output similar to the following:

```
Current time is: 1015363376897
Cached time is:  1015363376897

Current time is: 1015363385004
Cached time is:  1015363376897

...
```

The displayed cached time will remain unchanged in the output during subsequent page hits because the contents of the body, including the call to `System.currentTimeMillis()`, are not evaluated in the generated servlet. The `System.out.println()` log message in the body content will help confirm that the body is not evaluated on subsequent invocations. After 60 seconds, the cache will expire, the body content will be evaluated during the next page request, and the cached HTML response will be updated with the new output.

Even this simple behavior might be useful in a real application because the `wl:cache` tag can wrap any arbitrary JSP content, even directives such as `jsp:include`. Recall that `jsp:include` is used to include content generated by other JSP pages within the current page at page-processing time, often as an alternative to the page-generation-time `<%@ include file="..." %>` directive. If your display pages are built up from multiple component parts (header, footer, navigation bars, etc.) using many separate `jsp:include` directives to include the parts, a simple `wl:cache` tag placed around these directives can dramatically improve performance. The `CacheTest2.jsp` example program in Listing 1.6 illustrates this technique.

```
<%@ taglib uri="weblogic-tags.tld" prefix="wl" %>
<HTML>
<BODY>
<wl:cache timeout="5m">
<TABLE BORDER="1">
  <TR>
    <TD><jsp:include page="CacheTest2_header.jsp"/></TD>
  </TR>
  <TR>
    <TD><jsp:include page="CacheTest2_navbar.jsp"/></TD>
  </TR>
  <TR>
    <TD>
      <TABLE BORDER="1">
        <TR>
          <TD><jsp:include page="CacheTest2_leftside.jsp"/></TD>
</wl:cache>

<TD>This is the main content for the page..</TD>

<wl:cache timeout="5m">
          <TD><jsp:include page="CacheTest2_rightside.jsp"/></TD>
        </TR>
      </TABLE>
    </TD>
  </TR>
  <TR>
    <TD><jsp:include page="CacheTest2_footer.jsp"/></TD>
  </TR>
</TABLE>
</wl:cache>
</BODY>
</HTML>
```

Listing 1.6 CacheTest2.jsp.

The first time this page is executed, the HTML response generated by the content in the sets of `wl:cache` tags will be cached in memory. Subsequent page requests will avoid the multiple `jsp:include` operations during the page processing and the performance hit that goes with them.

BEST PRACTICE Look for opportunities to cache static, or relatively static, content using the `wl:cache` custom tag. Caching the results of `jsp:include` operations can improve performance significantly.

The first two example programs limited themselves to key-less caching, meaning that the content was cached and reused for the specified period of time regardless of client identity, or any parameter or value present during the page processing. In most cases, however, the generated page content depends on some contextual information such as a request parameter or scriptlet variable. Fortunately, the `wl:cache` tag includes a powerful and flexible mechanism for caching content based on parameters and other context information through the `key` attribute in the `wl:cache` tag definition:

```
<wl:cache key="[parameter|page|session|request|application].keyname" ...>
```

The important assumption is that the body content depends on the value of the key or keys, so caching must also depend on these values. For example, if the body content depends on the value of a request parameter called `howmany`, the `wl:cache` tag must include this parameter in the `key` attribute. The `CacheTest3.jsp` example program in Listing 1.7 illustrates this case.

```
<%@ taglib uri="weblogic-tags.tld" prefix="wl" %>
<HTML>
<BODY>
<wl:cache name="CacheTest3" key="parameter.howmany" timeout="5m">
<%
int jj = Integer.parseInt(request.getParameter("howmany"));
System.out.println("Inside cached body with howmany of " + jj);
%>
<H2>We're going to count from 1 to <%= jj %><H2>
<%
for (int ii = 1; ii <= jj; ii++) {
    out.print(ii + "<br>");
}
%>
</wl:cache>
</BODY>
</HTML>
```

Listing 1.7 CacheTest3.jsp.

Accessing this page with a specific value of `howmany` in the query string causes the body content, including the loop and `System.out.println()` code, to be executed one time. Subsequent page hits with the same `howmany` parameter value return the same content without reevaluating the content. Supplying a different value for `howmany` will cause the body to be evaluated for that value and the contents cached using that key value. In other words, if you hit the page five times with different `howmany` values, you've created five different cached versions of the body content using `howmany` as the key. This technique is very slick and very powerful for improving site performance.

Two of the optional attributes in the `wl:cache` tag provide important capabilities:

- The **size** attribute limits the size of the cache to a certain value. If the cache is key dependent and there are many possible key values, it is a good idea to limit the size of the cache to something reasonable (perhaps 500 to 1,000 entries) using this attribute.

- The **name** attribute is used to identify this cache within the overall set of caches managed by the wl:cache tag library. If you omit this attribute, the name will be a unique combination of the request URI and tag index in the page. This may be sufficient in simple cases. If the cache must be flushed, however, a name should be specified to allow a different wl:cache tag to be able to refer to the same name and flush the cache.

Content that depends on multiple parameters or context values can be cached by combining the parameters in the key attribute using a comma separator or by combining the multiple values ahead of time in a single scriptlet variable and placing that variable in the key attribute using the page.varname syntax. This code snippet uses multiple key parts:

```
<wl:cache key="parameter.howmany,parameter.color" timeout="5m">
...
</wl:cache>
```

This is effectively the same as this snippet:

```
<%
String ss = request.getParameter("howmany") + "," +
            request.getParameter("color");
%>
<wl:cache key="page.ss" timeout="5m">
...
</wl:cache>
```

In both cases, the content is cached and reused depending on the value of both the howmany and color request parameters.

How would caching work in a real application that displays business information using something like entity beans or value objects retrieved from a stateless session bean, two architectures common in J2EE applications? The JSP page used to display the bean content places the content-generation code in a wl:cache tag that depends on the value of the primary key for the bean. Subsequent page hits for the same bean information will then use the cached content.

The trick, of course, is that the underlying bean data may change, and the cached display page will continue to use the cached HTML output for that particular bean until the time-out period expires. You need to be able to flush the cache for a particular key value when the content is no longer valid in order to force the next page request to retrieve the bean and display the latest data. The wl:cache tag includes an optional attribute called flush for this purpose. You would flush the cache used by CacheTest3.jsp, for example, using a tag like this:

```
<wl:cache name="CacheTest3" key="parameter.howmany" flush="true" />
```

Note that there can be no body content when the wl:cache tag is used to flush a cache.

Generally speaking, this tag should be executed immediately after the bean is updated in the database. As we will discuss in Chapter 2, most large Web applications use servlets rather than JSP pages for processing bean changes. It is awkward, if not impossible, to call a JSP custom tag within a servlet to perform an activity like flushing the cached content for this particular bean.

One reasonable solution is to include logic in the display JSP page to sense a particular `flushcache` request parameter and conditionally perform the flush early in the processing of the page if this parameter is present. The servlet that performed the bean update will normally forward processing to the display JSP page after completing the update, and it is easy enough to include the `flushcache` parameter in the request before forwarding.

BEST PRACTICE **Use the key-specific caching capability of the `wl:cache` custom tag to cache page content for specific request parameters and beans whenever possible.**

Use Servlet Filtering for Common Behaviors

Servlet filtering, a new feature of servlets introduced in the Servlet 2.3 specification, provides a declarative technique for intercepting HTTP requests and performing any desired preprocessing or conditional logic before the request is passed on to the final target JSP page or servlet. Filters are very useful for implementing common behaviors such as caching page output, logging page requests, providing debugging information during testing, and checking security information and forwarding to login pages. Figure 1.2 illustrates the basic components of the filtering approach and shows the incoming HTTP request passing through one or more `Filter` classes in the `FilterChain` collection defined for this page request.

Placing a filter in the path of a particular servlet or JSP request is a simple two-step process: Build a class that implements the `javax.servlet.Filter` interface, and register that class as a filter for the desired pages and servlets using entries in the `web.xml` descriptor file. To illustrate this process, we will build and deploy a simple but useful filter that intercepts servlet and JSP requests and logs `HttpServletRequest` information before passing the request on to the intended JSP page or servlet. We'll call the filter `SnoopFilter` because it is very similar to the `SnoopServlet` discussed previously.

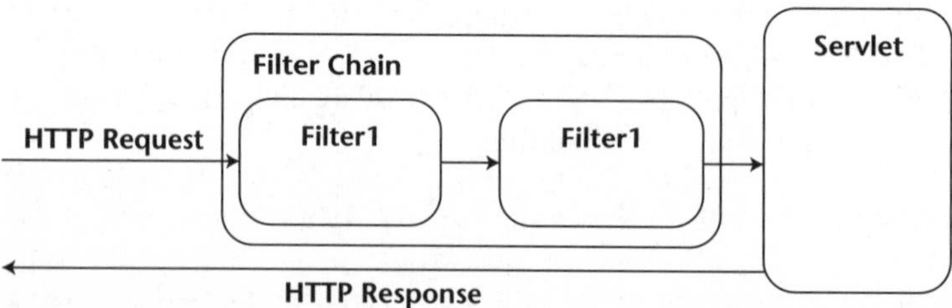

Figure 1.2 Servlet filtering.

Building a Simple SnoopFilter Filter Class

The first step is the construction of a filter class called SnoopFilter that implements the javax.servlet.Filter interface and performs the desired logging of request information. Simply put, the doFilter() method writes information from the HttpServletRequest object to System.out before forwarding to any additional filters in the filter chain. The source for SnoopFilter is available from the companion Web site (http://www.wiley.com/compbooks/masteringweblogic).

Registering SnoopFilter in the web.xml Descriptor File

Registering a filter requires a set of elements in the Web application descriptor file, web.xml. These elements declare the filter class and define the pages or servlets to which the filter should be applied. In this simple example, you want all pages and servlets in the application to be filtered through SnoopFilter, and the web.xml file includes the following elements:

```
<filter>
  <filter-name>SnoopFilter</filter-name>
  <display-name>SnoopFilter</display-name>
  <description></description>
  <filter-class>
    mastering.weblogic.ch01.example1.SnoopFilter
  </filter-class>
</filter>

<filter-mapping>
  <filter-name>SnoopFilter</filter-name>
  <url-pattern>/*</url-pattern>
</filter-mapping>
```

The <url-pattern>/*</url-pattern> element declares that all pages and servlets in the application should be filtered using SnoopFilter, so every page request will go through the filter before normal processing begins. The server's stdout stream will therefore contain detailed request information for every page request, which is potentially very useful during development and debugging.

Clearly the same general logging capability could have been placed in a helper class, custom tag, or simple scriptlet included in each JSP page or servlet, but the ability to control the specific pages or groups of pages using the SnoopFilter in a declarative manner (via url-pattern elements) has significant advantages.

Although this is obviously a simple example, SnoopFilter illustrates the value of filters for preprocessing activities such as logging, auditing, or debugging in J2EE Web applications. Filters are not limited to writing output to stdout; they can easily write information to separate log files, insert rows in database tables, call EJB components, add or modify request attributes, forward the page request to a different Web application component, or perform any other desired behavior unconditionally or based on specific request information. They are a very powerful addition to the J2EE servlet specification.

BEST PRACTICE Use filters to implement common behaviors such as logging, auditing, and security verification for servlets and JSP pages in your Web applications.

Response Caching Using the CacheFilter

WebLogic Server includes a filter called `CacheFilter` that provides page-level response caching for Web applications. This filter is very similar to the `wl:cache` custom tag, discussed earlier in this chapter, except that it operates at the complete page level rather than surrounding and caching only a section of JSP content in a page. The `CacheFilter` may also be used with servlets and static content, unlike the custom tag, which works only for JSP pages.

The `CacheFilter` is registered like any other servlet filter. Define the filter in the `web.xml` file, and specify the `url-pattern` of the page or pages to cache. Use initialization parameters in the filter registration to define time-out criteria and other cache control values similar to the `wl:cache` custom tag. For example, to cache the response from a specific JSP page for 60 seconds, register the `CacheFilter` using elements similar to the following:

```
<filter>
  <filter-name>CacheFilter1</filter-name>
  <filter-class>weblogic.cache.filter.CacheFilter</filter-class>
  <init-param>
    <param-name>timeout</param-name>
    <param-value>60</param-value>
  </init-param>
</filter>
...
<filter-mapping>
  <filter-name>CacheFilter1</filter-name>
  <url-pattern>CacheFilterTest1.jsp</url-pattern>
</filter-mapping>
```

The JSP page will execute the first time the URL is accessed by any client, and the content of the HTTP response will be cached by the filter and used for all subsequent access requests for 60 seconds.

Additional initialization parameters for the `CacheFilter` include the following:

Name. The name of the cache. The `wl:cache` tag may be used to flush the `CacheFilter` cache using this name and the `flush="true"` attribute. It defaults to the request URI.

Timeout. Timeout period for the cached content. It defaults to seconds, but it may be specified in units of `ms` (milliseconds), `s` (seconds), `m` (minutes), `h` (hours), or `d` (days).

Scope. The scope of the cached content. Valid values are request, session, application, and cluster. Note that `CacheFilter` does not support page scope. It defaults to application scope.

Key. The name of request parameters, session attributes, and other variables used to differentiate cached content. It is similar in function to the key attribute in the wl:cache custom tag.

Size. The maximum number of unique cache entries based on key values. It defaults to unlimited.

As a final example, recall that the CacheTest3.jsp page examined earlier used the wl:cache tag to cache the generated content based on the howmany request parameter because the page response depended on the value of that parameter (see Listing 1.7). The equivalent CacheFilter implementation would require the following entries in the web.xml file:

```
<filter>
  <filter-name>CacheFilter3</filter-name>
  <filter-class>weblogic.cache.filter.CacheFilter</filter-class>
  <init-param>
    <param-name>timeout</param-name>
    <param-value>5m</param-value>
  </init-param>
  <init-param>
    <param-name>key</param-name>
    <param-value>parameter.howmany</param-value>
  </init-param>
</filter>
...
<filter-mapping>
  <filter-name>CacheFilter3</filter-name>
  <url-pattern>CacheFilterTest3.jsp</url-pattern>
</filter-mapping>
```

The key parameter indicates that the page-level cache should be segregated based on the value of the howmany parameter in the request. A separate cached response will be created for each value of this parameter and used for five minutes before reevaluating the underlying page. Note that the CacheFilter class must be registered using a different filter-name element each time in order to supply different initialization parameters. The CacheFilterTest3.jsp page is very similar to CacheTest3.jsp (Listing 1.7), but it no longer requires the wl:cache custom tags:

```
<HTML>
<BODY>
<%
int jj = Integer.parseInt(request.getParameter("howmany"));
System.out.println("Inside cached body with howmany of " + jj);
%>
<H2>We're going to count from 1 to <%= jj %><H2>
<%
for (int ii = 1; ii <= jj; ii++) {
    out.print(ii + "<br>");
}
```

```
%>
</BODY>
</HTML>
```

The CacheFilter approach has an obvious advantage over the wl:cache technique in this example: Caching is performed using a declarative technique rather than embedding custom tags in the page itself. This defers the definition of caching behavior to deployment time and allows easier control of the caching parameters and scope using the web.xml descriptor elements.

BEST PRACTICE Use the CacheFilter instead of wl:cache tags for page-level response caching whenever possible to provide better flexibility during deployment.

Note that a JSP page included using the jsp:include element is considered a separate page for the purposes of caching. Configuring the CacheFilter to cache the contents of the included JSP page represents a viable alternative to surrounding the jsp:include element with wl:cache tags.

Using Custom JSP Base Classes

Recall that JSP pages are processed by the JSP engine and converted to a servlet. In WebLogic Server, the resulting servlet is a subclass of weblogic.servlet.jsp.JspBase by default. JspBase is a WebLogic-provided class that extends HttpServlet and forwards service calls to a method called _jspService(). You may create your own custom JSP base class that extends JspBase and configure the JSP engine to use your base class for generated servlets by including the extends attribute in the <%@ page ... %> directive on the JSP page.

The ability to define a custom JSP base class provides an alternative to static include directives for defining helper functions and utilities in the page. For example, if you want to provide a simple helper method called formatDate() to format a java.util.Date object, the method should probably be placed in a custom JSP base class rather than defining it in a separate file included using the <%@ include file="..." %> directive.

Using Run-Time Expressions in JSP Directives

Most of the attributes in JSP directives may be set using static information or using the contents of scriptlet expressions at run time. For example, the following simple jsp:include directive uses a statically defined target page:

```
<jsp:include page="welcome.jsp" />
```

The following version of the directive uses the value of the scriptlet variable mypage to determine which page to include at run time:

```
<jsp:include page="<%= mypage %>" />
```

The syntax used in these dynamic expressions is very similar to the normal use of the `<%= %>` expression scriptlets used to generate content in the HTTP response with one notable exception: The parser cannot handle expressions with unescaped double quotes. For example, the following directive will fail during page parsing and compilation:

```
<jsp:include page="<%= mypage + ".jsp" %>" />
```

The expression should be written this way using escaped double quotes:

```
<jsp:include page="<%= mypage + \".jsp\" %>" />
```

If this becomes too confusing for complex expressions, simply create a temporary scriptlet variable before the directive and refer to that variable in the directive, as shown here:

```
<% String fullname = mypage + ".jsp"; %>
<jsp:include page="<%= fullname %>" />
```

The example application built in Chapters 3 and 4 will make use of run-time expressions in `jsp:include` directives as part of its page-presentation architecture.

Creating Excel Files Using Servlets and JSP Pages

Creating spreadsheets using servlets and JSP pages is a useful way to provide users with results they can sort, manipulate, and print using Microsoft Excel or other spreadsheet applications. Servlets are the preferred mechanism, but JSP pages can also be used if you take steps to avoid unintended newline characters in the output stream.

To create a spreadsheet using a servlet, build the servlet in the normal manner but set the content type to `application/vnd.ms-excel` in the response header to indicate that the response should be interpreted as a spreadsheet. Data written to the response `Writer` object will be interpreted as spreadsheet data, with tabs indicating column divisions and newline characters indicating row divisions. For example, the `SimpleExcelServlet` servlet in Listing 1.8 creates a multiplication table using simple tabs and newlines to control the rows and columns in the result.

```
package mastering.weblogic.ch01.example1;

import java.io.*;
import javax.servlet.*;
import javax.servlet.http.*;

public class SimpleExcelServlet extends HttpServlet
{
    public static final String CONTENT_TYPE_EXCEL =
```

Listing 1.8 SimpleExcelServlet.java. *(continued)*

```
        "application/vnd.ms-excel";

    public void doGet(HttpServletRequest request,
                      HttpServletResponse response)
        throws IOException
    {
        PrintWriter out = response.getWriter();
        response.setContentType(CONTENT_TYPE_EXCEL);

        out.print("\t"); // empty cell in upper corner
        for (int jj = 1; jj <= 10; jj++) {
            out.print("" + jj + "\t");
        }
        out.print("\n");

        for (int ii = 1; ii <= 10; ii++) {
            out.print("" + ii + "\t");
            for (int jj = 1; jj <= 10; jj++) {
                out.print("" + (ii * jj) + "\t");
            }
            out.print("\n");
        }
    }
}
```

Listing 1.8 *(continued)*

Normal registration of this servlet in `web.xml` is all that is required in most cases:

```
<servlet>
  <servlet-name>SimpleExcelServlet</servlet-name>
  <servlet-class>
    mastering.weblogic.ch01.example1.SimpleExcelServlet
  </servlet-class>
</servlet>

<servlet-mapping>
  <servlet-name>SimpleExcelServlet</servlet-name>
  <url-pattern>/SimpleExcelServlet</url-pattern>
</servlet-mapping>
```

Users accessing the `/SimpleExcelServlet` location will be presented with a spreadsheet embedded in their browser window. The servlet may also be registered for a `url-pattern` that includes a `.xls` file extension to assist the user by providing a suitable default file name and type if they choose to use `Save As...` from within the browser:

```
<servlet-mapping>
  <servlet-name>SimpleExcelServlet</servlet-name>
```

```
    <url-pattern>/multitable.xls</url-pattern>
  </servlet-mapping>
```

Simple tab- and newline-based formatting may be sufficient in many cases, but you can achieve additional control by building HTML tables and using HTML formatting options such as <b> and <i> in the generated output. Because the content type was specified as `ms-excel`, these HTML tags are interpreted by the browser and spreadsheet application as equivalent spreadsheet formatting options.

The `FancyExcelServlet` example servlet in Listing 1.9 builds the same multiplication table as `SimpleExcelServlet` but uses HTML to control formats and cell sizes.

```
package mastering.weblogic.ch01.example1;

import java.io.*;
import javax.servlet.*;
import javax.servlet.http.*;

public class FancyExcelServlet extends HttpServlet
{
    public static final String CONTENT_TYPE_EXCEL =
        "application/vnd.ms-excel";

    public void doGet(HttpServletRequest request,
                      HttpServletResponse response)
        throws IOException
    {
        PrintWriter out = response.getWriter();
        response.setContentType(CONTENT_TYPE_EXCEL);

        out.print("<table border=1>");
        out.print("<tr>");
        out.print("<td> </td>"); // empty cell in upper corner
        for (int jj = 1; jj <= 10; jj++) {
            out.print("<td><b>" + jj + "</b></td>");
        }
        out.print("</tr>");

        for (int ii = 1; ii <= 10; ii++) {
            out.print("<tr>");
            out.print("<td><b>" + ii + "</b></td>");
            for (int jj = 1; jj <= 10; jj++) {
                out.print("<td>" + (ii * jj) + "</td>");
            }
            out.print("</tr>");
        }
        out.print("</table>");
    }
}
```

Listing 1.9 FancyExcelServlet.java.

You can also use JSP pages to create spreadsheets with one complication: The output of a JSP page often contains many spurious newline characters caused by extra white-space around directives and scriptlet tags, making it difficult to control the spreadsheet formatting when using simple tab and newline techniques. HTML formatting similar to the `FancyExcelServlet` works better in JSP pages used to create spreadsheets. Listing 1.10 presents the JSP equivalent to the `FancyExcelServlet`.

```
<% response.setContentType("application/vnd.ms-excel"); %>
<html>
<body>
<table border=1>
<tr>
  <td> </td>
  <% for (int jj = 1; jj <= 10; jj++) { %>
    <td><b><%= jj %></b></td>
  <% } %>
</tr>
<% for (int ii = 1; ii <= 10; ii++) { %>
  <tr>
    <td><b><%= ii %></b></td>
    <% for (int jj = 1; jj <= 10; jj++) { %>
      <td><%= (ii * jj) %></td>
    <% } %>
  </tr>
<% } %>
</table>
</body>
</html>
```

Listing 1.10 FancyExcelPage.jsp.

Viewing Generated Servlet Code

Viewing the servlet code generated for a particular JSP page can be instructive while learning JSP technology and useful during the testing and debugging process. Often the error report received during the execution of the JSP page indicates the line in the generated servlet code, but finding the JSP scriptlet code or tag that caused the error requires inspection of the Java code.

Generated Java servlet code will be kept alongside the generated servlet class files if the `keepgenerated` parameter is set to `true` in the `jsp-descriptor` section of the `weblogic.xml` descriptor file. The equivalent option for keeping the generated Java code for JSP pages compiled using the `weblogic.jspc` utility is `-keepgenerated` placed on the command line used to execute `weblogic.jspc`.

By default, the generated servlet classes and Java code will be placed in a temporary directory structure located under the domain root directory. The name of this temporary directory depends on the names of the server, enterprise application, and Web application, and it typically looks something like /myserver/.wlnotdelete /_appsdir_masterapp_dir_webapp_myserver/jsp_servlet. This default location may be overridden using the workingDir option in the weblogic.xml descriptor file.

Programmatic Authentication in Web Applications

The J2EE specification provides a declarative mechanism for controlling access to resources in the Web application. This mechanism uses elements in the web.xml file to define collections of resources and specify the roles required to access these resources. Users are asked for their logon identifier and password via a pop-up HTTP challenge window or special form configured for this purpose; upon submission of valid credentials, the user will be authenticated in the Web application security context and will be able to access secured resources. Chapter 10 of this book will cover many different aspects of WebLogic Server security including this simple declarative security for Web applications.

This declarative mechanism can occasionally fall short of the desired functionality, and many developers have resorted to building their own authorization mechanisms. In many of these designs the users are never actually authenticated in the Web application security context, and access to business-tier resources like EJB components is accomplished through the default, or <anonymous>, user. This is a poor practice for at least two reasons:

- Anyone with knowledge of the server listening port can connect to WebLogic Server as the <anonymous> user and gain access to the EJB components.
- The Web application does not forward a useful security context to the EJB container, thereby eliminating the value of methods such as getCallerPrincipal() and isCallerInRole() in the EJB components for security and auditing purposes.

WebLogic Server provides a little-known interface to programmatically authenticate the user and establish a proper security context for this client in the Web application. The method is located in the weblogic.servlet.security.ServletAuthentication class and is called simply weak(). The example page shown in Listing 1.11 takes parameters passed in through the HttpServletRequest and authenticates the user using the weak() method.

```
<%@ page import="weblogic.servlet.security.ServletAuthentication" %>
<HTML>
<HEAD>
<TITLE>Login Tester JSP Page</TITLE>
</HEAD>

<BODY>
<H2>User name before login is:
```

Listing 1.11 WeakLoginTest.jsp. *(continued)*

```
  <%= weblogic.security.acl.Security.getThreadCurrentUserName() %>
</H2>
<%
    // logs out if already logged in
    ServletAuthentication.logout(request);

    String username = request.getParameter("username");
    String password = request.getParameter("password");

    int retcode = ServletAuthentication.weak(username,
                                          password, session);
    if (retcode == ServletAuthentication.AUTHENTICATED) {
        out.print("Successful login using " +
                  username + " and " + password + ".<br>");
    }
    else {
        out.print("Bad login/password.<br>");
    }
%>
<H2>User name after login is:
  <%= weblogic.security.acl.Security.getThreadCurrentUserName() %>
</H2>
</BODY>
</HTML>
```

Listing 1.11 *(continued)*

Subsequent page requests by the same client will continue to use this newly established security context, and any communication with the EJB container will pass this context information along and make it available via `getCallerPrincipal()` or other normal methods.

Chapter Review

In this chapter we reviewed the key concepts related to Web applications in WebLogic Server and presented a number of important best practices designed to improve the quality and performance of your Web applications.

Most of this chapter has been at the detailed design and implementation level, the *trees* in a sense. In the next two chapters we will step back and look at the *forest* for a few minutes by examining the importance of the overall Web application architecture, the selection of a suitable presentation template technique, and the application of a model-view-controller pattern and framework for form and navigation handling.

CHAPTER

2

Choosing a Web Application Architecture

The J2EE specification defines many different technologies in great detail, but it does not actually define the architecture of a J2EE application. For example, the EJB specification describes the behaviors and characteristics of both entity beans and session beans and the rules that dictate how they are to be managed by the application server, but the specification does not define the proper choice for a given application. It is up to the system architect on the project to define rules governing the use of entity beans, session beans, and other EJB components.

Similarly, the J2EE specification defines the two key technologies for Web applications, Java servlets and JSP pages, but it does not specify how they should be used in an application. As a result, the J2EE community has adopted a wide variety of de facto standards and design patterns for architecting Web applications based on lessons learned by early adopters.

This chapter examines the presentation requirements that drive Web application architectures and makes specific recommendations to help you choose an appropriate architecture for your WebLogic Server application.

Architecture Key Concepts

Before embarking on a discussion of presentation requirements and architecture drivers, we need to step back and review some key concepts related to J2EE architecture.

J2EE Application Tiers

The J2EE specification and related documentation from Sun describe the J2EE platform as a distributed application environment organized in three tiers: client, business, and enterprise information systems (EIS) or data. Although this is a useful organization, it lumps all of the application-server-hosted components in the business tier. It is more common to break up this middle tier into two separate tiers, presentation and business, containing presentation-related components and business-related components, respectively. This organization is depicted in Figure 2.1.

A related rule of thumb states that a component in a given tier may communicate directly only with components in adjacent tiers. JSP pages may not access the database directly, for example. Presentation-tier components must request information from components in the business tier, which then request data from the database or other data-tier systems as required. The advantages of this approach include the flexibility to leverage the same business components across multiple presentation-tier components and the reduction in coupling between nonadjacent layers.

There is nothing particularly new or revolutionary about organizing components in tiers. Three-tier and *n*-tier client/server technologies have followed this model for years, and even so-called two-tier systems often had stored procedures and other middle-tier business services. The benefits of organizing components in tiers or layers are well known and accepted in the industry, but this layered organization hardly defines an application architecture.

Model-View-Controller Architecture

One design pattern often cited as a Web application architecture is the model-view-controller (MVC) pattern. This pattern has its roots in the Smalltalk world, where applications often use sophisticated techniques for viewing business information (the model) using interfaces (views) that are updated and managed automatically by controller objects whenever business objects change state.

When architects discuss the model-view-controller pattern today, they usually mean a watered-down version of the original. Essentially, the MVC pattern has become another layered architecture, where view components must interact with a controller component to gain access to model data. As shown in Figure 2.2, the J2EE technologies have shuffled around a bit, but the left-to-right interactions implicit in a tiered architecture are still present.

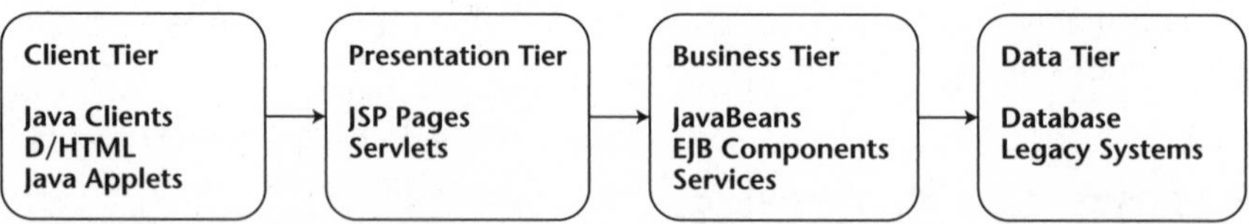

Figure 2.1 J2EE application tiers.

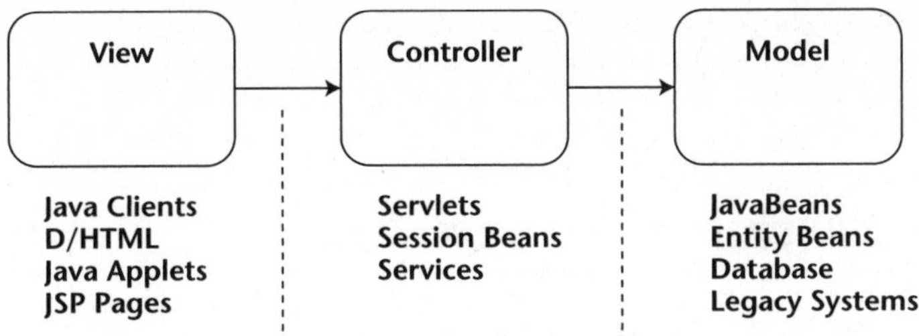

Figure 2.2 J2EE components mapped to MVC pattern.

There is more to the model-view-controller pattern than simply layering components and mandating left-to-right communication paths, of course. The MVC design pattern also commonly defines an approach for important presentation-tier behaviors such as defining navigational flow through the site and processing HTML form submissions.

Common J2EE Design Patterns

The J2EE architectural community has begun to rally around a number of important design patterns based on the seminal work on design patterns presented in *Design Patterns* by Erich Gamma, Richard Helm, Ralph Johnson, and John Vlissides (Addison-Wesley, 1995) and more recent books such as *Core J2EE Patterns: Best Practices and Design Strategies* by Deepak Alur, John Crupi, and Dan Malks (Prentice Hall PTR, 2001) and *EJB Design Patterns: Advanced Patterns, Processes, and Idioms* by Floyd Marinescu (John Wiley & Sons, 2002). Patterns such as the *session façade* and *value object* are so prevalent now in application design that they have become, in a sense, part of the J2EE platform. Every J2EE architect should read these works and be well versed in the advantages and disadvantages of each design pattern before sitting down to architect a system.

There are still some rough edges in these common J2EE design patterns, however. Often they tackle problems individually, leaving the proper combination of many different (and possibly conflicting) patterns as an exercise for the architect. Some of the patterns introduce additional layers in the architecture, ostensibly to reduce coupling between the layers already defined. We wonder how much decoupling is truly advantageous to the development and maintenance effort taken as a whole. By the time you implement the *business delegate, service locater, session façade, value object assembler,* and *composite entity* patterns in the business tier, for example, the resulting system may not be an improvement over the starting point.

The J2EE community has not yet reached the point where complete, end-to-end architectures incorporating a select set of well-understood design patterns are documented and available for new architectural efforts. We hope to address this deficiency in some small way in this chapter and subsequent chapters on EJB architecture by presenting complete, realistic example applications employing a consistent set of J2EE design patterns. The success or failure of your WebLogic project may depend more on the proper selection of architecture than on any other decision you make during development, so take the time to understand the issues involved before you start designing or coding.

Now that we have discussed some basic concepts related to Web application architecture, it is time to dig in and discuss the issues that drive presentation-tier architecture design decisions.

Presentation-Tier Architecture Selection

The high-level depiction of J2EE application tiers in Figure 2.1 defined the presentation tier as containing Java servlets and JSP pages. When we talk about presentation-tier architecture, we are essentially defining the manner in which these two types of components will be combined to create a user interface that meets the explicit and implicit requirements for the presentation tier of the application.

Understanding these explicit and implicit requirements is the goal of the next section.

Presentation-Tier Requirements

Defining the presentation-tier architecture is much like designing the application itself: It must depend on the requirements. You don't build a customer management system if the users want an accounting system, and you shouldn't design the presentation tier without understanding presentation-tier requirements.

We're not talking about understanding the user-interface requirements of the system, but rather the general requirements of any well-behaved Web application. Examples include good form validation and error handling, robust handling of bookmarks and browser *Back* buttons, ability to change graphics or page arrangements quickly, and helpful pop-ups and dialogs. Users are becoming more familiar and comfortable with the Web and are demanding robust behavior from their custom-built Web applications. Meanwhile, the large commercial sites keep raising the bar with respect to usability. Users see constant improvements in areas such as page layout customization, form validation, pick lists and pop-ups, and many other areas, and they wonder why you can't implement something similar for their project.

A detailed discussion of state-of-the-art JavaScript technologies and site design is beyond the scope of this book. If you are interested in user-controlled page layout and content customization, you should investigate BEA's WebLogic Portal product. Our focus is presentation-tier architecture rather than detailed site design and human factors engineering.

Achieving many of the basic usability and flexibility requirements of a site can be helped or hindered a great deal by the choice of presentation-tier architecture. These are some of the presentation-tier requirements:

- Display requirements
- Form/update requirements
- Navigation requirements

The following sections document these requirements and the ways they affect the required architecture.

Display Requirements

Display requirements include all of the user-interface requirements related to the presentation of data on Web pages. As discussed in Chapter 1, JSP pages are considered the best mechanism for creating HTML responses containing dynamic content. We will assume you're using JSP pages for display behavior unless otherwise noted.

In this section, we discuss some of the key display-related requirements that affect presentation-tier architecture decisions. At a minimum, the architecture must support the following:

- *Displaying model data* in various modes and forms
- *Displaying lists* of objects with flexible sorting, paging, and form-input capabilities
- *Controlling page availability and model data presentation* based on user authorization
- *Internationalization* of all appropriate content on pages
- *Producing flexible and maintainable pages* allowing for multiple deployments and efficient future modifications

Displaying Model Data

Applications must be able to display model data on view-only Web pages for inspection by the user. The architecture must provide a straightforward mechanism to retrieve the model object and place properly formatted attribute values in the HTML response. JSP pages offer expression scriptlets and `jsp:useBean`-related `jsp:getProperty` tags for the purpose of embedding the model data in the response, and they require only some mechanism for retrieving the proper model object and making it available in the proper context for display.

Displaying Model Data in a Form

You will often want to allow the creation and modification of model objects through an HTML form with input elements corresponding to the model object attributes. The presentation-tier architecture must provide a mechanism to retrieve the proper model object (or create an empty object) and populate the form elements with the properly formatted attribute values. The same JSP techniques used for viewing model data are appropriate in this case, namely expression scriptlets and `jsp:getProperty` tags.

Techniques for populating form elements with model data are simple enough for text input fields, requiring a snippet in the JSP page something like this:

```
<tr>
  <td nowrap>Middle name:</td>
  <td><INPUT TYPE="text" NAME="middleName"
       value="<%= person.getMiddleName() %>" size="50"></td>
</tr>
```

Techniques become more challenging when the form elements are formatted dates, select lists, checkboxes, radio buttons, and other fields requiring some form of mapping from the attribute value in the model object to the proper display format or selected value on the page. Your presentation-tier architecture must recognize the need for these complex form elements and provide convenient and reliable mechanisms for producing them.

Displaying a List of Model Objects

No Web application is complete without a search page for choosing criteria and a results page showing a list of model objects meeting the search criteria. Search criteria pages are typically straightforward HTML forms with no new requirements for the presentation-tier architecture. Search result pages, on the other hand, can often present a host of interesting challenges for the presentation tier:

- You should be able to sort results by different columns, perhaps by clicking on the desired column title.
- You may need to buffer and page results, presenting only a subset of the results on the page at one time and allowing the user to scroll through the results via Previous and Next buttons.
- Although most search result pages are simple views of the model data with perhaps a link to drill in and edit the corresponding object, some list pages may require form elements such as checkboxes or input fields associated with each row. The architecture should therefore support the creation of HTML forms containing multiple model objects in a list.

Creating search result pages containing lists of model objects can be accomplished with JSP pages using straightforward scriptlet looping code or iterator custom tags without much trouble. You can also accommodate sorting, results pagination, and multiobject forms through relatively simple techniques. The presentation-tier architecture should define the standard approach for accomplishing these tasks in a manner consistent with the solutions for other display-related requirements.

Presenting Role-Based Views of Data

Most Web applications require user authentication in some form or another, and many applications limit or modify the data presented to the user depending on their authorization. It may be as simple as identifying pages in the site available to particular users and using the declarative security provided through the `web.xml` descriptor file for the Web application. If that's the case for you, consider yourself fortunate. Web applications commonly require much more sophisticated role- or user-based control of the pages and data presented. Some typical requirements include the following:

- Selected pages or whole areas of the site are available or off limits based on user or role.
- Navigation devices such as menus, navigation bars, and hyperlinks must reflect the user or role by eliminating or disabling links leading to off-limit pages.
- Pages may be available to certain users or roles but exhibit display differences or limited functionality depending on the user. Forms may treat some fields as read-only for certain users, for example, or omit certain information completely.

- Page display and functionality may differ depending on both user information and attribute information in the model object itself. For example, modifying customer information might require that the user be a salesperson in that customer's region.

Are you beginning to get the picture? Many application-development efforts have abandoned the simplistic declarative security model offered by J2EE in favor of a custom-built authorization framework providing some or all of these features. The presentation-tier architecture you select should provide a mechanism for integrating with your chosen security system and meeting your role- and user-based display requirements.

Of course, writing your own authorization framework comes at a price. You are depending on your developers not only to understand all of the facets of writing a security framework but also to use it properly to protect your application's resources. Chapter 10 describes the WebLogic Server security model in detail, including the WebLogic Server extensions that allow you to address some of these authorization flexibility issues without writing your own security framework.

Internationalization

Your Web application may need to support internationalized content and display formats as part of a comprehensive globalization, localization, and internationalization (GLI) strategy.

Internationalization, often abbreviated as I18N, requires the removal of all language- and culture-specific items from the application source code and display pages. All displayed text, images with embedded text, informational and error messages, button labels, and other language-specific resources should be packaged independently from the application and presented using language-specific mechanisms in the display pages. Date formats, monetary and numeric formats, and other display formats may also require internationalization.

Localization, abbreviated L10N, takes this process one step further by tailoring the application look and feel, site content, currency conversions, business processes, and design considerations based on language and cultural considerations. More than just translating content, localization ensures that users feel the site has been designed specifically for them. Applications cannot be localized unless they are first internationalized.

Globalization seeks to ensure that all customers receive a similar quality of experience regardless of language, culture, and location. It builds on internationalization and localization and ensures the proper language- and location-specific handling of customer interactions at all levels in the system. This might include global site hosting, global content management, multilingual customer support facilities, global invoicing and fulfillment, and many other issues not directly related to the Web application itself.

A complete discussion of internationalization is beyond the scope of this book. We will consider internationalization requirements when choosing a Web application architecture, but we will not include internationalized content or behavior in our example applications.

Display Flexibility and Maintainability

The final display-related requirement emphasizes planning for the future in the design of the Web application.

First, unless the application is a short-lived throwaway, it will undergo maintenance and enhancement at some time in the future. Plan for this eventuality by designing in the right level of flexibility and modularity from the start.

Next, don't assume that the layout, look and feel, style sheets, images, logos, or any other visual elements will remain constant over time. Customer-facing Web sites are part of the brand image of the company, and companies are continually updating their sites to adopt the latest marketing and branding directions. Even internal sites can undergo significant modification in display characteristics when functionality is added or removed—for example, if new groups of users are given access or usability issues require major changes.

Finally, your site may need to be flexible enough to use in an application service provider (ASP) environment. The site appearance, colors, behaviors, and even layout may need to be easily customizable for multiple clients. You cannot copy the site and tweak it for the new client; you'll end up with multiple copies of the site to maintain, enhance, and update with desired functionality and look-and-feel changes. That's not where you want to be.

How might these relatively fuzzy requirements for flexibility and maintainability affect the presentation-tier architecture?

- Style sheets are critical for defining fonts, sizes, colors, and other display attributes. Every single table cell, input field, and piece of text on the site should use a `class` attribute.
- Define page layout details such as the overall HTML table structure in a way that allows modification in the future. For example, if the header, body, footer, and gutter contents and sizes are specified on every page in the site (a technique often referred to as the *composite view pattern*), how easy will it be to shuffle the table structure around and move advertisements from the left to the right gutter? Not easy at all if you must edit every page to change the `<jsp:include .../>` elements.
- Modularity of display content is important. Any common element, whether it is a copyright message or a navigation bar, should be separated from surrounding content and placed in its own JSP page for inclusion via `jsp:include` elements or `<%@ include file ... %>` directives.

We discuss various template and page-assembly options in Chapter 3 to provide some best practices related to display flexibility and maintainability, and in Chapter 4 we build an example Web application that demonstrates many of the topics outlined here.

Form/Update Requirements

The requirements in the previous section dealt primarily with the flow of data from the model to the view and with the proper formatting and display of that data. This next set of presentation-tier requirements deals with data flow in the opposite direction, from the view back to model components, normally through the posting of HTML forms. Figure 2.3 illustrates the basic flow of this data and the role of the presentation tier in the transfer process. Remember that we're talking about only presentation-tier requirements in this section, so this discussion will not cover business-tier requirements, such as transactional behavior or object-relational mapping.

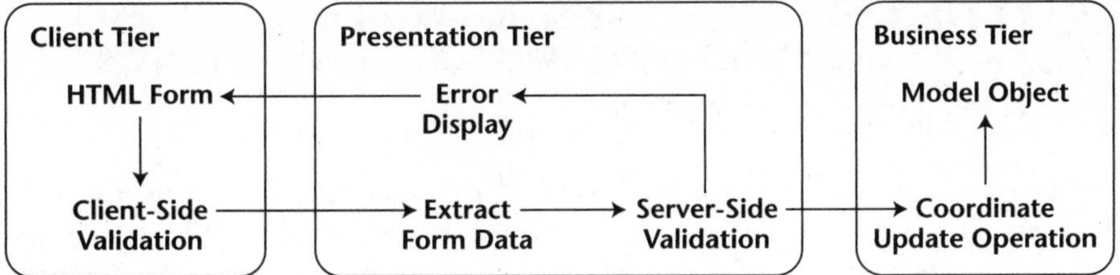

Figure 2.3 Steps required during form processing.

In this section we walk through the process from the HTML form to the model object, highlighting the presentation-tier requirements. At a minimum, the architecture must support the following:

- *Client-side validation* to provide immediate feedback to users when input does not meet constraints
- *Extraction of HTML form data* to facilitate subsequent validation and transfer steps
- *Server-side validation* to catch input errors before transferring data to model objects
- *Display of errors and original data* in the HTML form to allow user correction and resubmission
- *Efficient interaction with the business tier* to coordinate transactions properly and meet the interface requirements imposed by the business-tier architecture without undue complexity

Client-Side Validation

Although client-side validation is not strictly part of the presentation-tier architecture, it's commonly used, and it's important in the overall design of the view-to-model transfer process. Users expect form pages to warn them if required fields are left blank or inconsistent selections are made, without requiring a round trip to the server. You can apply client-side validation techniques in a light manner, perhaps checking only for required fields, or your design can include heavier levels of validation, such as checking fields for valid formats and content consistent with other fields.

Client-side validation is almost universally performed with JavaScript code that is executed just before submitting the form contents to the target. Errors are often displayed in a JavaScript alert window, and the cursor is placed in the offending field. A detailed examination of the mechanisms for providing client-side validation is beyond the scope of this book.

You should recognize that including client-side validation of fields in your application does not eliminate the need for server-side validation of the same required fields and formatting rules. Users may turn off JavaScript in their browsers or bypass the validation in other ways, causing invalid data to be passed to the server for processing.

BEST PRACTICE Use client-side validation to enhance the usability of the application, but do not rely solely on it for field validation. Perform the same validation in the server-side processing.

Remember that all fields appearing on the HTML form are visible to the user if he or she looks at the HTML source, so creating spurious form submissions with bad input data or even different hidden field values is a trivial matter for someone who wants to bypass your validation and security requirements. Design accordingly.

Extracting Form Data

The HTML form data is presented to the server-side processing component, normally a servlet or JSP page, as a series of parameters in the `HttpServletRequest` object. The first step in server-side processing is normally extracting the form data and placing it in an intermediate Java object appropriate for server-side validation and subsequent transfer operations. The type of Java object is determined by the presentation-tier architecture, but it is often a simple JavaBean, Value Object, or other straightforward data structure. Normally the form data is not extracted directly into a model object if the model is implemented using EJB components because of the overhead of creating and discarding temporary entity beans.

Note that you can perform most server-side validation by examining the `HttpServletRequest` parameters themselves without first extracting the data to an intermediate object, but this direct-inspection technique has at least two negative effects:

- Directly examining request parameters places the validation logic in the presentation-tier component itself rather than encapsulating the validation rules in an object used exclusively for this purpose. Many server-side validation rules involve multiple form fields and their interrelationships, and this logic is best encapsulated in the object containing all the attributes.
- If errors are encountered during server-side validation, the intermediate object plays a valuable role in preserving the original form input data for redisplaying it to the user. Without this object, it can be difficult to redisplay the HTML form properly to the user. We'll discuss this requirement in more detail in a moment.

BEST PRACTICE Extract HTML form data to a special-purpose intermediate object before performing server-side validation to improve encapsulation and assist in redisplaying the form data in case of validation errors.

You can extract HTML form data with an ugly and error-prone process of retrieving the parameter values field by field from the `HttpServletRequest` and placing them in the corresponding attributes of the intermediate object using code like this:

```
person.setLastName(request.getParameter("lastName"));
```

Instead, the presentation tier should provide helper methods or standard techniques for extracting form data and placing it in the intermediate object. One example is the

`<jsp:setProperty ... />` element discussed in Chapter 1. An asterisk in the `property` attribute signals that the run-time processing should use reflection to examine the `HttpServletRequest` and call set methods on the bean for each matching parameter in the request.

Server-Side Validation

Once the HTML form data has been placed in an intermediate object, the presentation-tier components should perform server-side validation to identify problems with the incoming data, collect all of the resulting error messages, and display them to the user. Server-side validation should include simple required-field checks as well as all formatting validation, interrelated field rules, and foreign-key constraints.

Do not use the database constraints to perform input validations. The database may very well have the same validation rules embedded in constraints, but you should not use these constraints as the primary line of defense against such data errors. Catching the problems during server-side validation will avoid starting and rolling back transactions in the business tier of your application. This will improve system performance and reduce database-related exceptions, which might mask or be confused with true errors needing attention during testing or production operation.

BEST PRACTICE **Perform all server-side validation in application code rather than by relying on database constraints. This improves performance and reduces confusion during testing.**

Don't stop performing server-side validation upon encountering the first error. The validation process should collect all errors encountered and make them available for display to the user for input correction and resubmission, as discussed next.

BEST PRACTICE **Server-side validation should collect and return all errors encountered in the submitted data rather than stopping with the first error. This provides a clearer picture of the validation requirements and reduces user frustration.**

Displaying Errors

Errors discovered in server-side processing must be sent back to the client for display. This is easier said than done because users expect to see the original form and input data along with the error messages. The presentation-tier architecture must therefore include a mechanism for displaying the errors on the original HTML form and allowing resubmission through the same validation process.

Note that normally the input data is not contained in a model object yet, so the redisplayed form cannot simply be an instance of the typical HTML form display of a model object (a requirement outlined earlier in this chapter). Instead, you need to display the input data submitted during the previous iteration without having created a model object. This represents a new display requirement not previously identified because previously you always displayed the contents of a model object in the HTML form. How the presentation tier preserves the submitted input data and makes it available for the redisplay of the HTML form depends on the architecture.

The error messages themselves may be presented in a separate section of the redisplayed form, as shown in Figure 2.4, or may cause individual error messages to appear near the offending fields. Other designs may present the errors as a pop-up alert window and highlight offending fields with appropriate colors or formats. The type of error display is an application-specific requirement negotiated with the users, but the presentation-tier architecture may need to support general or field-specific errors and should be selected with this flexibility in mind.

Interacting with the Business Tier to Update Model Objects

Once the form data has been extracted and validated, the presentation tier must interact with the business-tier components to perform the desired object creation, update, or deletion. The details of this interaction will depend greatly on the business-tier architecture and the type of intermediate object created during HTML form extraction.

For example, if the intermediate object is serializable and the business-tier architecture leans toward a stateless-service approach, the presentation tier may simply pass the intermediate object to the business-tier services for processing. In this case, the requirement for the presentation-tier architecture is minimal beyond creating the intermediate object.

On the other hand, if the business-tier architecture uses entity bean EJB components as model objects, the data in the intermediate object must be transferred to the entity bean attributes in a user- or container-demarcated transaction in some tier of the application. This transfer may be performed in a business-tier component, such as a façade or service that accepts the intermediate object as input and performs all the necessary steps, in which case the presentation tier again doesn't have much to do. If the transfer from intermediate object to entity bean is a requirement of the presentation tier, however, it does represent a significant design requirement for the presentation-tier architecture.

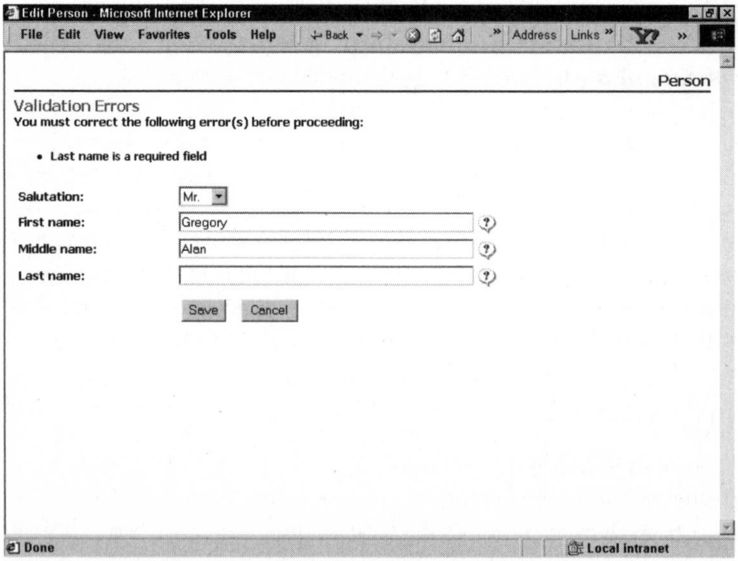

Figure 2.4 Typical validation error display.

Confused? It boils down to this: Depending on the specifics of the business-tier architecture and interfaces, the presentation-tier requirements may include more or less work associated with preparing the model objects for update. You need answers to questions such as these:

- Does the business tier provide a set of services using simple beans or data structures as parameters? Can you use the same beans or structures for the intermediate objects used during parameter extraction and server-side validation?
- Must the presentation tier coordinate transactions and transfer data directly to entity-bean model components? Can the business tier provide a façade or service that performs this task?

You must consider business-tier and presentation-tier architecture together to produce a good, efficient design. A key goal is to provide the right level of separation and encapsulation of the work required to perform the overall HTML form-to-model object transfer process without requiring numerous extra bean objects and hundreds of lines of related get/set transfer code. Don't lose sight of this goal in your zeal to minimize coupling between the tiers or create reusable services.

BEST PRACTICE Presentation-tier architecture requirements depend on the business-tier architecture and interfaces. Design the overall architecture with the requirements of both tiers in mind to avoid unnecessary complexity.

Obviously, the presentation-tier architecture is a little more complicated than just some JSP pages and a servlet for handling forms. The next few sections will round out the presentation-tier requirements.

Navigation Requirements

The previous sections outlined the requirements for the presentation of model data and the processing of form submissions as an isolated event. But in a large Web application, the individual search pages, results pages, model display pages, HTML forms, and other pages are all connected to form the overall Web site. Users navigate through the Web site performing the desired activities and receiving the proper display pages by clicking on appropriate hyperlinks or navigation-control elements in the site. These navigation activities impose significant requirements on the presentation-tier architecture.

Defining the related presentation-tier requirements depends less on how navigation is accomplished visually than on the answers to questions such as these:

- How are these navigational controls and links established? Does each page have hard-coded links representing all of the paths available to the user?
- Will individual pages or sections of pages be reused in multiple areas of the current application or in other applications?
- Does the presence or absence of navigation links depend on some state in the system, such as an attribute of a model object or the identity of the user? Where are these rules implemented?

- On which page does the user end up after submitting a form and performing a processing step? Is this target page hard-coded in the processing component? How is branching logic that depends on the outcome of the processing implemented?
- Does the site guard against multiple form submissions and improper use of the back/forward capability of browsers? Can the user safely bookmark pages deep within the site?

These are significant and involved questions. The answers applicable in your application may drive your presentation-tier architecture in many different ways and require significant infrastructure development. We'll boil these questions and issues down to three main requirements: basic navigation definition, outcome-based navigation, and submission/bookmark controls.

Basic Navigation Definition

Web applications are complex, interconnected sets of pages tied together with hyperlinks and other navigational controls. The specific target page for each link or control must obviously be specified somewhere in the architecture, but not necessarily in the JSP pages themselves. It may be more consistent with good maintainability and flexibility to defer the actual page name definition to some other component in the presentation-tier architecture.

Consider the following example snippet from a display JSP page that establishes a simple link to edit a particular person:

```
...
Display person elements
...
<a href="EditPerson.jsp?id=...">[Edit]</a>
```

The target page, `EditPerson.jsp`, is hard-coded in the JSP page, making it painful to change the name of the target page without affecting every page that links to this target page. Reusing this display page elsewhere in this application or subsequent applications is also made more difficult. The coupling between pages is strong and implemented in the pages themselves.

Contrast that snippet with a different JSP snippet using a general servlet as a controller to accept requests and pass the user to the proper page:

```
...
Display person elements
...
<a href="ActionServlet?action=editperson&id=...">[Edit]</a>
```

The `ActionServlet` would receive the `action` parameter in the `HttpServletRequest` and perform a lookup or conditional branching of some sort to determine the name of the target page, forwarding or redirecting the user to that page, as appropriate. The specific technique used to perform this activity is determined by the presentation-tier architecture.

We recommend that you use some form of controller servlet or other similar mechanism outside of the JSP pages themselves to define basic site navigation. Therefore, the presentation-tier architecture must enable and support this capability.

BEST PRACTICE Avoid hard-coding navigational links and controls in JSP pages. Use controller servlets or other presentation-tier components to define basic navigational logic.

Outcome-Based Navigation

Defining outcome-based navigation is, in some ways, the flip side of the previous section. In the previous section, the navigational information was removed from the JSP pages and placed in a controller layer of some sort. In this section, the outcome of a processing step defines the next page displayed for the user, and this navigational information too must be removed from an inappropriate place and delegated to the controller layer.

For example, a processing step that creates new users on the site may want to send a user to the `CreationComplete.jsp` page if the creation was successful and to the `CreationProblem.jsp` page if not. Where are these specific page names defined in the application? The name could be embedded in the processing component itself, as indicated by the following code snippet:

```
public void service(HttpServletRequest request,
                    HttpServletResponse response)
    throws ServletException, IOException
{
    ...
    boolean result = service.createUser(userinfo);
    String nextpage =
        (result ? "CreationComplete.jsp" : "CreationProblem.jsp");
    RequestDispatcher disp = request.getRequestDispatcher(nextpage);
    disp.forward(request, response);
}
```

In this crude example, the processing servlet will forward control depending on the outcome of the call to the service. Clearly, the hard-coding of the target pages in the servlet affects the maintainability and reusability of this component, making the coupling with the JSP page names and locations very strong. Although the controller or processing servlet is the right layer to determine the target page, hard-coding the names in the servlet is not appropriate.

We recommend that navigation information that depends on outcomes of processing steps, model object states, or other branching conditions should be defined in the controller layer using an external definition mechanism, such as a properties file or XML descriptor, to define the target page names. This minimizes coupling between controller-layer components and the display pages and allows for efficient maintenance and reuse of both controller and display components.

BEST PRACTICE Avoid hard-coding page names in controller servlets and other components. Use an external file or descriptor to define page names based on outcomes or branch conditions.

Submission/Bookmark Controls

It's a common lament for Web application designers: Site development would be easy if it weren't for the users! Users will explore every corner of the site, set and use bookmarks deep in the site, and make use of the Back and Forward functions of their browsers with wild abandon. Be prepared for the worst!

Although a complete discussion of this topic is beyond the scope of this book, there is at least one concrete requirement that you should impose on the presentation-tier architecture: The site must guard against multiple submissions or out-of-order submissions of HTML forms. Users may, by accident or intent, submit a form one time and perhaps continue to navigate through the site, then back up to the HTML form page again, and resubmit the form with the same or modified data. How will your site react if the form was used to place an order or create a new record?

Solutions to this problem vary from architecture to architecture, but they normally employ some form of token or timestamp in the form that is good for only a single submission. Preventing multiple form submissions and handling them properly when they occur represent important requirements for the presentation-tier architecture.

BEST PRACTICE Include safeguards in your presentation-tier components to prevent erroneous form submissions and handle user bookmarking and back/forward navigation properly.

We've barely scratched the surface of issues related to navigation definition and the handling of special situations and conditions caused by user activity. Clearly, additional requirements might affect the presentation-tier architecture, such as support for navigation bars or menus, security-based navigation behavior, customizing navigation on a per-user basis, and many others. The important thing to note is that achieving good maintainability and reusability of presentation-tier components imposes significant requirements on the presentation-tier architecture, which must be taken into consideration during architecture selection and design.

Building a Presentation-Tier Architecture

The preceding sections identified a number of important requirements imposed on the presentation-tier architecture based on typical user-interface requirements and good design principles. These requirements represent a tall order for any architecture and may seem somewhat daunting at this point.

Fortunately, you don't have to build a presentation-tier architecture from scratch unless you feel compelled to do so. Some kind folks in the open-source community have already built it for you; it's called Struts.

We need to finish up our general discussion of the presentation-tier architecture selection process with a few additional items, and then we will present a brief comparison of a typical hand-made presentation-tier architecture and the Struts architecture using the requirements discussed so far as the basis for comparison.

Other Architecture Considerations

Requirements imposed on the presentation-tier architecture are important but are not the only considerations that affect the selection or design of an architecture. Essentially, the requirements specify a minimum set of behaviors for the presentation tier but do not actually define the solution. The solution itself should take into account other factors, such as the following:

- How important is the separation of roles between so-called *creative* resources working with site visual design, page layout, and overall look and feel and the J2EE development resources? Is JSP scriplet code completely off limits or simply discouraged and replaced with `jsp:useBean` elements or custom tags where possible?
- What is the experience level of the J2EE development team? What about the team expected to perform ongoing maintenance and enhancements after the application rolls out? There is almost always a trade-off between flexibility and maintainability of the design and the apparent complexity of the original development. Find the right balance.
- Does it make sense to impose requirements such as the elimination of hard-coded navigation links based on the site size, need for reuse, and other factors? Can a compromise set of rules be established that mandates the use of controller navigation control in some areas but not others?
- Will performance be adversely affected by presentation-tier design decisions? Creating additional layers in the architecture and steps in processes such as form submission have a performance cost associated with them. Weigh this cost against the benefits of the additional design elements to justify the design.
- Is the design consistent with WebLogic Server clustering and other production-environment deployment practices and options? Don't preclude the use of clustering through some design feature or assumption, for example, or assume that the Web application will always be collocated with the EJB components if this is not true.

In the end, the presentation-tier architecture design or selection process comes down to a judgment call based on all of the available information and requirements. There is no single correct answer or even a set of hard-and-fast rules to go by. What makes sense for one application or development team may not make sense for a different development effort.

One fact remains: The presentation tier defines the behaviors closest to the user, and because of this it is subject to the highest variability of inputs, must react to the need for constant change, and can make or break your development effort. Don't rush the design decisions or jump on any given framework bandwagon unless you understand the details and have a clear picture of the costs and benefits for your application.

Candidate Presentation-Tier Architectures

In this section, we briefly compare two candidate presentation-tier architectures, summarizing their individual solutions to the presentation-tier requirements outlined in the previous section. The first architecture, a *JSP-centric architecture,* uses JSP pages alone to meet the presentation-tier requirements in a fairly *low-tech* approach to the problem. The second architecture, a *servlet-centric architecture,* uses JSP pages and servlets in a more complex and flexible model-view-controller design and represents a more state-of-the-art presentation-tier architecture.

The comparison will be performed by examining the components and techniques necessary to build a simple *Person Tracker* Web application using each architecture. The Person Tracker application maintains a list of people and allows users to view the list and edit individuals. It employs a simple stateless service Java object, `Person-Service`, as the business-tier component responsible for managing model objects. `PersonService` is a simple Java class that maintains a list of `Person` objects in memory and provides a straightforward interface for retrieving, creating, and updating people.

The complete source code for both solutions, along with a detailed walkthrough of their construction in each architecture, is available on the companion Web site (http://www.wiley.com/compbooks/masteringweblogic). This bonus material is also very valuable as an introduction to the Struts framework if you are unfamiliar with it. We'll be using Struts to build our main example program in the book, so we encourage you to download and examine the bonus material and the source code for the Person Tracker example program.

JSP-Centric Architecture

The JSP-centric architecture we chose for this comparison uses only a single presentation-tier technology, JSP pages, to produce a Web application meeting the presentation-tier requirements. The emphasis is on reducing complexity by eliminating all layers, technologies, and components not absolutely necessary to the design.

Figure 2.5 presents a high-level picture of the JSP components and their interactions in the architecture. Note that although everything in the presentation tier is implemented as JSP pages, there is still a controller component (called an *action page* in this architecture). This approach is basically an all-JSP implementation of the model-view-controller architecture.

The following list summarizes the JSP-centric solution according to the major presentation-tier requirements outlined in the previous section. See the downloadable example programs and bonus material for a detailed discussion of each of these areas.

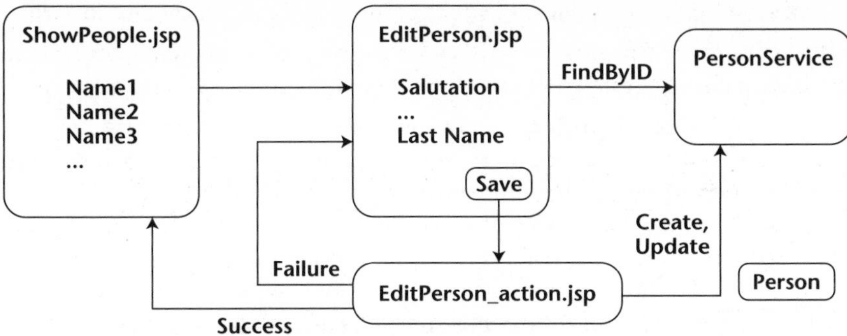

Figure 2.5 JSP-centric architecture components.

JSP pages perform display tasks. JSP pages are responsible for all of the display-related requirements outlined in the previous section. JSP pages fetch data from the service, create list displays by looping through collections of model objects, and create HTML forms containing model data for display and modification.

Action JSP pages process form submissions. Specialized JSP pages, called action pages, are used to process HTML form submissions. Action pages extract form data using `jsp:getProperty` or similar techniques, validate the data, and interact with the business-tier components. Errors are handled by forwarding back to the form page after creating a list of errors in the `HttpServlet-Request`. Form data is redisplayed on the form for correction by special code that looks for it in the request.

Navigation controlled by view and action pages. Basic navigation definition and outcome-based navigation are implemented in the JSP display pages and action pages using straightforward links and URLs. Navigation information could be stored in external files to reducing coupling at the expense of complexity. Submission controls are implemented using a custom token-based approach involving a hidden HTML form field and matching session attribute. HTTP redirects are used after form submissions, where possible, to alleviate bookmark and browser-navigation issues.

The benefits of the JSP-centric approach include the following:

- The number of components required to build a given application is small.
- The number of technologies used is small, reducing the learning curve for inexperienced developers.

The drawbacks include the following:

- Architecture tends to produce a tightly coupled application with hard-coded page names.
- Action JSP pages are primarily Java code but cannot be developed, compiled, and debugged as easily as pure Java code.

- Reuse of processing and validation logic is hampered by its placement in form-specific action JSP pages.

We recommend the JSP-centric architecture for small to medium-sized Web applications having a relatively static organization and a low potential for reuse of presentation-tier components, especially for development teams lacking the experience and skills required to implement more complex architectures properly. In these types of applications, the coupling and reuse drawbacks of the JSP-centric approach are outweighed by the benefits.

BEST PRACTICE **Consider a simple JSP-centric approach for small to medium-sized projects if the benefits of simplicity and reduced learning curve outweigh the reuse and flexibility drawbacks.**

Servlet-Centric Architecture

The servlet-centric architecture chosen for this comparison leverages the open-source servlet-centric framework called Struts to avoid building the required support components and logic from scratch. We're going to use a small subset of the components and features in the Struts framework, concentrating primarily on the features related to form handling and navigation.

Figure 2.6 presents a high-level view of the JSP, servlet, form, and model components and their interactions in the servlet-centric architecture chosen for this application.

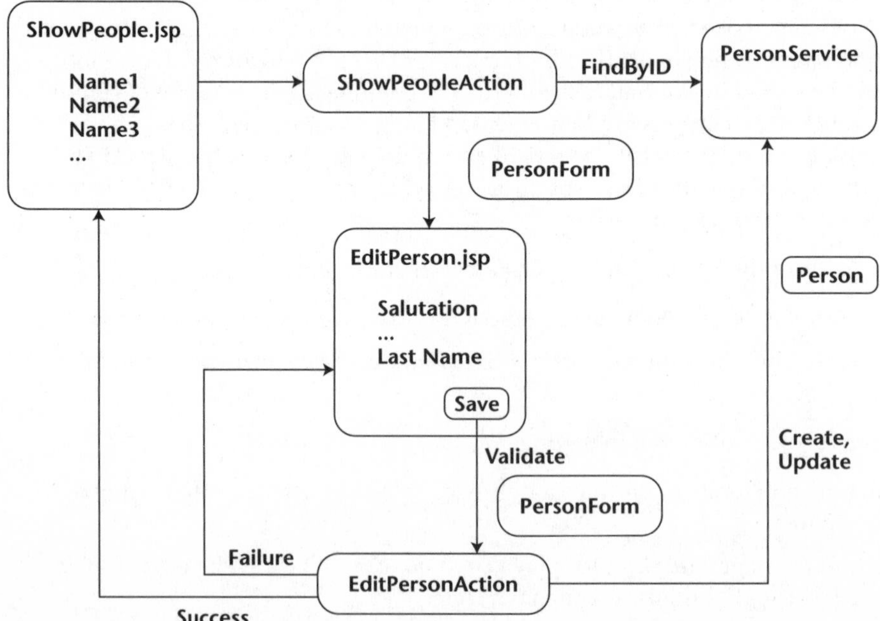

Figure 2.6 Servlet-centric architecture components.

There are still two main JSP pages, `ShowPeople.jsp` and `EditPerson.jsp`, but the components responsible for processing forms and controlling navigation have changed considerably in the new architecture. A new `PersonForm` object has been introduced for use by the `EditPerson.jsp` page and related processing, and the diagram does not include configuration and properties files required by the architecture. More components are required in the servlet-centric approach, overall, than in the JSP-centric architecture depicted in Figure 2.5.

Let's list the presentation-tier requirements in the same manner as before and examine how the servlet-centric architecture meets them in our example application. We again refer you to the downloadable source code and bonus material for a detailed examination of this solution.

JSP pages perform display tasks. JSP pages are again responsible for all of the display-related requirements. JSP pages use special Struts custom tags to create HTML forms, favor retrieving model data from the `HttpServletRequest` rather than fetching it directly, and avoid hard-coding links to other pages by referencing controllers rather than display pages. Struts also provides tags for internationalization and simple role-based conditional logic.

Controller components process form submissions. A centralized controller servlet invokes *action* classes to process HTML form submissions and interact with business-tier components. Specialized Java objects, called *form beans*, are used to extract and validate the HTML form data. Errors are handled by forwarding back to the form page after creating a list of errors in the `HttpServletRequest` for display by Struts tags on the form. Form data is automatically redisplayed on the form for correction.

Navigation controlled by configuration files. Basic and outcome-based navigation information is stored in an external configuration file, `struts-config.xml`. This file is also used by the controller servlet to relate JSP display pages, form beans, and action classes across the application. Submission controls are implemented using a built-in token-based approach involving a hidden HTML form field and matching session attribute. HTTP redirects are used after form submissions, where possible, to alleviate bookmark and browser-navigation issues.

The benefits of the Struts-based servlet-centric approach include the following:

- Display logic, processing logic, and form validation are encapsulated in different components, improving application flexibility and reuse.
- Pure Java code in controller components is easier to develop with IDE tools than JSP action pages.
- Navigation information is external to the components and code, improving flexibility and reuse.
- Developers can be found with experience using the Struts framework, jump-starting your development effort.

Drawbacks of this approach include the following:

- The learning curve increases, due to additional components and files required for operation.

- Dependence on an open-source framework such as Struts may become an issue in the long term.

We recommend the servlet-centric architecture for medium-sized to large Web applications, especially if they require flexible organization and have a substantial potential for component reuse. Using a prebuilt framework such as Struts helps reduce the development effort and complexity of the application and is important in long-term maintenance.

BEST PRACTICE Favor the servlet-centric approach for medium-sized to large projects unless there are strong arguments related to complexity or learning curve. The flexibility and reuse benefits of a servlet-centric approach almost always exceed the costs of learning and adopting the architecture for all but the simplest projects.

Additional Frameworks

In this section we've explored two candidate presentation-tier architectures, but clearly there are many more options to choose from. Custom-built architectures might combine elements from the JSP-centric approach and servlet-centric approach, or even adopt different approaches in different areas of the application. Remember, however, that custom-built architectures have an inherent disadvantage relative to standard frameworks such as Struts when it comes time to introduce new developers to a project or hand the code off to others for long-term maintenance and enhancements: No external developer is going to know your custom-built framework on day one.

There are also very good alternative open-source frameworks available if the Struts framework does not meet your particular needs:

- *Turbine* is an open-source framework from the same organization that developed the Struts architecture. Turbine represents a very strong implementation of the model-view-controller architecture providing enhanced flexibility, but it is arguably more complex than other controller-centric architectures such as Struts. Visit the Turbine home page at http://jakarta.apache.org/turbine for more information.
- *WebWork* is a recent addition to the open-source architecture offerings. Developed by a group of people at `SourceForge.net`, headed by the prolific designer and programmer Rickard Öberg, the WebWork framework supports both JSP-centric and servlet-centric development. Like Struts, it provides a custom-tag library for use in display JSP pages, an `Action`-based controller architecture, and facilities for internationalization and external message catalogs. It also provides a powerful Expression Language allowing very compact expressions in the place of unwieldy JSP scriptlet code and `jsp:useBean` elements. See http://www.opensymphony.com/webwork for more information on WebWork.

We've barely scratched the surface of what's out there today. If you are making Web application architecture decisions for a large project, avail yourself of all the information and resources available on the Internet to make a well-informed decision appropriate for your organization and project. Don't choose an architecture based on immediate reactions or previous experience. It's very important to the project that you choose well and get started in the right direction.

Chapter Review

We've covered a lot of information in this chapter. We began by defining some key architecture concepts and design patterns related to Web applications, including the model-view-controller pattern.

We then defined the requirements of a robust presentation-tier architecture in terms of display capabilities, form submission and processing requirements, and navigation controls. We discussed how meeting these requirements represents a significant design challenge for a home-grown, custom-developed architecture, thereby leading us to search for a prebuilt presentation-tier framework to speed development and improve maintenance.

Two candidate architectures were then compared in the context of the presentation-tier requirements defined earlier, and recommendations were provided to guide your selection of presentation-tier architecture based on project and team attributes.

It's time to apply what you learned in Chapters 1 and 2. In the next two chapters, we will design and build the presentation-tier components of a larger example application. This example program, a hotel reservation Web site, will provide a realistic platform for our examination of deployment issues, JMS best practices, security, application management, Web Services, and business-tier architecture selection in succeeding chapters.

CHAPTER

3

Designing an Example J2EE Application

In this chapter and the next, we explore the design and construction of a realistic example application. By realistic, we mean an example of sufficient size and complexity that key technology elements are useful and demonstrated in the example. The example will also help us explore decisions you must make during application development in WebLogic Server and will provide a context for sidebars and notes on best practices.

This chapter details the design of the presentation-tier layer of a fairly large and complex J2EE application. We'll cover different topics related to the example program throughout the book. For example, Chapter 4 walks through many of the presentation-tier components and discusses the techniques used in their construction. Chapter 7 details the design and development of the business-tier components and their interaction with the database.

We'll discuss issues and decisions in roughly the same order they were encountered during the actual design and development of the example application. We'll begin by examining the system requirements for the example application, a Web-based hotel reservation system.

Application Requirements

The example application is a Web-based reservation system for hotels, bed-and-breakfasts, and resorts, suitable for hosting in an application service provider (ASP) environment.

Specific requirements include the following:

- The system must provide a user site with a basic property search, pricing, room availability, and reservation capability.
- Property information must be created and maintained through an administration site providing pages for maintenance of property data including basic property information, room types, rate, inventory, and targeted marketing offers. Properties must be able to view and maintain their own information through the administration site.
- The visual appearance of the site must be easily configured to support multiple installations in an ASP environment.
- Users must be able to create profiles containing guest information to speed subsequent reservations.
- Marketing offers should be targeted to users based on the last property search performed or hotel selected.
- The application must employ a relational database to store all property, guest, and reservation information.

Sound challenging enough? Don't forget the ever-present requirements for high performance and good scalability, maintainability, and reliability. Sounds like a job for J2EE and WebLogic Server!

We're going to call our Web-based reservation application *bigrez.com*.

Business Domain Models

The *bigrez.com* system employs a relational database to store all business domain objects. Although Chapter 7 provides object models and discusses the business domain and business-tier components in more detail, we'll present the database model at this point to illustrate the scope of the business domain and provide a framework for discussing presentation-tier design. Figure 3.1 shows the logical database design of *bigrez.com*.

The data model in Figure 3.1 illustrates the key objects and relationships present in the business domain of this system. For example, each property has a set of room types, with related inventory and rate records defining the availability and price for that type of room for a particular date.

Our task in the user-facing Web application portion of *bigrez.com* is to hide this complex set of business objects and related processes and give the user an easy-to-use, step-by-step process for finding and booking the right room on the right dates. The administration site will present a view of this data more directly related to the database design.

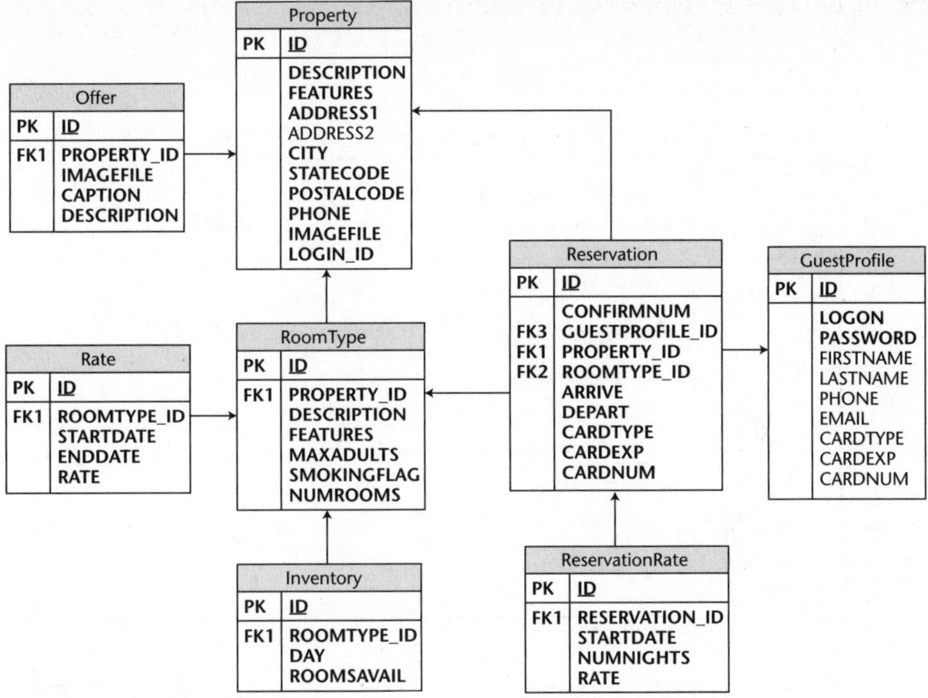

Figure 3.1 bigrez.com logical database design.

Presentation Requirements

The *bigrez.com* user-facing site must walk the user through the reservation process by presenting forms and pages in a logical order and building the reservation visually on one side of the screen. Although the specific appearance and layout of the site may vary from installation to installation, the basic layout illustrated in Figure 3.2 shows the key elements of the display.

The user will interact primarily with HTML forms and content presented in the work area, while the progress of the reservation is displayed in the reservation information area. The reservation information area can also be used as a navigation device to revisit a previous page in the process (for example, to change dates) by clicking on links in the area.

The basic reservation process is illustrated by Figure 3.3. This diagram represents the basic course through the reservation process. The actual process is subject to many detours and alternate courses not depicted in this figure, based on user navigation decisions. We'll cover some of these alternate courses during the discussion of the reservation information area later in the chapter.

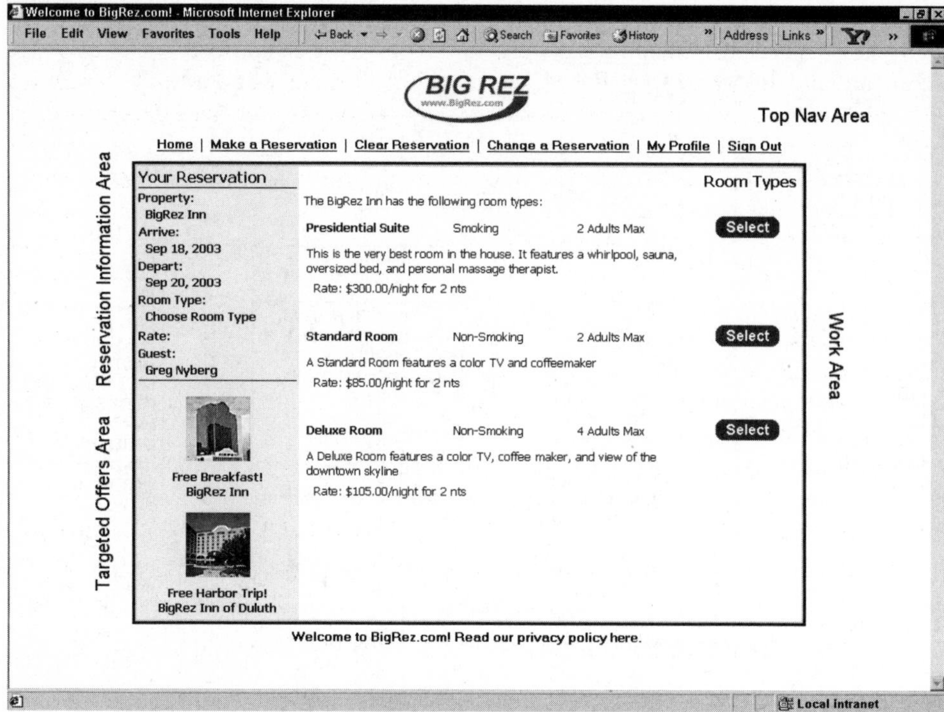

Figure 3.2 bigrez.com basic presentation layout.

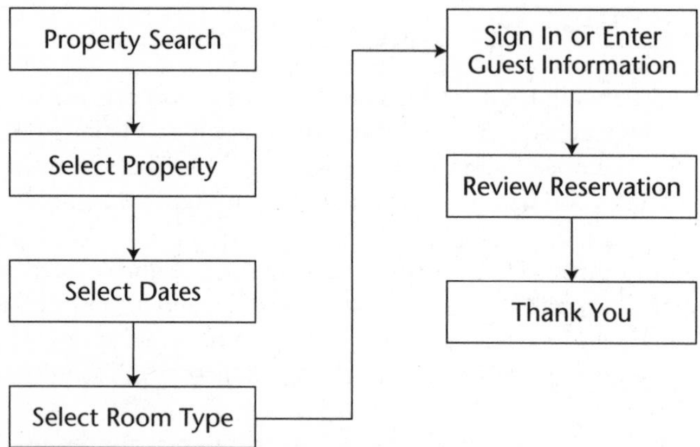

Figure 3.3 bigrez.com reservation process.

We must implement many business rules related to site navigation and the reservation process in the presentation tier of the application. For example, the user may not skip ahead and choose a room type before selecting a property and arrival/departure dates because the available room types are dependent on these choices. The user may, however, skip ahead and sign in or provide guest information at any point in the process. Note that the Web application architecture defines, among other things, where business rules such as these are implemented in the presentation tier.

The *bigrez.com* application also requires an administration site allowing authorized users to create and maintain the properties and related information used by the reservation process. Figure 3.4 presents an example page in the administration site, showing the basic structure of a page.

Both the user site and the administration site must meet all of the presentation-tier requirements discussed in Chapter 2, including display-related requirements, form/update requirements, and navigation requirements.

The *bigrez.com* site is not a small application. There are more than 20 JSP pages in the user site and another 15 pages in the administration site. We believe an example application of this size provides a more realistic platform for the construction, deployment, and management discussions to follow.

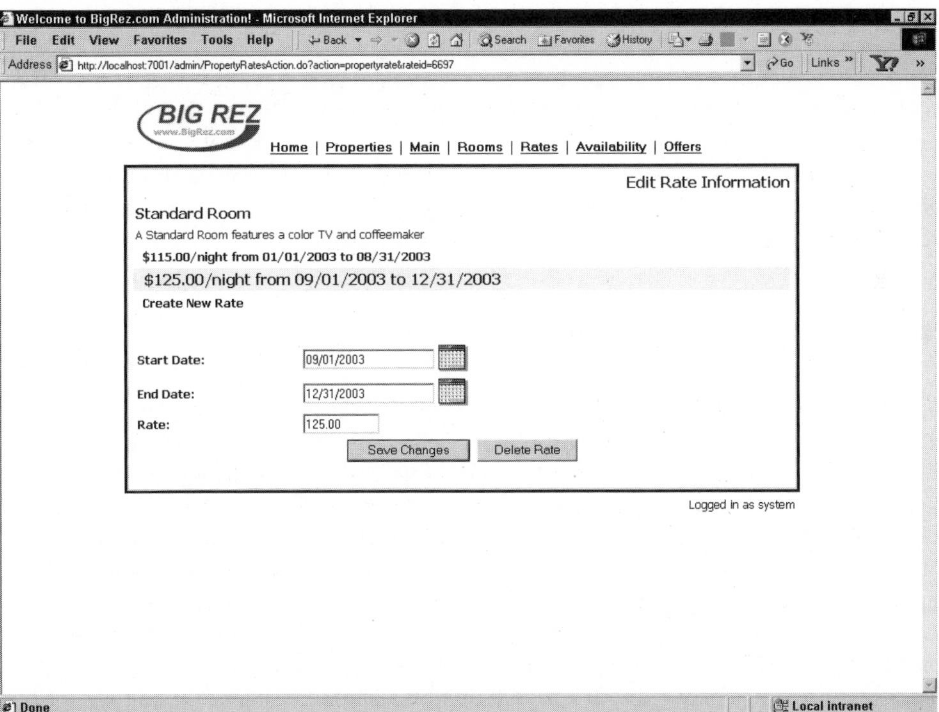

Figure 3.4 bigrez.com administration site example page.

Web Application Architecture

Chapter 2 discussed the selection of a Web application architecture and presented a brief comparison of two specific architectures: JSP-centric and servlet-centric. We need to choose an architecture for *bigrez.com* that will meet the requirements and provide good maintainability and flexibility.

As discussed in Chapter 2, there are advantages and disadvantages to both architectures. Although the JSP-centric approach is simpler, and might make our job easier in this chapter and the next as we design and construct the example application, the resulting architecture would not be suitable for many medium-sized to large applications. We're focusing on best practices in this book, and we feel a servlet-centric approach should be considered a best practice for most production applications.

The Web application architecture for *bigrez.com* will therefore adopt the servlet-centric architecture described in Chapter 2 and implemented in the Person Tracker example program, available in the bonus material on the companion Web site (http://www.wiley.com/compbooks/masteringweblogic). Display JSP pages will present beans, forms, and business data to the user, and user actions and submitted HTML forms will be processed by the `execute()` method in page-specific `Action` classes. The difference is that *bigrez.com* requires much more sophistication both in terms of navigation and interaction with the business-tier layer. We'll discuss both of these areas in detail in a later section.

One key aspect of the chosen architecture is that controller components are responsible for loading required data into the proper context for display in the JSP pages. `Action` classes should interact with the business-tier components to retrieve the desired data and place it in the `HttpServletRequest` before forwarding to the next display JSP page. If the JSP page includes an HTML form, the `Action` class will create a form bean and place it in the request for use by the page.

Presentation Approach

The servlet-centric architecture selected for *bigrez.com* uses JSP pages for all display-related components. JSP pages will therefore be used to display business data, forms, search results, and all visual elements that define the overall design of the site. As shown in Figure 3.2, the site includes navigation bars, headers and footers, and a left-side gutter containing the current reservation information and targeted offers. We must now decide how this overall table structure will be defined and who will be responsible for assembling the generated HTML into a single response to the user.

A very common design pattern, the *composite view pattern*, is often used for this purpose. This pattern recognizes the importance of placing individual pieces of content in separate view components, in our case either stand-alone JSP pages or snippets of JSP code. As discussed in the literature, the overall page is then assembled by some manager or controller in the architecture that knows the proper placement of each view component on the final page and is responsible for creating the top-level HTML tags and structure for the page. The specific technique used to include the separate view components is not defined by the pattern and can include translation-time `<%@ include ... %>` directives, dynamic `jsp:include` techniques, or more sophisticated techniques using helper objects or custom tags.

We'll employ the composite view pattern in the construction of our example application by breaking the overall page into six different view components, as illustrated by Figure 3.5. Each of these view components will be a separate, stand-alone JSP page included in the overall HTML response using the `jsp:include` dynamic include capability. The information generated by the primary display page will be located in the framed area to the right of the reservation information and offers areas in the left gutter.

So far, so good, but we're not done yet. Which component or page, exactly, is going to define the overall page structure, generate the top-level HTML tags such as `<body>` and `<table>`, and use `jsp:include` elements to assemble the page? Will each display page in the site include the proper view components to assemble the overall response, a commonly used technique we've labeled *self-assembly*? Or will some master page or template be responsible for creating the overall HTML response and including the specific display page in the response, a technique we've called *master page assembly*? Let's examine these two options in more detail and make a design decision for the *bigrez.com* example application.

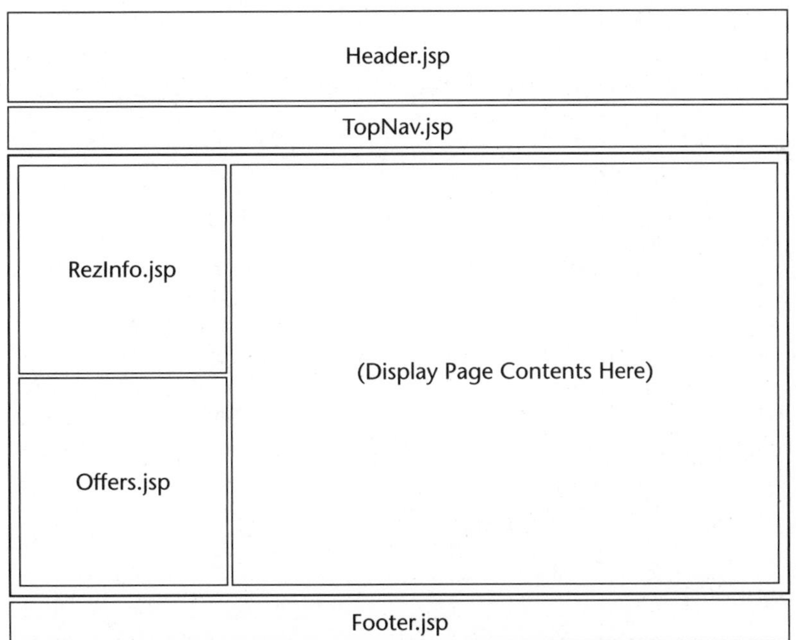

Figure 3.5 bigrez.com primary view components and layout.

Self-Assembly

In the self-assembly technique, the display page assembles all of the supporting pieces of the overall response. The display page basically includes the view components or code snippets required to create the proper HTML table structure and embed all of the headers, footers, and other visual elements in their proper locations. The `SimpleHome_SA.jsp` page, presented in Listing 3.1, illustrates how the *bigrez.com* home page might be constructed using the self-assembly technique.

```
<%@ page extends="com.bigrez.ui.MyJspBase" %>

<!DOCTYPE HTML PUBLIC "-//W3C//DTD HTML 4.0 Transitional//EN">

<html>
<head>

  <title>Welcome to BigRez.com!</title>

  <link rel=stylesheet type="text/css" href="css/StyleMaster.css">
  <script src="/js/DatePicker.js"></script>

</head>

<body bgcolor="#FFFFFF">

<table align="center" width="725" cellpadding="0" cellspacing="0"
       border="0">
  <tr>
    <td>
      <table align="center" cellpadding="0" cellspacing="10">
        <tr>
          <td align="center">
            <jsp:include page="/Header.jsp"></jsp:include>
          </td>
        </tr>
        <tr>
          <td>
            <jsp:include page="/TopNav.jsp"></jsp:include>
          </td>
        </tr>
      </table>
    </td>
  </tr>
</table>

<table align="center" width="725" cellpadding="0" cellspacing="0"
       border="0">
  <tr>
    <td width="175" valign="top" bgcolor="#EEEEEE">
```

Listing 3.1 SimpleHome_SA.jsp showing self-assembly.

```
        <table width="175" border="0" cellpadding="0" cellspacing="0">
        <tr>
          <td><jsp:include page="/RezInfo.jsp"/></td>
        </tr>
        <tr>
          <td><jsp:include page="/Offers.jsp"/></td>
        </tr>
        </table>
      </td>
      <td width="1" >
        <img src="images/space.gif" width="1" height="1">
      </td>
      <td width="550" valign="top">
        Home Page Contents Here..
      </td>
    </tr>
  </table>

  <table align="center" width="725" cellpadding="0" cellspacing="0"
         border="0">
    <tr>
      <jsp:include page="/Footer.jsp"/>
    </tr>
  </table>

  </body>
  </html>
```

Listing 3.1 *(continued)*

The five common components (Header.jsp, TopNav.jsp, RezInfo.jsp, Offers.jsp, and Footer.jsp) are included in the HTML response at the proper location in the overall page structure and table layout. In this simple technique, a large amount of the structure and layout would have to be copied to all display pages in the site, making maintenance and customization for different installations difficult. This simple type of self-assembly is suitable for only the smallest Web applications.

The basic self-assembly approach can be improved by combining the sections above and below the display page content itself in additional intermediate view components, as illustrated in the BetterHome_SA.jsp example in Listing 3.2.

```
<%@ page extends="com.bigrez.ui.MyJspBase" %>

<jsp:include page="/Top_SA.jsp">
  <jsp:param name="title" value="Welcome to BigRez.com!"/>
</jsp:include>

<table align="center" width="725"
```

Listing 3.2 BetterHome_SA.jsp showing improved self-assembly. *(continued)*

```
        cellpadding="0" cellspacing="0" border="0">
  <tr>
    <jsp:include page="/LeftSide_SA.jsp"/>
    <td width="1" >
      <img src="images/space.gif" width="1" height="1">
    </td>
    <td width="550" valign="top">
      Home Page Contents Here..
    </td>
  </tr>
</table>

<jsp:include page="/Bottom_SA.jsp"/>
```

Listing 3.2 *(continued)*

These new intermediate view components, `Top_SA.jsp`, `LeftSide_SA.jsp`, and `Bottom_SA.jsp`, basically contain the HTML and lower-level `jsp:include` tags previously contained in the display page itself, thereby reducing the amount of content copied on each display page. This technique represents a significant improvement over the simple technique, although it too has limitations as the complexity of the page structure surrounding the display content increases.

Because the title of the HTML page is now defined in the common `Top_SA.jsp`, each display page must provide the title to the included JSP using a request parameter:

```
<jsp:include page="/Top_SA.jsp">
  <jsp:param name="title" value="Welcome to BigRez.com!"/>
</jsp:include>
```

The `Top_SA.jsp` page must define the title using the passed-in request parameter:

```
<head>
  <title><%= request.getParameter("title") %></title>
  ...
</head>
```

Note that these self-assembly examples did not include all of the visual elements desired for the *bigrez.com* site (see Figure 3.2) in order to keep the examples simple. For example, the table containing the `LeftSide_SA.jsp` component and the actual display page content should have been surrounded by a two-color border. This would complicate the table structure copied in each display page.

Some form of self-assembly would probably work for the *bigrez.com* site, but we're looking for a technique that provides more flexibility and is easier to maintain. Imagine, for example, that we want to move the reservation information and targeted offers from the left gutter to the right gutter or that we need to add a completely new view component, perhaps something like a bread-crumb navigator, in the table containing the display page. Both of these changes would require touching all of the display pages to modify the table structure and `jsp:include` directives to reflect the new layout and components.

We'd also like to be able to deploy the same application for multiple hotel chains or customers. What if a potential new customer demands a different layout? The display pages or intermediate view components would have to be copied and edited to create a new layout, hurting maintainability, or would require conditional code to assemble the page differently based on the client, adding complexity. Neither solution provides a clean, easy mechanism to reuse the application in the face of significant layout changes.

No matter how sophisticated the include process becomes through the use of custom tags, view helpers, or even framework components meant for this purpose, the basic concept of self-assembly is inherently flawed. The individual display pages should know little or nothing about the way in which they are assembled to form the overall page, and self-assembly in all its forms breaks this rule.

What we need is an implementation of the *composite view* pattern that completely separates the overall structure and layout of the page from the contents of the display area. In the next section, we'll discuss one useful solution: *master page assembly*.

Master Page Assembly

The self-assembly approach, discussed in the previous section, separated the complete page contents into individual view components and made it the responsibility of the display page itself to include these components in the correct manner to build the full HTML response. The display page was in charge of the assembly process. In the master page assembly approach, on the other hand, the display page is simply another piece of content included in the overall response by a *master* page. As shown in Figure 3.6, the master page is now in charge of the assembly process and defines the overall page structure and layout.

This seems simple enough as a concept, but how can the same master page be used for all the different display pages in the site? How does the master page know which display page to include?

The trick to making this technique work is the run-time evaluation of a `jsp:include` directive placed in the master page to include the proper content page. Recall that the `jsp:include` directive had two basic forms. The first is a version using a statically defined page name:

```
<jsp:include page="/Home.jsp" />
```

The second is a version with the page name defined using a run-time expression:

```
<jsp:include page="<%= variablename %>" />
```

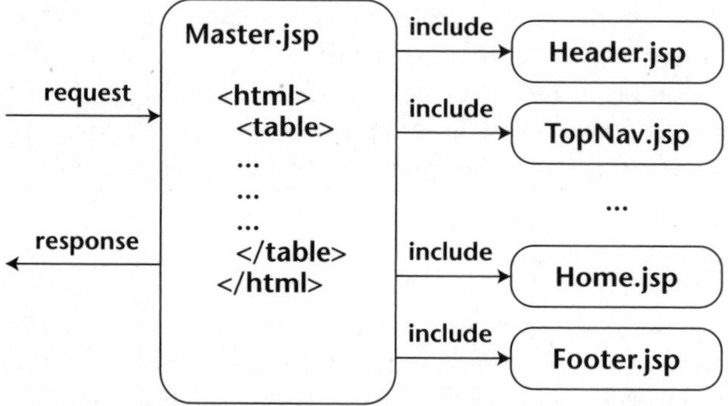

Figure 3.6 Comparison of self-assembly and master page assembly.

The version using a run-time expression as the page name provides one straightforward way to share the same master page across many display pages. In its simplest form, the `Master.jsp` page looks for a particular request parameter, `page`, and uses it in a `jsp:include` directive to include the proper page in the display area in the overall template defined in the master page:

```
...
<% String pagename = request.getParameter("page"); %>
...
<body>
<table>
...
      <% try { %>
      <jsp:include page="<%= pagename %>"/>
      <% }
         catch (IOException e) {
      %>
        <jsp:include page="Blank.jsp"/>
      <% } %>
...
</table>
</body>
```

All of the display pages are then accessed using URLs with the master page name and a query-string parameter defining the display page. For example, http://servername:port/Master.jsp?page=Home.jsp would invoke the `Master.jsp` master page and provide the name of the display page to include, `Home.jsp`. Hyperlinks within the pages would likewise specify URLs containing this syntax:

```
<A HREF="Master.jsp?page=ViewProperty.jsp">...</A>
```

Because we're using Struts to control navigation, if we choose this technique for *bigrez.com*, the mapping elements in `struts-config.xml` must also reflect this syntax:

```
...
<action path="/PropertyListAction"
        type="com.bigrez.ui.PropertyListAction"
        name="PropertyForm"
        scope="request"
        validate="false"
        input="/Master.jsp?page=PropertyList.jsp">
  <forward name="viewproperty"
           path="/Master.jsp?page=ViewProperty.jsp" redirect="false"/>
  <forward name="success"
           path="/Master.jsp?page=SelectDates.jsp" redirect="false"/>
</action>
...
```

We can now make changes to the overall site look and feel by modifying a single page, `Master.jsp`, without touching any of the display pages. These changes can include a wholesale rearranging of the page structure, the addition or deletion of included view components, and any other desired changes. The master page assembly technique is also forgiving during development because it reacts to a missing display page by displaying a blank page in the display area rather than causing an HTTP 404 error.

The use of URLs containing the master page name plus a parameter defining the included display page is a viable and useful approach for achieving the master page assembly technique in JSP-based Web applications. We could select this approach for *bigrez.com* and be perfectly content, but before we do, let's examine an alternative technique with some distinct advantages.

Master Page Assembly with Page Display Servlet

Including the `page` parameter on every request for a display page is not ideal. The full URL appears to the user in the browser, thereby exposing our technique, and all of the `path` elements in the `struts-config.xml` file must include the full *Master.jsp?page=...* syntax. In addition, hard-coding the name of the master page everywhere in the system makes it more difficult to use different master pages depending on some run-time variable or user characteristic. What we need is a mechanism to invoke the master page as if the URL contained the full syntax without requiring that all links and navigation paths contain this syntax.

We recommend the use of a *page display servlet* mapped to a particular file extension as the best mechanism to achieve the desired master-page-assembly behavior without requiring the full syntax on every link. Essentially, the desired display page is requested using an URL such as *Home.page*, and the `.page` extension causes WebLogic Server to invoke a particular servlet, `PageDisplayServlet`, which translates the request for *Home.page* into the equivalent request for *Master.jsp?page=Home.jsp* automatically.

Configuring this technique requires a few simple steps and components. First, the `PageDisplayServlet` is created to perform the desired mapping. As shown in Listing 3.3, this is a simple servlet that forwards the request to the `Master.jsp` page and includes the desired display page as a request parameter.

```
package com.bigrez.ui;

import java.io.IOException;
import javax.servlet.RequestDispatcher;
import javax.servlet.ServletException;
import javax.servlet.http.HttpServlet;
import javax.servlet.http.HttpServletRequest;
import javax.servlet.http.HttpServletResponse;

public class PageDisplayServlet extends HttpServlet
{
    private static org.apache.log4j.Category LOG =
        org.apache.log4j.Category.getInstance("PageDisplayServlet");

    private void handlePageRequest(HttpServletRequest request,
                                   HttpServletResponse response)
        throws ServletException, IOException
    {
        String page = request.getRequestURI();
        // drop leading / and .page suffix
        String newpage =
            page.substring(1, page.indexOf(".page")) + ".jsp";
        LOG.info("Forwarding to /Master.jsp?page=" + newpage);
        RequestDispatcher dispatch =
            request.getRequestDispatcher("/Master.jsp?page=" +
                                         newpage);
        dispatch.forward(request,response);
    }

    public void doGet (HttpServletRequest request,
                       HttpServletResponse response)
        throws ServletException, IOException
    {
        handlePageRequest(request,response);
```

Listing 3.3 PageDisplayServlet.java.

```
    }

    public void doPost (HttpServletRequest request,
                        HttpServletResponse response)
        throws ServletException, IOException
    {
        handlePageRequest(request,response);
    }
}
```

Listing 3.3 *(continued)*

Next, we configure WebLogic Server to invoke this servlet for requests such as *Home.page* by mapping the `.page` file extension to the `PageDisplayServlet` servlet in the `web.xml` descriptor file:

```
<servlet>
  <servlet-name>pagedisplay</servlet-name>
  <servlet-class>com.bigrez.ui.PageDisplayServlet</servlet-class>
</servlet>
...
<servlet-mapping>
  <servlet-name>pagedisplay</servlet-name>
  <url-pattern>*.page</url-pattern>
</servlet-mapping>
```

That's it! We can now employ the `.page` syntax for all of the hyperlinks in the system and leave the mapping from *Something.page* to *Master.jsp?page=Something.jsp* up to the `PageDisplayServlet` at request time. This change also simplifies the mapping elements in the `struts-config.xml` file:

```
<action path="/PropertyListAction"
        type="com.bigrez.ui.PropertyListAction"
        name="PropertyForm"
        scope="request"
        validate="false"
        input="/PropertyList.page">
  <forward name="viewproperty"
           path="/ViewProperty.page" redirect="false"/>
  <forward name="success"
           path="/SelectDates.page" redirect="false"/>
</action>
```

We could also use multiple master pages and have the `PageDisplayServlet` choose the correct master page based on user preferences or other run-time criteria.

We selected this version of the master-page-assembly approach for *bigrez.com* because of the benefits related to maintainability and customization. As you'll see when we walk through the example program in detail, the use of the `PageDisplay Servlet` helps keep the configuration files and links clean and simple.

Business-Tier Interfaces

Now that we've identified the mechanisms for displaying data and handling navigation and form submission, it is time to discuss the heart of any presentation-tier architecture: interfacing with business-tier components.

First, we need to look ahead a bit to Chapter 7, where we discuss the design and development of the EJB components for this application. Clearly the business-tier interfaces available to the Web application depend on the architecture of the business tier. Although we thoroughly discuss the choice of business-tier architecture in Chapter 7, what you need to know here is that we decided to make heavy use of entity beans and container-managed persistence (CMP) throughout the business tier. Queries will be implemented as finder methods on the bean home interfaces, and all relationships between beans will be defined and managed using the EJB 2.0 CMP techniques. There will be a few stateless session beans acting as façades for complex business logic not appropriate for placement in entity beans.

What does the decision to emphasize entity beans and CMP in the business tier mean to the presentation tier? Depending on the detailed design of the business-tier interfaces, perhaps very little. We need to examine some alternatives for the interaction with the business tier and make a selection.

Although we have many options available, we're going to narrow the choice of business-tier interface down to two basic approaches: *indirect interaction* with the entity beans via session beans and value objects and *direct interaction* with the entity beans. Note that many interface techniques making use of business delegates, command classes, data transfer objects, and other design patterns essentially fall in to the approach we're calling indirect interaction.

In the first approach, indirect interaction, presentation-tier components are insulated from the entity beans completely by introducing a stateless session bean or other component that acts as a session façade to encapsulate the entity beans and all business-tier behaviors. Communication with the session bean is normally performed using a *value object*, a separate Java class containing the same basic information as the entity bean. JSP pages and controller components never access the entity beans directly or perform any finder methods to obtain collections of beans.

In the second approach, direct interaction, presentation-tier components are allowed to interact directly with entity beans in the business tier. JSP pages and controller components may retrieve data elements directly from the beans, traverse relationships in the entity beans to access other beans, perform finder queries to obtain collections of beans, and update bean information by calling set methods directly on the entity beans.

Many of the common design alternatives are simply offshoots of these basic techniques. For example, XML documents or JDBC `RowSet` objects might be used instead of value objects in the indirect approach, or entity beans might return value objects containing all of their data rather than allowing direct interaction from presentation-tier components. Both of these alternatives are indirect interaction in our way of thinking because the key element of the direct interaction approach is the ability for the presentation-tier components simply to call entity bean get and set methods when desired without any additional layers or objects used for communication.

Chapter 7 discusses these alternatives in detail and explains the decision-making process that led us to choose the direct interaction approach for *bigrez.com*. Surprised? Clearly this approach is not the normal technique employed in the J2EE community today.

The following sections highlight some of the important implications of this decision on the presentation-tier components. These implications include the following:

- Presentation-tier components may access entity bean attributes directly, through get and set methods, during both the display of bean data and the processing of forms.
- Presentation-tier components may traverse and manipulate relationships between entity beans using relationship get and set methods on the beans.
- Action classes continue to place value objects and form beans in the `HttpServletRequest` context prior to forwarding to JSP pages, but they may also place entity bean references in that context to support direct interaction by the pages.

Displaying Bean Attributes on JSP Pages

The primary role of display JSP pages in the servlet-centric architecture is the display of data placed in the `HttpServletRequest` or other context by controller components. In the indirect interaction approach, the object placed in the request is often a value object or other simple data structure, but in the direct interaction approach the object is normally a local reference to an entity bean. In either approach, the JSP page declares the existence of the bean in the page using `jsp:useBean` and displays data from the bean using `jsp:getProperty` tags or the equivalent `bean:write` tags in Struts. Although the JSP may look similar in both approaches, there is a significant difference behind the scenes.

First, the `jsp:useBean` tag that declares the existence of the bean in the JSP page must obviously reflect the correct data type of the object in the request. For example, if a JSP page was displaying information in a simple `PropertyInfo` value object, the `jsp:useBean` tag would look something like this:

```
<jsp:useBean id="prop" type="com.bigrez.val.PropertyInfo"
             scope="request"/>
```

The page accessing the entity bean directly would use the type of the local reference:

```
<jsp:useBean id="prop" type="com.bigrez.ejb.PropertyLocal"
             scope="request"/>
```

One important difference is the way the `jsp:useBean` tag handles the case where the desired bean is not found in the specified context. Recall that in this case, the tag will attempt to create an instance of the specified class using the default constructor, an operation that normally succeeds for value objects but is not valid for `PropertyLocal` or any other entity bean interface because they are, in fact, interfaces rather than concrete classes. Note that placing the proper `findByPrimaryKey()` or other initialization code in the body of the jsp:useBean tag does not help because the tag still attempts to call a default constructor prior to executing any scriptlet code placed in the tag body. Therefore, the bean reference must already be in the required scope before the jsp:useBean tag is executed to avoid a run-time exception. In most cases, the bean will be placed in the proper context by the controller component prior to forwarding to the page, so this is not a big problem.

Accessing the data in the bean is identical in both approaches, assuming the value object and entity bean both have get methods for the desired data. For example, the following tag calls the getDescription() method on the underlying object (either value object or bean) and places the result in the generated HTML response:

```
Description: <jsp:getProperty name="prop" property="description"/>
```

Bean attributes that require formatting during display might use the View Helper pattern, by invoking a formatting helper object in an expression scriptlet:

```
<%= DateHelper.format(rez.getArrive()) %>
```

They can also employ a custom tag that includes the ability to specify a format, as does the bean:write tag in the Struts framework:

```
<bean:write name="rez" property="arrive" formatKey="date.format1"/>
```

Formatting helper classes and tags such as these are critical in the direct interaction approach. There may be a large number of fields that should appear differently on the displayed HTML page than they do in their internal representation in the entity bean.

Note that this need for formatting does not argue for value objects because value objects may also require formatting for display. Value objects should normally be exact replicas of the attributes and formats in the corresponding entity beans. If the value object includes attributes preformatted for display, it is not a true generic value object, but instead reflects presentation-tier formatting requirements, reducing its potential for reuse. Don't fall into this trap of preformatting data in business objects when using either entity beans or value objects. Formatting must be done by presentation-tier components using helper classes or tags depending on the requirements of that particular display component.

BEST PRACTICE Do not perform display formatting in entity beans or value objects. Use presentation-tier components such as helper classes or custom tags to map business data to display formats where required.

The final nuance in the direct interaction approach of accessing entity bean attributes directly deals with the EJB life cycle and transactions. Depending on your experience level using entity beans, you might have some significant reservations about executing get methods against the beans from within a JSP page. Normally, each get request causes a full ejbLoad()/ejbStore() life cycle of the bean, but not if you are careful, as we will explain in a moment.

One of the first things you learn about entity beans when starting out with EJB technology is the importance of accessing them efficiently, rather than one get method at a time. Most of us have written a Java client program something like this at one point in our careers:

```
...
Integer pk = new Integer(1);
CabinRemote cabin_2 = home.findByPrimaryKey(pk);
System.out.println(cabin_2.getName());
System.out.println(cabin_2.getDeckLevel());
System.out.println(cabin_2.getShipId());
System.out.println(cabin_2.getBedCount());
...
```

If you put a log statement in the `ejbLoad()` method on the bean, you may be surprised to discover that the bean is being read from the database four times, once for each get method called on the bean. At this point, you might either give up on EJB completely in disgust (perhaps switching to something easier?) or read a little more and realize your mistake. Transactions control entity bean life cycles in EJB, requiring an `ejbLoad()` at the start of a transaction and an `ejbStore()` at the end, and this example begins and ends four separate transactions by calling get methods from a client program outside the scope of a transaction.

You can make this simple Java client program much more efficient by starting an explicit transaction before the `findByPrimaryKey()` method and ending it after the final get method:

```
Context ctx = getInitialContext();
UserTransaction tran =
    (UserTransaction) ctx.lookup("java:comp/UserTransaction");
try {
    tran.begin();
    ...
    Integer pk = new Integer(1);
    CabinRemote cabin_2 = home.findByPrimaryKey(pk);
    System.out.println(cabin_2.getName());
    System.out.println(cabin_2.getDeckLevel());
    System.out.println(cabin_2.getShipId());
    System.out.println(cabin_2.getBedCount());
    ...
    tran.commit();
}
catch (Exception e) {
    ...
    tran.rollback();
    throw e;
}
```

The first get method now causes the bean to be loaded via `ejbLoad()` and kept in memory for the duration of the transaction, allowing the subsequent get methods to access the data more efficiently.

To apply this lesson to display JSP pages that need to get and display many bean attributes without incurring multiple transaction cycles, you simply place transaction-control code similar to the `begin()` and `commit()` code shown here in your JSP pages surrounding the tags that access the entity bean. In *bigrez.com*, we've placed this code in two JSP scriptlet snippets, `BeginTrans.jspf` and `EndTrans.jspf`, shown in Listing 3.4 and Listing 3.5. These snippets are included on appropriate pages at the top and bottom of the page. This technique ensures that the transaction is properly committed or rolled back regardless of run-time exceptions thrown by the page, and it ensures that all access to beans in the page is done in the context of a transaction.

```
<%
// We create a block here to allow multiple transactions per page
{
    Context utJNDIContext = getInitialContext();
    UserTransaction tran = (UserTransaction)
        utJNDIContext.lookup("java:comp/UserTransaction");
    try {
        tran.begin();
%>
```

Listing 3.4 BeginTrans.jspf starts the transaction.

```
<%
// This include file terminates a transaction start block

        tran.commit();
    }
    catch (Exception e) {
        e.printStackTrace();
        tran.rollback();
        throw e;
    }
}
//end trans block
%>
```

Listing 3.5 EndTrans.jspf ends the transaction.

BEST PRACTICE **Wrap all direct access to entity beans made by presentation-tier components in explicit transactions created using the** `UserTransaction` **interface. This rule applies to JSP pages and controller components.**

The JSP scriptlet files listed in Listing 3.4 and Listing 3.5 represent a low-tech solution to the problem of wrapping entity bean access in a transaction. You might consider creating a custom tag that starts the transaction in `doStartTag()` and ends it in `doEndTag()` as an alternative, but take care to trap and handle exceptions occurring in the tag body by implementing the `TryCatchFinally` interface in your tag class and overriding the `doCatch()` method.

You could also modify the `PageDisplayServlet` itself, wrapping the `forward()` invocation in transaction-control logic to place all included display JSP pages in an explicit transaction automatically:

```
...
RequestDispatcher dispatch =
    request.getRequestDispatcher("/Master.jsp?page="+newpage);
Context utJNDIContext = getInitialContext();
UserTransaction tran = (UserTransaction)
    utJNDIContext.lookup("java:comp/UserTransaction");
try {
    tran.begin();
    dispatch.forward(request,response);
    tran.commit();
}
catch (Exception e) {
    tran.rollback();
    ...
}
```

This technique has the advantage of being automatic, requiring no explicit tags or included files in display JSP pages, but it also reduces performance by creating a transaction for all pages regardless of their need for one.

We've chosen to include the simple transaction-control `.jspf` files in appropriate JSP pages rather than use a more advanced technique to keep the implementation simple and transparent. This simple technique has its limitations, the chief one being that all transaction control occurs at the individual page level. Because the overall HTML response is generated by a series of JSP pages in our master-page-assembly approach, multiple transactions may be required to create the response. This simple technique will also fail if a page starts a transaction and includes another page that attempts to start its own transaction. Consider using a more advanced technique, such as creating a transaction in the `PageDisplayServlet` or master JSP page, if these limitations are unacceptable to you.

The need to wrap all entity bean access in an explicit transaction represents the biggest weakness of the direct interaction approach. The actual performance cost of this requirement is fairly small given the basic approach of collocating Web application components and EJB components in the same enterprise application archive (`.ear`) file and using only local interfaces. We contend that the benefits of direct interaction outweigh the drawbacks in certain applications, and we discuss this in more detail in Chapter 7. Remember that patterns such as session façade grew out of the limitations of the EJB 1.1 entity bean model and the absence of local interfaces; perhaps it is time to revisit the need for that pattern for simple entity bean interaction.

In summary, the choice of direct interaction affects display JSP pages in two primary ways:

- Bean references must be present in the required scope before the corresponding `jsp:useBean` tag is encountered in the page to avoid run-time exceptions.
- Pages that access entity bean attributes directly must perform this activity in a transaction by including `BeginTrans.jspf` and `EndTrans.jspf` at the top and bottom of the page, respectively.

Relationships in Presentation Components

One of the significant benefits of the direct interaction approach is the ability of presentation-tier components such as JSP pages and `Action` classes to work directly with the object lattice and relationships implemented in the entity beans themselves. There is no need to write session bean methods that fetch and return lattices of value objects simulating the entity bean relationships or implement some form of lazy instantiation of relationship collections in parent value objects. When the entity beans are used directly, all retrieving of relationships and related beans is managed automatically by the CMP code in the container, and in WebLogic Server, this relationship management code has been optimized for performance. Chapter 6 discusses these caching and relationship management features of WebLogic Server and provides best practices for their use.

If a JSP page or `Action` class has a reference to a particular `RoomType` bean, for example, it can simply use the `getRates()` method on the bean to obtain a collection of related `Rate` entity bean references. Relationships can be traversed in the opposite direction with equal ease because we're implementing bidirectional relationships for all entity beans in the system.

The result is clean, natural code in the presentation-tier components without any additional development of specialized session bean methods and data transfer objects to retrieve and manage relationships. For example, a page that displays information about a particular property and the room types defined in that property needs only the property bean reference placed in the `HttpServletRequest`, and it can use the `getRoomTypes()` relationship method on the property bean to iterate through the room types for display:

```
<jsp:useBean id="prop" scope="request"
             type="com.bigrez.ejb.PropertyLocal"/>
...
<logic:iterate id="roomtype" type="com.bigrez.ejb.RoomTypeLocal"
               collection="<%= prop.getRoomTypes() %>">
  <tr>
    <td width="30%" align="left">
      ...
      <jsp:getProperty name="roomtype" property="description"/>
```

```
      </td>
    </tr>
  ...
  </logic:iterate>
```

Don't let the <logic:iterate> tag confuse you. It's another tag in the Struts framework that we'll be using in the *bigrez.com* site to iterate through a collection and define a page bean for each element in the collection. In this case, roomtype will be a reference to each room type entity bean related to the property. Check out the Struts home page at http://jakarta.apache.org/struts for more information on this and many other useful custom tags.

Code in the Action classes can also traverse relationships naturally to improve readability. For example, when the user clicks on an offer, we must load the correct property bean in the request before forwarding to the next page. This code snippet in OfferAction.java is made much clearer by traversing the relationship between an offer and its related property directly using getProperty():

```
String offer_id = request.getParameter("id");
int id = Integer.parseInt(offer_id);
OfferLocal offer = (OfferLocal) Locator.getBean("OfferLocal", id);
PropertyLocal prop = offer.getProperty();
ActionUserHelper.loadPropertyBean(request, prop);
```

Some of the helper methods and utility classes present in this code have not been covered yet, but you should get the idea. In a session bean architecture, we would likely use two calls to the façade bean: the first to fetch the offer-related value object containing the property ID and the second to fetch the property-related value object associated with the offer. The code here represents the better option in terms of clarity.

So far we've talked only about retrieving and traversing relationships with presentation-tier components. The benefits of direct interaction during these operations are relatively minor, as it turns out, compared to the benefits during updates. For example, you can manipulate relationships between EJB 2.0 CMP entity beans by simply manipulating the Collection classes returned by the bean methods. Chapter 7 will describe why this feature is important for the *bigrez.com* administration site and how direct interaction represents a significant improvement over alternative indirect techniques when it comes to managing complex relationships.

In summary, the use of direct interaction simplifies the traversal and management of relationships between business objects by allowing the presentation-tier components access to the relationship methods available on the entity beans themselves.

Action Classes Load Beans and Forms for Display

The servlet-centric architecture we've chosen for *bigrez.com* requires that controller components load required objects in the HttpServletRequest prior to forwarding control to the display JSP page. The objects loaded in the request are typically one of three types:

Entity bean local references. Because we are using the direct interaction approach, the objects loaded in the request will often be local references to entity beans required by the display page.

Form beans. If the display JSP page is a Struts form, the controller must load an appropriate `ActionForm` object in the request containing the current attributes of the corresponding bean.

Value objects or collections. Some pages in the site require specialized collections or complex data structures best prepared ahead of time by the controller rather than created in the JSP page itself.

To load a local bean reference in the request, the controller components (`Action` classes in Struts) simply locate the desired bean and place the reference in the `HttpServletRequest` using code similar to the following:

```
PropertyHomeLocal propertyhome = (PropertyHomeLocal)
    ctx.lookup("java:comp/env/ejb/PropertyHomeLocal");
PropertyLocal prop = propertyhome.findByPrimaryKey(pk);
request.setAttribute("prop", prop);
```

The display JSP page may now obtain this bean reference using `jsp:useBean` tags or equivalent Struts tags to retrieve bean attribute data:

```
<jsp:useBean id="prop" type="com.bigrez.ejb.PropertyLocal"
             scope="request"/>
...
Description: <jsp:getProperty name="prop" property="description"/>
```

Form beans required by Struts forms are loaded in the request by the controller class in a similar manner. For example, if a `Property` was being edited on a form page, the code to fetch the entity bean, create the form bean, and place the form bean in the request might look like this:

```
PropertyHomeLocal propertyhome = (PropertyHomeLocal)
    ctx.lookup("java:comp/env/ejb/PropertyHomeLocal");
PropertyLocal prop = propertyhome.findByPrimaryKey(pk);
PropertyMainForm pform = new PropertyMainForm();
pform.setId(prop.getId());
pform.setDescription(prop.getDescription());
...
pform.setFeatures(prop.getFeatures());
request.setAttribute("PropertyMainForm", pform);
```

The target page can now locate the required form bean and display the form with values representing the current attributes of the property. Note that locating entity beans and copying attribute data from entity beans to form beans are straightforward tasks but require a fair number of lines of code. In *bigrez.com* these tasks are handled by two helper objects, `Locator` and `CopyHelper`, which shrinks the required code substantially:

```
PropertyLocal prop =
    (PropertyLocal) Locator.getBean("PropertyLocal", pk);
PropertyMainForm pform = new PropertyMainForm();
CopyHelper.copy(prop, pform);
request.setAttribute("PropertyMainForm", pform);
```

The `Locater` and `CopyHelper` classes are detailed in subsequent chapters. Note that all get method invocations on the entity bean, whether explicit in the code or performed in the helper class, must be performed in a transaction for the same reasons described earlier in this chapter. As you'll see when we examine some sample code from the application, utility methods comparable to `BeginTrans.jspf` and `EndTrans.jspf` are used to begin and end transactions in `Action` classes.

Value objects and specialized collections of objects or references are also precreated and placed on the `HttpServletRequest` for use by display JSP pages requiring this type of data. A good example of this technique is the `PropertyList` display page that displays property information for hotels matching the user's search criteria. The controller performs the search and loads the collection of matching properties in the request using code similar to the following:

```
PropertyHomeLocal propertyhome =
    (PropertyHomeLocal) Locator.getHome("PropertyHomeLocal");
props = propertyhome.findByCityState(city, stateCode);
request.setAttribute("props", props);
```

Note that the controller uses a finder defined on the home interface for `Property` to perform the search rather than a specialized method defined on a stateless-session bean or other façade. The direct interaction approach allows the direct invocation of entity bean finder methods in presentation-tier components. Although there are occasions in *bigrez.com* when the presentation tier must use a façade to perform complex business logic, simple finder methods do not warrant another layer of abstraction in our opinion.

The direct interaction approach requires that controller components place entity bean references on the `HttpServletRequest` along with the usual `ActionForm` classes and value objects required in any servlet-centric architecture using Struts.

BEST PRACTICE **Controller components should generally prepare the request or session context before forwarding to display JSP pages rather than allowing JSP pages to obtain bean references themselves.**

Action Classes Perform Bean Updates

The servlet-centric architecture dictates that controller components are responsible for processing HTML form submissions and performing the required updates to the underlying business objects. In the direct interaction approach, the controller components are therefore allowed to modify the underlying entity beans and relationships modeling the business data directly.

For example, in *bigrez.com* the `PropertyMainAction` class is the controller responsible for taking changes made in the main property information form and applying them to the database. We'll examine this class in detail later, but for now, look at just the key lines that perform the transfer from the form bean to the entity bean:

```
PropertyMainForm pform = (PropertyMainForm)form;
...
PropertyLocal prop =
    (PropertyLocal) Locator.getBean("PropertyLocal", id);
CopyHelper.copy(pform, prop); // calls set methods on entity bean
```

This process is really just a mirror image of the code in the previous section that created the form bean from the entity bean before displaying the form page. The controller, a presentation-tier component, is allowed to locate and modify the contents of the `PropertyBean` entity bean directly through this code. As before, it must be done in a transaction.

In a similar way, the controllers that create new beans or add beans to relationships simply perform these tasks using the entity bean home interfaces or relationship get and set methods, as appropriate. You could encapsulate these functions in façade beans to avoid direct manipulation of the beans, but there are some benefits to avoiding the creation of additional layers in the architecture solely for encapsulation.

Note that selected operations in *bigrez.com* are complex enough to warrant a façade bean with methods encapsulating the behavior. For example, the creation of a reservation bean and all related entity beans is best implemented in a session bean and accessed from the presentation-tier components through that façade. This technique is the exception rather than the rule in the direct interaction approach, however.

Chapter Review

The following list summarizes the design decisions we've made for the *bigrez.com* application:

- The *bigrez.com* application includes a separate user site and administration site, with different processes and visual designs.
- The application meets the presentation-tier requirements for basic display, navigation, and form validation and submission outlined in Chapter 2.
- We'll use master page assembly to control the overall structure of pages in the site, with a page display servlet used to invoke the master page for `.page` file extensions.
- We'll use a servlet-centric architecture with the Struts framework to implement a model-view-controller approach in the presentation tier.
- Presentation-tier components access business-tier components directly, with a minimal number of additional value objects and session bean façade components, representing an interface technique we've called direct interaction.

Are you ready to look at the code and see how it all comes together? Turn to the next chapter, and let's get to it!

CHAPTER

4

Building an Example Web Application

In this chapter, we walk through the construction of a realistic example Web application, *bigrez.com.* Because this book is intended for intermediate- to advanced-level developers and architects, we assume that you understand the basic steps required to construct a J2EE Web application. Our emphasis is on any construction techniques unique to WebLogic Server as well as the components and techniques required for the *bigrez.com* application resulting from the choice of presentation approach, Web application architecture, and the use of direct interaction with the business-tier components.

The construction of the Web application portion of *bigrez.com* involves the following steps:

1. Constructing the application skeleton, including master pages, page display servlets, descriptor files, build files, and all required directory structures and configuration files
2. Identifying and constructing the specific JSP display pages, form beans, and controller components required to implement the user and administration site behaviors

Additional steps are required to construct the necessary business-tier components and related persistence logic. These steps are covered in Chapter 7.

Overview of Application Components

The *bigrez.com* example is large enough that we will start our discussion of its contents by presenting a list of the major groups of components in the application and a high-level picture of the work directory structure. These will help you understand the role of the components listed in this chapter in the overall application design. Note that complete source listings of all components would require a prohibitive amount of space, so we are including only listings of key components that emphasize steps and techniques covered in the text. You are encouraged to download the complete example program and installation instructions from the companion Web site (http://www.wiley.com/compbooks/masteringweblogic).

The application components have been split into six separate groups:

- **User site display components** including display JSP pages, JSP include files, style sheets, and key configuration and descriptor files, located in the `web-user` subdirectory
- **Administration site display components** including the same types of components for the administration Web application, located in the `web-admin` subdirectory
- **Form beans** used by form pages in both sites for entry and update of business data, located in the `com/bigrez/form/*` subdirectories
- **Action classes and helpers** representing the controller components in the architecture and any controller helper classes, located in the `com/bigrez/ui/*` subdirectories
- **Utilities and value objects** including classes shared by the Web application- and business-tier layers of the architecture, located in the `com/bigrez/utils/*` and `com/bigrez/val` subdirectories
- **EJB components** used by both sites to encapsulate persistence services and complex business logic, located in the `com/bigrez/ejb/*` subdirectory

These groups are reflected in the overall structure of the working directory shown in Figure 4.1. This structure incorporates the development environment best practices discussed in Chapter 13.

Some of the directories shown in Figure 4.1 contain components required during the build and packaging process, topics we'll cover in Chapters 5 and 8. This chapter will emphasize the presentation-tier components in the `web-user` and `web-admin` directories along with form, user interface, value, and utility components in selected directories in the `java` directory structure.

All source code, Web components, images, and key configuration files are located in the working directory structure. The build process, driven by the `build.xml` file, assembles the components appropriately and places them in the WebLogic Server domain during the build process. Chapter 5 discusses deployment and management of WebLogic Server Web applications and details the steps required to package and deploy the *bigrez.com* application.

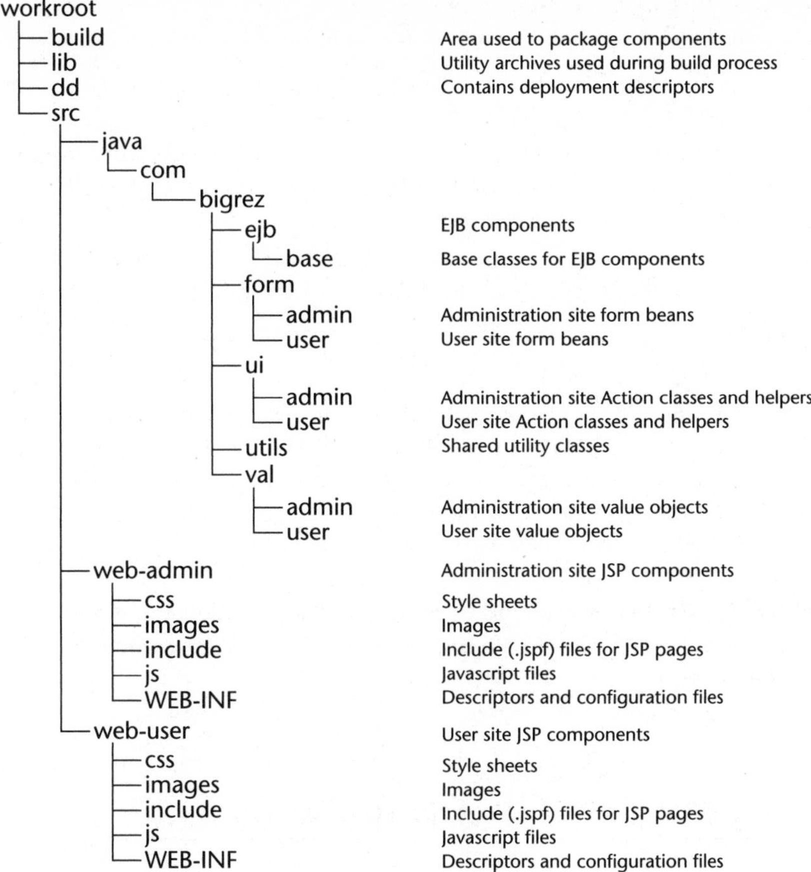

Figure 4.1 Working directory structure for the bigrez.com application.

Constructing the Application Skeleton

The first step when creating a new Web application is the construction of the application skeleton. In the *bigrez.com* Web application, this skeleton consists of the minimum components required to configure and boot the user and administration Web sites and display their respective home pages. This is not simply a `Home.jsp` page for each site, remember. We are using a Struts servlet-centric architecture and a master-page-assembly presentation approach, so the skeleton must include the basic configuration files and components required to implement our chosen approach.

The skeleton Web applications for both sites consist of the following components:

- The `Master.jsp` template page for the site, defining the overall page layout and included components

- Supporting view components such as Header.jsp, TopNav.jsp, Footer.jsp, and placeholder versions of view components such as RezInfo.jsp and Offers.jsp
- The PageDisplayServlet, used in page assembly
- The web.xml and weblogic.xml descriptor files, including JSP configuration elements and the servlet mappings from *.do to the Struts ActionServlet and *.page to the PageDisplayServlet
- A placeholder struts-config.xml file with sufficient configuration information, to start the ActionServlet on Web application boot
- Placeholder Home.jsp page, to use as a test page to validate skeleton configuration

These skeleton components, once deployed to the appropriate Web applications in the domain, are sufficient to present the Home.jsp page in the display area of the layout when the *Home.page* URL is accessed from a browser. On a typical development project, the skeleton components are then placed in source code control to form the starting point for the Web application construction tasks to follow.

BEST PRACTICE Begin construction by building an application skeleton containing the minimum number of components necessary to configure and start the Web application.

Constructing the User Site Components

Once the application skeleton is in place, additional view components are added in a piecewise fashion to flesh out the application. The construction of the user site in *bigrez.com* was broken down into three primary sections:

- *Reservation information components* responsible for the display of the reservation information area on the page and for the handling of user actions in that area
- *Core reservation process components* providing the main site functionality of finding properties, selecting dates, room types, and rates and making reservations
- *Targeted offers components* generating the targeting marketing offers in the left gutter depending on the user's recent search results and selections

In the following sections, we'll examine each of these sections of the user site in some detail, highlighting key components and techniques in each section.

Reservation Information Components

Creating a reservation requires a multiple-step process. Intermediate results must be stored in the HttpSession on behalf of the user, a technique much like a shopping cart in an e-commerce site. The *bigrez.com* application uses a serializable value object called `ReservationInfo` to store this information in the session. As the user selects a property, selects dates, selects a room type, and signs in to the site, the related information is saved in the `HttpSession` in the `ReservationInfo` object and its child `ReservationRateInfo` objects. These classes are simple value objects with private attributes and appropriate get and set methods, so complete listings are not required. For reference, the `ReservationInfo` class has the following attributes:

```
private String lastSearchCity;
private String lastSearchState;
private int propertyId;
private String propertyDescription;
private int roomTypeId;
private String roomTypeDescription;
private int guestProfileId;
private String firstName;
private String lastName;
private String phone;
private String email;
private String cardType;
private String cardExp;
private String cardNum;
private Date arriveDate;
private Date departDate;
private Collection rezRates;
```

The `ReservationRateInfo` class has these attributes:

```
private Date startDate;
private int numNights;
private float rate;
```

The current reservation information is displayed on the left side of the screen on every page in the user site in a small reservation information area generated by the `RezInfo.jsp` display JSP page. Figure 3.2 in the previous chapter showed this reservation information area in the context of the overall display. As the user selects a property, selects dates, or completes additional steps in the process, the reservation information area changes to reflect these selections.

The `RezInfo.jsp` page generates this area using a `jsp:useBean` tag to declare the existence of the `ReservationInfo` object in the `HttpSession` and provide a local page variable, `rezinfo`, for accessing the attributes of the object:

```
<jsp:useBean id="rezinfo" scope="session"
             class="com.bigrez.val.user.ReservationInfo" />
```

The `rezinfo` variable may now be used in simple `jsp:getProperty` tags to retrieve specific attributes from the object and display them on the page:

```
<jsp:getProperty name="rezinfo" property="propertyDescription"/>
```

Collections contained in the `rezinfo` variable may be examined using Struts `logic:iterate` tags:

```
<jsp:useBean id="rezrates" class="java.util.ArrayList" scope="page">
  <% rezrates = (ArrayList) rezinfo.getRezRates(); %>
</jsp:useBean>
...
<tr>
  <td>
    <span class="sidebar-title">Rate:</span>
    <logic:iterate id="rezrate"
        type="com.bigrez.val.user.ReservationRateInfo"
        collection="<%= rezrates %>">
      <br> <span class="sidebar-data">
      <jsp:getProperty name="rezrate" property="numNights"/>
      nts @ $
      <jsp:getProperty name="rezrate" property="rate"/>/nt</span>
    </logic:iterate>
  </td>
</tr>
```

The `rezinfo` variable may also be used in `logic:equal` or `logic:notEqual` tags to display information conditionally. For example, we want to display the string `Choose Property` for the property description if the user has not yet selected a property for this reservation. Rather than performing this logic in the `ReservationInfo` value object or creating a separate `Helper` class, we've made use of these `logic` tags to control the display:

```
<a class="sidebar-link" href="/RezInfoAction.do?action=property">
  <logic:equal name="rezinfo" property="propertyId" value="0">
    Choose Property
  </logic:equal>
  <logic:notEqual name="rezinfo" property="propertyId" value="0">
    <jsp:getProperty name="rezinfo" property="propertyDescription"/>
  </logic:notEqual>
</a>
```

BEST PRACTICE Do not place conditional display logic, such as replacing empty values with default messages, in value objects. Use custom tags or other view components to create conditional displays.

The displayed values in the reservation information area are also used as navigation links, allowing the user to jump back to a previous decision or log in early. As the code snippet shows, the target URL for the property description is *RezInfoAction.do*. All hyperlinks in this JSP page and every other JSP page in the site use this *<PageName>Action.do* approach rather than hard-coding page names in the display JSP pages. As discussed in Chapter 2, these **.do* locations are mapped in the `web.xml` file to the default `ActionServlet` in Struts, which then instantiates and uses an `Action` class—in this case `RezInfoAction`—to handle the request.

The `execute()` method in `RezInfoAction` interrogates the request to determine the proper action and performs the required preparation and forwarding steps:

```
public ActionForward execute(ActionMapping mapping,
                             ActionForm form,
                             HttpServletRequest request,
                             HttpServletResponse response)
    throws IOException, ServletException
{
    String action = request.getParameter("action");
    ReservationInfo rezinfo = getRezInfo(request);
    ...
    if (action.equals("dates")) {
        if (rezinfo.getPropertyId() == 0) {
            action = "property"; // can't do dates before property
            ActionErrors errors = new ActionErrors();
            errors.add(ActionErrors.GLOBAL_ERROR,
                new ActionError("error.rezinfo.propertybeforedates"));
            saveErrors(request, errors);
        }
        else {
            // prepare the request with a SelectDatesForm object
            // to populate fields
            ActionUserHelper.loadSelectDatesForm(request, rezinfo);
        }
        return mapping.findForward(action);
    }
    ...
}
```

This simple controller behavior of the `RezInfoAction` class is depicted in Figure 4.2.

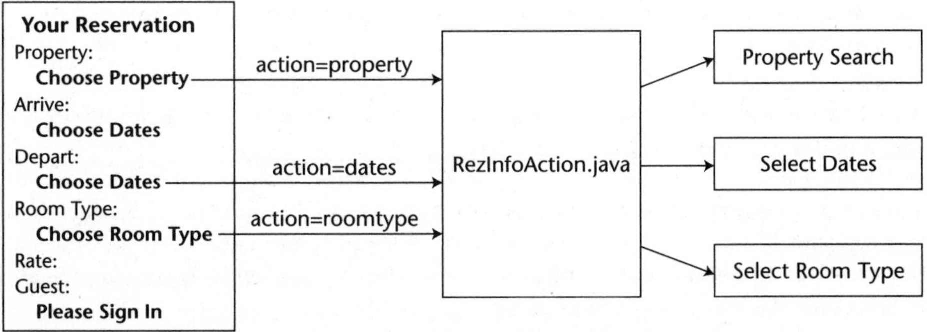

Figure 4.2 The RezInfoAction controller determines the display page.

As the code snippet indicates, there are many business rules in each `if (action.equals(...))` block in the class that modify this simple controller behavior. For example, if the user has not yet selected a property, the property search page must be displayed before selecting dates or room types. The key is that none of these business rules are contained in the `RezInfo.jsp` display page. Consistent with the model-view-controller approach, the controller component `RezInfoAction` is responsible for both navigation and the application of presentation-related business rules.

The `RezInfoAction` class also illustrates an important implementation detail. As discussed earlier, controller components are responsible for placing the required beans, forms, or value objects in the proper scope before forwarding control to the display JSP page. The `RezInfoAction` class forwards control to many different pages in the action-specific branching logic, so it must be capable of preparing many different types of objects before forwarding. The class uses a series of helper methods in the `ActionUserHelper` class to perform this preparation, thereby encapsulating the required business-tier interaction in these methods to foster reuse. For example, the following code prepares for the JSP page that displays a particular property by loading the `PropertyBean` local reference in the request:

```
ActionUserHelper.loadPropertyBean(request, rezinfo.getPropertyId());
```

The `loadPropertyBean()` method in the helper class performs the key operations:

```
...
PropertyLocal prop =
    (PropertyLocal) Locator.getBean("PropertyLocal", id);
request.setAttribute("prop", prop);
...
```

We'll discuss specific display pages, their preparation requirements, and the contents of the `ActionUserHelper` class in more detail in the next section.

BEST PRACTICE Preparation of the request or session context prior to forwarding to a display JSP page should be performed in a common helper method. There may be multiple paths to the same display page, and all controllers leading to that page should use the same helper method to prepare the request or session.

One other interesting technique demonstrated in `RezInfoAction` is the use of the standard Struts error-handling functions to place messages on subsequent display JSP pages. If the user clicks on the `Choose Dates` link before a property is selected, we must display the property search page rather than the select dates page. Rather than simply sending the user to the property search screen without explanation, we will place a message in the normal location used for form-validation or form-submission errors and proceed to the new target page:

```
if (action.equals("dates")) {
    if (rezinfo.getPropertyId() == 0) {
        action = "property"; // can't do dates before property
        ActionErrors errors = new ActionErrors();
        errors.add(ActionErrors.GLOBAL_ERROR,
            new ActionError("error.rezinfo.propertybeforedates"));
        saveErrors(request, errors);
    }
    else {
        // prepare the request with a SelectDatesForm to populate fields
        ActionUserHelper.loadSelectDatesForm(request, rezinfo);
    }
    return (mapping.findForward(action));
}
```

The target page displays these errors by including the standard `<html:errors/>` tag in the page definition.

In summary, the reservation information area of the *bigrez.com* user site is designed to display the current status of the reservation process and allow the user to jump directly to certain steps in the process, subject to business rules enforced in the `RezInfoAction` controller component. The display area is created by the `RezInfo.jsp` display JSP page using data stored in the `HttpSession` in the `ReservationInfo` and `ReservationRateInfo` value objects. All hyperlinks invoke the `RezInfoAction` controller class through the normal Struts action-mapping facilities, and this controller class is responsible for determining the proper JSP page to display.

The reservation information area design and the chosen implementation techniques provide a good model for a shopping cart or other multiple-step process in your J2EE Web applications.

Core Reservation Process Components

The core reservation process, illustrated in Figure 3.3, walks the user step-by-step through the selection of required elements of a reservation. In this section, we examine a few of the presentation-tier components in detail to illustrate the solutions employed for common requirements in J2EE Web applications.

Defining Navigation Paths

The reservation process involves a fair number of separate display JSP pages, controller `Action` classes, and related form beans and value objects. Table 4.1 provides a list of the primary components in the process. Note that not all display pages have form beans and that all pages, except the final `ReservationThankYou` page, have their own controller `Action` class for processing user actions on the page.

Table 4.1 Core Reservation Process Primary Components

DISPLAY COMPONENT	RELATED CONTROLLER COMPONENT	FORM BEAN
PropertySearch.jsp	PropertySearchAction .java	PropertySearchForm .java
PropertyList.jsp	PropertyListAction .java	
SelectDates.jsp	SelectDatesAction .java	SelectDatesForm .java
SelectRoomType.jsp	SelectRoomTypeAction .java	
GuestInformation.jsp	GuestInformation Action.java	GuestInformation Form.java
ReviewReservation .jsp	ReviesReservation Action.java	
ReservationThankYou .jsp		

BEST PRACTICE Use a standard naming convention for display pages, `Action` **controller classes, and form beans to make relationships between components clear without inspecting the configuration file. The chosen convention of appending** `Action` **and** `Form` **to the display page name is a reasonable choice.**

As discussed in Chapter 2, the servlet-centric Web application architecture dictates certain rules and principles related to presentation-tier components and their relationships. One key principle is the separation of roles between display components, controller components, and navigational control facilities. The *bigrez.com* application meets the requirements by adopting the following rules:

- Display JSP pages must use *<PageName>Action.do* controller invocations for all hyperlinks and form-posting targets. The controller is always responsible for determining the next page in the process based on the user's action, the current state, and navigation control information.
- Controller components do not refer directly to display JSP page names when specifying the next page for display. Logical page names are used in controller code, and these logical names are mapped to actual page names in the Struts configuration files.

A critical aspect of this design is the Struts configuration file, `struts-config.xml`. This file defines the mapping between logical and actual JSP page names as well as the relationships between pages, form beans, and their controllers. Please download the struts-config.xml file for *bigrez.com* from the companion web site (http://www.wiley.com/compbooks/masteringweblogic) and review it before proceeding.

We've also used the struts-config.xml file to define the basic course, or *happy path*, through the reservation process by defining success mappings in each core reservation page. For example, the next page after SelectDates is SelectRoomType, but rather than hard-coding this relationship in any JSP or controller component, the mapping is placed in the definition of the SelectDatesAction controller component and given the logical name success:

```
<action path="/SelectDatesAction"
        type="com.bigrez.ui.user.SelectDatesAction"
        name="SelectDatesForm"
        scope="request"
        validate="true"
        input="/SelectDates.page">
  <forward name="success" path="/SelectRoomType.page" redirect="false"/>
</action>
```

As we'll examine in a moment, the controller component may now indicate that processing may continue with the next page in the reservation process by simply returning this mapping using the logical name:

```
return (mapping.findForward("success"));
```

In theory, you can change the order of the reservation process by simply modifying the entries in struts-config.xml to indicate the new success pages for each page in the process. Unfortunately, modifying the page flow also requires some changes in related controller classes to prepare the request properly, given the new success page. These kinds of controller changes demonstrate one problem inherent in the external definition of page flows: There are likely to be dependencies in the flow not represented in the page-flow definition. The *bigrez.com* application uses helper methods to prepare for subsequent pages, thereby reducing the amount of work required to change the flow. Other options include forwarding to *preparation* controller components capable of preparing the request for a particular new page, rather than preparing the request and forwarding directly to the page. A detailed discussion of these options is beyond the scope of this book.

Controller components that do not follow this simple success chain or that need to indicate a different target page also use logical page mappings defined in the configuration file. The RezInfoAction class already discussed had many examples of this technique.

Now that we've discussed the basic approach to navigation in the user site, let's examine selected pages and controller components in the site to learn more about its construction.

Property Search/Selection Pages

As indicated in Table 4.1, the first page in the reservation process is PropertySearch.jsp, a simple search page allowing the user to pick the desired city or state to use in finding a property. This page uses a form bean and the standard Struts tags for creating HTML forms and input elements, as you can see in Listing 4.1.

```
<%@ page extends="com.bigrez.ui.MyJspBase" %>

<%@ taglib uri="/WEB-INF/struts-html.tld" prefix="html" %>

<html:form action="/PropertySearchAction" method="get">

<table width="100%" cellspacing="5" cellpadding="0">
  <tr>
    <td class="page-header" align="right">Find a Property</td>
  </tr>
  <tr><td><html:errors/></td></tr>
  <tr>
    <td class="page-text">
      Please enter the state or city you plan to visit:
    </td>
  </tr>
  <tr><td> </td></tr>
  <tr>
    <td>
      <table width="100%" cellspacing="6" cellpadding="0">
        <tr>
          <td width="25%" class="page-label" nowrap>State Code:</td>
          <td width="75%">
            <html:select property="stateCode">
              <html:option value="">Choose...</html:option>
              <html:options collection="stateCodeList"
                            property="value" labelProperty="label"/>
            </html:select>
          </td>
        </tr>
        <tr>
          <td class="page-label" nowrap>City:</td>
          <td>
            <html:select property="city">
              <html:option value="">Choose...</html:option>
              <html:options collection="cityList"
                            property="value" labelProperty="label"/>
            </html:select>
          </td>
        </tr>
        <tr><td> </td></tr>
        <tr>
          <td colspan="2" align="left">
              <input type="submit" value="Find Properties">
          </td>
        </tr>
```

Listing 4.1 PropertySearch.jsp.

```
        </table>
      </td>
    </tr>
  </table>
  </html:form>
```

Listing 4.1 *(continued)*

The drop-down list elements of valid state codes and city codes are generated using the `html:select` and `html:option` Struts tags. These tags look for the specified collections, either `stateCodeList` or `cityList`, in all of the scopes available to the page. In this case, we've preloaded these collections in the `application` scope using an `InitializationServlet` loaded during application startup.

The `PropertySearch.jsp` page submits the contents of the HTML form to the standard `ActionServlet` defined in the Struts framework. The `ActionServlet` then forwards the contents to the `PropertySearchAction` controller class using the form bean defined for this page, `PropertySearchForm`. Note that the `html:form` tag in the page defines the `method` attribute to be a `GET` rather than a `POST`. We've used the `GET` method on a number of the forms in the user site to allow more natural browser navigation without warning messages caused by `POST` actions.

BEST PRACTICE **Use `GET` rather than `POST` when possible in form pages. Users will be able to navigate more freely and will be able to refresh pages without receiving form-posting warning messages from their browsers.**

As before, the `PropertySearchForm` form bean is first given a chance to validate the HTML form contents using its `validate()` method:

```
public ActionErrors validate(ActionMapping mapping,
                             HttpServletRequest request)
{
    ActionErrors errors = new ActionErrors();
    if (isEmpty(city) && isEmpty(stateCode))
        errors.add(ActionErrors.GLOBAL_ERROR,
                   new ActionError("error.propertysearch.nocriteria"));
    return errors;
}
```

If the form-bean validation returns no errors, the `execute()` method in the controller class is invoked to complete the processing of this form submission. As shown in Listing 4.2, the `execute()` method uses the selected values of `city` and `stateCode` to execute a finder method directly on the `PropertyHomeLocal` interface:

```
PropertyHomeLocal propertyhome =
(PropertyHomeLocal) Locator.getHome("PropertyHomeLocal");
Collection props = null;
```

```
...
LOG.debug("Finding properties using city " + city);
props = propertyhome.findByCity(city);
...
```

This direct invocation of the entity bean finder method to retrieve a list of matching properties is consistent with the direct interaction approach we've adopted for this application. The returned collection is actually a collection of local references, implementing the `PropertyLocal` interface, representing the related `PropertyBean` objects. Chapter 7 describes the declaration and definition of finder methods, such as this one, using EJB generation tools.

```
package com.bigrez.ui.user;

import java.io.IOException;
import java.util.Collection;
import javax.ejb.FinderException;
import javax.naming.NamingException;
import javax.servlet.ServletException;
import javax.servlet.http.HttpServletRequest;
import javax.servlet.http.HttpServletResponse;
import org.apache.struts.action.ActionForm;
import org.apache.struts.action.ActionForward;
import org.apache.struts.action.ActionMapping;

import com.bigrez.ejb.PropertyHomeLocal;
import com.bigrez.form.user.PropertySearchForm;
import com.bigrez.utils.Locator;
import com.bigrez.val.user.ReservationInfo;

public final class PropertySearchAction extends BigRezUserAction
{
    public ActionForward execute(ActionMapping mapping,
                                 ActionForm form,
                                 HttpServletRequest request,
                                 HttpServletResponse response)
        throws IOException, ServletException
    {
        LOG.info(">>> PropertySearchAction::execute()");
        PropertySearchForm pform = (PropertySearchForm)form;
        try {
            String city = pform.getCity();
            String stateCode = pform.getStateCode();
            ReservationInfo rezinfo = getRezInfo(request);
            rezinfo.setLastSearchCity(city);
            rezinfo.setLastSearchState(stateCode);
            PropertyHomeLocal propertyhome = (PropertyHomeLocal)
                Locator.getHome("PropertyHomeLocal");
```

Listing 4.2 PropertySearchAction.java.

```
            Collection props = null;
            if (!isEmpty(city)) {
                if (!isEmpty(stateCode)) {
                    LOG.debug("Finding properties using city " + city +
                              " and state " + stateCode);
                    props =
                      propertyhome.findByCityState(city, stateCode);
                }
                else {
                    LOG.debug("Finding properties using city " + city);
                    props = propertyhome.findByCity(city);
                }
            }
            else {
                LOG.debug("Finding properties using state " +
                          stateCode);
                props = propertyhome.findByState(stateCode);
            }
            ActionUserHelper.loadPropertyBeans(request, props);
        }
        catch (NamingException ne) {
            LOG.error("NamingException searching for properties", ne);
            ActionUserHelper.loadJSPException(request, ne);
            return (mapping.findForward("error"));
        }
        catch (FinderException fe) {
            LOG.error("FinderException searching for properties", fe);
            ActionUserHelper.loadJSPException(request, fe);
            return (mapping.findForward("error"));
        }
        return mapping.findForward("success");
    }
}
```

Listing 4.2 *(continued)*

The final step in handling the search request is placing the necessary objects in the `HttpServletRequest` context to prepare for the display JSP page showing the results. The display page, `PropertyList.jsp`, expects the matching properties to be located in the request using the `props` identifier, so we could easily place our collection of matching properties in the request manually using:

```
request.setAttribute("props", props);
```

The best practice presented earlier indicated that helper methods should be used for this purpose, so we'll delegate this preparation step to the `ActionUserHelper` class using the following invocation:

```
ActionUserHelper.loadPropertyBeans(request, props);
```

If you examine the code in `ActionUserHelper` you'll notice that `loadPropertyBeans()` performs the same `request.setAttribute(...)` statement in this simple case:

```
public static void loadPropertyBeans(HttpServletRequest request,
                                     Collection props)
    throws FinderException, NamingException
{
    request.setAttribute("props", props);
    return;
}
```

Many other preparation methods in `ActionUserHelper` are more involved, as evidenced by the length and complexity of the code in the class. We make heavy use of these helper methods in other controller classes.

The `PropertySearchAction` controller forwards the request to the `success` mapping for this page, which according to the `struts-config.xml` file is `PropertyList.page`. WebLogic Server's servlet container intercepts this `*.page` request and passes it to the `PageDisplayServlet` according to the `servlet-mapping` information in `web.xml`. The `Master.jsp` page is then invoked with the `page` request parameter set appropriately, and finally the user sees the matching properties displayed by `PropertyList.jsp`, as shown in Figure 4.3.

The `PropertyList.jsp` page is fairly straightforward, so rather than including a listing of the entire page, we'll examine a few key sections.

First, the page gains access to the collection of matching property references using the `jsp:useBean` element:

```
<jsp:useBean id="props" type="java.util.Collection" scope="request"/>
```

Note that the collection must be present under the ID `props`, or this tag will fail attempting to instantiate a `Collection` object. This fact emphasizes again the importance of preparing data in the controllers before forwarding requests to the display JSP pages.

The collection is iterated through using the `logic:iterate` tag in Struts:

```
<logic:iterate id="prop" type="com.bigrez.ejb.PropertyLocal"
               collection="<%= props %>">
...
</logic:iterate>
```

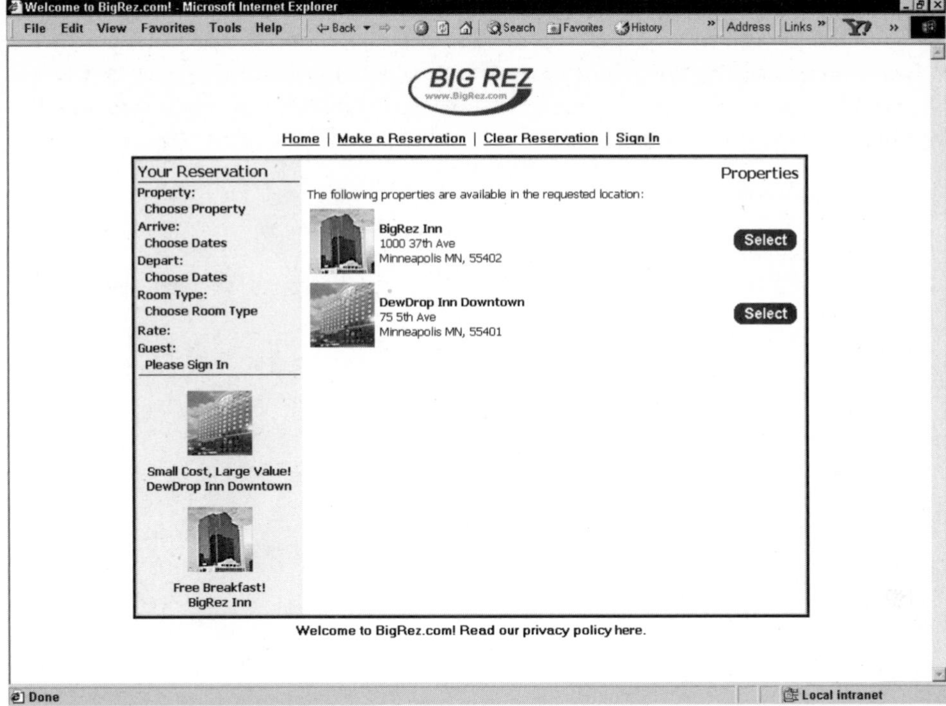

Figure 4.3 Property list page.

In this loop, the attributes of each `PropertyBean` are displayed using `jsp:getProperty` elements and the `prop` reference created by the iteration tag. Because we are interacting directly with the entity beans, all of this activity must be performed in the context of a transaction. The `BeginTrans.jspf` and `EndTrans.jspf` files are included at the top and bottom of the page, respectively, to ensure that we are in a transaction.

Consistent with our servlet-centric approach, all of the links on this page use *PropertyListAction.do* as the primary target, with different links specifying different `action` values and any required parameters. For example, the Select button for a property is defined in the page as follows:

```
<a href="PropertyListAction.do?action=select&id=<jsp:getProperty
         name="prop" property="id"/>">
  <img src="/images/selectbutton.gif" alt="" border="0">
</a>
```

Clicking Select for a given property invokes the PropertyListAction class, passing in the parameter action with a value of select and the parameter id with a value equal to the property primary key. The PropertyListAction class saves this property information in the ReservationInfo object in the session, prepares the necessary beans or forms, and forwards to the next page in the process:

```
beginTrans(request);
String propertyId = request.getParameter("id");
int id = Integer.parseInt(propertyId);
PropertyLocal prop = ActionUserHelper.loadPropertyBean(request, id);
if (action.equals("select")) {
    ReservationInfo rezinfo = getRezInfo(request);
    if (id != rezinfo.getPropertyId()) {
        rezinfo.setPropertyId(id);
        rezinfo.setPropertyDescription(prop.getDescription());
        rezinfo.clearRoomType();
        rezinfo.clearRates();
    }
    ActionUserHelper.loadSelectDatesForm(request, rezinfo);
    action = "success"; // next step in process
    setRezInfo(request, rezinfo);
}
commitTrans(request);
```

Note the use of helper classes and utility methods, such as getRezInfo() and setRezInfo(), rather than accessing attributes directly in the HttpServletRequest and HttpSession. It is always a good idea to reduce the number of places in your code that access these objects using key values to avoid unnecessary search-and-replace tasks whenever these key values need to change. String constants defined in a convenient location can also help minimize the effect of key changes.

The call to setRezInfo() (defined in the BigRezUserAction base class) performs a setAttribute() in the HttpSession to place the ReservationInfo object in the session:

```
protected void setRezInfo(HttpServletRequest request, Object rezinfo)
{
    // set the information in the session again to ensure replication
    request.getSession(true).setAttribute("rezinfo", rezinfo);
}
```

Why do we have to do this again when the ReservationInfo object is already in the session and the only activity in this method was changing some of the attributes in the object? Calling setAttribute() is important when using session persistence because it tells WebLogic Server that you have changed something in the object stored in the HttpSession. You must call setAttribute() at some point during the processing to ensure that changes made to the object will be saved to the JDBC persistence store or propagated to the backup server.

BEST PRACTICE Make sure to call `setAttribute()` on any session variables that have changed during the processing of the request. WebLogic Server relies on this signal to persist session changes properly to the JDBC datastore or backup server in the cluster.

As shown in this partial source listing for `ActionUserHelper.java`, the `loadSelectDatesForm()` method prepares for the `SelectDates.jsp` page by creating a `SelectDatesForm` form bean and placing it in the request:

```
public static void loadSelectDatesForm(HttpServletRequest request,
                                       ReservationInfo rezinfo)
{
    LOG.info(">>> loadSelectDatesForm");
    // prepare the request with a SelectDatesForm to populate fields
    SelectDatesForm sdform = new SelectDatesForm();
    if (rezinfo.getArriveDate() != null) {
        sdform.setArriveDate(
            DateHelper.format1(rezinfo.getArriveDate()));
        sdform.setDepartDate(
            DateHelper.format1(rezinfo.getDepartDate()));
    }
    else {
        Calendar now = Calendar.getInstance();
        now.set(Calendar.HOUR, 0);// get midnight date/time
        now.set(Calendar.MINUTE, 0);
        now.set(Calendar.SECOND, 0);
        sdform.setArriveDate(DateHelper.format1(now.getTime()));
        now.add(Calendar.DAY_OF_MONTH, 1);
        sdform.setDepartDate(DateHelper.format1(now.getTime()));
    }
    request.setAttribute("SelectDatesForm", sdform);
}
```

Note that the `loadSelectDatesForm()` method prepopulates the form bean with dates based on the current date if no values are present in the `ReservationInfo` value object. We are now ready to proceed to the `SelectDates` page and obtain the user's desired arrival and departure dates.

Date Selection and Availability Display Pages

The `SelectDates.jsp` page presents the user with a simple form requesting an arrival and departure date (see Figure 4.4). Calendar icons next to each field use JavaScript to pop up a calendar window allowing the user to pick dates. We're not going to cover this feature in the book, but feel free to look at `DatePicker.js` in the downloadable code if you're interested in how these buttons work.

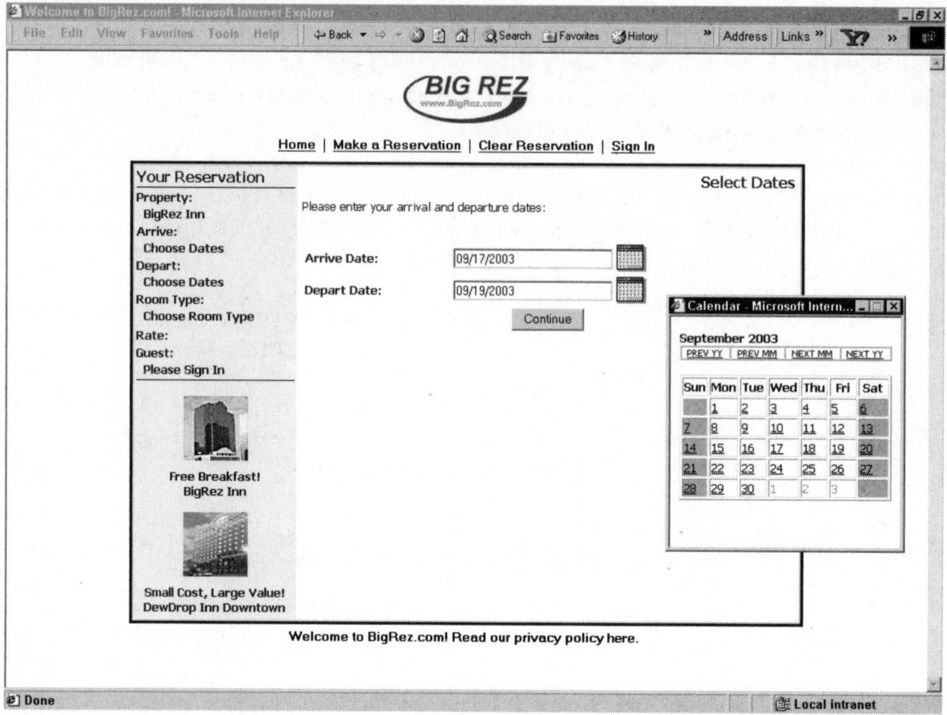

Figure 4.4 Select dates page.

The user chooses the desired dates and submits the form to the `SelectDatesAction` controller class. This form again uses the `GET` method rather than `POST` to improve browser navigation. Consistent with the servlet-centric architecture, all field validation takes place in the form bean `validate()` method or in the controller class. The `validate()` method in `SelectDatesForm` checks for empty or invalid dates, as well as reversed dates, and returns appropriate `ActionError` objects representing these errors:

```
public ActionErrors validate(ActionMapping mapping,
                             HttpServletRequest request)
{
    LOG.info(">>> SelectDatesForm::validate()");
    ActionErrors errors = new ActionErrors();
    if (assertNonEmpty(errors, arriveDate,
                       "error.selectdates.arriveempty")) {
        assertValidDate(errors, arriveDate,
                        "error.selectdates.arriveinvalid");
    }
    if (assertNonEmpty(errors, departDate,
                       "error.selectdates.departempty")) {
        assertValidDate(errors, departDate,
                        "error.selectdates.departinvalid");
```

```
        }
        try {
            Date arrive = DateHelper.parse(arriveDate);
            Date depart = DateHelper.parse(departDate);
            if (arrive.equals(depart) || arrive.after(depart)) {
                errors.add(ActionErrors.GLOBAL_ERROR, new ActionError(
                           "error.selectdates.arriveafterdepart"));
            }
        }
        catch (ParseException e) {
            LOG.error("ParseException validating SelectDatesForm", e);
            errors.add(ActionErrors.GLOBAL_ERROR,
                       new ActionError("error.validationproblem"));
        }
        return errors;
    }
```

If the `validate()` method succeeds, the dates must be present and properly formatted. Processing can then continue in the `execute()` method of the `SelectDatesAction` class:

```
    public ActionForward execute(ActionMapping mapping,
                                 ActionForm form,
                                 HttpServletRequest request,
                                 HttpServletResponse response)
        throws IOException, ServletException
    {
        LOG.info(">>> SelectDatesAction::execute()");
        SelectDatesForm sdform = (SelectDatesForm)form;
        try {
            // save the selected dates in the ReservationInfo object
            ReservationInfo rezinfo = getRezInfo(request);
            // safety checks that we have property selection already
            if (rezinfo.getPropertyId() == 0) {
                return (mapping.findForward("property"));
            }
            rezinfo.setArriveDate(
                      DateHelper.parse(sdform.getArriveDate()));
            rezinfo.setDepartDate(
                      DateHelper.parse(sdform.getDepartDate()));
            rezinfo.setRezRates(new ArrayList());
            setRezInfo(request, rezinfo);
            // prepare the information required for next page
            ActionUserHelper.loadPropertyBean(
                             request, rezinfo.getPropertyId());
            ActionUserHelper.loadRateAvailabilityInfos(request, rezinfo);
        } catch (ParseException e) {
            LOG.error("ParseException setting dates", e);
            ActionUserHelper.loadJSPException(request, e);
            return (mapping.findForward("error"));
```

```
        } catch (NamingException e) {
            LOG.error("NamingException setting dates", e);
            ActionUserHelper.loadJSPException(request, e);
            return (mapping.findForward("error"));
        }
        return mapping.findForward("success");
    }
```

The `execute()` method has two primary tasks: save the selected dates in the `ReservationInfo` object in the session and prepare the necessary beans in the request for the next page, `SelectRoomType.jsp`.

Saving the selected dates is a task made easy by the `DateHelper` helper class used to format the form attributes and by the `getRezInfo()` and `setRezInfo()` methods used to retrieve and set the information in the session.

Preparing for the next display page looks like another simple task, involving only two calls to the `ActionUserHelper` class to perform the preparation. But looks can be deceiving. The call to `loadPropertyBean()` simply places a local reference to the currently selected property bean in the request, but the call to `loadRateAvailabilityInfos()` does something we haven't encountered yet in our discussion:

```
public static void loadRateAvailabilityInfos(
                HttpServletRequest request, ReservationInfo rezinfo)
    throws NamingException
{
    LOG.info(">>> loadRateAvailabilityInfos");
    ReservationSessionLocal rezsession = (ReservationSessionLocal)
        Locator.getSessionBean("ReservationSessionLocal");
    PropertyLocal prop = (PropertyLocal)
        Locator.getBean("PropertyLocal", rezinfo.getPropertyId());
    Collection rainfos =
        rezsession.calculateAllRateAvailabilityInfo(
            prop, rezinfo.getArriveDate(), rezinfo.getDepartDate());
    request.setAttribute("rainfos", rainfos);
}
```

This method makes use of a session bean called `ReservationSession` to retrieve a collection of objects for the given property and dates. The returned collection contains `RateAvailabilityInfo` objects, a class encapsulating information about the price and availability of a given room type in the selected hotel for the dates requested by the user. Rather than list the entire class, here are the attributes of a `RateAvailabilityInfo` object:

```
private RoomTypeLocal roomType;
private boolean availableFlag;
private Collection rates;
private Collection blockingControls;
```

Each attribute of the RateAvailabilityInfo object plays a different role:

- The roomType attribute is a reference to the RoomType entity bean this object represents.
- The availableFlag attribute is a simple Boolean value indicating whether the room is available for the requested dates.
- The rates collection contains RaeservationRateInfo objects representing date ranges and rates for this room type during the requested dates (recognize that rates could change during the length of the stay).
- The blockingControls collection contains a list of Inventory entity bean references for days that cannot be booked at this hotel during the date range.

The creation of these objects and collections is covered in Chapter 7 when we examine the ReservationSession bean and the calculateAllRateAvailability-Info() method.

Why did we use a session bean here, and does this argue that the direct interaction approach is inappropriate for our application because it cannot be used for all business-tier interaction? We believe a session bean makes sense in this case because the work required to determine the rates and availability is complex enough to warrant some form of delegation, whether it be via a business delegate pattern, helper pattern, or the chosen session façade pattern. A session bean is favored over these alternative delegation options because it provides pooling for efficiency and automatic, declarative transaction control through standard EJB descriptors. We'll use a session bean because it best accomplishes the goal of retrieving and returning a collection of objects suitable for the next step in the reservation process.

BEST PRACTICE Favor encapsulating complex business logic in session beans, even when using the direct interaction approach, to improve efficiency and maintainability.

Notice that the RateAvailabilityInfo objects returned by the session bean are hybrids rather than pure value objects because they contain entity-bean references rather than additional value objects where it is convenient to do so. This collection of objects is placed in the HttpServletRequest, just like any other entity bean or form bean, to make it available for use in the next page in the process, the SelectRoom-Type page.

As shown in Figure 4.5, the SelectRoomType page presents the user with a list of room types, rates, and availability information to assist them in choosing the desired room for their stay. Rooms that are not available for the entire duration of the stay are not available for selection and indicate the specific nights they are unavailable below their normal rates. We'll talk more about rates and availability when we walk through some pages in the administration site, so for now let's concentrate on how this content is built by the display JSP page.

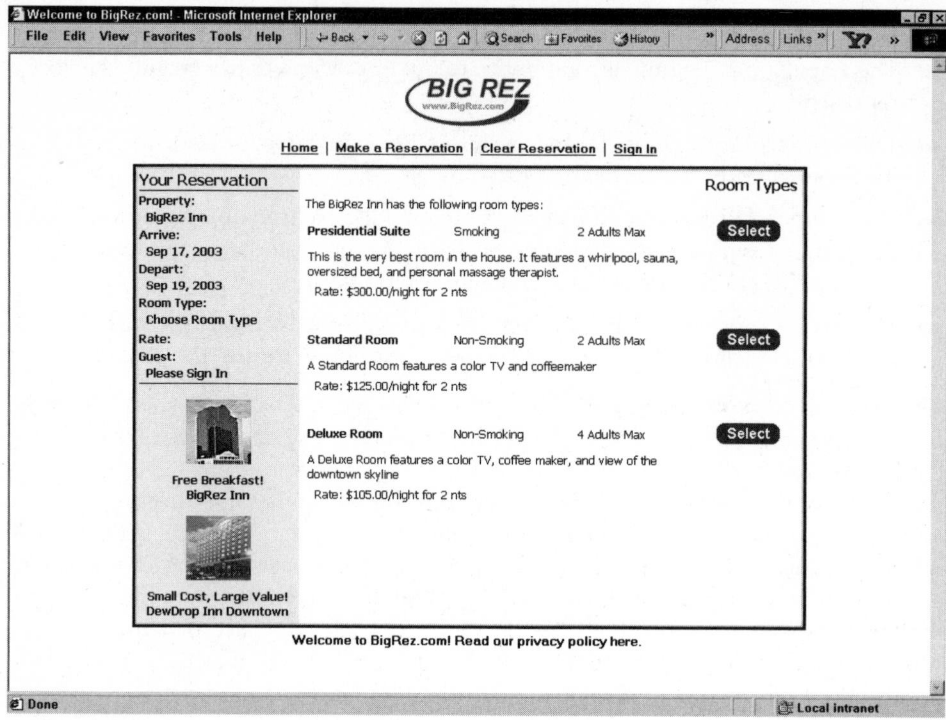

Figure 4.5 Select room type page.

The `SelectRoomType.jsp` page is listed in Listing 4.3 in its entirety because it contains many interesting features and highlights some limitations of the JSP tag library when dealing with complex nested data structures.

```
<%@ page import="com.bigrez.ejb.*" %>
<%@ page extends="com.bigrez.ui.MyJspBase" %>

<%@ taglib uri="/WEB-INF/struts-bean.tld" prefix="bean" %>
<%@ taglib uri="/WEB-INF/struts-logic.tld" prefix="logic" %>

<%@ include file="include/BeginTrans.jspf" %>
<jsp:useBean id="prop" scope="request"
             type="com.bigrez.ejb.PropertyLocal" />
<jsp:useBean id="rainfos" scope="request"
             type="java.util.Collection" />

<table width="100%" cellspacing="5" cellpadding="0">
  <tr>
    <td class="page-header" align="right">Room Types</td>
  </tr>
  <tr>
```

Listing 4.3 SelectRoomType.jsp.

```
    <td class="page-text">The <jsp:getProperty name="prop"
        property="description"/> has the following room types:
    </td>
  </tr>

  <tr>
  <td>
  <table width="100%" cellspacing="0" cellpadding="3" border="0">
  <logic:iterate id="rainfo" collection="<%= rainfos %>"
                 type="com.bigrez.val.user.RateAvailabilityInfo">
    <tr>
      <td width="30%" align="left">
        <a class="table-link"
           href="SelectRoomTypeAction.do?action=select&id=<bean:write
                 name="rainfo" property="roomType.id"/>">
          <bean:write name="rainfo" property="roomType.description"/>
        </a>
      </td>
      <td width="25%" class="table-data">
        <bean:message key="<%= \"smoking\" +
                          rainfo.getRoomType().getSmokingFlag() %>"/>
      </td>
      <td width="25%" class="table-data">
        <bean:write name="rainfo"
                    property="roomType.maxAdults"/> Adults Max
      </td>
      <logic:equal name="rainfo" property="availableFlag" value="true">
        <td width="20%" align="center">
          <a href="SelectRoomTypeAction.do?action=select&id=<bean:write
            name="rainfo" property="roomType.id"/>">
            <img src="/images/selectbutton.gif" alt="" border="0">
          </a>
        </td>
      </logic:equal>
      <logic:equal name="rainfo"
                   property="availableFlag" value="false">
        <td class="table-header" width="20%" align="center">
          Unavailable
        </td>
      </logic:equal>
    </tr>
    <tr>
      <td colspan="3" class="table-data">
        <bean:write name="rainfo" property="roomType.features"/>
      </td>
    </tr>
    <logic:iterate id="rate" collection="<%= rainfo.getRates() %>"
                   type="com.bigrez.val.user.ReservationRateInfo" >
      <tr>
```

Listing 4.3 *(continued)*

```
            <td colspan="3" class="table-data">
                Rate: $<bean:write name="rate"
                  property="rate" formatKey="float.price"/>/night
              for 
              <jsp:getProperty name="rate" property="numNights"/> nts
            </td>
        </tr>
      </logic:iterate>
      <logic:iterate id="blocker" type="com.bigrez.ejb.InventoryLocal"
                     collection="<%= rainfo.getBlockingControls() %>">
        <tr>
            <td colspan="3" class="table-data">
                Not Available on <bean:write name="blocker"
                  property="day" formatKey="date.format1"/>
            </td>
        </tr>
      </logic:iterate>
      <tr><td> </td></tr>
    </logic:iterate>
    </table>
    </td>
    </tr>
  </table>

  <%@ include file="include/EndTrans.jspf" %>
```

Listing 4.3 *(continued)*

The SelectRoomType page first declares the existence of prop and rainfos beans using jsp:useBean tags:

```
<jsp:useBean id="prop" scope="request"
             type="com.bigrez.ejb.PropertyLocal" />
<jsp:useBean id="rainfos" scope="request" type="java.util.Collection"/>
```

These variables are now available for use in either jsp:getProperty tags or Struts custom tags. The page next uses the logic:iterate tag to iterate through the rainfos collection, defining a new page bean called rainfo in the loop:

```
<logic:iterate id="rainfo" collection="<%= rainfos %>"
               type="com.bigrez.val.user.RateAvailabilityInfo">
...
</logic:iterate>
```

Recall that each object in the rainfos collection is a RateAvailabilityInfo value object containing a reference to the related RoomType entity bean as well as rate and availability information. These other objects are “nested” in the RateAvailabilityInfo object, in a sense, so the page must traverse these internal nesting links to display the data related to the nested objects.

In the main loop, the page displays basic room type information by traversing the nested link in the `RateAvailabilityInfo` object to the `RoomType` bean using the `bean:write` tag provided by Struts:

```
<bean:write name="rainfo" property="roomType.description"/>
```

The `bean:write` tag, unlike the normal `jsp:getProperty` tag, allows nested attribute names in the `property` attribute of the tag. If a standard `jsp:getProperty` tag was used to display the nested data, the simple syntax you just saw would be replaced with the following code:

```
<% loadPageObject(pageContext, "roomType", rainfo.getRoomType()); %>
<jsp:useBean id="roomType" type="com.bigrez.ejb.RoomTypeLocal"/>
<jsp:getProperty name="roomType" property="description"/>
```

The scriptlet code calls the `loadPageObject()` method in the JSP page base class, `MyJspBase`, in order to place the `RoomType` reference from the current `rainfo` object in the page context. This step is required because the `jsp:useBean` tag must find the variable already located in the desired scope, a limitation discussed earlier in this chapter. The `jsp:useBean` tag then declares the `roomType` variable, making it available for use by the subsequent `jsp:getProperty` tag. Finally, the `jsp:getProperty` tag displays the description value. This three-step process for accessing nested attributes in page beans argues strongly for the use of a custom-tag library, such as the `bean` or `nested` libraries in Struts, when accessing nested attributes.

BEST PRACTICE **Use Struts'** `bean:write` **or** `nested` **tags to access nested attributes and components in display JSP pages rather than standard** `jsp:getProperty` **tags to avoid complexity caused by the limitations of the standard** `jsp:useBean` **and** `jsp:getProperty` **tags.**

Unlike some Struts applications, the *bigrez.com* application does not make heavy use of the `bean:message` tag to parameterize display strings and retrieve them from the `ApplicationResources.properties` file. This was a conscious decision to help maintain clarity by retaining actual display messages in the example JSP pages. So far, the only messages placed in the `ApplicationResources.properties` file have been error messages used by server-side form validation and other controller logic.

The `SelectRoomType` page uses the `bean:message` tag to demonstrate an interesting technique for converting Boolean bean attributes to a corresponding message in the JSP page. The `RoomType` bean in the `rainfo` object includes a `smokingFlag` Boolean attribute, and this page must display either `Smoking` or `Non-Smoking` depending on the value of this attribute. There are many ways to accomplish this, of course, including the ternary operator in JSP scriptlet code:

```
<%= rainfo.getRoomType().getSmokingFlag().booleanValue()
```

```
? "Smoking":"Non-Smoking" %>
```

A verbose set of `logic` tags would also work:

```
<logic:equal name="rainfo" property="roomType.smokingFlag" value="true">
  Smoking
</logic:equal>
<logic:equal name="rainfo" property="roomType.smokingFlag"
value="false">
  Non-Smoking
</logic:equal>
```

We've chosen to employ the `bean:message` tag to accomplish this task by placing two entries in the `ApplicationResources.properties` file representing the strings to display for true and false conditions:

```
smokingtrue=Smoking
smokingfalse=Non-Smoking
```

We then provide the `bean:message` tag a `key` containing the value of the smoking flag:

```
<bean:message
   key="<%= \"smoking\"+rainfo.getRoomType().getSmokingFlag() %>"/>
```

This solution is not much better than the JSP scriptlet technique, but it does illustrate the potential for displaying conditional messages using the `bean:message` tag. Note that the run-time expression defining the value for the `key` attribute includes a literal, `"smoking"`, requiring escaped double quotes to avoid JSP parsing errors.

The `SelectRoomType` page also demonstrates a more standard use of the `ApplicationResources.properties` file by performing the formatting of bean attributes using `bean:write` tags with display formats defined in the properties file. For example, the `ApplicationResources.properties` file contains the following entries:

```
date.format1=MM/dd/yyyy
date.format2=MMM dd, yyyy
float.price=#.00
```

Dates and prices are then displayed on the page using these formats in the `bean:write` tags:

```
<bean:write name="rate" property="rate" formatKey="float.price"/>
...
<bean:write name="blocker" property="day" formatKey="date.format1"/>
```

Alternative techniques using `ViewHelper` objects are possible, but they require scriptlet code embedded in the HTML and appropriate `<%@ page import ... %>` directives at the top of the page, while the `bean:write` mechanism provides a cleaner and more flexible solution.

BEST PRACTICE **Use** `bean:write` **tags with display formats defined in the application properties file to format display values such as dates and amounts.**

The user examines the room types and rates displayed on this page and selects the desired room by clicking one of the `Select` buttons on the right side of the page. These buttons, like every other hyperlink in *bigrez.com*, are mapped to an `Action` controller class:

```
<a href="SelectRoomTypeAction.do?action=select&id=
        <bean:write name="rainfo" property="roomType.id"/>">
  <img src="/images/selectbutton.gif" alt="" border="0">
</a>
```

A partial listing of the target `SelectRoomTypeAction` controller class is shown below:

```
public ActionForward execute(ActionMapping mapping,
                             ActionForm form,
                             HttpServletRequest request,
                             HttpServletResponse response)
    throws IOException, ServletException
{
    LOG.info(">>> SelectRoomTypeAction::execute()");
    try {
        int roomTypeId = Integer.parseInt(request.getParameter("id"));
        ReservationInfo rezinfo = getRezInfo(request);
        // safety checks that we have property and dates already
        if (rezinfo.getPropertyId() == 0) {
            return mapping.findForward("property");
        }
        else if (rezinfo.getArriveDate() == null) {
            ActionUserHelper.loadSelectDatesForm(request, rezinfo);
            return mapping.findForward("dates");
        }
        beginTrans(request);
        ReservationSessionHomeLocal home =
            (ReservationSessionHomeLocal)
                Locator.getHome("ReservationSessionHomeLocal");
        ReservationSessionLocal rezsession = home.create();
        RoomTypeLocal roomtype = (RoomTypeLocal)
            Locator.getBean("RoomTypeLocal", roomTypeId);
        Collection rezrates =
            rezsession.calculateRates(roomtype,
                                      rezinfo.getArriveDate(),
                                      rezinfo.getDepartDate());
        rezinfo.setRoomTypeId(roomTypeId);
        rezinfo.setRoomTypeDescription(roomtype.getDescription());
        rezinfo.setRezRates(rezrates);
        setRezInfo(request, rezinfo);
        // prepare the request with a GuestInformationForm object
```

```
            ActionUserHelper.loadGuestInformationForm(request, rezinfo);
            commitTrans(request);
        }
        catch (Exception e) {
            ...
        }
        return mapping.findForward("success");
    }
```

`SelectRoomTypeAction` processes the room type selection by calling the `ReservationSession` bean to retrieve rate information, placing the selected room and rate information in the `ReservationInfo` session variable, preparing the required form bean, and forwarding to the next page in the reservation process.

The next page in the reservation process, `GuestInformation`, is a fairly straightforward HTML form used to collect guest information and credit-card information for the reservation. It is a typical Struts form using the `GuestInformationForm` form bean and submitting the data to the `GuestInformationAction` controller class, a pattern we've already covered in some detail. You may examine these components in the downloaded example code if desired, but we will not discuss the `GuestInformation` page in this text.

Reservation Creation Process

The final step in the reservation process begins with a confirmation page, `ReviewReservation`, shown in Figure 4.6. The `ReviewReservation.jsp` display page simply displays information from the `ReservationInfo` object located in the `HttpSession` along with the standard property information from a `PropertyLocal` reference placed in the request by the controller responsible for forwarding to this page. The user examines the contents and clicks on the confirmation button to officially make the reservation.

The only wrinkle introduced on this page is the use of an HTML form, created using Struts form tags, even though there are no apparent input fields in the form. We will make use of the token-based form-posting logic built in to Struts to ensure that this form is submitted for processing once and only once. Rather than building this logic ourselves, the `GuestInformationAction` controller responsible for preparing the request for this page places a token in the request using the standard mechanism:

```
saveToken(request)
```

The controller component this page submits to, `ReviewReservationAction`, checks for the token during form processing:

```
// Check for the transaction token set in previous action class
if (!checkToken(request, "error.transaction.token")) {
    return mapping.findForward("systemproblem");
}
```

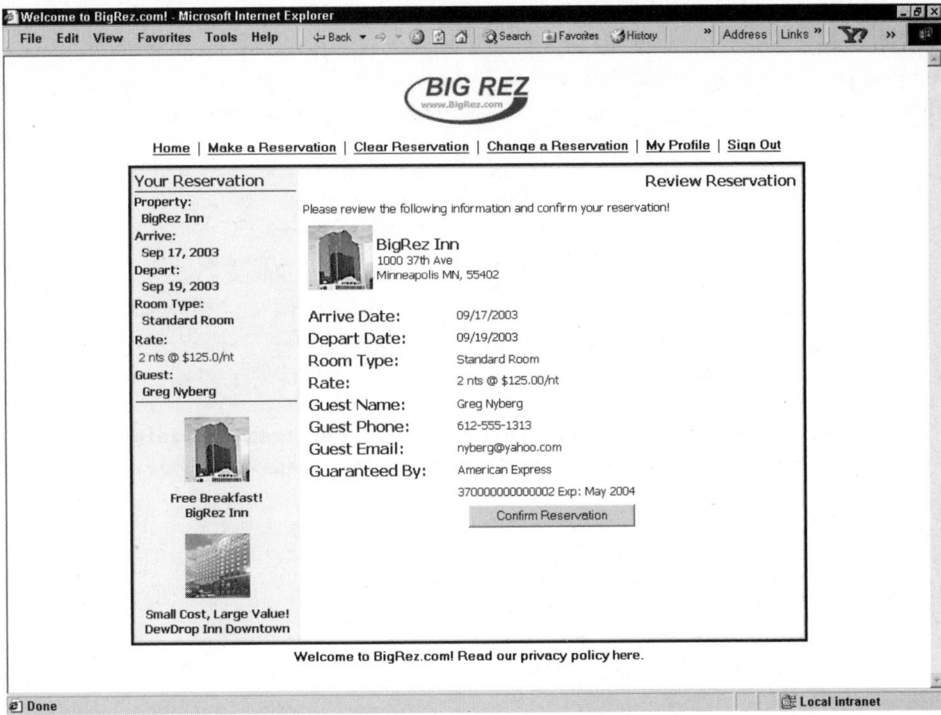

Figure 4.6 Review reservation page.

We've used a helper method, `checkToken`, defined in the `BigRezAction` base class for all `Action` classes:

```
protected boolean checkToken(HttpServletRequest request,
                             String errorkey) {
    if (!isTokenValid(request)) {
        ActionErrors errors = new ActionErrors();
        errors.add(ActionErrors.GLOBAL_ERROR,
                   new ActionError(errorkey));
        saveErrors(request, errors);
        return false;
    }
    else {
        resetToken(request);
        return true;
    }
}
```

If the token is not present or is not valid, the form submission is not accepted and the user is presented with an error message stating that the form may be submitted only once.

After validating and clearing the token, the `ReviewReservationAction` controller class is responsible for invoking the proper business components to create the final, persistent reservation. It passes a copy of the `ReservationInformation` value object to the `ReservationSession` session bean responsible for this task:

```
public ActionForward execute(ActionMapping mapping,
                             ActionForm form,
                             HttpServletRequest request,
                             HttpServletResponse response)
    throws IOException, ServletException
{
    LOG.info(">>> ReviewReservationAction::execute()");
    try {
        ...
        ReservationSessionLocal rezsession = (ReservationSessionLocal)
            Locator.getSessionBean("ReservationSessionLocal");
        ReservationLocal reservation =
            rezsession.createReservation(rezinfo);
        // prepare for the thankyou page before clearing rezinfo
        HttpSession session = request.getSession(true);
        session.setAttribute("rezid", reservation.getId());
        rezinfo.clearAllButProfile();
        setRezInfo(request, rezinfo);
    }
    catch (BigRezBusinessException e) {
      ...
    }
    catch (NamingException e) {
      ...
    }
    catch (EJBException e) {
      ...
    }
    return mapping.findForward("success");
}
```

We have adopted the value object and session façade pattern for the complex reservation creation operation for reasons we've discussed previously. Note that the primary key of `Reservation` entity bean created and returned by the `createReservation` method is placed in the `HttpSession` rather than the `HttpServletRequest` in preparation for the `ReservationThankYou` page. This unusual choice was made to allow a `redirect="true"` in the `success` mapping from this action to the `ReservationThankYou` page, thereby causing the transfer from the controller to the next page to be an HTTP redirect rather than a server-side forward operation. The resulting page display is better behaved should the user refresh the page or attempt to back up to it in the browser after moving somewhere else. A reference to the `Reservation` entity bean itself may not be placed on the `HttpSession` because local references are not serializable.

Before redirecting to the next page, all previous information in the session-based `ReservationInfo` object is cleared to indicate that the reservation process is complete. The user is now presented with the `ReservationThankYou` page presenting the data contained in the final `Reservation` bean. The process is complete!

Targeted Offers Components

To round out our discussion of the user site in *bigrez.com,* we will briefly examine the targeted offers area on the left side of the page. As shown in Figure 3.2 in the previous chapter, this area presents a small number of offers containing a graphic, caption, and related property name. Clicking an offer simply displays the normal property information page for the given hotel, a simplification we chose for this example application. In a real site, clicking an offer might display a special page with detailed information about the offer and provide a shortcut for selecting a specific rate or room type in the hotel, for example.

There are two interesting techniques demonstrated by the offers area:

- Determining the offers to be displayed using a stateless session bean with method invocations placed directly on the display JSP page
- Caching the displayed offers using WebLogic Server `wl:cache` custom tags

The specific offers presented to the user depend on the last city and state searched by the user and the current selected property, if any, in the `ReservationInfo` object. The business logic for selecting and ordering the offers is complex and is therefore encapsulated in a session bean, the `OfferSessionBean`, in a method called `getOffersForDisplay()`. The business-logic contained in this session bean is discussed in Chapter 7. The source code for `Offers.jsp` is shown in Listing 4.4.

```
<%@ page import="com.bigrez.utils.*, com.bigrez.ejb.*" %>
<%@ page extends="com.bigrez.ui.MyJspBase" %>

<%@ taglib uri="/WEB-INF/struts-logic.tld" prefix="logic" %>
<%@ taglib uri="/WEB-INF/struts-bean.tld" prefix="bean" %>
<%@ taglib uri="/WEB-INF/weblogic-tags.tld" prefix="wl" %>

<jsp:useBean id="rezinfo" scope="session"
             class="com.bigrez.val.user.ReservationInfo" />

<% loadPageObject(pageContext, "offerhash", rezinfo.getOfferHash());%>
<wl:cache name="Offers" key="offerhash" timeout="30s" scope="session">
<% LOG.info("Creating Offers.jsp display for hash "+offerhash);%>
<%@ include file="include/BeginTrans.jspf" %>
<% loadSessionBean(pageContext, "offersession", "OfferSessionLocal");%>
<jsp:useBean id="offersession" scope="page"
             class="com.bigrez.ejb.OfferSessionLocal"/>

<table width="100%" cellpadding="0" cellspacing="0" bgcolor="#EEEEEE">
```

Listing 4.4 Offers.jsp. *(continued)*

```
  <tr valign="top">
    <!-- force offer block to be at least 200 high -->
    <td width="1" bgcolor="#EEEEEE">
      <img src="images/space.gif" width="1" height="200"></td>
    <td>
      <table width="100%" align="center" cellpadding="0"
             cellspacing="5" bgcolor="#EEEEEE">
      <logic:iterate id="offer" type="com.bigrez.ejb.OfferLocal"
          collection="<%=
              offersession.getOffersForDisplay(rezinfo, 2) %>">
        <tr><td>
          <img src="images/space.gif" width="1" height="5">
        </td></tr>
        <tr align="center">
          <td>
            <img src="/images/<jsp:getProperty name="offer"
                                        property="imageFile"/>"
                 alt="<jsp:getProperty name="offer"
                                    property="description"/>"
                 width="70" height="70">
          </td>
        </tr>
        <tr align="center">
          <td>
            <a class="sidebar-link"
               HREF="/OffersAction.do?id=<jsp:getProperty
                     name="offer" property="id"/>">
              <jsp:getProperty name="offer" property="caption"/><br>
              <bean:write name="offer"
                          property="property.description"/>
            </a>
          </td>
        </tr>
      </logic:iterate>
      </table>
    </td>
  </tr>
</table>
<%@ include file="include/EndTrans.jspf" %>
</wl:cache>
```

Listing 4.4 *(continued)*

Unlike most display JSP pages in the site, there is no controller responsible for preparing the required `Offer` objects in the `HttpServletRequest` prior to forwarding to this page. The `Offers.jsp` display page is actually included by the `Master.jsp` page-assembly template on every page request, so every controller would be responsible for creating the necessary data in the request if we adopted the normal design pattern. Instead, we allow the `Offer.jsp` page to call the stateless session bean directly to retrieve the collection of `Offer` objects to display based on the current `ReservationInformation` contents:

```
<% loadSessionBean(pageContext, "offersession", "OfferSessionLocal");%>
<jsp:useBean id="offersession" scope="page"
             class="com.bigrez.ejb.OfferSessionLocal" />
...
<logic:iterate id="offer" type="com.bigrez.ejb.OfferLocal"
    collection="<%= offersession.getOffersForDisplay(rezinfo,2) %>">
...
</logic:iterate>
```

Note that we could have used a business delegate pattern at this point by encapsulating the session bean invocation in a page bean or other helper, but in the spirit of direct interaction, we will avoid introducing intermediate objects and helpers unless they encapsulate significant complexity or foster reuse. The code required to access the bean directly is fairly straightforward, the only trick being the use of a helper method defined on the JSP base page to create the stateless session bean and make it available in the `PageContext` before declaring it with a `jsp:useBean` element. The `loadSessionBean()` helper method is defined on `MyJspBase.java`, as shown here:

```
protected void loadSessionBean(PageContext context,
                               String name, String localname)
    throws NamingException
{
    Object _temp = Locator.getSessionBean(localname);
    context.setAttribute(name, _temp);
}
```

Once the JSP page has the `offersession` bean reference, the `logic:iterate` tag is employed to loop through the list returned by the `getOffersForDisplay()` method and display the contents of each `Offer` in the list. The objects returned in this list are actually local references to `OfferBean` entity beans, so the access must be within the context of a transaction. Displaying the offer data is performed with straightforward `jsp:getProperty` elements in the loop as well as a single `bean:write` tag used to access the description (name) of the property related to this offer:

```
<bean:write name="offer" property="property.description"/>
```

The second interesting technique demonstrated by `Offers.jsp` is the use of the WebLogic Server `wl:cache` tag to improve the performance of this page. We discussed the capabilities and limitations of the `wl:cache` tag in some detail in Chapter 1. The tag basically caches the HTML response created within the body of the tag for a specific duration, using the cached version of the response rather than evaluating the body on subsequent page requests. The goal in `Offers.jsp` is to reduce the number of hits to the session bean and the related `Offer` beans to improve performance.

If the offers displayed to the user were completely random and unrelated to the current `ReservationInformation` context, we might be tempted simply to surround the bulk of the `Offer.jsp` page with caching tags similar to the following:

```
<wl:cache name="Offers" timeout="30s" scope="application">
...
// Generate all HTML output
...
</wl:cache>
```

In this scenario, the cached content would expire after 30 seconds. The next page request would cause a reevaluation and recaching of the content, and all users would see a different set of offers for the next 30 seconds. Unfortunately, this simple caching isn't sufficient for our purposes. According to the business rules for the site, the displayed offers depend on selections made by the user. If the user chooses a particular city, state, or property during the reservation process, the offers must reflect these choices. How can we cache the list of displayed offers whenever possible while meeting this business requirement?

We could flush the cache every time the user makes a selection that affects the displayed offers. This technique was described in Chapter 1 and might be required in certain circumstances. There is, however, a better way: cache the response based on the current selection data.

As described in Chapter 1, the `wl:cache` tag includes a `key` attribute that can be used to specify the variables whose values should be used as the key for the cached contents. Essentially, the cached contents should depend on the values stored in the variables defined in the `key` attribute. In our case, the cached content depends on the recent city, state, and property selections made by the user. Rather than expose all of this complexity in the key definition, we've introduced a hash function on the `ReservationInfo` class and used this hash as the key for the caching tag:

```
<% loadPageObject(pageContext, "offerhash", rezinfo.getOfferHash()); %>
<wl:cache name="Offers" key="offerhash"
          timeout="30s" scope="application">
```

The `getOfferHash()` method in `ReservationInfo` simply appends the selection values together to form a `String` value representing the current user selections:

```
public String getOfferHash()
{
    // return a hash string of data used to fetch offers
    return "[" + lastSearchCity + "," + lastSearchState + "," +
           propertyId + "]";
}
```

This string is placed in the page context by `loadPageObject()` using the name `offerhash`, and the `wl:cache` tag is then configured to control caching using this variable. If the application already has a response cached for that particular hash of selection information, the tag will use the previous response. If the cache does not contain a response for that selection information, the body of the tag will be evaluated and the response cached using the key. The response will therefore be generated each time the user changes a selection, but as long as that selection remains in effect the response will be retrieved from the cache, subject to the `timeout` value, of course.

Note that we've defined `scope="application"` in the tag, so response data will be cached at the application level. The application will therefore present the same set of selection-specific offers to every user of the site for the entire 30 seconds. In other words, every user who does a search for properties in a particular city or chooses a particular hotel will see the same offers during that 30-second period of time. Offers could also be cached on a per-user basis using the `session` scope, but placing cached information in the session impacts performance if session persistence is employed and should be avoided if possible.

BEST PRACTICE **Avoid using `session` scope for response data cached using `wl:cache` tags. If session persistence is being employed in the application, the cached data will be treated like other session data and persisted to the JDBC datastore or replicated to backup servers, hurting performance. Consider an `application`-scope cache with a `key` that includes the session ID as one alternative.**

Finally, the hyperlinks in the offers area invoke the controller object for this page, `OffersAction`, just like any other JSP page in the application. The controller retrieves the offer identifier from the request parameter, acquires a reference to the `OfferBean` entity bean, and uses the relationship get method on the `OfferBean` to determine the property to load in the request before forwarding to the property display page:

```
String offerId = request.getParameter("id");
int id = Integer.parseInt(offerId);
OfferLocal offer = (OfferLocal)Locator.getBean("OfferLocal", id);
PropertyLocal prop = offer.getProperty();
ActionUserHelper.loadPropertyBean(request, prop);
```

That's it! We are now ready to proceed to the construction of the administration site components including pages for entering, updating, and deleting all of the information used by the *bigrez.com* user site.

Construction of Administration Site Components

The construction of the administration site in *bigrez.com* is broken down into two primary sections:

- *Authorization/authentication components* controlling access to site components and allowing properties to view and manage only their own information
- *Property maintenance components* providing pages for creating, modifying, and deleting all of the property information required to drive the user site

Note that the administration site is designed to be a completely separate Web application deployed to WebLogic Server alongside the user site. The administration site has its own web.xml file, struts-config.xml file, and a completely independent set of display components.

We will now examine the two sections of the administration site, highlighting key components and techniques in each section as appropriate.

Authorization/Authentication Components

The administration site in *bigrez.com* is not available to the general user community. Two classes of users are allowed to access the administration site: hotel administrators and system administrators. Hotel administrators are allowed to maintain information for their own hotels, while system administrators are allowed to maintain information for all hotels as well as create new hotels and remove existing hotels.

We've employed the standard J2EE Web application security mechanisms provided by WebLogic Server as a starting point for this application. More advanced WebLogic Server-specific security mechanisms will be discussed in Chapter 10. Standard Web application security relies on three primary components:

- The definition of users and groups in the application server environment using administration tools provided by WebLogic Server
- Declaring Web application security in the web.xml file for the application and specifying the roles having access to specific Web components
- Defining the mapping between the roles defined in the web.xml file and the principals, either users or groups, defined in the environment

Using the WebLogic Server administration console, a HotelAdministrators group is created and a small set of hotel administrator users are added to the default realm for the application and made members of this group. A separate BigRezAdministrators group is also created in the realm, and a single administrator user is created and made a member of that group. Chapter 5 walks through this process in detail.

Web application security is then declared and configured in the web.xml descriptor file for the administration site using the standard descriptor elements. First, all of the pages and servlets in the administration site are secured by defining a security-constraint element containing all display resources and indicating with the auth-constraint tag that only the admin and hoteladmin roles may access these resources:

```
<security-constraint>
  <web-resource-collection>
    <web-resource-name>Admin Pages</web-resource-name>
    <url-pattern>*.jsp</url-pattern>
    <http-method>GET</http-method>
    <http-method>POST</http-method>
  </web-resource-collection>
  <web-resource-collection>
    <web-resource-name>Page Display Servlet</web-resource-name>
    <url-pattern>*.page</url-pattern>
    <http-method>GET</http-method>
    <http-method>POST</http-method>
  </web-resource-collection>
```

```
    <web-resource-collection>
      <web-resource-name>Action Servlets</web-resource-name>
      <url-pattern>*.do</url-pattern>
      <http-method>GET</http-method>
      <http-method>POST</http-method>
    </web-resource-collection>
    <auth-constraint>
      <role-name>admin</role-name>
      <role-name>hoteladmin</role-name>
    </auth-constraint>
  </security-constraint>
```

Next, the Web application is configured to use form-based authentication by including a `login-config` element defining the authentication method and the pages to use for requesting login information from the user and for reporting login problems:

```
  <login-config>
    <auth-method>FORM</auth-method>
    <form-login-config>
      <form-login-page>/Login.page</form-login-page>
      <form-error-page>/Login.page?error=true</form-error-page>
    </form-login-config>
  </login-config>
```

The Web container is responsible for displaying the specified login page whenever a user requests a resource in the site for which they are not authorized. Note that the *Login.page* URL specified for this page will actually cause the `PageDisplayServlet` to be invoked, which will then forward to the `Master.jsp` assembly page, which then finally includes the actual login page, `Login.jsp`, in the standard template for the site. We'll examine `Login.jsp` in a moment, but first let's finish the required descriptor entries in `web.xml`:

```
  <security-role>
      <role-name>admin</role-name>
  </security-role>
  <security-role>
      <role-name>hoteladmin</role-name>
  </security-role>
```

These elements simply declare the existence of the security roles used in the `auth-constraint` elements earlier in the descriptor. Note that these security roles are not the same as the `BigRezAdministrators` and `HotelAdministrators` groups defined in the WebLogic Server realm. Although WebLogic Server will automatically map roles to groups in the realm if the names are identical, this is not a best practice. As discussed in Chapter 10, a separate set of elements in `weblogic.xml` should be used to map roles to principals, either groups or users, in the realm. For *bigrez.com*, these mapping elements in `weblogic.xml` look like this:

```
  <security-role-assignment>
    <role-name>admin</role-name>
```

```
    <principal-name>BigRezAdministrators</principal-name>
  </security-role-assignment>
  <security-role-assignment>
    <role-name>hoteladmin</role-name>
    <principal-name>HotelAdministrators</principal-name>
  </security-role-assignment>
```

BEST PRACTICE **Always map the roles defined in** `web.xml` **to principals (groups or users) defined in the realm using explicit** `security-role-constraint` **entries in** `weblogic.xml` **rather than relying on automatic matching of role names to principal names.**

As shown in Listing 4.5, the `Login.jsp` page follows the basic rules of form-based authentication. It defines an HTML form with the action `j_security_check` containing input fields `j_username` and `j_password`. This page will be displayed automatically by the Web container whenever a user attempts to access any controlled resource in the application.

```
<%@ page extends="com.bigrez.ui.MyJspBase" %>

<%@ taglib uri="/WEB-INF/struts-bean.tld" prefix="bean" %>
<%@ taglib uri="/WEB-INF/struts-logic.tld" prefix="logic" %>

<table width="100%" cellspacing="5" cellpadding="0">
  <tr>
    <td class="page-header" align="right">Login</td>
  </tr>
  <tr>
    <td class="page-text">Please log in to Administration Site:</td>
  </tr>
  <logic:present parameter="error">
    <tr><td> </td></tr>
    <tr><td class="error-header2">
      Invalid Administrator ID or Password. Please try again.
    </td></tr>
  </logic:present>
  <tr><td> </td></tr>
  <tr>
    <td>
      <form method="POST" action="j_security_check">
        <table width="50%" border="0" cellspacing="0" cellpadding="0">
          <tr>
            <td width="50%" class="page-label">Administrator ID:</td>
            <td width="50">
              <input type="text" name="j_username" size="15"
                     maxlength="15"
```

Listing 4.5 Login.jsp.

```
                  value="<%= getr(request, "j_username") %>">
          </td>
        </tr>
        <tr>
          <td class="page-label">Password:</td>
          <td>
            <input type="password" name="j_password" size="15"
                  maxlength="15"
                  value="<%= getr(request, "j_password") %>">
          </td>
        </tr>
        <tr><td colspan="2"> </td></tr>
        <tr>
          <td align="center" colspan="2">
             <input type="submit" value="Submit">
          </td>
        </tr>
      </table>
    </form>
  </td>
 </tr>
</table>
```

Listing 4.5 *(continued)*

When the user submits the form, the container intercepts the request and attempts to authenticate using the default security realm and the supplied username and password. If the supplied data is not correct, the container forwards the user to the page defined in the `web.xml` file in the `form-error-page` element, normally an error page of some sort. We've added a twist here by defining the error page to be the `Login.jsp` page again with an `error` parameter:

```
<form-error-page>/Login.page?error=true</form-error-page>
```

In the `Login.jsp` page, we can now sense the presence of this `error` request parameter, using standard Struts tags or any normal scriptlet-based mechanism, and conditionally display an error message at the top of the page:

```
<logic:present parameter="error">
  <tr><td> </td></tr>
  <tr><td class="error-header2">
    Invalid Administrator ID or Password. Please try again.
  </td></tr>
</logic:present>
```

The login form will therefore be redisplayed to the user in the case of login errors with this additional error message at the top. We added one final touch to the page by including in the input fields the previous submitted values using simple expression scriptlets:

```
<input type="text" name="j_username" size="15" maxlength="15"
       value="<%= getr(request, "j_username") %>">
```

`getr()` is a simple utility method in the JSP base class that returns the given request parameter as a `String`, with missing parameters returning an empty string. The page will now display the previous values in the form after an authentication error.

All of these components and configuration entries essentially define the authentication side of the security system. Only users who have a valid login and password in the default security realm and belong to one of the proper groups will be able to access administration site resources. This represents only half of the solution, however. We still need to define authorization logic restricting certain actions and allowing access to property data based on the user's group membership and other criteria.

Recall that there are two different types of users: hotel administrators and system administrators. Hotel administrators should be able to view and maintain only the data for their property, whereas system administrators have complete authority over all properties and related functions. We've elected to implement substantially all of this authorization logic in our presentation-tier components as a starting point.

We'll examine some of the authorization logic built into various maintenance pages in the next section as we examine the specific pages, but let's look at a typical example before moving on. The `PropertyList` page shows a list of all properties in the system, filtered according to authorization. System administrators, for example, see all properties in the system. The controller component responsible for preparing the `HttpServletRequest` prior to forwarding to this page fills the request with a collection of `PropertyLocal` references using one of two different versions of the finder method:

```
String username = request.getRemoteUser().toUpperCase();
...
if (request.isUserInRole("admin")) {
    props = phome.findAll();
}
else {
    props = phome.findByLoginId(username);
}
request.setAttribute("props",props);
```

The `findByLoginId()` finder method filters the returned property references using the `loginId` attribute in the property bean, thereby limiting the result set to those properties that have this user's name in that attribute. Hotel administrators will typically see only a single property displayed in the list, although there is no reason why multiple properties could not be managed by the same user by setting the `loginId` attribute in multiple properties to that user's name.

In the `PropertyList` display JSP page, we also want to prohibit hotel administrators from creating new properties. System administrators see a complete list of properties, as stated earlier, but also have a link available at the bottom of the page to create a new property. We simply place the hyperlink used to create a new property in conditional logic requiring a specific role using standard Struts tags:

```
<logic:present role="admin">
  <tr>
    <td>
  <a class="table-link" href="PropertyListAction.do?action=create">
        Create New Property
      </a>
    </td>
  </tr>
</logic:present>
```

Clearly, we must also check authorization in the related controller classes to supplement this display-side logic and avoid back-door attempts to access unauthorized functions. The `PropertyListAction` controller, for example, includes the following role check in the code that handles the creation of a new property:

```
// we must check for proper role first
if (!isAdminUser(request)) {
    ActionErrors errors = new ActionErrors();
    errors.add(ActionErrors.GLOBAL_ERROR,
               new ActionError("error.propertylist.createnotadmin"));
    saveErrors(request, errors);
    return mapping.findForward("systemproblem");
}
... process the create request ...
```

`isAdminUser()` is defined in the `BigRezAdminAction` base class as follows:

```
protected boolean isAdminUser(HttpServletRequest request) {
    // check for administrator role by name
    return request.isUserInRole("admin");
}
```

BEST PRACTICE **The `logic:present` Struts tags provides a convenient mechanism for checking a user's authorization level in JSP pages. Make sure to supplement any role checks in JSP pages with verification checks in controller components to avoid back-door access to prohibited data or functions.**

Now let's move on to discuss a few of the property maintenance components in the administration site to complete our examination of the *bigrez.com* Web application.

Property Maintenance Components

Table 4.2 lists the primary presentation-tier components responsible for maintenance of property information in the administration site. Once a property is chosen using the `PropertyList` page, the user may update five different types of information: main property information, room types in the property, rates for a given room type, availability of a given room type, and the targeted offers for the property.

Table 4.2 Property Maintenance Primary Components

DISPLAY COMPONENT	RELATED CONTROLLER COMPONENT	FORM BEAN
PropertyList.jsp	PropertyListAction .java	
PropertyMain.jsp	PropertyMainAction .java	PropertyMainForm .java
PropertyRooms.jsp	PropertyRoomsAction .java	
PropertyRoom.jsp	PropertyRoomAction .java	PropertyRoomForm .java
PropertyRates.jsp	PropertyRatesAction .java	
PropertyRate.jsp	PropertyRateAction .java	PropertyRateForm .java
PropertyAvails.jsp	PropertyAvailsAction .java	
PropertyAvail.jsp	PropertyAvailAction .java	PropertyAvailForm .java
PropertyOffers.jsp	PropertyOffersAction .java	
PropertyOffer.jsp	PropertyOfferAction .java	PropertyOfferForm .java

These maintenance components are intended to demonstrate proper use of the Struts framework and the direct interaction approach across a variety of different form types and update requirements. As shown in the table, all of the display JSP pages use a similarly named `Action` controller class, and all form pages use form beans. Consistent with the standard Struts approach, all relationships between these components are defined in the administration site `struts-config.xml` file.

The following sections examine selected pages in the administration site to highlight additional techniques and best practices.

Property Main Form

The main property maintenance page, `PropertyMain.jsp`, is a standard Struts HTML form page using a form bean and `Action` controller class to process updates. As shown in Figure 4.7, the page presents all of the basic property information for update by the user. System administrators may also delete the property completely or change the `loginId` attribute through this page.

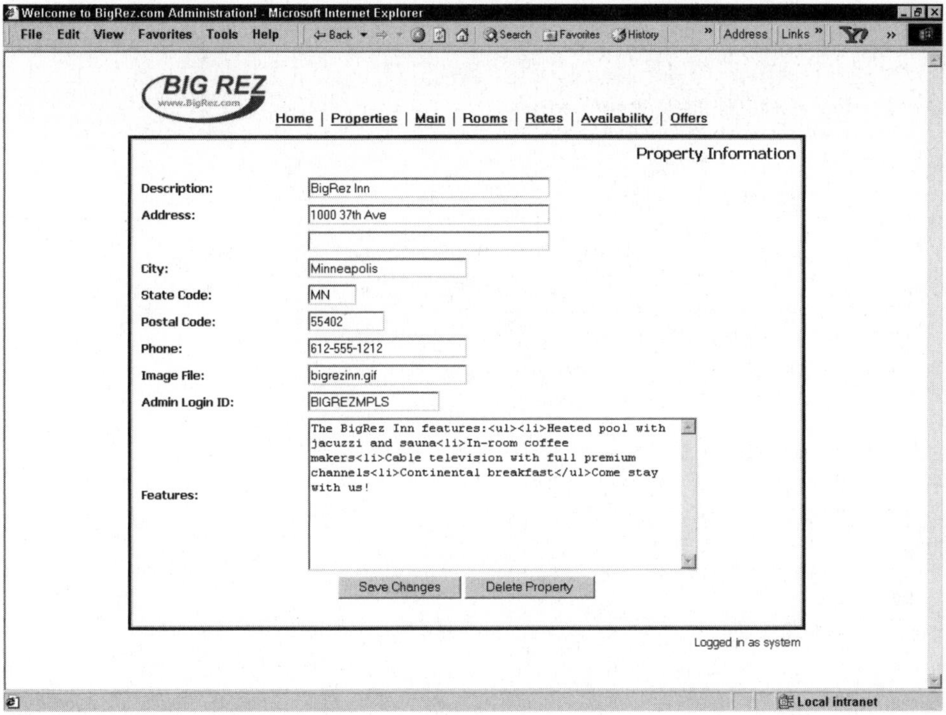

Figure 4.7 Property main page.

The `PropertyMain.jsp` display page uses the Struts `html:form` tags and related input tags to create the HTML form. No JavaScript field validation was employed in these pages to keep them simple. The `loginId` field, editable only by system administrators, is defined in conditional logic based on the user's role:

```
<tr>
  <td class="page-label">Admin Login ID:</td>
  <td>
    <logic:present role="admin">
      <html:text property="loginId" size="20" maxlength="20" />
    </logic:present>
    <logic:notPresent role="admin">
      <span class="table-data">
        <bean:write name="PropertyMainForm" property="loginId"/>
      </span>
      <html:hidden name="PropertyMainForm" property="loginId"/>
    </logic:notPresent>
  </td>
</tr>
```

Form validation is performed by the `validate()` method in the form bean in a similar manner to previous form beans. The `Action` controller class, `PropertyMainAction`, accepts the submitted form once it has been validated and processes the changes in the `execute()` method, as shown in Listing 4.6.

```
package com.bigrez.ui.admin;

import org.apache.struts.action.*;

import java.io.IOException;
import javax.servlet.ServletException;
import javax.servlet.http.HttpServletRequest;
import javax.servlet.http.HttpServletResponse;
import org.apache.struts.action.ActionForm;
import org.apache.struts.action.ActionForward;
import org.apache.struts.action.ActionMapping;
import org.apache.struts.action.ActionForm;
import org.apache.struts.action.ActionForm;

import com.bigrez.form.admin.PropertyMainForm;
import com.bigrez.ejb.PropertyLocal;
import com.bigrez.ejb.PropertyHomeLocal;
import com.bigrez.utils.Locator;
import com.bigrez.utils.CopyHelper;

public final class PropertyMainAction extends BigRezAdminAction
{
    public ActionForward execute(ActionMapping mapping,
                                 ActionForm form,
                                 HttpServletRequest request,
                                 HttpServletResponse response)
        throws IOException, ServletException
    {
        String action = request.getParameter("action");
        LOG.info(">>> PropertyMainAction::execute() with action " +
                 action);
        PropertyMainForm pform = (PropertyMainForm)form;
        // Check for the transaction token set in previous action class
        if (!checkToken(request, "error.transaction.token")) {
            return mapping.findForward("systemproblem");
        }
        try {
            beginTrans(request);
            PropertyLocal prop = null;
            if (action.equals("update")) {
                if (pform.getId() == null ||
                    pform.getId().intValue() == 0) {
                    // create new property
                    PropertyHomeLocal propertyhome = (PropertyHomeLocal)
                        Locator.getHome("PropertyHomeLocal");
                    prop = propertyhome.create(pform.getDescription(),
                                               pform.getFeatures(),
                                               pform.getAddress1(),
                                               pform.getCity(),
```

Listing 4.6 PropertyMainAction.java.

```
                                pform.getStateCode(),
                                pform.getPostalCode(),
                                pform.getPhone(),
                                pform.getImageFile(),
                                pform.getLoginId());
                prop.setAddress2(pform.getAddress2());
                ActionAdminHelper.setPropertyId(request,
                    prop.getId().intValue());
            }
            else {
                // update existing property
                int id = pform.getId().intValue();
                prop = (PropertyLocal)
                    Locator.getBean("PropertyLocal", id);
                CopyHelper.copy(pform, prop);
                ActionAdminHelper.setPropertyId(request, id);
            }
        }
        else if (action.equals("delete")) {
            if (!isAdminUser(request)) {
                ActionErrors errors = new ActionErrors();
                errors.add(ActionErrors.GLOBAL_ERROR,
                           new ActionError(
                               "error.property.deletenotadmin"));
                saveErrors(request, errors);
                commitTrans(request);
                return mapping.findForward("systemproblem");
            }
            // delete the property
            int id = pform.getId().intValue();
            prop = (PropertyLocal)
                Locator.getBean("PropertyLocal", id);
            if (prop.getReservations().size() > 0) {
                ActionErrors errors = new ActionErrors();
                errors.add(ActionErrors.GLOBAL_ERROR,
                           new ActionError(
                              "error.property.reservationsexist"));
                saveErrors(request, errors);
                commitTrans(request);
                saveToken(request);
                return new ActionForward(mapping.getInput());
            }
            prop.remove(); // delete the property and cascade...
            ActionAdminHelper.clearPropertyId(request);
        }
        commitTrans(request);
        ActionAdminHelper.loadPropertyList(request);
    }
```

Listing 4.6 *(continued)*

```
            catch (Exception e) {
                LOG.error("Exception saving property changes", e);
                try {
                    rollbackTrans(request);
                }
                catch (Exception ee) {
                    LOG.error("Exception rolling back ",ee);
                }
                ActionAdminHelper.loadJSPException(request,e);
                return mapping.findForward("error");
            }
            return mapping.findForward("success");
        }
    }
```

Listing 4.6 *(continued)*

The `execute()` method is a fairly complex method because it handles the creation, update, and deletion of properties while checking for valid submit tokens, the proper user role, and the presence of any reservations for this property. We can't provide a complete walkthrough of the code here, so we will touch on a few highlights that might not be obvious from the source code.

First, notice that the creation of a new `Property` bean is performed in this code rather than through a session bean façade or other helper class. In the direct interaction approach, we are allowed to call the `create()` method for a bean directly.

Next, examine the code responsible for updating the `Property` bean with the form contents:

```
// update existing property
int id = pform.getId().intValue();
prop = (PropertyLocal)Locator.getBean("PropertyLocal", id);
CopyHelper.copy(pform, prop);
```

It doesn't seem long enough, does it? One of the benefits of the direct interaction approach is the simplicity of updates, where all that is required is a reference to the entity bean and the calling of its set methods. So where are the set method calls transferring the data from the `PropertyMainForm` form bean to the `Property` entity bean? We've employed a handy helper class called `CopyHelper` for this purpose.

`CopyHelper` has a single static method, `copy()`, which uses reflection to find matching get and set methods on the two input `Object` references and transfer data using these matched methods. The class actually caches the matching set of methods using the two class names as a key to allow faster operation on subsequent calls. As long as attribute names and data types match in the beans, a single call to `copy()` is the only operation required to transfer all of the form bean data to the entity bean.

When the transaction commits, `ejbStore()` will be called on the entity bean by the container, and all of the changes will be saved.

BEST PRACTICE Consider using a reflection-based utility, such as the `CopyHelper` class used in *bigrez.com*, to simplify the transfer of data between forms, entity beans, and value objects.

The last piece of code to examine in `PropertyMainAction` is the code to delete a property. After checking that the property does not have existing reservations, the property is simply deleted using the `remove()` method on the local interface:

```
prop.remove();
```

What about all of the related beans such as `RoomType`, `Rate`, and `Offer` that have relationships and foreign-key constraints with this property? How can we delete the property without first deleting all of its children? As we will discuss in Chapter 7, the relationships between the `Property` bean and its children are all defined with a `cascade-delete` option on the child end of the relationship. WebLogic Server is responsible for traversing all relationships and automatically deleting all children and grandchildren objects before deleting the `Property` bean itself. All you have to do is call `remove()` on the `Property` bean interface.

One of the child beans of the `Property`, the `Reservation` bean, is not configured using `cascade-delete` in the relationship. In other words, existing reservations at a property are not automatically deleted by the container when the property is deleted. Because the database includes foreign-key constraints between the related tables, the database will throw an exception if the property is deleted leaving orphan reservation records. We avoid this error by including code in the `PropertyMainAction` class to ensure that a property has no reservations before attempting the deletion:

```
// delete the property
int id = pform.getId().intValue();
prop = (PropertyLocal) Locator.getBean("PropertyLocal", id);
if (prop.getReservations().size() > 0) {
    ActionErrors errors = new ActionErrors();
    errors.add(ActionErrors.GLOBAL_ERROR,
               new ActionError("error.property.reservationsexist"));
    saveErrors(request, errors);
    commitTrans(request);
    saveToken(request);
    return (new ActionForward(mapping.getInput()));
}
prop.remove(); // delete the property and cascade...
```

Now let's move on to a form page that demonstrates some date-handling logic and a few other tricks, the `PropertyRate` page.

Rate Maintenance Pages

The PropertyRates page displays a complete set of room types and rates available for the current property, as shown in Figure 4.8. Users click on any one of the existing rate entries for a given room type or on the link to create a new room type. All of this data is created in the display JSP page itself from a single object, the Property bean reference, placed in the HttpServletRequest by the upstream controller class. The property's getRoomTypes() method is used to retrieve room types and display their information, and the getRates() method is used in each room type to create the complete display of data.

As usual, all hyperlinks on this page invoke actions on the PropertyRatesAction controller class, which loads the request with the proper information before forwarding to the PropertyRate page. As shown in Figure 4.9, the PropertyRate page combines the properties of a list page and a form page, allowing the user to modify or delete the currently selected rate or navigate to a different rate in the current room type by clicking on a different rate in the list.

A complete examination of this page is beyond the scope of the discussion, but you are encouraged to examine the PropertyRate.jsp source code in the downloadable example code to gain additional insight. We'll jump ahead to the PropertyRateAction controller class to examine briefly how the dates and other unique aspects of this page are handled in the execute() method in that class. Please download and examine the source code for the PropertyRateAction controller class before proceeding.

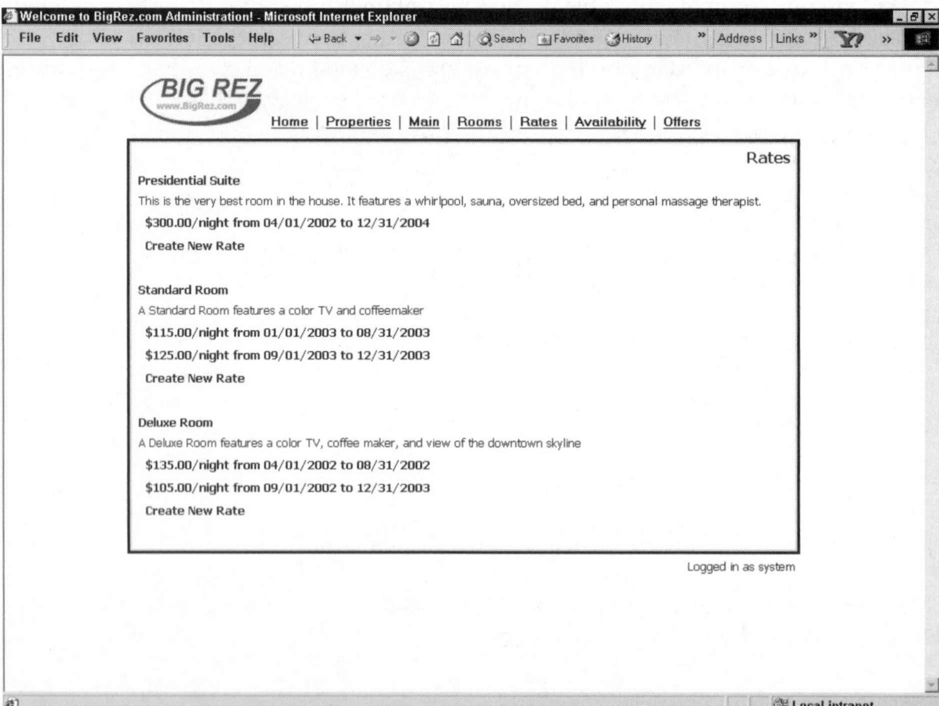

Figure 4.8 Property rates page.

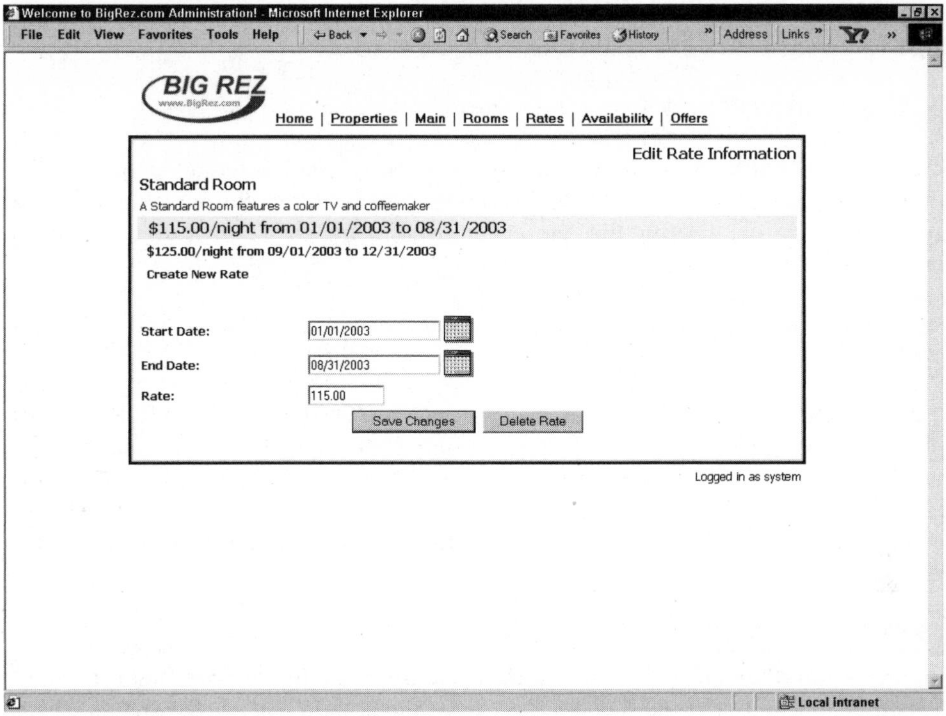

Figure 4.9 Property rate page.

The `execute()` method in `PropertyRateAction` must handle many special cases and perform all create, update, and delete functionality for the associated `PropertyRate` form page. It's a long and complex method, so we'll just look at a couple of interesting sections.

First, note that form validation is being performed in the `execute()` method rather than in the form bean. We've decided to bypass normal input validation for the `delete` action to avoid validation errors that do not matter during a delete, and this is one easy way to do it.

Next, notice that the update logic does not make use of the `CopyHelper` class in this particular case, but instead copies the data manually from the form bean to the entity bean:

```
int id = prform.getId().intValue();
rate = (RateLocal) Locator.getBean("RateLocal", id);
rate.setStartDate(startDate);
rate.setEndDate(endDate);
rate.setRate(prform.getRate());
```

The form bean uses `String` attributes to hold the `start` and `end` dates, and the `Rate` entity bean uses `Date` attributes, so the `CopyHelper` reflection mechanism will fail to transfer the date information properly between these beans because it cannot perform the necessary type conversions. We must transfer the data manually.

Finally, the delete logic removes the `Rate` bean from the system completely using a simple call to the `remove()` method on the bean reference:

```
rate.remove(); // delete the rate completely..
```

This has the side effect of removing the `Rate` bean from its relationship with the parent `RoomType` bean automatically. In fact, if you attempt to eliminate the relationship manually before deleting the `Rate` bean itself, using code something like this, it won't work:

```
roomtype.getRates().remove(rate); // this causes foreign-key error!
rate.remove();
```

A foreign-key constraint error will be raised by the database. It turns out that WebLogic Server performs the `update` SQL statement required to eliminate the relationship before performing the `delete` SQL statement, and because the `Rate` table does not allow the `ROOMTYPE_ID` to be null, an error is raised. Remove children beans directly using their `remove()` method rather than trying to perform the delete in two steps.

BEST PRACTICE **Remove child entity beans in one step by calling the `remove()` method on their local interface. Attempts to first remove them from relationships and then remove the bean from the system will cause foreign-constraint errors in databases employing these constraints.**

Availability Maintenance Pages

We're down to one more set of maintenance pages to examine: the `PropertyAvails` list page and the `PropertyAvail` availability update page. These pages are designed to present the user with a high-level view of room availability at the current property and provide a mechanism for modifying that availability. Availability may be modified by closing out rooms on certain dates or limiting the number of rooms available on certain dates.

Availability in the *bigrez.com* system is stored in the `Inventory` table as a sparse series of rows linked to room types. For example, if the `Deluxe` room type is not available for the date 11/15/2003, there will be a row in the `Inventory` table linked to that room type having a date stamp of 11/15/2003 with a `ROOMSAVAIL` value of zero. The term *sparse* in the previous sentence indicates that the absence of a row in the database for a particular room type and date means no limit or problem with that date instead of implying that there is no inventory available on that date. Chapter 7 will discuss how this inventory data is queried and used to create the availability information employed by the reservation process itself as well as the maintenance pages in this section.

Let's look at the list page for availability, `PropertyAvails.jsp`. As shown in Figure 4.10, the `PropertyAvails` page presents the user with a high-level view of availability over a nine-month period, providing counts of closed days (days with zero inventory) and days with some control (either closed or limited remaining inventory).

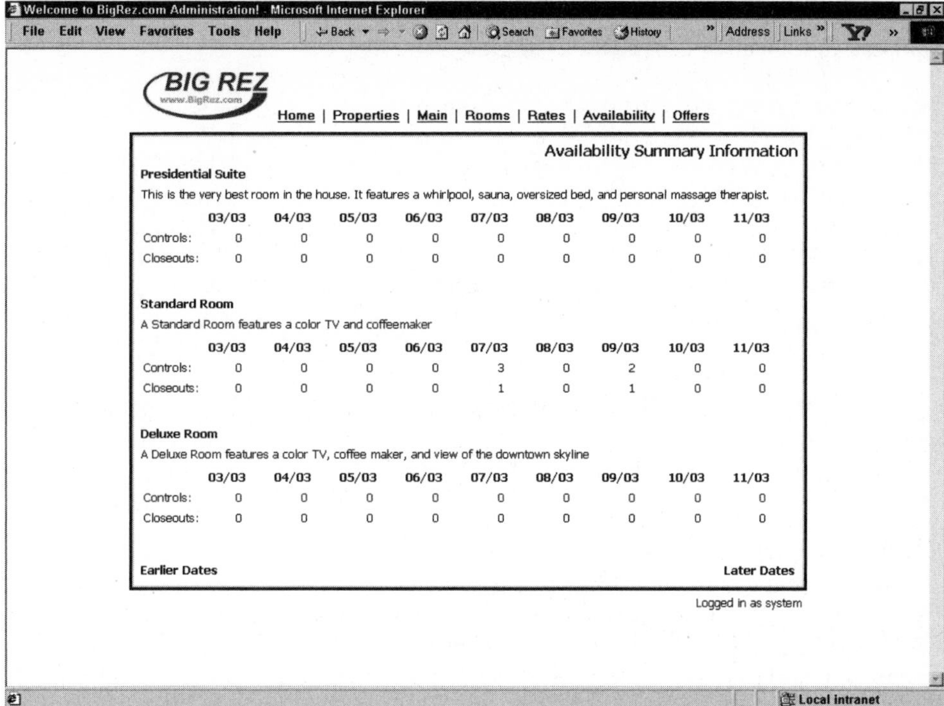

Figure 4.10 Availability list page.

This display represents a great deal of information and a fair number of calculations, so we've chosen to implement the business logic required to collect all of these counts as a session bean façade and value object. Consistent with other pages in the site requiring complex value objects for display, the `Action` controller class responsible for preparing the request invokes the proper calculation method on the session bean and places the result on the `HttpServletRequest` before forwarding to the list page.

For example, in the controller class-handling actions for the top navigation bar, `TopNavAction`, the code appears as follows:

```
Date start = DateHelper.getFirstDayOfMonthNoTime();
ActionAdminHelper.loadAvailSummaryInfos(request, start, id);
```

The `loadAvailSummaryInfos()` method simply calls the `InventorySession` session bean to retrieve a collection of `AvailabilitySummaryInfo` value objects and places them on the request using the `asinfos` key value:

```
InventorySessionLocal isession = (InventorySessionLocal)
    Locator.getSessionBean("InventorySessionLocal");
PropertyLocal prop = (PropertyLocal)
    Locator.getBean("PropertyLocal", propertyid);
Collection asinfos =
    isession.calculateAllAvailSummaryInfo(prop, startDate, 9);
request.setAttribute("asinfos", asinfos);
request.setAttribute("startDate", AvailHelper.format(startDate));
```

The `AvailabilitySummaryInfo` object is a standard value object containing the following attributes with corresponding get and set methods:

```
private RoomTypeLocal roomType;
private Date startDate;
private Collection controlCounts;
private Collection closeoutCounts;
```

To display the summary information, the `PropertyAvails.jsp` page gains access to the collection on the request with a `jsp:useBean` element and iterates through the `AvailabilitySummaryInfo` value objects:

```
<jsp:useBean id="asinfos" scope="request"
             class="java.util.Collection" />
...
<logic:iterate id="asinfo" collection="<%= asinfos %>"
               type="com.bigrez.val.admin.AvailabilitySummaryInfo">
...
</logic:iterate>
```

Typical `bean:write` tags are then used inside the loop to access and display the room-type `description` and `feature` attributes from the `RoomType` bean nested in the `asinfo` object:

```
<tr>
  <td>
    <a class="table-link" href="...">
      <bean:write name="asinfo" property="roomType.description"/>
    </a>
  </td>
</tr>
<tr>
  <td class="table-data">
    <bean:write name="asinfo" property="roomType.features"/>
  </td>
</tr>
```

Finally, nested `logic:iterate` tags are used to iterate over the collections stored in the `asinfo` object and create the summary information:

```
<tr>
  <td class="table-data">Controls:</td>
  <logic:iterate id="controlCount" type="java.lang.Integer"
                 collection="<%= asinfo.getControlCounts() %>">
    <td class="table-data" align="center"><%= controlCount %></td>
  </logic:iterate>
</tr>
<tr>
  <td class="table-data">Closeouts:</td>
```

```
  <logic:iterate id="closeoutCount" type="java.lang.Integer"
                 collection="<%= asinfo.getCloseoutCounts() %>">
    <td class="table-data" align="center"><%= closeoutCount %></td>
  </logic:iterate>
</tr>
```

There are also hyperlinks on this page designed to drill in on a given month to view the details for the month and edit the availability as well as links to scroll forward and backward in time. Examine the source code for `PropertyAvails.jsp` in the downloadable example code to see how these links are created in the page.

For this discussion, we'll simply state that the user clicks a hyperlink on the summary page, which provides the underlying controller class, `PropertyAvailsAction`, with the parameters necessary to prepare the proper information in the request to forward to the maintenance page, `PropertyAvail.jsp`. This page uses the form bean `PropertyAvailForm`, which contains date attributes used for navigation and an `ArrayList` of values representing the inventory values for each day in the month:

```
private String currentDate;
private String editDate;
private ArrayList control;
```

The controller prepares the `PropertyAvailForm` form bean by copying the values from the appropriate `Inventory` beans to the proper locations in the `control` collection, a task contained in the `loadPropertyAvailForm()` method in the `AdminActionHelper` helper class:

```
public static PropertyAvailForm loadPropertyAvailForm(
                HttpServletRequest request, int roomid,
                Date currentDate, Date editDate)
    throws NamingException
{
    LOG.info(">>> loadPropertyAvailForm with roomid " +
             roomid + " and editDate "+editDate);
    InventorySessionLocal isession = (InventorySessionLocal)
        Locator.getSessionBean("InventorySessionLocal");
    RoomTypeLocal roomtype = (RoomTypeLocal)
        Locator.getBean("RoomTypeLocal", roomid);
    Collection availList =
        isession.calculateAvailList(roomtype, editDate);
    PropertyAvailForm paform = new PropertyAvailForm();
    // MM/YY format
    paform.setCurrentDate(AvailHelper.format(currentDate));
    // MM/DD/YYYY format
    paform.setEditDate(DateHelper.format1(editDate));
    paform.setControl((ArrayList)availList);
    request.setAttribute("PropertyAvailForm", paform);
    return paform;
}
```

As shown in the listing, a method called `calculateAvailList()` on the `InventorySession` session bean does the real work of creating the list of values for the given room type and month. The helper simply copies the list to the form bean in preparation for display.

The request now contains a `PropertyAvailForm` with an `ArrayList` of `String` objects suitable for display in the availability maintenance page, `PropertyAvail.jsp`. The Struts framework provides a mechanism for iterating through a `List` in a form bean and creating multiple input fields on the page. We've added logic to break the list of days into columns for better usability, the net result being the form page shown in Figure 4.11. Examine the source code for the `PropertyAvail.jsp` page in the downloadable example code to see how this display is created using `logic:iterate` tags and nested `html:input` tags.

BEST PRACTICE Generate HTML forms containing a list of inputs using Struts `logic:iterate` tags with nested `html:input` tags. These tags provide automatic mapping to a `List` in a form bean and greatly simplify the process.

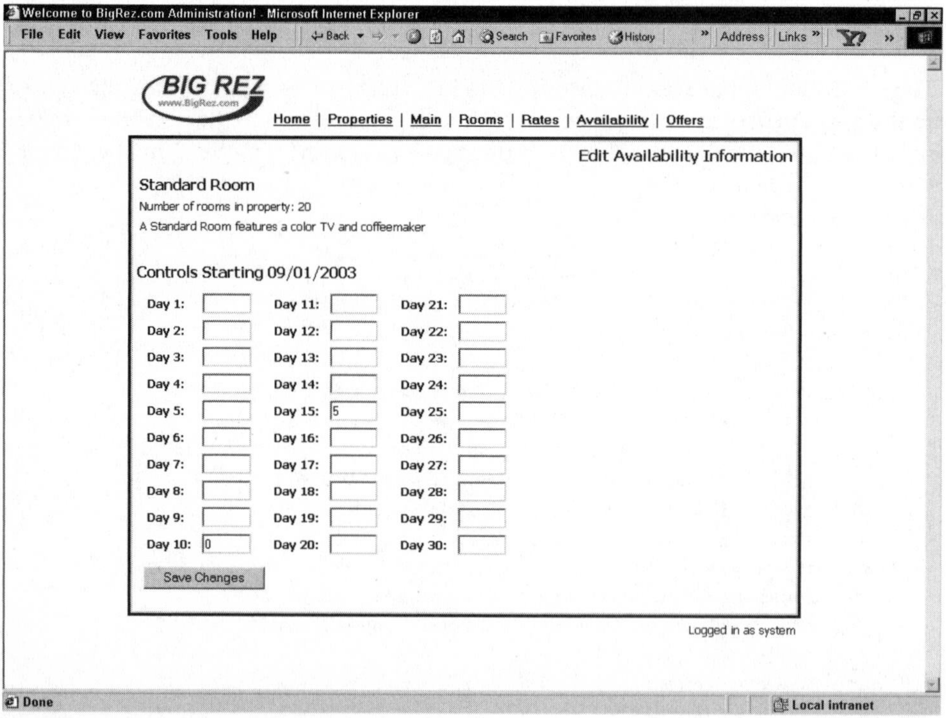

Figure 4.11 Availability maintenance page.

The HTML form is submitted to the controller class for this page, PropertyAvail Action. The Struts framework takes care of populating the form bean with the contents of the HTML form, including the placement of each availability value on the form in the correct location in the control list in the form bean. The form is then validated by the validate() method within PropertyAvailForm:

```
public ActionErrors validate(ActionMapping mapping,
                             HttpServletRequest request)
{
    LOG.info(">>> PropertyAvailForm::validate()");
    ActionErrors errors = new ActionErrors();
    Iterator i = control.iterator();
    while (i.hasNext()) {
        String value = (String)i.next();
        if (!isEmpty(value)) {
            try {
                Integer.parseInt(value);
            }
            catch (NumberFormatException e) {
                errors.add(ActionErrors.GLOBAL_ERROR,
                           new ActionError("error.avail.nonnumeric"));
            }
        }
    }
    return errors;
}
```

Once the form is validated, the execute() method in the PropertyAvailAction controller class is invoked to process the submission:

```
public ActionForward execute(ActionMapping mapping,
                             ActionForm form,
                             HttpServletRequest request,
                             HttpServletResponse response)
    throws IOException, ServletException
{
    LOG.info(">>> PropertyAvailAction::execute()");
    PropertyAvailForm paform = (PropertyAvailForm)form;

    // Check for the transaction token set in previous action class
    if (!checkToken(request, "error.transaction.token")) {
        return mapping.findForward("systemproblem");
    }
    try {
        int propertyid = ActionAdminHelper.getPropertyId(request);
        int roomid = Integer.parseInt(request.getParameter("id"));
        Date editDate = DateHelper.parse(paform.getEditDate());
        Date currentDate = AvailHelper.parse(paform.getCurrentDate());
        ArrayList controls = paform.getControl();
        LOG.info("controls: " + controls);

        beginTrans(request);
```

```
            InventorySessionLocal isession = (InventorySessionLocal)
                Locator.getSessionBean("InventorySessionLocal");
            RoomTypeLocal roomtype = (RoomTypeLocal)
                Locator.getBean("RoomTypeLocal", roomid);
            // Perform the real update work here
            isession.updateInventory(roomtype, editDate, controls);
            // must commit before reloading data for next page!
            commitTrans(request);

            beginTrans(request);
            ActionAdminHelper.loadPropertyBean(request, propertyid);
            ActionAdminHelper.loadAvailSummaryInfos(request, currentDate,
                                                    propertyid);
            commitTrans(request);
        }
        catch (Exception e) {
            ...
        }
        return mapping.findForward("success");
    }
```

We've elected to use a method on the `InventorySession` stateless session bean to perform the update operation rather than creating, updating, and removing `Inventory` beans directly in the controller component.

Note that the transaction containing the bean data must be committed before attempting to load the HTTP request with new summary information. The queries used by `loadAvailSummaryInfos()` will not reflect the newly inserted or updated bean data until the transaction is committed and the `ejbStore()` methods have been called for the beans involved in the current transaction.

BEST PRACTICE **Be careful when executing finder methods or other queries from within transactions affecting the beans in the query. Either commit the transaction before executing the queries to update the database and ensure accurate queries, or use the** `include-updates` **capability of WebLogic Server to flush the updates in the transaction for selected finders. See Chapter 6 for a discussion of the** `include-updates` **feature.**

Chapter Review

This chapter examined the construction process for the *bigrez.com* example application and presented a detailed discussion of selected presentation-tier components. Key concepts such as navigation control, presenting the progress through the reservation process, form validation techniques, handling errors, securing the administration site, and caching HTML responses were included in the discussion.

In the next chapter, we'll talk about packaging and deploying Web applications in WebLogic Server and walk through the packaging and deployment of the *bigrez.com* Web application components.

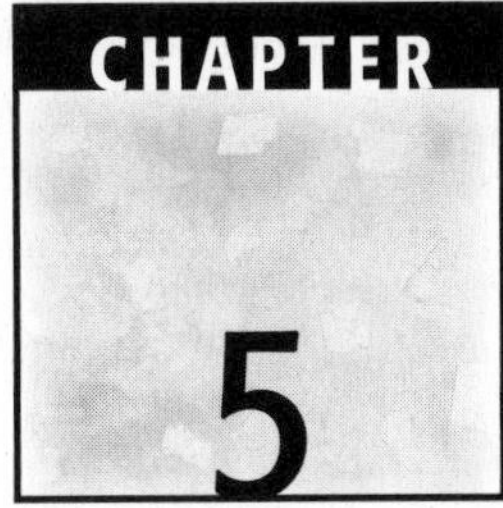

Packaging and Deploying WebLogic Web Applications

This chapter discusses the steps required to package and deploy a WebLogic Server Web application. Consistent with the intermediate to advanced nature of this book, we assume that you have some knowledge of the J2EE specification and the required elements in a well-structured Web application. Our emphasis will be on the techniques applicable to a WebLogic Server deployment rather than a generic J2EE environment. We also assume a basic level of experience with the Ant build tool provided by the Apache Software Foundation. See the Ant home page at http://jakarta.apache.org/ant for online documentation.

Figure 5.1 presents the basic process for packaging and deploying a Web application using WebLogic Server. The basic steps in the process are as follows:

1. Create `web.xml` and `weblogic.xml` descriptor files.
2. Organize the Web application components in the proper directory structure.
3. Precompile JSP pages and place generated class files in Web application structure.
4. Deploy the application to WebLogic Server as an exploded or archived Web application.

The rest of this chapter discusses each of the steps in this process and the tools available in WebLogic Server to perform each activity.

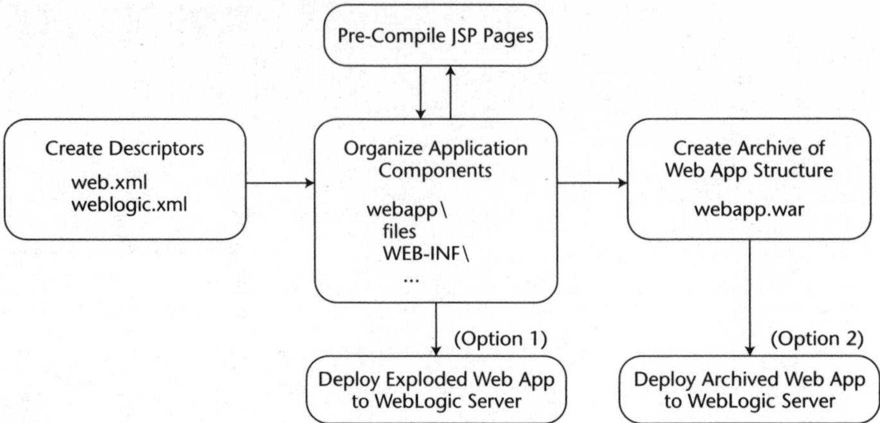

Figure 5.1 Basic packaging and deployment process.

Packaging Web Applications

You package Web applications for deployment in WebLogic Server by creating the correct Web application directory structure and placing in that structure the view components, images, class libraries, and descriptor files required for the application. In this section, we will briefly review the structure of a standard J2EE Web application, examine key elements in the `web.xml` and `weblogic.xml` descriptor files, and present a build process for creating Web applications using the Ant utility.

Web Application Directory Structure

The standard Web application directory structure, depicted in Figure 5.2, defines the proper location for all of the components required for the application. Viewable components, such as JSP pages, static HTML pages, images, and other content intended for viewing by client browsers, are placed directly below the root directory in the structure. Internal files, such as Java classes, libraries, and descriptors, are placed in the `WEB-INF` directory.

The viewable components can be placed directly in the root directory of the Web application or in subdirectories below the root directory to improve the overall organization of the site. It is very common, for example, to have supporting content such as images, style sheets, or JavaScript functions located in separate directories, as shown in Figure 5.3.

HTML and JSP files can also be placed in separate directories to improve organization, as shown in Figure 5.4.

```
webapp
├─.html files
├─.jsp files
├─images, style sheets, javascript files, etc.
└─WEB-INF
   ├─web.xml                    Standard web-app descriptor file
   ├─weblogic.xml               Weblogic-specific descriptor file
   ├─.tld files, .xml files     Other descriptors and configuration files
   ├─classes
   │  └─ .class files           Web-application classes in package hierarchy
   └─lib
      └─ .jar files             Archived utility and client libraries
```

Figure 5.2 Standard Web application directory structure.

```
webapp
├─.html files
├─.jsp files
├─images
│  └─ .gif files, .jpg files, etc.
├─css
│  └─ style sheets
├─js
│  └─ JavaScript files
└─WEB-INF
   └─ ...
```

Figure 5.3 Place supporting files in separate directories.

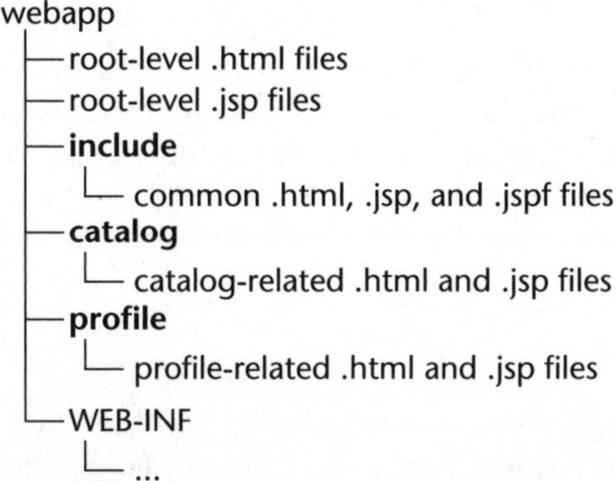

Figure 5.4 Use directories to organize the application.

Hyperlinks and directives, such as `jsp:include`, in the view pages must reflect any directory structure present in the Web application, so it is important to make these organizational decisions early in the development process. Recognize that a good hierarchical organization allows the use of directories in the `url-pattern` descriptor elements to better configure security, servlet mapping, filter mapping, and other features.

When organizing your Web applications, be aware of the important difference between separate directories in a Web application and separate Web applications:

- *Separate directories* in the same Web application represent a purely organizational structure. Components in all directories of a Web application share the same `HttpSession` data, classloader, application-scoped variables, authentication information, servlet and JSP configuration, and all parameters defined at the Web application level in the `web.xml` or `weblogic.xml` descriptors.
- *Separate Web applications* may look similar to separate directories from the point of view of the user, differing only by the context path in the URL (for example, */user/main.jsp* versus */admin/main.jsp*). In the application server, however, separate Web applications are treated much differently than separate directories in the same Web application. Each Web application will use a different classloader, have its own set of descriptor files and application-scoped variables, and store separate `HttpSession` data for the user. The only information shared by both Web applications, essentially, is authentication information. Even this can be scoped to each Web application separately, if desired, creating completely independent applications.

Use separate directories in a single Web application when the directories represent different areas of the same site and you need a single `HttpSession` preserved across the directories. Use separate Web applications when there is a strong need to isolate the sections of the overall application from each other and there is no need to share `HttpSession` information.

BEST PRACTICE Use separate directories in a single Web application to share context and session information. Choose separate Web applications to provide the maximum isolation between the sections of the overall application.

The *bigrez.com* application uses two separate Web applications, `user` and `admin`, rather than a single Web application with separate directory structures. We made this choice because the two sites are intended for completely different sets of users and have different security and auditing rules, and because there is no requirement to share `HttpSession` data across the two sites.

Internal Components

The `WEB-INF` directory contains all of the internal components, including configuration and supporting files for the application. Files located in `WEB-INF` are not accessible directly by the client browser.

As described in Chapter 1, any Java class files or resource files located in the WEB-INF/classes directory are loaded automatically by the Web application classloader and made available to all components in the Web application. In a similar manner, all Java archive (.jar) files placed in WEB-INF/lib are loaded automatically and made available to the Web application. Note that class files located in /classes are loaded before archives in /lib, an important distinction if individual classes are defined in both locations.

NOTE **Class files located in** WEB-INF/classes **are loaded before archives in** WEB-INF/lib. **If the same class is located in both places, the version in** WEB-INF /classes **will be used in the application.**

The remaining files in WEB-INF are descriptor files used by the container to deploy and configure the Web application properly at run time. These files are discussed in the following section.

Web Application Descriptor Files

WebLogic uses two primary descriptor files to deploy the Web application properly: web.xml and weblogic.xml. See the online documentation available at http://edocs.bea.com/wls/docs81/webapp/deployment.html for a complete listing of the elements and structure of these files. We'll examine the descriptor files in *bigrez.com* to help you understand key elements and best practices related to these files.

Standard web.xml Descriptor File

The web.xml descriptor file is defined by the J2EE specification and is used by WebLogic Server to control basic configuration and deployment of the application. Table 5.1 outlines the high-level sections of the web.xml file and lists the key elements used in each section.

Table 5.1 Sections of the web.xml Descriptor File

WEB.XML SECTION	PURPOSE AND KEY TOP-LEVEL XML ELEMENTS
Deployment attributes	Defines graphics and descriptions used by deployment and management tools. <icon>, <display-name>, <description>, <distributable>
Context parameters	Defines parameters and values placed in a Web application context, making them available in application components. <context-param>

(continued)

Table 5.1 *(continued)*

WEB.XML SECTION	PURPOSE AND KEY TOP-LEVEL XML ELEMENTS
Filter information and mapping	Provides deployment information, name, class, initialization parameters, and URL mappings for filters in the application. `<filter>`, `<filter-mapping>`
Application listeners	Defines listener classes used to intercept application events. `<listener>`
Servlet information and mapping	Provides deployment information, name, class, initialization parameters, security roles, and URL mappings for servlets in the application. `<servlet>`, `<servlet-mapping>`
Session configuration	Defines the time-out value for `HttpSession` information. `<session-config>`
MIME mapping	Defines MIME types for file extensions. `<mime-mapping>`
Welcome pages	Provides a list of default pages for unspecified page requests. `<welcome-file-list>`
Error pages	Defines the error page to be displayed in case of specific HTTP error code or Java exception. `<error-page>`
JSP tag libraries	Identifies and maps tag library definition (`.tld`) file to a specific URI name. `<taglib>`
Resource references	Defines an external resource available in the Web application. `<resource-ref>`
Security information	Defines the security authorizations required to access sets of Web pages, the technique used to authenticate a user, and security roles valid in the application. `<security-constraint>`, `<login-config>`, `<security-role>`

Table 5.1 *(continued)*

WEB.XML SECTION	PURPOSE AND KEY TOP-LEVEL XML ELEMENTS
Environment entries	Defines a data value available in the environment. `<env-entry>`
EJB references	Defines EJB components available to Web application components using environment lookups. `<ejb-ref>, <ejb-local-ref>`

The *bigrez.com* application consists of two separate Web applications, `user` and `admin`. Each application has a `web.xml` descriptor file containing the elements required for proper operation of the Web components in the application. Please download these files from http://www.wiley.com/compbooks/masteringweblogic and examine them before proceeding.

We'll now walk through the `web.xml` file for the administration site and highlight some sections worth noting in that file. We won't examine the `web.xml` file for the user site because it contains a subset of the elements in the administration version.

The first section in `web.xml` defines a filter used to log all activity on the administration site:

```
<!-- define auditing filter to log all admin activity -->
<filter>
  <filter-name>AuditFilter</filter-name>
  <display-name>AuditFilter</display-name>
  <description></description>
  <filter-class>com.bigrez.ui.admin.AuditFilter</filter-class>
</filter>

<filter-mapping>
  <filter-name>AuditFilter</filter-name>
  <url-pattern>/Master.jsp</url-pattern>
</filter-mapping>

<filter-mapping>
  <filter-name>AuditFilter</filter-name>
  <url-pattern>*.do</url-pattern>
</filter-mapping>
```

The `AuditFilter` is invoked for all requests matching the URL patterns `/Master.jsp` or `*.do`. The pattern `Master.jsp` is used rather than `*.jsp` to avoid invoking the filter for all JSP pages included using `jsp:include` directives. The `doFilter` method in the `AuditFilter` class simply logs the request and its parameters to the standard logging facility and invokes the next filter, if any, in the chain:

```
public void doFilter(ServletRequest request,
                     ServletResponse response, FilterChain chain)
    throws IOException, ServletException
{
    HttpServletRequest req = (HttpServletRequest)request;
    StringBuffer auditentry = new StringBuffer();
    auditentry.append(req.getRemoteAddr() + " " + req.getRemoteUser() +
                      " " + req.getRequestURI());
    Enumeration e = req.getParameterNames();
    if (e.hasMoreElements()) {
        while (e.hasMoreElements()) {
            String name = (String)e.nextElement();
            auditentry.append(" " + name + "=" +
                              req.getParameter(name));
        }
    }
    LOG.info(auditentry.toString());
    // continue processing any other filters
    chain.doFilter(request, response);
}
```

The next section of the administration `web.xml` file defines the three servlets active in the application and provides the required startup and mapping information:

- `ActionServlet` is the standard controller servlet used by Struts to process HTML form submissions and other actions. We've mapped this servlet to the URL pattern **.do*, provided the location of the file containing application resources, provided the location of the `struts-config.xml` file, and configured the servlet to load during startup in order to preload the configuration information.
- `PageDisplayServlet` was discussed in detail in Chapter 3 as our solution for page assembly. This servlet is mapped to the URL pattern **.page* to implement the assembly technique described in that discussion.
- `InitializationServlet` is used as a startup class to preload selected information in to the Web application context for use in drop-down lists in the display pages. Note that the servlet is not mapped to any URL patterns, so it will never be accessed from a client HTTP request.

We've used a servlet as an initialization or startup class rather than defining a server-level `StartupClass` object for a number of reasons:

1. A server-level startup class must be defined in the system classpath for the class to be available during server startup. Application classes should generally not be loaded in the system classpath because this practice inhibits redeployment of the application and is the root cause of many `NoClassDefFoundError` exceptions.
2. A class located in the system classpath can use only classes that are available in that classloader. This restriction often necessitates moving additional classes to the system classpath, which in turn use other classes that must also be promoted to the system classpath, a vicious cycle that is difficult to break.

3. Classes present in the system classpath cannot be deployed automatically by WebLogic Server to managed servers in the domain (Chapter 11 discusses these concepts). The classes must be manually copied to each server in the domain and made available in the system classpath during server startup.

Servlets are a much better alternative for startup classes because they avoid the system classpath issues completely, have visibility to all classes defined or available in the Web application, and are reinitialized whenever their hosting Web application is redeployed. The Web application containing the initialization servlet may also be configured to always deploy after any EJB components in the same overall application, thereby allowing the initialization servlet to access the EJB components reliably. Use the `Deployment Order` attribute associated with each application component to control the order of deployment in a combined EJB and Web application.

BEST PRACTICE Use servlets as startup or initialization classes rather than defining server-level `StartupClass` classes. Servlet-based initialization classes reload when the Web application is redeployed and avoid the problems associated with classes located in the system classpath.

In the next section of `web.xml` we define the default welcome page, `Home.page`, and the error page to display when an HTTP 500 error code falls out of a servlet or JSP invocation:

```
<welcome-file-list>
  <welcome-file>Home.page</welcome-file>
</welcome-file-list>

<error-page>
  <error-code>500</error-code>
  <location>/Master.jsp?page=ErrorPage.jsp</location>
</error-page>
```

Note that although the welcome page definition can use the `.page` syntax, the error page must invoke the `Master.jsp` directly to avoid losing the error information in the HTTP request.

The next section declares the existence of specific JSP tag libraries and indicates the location of each tag library descriptor (`.tld`) file in the `WEB-INF` directory. The format of these tag library descriptor files is beyond the scope of this discussion. Consistent with our best practices from Chapter 1, we are using libraries supplied by other sources, and we have not created any custom tag libraries of our own, so these files are simply copies of the `.tld` files supplied with the Struts framework.

The administration site employs standard J2EE security to control access to pages in the application, and the next few sections of `web.xml` contain the elements necessary to enable and configure this security. These elements, `security-constraint`, `login-config`, and `security-role`, are explained in detail in Chapter 4 and will not be discussed here. The login page, `Login.jsp`, is also listed and described in Chapter 4.

That's all there is to the administration site `web.xml` file.

Locating EJB Components

Home interfaces for EJB components are looked up by the application using an `InitialContext` object and a string representing either the global JNDI name or the reference name given to the component in the JNDI Environment Naming Context (ENC). Avoid hard-coding global JNDI names in the application code because this ties the code directly to the deployment details and limits the flexibility to change JNDI names. Instead, use lookups similar to the following:

```
Context jndiContext = new InitialContext();
Object obj = jndiContext.lookup("java:comp/env/ejb/RateHomeLocal");
```

The `java:comp/env/ejb/...` ENC syntax requires a mapping element in the `web.xml` file to map this reference name to an actual bean in the application. An element similar to the following is therefore required for each EJB component referenced using the ENC syntax:

```
<ejb-local-ref>
  <ejb-ref-name>ejb/RateHomeLocal</ejb-ref-name>
  <ejb-ref-type>Entity</ejb-ref-type>
  <local-home>com.bigrez.ejb.RateHomeLocal</local-home>
  <local>com.bigrez.ejb.RateLocal</local>
  <ejb-link>RateEJB</ejb-link>
</ejb-local-ref>
```

The mapping may be accomplished using `ejb-link` elements in `web.xml`, as shown here, or may use `reference-descriptor` elements in `weblogic.xml` to map the reference names to global JNDI names. We recommend the easier and more portable `ejb-link` elements.

BEST PRACTICE **Use the `java:comp/env/ejb/...` ENC syntax to look up EJB home interfaces to eliminate strong coupling between application code and JNDI names. Map the reference names to deployed beans using `ejb-link` elements in the `web.xml` descriptor file.**

The *bigrez.com* application uses a `Locator` utility class to acquire and cache references to EJB home interfaces in Web application components and business-tier code. Many examples in the previous chapter looked similar to this:

```
RateHomeLocal ratehome =
    (RateHomeLocal) Locator.getHome("RateHomeLocal");
```

The `Locator` class is very useful in the application code because it abstracts the process for retrieving and caching home interfaces and provides a simple syntax requiring no knowledge of the EJB deployment. The `Locator` class looks for the specified home interface in two ways:

- It prepends `java:comp/env/ejb/` to the supplied name and searches in the JNDI ENC for the desired home interface.
- It searches for the supplied name as a global JNDI name.

As a Web application deployer, you therefore have a choice: allow the Locator class to find EJB home interfaces using the JNDI names directly or include ejb-ref and ejb-local-ref descriptor elements in the web.xml descriptor file to make home interfaces available using the java:comp/env/ejb/... syntax. The application code does not change based on your decision; it is simply a matter of deployment preference.

The web.xml files for *bigrez.com* do not include ejb-local-ref elements for EJB components, so Locator lookups will rely on global JNDI names by default. The two-step nature of the Locator utility gives us the flexibility to add selected ejb-local-ref elements in the future if there is a need to map the original name to a different bean, but there is no need to precreate all of these elements initially. A performance penalty is associated with this two-step process, naturally. The JNDI lookup throws an exception if the first search, using the java:comp/env/ejb/... syntax, fails to find the home interface, and the lookup must then be repeated using the global JNDI name. Repeating this two-step process for every request would have serious repercussions on performance. Caching of home interfaces in the Locator class eliminates this inefficiency on all subsequent requests for the same home interface.

The bottom line is that application code should not be aware of the referencing technique used to map names to EJB home interfaces. It is generally best to use the java:comp/env/ejb/... syntax in your home lookup code and create the necessary mapping elements in web.xml, as described in the best practice. Using a Locator class that tries to find the home interface multiple ways is also a reasonable solution.

weblogic.xml Descriptor File

The weblogic.xml descriptor file is a WebLogic Server-specific file used to control WebLogic Server-specific features and provide extensions to the basic configuration and deployment features in web.xml. Table 5.2 outlines the high-level sections of the weblogic.xml file and lists the key elements used in each section. See the online documentation at http://edocs.bea.com/wls/docs81/webapp/deployment.html for a complete listing.

Table 5.2 Sections of the weblogic.xml Descriptor File

WEBLOGIC.XML SECTION	PURPOSE AND KEY TOP-LEVEL XML ELEMENTS
Deployment attributes	Defines information used by deployment and management tools. <description>, <weblogic-version>
Context root information	Defines the context root for the Web application. Used when the Web application is not deployed in an enterprise application (.ear) file. <context-root>

(continued)

Table 5.2 *(continued)*

WEBLOGIC.XML SECTION	PURPOSE AND KEY TOP-LEVEL XML ELEMENTS
Security role/principal mapping	Assigns specific principals in the security realm to a role defined in the `web.xml` descriptor, supplementing any realm assignments. `<security-role-assignment>`
Resource references	Provides the physical location (JNDI name) of resources and EJB components declared in the `web.xml` file using `resource-ref`, `ejb-ref`, and `ejb-local-ref` elements. `<reference-descriptor>`
Directory mapping information	Defines alternate locations for files matching specific URL patterns. `<virtual-directory-mapping>`
URL matching class	Defines the class used to map URLs to servlets with additional path information. `<url-match-map>`
Session configuration	Defines detailed `HttpSession` configuration parameters such as persistence technique, cookie name, and so on. `<session-descriptor>`
JSP configuration	Defines configuration parameters for JSP generation and compilation. `<jsp-descriptor>`
Container configuration	Defines miscellaneous parameters controlling container behavior for forwards and HTTP redirects. `<container-descriptor>`
Character set parameters	Defines character set mappings for incoming request data. `<charset-params>`

The `weblogic.xml` descriptors for both sites in `bigrez.com` require only a handful of elements to configure their respective Web applications properly. Listing 5.1 presents the administration site version of this file.

```
<!DOCTYPE weblogic-web-app PUBLIC
"-//BEA Systems, Inc.//DTD Web Application 8.1//EN"
"http://www.bea.com/servers/wls810/dtd/weblogic-web-jar.dtd">

<weblogic-web-app>
  <security-role-assignment>
    <role-name>admin</role-name>
    <principal-name>BigRezAdministrators</principal-name>
  </security-role-assignment>
  <security-role-assignment>
    <role-name>hoteladmin</role-name>
    <principal-name>HotelAdministrators</principal-name>
  </security-role-assignment>

  <session-descriptor>
    <session-param>
      <param-name>PersistentStoreType</param-name>
      <param-value>memory</param-value>
    </session-param>
  </session-descriptor>

  <jsp-descriptor>
    <jsp-param>
      <param-name>pageCheckSeconds</param-name>
      <param-value>1</param-value>
    </jsp-param>
    <jsp-param>
      <param-name>debug</param-name>
      <param-value>true</param-value>
    </jsp-param>
    <jsp-param>
      <param-name>keepgenerated</param-name>
      <param-value>true</param-value>
    </jsp-param>
  </jsp-descriptor>
</weblogic-web-app>
```

Listing 5.1 Administration site weblogic.xml descriptor file.

We've defined only three sections in this file, and within these sections only a small number of elements. We'll walk through these sections first and then briefly describe why none of the other sections applies to the *bigrez.com* application.

The `security-role-assignment` section maps the roles defined in the `web.xml` file to principals, either groups or users, in the WebLogic Server environment. This topic is discussed in more detail in Chapters 4 and 10.

The `session-descriptor` section contains a single element defining the `PersistenceStoreType` to be `memory`:

```
  <session-descriptor>
    <session-param>
```

```
    <param-name>PersistentStoreType</param-name>
    <param-value>memory</param-value>
  </session-param>
</session-descriptor>
```

We're willing to accept the default values for all of the other session-related parameters defined in this section. In fact, `memory` itself is the default value for the `PersistentStoreType` parameter, but we've included it in this file as a reminder to ourselves to change the value to `replicated` when we get ready for a clustered production release of the application.

The `jsp-descriptor` section contains some parameters defining both nondefault values and values we must revisit and modify when making a production release. The `pageCheckSeconds` parameter, for example, should be set to the value -1 in production to disable all page checking and recompilation.

The following list identifies sections we did not require in the `weblogic.xml` file and explains our rationale for excluding them to give you an idea about when they might be required in your development efforts:

Context root information. We will be deploying the user and administration Web applications in an enterprise application (`.ear`) file. The context root will be defined in the `application.xml` file.

Resource references. We've chosen to access EJB components using JNDI names and a `Locator` utility class, so no `ejb-ref` or `ejb-local-ref` elements are necessary in `web.xml`, and no matching `ejb-reference-description` elements are required here.

Directory mapping information. Images are placed in the user and administration Web applications rather than mapped to a separate directory using this section.

Most Web applications require very little configuration information in the `weblogic.xml` file. Unlike the WebLogic Server-specific EJB descriptors, which are almost always necessary and are usually very long and complex, the default values for `weblogic.xml` are often sufficient.

Precompiling JSP Components

At some point in the packaging process you have a decision to make: Should JSP pages in the application be processed and compiled by the server when the page is first accessed by a user, or should all pages be precompiled before deploying the application? Precompiling improves site performance and ensures that all JSP pages in the site compile before deployment takes place. Without precompiling the JSP pages, syntax errors in scriptlet code and custom-tag elements will not be caught until a user accesses the page.

BEST PRACTICE All production and test deployments should include precompiled JSP pages. Development deployments intended for use on the developer's workstation may use precompiled pages or on-the-fly compilation.

As discussed in Chapter 1, WebLogic Server provides a utility called `weblogic.jspc`, which can be used to precompile JSP pages in the Web application. Precompiling pages essentially simulates the page parsing, servlet generation, and servlet compiling that occur when a JSP page is accessed during site operation.

Although you can use the `weblogic.jspc` utility on a deployed, exploded Web application located in the `applications` directory of a WebLogic Server domain, a better technique includes the precompilation step in the build process used to create and package the Web application. In this technique, the precompiled JSP classes are created in a staging area for the application and packaged in a manner very similar to other Java classes.

The *bigrez.com* example application contains two separate Web applications, `user` and `admin`. As shown in Figure 5.5, these Web applications are located in the directories `web-user` and `web-admin` below the root working directory for the overall application.

This type of development environment structure is documented and described in Chapter 13 when we cover development best practices. For the purposes of this discussion, the key item to note is that the Web applications themselves are located in the working directory hierarchy. All JSP files, descriptors, and other files are in the `web-user` and `web-admin` directories, providing a natural staging area for precompiling JSP pages and for packaging the Web applications.

WebLogic Server 8.1 introduces a new application compiler, `weblogic.appc`, capable of compiling enterprise-application (`.ear`) files, EJB archive (`.jar`) files, Web application (`.war`) files, and exploded versions of these files. You can use `weblogic.appc` to validate the descriptors and precompile the JSP files in a Web application by invoking the utility and passing it the root directory for the application:

```
java -classpath ... weblogic.appc src/web-user
```

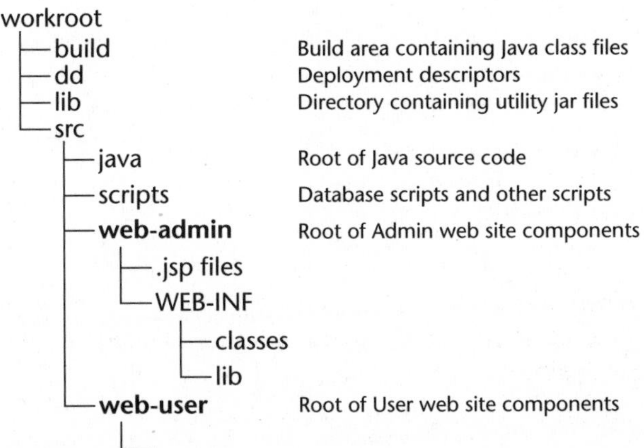

Figure 5.5 Web applications located in working directory structure.

Many options and parameters are available with `weblogic.appc`; see the BEA online documentation at http://edocs.bea.com/wls/docs81/webapp/basics.html for details.

Integrating `weblogic.appc` in your `build.xml` file is accomplished using a new Ant task, `wlappc`, also introduced in WebLogic Server 8.1. The `build.xml` file for *bigrez.com* includes targets for precompiling the JSP files in the `web-user` and `web-admin` directories using this new `wlappc` task:

```
<taskdef name="wlappc" classname="weblogic.ant.taskdefs.j2ee.Appc"/>
<target name="jspc-user">
  <!-- Pre-compile JSP pages to src/web-user/WEB-INF/classes -->
  <wlappc source="${webuser}"
          classpathref="jspc.user.classpath" verbose="true">
  </wlappc>
</target>

<target name="jspc-admin">
  <!-- Pre-compile JSP pages to src/web-admin/WEB-INF/classes -->
  <wlappc source="${webadmin}"
          classpathref="jspc.admin.classpath" verbose="true">
  </wlappc>
</target>
```

In previous versions of WebLogic Server these targets would have invoked the `weblogic.jspc` utility as shown here:

```
<target name="jspc-user">
  <java classname="weblogic.jspc" fork="yes"
        classpathref="jspc.user.classpath">
    <arg line="-depend -compileAll -k -webapp ${webuser}
       -d ${webuser}/WEB-INF/classes"/>
  </java>
</target>

<target name="jspc-admin">
  <java classname="weblogic.jspc" fork="yes"
        classpathref="jspc.admin.classpath">
    <arg line="-depend -compileAll -k -webapp ${webadmin}
       -d ${webadmin}/WEB-INF/classes"/>
  </java>
</target>
```

The `webuser` and `webadmin` properties are defined in `build.xml` to reference the appropriate subdirectories of the root directory:

```
<property name="webuser" value="${src}/web-user"/>
<property name="webadmin" value="${src}/web-admin"/>
```

These `jspc` targets scan the Web application directories for all files ending in `.jsp` and perform the same servlet-generation and compilation steps performed by the application server at run time. The `weblogic.appc` compiler requires the same descriptor files, library archive files, and Java class files as the run-time container requires. The `WEB-INF` directory must therefore contain the appropriate descriptors, and the classpath for `weblogic.appc` must include all required directories and archive files.

The `jspc` tasks create a set of `.class` files in the `WEB-INF/classes/jsp_servlet` directory under each Web application. These files are the precompiled JSP servlet classes and should be packaged and deployed in this same location in the final Web application archive file or exploded structure.

Note that the generated code in the precompiled class is very picky about the timestamp of the associated JSP file. If the JSP file in the deployed Web application is older or newer than the file used to create the precompiled class, the precompiled class will be ignored at run time, and the normal on-the-fly JSP compilation will occur. To avoid this problem, be careful to preserve the file timestamp when copying JSP files from the area used to create the precompiled classes to an exploded application structure or staging area. In the `dist` task in the *bigrez.com* build process, for example, the `preservelastmodified` attribute is included in the `copy` task to ensure that the JSP files retain the proper timestamps:

```
<target name="dist" depends="compile">
  <!-- Copy all of the webapplication files to the proper webapps -->
  <copy todir="${webapp.user.dir}" preservelastmodified="true">
    <fileset dir="${webuser}" includes="**/*.*"/>
  </copy>
  <copy todir="${webapp.admin.dir}" preservelastmodified="true">
    <fileset dir="${webadmin}" includes="**/*.*"/>
  </copy>
  ...
</target>
```

BEST PRACTICE Preserve JSP file timestamps when copying to the staging area or exploded Web application to ensure precompiled classes are used at run time.

The complete *bigrez.com* build file, `build.xml`, is available in the downloadable example code for your reference. Chapter 8 discusses the packaging and deployment of the entire *bigrez.com* enterprise application using the targets in `build.xml`.

There is one additional best practice to discuss related to precompiling JSP pages. It is a rather mundane recommendation, but it can be costly if you do not follow it. Any partial pages or snippets of scriplet code included in the actual JSP pages using `<%@ include file="..." %>` should have a file extension other than `.jsp`. The `.jspf` file extension is recommended in the JSP specification, but any extension will work.

Why is using a different extension important? The `weblogic.appc` compiler typically scans the Web application directory and compiles all files that match the desired file name (`*.jsp`) and will probably not be able to compile any partial pages it encounters. They were never intended to be stand-alone pages yielding their own servlet classes—they are simply snippets of HTML or JSP code included in a master JSP page.

Many developers wait to begin precompiling their JSP pages until late in the development cycle and learn this lesson the hard way.

Note that this practice applies only to the static `<%@ include file="snippet.jspf" %>` directive and not to the dynamic `<jsp:include file="header.jsp"/>` directive. The dynamic directive assumes the target page is a stand-alone JSP page capable of being converted to a Java servlet, so the target page should be included in the precompilation process and should retain the `.jsp` file extension.

BEST PRACTICE **Use the `.jspf` file extension for all partial pages and JSP snippets included in JSP pages using the static `<%@ include file="..." %>` directive to avoid precompilation problems.**

Creating an Exploded Web Application

To create an exploded Web application, you basically copy the Web application directory structure contained in the work area of your application to the appropriate location in the WebLogic Server domain. The deployed version of the application therefore retains all of the structure and individual files discussed in the previous sections.

Typically, a set of `copy` tasks is created in the `build.xml` script for the application that copy the Web application components, along with appropriate Java classes compiled to a `build` directory, to the destination directory in the WebLogic Server directory structure.

In *bigrez.com*, we are deploying the user and administration Web applications in exploded format in an exploded enterprise application (`.ear`) file as part of the development build process. We'll defer the discussion of the exploded `.ear` format to Chapter 8 and simply state that the proper locations for the two exploded Web applications become the following:

```
/mastering/user_projects/bigrezdomain/applications/rezapp/user
/mastering/user_projects/bigrezdomain/applications/rezapp/admin
```

These locations are defined at the top of the `build.xml` file using properties defined in `build.properties`:

```
build.xml:

  <property name="domain.dir" value="${DOMAIN_HOME}/${DOMAIN}"/>
  <property name="applications" value="${domain.dir}/applications"/>
  <property name="deploy.dir" value="${applications}/${APPLICATION}"/>
  <property name="webapp.user.dir" value="${deploy.dir}/user"/>
  <property name="webapp.admin.dir" value="${deploy.dir}/admin"/>

build.properties:

  WEBLOGIC_HOME=c:/bea/weblogic81
  DOMAIN_HOME=c:/mastering/user_projects
  DOMAIN=bigrezdomain
  APPLICATION=rezapp
```

Note that a Web application deployed as a stand-alone application in the WebLogic Server domain, rather than as a part of an enterprise application (`.ear`) file, would be deployed directly to the `applications` directory.

The `copy` tasks used by *bigrez.com* to deploy the exploded Web applications are part of the `dist` task:

```
<target name="dist" depends="makeapp,ejbjar">
  <!-- Copy all of the webapplication files to the proper webapps -->
  <copy todir="${webapp.user.dir}" preservelastmodified="true">
    <fileset dir="${webuser}" includes="**/*.*"/>
  </copy>
  <copy todir="${webapp.admin.dir}" preservelastmodified="true">
    <fileset dir="${webadmin}" includes="**/*.*"/>
  </copy>
  <!-- Copy the user webapp classes to the user/WEB-INF/classes -->
  <copy todir="${webapp.user.dir}/WEB-INF/classes">
    <fileset dir="${build}"
             includes="**/ui/**/*.class,**/form/**/*.class"
             excludes="**/admin/**/*.class" />
  </copy>
  <!-- Copy the admin webapp classes to the admin/WEB-INF/classes -->
  <copy todir="${webapp.admin.dir}/WEB-INF/classes">
    <fileset dir="${build}"
             includes="**/ui/**/*.class,**/form/**/*.class"
             excludes="**/user/**/*.class" />
  </copy>
  <!-- Copy the EJB jar file  -->
  <copy file="${ejb.jar.filename}" todir="${deploy.dir}" />
  <!-- Copy properties files to the webapp/WEB-INF/classes -->
  <copy todir="${webapp.user.dir}/WEB-INF/classes">
    <fileset dir="${src}" includes="**/ui/user/*.properties" />
  </copy>
  <!-- Copy properties files to the webapp/WEB-INF/classes -->
  <copy todir="${webapp.admin.dir}/WEB-INF/classes">
    <fileset dir="${src}" includes="**/ui/admin/*.properties" />
  </copy>
  <!-- Copy EAR descriptor files to application META-INF -->
  <copy todir="${deploy.dir}/META-INF">
    <fileset dir="${basedir}/dd">
       <include name="application.xml,weblogic-application.xml" />
    </fileset>
  </copy>
  <!-- Copy utility archives to application lib directory -->
  <copy todir="${deploy.dir}/lib">
    <fileset dir="${basedir}/lib" includes="log4j.jar" />
  </copy>
</target>
```

These `copy` tasks are responsible for moving all of the Web application components, descriptors, properties files, precompiled JSP classes, and supporting Java classes from the working area to the proper deployment directory. Note that the `copy` tasks for the user and admin support classes are careful to copy only the appropriate package hierarchies to the destination directory. We developed both types of support classes in a single work area directory structure, segregated only by the user or admin in the package name, and we use that package name difference to copy the correct files to each Web application destination.

Creating a Web Application Archive File

A Web application archive file, or .war file, contains all of the Web application components, descriptors, and supporting classes in a single file. The internal structure of the .war file is identical to the equivalent exploded Web application deployment directory.

Creating a .war file is easy enough in theory: You simply execute the appropriate jar command to include all of the desired Web application components and supporting files in the archive. In practice, you need a mechanism to assemble the proper components and files in a staging area in preparation for the standard jar utility, or you need a better jar technique that allows you to piece together components and supporting classes from various locations in a single archive. Either solution works, but we prefer the latter.

The recommended archive technique uses the war task in Ant to build the archive from a variety of files. The war task, like the basic jar Ant task, allows the definition of multiple fileset embedded elements, each with flexible and powerful controls for including and excluding files from the archive. The war task adds a number of special elements that automatically place the specified files in their proper locations in the Web application directory structure.

In the *bigrez.com* build process, the .war files for each Web application are created using the following two tasks in the build.xml file:

```
<target name="war-user" depends="compile">
  <!-- Create user.war webapp archive file -->
  <war destfile="${basedir}/user.war"
       webxml="${webuser}/WEB-INF/web.xml">
    <fileset dir="${webuser}"
             includes="**/*.*"
             excludes="**/*.java, WEB-INF/web.xml"/>
    <classes dir="${build}"
             includes="**/ui/**/*.class, **/form/**/*.class"
             excludes="**/admin/**/*.class" />
    <classes dir="${srcjava}"
             includes="**/ui/user/*.properties" />
  </war>
</target>

<target name="war-admin" depends="compile">
  <!-- Create admin.war webapp archive file -->
  <war destfile="${basedir}/admin.war"
       webxml="${webadmin}/WEB-INF/web.xml">
    <fileset dir="${webadmin}"
             includes="**/*.*"
```

```
               excludes="**/*.java, WEB-INF/web.xml"/>
      <classes dir="${build}"
               includes="**/ui/**/*.class, **/form/**/*.class"
               excludes="**/user/**/*.class" />
      <classes dir="${srcjava}"
               includes="**/ui/admin/*.properties" />
    </war>
  </target>
```

That's all you need to create the Web application archive from the Web application components in our work area and the supporting classes in the build area. The simplicity of this step is a direct result of the directory structure and practices we've adopted in the development environment.

Deploying Web Applications

Now that we've reviewed the structure of a Web application, the contents of its descriptor files, and the techniques available for creating an exploded Web application and archive file, it is time to examine the options for deploying Web applications to WebLogic Server. This part of the chapter concentrates on the techniques from the developer's point of view—how to deploy the application in a single server or workstation environment for the purposes of development and unit testing. Chapter 11 describes techniques and best practices in a multiserver, managed, clustered environment.

There are three basic ways to deploy a Web application, or any other J2EE application, in a WebLogic Server environment:

- Automatic deployment
- WebLogic deployer utility or Ant task
- WebLogic Console deployment

This list represents our order of preference for deploying applications in a single server or workstation environment. We'll examine each option in the following sections, followed by a brief discussion of the steps required to configure security information for proper admin site operation.

Automatic Deployment

Automatic deployment is the simplest technique available for deploying an application to an administration server or a combined administration/managed server. If automatic deployment is enabled during the startup process, the administration server will constantly scan the applications directory for new applications as well as modifications to existing applications. When a new application is placed in the applications directory, the administration server immediately attempts to load and deploy the application. When an existing, deployed application is modified, the server immediately attempts to undeploy the old version and deploy the new version of the application.

This is exactly the sort of behavior a developer prefers during development and unit testing. Changes can be made to the application and redeployed rapidly to a running server without requiring a complete restart of the server, a big advantage in an iterative development and testing process.

Two steps are required to deploy an application using automatic deployment.

First, automatic deployment must be enabled for the administration server. In the `startWebLogic` command or shell script used to start the server, make sure that the `PRODUCTION_MODE` variable is either set to `false` or not set, which is the default. This variable is used by the script to control the value of the `weblogic.ProductionModeEnabled` property in the `java` command line used to start the server. A value of `true` means `production` mode, and `false` means `development` mode, which will enable auto-deployment, among other things. Note that this variable was `STARTMODE` in previous versions of WebLogic Server.

Next, copy the Web application archive file or exploded Web application directory structure to the `applications` directory in the domain. Although applications can be located almost anywhere in the directory structure in general, automatic deployment works only for applications placed in the `applications` directory. As indicated in Figure 5.6, an archive file should be located directly in the `applications` root directory, not in a subdirectory, and an exploded application should include a top-level directory.

The archive root name, `webapp1`, and top-level directory name, `webapp2`, will be used by the server as the initial name and root context for the deployed applications. Users will access pages in the applications using http://localhost:port/webapp1/... and http://localhost:port/webapp2/... URL locations.

When the new file or directory structure appears in the `applications` directory the administration server will immediately sense the new application and attempt to deploy it. Assuming the archive or directory is well structured and contains the required descriptor files, the new application will be deployed and ready for use. Mission accomplished!

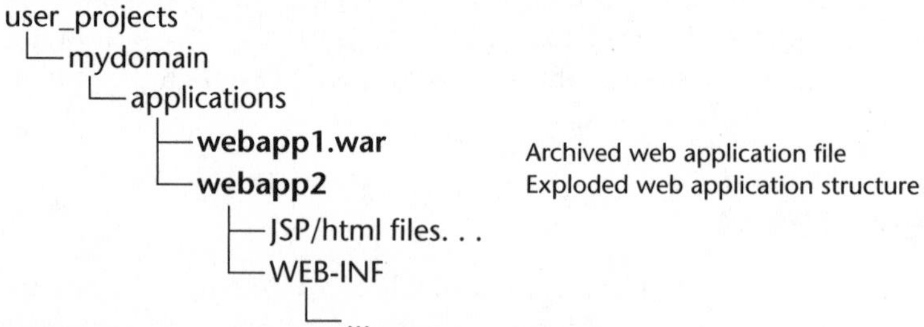

Figure 5.6 Web applications deployed in applications directory.

WARNING Depending on the size of your Web application, it is possible that the server will begin deploying the application before the copying process is complete. The server is smart enough to sense this race condition and wait in the case of an archive file, but there is no way for it to know when the copying process is complete for an exploded application. It is safer to copy a new, exploded application directory structure to the `applications` directory while the administration server is shut down. When the server is started, the new application will be sensed and automatically deployed.

The *bigrez.com* application uses this automatic deployment technique. The `dist` task in the `build.xml` file places the exploded application files in the `applications` directory in preparation for automatic deployment. No additional steps or tasks are required to deploy the application or modify the contents of the deployed application, although for reasons we'll describe in a moment, you need to signal the server when a modification is made to the exploded application to force a redeployment.

Applications deployed using archive files can be redeployed automatically by simply overwriting the existing version of the archive file in the `applications` directory. This rule holds for all archive types, including Web application `.war` files, EJB `.jar` files, and enterprise application `.ear` files. The server senses the timestamp change for the file and automatically undeploys the old application and deploys the new version of the application.

Applications deployed using exploded formats present a problem for the server: Which file timestamp should be monitored to sense a change in the application and force a redeployment? There could be hundreds or thousands of files in the exploded directory structure, making it impossible to monitor all of them for changes. WebLogic Server chose to introduce a special file, `REDEPLOY`, for this very purpose. The contents of this file do not matter; only the timestamp matters. If you `touch` the file or otherwise modify its timestamp, the server redeploys the application. The `REDEPLOY` file is located in the `META-INF` directory in enterprise applications and in the `WEB-INF` directory in Web applications.

The *bigrez.com* application uses an enterprise application, so there is a `REDEPLOY` file located in the `META-INF` directory used for this purpose. A `redeploy` task in the `build.xml` file touches the `REDEPLOY` file to cause a redeployment of the exploded application:

```
<target name="redeploy">
  <touch file="${deploy.dir}/META-INF/REDEPLOY"/>
</target>
```

Recognize that the new versions of the application files in the exploded directory structure must already be present before requesting the redeployment, or a race condition could occur.

Given the added complexity described here, why would you choose to deploy to a workstation or single-server environment using an exploded Web application? Simply put, the ability to modify JSP pages without redeploying the Web application, or the enclosing enterprise application, provides a big benefit in an iterative development process. In previous versions of WebLogic Server, redeploying the application for a simple page change caused all `HttpSession` objects and user login contexts to be dropped. This was a strong reason to avoid redeployment for a simple page change. Although WebLogic Server 8.1 has improved the redeployment process for Web applications by retaining session and user authentication information during the process, there can still be a significant overhead associated with redeployment. For example, if the Web application is part of an enterprise application, all of the EJB components in the application must also be undeployed and redeployed. This is clearly a lot of effort to make a simple JSP change.

With an exploded deployment, you simply edit the JSP pages in the working area and invoke a copying function, like the `dist` task in *bigrez.com*'s build script, to copy the modified pages to the exploded Web application. As you continue browsing the site, new pages will be recompiled by the server when they are accessed by the browser because the timestamp on the JSP file no longer matches the timestamp in the generated class file. WebLogic Server keeps track of files included using the `<%@ include file="..." %>` directive as well, so changes to `.jspf` files will also cause the correct JSP pages to be recompiled as they are accessed. Remember that this timestamp checking is controlled by the `pageCheckSeconds` parameter set in `weblogic.xml`. The default value is one second, so the behavior described here will apply unless you disable it using that parameter.

This all adds up to a clear advantage to using an exploded application structure during development.

BEST PRACTICE Use exploded application structures for deployment on developer workstations to allow fine-grained updates to JSP pages without requiring a complete redeployment of the enclosing application. Automatic deployment is sufficient for these installations if you have a good technique for touching the `REDEPLOY` file to cause redeployments on demand.

WebLogic Deployer Utility and Ant Task

The default WebLogic Server installation includes a utility, `weblogic.Deployer`, providing a command-line technique for deploying and managing applications. The `weblogic.Deployer` utility mirrors the deployment functions available through the WebLogic Console, including the deployment of new applications, redeployment of modified applications, undeploying existing applications, and modifying the targeted servers for an application. The `weblogic.Deployer` utility also provides an upload capability to move applications from a staging directory to the proper directory in the administration server in preparation for deployment.

The `weblogic.Deployer` utility is invoked using the following basic syntax:

```
java weblogic.Deployer [options] [action] [files]
```

As before, we'll concentrate here on the actions and options necessary to deploy and redeploy an application to a stand-alone server instance in a simple development environment. Chapter 11 discusses deployment of applications in production environments.

The following steps are required to deploy a Web application manually using the `weblogic.Deployer` utility:

1. Start the WebLogic Server instance in production mode by including `PRODUCTION_MODE=true` in the `startWebLogic` script.
2. Copy the exploded enterprise application or Web application directory structure to the `applications` directory or any other desired directory. The `weblogic.Deployer` utility includes an upload feature that can perform this step if desired, although there is little reason to use it for a stand-alone server on a developer workstation.
3. Deploy the application using the `activate` action in the `weblogic.Deployer` utility.

The first two steps are self-explanatory. Using production mode disables the automatic deployment of archives and directory structures placed in the `applications` directory, allowing you to control this deployment manually. The application may be placed in the `applications` directory, as in the automatic deployment case, or it may be placed in any desired directory on the server. We suggest a directory such as `myapps` in the domain directory structure to avoid confusion.

The `webapp1` application may now be deployed from the Web archive file `webapp1.war` using the command:

```
java weblogic.Deployer -adminurl http://localhost:7001 -name webapp1
  -source /myapps/webapp1.war -targets myserver -activate
```

Note that the directory specified in the `source` option is relative to the domain root directory for the server unless you're using the upload feature, in which case it is relative to the current directory.

You can deploy exploded applications such as `webapp2` in this manner by referring to the root directory of the exploded Web application in the `source` option:

```
java weblogic.Deployer -adminurl http://localhost:7001 -name webapp2
  -source /myapps/webapp2 -targets myserver -activate
```

Redeploying a modified application is accomplished using basically the same command and options with the exception of the `targets` option. The `targets` option should be removed for a redeployment request because the option works like a toggle: If an application is already deployed to the targeted server, it will be undeployed. The `source` option again refers to the archive file or root directory of the exploded application.

The example command lines shown so far require you to enter the administrator's username and password to complete the operation. You can specify these values on the command line with the `user` and `password` options:

```
java weblogic.Deployer -user system -password weblogic ...
```

Other useful options include debug and verbose, providing details during the deployment operations to assist in troubleshooting problems.

Using the weblogic.Deployer utility to deploy Web applications replaces the automatic deployment performed by WebLogic Server when running in development mode. Once the application is deployed, however, many of the same redeployment and modification rules apply. For example, changes to JSP pages in exploded Web applications will still cause automatic recompilation of the page when a user accesses it.

The behavior of the server in response to a timestamp change in the REDEPLOY file or archive file itself depends on the setting of PRODUCTION_MODE in the startWebLogic script and the choice of directory containing the application, as shown in Table 5.3. In some cases, the server will automatically redeploy the application, and in other cases you must manually redeploy the application using the weblogic.Deployer utility.

Because the automatic deployment feature affects only applications placed in the applications directory, you may combine automatic and manual deployment in the same domain. Leave PRODUCTION_MODE set to false in the start script, place applications using automatic deployment in the applications directory, and place applications using manual deployment in an alternate directory such as myapps.

WebLogic Server 8.1 introduces a new Ant task, wldeploy, providing the same basic functions as the weblogic.Deployer utility. Deploying the exploded webapp2 Web application from the /myapps directory requires an Ant target similar to the following:

```
<target name="deploy">
  <wldeploy user="system" password="weblogic"
            action="deploy" source="${domain.dir}/myapps/webapp2" />
</target>
```

BEST PRACTICE **Favor the new wldeploy Ant task over the command-line weblogic.Deployer utility when manually deploying or redeploying applications. It provides the same functionality and is much easier to integrate in the overall build and deployment process.**

Table 5.3 Redeployment Behavior Depends on Production Mode and Application Location

PRODUCTION MODE	APPLICATION DIRECTORY	REDEPLOYMENT BEHAVIOR
TRUE	applications directory or alternate location	Timestamps are ignored. Modified application must be manually redeployed.
FALSE	applications directory	The server monitors the timestamp of the archive file or REDEPLOY file and automatically redeploys applications.
FALSE	alternate location	Timestamps are ignored. Modified application must be manually redeployed.

See the BEA online documentation at http://edocs.bea.com/wls/docs81/deployment/tools.html for more information on both the `weblogic.Deployer` utility and the new `wldeploy` Ant task.

WebLogic Console Deployment

You can use the WebLogic Console to deploy and manage Web applications in a combined administration/managed server instance or across complex clusters of managed servers. In this chapter, we're interested in the simple case of a combined or stand-alone server instance suitable for development and unit testing on a workstation. Deploying a Web application to a stand-alone server instance involves the following steps:

1. Start the WebLogic Server instance in production mode by setting `PRODUCTION_MODE=true` in the `startWebLogic` script.
2. Copy the exploded archive file or Web application directory structure to the `applications` directory or any other desired directory.
3. Deploy the application using the WebLogic Console.

Using production mode disables the automatic deployment of archives and directory structures placed in the `applications` directory, allowing you to control this deployment manually through the console. The application may be placed in the `applications` directory or any desired directory on the server. We suggest a directory such as `myapps` in the domain directory structure to avoid confusion.

Once the server is running and the applications to be deployed are in place, open the WebLogic Console and click the Deployments->Web Application Modules folder in the left-hand navigation bar. Click the `Deploy a new Web Application Module` link. The right pane will refresh and display some text describing the deployment process along with an HTML-based directory listing starting at the domain root directory. You should see the standard `applications` directory, the `myapps` directory containing your Web applications, and any other directories present at the domain root level. Click the `myapps` directory link to drill down to that directory and examine its contents. Your application archive files or exploded directory structures should be listed, as shown in Figure 5.7.

Select one of the displayed Web applications using the radio buttons. The console now displays a form allowing you to choose the servers and clusters on which this application should be deployed, if applicable.

Target your application to the current server, `myserver`, and click the `Deploy` button to complete the deployment of the new Web application. The display will refresh to present the normal deployment status window for an application containing status information and controls used to manage the application. The new application has now been deployed to the server and is ready for use.

Once the application is deployed using the WebLogic Console, redeployment and modification behavior follow the same rules outlined in the previous section; see Table 5.3 for the behavior under different combinations of deployment mode and application location. Note that the WebLogic Console can also be used to redeploy an exploded, automatic deployment application in lieu of modifying the timestamp on the `REDEPLOY` file or using one of the utilities described in the previous section.

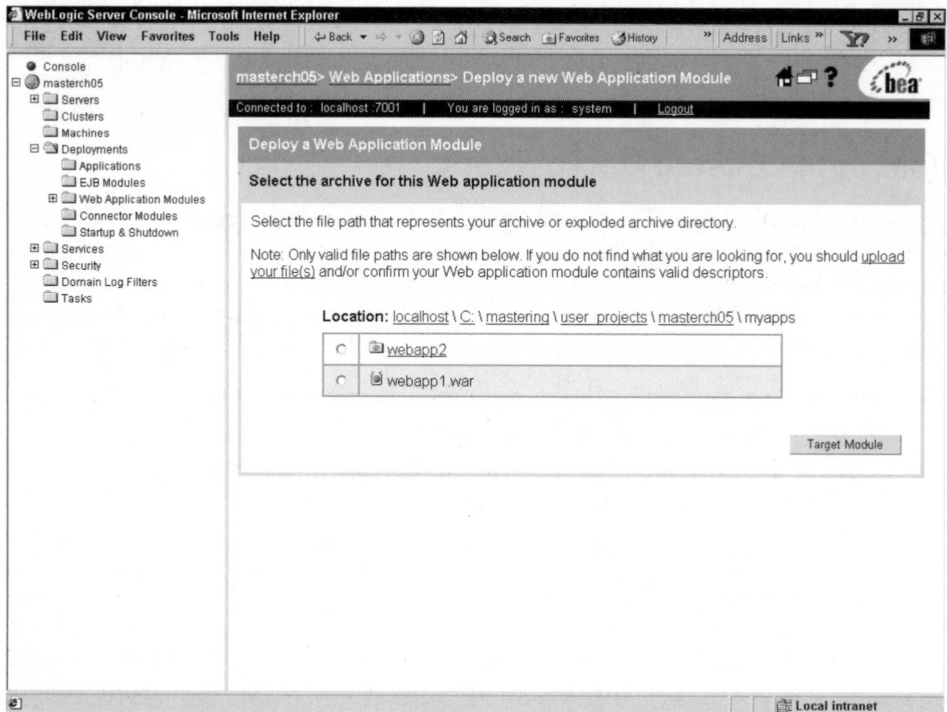

Figure 5.7 Contents of the MyApps directory.

BEST PRACTICE Manual application deployment using the administration console requires a number of steps to perform and is not required for developer workstation deployments. Use automatic deployment or one of the deployment utilities outlined in the previous section in these environments.

Creating Required Users and Group for BigRez.com

The *bigrez.com* application includes two separate Web applications, `user` and `admin`. As we discussed in Chapter 4, the `admin` Web application uses standard J2EE security features to control access to the property maintenance pages. The required users and groups must be created in the default security realm in WebLogic Server to complete the deployment of the *bigrez.com* Web applications.

After starting the domain, open the WebLogic Console and navigate to the `Security` folder in the navigation pane on the left. Open the default realm, normally called `myrealm`, and click on the `Groups` folder. You should see a list on the right side containing the default groups in the security realm, as shown in Figure 5.8.

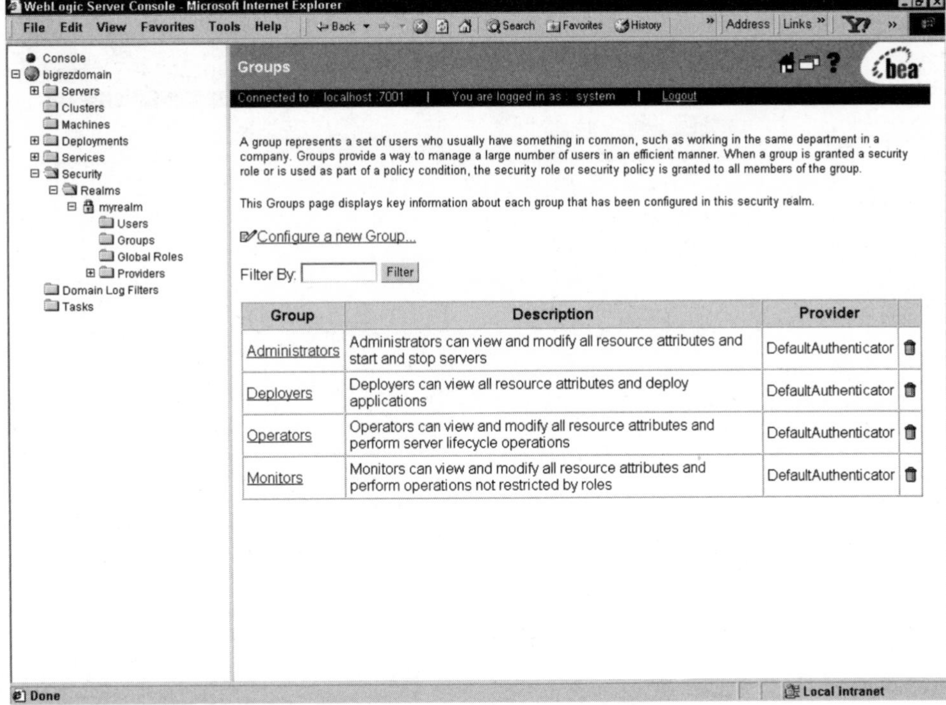

Figure 5.8 Groups in the default security realm.

Click on `Configure a New Group`, and fill out the form, as shown in Figure 5.9, to create the new `HotelAdministrators` group required by the `admin` Web application. Click on `Apply` to create the group. Repeat this process to create the new `BigRezAdministrators` group as well.

Next, click on the Users folder on the left side of the screen. The list on the right should show only the `system` user and any other users you may have created for testing purposes. Click on `Configure a New User` and create users with names `BIGREZMPLS`, `BIGREZDUL`, and `DEWDROP1` using any convenient passwords. These three usernames correspond to the `loginId` values for the three properties defined in the *bigrez.com* application and are used to log in as hotel administrators for these hotels. Make these users members of the `HotelAdministrators` group by adding them to the group one at a time through the `Groups` tab in each user display. Repeat this process to create a `BIGREZADMIN` user and assign it to the `BigRezAdministrators` group.

The required users and groups are now available in the security realm. Hotel managers may log in to the `admin` site using these hotel-specific usernames and passwords to access and maintain property information for the corresponding hotels. System administrators log in to the `admin` site using the `BIGREZADMIN` username and password and have access to all properties.

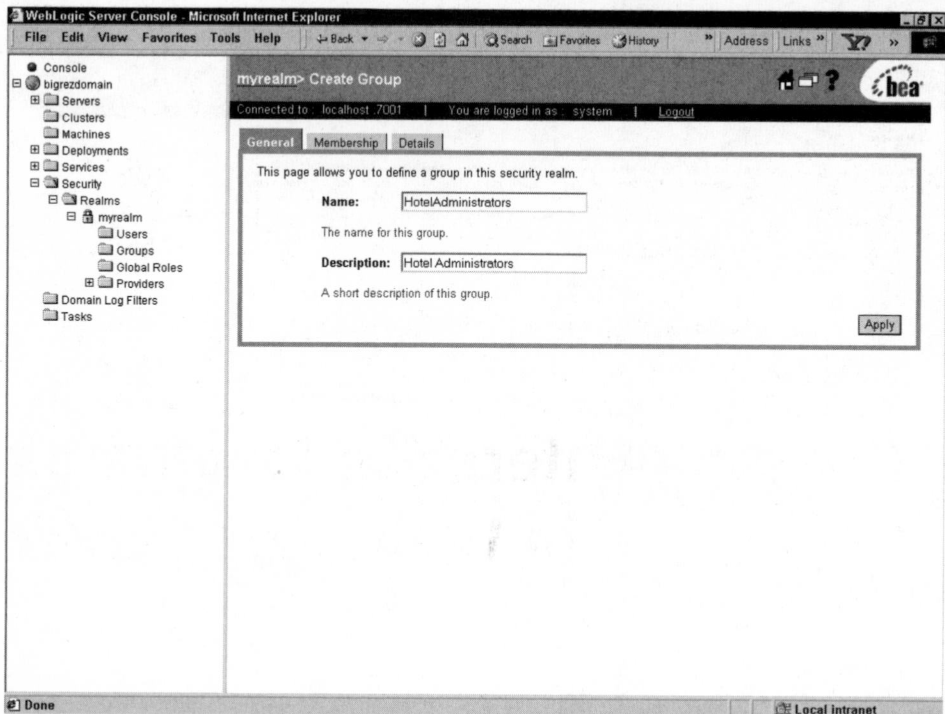

Figure 5.9 Create the HotelAdministrators group for the admin site.

Chapter Review

This chapter discussed the steps required to package and deploy a Web application to the WebLogic Server environment.

The first half of the chapter reviewed the structure of a Web application and the contents of the Web application descriptor files `web.xml` and `weblogic.xml`. Ant-based techniques for assembling Web applications, precompiling JSP components, and creating exploded and archived Web applications were then presented. Some portions of the *bigrez.com* build process were also presented to illustrate best practices in these areas.

The second half of the chapter discussed techniques available for deploying and redeploying Web applications using WebLogic Server features and utilities. The emphasis in this chapter was on the best way to deploy applications to a developer workstation or stand-alone server in support of the development and unit-testing process rather than deploying and managing a production server environment.

The next two chapters complete the design and construction of the *bigrez.com* example application by discussing the EJB components required in the business tier to support the application requirements. Chapter 8 revisits packaging and deployment of enterprise applications, including EJB components, and will provide a complete walkthrough of the *bigrez.com* build and deployment process.

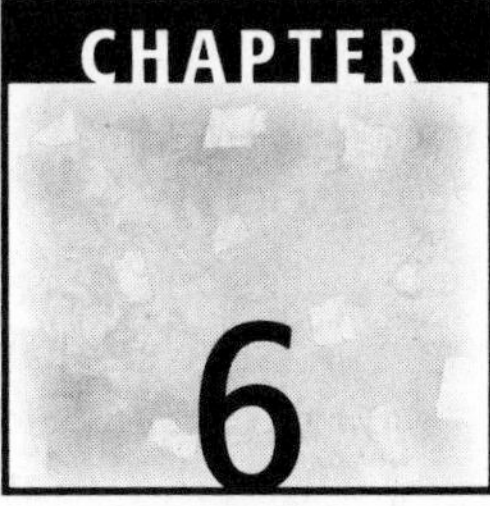

Building Enterprise JavaBeans in WebLogic Server

In this chapter, we examine best practices related to the implementation of Enterprise JavaBeans (EJB) technology in the WebLogic Server product. Chapters 7 and 8 walk through the development and deployment of an example EJB application to highlight related best practices.

This chapter is not intended as a primer, introduction, or reference for EJB technology. Our primary emphasis is the EJB container in WebLogic Server and its unique features and capabilities. If you're unfamiliar with the basics of EJB, we suggest you study *Mastering Enterprise JavaBeans*, 2nd Edition, by Ed Roman, Scott Ambler, and Tyler Jewel (John Wiley & Sons, 2001), a complete treatment of EJB technology. The book *Enterprise JavaBeans*, 3rd Edition, by Richard Monson-Haefel (O'Reilly & Associates, 2001) is another strong EJB reference.

We begin by briefly reviewing some EJB terms and key concepts to support the discussions that follow. The second half of the chapter discusses EJB features that are specific to WebLogic Server.

EJB Technology Overview

The Enterprise JavaBeans (EJB) specification defines a server-side component technology designed to support the construction of distributed enterprise-class applications. We'll break apart the definition of EJB and examine key concepts:

EJB is a specification. It is not a set of classes, code, or reference implementation components. Vendors such as BEA are expected to build application servers that implement EJB technology according to that specification.

EJB is a component technology. Component technologies emphasize the encapsulation of business logic in *components* deployed and managed in a *container*. The EJB specification carefully defines the interactions between components and their containers to ensure portability and consistency between EJB container vendors.

EJB supports distributed applications. EJB components may be distributed across multiple servers or processes with a limited impact on component developers, a concept known as *location transparency*.

EJB is designed for enterprise-class applications. The EJB specification is very concerned with transactions, security, concurrency, and memory management because these areas are important for large, mission-critical applications.

To remain consistent with the target audience for this book, intermediate- to advanced-level developers and architects, we will not discuss the basic development approach for EJB components. We assume that you have already built some simple EJB components and are familiar with the key steps and concepts involved, and that you would rather learn about more advanced topics and best practices for developing EJB applications.

The next chapter discusses the development and packaging of the *bigrez.com* example EJB application and will cover some of the tools and best practices related to the development process. Chapter 13 is also dedicated to development best practices, so there is no lack of information on this topic in this book.

EJB Component Types

The EJB 2.0 specification defines the following types of EJB components:

- Stateless session bean (SLSB)
- Stateful session bean (SFSB)
- Entity bean
- Message-driven bean (MDB)

Each of these component types fulfills a different design requirement for enterprise-class distributed systems. The following sections review each of these types and look at a few simple examples to complete our discussion of EJB key concepts.

Stateless Session Beans

Stateless session bean (SLSB) components are designed to service requests using a classic stateless request/response style. Setting aside complexities related to bean life cycle and pooling, an SLSB is not unlike a shared static class used as a service (like the

PersonService class in Chapter 2). The SLSB has a set of methods, exposed through local or remote interfaces, that can be called by clients to request particular services. Data is passed to the SLSB methods using method parameters, and results are returned, typically, through the return type of the method. This is classic request/response design.

Generally speaking, SLSB components are suitable for encapsulating business processes rather than business data. SLSB components often have names like AccountingService or ContractManager, signifying their role as managers or services related to certain business domains. Method names normally make clear the particular service exposed by the interface:

```
AccountingServiceLocal aservice = ... // Obtain reference to SLSB
float tax = aservice.calculateTax(income, expenses);
System.out.println("The IRS is only taking $" + tax + " this year!");
```

SLSB components have distinct advantages over simple static classes:

- EJB developers do not have to write thread-safe code. The EJB container prevents more than one thread in a given bean instance.
- EJBs provide location transparency in that they can be invoked from other processes.
- Transaction control and security constraints are implemented by the EJB container and declared using standard descriptor elements. Transaction and security contexts are automatically propagated to SLSB methods without requiring extra method parameters, a common approach in a static class.

Clients are given a particular instance of the SLSB for use during the single request/response cycle, and there is no guarantee that subsequent requests from the same client will be handled by the same instance of the SLSB. In general, SLSB components should not have client-associated instance variables, although it is possible to use instance variables to cache connections to shared resources or shared read-only data if desired. Just recognize that each invocation to the SLSB is independent from past and future invocations from the same client, and you can't make assumptions about the contents of the instance variables.

SLSB components are often used to implement the session façade design pattern discussed briefly in Chapter 3. The business process encapsulated by the SLSB may include complex calculations and interactions with additional EJB components, including both SLSB and entity beans, and the single method defined on the SLSB provides a simplifying façade for this complex process. The SLSB-based façade also provides a convenient mechanism for ensuring transactional integrity. The container is often configured to require or create a transaction whenever the SLSB method is invoked, thereby ensuring that all operations in the method are part of the same transaction.

We'll make use of SLSB and the session façade pattern in the example application in Chapter 7 for selected business processes requiring complex calculations and interactions with multiple EJB components.

Stateful Session Beans

Stateful session bean (SFSB) components combine the request/response mechanism of stateless session beans with the storage of state information between method invocations. Clients are given a dedicated instance of the SFSB to use for multiple method invocations, and subsequent requests from the same client are guaranteed to be handled by the same instance of the SFSB bean. These beans should generally have instance variables that store the intermediate state of the process being modeled by the SFSB. If there are no instance variables, there's no reason to use a stateful session bean.

SFSB components are normally used to implement multistep business processes that require retention of state information from step to step. They fall somewhere between SLSB and entity beans in terms of function and naming, and they often have names like `Reservation` or `ReservationProcess`. Method names on SFSB components also tend to fall somewhere between SLSB and entity beans, and they may have set methods for updating the state information in the bean as well as methods that perform business processing:

```
ReservationLocal rez = ... // Obtain reference to SFSB component
rez.setProperty(...);
...
rez.setDates(...);
...
rez.setGuestInformation(...);
...
String confirmnum = rez.performBooking();
System.out.println("Your confirmation number is: " + confirmnum);
```

In this example code, we've used an SFSB to maintain information about the customer's selections during the reservation process before invoking the final `performBooking()` method to make the reservation. The set method invocations are shown as if they occurred in the same block of code, but this is not required. As long as the client holds on to and uses the same SFSB reference, the invocations will be processed by the same instance of the SFSB.

Note that the *bigrez.com* example application, introduced in Chapters 3 and 4, uses a value object placed in the `HttpSession` to store intermediate results and passes this value object to a method on a stateless session bean to perform the final booking. Essentially, we store the intermediate data in the session rather than just storing a reference to a client-specific SFSB. Both techniques are viable ways to achieve the same effective result, and the choice is up to the architect. When the client is a Web application, we tend to lean toward the `HttpSession` approach for the simple reason that SFSB components increase the complexity of the overall system and may introduce unnecessary transaction and security processing mandated by the EJB specification. SFSBs really are more appropriate for maintaining a client's server-side state for remote clients—that is, clients not in the same JVM.

WebLogic Server includes the replication of SFSB data in a cluster, a topic discussed later, so both techniques have the same failover capability as well. When you try to use an SFSB from a Web application client where both the `HttpSession` and the SFSB are using in-memory replication, the failover scenarios can get a little bit complex. As a result, we tend to recommend using `HttpSession` objects to hold client session state for Web applications and SFSB only for applications where the client is not a Web application.

BEST PRACTICE **Avoid using stateful session beans for Web application client data more readily stored in the `HttpSession`. Although both SFSB and `HttpSession` data are replicated for failover in WebLogic Server, complexity considerations favor the use of `HttpSession` storage when possible. Use an SFSB for situations where the client is not a Web application.**

You should consider three issues with stateful session beans before using them:

- SFSB components normally disallow concurrent access, although WebLogic Server does include a flag to allow concurrent invocations to block rather than cause an exception. In a Web application multiple requests from the same user may be processed simultaneously, a condition that might require simultaneous access to the client-associated SFSB.
- If an SFSB throws a `RuntimeException` the container destroys the instance of the bean and all associated state information is lost, as required by the EJB specification.
- SFSB components are not appropriate for long-term storage of state. Use entity beans to store data that must survive the client restarting the browser session or returning to the application after an extended period of time.

While there may be specific applications for which the SFSB component is well suited, it is generally best to use `HttpSession` objects for short-lived, client-specific data and entity beans or other database-backed storage for long-lived data.

Entity Beans

Entity bean components are designed to encapsulate state information and manage the persistence of that state information. Entity beans seem straightforward on the surface: Clients obtain a reference to an entity bean instance representing some persistent business data and invoke get and set methods on the bean to interact with the data. When the client is done with the bean, any changes in state are flushed back to the persistent store. What could be simpler?

The reality is bit more complicated, of course. Before we dive in and review some entity bean details, let's examine the steps in this simple scenario to begin identifying the required methods in an entity bean from the developer's point of view:

1. First, obtaining a reference to the proper entity bean instance is normally accomplished using a *finder* method. Finder methods, defined in the *home* interface and implemented in the bean class, may look up beans by primary key or by any other criteria. Finder methods may return single bean references or collections of beans.

2. Next, the client interacts with the bean instance using get and set methods or any other methods defined on the bean's interface. The bean state must be loaded from the persistent store before the methods are called, a task that the container either performs itself or tells the bean class to perform by invoking the `ejbLoad()` method defined in the bean class. Method invocations may alter the state information in the bean instance, and subsequent calls to the same instance will reflect these changes.
3. Finally, when the client is done with the bean, its contents are flushed back to the persistent store, either automatically by the container or by the container telling the bean to do it via the `ejbStore()` method defined in the bean class.

Notice that two different mechanisms are used to load and store bean data. These operations are performed automatically by the container, a technique known as container-managed persistence, or by calling methods in the bean class, an option known as bean-managed persistence. The next two sections will describe and contrast these options in more detail.

This simple scenario does not include the creation of a new entity bean or the deletion of one. Once again, the exact mechanism depends on the bean's chosen persistence mechanism. For container-managed persistence (CMP), the container does these automatically; for bean-managed persistence (BMP), the container tells the bean to do it via the `ejbCreate()` and `ejbRemove()` life-cycle methods on the bean class.

That's it! From a developer's point of view, entity beans require only a small set of methods on the bean class to perform all of the functions required to encapsulate business data in the entity bean. There are additional life-cycle methods, such as `ejbActivate()` and `ejbPassivate()`, required by the EJB container to help manage bean life cycles and instance pooling. Often, these methods do not require any bean-specific code and are defined or stubbed out in a common base class. Table 6.1 outlines the minimum required methods for entity beans and summarizes their role in the process.

Table 6.1 Methods Required in Entity Bean Classes

METHOD	CMP DESCRIPTION	BMP DESCRIPTION
`ejbCreate(...)`	Implementations of the `create` methods defined on the home interface. Used to initialize the bean attributes (by calling the set methods) before the container inserts them into the database. The CMP bean must not manipulate the container-managed relationship fields until `ejbPostCreate()`.	Implementations of the `create` methods defined on the home interface. Used to initialize the bean attributes (by calling the set methods) and insert the data into the database.

Table 6.1 *(continued)*

METHOD	CMP DESCRIPTION	BMP DESCRIPTION
`ejbPostCreate(...)`	Matches the `ejbCreate (...)` method. Called by the EJB container after the bean instance has been associated with a primary key and an `EJBObject`. Normally used to set relationship attributes because these may require the `EJBObject` reference.	Same as CMP.
`ejbFind`*`XXX`*`(...)`	Implementations of the finder methods defined on the home interface. Used to obtain a reference to a single bean or a collection of beans matching the desired criteria. Automatically generated by the container from the deployment descriptors.	Implementations of the finder methods defined on the home interface. Used to obtain a reference to a single bean or a collection of beans matching the desired criteria. Must be written to perform the appropriate SQL `SELECT` statement to return the matching bean(s).
`ejbLoad()`	Called by the EJB container just after the bean's state has been read from the database. Can be used to modify the representation of the data before methods are invoked.	Called by the EJB container when an instance should read its state information from the persistent store. Must include the necessary SQL `SELECT` statement code to read data from the database and update the bean attributes to match the database state.
`ejbRemove()`	Called by the EJB container just before it removes the bean from memory.	Called by the EJB container when an instance should remove itself from the persistent store. Must contain the appropriate SQL `DELETE` statement code to remove the bean's data from the database.

(continued)

Table 6.1 *(continued)*

METHOD	CMP DESCRIPTION	BMP DESCRIPTION
`ejbStore()`	Called by the EJB container just before the bean's state will be written back to the database. Can be used to modify the data representation before it is saved to the database.	Called by the EJB container when an instance should save its state information to the persistent store. Must include the appropriate SQL `UPDATE` statement code to save the bean's current state to the database.
`ejbPassivate()`	Called by the EJB container just before the bean is passivated because of inactivity or a lack of resources in the bean instance pool.	Same as CMP.
`ejbActivate()`	Called by the EJB container after the bean is reactivated from a passive state.	Same as CMP.
`setEntityContext()`	Called by the EJB container at the beginning of the bean life cycle to provide context information.	Same as CMP.
`unsetEntityContext()`	Called by the EJB container at the end of the bean life cycle just prior to removal from the bean pool.	Same as CMP.
Attribute Get and Set Methods	Requires abstract get and set method declarations rather than attribute definitions. The container will generate the actual concrete bean class.	Optional. The bean can do whatever it wants because it controls its own state.
`ejbSelect`***XXX***`()`	Optional. Only for internal use in the bean class and never exposed directly via remote or local interfaces. Methods are automatically generated from deployment descriptors.	Not applicable.

Table 6.1 *(continued)*

METHOD	CMP DESCRIPTION	BMP DESCRIPTION
`ejbHome`*XXX*`()`	Optional. Allows adding stateless methods to a bean's home interfaces that return something other than bean references to the current bean. Methods are automatically generated from deployment descriptors.	Optional. Allows adding stateless methods to a bean's home interfaces that return something other than bean references to the current bean. Must include any SQL code necessary to process the request. Must not access any bean instance variables.

In addition to the required methods in Table 6.1, entity bean classes may include get and set methods for attributes (required for CMP), additional methods allowing clients to request data in other forms such as XML or `Composite Value Objects`, and *home* and *select* methods introduced in the EJB 2.0 specification. We'll build some typical entity beans later in this chapter as examples, and there are some example beans available in the samples installed with the WebLogic Server product. There are also many good books available on EJB with examples of simple entity beans.

Building simple entity beans is not very difficult. The real challenge is building high-performance entity bean applications for complex, realistic business models with many interrelated business objects. The entity bean life cycle that works so well in theory breaks down when you're trying to achieve high transaction rates with complex graphs of business objects unless you are careful to optimize the process using proper transactional controls and all of the tools and features available in your EJB container. As you'll learn when we examine some of the latest features of the WebLogic Server EJB container, achieving high performance with entity beans is all about understanding the bean access patterns, caching, and efficient queries. Features that reuse cached instances of beans and combine multiple operations in a single database invocation yield big performance gains.

We will cover many advanced topics and WebLogic Server-specific features related to entity beans in this chapter. Before we do, however, we need some straightforward entity beans as a foundation for these discussions. Therefore, we'll examine some simple entity beans built using the two techniques available for implementing the required persistence management methods: *bean-managed persistence* and *container-managed persistence.*

Bean-Managed Persistence

Bean-managed persistence (BMP) entity beans are beans whose required persistence management methods have been implemented by the developer in the bean class itself. The bean is responsible for managing its own persistence, hence the name. In its simplest form, the bean class implements the required methods using JDBC calls to

SELECT, UPDATE, INSERT, or DELETE the persistent data as appropriate. A detailed discussion of the required methods and techniques for developing BMP entity beans is beyond the scope of this book.

The download site (http://www.wiley.com/compbooks/masteringweblogic) contains an example with a simple BMP entity bean, PersonBMPBean, which will be useful as a starting point for the discussions that follow. The example contains the PersonBMPBean class and supporting files along with JSP pages that test the basic create, load, update, and remove behaviors of this BMP entity bean and illustrate both good and bad techniques for interacting with beans from JSP pages. For example, in the efficient page, PersonBMPTest.jsp, the access to the bean is wrapped in a transaction using techniques discussed in Chapter 3:

```
<%@ include file="include/BeginTrans.jspf" %>
<%
  out.print("<H2>Looking up Person 101 again..</H2>");
  PersonBMPLocal person101b = home.findByPrimaryKey(new Integer(101));
  out.print("Name: " + person101b.getSalutation() + " " +
            person101b.getFirstName() + " " +
            person101b.getLastName() + "<br>");
  out.print("<H2>Changing data in person bean</H2>");
  person101b.setFirstName("John");
  person101b.setLastName("Smith");
%>
<%@ include file="include/EndTrans.jspf" %>
```

By including this activity in a transaction the bean is loaded only once at the beginning of the transaction and stored only once at the end of the transaction, and all get and set calls use the same bean instance in memory. The calls made to the bean instance by the container are limited to the following:

```
ejbFindByPrimaryKey(101)
ejbLoad()
ejbStore()
```

The other JSP page, PersonBMPTestNoTrans.jsp, performs the same basic code without the use of a transaction. The bean is loaded and stored for each container-managed transaction created as get and set methods are called, resulting in a large number of ejbLoad() and ejbStore() calls.

This example drives home the importance of interacting with entity beans in the context of a transaction, either explicitly created on the client or automatically created by the container in a session façade method declared to use transactions.

BEST PRACTICE **Always access entity beans in the context of a transaction, either created explicitly using the** UserTransaction **interface or created automatically by the container. Failure to do so will result in multiple load/store cycles and poor performance.**

The use of bean-managed persistence is not recommended as a best practice for the majority of applications. There are several reasons, including the following:

JDBC code complexity. With BMP, the onus of writing all of the database access code is left to the bean developer. At first glance, you might mistake this for a good thing, thinking that you can write better SQL than the container. In some cases, you might even be right. The problem is that JDBC coding can be error-prone and may involve insidious errors that you may not find until production; these errors often cause memory leaks that can crash your application server when the JVM runs out of memory.

Limited ability for optimizations. The container must treat the BMP entity EJB as a black box because it has no knowledge about the bean's implementation. As such, it must always call the life-cycle methods at the predefined times because the container has no visibility into what happened to the bean during a particular transaction. For example, the container does not know whether the transaction only read data or actually updated it; therefore, it must always invoke `ejbStore()` at the end of the transaction to tell the bean to save its state. While this example can be overcome by adding intelligence to the bean code to know how to react to `ejbStore()` calls, we will explore more examples later in the chapter that cannot be overcome.

Maintainability. With BMP, you have to write all of the code yourself, including the SQL statements to access your database. While this may not seem like a big deal at first, think about a typical large development project where database changes can occur frequently. If the database schema changes, you have to modify your bean code to reflect the changes. With many CMP beans, you need to write very little actual Java code. All of the mapping between the bean attributes and the database is done in the deployment descriptor, making it easy to regenerate the database persistence code after a schema change. In addition, container-managed persistence can also manage relationships with other entity beans. Again, these relationships are described in the deployment descriptor rather than hard-coded in the bean's Java code, making it easier to adapt to change.

Container-managed persistence, the subject of the next section, is a much stronger alternative for entity bean persistence and should be used whenever possible.

Container-Managed Persistence

Container-managed persistence (CMP) entity beans use persistence-related methods generated by the EJB container rather than methods provided by the bean developer, as was the case in BMP entity beans. Both types of beans define the same methods, such as `ejbCreate()`, `ejbLoad()`, and `ejbStore()`, but in CMP entity beans these methods no longer perform the actual persistence operations. Instead, the container calls these standard methods on the bean instance to signal that associated persistence operations have occurred or are about to occur, giving you an opportunity to modify any internal state or log the operation. The actual persistence operations take place in separate, internal bean methods that are code-generated by the EJB container or tools provided by the container vendor.

Bean classes in BMP entity beans were concrete classes with attributes, get and set methods to access those attributes, and a full set of persistence-related methods. In CMP beans, however, the bean class is actually an abstract class with abstract get and set methods, and it has no requirements for any persistence-related methods. The EJB compiler provided by WebLogic Server uses mapping information in descriptor files provided by the developer to generate a concrete subclass of the entity bean class. The code-generated concrete class implements all of the internal persistence-related methods and provides the actual instance attributes and concrete get and set methods.

A complete discussion of CMP entity beans is beyond the scope of this book. The following simple example illustrates the basic requirements for a CMP entity bean and provides a basis for many of the complex topics and WebLogic Server-specific discussions that follow. The *bigrez.com* example program also uses CMP entity beans for all business objects and relationships and provides a more realistic example.

Listing 6.1 presents the source listing for the CMP entity bean class `PersonCMPBean.java`. This CMP bean class and all supporting classes and files are available from the download site for your reference.

```
package mastering.weblogic.ch06.example2.ejb;

import java.util.Collection;
import javax.ejb.EJBException;
import javax.ejb.EntityContext;
import javax.ejb.FinderException;

public abstract class PersonCMPBean extends
    mastering.weblogic.ch06.example2.ejb.base.BaseEntity
{
    private static org.apache.log4j.Category LOG =
        org.apache.log4j.Category.getInstance("PersonCMPBean");

    public java.lang.Integer ejbCreate(Integer pId, String pSalutation,
                                       String pFirstName,
                                       String pMiddleName,
                                       String pLastName)
    {
        LOG.info("ejbCreate()");
        setId(pId);
        setSalutation(pSalutation);
        setFirstName(pFirstName);
        setMiddleName(pMiddleName);
        setLastName(pLastName);
        return null; // CMP returns NULL
    }

    public void ejbPostCreate(Integer pId, String pSalutation,
                              String pFirstName, String pMiddleName,
                              String pLastName)
    {
```

Listing 6.1 PersonCMPBean.java.

```
        LOG.info("ejbPostCreate()");
    }

    // define abstract accessor methods for all bean attributes
    public abstract Integer getId();
    public abstract void setId(Integer pId);
    public abstract String getSalutation();
    public abstract void setSalutation(String pSalutation);
    public abstract String getFirstName();
    public abstract void setFirstName(String pFirstName);
    public abstract String getMiddleName();
    public abstract void setMiddleName(String pMiddleName);
    public abstract String getLastName();
    public abstract void setLastName(String pLastName);
}
```

Listing 6.1 *(continued)*

Comparing the size of this file with the equivalent BMP source file, PersonBMP-Bean.java, provides a clear example of the reduction in Java code inherent in the CMP approach. There are some key differences between the BMP and CMP bean classes:

- PersonCMPBean is defined as an abstract class; PersonBMPBean is concrete.
- PersonCMPBean defines only abstract get and set methods with no instance variables. The BMP version defined the instance variables themselves as well as concrete get and set methods.
- PersonCMPBean defines only ejbCreate() and ejbPostCreate() and does not perform any SQL operations in these methods. The other standard entity bean methods can be defined in a base class, in this case BaseEntity, because they are simply callbacks that typically require little or no application code. The BMP version defined all of the required methods and performs all required SQL operations in the bean class.

Listings 6.2 presents the local interface for the CMP entity bean, essentially unchanged from its BMP counterpart.

```
package mastering.weblogic.ch06.example2.ejb;

import javax.ejb.EJBLocalObject;

public interface PersonCMPLocal extends EJBLocalObject
{
    public Integer getId();
    public String getSalutation();
    public void setSalutation(String pSalutation);
    public String getFirstName();
```

Listing 6.2 PersonCMPLocal.java. *(continued)*

```
    public void setFirstName(String pFirstName);
    public String getMiddleName();
    public void setMiddleName(String pMiddleName);
    public String getLastName();
    public void setLastName(String pLastName);

}
```

Listing 6.2 *(continued)*

Listing 6.3 presents the home interface for the CMP entity bean, also essentially unchanged from its BMP counterpart.

```
package mastering.weblogic.ch06.example2.ejb;

import javax.ejb.CreateException;
import javax.ejb.EJBLocalHome;
import javax.ejb.FinderException;

public interface PersonCMPHomeLocal extends EJBLocalHome
{
    public PersonCMPLocal findByPrimaryKey(Integer primaryKey)
        throws FinderException;
    public PersonCMPLocal create(Integer pId, String pSalutation,
                                 String pFirstName, String pMiddleName,
                                 String pLastName)
        throws CreateException;
}
```

Listing 6.3 PersonCMPHomeLocal.java.

Listing 6.4 presents the standard `ejb-jar.xml` descriptor file for the CMP entity bean. Like the BMP version, this file contains basic configuration, security, and transaction information. The CMP version also defines the bean attributes, using `cmp-field` elements, and the primary key for the bean.

```
<?xml version="1.0"?>

<!DOCTYPE ejb-jar PUBLIC
"-//Sun Microsystems, Inc.//DTD Enterprise JavaBeans 2.0//EN"
"http://java.sun.com/dtd/ejb-jar_2_0.dtd">

<ejb-jar>
  <enterprise-beans>
    <entity>
```

Listing 6.4 ejb-jar.xml.

```
      <ejb-name>PersonCMPEJB</ejb-name>
      <local-home>
        mastering.weblogic.ch06.example2.ejb.PersonCMPHomeLocal
      </local-home>
      <local>
        mastering.weblogic.ch06.example2.ejb.PersonCMPLocal
      </local>
      <ejb-class>
        mastering.weblogic.ch06.example2.ejb.PersonCMPBean
      </ejb-class>
      <persistence-type>Container</persistence-type>
      <prim-key-class>java.lang.Integer</prim-key-class>
      <reentrant>False</reentrant>
      <cmp-version>2.x</cmp-version>
      <abstract-schema-name>PersonCMPEJB</abstract-schema-name>
      <cmp-field><field-name>id</field-name></cmp-field>
      <cmp-field><field-name>salutation</field-name></cmp-field>
      <cmp-field><field-name>firstName</field-name></cmp-field>
      <cmp-field><field-name>middleName</field-name></cmp-field>
      <cmp-field><field-name>lastName</field-name></cmp-field>
      <primkey-field>id</primkey-field>
      <security-identity><use-caller-identity/></security-identity>
    </entity>
  </enterprise-beans>
  <assembly-descriptor>
    <security-role>
      <role-name>Anonymous</role-name>
    </security-role>
    <method-permission>
      <role-name>Anonymous</role-name>
      <method>
         <ejb-name>PersonCMPEJB</ejb-name>
         <method-name>*</method-name>
      </method>
    </method-permission>
    <container-transaction>
      <method>
        <ejb-name>PersonCMPEJB</ejb-name>
        <method-name>*</method-name>
      </method>
      <trans-attribute>Required</trans-attribute>
    </container-transaction>
  </assembly-descriptor>
</ejb-jar>
```

Listing 6.4 *(continued)*

Listing 6.5 presents the WebLogic Server-specific descriptor file, `weblogic-ejb-jar.xml`, a file used to configure EJB deployments and map generic resource names in `ejb-jar.xml` to specific names in the environment. In the case of CMP entity beans, the weblogic-ejb-jar.xml file is basically identical to the BMP version except for a persistence element added to indicate the type of persistence being employed in the bean.

```
<?xml version="1.0"?>

<!DOCTYPE weblogic-ejb-jar PUBLIC
'-//BEA Systems, Inc.//DTD WebLogic 8.1.0 EJB//EN'
'http://www.bea.com/servers/wls810/dtd/weblogic-ejb-jar.dtd'>

<weblogic-ejb-jar>
  <weblogic-enterprise-bean>
    <ejb-name>PersonCMPEJB</ejb-name>
    <entity-descriptor>
      <entity-cache>
        <max-beans-in-cache>1000</max-beans-in-cache>
      </entity-cache>
      <persistence>
        <persistence-use>
          <type-identifier>WebLogic_CMP_RDBMS</type-identifier>
          <type-version>6.0</type-version>
          <type-storage>META-INF/weblogic-cmp-rdbms-jar.xml
          </type-storage>
        </persistence-use>
      </persistence>
    </entity-descriptor>
    <local-jndi-name>PersonCMPHomeLocal</local-jndi-name>
  </weblogic-enterprise-bean>
  <security-role-assignment>
    <role-name>Anonymous</role-name>
    <externally-defined/>
  </security-role-assignment>
</weblogic-ejb-jar>
```

Listing 6.5 weblogic-ejb-jar.xml.

CMP entity beans also require a second WebLogic Server-specific descriptor file, weblogic-cmp-rdbms-jar.xml, providing the EJB compiler code-generation process with the required database mapping information. In this simple CMP example, the weblogic-cmp-rdbms-jar.xml descriptor file, shown in Listing 6.6, contains only two important elements: the data-source-name element providing the name of the JDBC DataSource to use for persistence and a table-map element with information defining the database table and column names for the bean attributes. Note that table-map was introduced in WebLogic Server 7.0. It was added to support multiple tables for CMP beans. In previous versions the table-name and field-map elements were direct children of weblogic-rdbms-bean.

```
<?xml version="1.0"?>

<!DOCTYPE weblogic-rdbms-jar PUBLIC
 '-//BEA Systems, Inc.//DTD WebLogic 8.1.0 EJB RDBMS Persistence//EN'
 'http://www.bea.com/servers/wls810/dtd/
                              weblogic-rdbms20-persistence-810.dtd'>

<weblogic-rdbms-jar>
  <weblogic-rdbms-bean>
    <ejb-name>PersonCMPEJB</ejb-name>
    <data-source-name>PersonDataSource</data-source-name>
    <table-map>
      <table-name>PERSON</table-name>
      <field-map>
        <cmp-field>id</cmp-field>
        <dbms-column>ID</dbms-column>
      </field-map>
      <field-map>
        <cmp-field>salutation</cmp-field>
        <dbms-column>SALUTATION</dbms-column>
      </field-map>
      <field-map>
        <cmp-field>firstName</cmp-field>
        <dbms-column>FIRSTNAME</dbms-column>
      </field-map>
      <field-map>
        <cmp-field>middleName</cmp-field>
        <dbms-column>MIDDLENAME</dbms-column>
      </field-map>
      <field-map>
        <cmp-field>lastName</cmp-field>
        <dbms-column>LASTNAME</dbms-column>
      </field-map>
    </table-map>
  </weblogic-rdbms-bean>
</weblogic-rdbms-jar>
```

Listing 6.6 weblogic-cmp-rdbms-jar.xml.

The example, available from http://www.wiley.com/compbooks/mastering weblogic, includes all of these CMP-related source files as well as two simple JSP pages used to test the resulting CMP beans. The `PersonCMPTest.jsp` performs the bean creation, find, load, update, and remove operations in the same way as the previous example page, including the use of a containing transaction. The `PersonCMPTestNoTrans.jsp` page performs the same steps without transactions. Again, the use of a transaction is critical to avoid unnecessary bean load and store operations.

Our simple example illustrates some of the advantages of CMP entity beans over BMP entity beans, advantages that only grow larger as the complexity of the object model increases and the need for performance becomes more critical. CMP beans should be favored in nearly all circumstances.

BEST PRACTICE Container-managed persistence (CMP) entity beans offer significant advantages over bean-managed persistence (BMP) entity beans. As the object-model complexity and need for sophisticated reading and writing behavior increase, the advantages of CMP beans become very compelling.

There are two ways to monitor persistence activity in CMP entity beans. The official way is JDBC logging in the WebLogic Server domain using the WebLogic Console. Enabling JDBC logging creates a very verbose output showing SQL operations, bound variables, and a great deal of driver-specific JDBC output.

A second, unofficial technique is available in CMP beans. WebLogic Server provides an undocumented mechanism to enable detailed logging of all persistence-related activity occurring in the generated concrete subclass of the bean class. To enable this logging, include the following option definitions in the `startWebLogic` start script used to boot the server:

```
set JAVA_OPTIONS=-Dweblogic.ejb20.cmp.rdbms.codegen.debug=true
                 -Dweblogic.ejb20.cmp.rdbms.codegen.verbose=true
```

WebLogic Server will generate verbose log messages in the code-generated methods, providing valuable information for tuning and debugging your CMP-based application. The actual SQL statements sent to JDBC will be listed, along with messages indicating when persistence-related methods are being invoked by the container. A detailed examination of this output for your application may provide important insights related to performance and tuning, especially if you notice many calls to persistence methods, indicating poor design of the interaction with the bean. Note that these flags are not officially supported by BEA and may change or be eliminated as some point.

BEST PRACTICE Use JDBC logging to view SQL operations performed by your application as a first step in debugging or tuning persistence activity. Alternately, include the `weblogic.ejb20.cmp.rdbms.codegen.debug` **and** `.verbose` **flags in the options used to start WebLogic Server to view CMP-related activity.**

Finder Methods

Entity beans represent individual business objects. Once you have a reference to an entity bean, you may interact with that bean using its public interface. These references are obtained, in many cases, using Finder methods.

Methods that query the persistent store to retrieve either a single bean reference or a collection of bean references based on search criteria are called *finder methods*. Clients call these methods through the entity bean home interface to obtain the desired reference or references.

The most common finder method is `findByPrimaryKey()`, a method designed to return a single bean reference given the primary key value. You can create other finder methods to satisfy particular needs of the application. In the simple BMP example earlier in the chapter, for example, we might add the ability to find `PersonBMPBean` references for all beans matching a specific last name. Adding this finder requires two changes. First, the new `ejbFindByLastName()` method is added to the `PersonBMPBean` class definition:

```
public Collection ejbFindByLastName(String lastname)
    throws FinderException
{
    LOG.info("ejbFindByLastName(" + lastname + ")");
    try {
        String stmnt = "SELECT ID FROM PERSON WHERE LASTNAME LIKE ?";
        ArrayList params = new ArrayList();
        params.add(lastname);
        ArrayList results =
            SQLHelper.executePreparedQuery(stmnt, params);
        return results;
    }
    catch (SQLException se) {
        LOG.error("SQLException", se);
        throw new FinderException(se.getMessage());
    }
}
```

Second, the `PersonBMPHomeLocal` interface is modified to include the public interface method mapped to this finder method:

```
public Collection findByLastName(String lastname)
    throws FinderException;
```

Note that finder methods are always prefixed by `ejbFind` in the bean class, while the home interface prefixes the name with `find` only. The EJB container knows to call the `ejbFind`*XXX*`()` method in the bean class to retrieve the primary keys whenever the `find`*XXX*`()` method is invoked through the home interface.

The implementation of a finder method is defined in the bean class for BMP entity beans only. If the entity bean uses CMP for persistence, the `ejbFind`*XXX*`()` method on the bean class is automatically created by the EJB container during the generation of the concrete bean class. The code-generation tools use information in the `ejb-jar.xml` and `weblogic-cmp-rdbms-jar.xml` descriptor files to generate the proper SQL in the `ejbFind`*XXX*`()` method. The `ejb-jar.xml` descriptor file must define the finder query using EJB-QL, the EJB Query Language, a cross between an object-based query language and SQL.

To add the same `ejbFindByLastName()` method to the CMP-based `PersonCMPBean` entity bean, for example, the following `query` element is added to the entity definition for the `PersonCMPEJB` bean in the `ejb-jar.xml` descriptor file:

```
<query>
  <query-method>
    <method-name>findByLastName</method-name>
    <method-params>
      <method-param>java.lang.String</method-param>
    </method-params>
  </query-method>
  <ejb-ql>
    <![CDATA[SELECT OBJECT(o) FROM PersonCMPEJB o WHERE
                                              o.lastName LIKE ?1]]>
  </ejb-ql>
</query>
```

The `PersonCMPHomeLocal` interface also needs to reflect the new method by including the same definition required in the BMP case:

```
public Collection findByLastName(String lastname)
    throws FinderException;
```

Details regarding basic EJB-QL syntax and usage are beyond the scope of this book; refer to the EJB references given earlier or consult BEA's online documentation at http://edocs.bea.com/wls/docs81/ejb/cmp_basic.html for more information. Although the use of EJB-QL and CMP provides reasonable flexibility in the definition of finder queries, including the ability to traverse bean relationships, you are likely to encounter some significant limitations in EJB-QL during development. Later in this chapter we'll discuss some of the WebLogic Server-specific extensions to EJB-QL designed to address these limitations.

Select Methods

CMP entity beans include an additional feature, *select* methods, allowing the definition of EJB-QL queries that return arbitrary data types or bean references. Unlike `ejbFindBy`*XXX*`()` methods, which are defined in the bean class but called through the public home interface via `find`*XXX*`()` methods, `ejbSelect`*XXX*`()` methods are private to the bean class itself and have no public interface. These `ejbSelect`*XXX*`()` methods are often used as helper methods by complex business logic defined in the bean class. Table 6.2 outlines some of the similarities and differences between select methods and finder methods.

Table 6.2 A Comparison of Select Methods and Finder Methods

SELECT METHODS	FINDER METHODS
Available for CMP entity beans only.	Available for CMP and BMP entity beans.
EJB-QL used to define query.	EJB-QL used to define query for CMP entity beans; custom SQL used for BMP entity beans.
Public method on bean class, not exposed to clients in local or remote interfaces.	Public method on bean class, included in home interface.
Allows parameters, including bean references.	Allows parameters, including bean references.
May return bean references or arbitrary data types, including collections. May return references to different entity beans.	Always returns a reference, or collection of references, to the specific entity bean defining the method. No arbitrary data types or references to other beans may be returned.

Adding a simple `ejbSelectXXX()` method to the `PersonCMPBean` entity bean requires an additional `query` element in the `ejb-jar.xml` descriptor file:

```
<query>
  <query-method>
    <method-name>ejbSelectFirstNames</method-name>
    <method-params>
      <method-param>java.lang.String</method-param>
    </method-params>
  </query-method>
  <ejb-ql>
    SELECT o.firstName FROM PersonCMPEJB o WHERE o.lastName = ?1
  </ejb-ql>
</query>
```

It also requires a corresponding abstract method definition in the `PersonCMPBean` bean class:

```
public abstract Collection ejbSelectFirstNames(String lastname)
    throws FinderException;
```

Other methods in the bean class may now call `ejbSelectFirstNames()` to retrieve a collection of `String` objects representing the first names of all beans with the specified last name.

This example doesn't begin to demonstrate the power and flexibility of select methods. Refer to the EJB references cited earlier, or see the BEA documentation and examples for additional information. We'll discuss some of the WebLogic Server-specific extensions to select methods, including the ability to return JDBC `ResultSet` objects containing multiple columns, later in this chapter.

Home Methods

The final type of entity-bean method, common to both BMP and CMP entity beans, is the *home* method. Home methods are defined in the bean class but accessed through the home interface, and they provide a mechanism for associating business logic to an entity bean class that is not specific to a particular bean instance. They are, in some ways, equivalent to methods on stateless session beans and can be used for the same types of stateless behaviors typically placed in such beans.

Clients invoke the home method through the bean's home interface, and the container uses an instance of the bean class and invokes the actual `ejbHome`*XXX*`()` implementation in the bean. This mechanism is particularly handy for accessing internal select methods on the bean class.

For example, to expose the `ejbSelectFirstNames()` method, discussed in the previous section, for use by clients, create an `ejbHomeGetFirstNames()` method on the bean class and have it forward the request to the internal `ejbSelectFirstNames()` method:

```
public Collection ejbHomeGetFirstNames(String lastname)
    throws FinderException
{
    // invoke the ejbSelect method to fetch the desired values
    return ejbSelectFirstNames(lastname);
}
```

The `ejbHomeGetFirstNames()` method is then exposed in the home interface using the mapped name `getFirstNames()`, a convention similar to the mapping of finder methods:

```
public Collection getFirstNames(String lastname)
    throws FinderException;
```

As shown in Figure 6.1, the client simply invokes the `getFirstNames()` method on the home interface to obtain the desired collection of `String` objects, and the EJB container and our forwarding code in `ejbHomeGetFirstNames()` take care of passing the request along to the `ejbSelectFirstNames()` method that performs the actual query.

Remember that home methods on the bean class are not called in the context of a particular bean instance. You should not access or modify attributes in the bean instance being used to invoke the `ejbHome`*XXX*`()` method. Home methods should be thought of as stateless methods of the bean class in that respect.

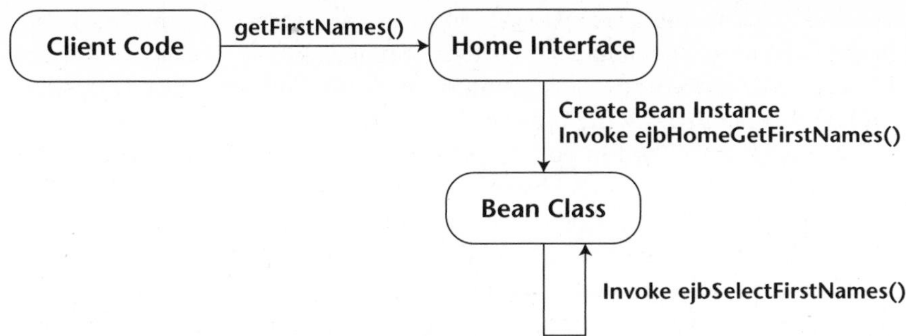

Figure 6.1 Using home methods to invoke select methods.

The real power of home methods is their ability to expose queries of bean data without the need to always create the underlying entity bean objects. For example, if your user submits a query to display all accounts in Texas, the last thing that you want to do is invoke a finder method to do this because you have no idea how many results the query will return or what they intend to do with this list. Using a finder method may cause a large number of objects to be brought into the container's cache, flushing out other objects that may be more important to cache. In this situation, use a home method to retrieve just enough data to create the list and associate each list entry with a primary key. This way, when the user wants to look at a particular entry, you can direct the container to find one entity bean and prevent filling the container's cache with beans that may not be used again. We will talk more about container caching later in this chapter.

TIP **Using home methods to populate large lists is often more efficient than using an equivalent finder method unless you are sure that the user is going to interact further with each and every matching bean.**

Message-Driven Beans

Message-driven bean (MDB) components were added in the EJB 2.0 specification to address a significant hole in the integration of EJB and Java Message Service (JMS) technology. EJB components are capable of acting as JMS *producers*, creating and sending messages to JMS destinations, but prior to EJB 2.0, there was no way for an EJB component to act as an asynchronous JMS *consumer*. There was nothing preventing a stateless session bean from invoking `receive()` and waiting for a message, of course, but this synchronous operation had the potential to block the thread indefinitely.

Architects typically addressed the problem by creating additional Java components, acting as JMS consumers that responded to incoming JMS messages by invoking particular methods on EJB components. The Java components provided the bridge between JMS and EJB by acting as asynchronous JMS consumers and synchronous EJB clients. Often these bridging components were run in their own Java threads using the server-initialization capability of the particular server product; in the case of WebLogic

Server, this was called a startup class. This technique, while acceptable in some cases, was not portable across vendors, had no built-in management or pooling capability, and forced you to place the bean's public interface classes in the server's classpath (making it impossible to redeploy the EJB without shutting down the server).

Message-driven beans are the EJB equivalent of these hand-built bridging components. Instances of the MDB are created by the container to use as listeners on the JMS destination configured for that particular bean. The bean instances are deployed, pooled, and managed much like stateless session beans. The MDB class implements the `onMessage()` method to process JMS messages delivered by the container. The `onMessage()` method typically invokes the EJB components to process the message, and all of this can be done in the context of a transaction that includes the delivery of the originating message to the MDB. This ability to use transactional behavior with asynchronous message consumers is one clear advantage of MDB components over previous hand-built JMS bridge components. We will talk more about JMS and MBDs in Chapter 9.

Now that we've completed our review of EJB key concepts and looked at a few generic EJB examples, it is time to dive in to the unique features and capabilities of the WebLogic Server EJB container.

WebLogic Server EJB Container

Our discussion of WebLogic Server EJB features will concentrate on features useful in the creation of classic *n*-tier J2EE applications using EJB components for the business tier of the application. We'll start with a brief review of the EJB container and the life cycle of EJB components in the WebLogic Server container implementation. The next section documents WebLogic Server EJB features common to many of the EJB component types. The bulk of the chapter is then spent discussing features applicable to specific types of EJB components.

There are so many EJB-related features and configuration parameters in WebLogic Server that we had to make some choices in the interest of space. The theme for this book is best practices, after all, and some advanced features and capabilities represent more useful and important concepts for typical J2EE applications than others. The next chapter is intended to apply the best practices discussed here in a realistic J2EE application.

EJB Container Basics

The EJB container is a fundamental part of the EJB architecture. In a nutshell, the EJB container provides the environment used to host and manage the EJB components deployed in the container. The container is responsible for providing a standard set of services, including caching, concurrency, persistence, security, transaction management, and locking services. The container also provides distributed access and lookup functions for hosted components, and it intercepts all method invocations on hosted components to enforce declarative security and transaction contexts.

The EJB container is not a single Java class, nor is it a single API or service accessible to the contained components or external client code. It is more of an abstract concept implemented by each server vendor in a unique fashion. Note that most of the unique features of WebLogic Server described in the remaining sections of this chapter are actually features of the EJB container itself.

EJB Life Cycle in WebLogic Server

One of the key responsibilities of the EJB container is the management of EJB component life cycles. Bean instances are pooled and reused by the container to host specific beans in an effort to reduce the number of object instantiations. Rather than spend time reviewing the complex and confusing processes involved in pooling, passivation, activation, and other memory-management issues, we'll take a more pragmatic approach by concentrating on the key life-cycle events of an EJB component from the point of view of a client of the component.

Given that approach, the life cycle of a standard entity bean, for example, becomes fairly simple:

1. The client obtains a reference to the entity bean in some way, possibly using a finder method or by traversing a bean relationship.
2. The client invokes a business method on the reference. We'll assume no transaction is active.
3. The container starts a transaction, if appropriate.
4. The container reuses an existing instance from the pool, if available, or instantiates a new bean instance and initializes its context by calling `setEntityContext()`.
5. The container loads the bean's state from the persistent store, either automatically or by calling `ejbLoad()`.
6. The container invokes a desired business method on behalf of the client. The bean performs the desired operation.
7. The container saves bean attributes to the persistent store, either automatically or by calling `ejbStore()`.
8. The container commits the transaction created for this life cycle, if appropriate.
9. The results of the business-method call are returned to the client.

Everything revolves around the transaction boundaries. By default, the container always loads and stores standard entity beans on transaction boundaries. The life cycle described here should be taken as the baseline or worst case for an entity bean, and many EJB optimization and caching techniques are intended to improve performance by reducing the work in each step or eliminating steps completely. Note that we've used the term *standard entity bean* in this section to indicate a normal, read-write entity bean with no special configuration flags or deployment descriptors used to modify the default life cycle, as described by the EJB specification.

The life cycle of a stateless session bean is simpler than an entity bean because there are no persistence requirements:

1. The client obtains a reference to the stateless session bean home interface.
2. The client uses the `create()` method on the home interface to create an SLSB and obtain a reference.

3. The client invokes a business method on the bean reference.
4. The container reuses an existing instance from the pool, if available, or instantiates a new bean instance and initializes its context by calling `setSessionContext()`.
5. If the bean instance was newly created in Step 4, the container invokes `ejbCreate()` on the bean instance; otherwise, it skips this step.
6. The container starts a transaction, if appropriate.
7. The container invokes a business method on the bean instance, and the bean performs the desired operation.
8. The container commits the transaction, if appropriate.
9. The results of the business-method call are returned to the client.
10. The client may invoke additional business methods on the bean reference, each of which may end up invoking methods on a different bean instance.
11. The client calls `remove()` on the bean reference when it is done with the SLSB as a way of letting the container know that the client is through with the reference.
12. At some point, if the container decides to reduce the size of the bean instance pool, the container invokes `ejbRemove()` on the bean instance. It is important to understand that this decision is not related to the client calling `remove()`.

Note that `setSessionContext()` or `ejbCreate()` are good places to preload cached data in an SLSB instance or perform other initialization steps such as JNDI lookups. Although SLSBs are stateless from the point of view of the client, the bean instances are reused and may take advantage of cached data in internal member variables.

The life cycle of a stateful session bean is controlled by the client explicitly through the `create()` and `remove()` methods:

1. The client obtains a reference to the stateful session bean home interface.
2. The client uses one of the `create()` methods on the home interface to create an SFSB and obtain a reference.
3. The container instantiates a new bean instance and initializes its context by calling `setSessionContext()`.
4. The container invokes the corresponding `ejbCreate()` method on the bean instance.
5. The client invokes a business method on the bean reference.
6. The container starts a transaction, if appropriate.
7. The container invokes a business method on the bean instance, and the bean performs the desired operation.
8. The container commits the transaction, if appropriate.
9. The results of the business-method call are returned to the client.
10. The client may invoke additional business methods on the bean reference and is assured that these additional calls will go to the same instance of the bean.

11. The client calls `remove()` on the bean reference when it is done with the SFSB.
12. The container calls `ejbRemove()` on the bean instance, allowing it to clean up any resources before it is removed.

Like SLSB components, `setSessionContext()` and `ejbCreate()` are called once when a SFSB instance is created and are appropriate places for creating internal caches or performing other initialization steps. Of course, the cache is specific to the particular client's session so you could just as easily use lazy initialization because, either way, the client will be waiting on the initialization work.

This very brief introduction to the life cycle of various EJB components represents a simplified view of the process. Additional complexities are introduced by limitations in the pool and cache sizes that you need to understand to configure your application properly. We'll cover some of these complexities in a subsequent section on setting pool sizes and configuring passivation.

General WebLogic Server EJB Features

This section discusses some of the important general features of the WebLogic Server EJB container related to all types of EJB components. Subsequent sections will detail WebLogic Server features related to specific EJB types.

EJB Deployment/Redeployment

One important feature of the WebLogic Server EJB container is the ability to deploy and redeploy EJB components easily. Chapter 8 discusses the basic EJB packaging and deployment process, and it compares various options for deploying EJB components in WebLogic Server.

Dynamic EJB Compiling

The normal packaging and deployment technique for EJB components involves the execution of the WebLogic Server EJB compiler utility, `weblogic.ejbc`, or the new application compiler, `weblogic.appc`, to create a complete EJB archive file containing all of the container classes required for the EJB components. These container classes include home object and EJB object implementation classes, plus concrete classes for the beans that are subclasses of the bean class provided. The complete EJB archive file is then deployed to WebLogic Server using one of the techniques discussed in Chapter 8.

WebLogic Server also allows the deployment of an intermediate EJB archive file that has not been processed through the `weblogic.ejbc` or `weblogic.appc` utility. This intermediate archive file must contain the EJB components and descriptor files required by the `weblogic.ejbc` or `weblogic.appc` utility, as in the normal packaging and deployment approach discussed in Chapter 8, but the actual compilation step can be deferred until the archive file is processed by the EJB container during the deployment of the application. Note that this same dynamic compilation approach will be employed by WebLogic Server to deploy EJB archive files created using a different version of the compiler, even if the difference is only a service pack. This makes it less painful for you.

Dynamic execution of the EJB compiler may be forced unconditionally for a given EJB archive during the deployment of the application by setting the `Force Generation` option. To configure this option, find the desired EJB archive underneath the `Deployments` folder hierarchy in the WebLogic Console's left-hand navigation bar and look in the `Compiler Options Configuration` tab.

Referencing Other EJB Components

WebLogic Server supports the standard referencing mechanisms defined in the EJB 2.0 specification, including the `ejb-link` element in the `ejb-jar.xml` file. In this section, we will discuss referencing EJBs in the same application and in other applications. We end this section with a discussion of the WebLogic Server pass-by-reference optimization.

Referencing EJB Components in the Same Application

It is very common for EJB components to reference other EJB components contained in the same J2EE application. All EJB components in the same EJB archive file are in the same application, as are all EJB components in different archive files in a single enterprise application (`.ear`) archive file or directory structure.

EJB components typically obtain a reference to other components in the same application using the normal `java:comp/env/ejb` JNDI lookup syntax:

```
Test2SessionHomeLocal homelocal2 =
    (Test2SessionHomeLocal)ctx.lookup("java:comp/env/ejb/Test2");
```

There are two primary ways to map this generic syntax to the actual home interface: mapping to a global JNDI name in the `weblogic-ejb-jar.xml` file or using `ejb-link` elements.

In the first approach, the referencing component includes a `ejb-local-ref` element in the `ejb-jar.xml` file declaring the reference:

```
<ejb-local-ref>
  <ejb-ref-name>ejb/Test2</ejb-ref-name>
  <ejb-ref-type>Session</ejb-ref-type>
  <local-home>
    mastering.weblogic.ch06.example3.ejb.Test2SessionHomeLocal
  </local-home>
  <local>
    mastering.weblogic.ch06.example3.ejb.Test2SessionLocal
  </local>
</ejb-local-ref>
```

The `ejb-local-reference-description` elements in the `weblogic-ejb-jar.xml` file map this reference to a particular JNDI name:

```
<ejb-local-reference-description>
  <!-- Matches entry in ejb-jar.xml file -->
  <ejb-ref-name>ejb/Test2</ejb-ref-name>
  <jndi-name>Test2SessionHomeLocal</jndi-name>
</ejb-local-reference-description>
```

In the second approach, the referencing component includes an `ejb-link` element in the `ejb-local-ref` element in `ejb-jar.xml`, specifying the name of the other EJB component:

```
<ejb-local-ref>
  <ejb-ref-name>ejb/Test2</ejb-ref-name>
  <ejb-ref-type>Session</ejb-ref-type>
  <local-home>
    mastering.weblogic.ch06.example3.ejb.Test2SessionHomeLocal
  </local-home>
  <local>
    mastering.weblogic.ch06.example3.ejb.Test2SessionLocal
  </local>
  <ejb-link>Test2SessionEJB</ejb-link>
</ejb-local-ref>
```

In this approach there is no need to map the `ejb/Test2` name to a specific JNDI name, so no `ejb-local-reference-description` elements are required in the `weblogic-ejb-jar.xml` descriptor. WebLogic Server automatically maps the `ejb/Test2` reference to the `Test2SessionEJB` home interface and makes it available for lookup using the `java:comp/env` syntax shown previously. The name `Test2SessionEJB` is the logical name assigned to the EJB in its deployment descriptor. The `ejb-link` element may also specify the name of the EJB archive file hosting the desired component:

```
<ejb-link>test2.jar#Test2SessionEJB</ejb-link>
```

This is required only if two EJBs in two different archive files use the same logical name. Components in the same application can, of course, look each other up directly using known global JNDI names:

```
Test2SessionHomeLocal homelocal2 =
    (Test2SessionHomeLocal) ctx.lookup("Test2SessionHomeLocal");
```

This technique increases the coupling between EJB components by requiring that code in all referencing components knows the JNDI name for the desired component, but eliminates the need for all `ejb-ref` elements in descriptor files. Although the number of `ejb-ref` elements can grow exponentially in applications with many components requiring references to each other, using tools such as EJBGen, described in the next chapter, to create these `ejb-ref` and related elements makes this technique more tenable for large applications.

BEST PRACTICE **Use `ejb-ref` elements, in conjunction with either `ejb-link` or `ejb-reference-description` elements, rather than direct lookup using global JNDI names, to reduce coupling between components in most applications.**

Referencing EJB External Components

EJB components located in different applications, whether different enterprise application archive (`.ear`) files or just other EJB jar files not part of the current application, whether running in the same WebLogic Server instance or not, are considered external components. These components do not share the same local JNDI tree, so the `ejb-link` mechanism for referencing other components is not available. Components must use either global JNDI names or include appropriate `ejb-ref` elements in `ejb-jar.xml` and `ejb-reference-description` elements in the `weblogic-ejb-jar.xml` descriptor to look up external components. Note that external components must be looked up and used by their remote interfaces rather than local interfaces.

Because the components are external to the current application and more likely to change their global JNDI names, we suggest you use `ejb-ref` and `ejb-reference-description` elements instead of global JNDI names in referencing bean code.

BEST PRACTICE **Use `ejb-ref` and `ejb-reference-description` elements to access EJB components in other applications.**

Calling Components by Reference

The J2EE specification requires that EJB components invoked through their remote interfaces must use pass-by-value semantics, meaning that method parameters are copied during the invocation. Changes made to the passed-in object in the bean method are not reflected in the caller's version of the object. Copying method parameters is required in the case of a true remote or external invocation, of course, because the parameters are serialized by the underlying RMI infrastructure before being provided to the bean method. Pass-by-value semantics are also required between components located in different enterprise applications in the same Java virtual machine due to classloader constraints.

EJB components located in the same enterprise-application archive (`.ear`) file are loaded by the same classloader and have the option of using pass-by-reference semantics for all invocations, eliminating the unnecessary copying of parameters passed during the invocation and improving performance. Set the `enable-call-by-reference` parameter to `true` in the `weblogic-ejb-jar.xml` descriptor file to enable this feature for each bean in your application. Local references always use pass-by-reference semantics and are unaffected by the `enable-call-by-reference` setting.

WARNING **The default value of** `enable-call-by-reference` **was** `true` **in WebLogic Server 7.0 but is now** `false` **in WebLogic Server 8.1 in order to comply with Sun's J2EE licensing policy changes that require all J2EE compatible servers to support the specification with their out-of-the-box configuration. Be sure to set** `enable-call-by-reference` **to** `true` **for all beans in your application that have remote interfaces to avoid parameter copying unless your application requires copying for functional correctness.**

Session Bean Features

The first set of WebLogic Server-specific features is related to session bean components and their management by the container.

Stateful Session EJB Cache Management

Stateful session bean instances are created by WebLogic Server as they are needed to service client requests. Between requests these instances reside in a bean-specific cache in the *active* state, ready for the next request. The size of the cache is limited by the `max-beans-in-cache` element in the `weblogic-ejb-jar.xml` deployment descriptor file. As long as your application never requires more than `max-beans-in-cache` instances of the SFSB at any given time to service all concurrent clients, there is no contention for the cache and performance is optimal. If you limit the number of beans in the cache, WebLogic Server may be forced to manage the cache in a fairly active manner using the following rules:

- If the cache is full, bean instances that are not being used at that moment for client requests are subject to passivation. Setting the `idle-timeout-seconds` has no effect on this rule because the server must make room for additional instances.
- If the cache is full and all instances are currently pinned in the cache fulfilling client requests, WebLogic Server throws a `CacheFullException`. It will not block and wait for an instance to become available for passivation. Note that this condition is unlikely to occur if the `max-beans-in-cache` setting is higher than the maximum number of execute threads because the number of simultaneous client requests is normally limited by the number of threads.
- Passivation logic is controlled by the `cache-type` and `idle-timeout-seconds` elements in the descriptor. The default setting for `cache-type`, not recently used (NRU), passivates beans only when the number of active beans approaches the `max-beans-in-cache` setting. It will not passivate based solely on time using the `idle-timeout-seconds` setting. An alternative `cache-type` value, least recently used (LRU), passivates based on both the maximum cache size and the time-out setting. While the LRU setting can be a convenient way of enforcing idle time-outs on the resources the objects encapsulate, it requires the container to keep track of the bean's access time and

maintain an ordered list that gets updated after each bean access. Unless you have a good reason to need idle time-outs strictly enforced, most applications should retain the default NRU algorithm and passivate only on memory pressure.

- Passivated instances that are unused for `idle-timeout-seconds` are subject to removal from disk storage during cache maintenance.
- If `idle-timeout-seconds` is set to zero, beans are simply removed when chosen for passivation and are never passivated to disk storage. This can be a useful option to avoid passivating old instances representing lost clients or transactions that were completed long before. Of course, this can also cause long-running clients to lose their sessions if the `max-beans-in-cache` is not properly tuned.

Recall that passivation of beans refers to the serialization of nontransient data in the bean to disk storage to release the memory used by the bean. The next request for the passivated bean will require activation, the reverse process, where bean attributes are read from the disk store and the active bean instance is recreated in memory. Needless to say, passivation and activation cycles are extremely expensive. You should monitor the amount of passivation activity occurring in your system using the WebLogic Console and tune the `max-beans-in-cache` setting to reduce or eliminate this activity to achieve high performance.

BEST PRACTICE **Avoid excessive passivation of stateful session beans by setting** `max-beans-in-cache` **high enough to meet the instance requirements for the expected maximum concurrent user count.**

Your application should always call `remove()` to delete the active bean instance from the cache when a client is through using the instance. Failure to call `remove()` leaves the bean instance in the active state and consumes one slot in the cache, requiring eventual passivation by WebLogic Server during cache management to make room for additional client beans.

BEST PRACTICE **Always call** `remove()` **on a stateful session bean after you are done using it to delete it from the bean cache.**

The `idle-timeout-seconds` setting is obviously very important in cache management. The bean is subject to passivation once the time-out expires, assuming the LRU algorithm is being used, and may be removed from storage completely after the time-out period passes again. The default time-out value, 600 seconds, may be too short if users are likely to pause between requests for a longer period of time. If you are using SFSBs with a Web application, it might make sense to set this time-out value equal to the `HttpSession` time-out value for your Web application, for example, to be more consistent. Otherwise, review your business requirements and set the `idle-timeout-seconds` to the lowest value possible that still meets your application's requirements.

BEST PRACTICE **Stateful session beans used to store session state for Web applications should have their** `idle-timeout-seconds` **set equal to the** `HttpSession` **time-out value. For non-Web clients, set the** `idle-timeout-seconds` **to the lowest value possible while still meeting your business requirements for the application.**

In-Memory Replication for Stateful Session EJBs

Stateful session bean components are used to encapsulate client-specific data and processes that must maintain state across multiple method invocations. These invocations may be separated by periods as short as milliseconds or as long as hours, subject to time-out settings. State that is maintained across multiple invocations would be lost if the SFSB was deployed to a single server instance that failed or became unavailable to the client. Fortunately, WebLogic Server provides failover for stateful session beans deployed in a cluster, just as it does for `HttpSession` data through the use of in-memory replication.

Figure 6.2 illustrates the basic in-memory replication scenario and shows communication paths before and after the failure of Server2. In this example, Client155 was using the SFSB155 component hosted on Server2 as the primary copy of the bean. When that server failed, Client155 was automatically redirected to the backup copy of the SFSB155 component hosted on the other server. This failover logic is provided by the replica-aware stub object used by the client for all communication with the bean. The stub acts as a proxy for the bean in much the same way the Web server plug-in acts as a proxy for Web applications and provides failover in the presentation tier.

Changes made to the primary copy of an SFSB component are copied to the replicated version on the backup server at the end of a committed transaction involving the SFSB component. Note that modified SFSB data may be lost if either server fails during the post-commit transfer of data to the backup server because the replication is done outside the scope of the transaction.

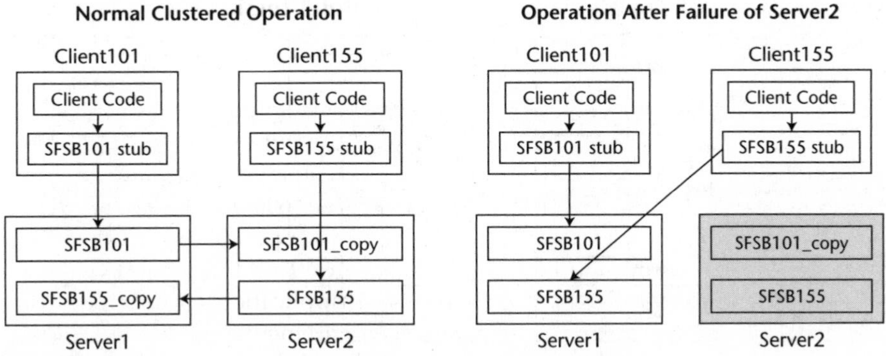

Figure 6.2 The replica-aware stub provides SFSB failover.

Although we generally recommend storing session data in the `HttpSession` and using `HttpSession` replication alone when possible, you might consider using SFSB replication to store business data or the intermediate results of a multistep process under some conditions. Figure 6.3 illustrates the Web application replication scenario using an `HttpSession` to store the replica-aware stub object and a replicated SFSB component to store the business data.

Note that both the Web application and EJB components are located on the same machine. Failure of that machine will cause the Web server plug-in to fail over to servlets and JSPs on the specific secondary machine saved in the cookie sent to the browser. How can you be sure that the backup copy of the SFSB data will be located on the same machine as the backup copy of the `HttpSession` data, as illustrated in Figure 6.3? Just as WebLogic Server always prefers to communicate with EJB components located in the same application as the Web application components, it normally configures the failover copies of both the `HttpSession` data and the replicated SFSB data on the same backup server.

Unfortunately, the collocation of both kinds of backup data is not guaranteed to occur in all conditions. If the `HttpSession` secondary and the SFSB secondary are located on different machines, you can easily get into a situation where a single client request involves calling from one WebLogic Server cluster member to another to process the request. Performance will suffer if this scenario occurs, and the large number of cross-server messages and the threads consumed by these messages also expose your application to a potential deadlock condition discussed in Chapter 12.

WARNING Be careful when storing SFSB references in the `HttpSession` because in-memory replication doesn't guarantee collocation of secondary objects and may lead to excessive server-to-server calls in the same cluster after a primary server failure. Not only will this kill your performance, but it also will expose your application to potential deadlock situations.

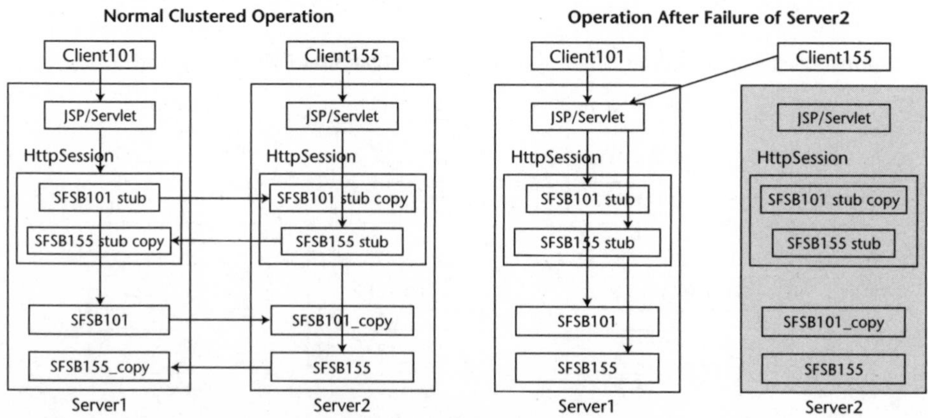

Figure 6.3 Replicated HttpSession and SFSB component.

Recognize that SFSB replication is more costly in terms of memory and performance than `HttpSession` replication because there is no simple way for the container to determine which portions of the bean have changed. While `HttpSession` replication relies on `setAttribute()` calls to determine the data that must be sent to the backup server, SFSB replication requires before and after images of the SFSB to determine changes requiring replication at the end of the transaction. For efficiency, the server keeps the after image from the last transaction to use as the before image for the next; this means that you have two copies of the bean in memory in the primary server and one in the secondary server.

Why would you use replicated SFSB components when `HttpSession` replication fills essentially the same role? Web applications should probably stick with `HttpSession` replication to maximize performance and avoid introducing additional complexity, but not all applications are Web applications. Replicated SFSB components allow non-Web applications to maintain state between method invocations in a fully clustered fashion as well.

Configuring SFSB components for in-memory replication requires a `replication-type` element in the descriptor for the stateless session bean in `weblogic-ejb-jar.xml`:

```
<stateful-session-clustering>
  ...
  <replication-type>InMemory</replication-type>
</stateful-session-clustering>
```

Entity Bean Features

The next set of WebLogic Server-specific features covers the capabilities related to entity beans. There are a large number of entity bean capabilities provided by WebLogic Server; far more than any other type of EJB component. In a sense, this reflects the complexity of the problem entity beans are being asked to solve and the need for features above and beyond the J2EE specification to create enterprise-class applications. There are many possible strategies for achieving good performance with proper transactional controls and concurrency. No single strategy is best is all situations, and the EJB container relies on the application developer to configure entity-bean persistence properly for best performance.

This section covers strategies and best practices in four major areas: concurrency, caching, tuning queries and persistence operations, and advanced CMP features. You should be aware of all possible strategies and their implications before choosing a strategy for your entity bean-based J2EE application.

Concurrency Strategies

The basic load-and-store cycle used to read and write entity-bean data on a per-transaction basis is sufficient, in theory, to ensure that clients always interact with a bean containing the latest data in the database. This simplistic approach might be sufficient for small applications with few users and limited performance requirements, but it fails to meet the needs of a true enterprise-class architecture for two reasons:

- No caching of bean data. In this simplistic approach, every transaction with an entity bean involves a database operation to retrieve bean data from the persistent store. You saw this behavior in the simple `PersonBMPBean` example application earlier. The bean-instance caching defined by the EJB specification does not cache the contents of the beans, only the *instance* created in the pool. You therefore need some facility for safely caching bean data to improve performance where appropriate.
- No concurrency support. The simplistic load-and-store cycle does not specify how to handle multiple clients interacting with the same entity bean during this life cycle. To make matters worse, if the application is clustered across multiple servers, the clients accessing the beans may be using different EJB containers running on different JVMs on different machines. Coordinating concurrent access to bean data across multiple containers is also a requirement for enterprise-class systems.

WebLogic Server provides a robust set of caching and concurrency options to address these two limitations. You should recognize that caching of data and controlling concurrent access to data are strongly interrelated. WebLogic Server combines approaches for both sides of the problem in a set of *concurrency strategies*:

- **Exclusive concurrency strategy**, or *exclusive locking*, addresses the concurrency side of the problem by using in-memory locking to serialize access to specific bean instances in an EJB container. Caching can be configured using the cache-between-transactions feature, described later in this chapter, in a nonclustered environment.
- **Database concurrency strategy**, or *database locking*, addresses the concurrency side of the problem by relying on the underlying database technology to reject changes made by two simultaneous transactions. Caching data between transactions is not possible with this strategy.
- **Read-only concurrency strategy** is more of a caching solution than a concurrency solution. Bean data is kept in memory and loaded from the database as a result of time-out or explicit invalidation. Concurrent access to bean data is allowed through the creation of multiple beans.
- **Optimistic concurrency strategy**, or *optimistic locking*, uses the classic client/server approach of ensuring that the underlying database rows have not been updated by any other client during the life cycle of the bean. Caching is possible using the cache-between-transactions feature in both clustered and nonclustered environments. Only CMP entity beans may use this strategy.

We'll discuss each of these concurrency strategies in detail in the sections that follow. The desired concurrency strategy is defined on a per-bean basis in the `weblogic-ejb-jar.xml` descriptor file in the `entity-cache` element in the entity descriptor:

```
<entity-descriptor>
    <entity-cache>
```

```
        ...
        <concurrency-strategy>Exclusive</concurrency-strategy>
    </entity-cache>
    ...
</entity-descriptor>
```

The default concurrency strategy in WebLogic Server 6.*x* and later is database concurrency. Prior versions used exclusive concurrency by default.

Exclusive Concurrency Strategy

The exclusive concurrency strategy uses in-memory locking to serialize access to bean instances in an EJB container. When a client enlists a specific entity bean instance in a transaction by calling a method on the bean interface, the EJB container creates an exclusive lock on that bean instance held for the duration of the transaction. Other clients attempting to enlist the same bean in a transaction are forced to wait for the first transaction to complete before acquiring the lock on the instance. Because the first client's lock is not released until the transaction completes and modified data is flushed to the database, the next client will always see the latest committed data when the container loads the data on its behalf.

Table 6.3 presents a simplified example of this process for two clients attempting to access the same entity bean at the same time. Clearly the activity becomes more complex if additional EJB components are involved in the transaction, but the example represents the primary activities in the process.

Table 6.3 Exclusive Concurrency Example

CLIENT #1 THREAD ACTIVITY	CLIENT #2 THREAD ACTIVITY
The client acquires a reference to bean 101.	The client acquires a reference to bean 101.
The client invokes a method on the bean interface.	
The EJB container intercepts the request, starts the transaction, enlists bean 101 in the transaction, and places an exclusive lock on bean 101 in the lock manager.	
The EJB container loads the data from the database into the bean instance.	The client invokes a method on the bean interface
The EJB container passes the request to a method on the bean instance.	The EJB container intercepts the request, starts the transaction, and blocks the thread, waiting to obtain an exclusive lock on bean 101.

(continued)

Table 6.3 *(continued)*

CLIENT #1 THREAD ACTIVITY	CLIENT #2 THREAD ACTIVITY
The bean instance processes the request and returns.	The thread is blocked.
The EJB container saves the bean instance's state to the database.	The thread is blocked.
The EJB container commits the transaction and removes the exclusive lock on bean 101.	The thread is blocked.
The results are returned to the client.	The EJB container enlists bean 101 in the transaction and places an exclusive lock on bean 101 in the lock manager.
	The EJB container loads the data from the database into the bean instance.
	The EJB container passes the request to a method on the bean instance.
	The bean instance processes the request and returns.
	The EJB container saves the bean instance's state to the database.
	The EJB container commits the transaction and removes the exclusive lock on bean 101.
	The results are returned to the client.

There are a number of problems with this concurrency strategy when applied to realistic, enterprise-class applications:

- Most enterprise-class applications are deployed in a cluster, and each server instance in the cluster will deploy the EJB components in a separate EJB container. Because exclusive locking is performed by each EJB container and is local to that container only, there is no concurrency control across servers in the cluster. In other words, if two clients were talking to bean instances representing the same business object on two different servers, the second client would not be blocked by the first client. In effect, clients going to different servers use database concurrency while clients going to the same server use exclusive concurrency.
- The EJB container does not discriminate between read and write operations for locking, so clients wishing to read data from the bean are blocked in the same way as clients performing updates. This can produce significant response-time degradation if contention occurs for the same entity beans.

- Exclusive locking brings with it the problem of potential deadlocks. Deadlocks occur when two clients access a set of entity beans in a different order, such that each client thread is blocked waiting for the other client thread to release the lock it needs to proceed. Such deadlocks are difficult to avoid unless you take extreme care to ensure that all access to multiple entity beans proceeds in a consistent order in every component of the application.

Some of these issues are the result of requiring the EJB container to maintain strong transactional and isolation controls, or ACID properties, for the underlying data. The container cannot, for example, allow read access to a bean instance involved in another transaction without violating basic isolation rules.

The exclusive concurrency strategy is no longer the default strategy in WebLogic Server. Use this strategy sparingly, if at all, and remember that the locking is on a per-container basis.

BEST PRACTICE Avoid exclusive concurrency unless synchronizing access to the underlying data source is critical to the correct operation of the system. Recognize that clustered environments generally defeat exclusive locking because of its per-container implementation. Be aware of potential deadlocks when using exclusive locking, and control the order of lock acquisition throughout your application to avoid deadlocks.

Configuring the exclusive concurrency strategy requires the following element in the `entity-descriptor` for the entity bean:

```
<entity-descriptor>
    <entity-cache>
        ...
        <concurrency-strategy>Exclusive</concurrency-strategy>
    </entity-cache>
    ...
</entity-descriptor>
```

There are no other options or elements associated with the exclusive concurrency strategy. Note that this strategy may be combined with the cache between transactions caching strategy described later in this chapter in a single server environment.

Database Concurrency Strategy

The database concurrency strategy relies on the underlying database technology to reject changes made by two simultaneous transactions. Rather than enforce exclusive access to a given bean, the container gives all clients their own copies of the entity bean at the start of their individual transactions and allows the database to catch and reject attempts to access the underlying data in ways that violate the isolation level in use. Essentially, the database concurrency strategy in its simplest form represents no concurrency control at all in the EJB container.

If multiple clients obtain references to the same bean and call only get methods, as opposed to set methods, this concurrency strategy has no effect on the life cycle of the bean instances. Each bean is loaded, processes the get requests, and is removed from the cache. Because the CMP logic is smart enough to avoid executing an update statement when only get methods are called, no database updates occur and no concurrency issues exist. Each bean life cycle is independent.

If multiple clients obtain references to the same bean and do call set methods on the bean, the final database-update step in the bean life cycle will be performed by one client before the others, and the database locking will prevent subsequent commits from succeeding under most conditions. Specific database technologies and isolation levels affect this behavior, of course, but Table 6.4 illustrates the normal case in more detail.

Table 6.4 Database Concurrency Example

CLIENT #1 THREAD ACTIVITY	CLIENT #2 THREAD ACTIVITY
The client acquires a reference to bean 101.	The client acquires a reference to bean 101.
The client invokes a method on the bean interface.	
The EJB container intercepts the request, starts the transaction, instantiates bean 101 in the cache, and enlists bean 101 in the transaction.	
The EJB container loads the data from the database into the bean instance.	The client invokes a method on the bean interface.
The EJB container passes the request to a method on the bean instance.	The EJB container intercepts the request, starts the transaction, instantiates bean 101 in the cache, and enlists bean 101 in the transaction.
The bean instance processes the request and returns.	The EJB container loads the data from the database into the bean instance.
The EJB container saves the bean instance's state to the database.	The EJB container passes the request to the method on the bean instance.
The EJB container commits the transaction.	The bean instance processes the request and returns.
The results are returned to the client.	The EJB container saves the bean instance's state to the database.
	The EJB container attempts to commit the transaction. The database raises an exception because of the previous commit by Client #1.
	The database exception is returned to the client.

Because Client #1 performs the commit before Client #2, the transaction in the Client #2 thread is doomed to fail during either the database update step or the final transaction commit step. Where it fails depends on the specific database technology.

The database concurrency strategy has two significant advantages over the exclusive strategy:

- No locking or synchronization is performed by the EJB container. This eliminates the potential for deadlocks in the EJB container and improves performance considerably for applications that suffer from contention related to certain entity beans.
- The database concurrency strategy works in a cluster because it relies on the RDBMS, a shared service, for concurrency control, rather than on the individual EJB containers.

There are three big disadvantages with the database concurrency strategy, however:

- Transactions may fail during the database update or commit step in the bean life cycle, raising a database-related exception to the client. Client code must catch this exception and decide if it is safe to retry the entire transaction again. The entire transaction rolls back, not just the portion related to the entity bean that caused the exception.
- WebLogic Server does not allow the use of the cache-between-transactions feature with this concurrency strategy. As you will see when this feature is covered later, cache-between-transactions eliminates the need to reload the data from the database for a bean found in the cache, potentially representing a large performance gain. Because the database concurrency strategy always provides and loads a new bean for each client, it is incompatible with this caching feature.
- You are essentially moving any potential deadlocks from the EJB container down to the database.

Despite these disadvantages, database concurrency represents a solid starting point and is preferred over exclusive concurrency in most applications.

BEST PRACTICE The database concurrency strategy is preferred over the exclusive strategy in most applications, but it suffers from the lack of support for caching data between transactions.

The database concurrency strategy is the default in WebLogic 6.*x* and later, so failing to explicitly set the caching strategy on a bean causes WebLogic Server to use database concurrency. You may also declare the strategy explicitly using this element:

```
<entity-descriptor>
    <entity-cache>
        ...
        <concurrency-strategy>Database</concurrency-strategy>
    </entity-cache>
    ...
</entity-descriptor>
```

Read-Only Concurrency Strategy

The read-only concurrency strategy in WebLogic 7.*x* and later is an improved version of the standard read-only entity beans available in WebLogic 5.*x* and 6.*x*. This improved read-only concurrency strategy provides a mechanism for the long-term caching of entity bean data in the EJB container, while eliminating the previous requirement for exclusive access to the cached bean instance.

When using this strategy, the container will populate a particular bean instance the first time it is referenced by a client by reading the bean's state from the database. Subject to `max-beans-in-cache` limitations, this bean instance then remains in memory indefinitely and is used by the container during subsequent invocations by new clients. In previous versions of WebLogic Server, this cached bean had to be accessed by clients using an exclusive locking scheme, creating the potential for deadlocks and performance bottlenecks. WebLogic Server 7.*x* and later changes the default behavior of read-only beans to avoid this exclusive locking by copying bean data from the cached bean instance to a separate instance for each client request.

The EJB container never tries to save the bean's state at the end of transactions involving read-only beans, so no changes can be made to the persistent data through these beans.

An entity bean is declared to be read-only by setting the `concurrency-strategy` element to `ReadOnly`. Beans with this setting use the new caching mechanism that avoids exclusive locks on the cached bean data. To configure beans to use exclusive locking on the cached bean data, thereby simulating the behavior of read-only beans in WebLogic 5.*x* and 6.*x*, use the `ReadOnlyExclusive` concurrency strategy.

The `read-timeout-seconds` element may also be included with both `ReadOnly` and `ReadOnlyExclusive` beans:

```
<entity-cache>
  ...
  <read-timeout-seconds>600</read-timeout-seconds>
  <concurrency-strategy>ReadOnly</concurrency-strategy>
</entity-cache>
```

This element adds another check during each method invocation on the cached bean to verify that the cached data has not expired. If the data is older than the time-out setting, the container reloads the bean's state from the persistent store to refresh the cache. The method invocation that caused the refresh, and all subsequent calls by clients, will receive bean instances containing a copy of the updated data. The default value of `read-timeout-seconds` is 0, meaning that no time-out checks will occur and the bean's state will be loaded from the persistent store only during initial bean creation and after explicit invalidation, a topic covered later in this chapter.

It is also possible to configure entire groups of entity beans to have the `ReadOnly` or `ReadOnlyExclusive` concurrency strategy using the `weblogic-application.xml` descriptor file. This capability is part of the combined-caching-support feature introduced in WebLogic Server 7.0, which will be discussed later in this chapter.

Optimistic Concurrency Strategy

The optimistic concurrency strategy enforces concurrency using the classic client/server approach of ensuring that the underlying database rows have not been updated by any other client during the transaction. This strategy is available only for CMP entity beans.

Optimistic locking schemes take advantage of the fact that most access to bean data is for read purposes. Each client thread is given its own copy of the entity bean, much like the database strategy, and checks are performed during the final database update to ensure that no changes have occurred in the database during the bean life cycle. We'll discuss the specific types of checks that can be performed and the techniques used by WebLogic Server to ensure concurrency in a moment.

Table 6.5 presents a simple example for two clients accessing and modifying the same bean.

Table 6.5 Optimistic Concurrency Example

CLIENT #1 THREAD ACTIVITY	CLIENT #2 THREAD ACTIVITY
The client acquires a reference to bean 101.	The client acquires a reference to bean 101.
The client invokes a method on the bean interface.	
The EJB container intercepts the request, starts the transaction, instantiates bean 101 in the cache, and enlists bean 101 in the transaction.	
The EJB container loads the data from the database into the bean instance and saves key attribute values in the bean for concurrency checks in the database update step.	The client invokes a method on the bean interface.
The EJB container passes the request to a method on the bean instance.	The EJB container intercepts the request, starts the transaction, instantiates bean 101 in the cache, and enlists bean 101 in the transaction.
The bean instance processes the request and returns.	The EJB container loads the data from the database into the bean instance and saves key attribute values in the bean for concurrency checks in the database update step.
The EJB container performs the database update using the previous key attribute values in the WHERE clause, verifies that the update modified the row, and completes successfully.	The EJB container passes the request to a method on the bean instance.

(continued)

Table 6.5 *(continued)*

CLIENT #1 THREAD ACTIVITY	CLIENT #2 THREAD ACTIVITY
The EJB container commits the transaction.	The bean instance processes the request and returns.
The results are returned to the client.	The EJB container performs the database update using the previous key attribute values in the WHERE clause, senses that the update didn't modify the database, rolls back the transaction, and raises an exception.
	An `OptimisticConcurrencyException` is returned to the client.

The optimistic concurrency strategy ensures that the row in the database has not changed during the life cycle of the bean. This is accomplished in WebLogic Server by saving, in the entity bean instance, the values of specific fields as they existed during the database read invocation. These saved values are then used in database update operations to verify that the database row has not changed by including them in the `WHERE` clause of the SQL `UPDATE` statement.

WebLogic Server supports four different techniques for checking the saved values in the bean instance against the current contents of the database row:

- **Check all fields read during transaction**, which requires that all of the fields read from the database during the transaction still have their original values in the database row.
- **Check fields modified during transaction**, which requires that any fields being modified by the `UPDATE` statement itself still have their original values in the database row.
- **Check a version column**, which requires that a specific numeric column in the mapped table still contains the value it did during the database read.
- **Check a timestamp column**, which requires that a specific timestamp column in the mapped table still contains the value it did during the database read.

The Optimistic strategy is declared in the `weblogic-ejb-jar.xml` file:

```
<entity-cache>
  ...
  <concurrency-strategy>Optimistic</concurrency-strategy>
</entity-cache>
```

The technique used to validate the bean values during the database update process is defined in the CMP descriptor file, `weblogic-cmp-rdbms-jar.xml`, in a `verify-columns` element inside the table mapping section:

```
<weblogic-rdbms-jar>
  <weblogic-rdbms-bean>
```

```
      <ejb-name>PersonCMPEJB</ejb-name>
      <data-source-name>MasteringDataSource</data-source-name>
      <table-map>
        <table-name>PERSON</table-name>
        <field-map>
          <cmp-field>id</cmp-field>
          <dbms-column>ID</dbms-column>
        </field-map>
        ...
        <field-map>
          <cmp-field>lastName</cmp-field>
          <dbms-column>LASTNAME</dbms-column>
        </field-map>
        <verify-columns>Modified</verify-columns>
      </table-map>
    </weblogic-rdbms-bean>
  </weblogic-rdbms-jar>
```

Valid values for verify-columns are Read, Modified, Version, and Timestamp.

The Read and Modified techniques require no other elements in the descriptor because the container will construct the WHERE clause used in the row update based on columns read or modified as appropriate. The Version and Timestamp techniques require an additional optimistic-column element in the table mapping section defining the table column used for these techniques:

```
<table-map>
  <table-name>PERSON</table-name>
  ...
  <verify-columns>Timestamp</verify-columns>
  <optimistic-column>LAST_MODIFIED</optimistic-column>
</table-map>
```

The column used for Version or Timestamp checking may be included in the container-managed fields for the CMP bean, but this is not required. You may not call the set method for this field.

BEST PRACTICE The Version and Timestamp techniques are the most direct implementations of optimistic concurrency and are recommended for most applications. The Read and Modified techniques work well if there are no timestamp or version columns available in the table, but they may create long WHERE clauses that must be parsed and evaluated by the underlying database system for every update, hurting performance.

Regardless of the technique you use, WebLogic Server includes appropriate additional criteria on the WHERE clause in the internal database update operation to enforce concurrency. For example, if the PersonCMPBean defined earlier in this chapter used optimistic locking with a Modified technique, and the firstName and lastName attributes were modified during the bean life cycle, the executed SQL statement would be as follows:

```
UPDATE PERSON SET FIRSTNAME = ? , LASTNAME = ?
              WHERE ID = ? AND FIRSTNAME = ? AND LASTNAME = ?
```

If this statement fails to update a row in the database, the EJB container assumes another client has either deleted the row or another client or process changed one of the modified fields. In either case, there is a concurrency problem, and the container throws an `OptimisticConcurrencyException`:

```
weblogic.ejb.OptimisticConcurrencyException:
Optimistic concurrency violation.
Instance of bean 'PersonCMPEJB' with primary key '101' was changed by
another transaction.
```

It is up to the caller performing the business method that caused the exception to determine if it is safe to retry the operation by starting the transaction again, reacquiring the bean instance with updated data from the database, and reapplying the desired changes. Normally, it is not safe simply to reapply the changes without asking for user permission. It may also be necessary to check that the row still exists in the database to determine the proper course of action. The safest technique is to report the concurrency exception to the user and ask him or her to determine the correct action.

BEST PRACTICE Include exception-handling code in client applications and session façade beans to trap and handle `OptimisticConcurrencyExceptions` **thrown by the container at the end of a bean life cycle. In some cases, the operation can simply be retried, but often the user must be informed of the error and given the opportunity to select a course of action.**

The optimistic strategy allows the use of the cache-between-transactions feature, discussed next, to eliminate unnecessary database reads if the bean is already present in the cache.

One final nuance related to optimistic concurrency and Web applications is worth discussing: There is a difference between enforcing concurrency in the context of a container transaction and ensuring that multiple Web users do not perform conflicting updates. To see the difference, consider a typical Web application having an HTML form used to edit bean data. The form might be populated with entity bean data during one transaction, sent to the user's browser for update, posted to a controller or action JSP page after changes are made, and used to modify bean data during a second transaction. Optimistic concurrency ensures integrity during each of the two transactions, but it does not preclude two users from viewing the same bean simultaneously and submitting conflicting changes one at a time. To understand why, recall that optimistic concurrency rereads the bean data from the database, including the version or timestamp column, at the start of each of the two transactions for each user individually. The second transaction will succeed for both users because the checked columns will not be changing during the duration of the second transaction.

If this scenario is a concern you need to supplement the optimistic concurrency behavior in WebLogic Server with one additional check: The version or timestamp in the database must not be different from the value read during the original HTML form generation. The easiest way to implement this check is to include on the HTML form a hidden field containing the version number or timestamp and then compare this value with the value read from the database at the start of the second transaction. If they are different, some other process modified the data between the time the form was created and the time it was submitted, exactly what you are trying to catch and prevent. The combination of this type of application-level check and the server-based optimistic concurrency logic provides a strong level of concurrency control for your application.

WARNING **Optimistic concurrency in WebLogic Server's EJB container handles concurrency issues only within a single transaction context. Most distributed applications may require some sort of optimistic concurrency control across multiple transactions to prevent data loss or corruption. Implement this cross-transaction checking by verifying that the version of the data displayed to the user hasn't changed. Perform this verification at the beginning of the update transaction before making any changes to the underlying data.**

Caching Strategies

The following sections describe caching techniques available in the WebLogic Server EJB container. Note that caching in the container will improve performance for applications with the right types of EJB operations, but it is no silver bullet. It may add complexity for little or no benefit in applications that perform mostly write operations, for example, or consume heap space better used by other components in the application. Our goal in this section is to help you understand the specific advantages, disadvantages, and ramifications of each caching technique to aid in your evaluation and implementation of these strategies.

Caching between Transactions

The normal life cycle of an entity bean includes a database read operation at the beginning and a database update operation at the end of the life cycle. The read-only concurrency strategy was one mechanism for avoiding the read operation for beans with data suitable for long-term caching. WebLogic Server also provides a second mechanism for avoiding database reads, the cache-between-transactions feature, which essentially caches bean data in the EJB container for use by multiple clients. This feature replaces the `db-is-shared` descriptor element available in WebLogic Server before version 7.0.

An entity bean configured to use caching between transactions will be loaded from the database only in the following circumstances:

- No bean instance containing cached data is available in the cache. This might be the first client to access the bean in this EJB container, or the cache management algorithms may have flushed the bean from the cache to manage memory.
- The entity bean is involved in a transaction that is rolled back. The container must reload the contents of the bean from the database because no backup copy is kept to reset the bean to its original state.
- A finder method other than `findByPrimaryKey()` is invoked to locate matching beans, and the bean is configured with `finders-loan-bean` set to `true`. This feature will be discussed later in this chapter.
- Optimistic concurrency is used in conjunction with caching between transactions in a clustered environment, and a different EJB container in the cluster has informed this container that a client updated the bean.

Configuring a bean to use caching between transactions is accomplished by setting the `cache-between-transactions` element in the `entity-cache` to true:

```
<entity-cache>
  <concurrency-strategy>Optimistic</concurrency-strategy>
  <cache-between-transactions>True</cache-between-transactions>
</entity-cache>
```

Caching between transactions is not available for all concurrency strategies in all deployment architectures. As Table 6.6 shows, only the optimistic concurrency strategy allows caching between transactions in both clustered and nonclustered environments.

The exclusive concurrency strategy may be combined with caching between transactions to eliminate the need to load bean data from the database at the start of the bean life cycle. This combination is available only in a single-server environment at the current time.

Table 6.6 Caching-between-Transactions

CONCURRENCY STRATEGY	CBT ALLOWED IN NONCLUSTERED ENVIRONMENT?	CBT ALLOWED IN CLUSTERED ENVIRONMENT?
Exclusive	Yes, and exclusive locking behavior is maintained on the cached bean instance.	No, containers have no mechanism to publish changes to others.
Database	No.	No.
Read-only	Not applicable; read-only beans have different rules for database reads based on time-outs.	Not applicable; read-only beans have different rules for database reads based on time-outs.
Optimistic	Yes.	Yes, containers inform each other via multicast when bean data changes.

The optimistic concurrency strategy, combined with caching between transactions, provides a very powerful mechanism for obtaining high performance with a minimal chance for data corruption. Recall that the optimistic strategy does not rely on locking, within either the EJB container or the database, to avoid concurrency conflicts proactively. Instead, the strategy senses conflicts during the database update process, using one of the four techniques described earlier, and works very effectively in a clustered environment or in the presence of other applications or processes performing updates to the database.

In addition, when bean changes are committed to the database in one EJB container, a multicast approach is used to invalidate cached beans in all other containers in the cluster. The next time a client in these containers uses an instance of the invalidated bean, its data will be retrieved from the database to ensure accuracy and avoid concurrency conflicts during subsequent updates.

The only serious problem with the combination of optimistic concurrency and caching between transactions is the potential for stale data in the cached beans if changes are made to the database through applications or processes not participating in the WebLogic Server cluster. The cached data will continue to be used by clients for read purposes, and the staleness of the data will not be sensed until a client attempts to update something in the database and produces a concurrency conflict. The potential for stale data is a price you pay for the performance benefits of caching, a fair trade in many cases.

BEST PRACTICE **Combining caching between transactions with optimistic concurrency provides a very powerful caching mechanism that is cluster-aware and very efficient. Use caching between transactions with optimistic concurrency as your default configuration for entity beans in WebLogic Server unless application requirements dictate otherwise.**

Read-Only Multicast Invalidation

Entity beans configured with read-only concurrency provide a convenient long-term caching facility and, as we will discuss in the next section, can be combined with standard entity beans to form a matched pair of beans in what is called a *read-mostly* pattern. Before discussing this pattern, however, we want to address the simpler case of read-only beans deployed alone and identify the mechanisms available for invalidating cached data.

The first invalidation mechanism, the `read-timeout-seconds` configuration parameter, was discussed earlier in this chapter. The `read-timeout-seconds` parameter provides a mechanism for automatic, periodic invalidation of cached data. After the time-out period expires, the next client request will cause the bean data to be reloaded from the database during that request. Note that `read-timeout-seconds` is not a timer; Nothing actually happens when the time-out expires. The bean is simply invalid the next time it is used. No database read activity will take place until a client uses a reference to the bean with expired contents.

The second invalidation mechanism, *multicast invalidation*, allows the programmatic invalidation of cached entity bean data on all servers in the WebLogic Server cluster. Invalidation is accomplished by obtaining a reference to the home or local home interface for the read-only entity bean and using one of the `invalidate` methods defined in the `CachingHome` or `CachingLocalHome` interfaces:

```
package weblogic.ejb;
public interface CachingHome
{
    public void invalidate(Object pk) throws RemoteException;
    public void invalidate(Collection pks) throws RemoteException;
    public void invalidateAll() throws RemoteException;
}
```

As indicated in this interface definition, you may invalidate one bean, a collection of beans, or all read-only beans of the type associated with this `home` interface. For example, the following code invalidates a specific read-only `PersonCMPROBean` instance using the `CachingLocalHome` for the bean:

```
CachingLocalHome home =
    (CachingLocalHome)ctx.lookup("PersonCMPROHomeLocal");
home.invalidate(new Integer(101));
```

The home interface will not extend the `CachingHome` or `CachingLocalHome` interface unless the bean uses read-only concurrency. This multicast invalidation technique is not available for any other concurrency strategies. The ability to invalidate cached data programmatically is one of the only reasons to consider read-only concurrency and its close relative, the read-mostly pattern.

Read-Mostly Pattern

The read-mostly pattern is a specific entity bean deployment approach in which a matched pair of entity beans, one using read-only concurrency and one using exclusive, database, or optimistic concurrency, represents the same persistent data. As illustrated in Figure 6.4, clients requiring read access to bean data use the read-only bean to take advantage of the automatic caching provided by that strategy. Clients requiring traditional read and write access to bean data use the standard entity bean deployed with one of the other types of concurrency. Sounds great, but how is the read-only data kept in synch with the actual data being modified through the standard entity bean?

A key element of this deployment approach is the automatic invalidation facility provided by WebLogic Server. Based on the multicast invalidation capability discussed in the previous section, automatic invalidation ensures that attribute changes made through the standard entity bean are reflected in the read-only bean the next time it is accessed by a client. The standard bean is linked to the read-only bean through an `invalidation-target` element in the `weblogic-ejb-jar.xml` file:

```
<weblogic-enterprise-bean>
  <ejb-name>PersonCMPEJB</ejb-name>
  <entity-descriptor>
    <entity-cache>
      <concurrency-strategy>Optimistic</concurrency-strategy>
    </entity-cache>
    <persistence>
      ...
    </persistence>
    <invalidation-target>
      <ejb-name>PersonCMPROEJB</ejb-name>
    </invalidation-target>
  </entity-descriptor>
  <local-jndi-name>PersonCMPHomeLocal</local-jndi-name>
</weblogic-enterprise-bean>

<weblogic-enterprise-bean>
  <ejb-name>PersonCMPROEJB</ejb-name>
  <entity-descriptor>
    <entity-cache>
      <read-timeout-seconds>600</read-timeout-seconds>
      <concurrency-strategy>ReadOnly</concurrency-strategy>
    </entity-cache>
    ...
  </entity-descriptor>
  <local-jndi-name>PersonCMPROHomeLocal</local-jndi-name>
</weblogic-enterprise-bean>
```

After the transaction involving the standard bean commits, the EJB container uses multicast to invalidate the read-only bean on all servers in the cluster. This invalidation operation occurs after the transaction is committed, to eliminate the potential for race conditions in which a read-only bean reloads its data from the database before the updates are committed, possibly loading old values again.

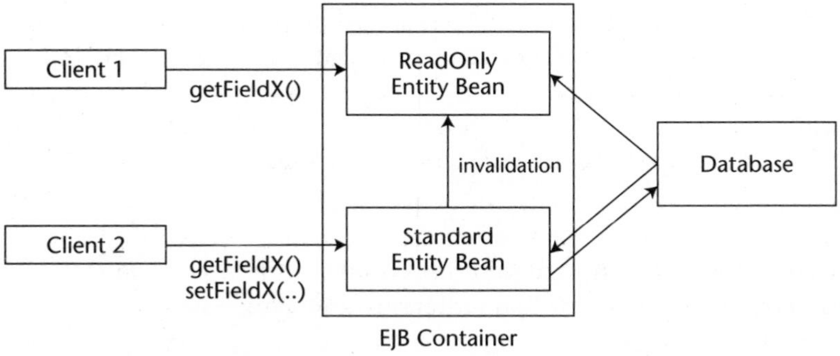

Figure 6.4 Read-mostly pattern.

Implementing the Read-Mostly Pattern

The read-mostly pattern is commonly implemented using two separate CMP entity beans configured to read from and write to the same database table. This dual-bean-class technique is fairly straightforward and won't be covered in this text.

As an alternative to the dual-bean-class technique, the read-mostly pattern can also be implemented by deploying the same bean twice, once as a standard bean and once as a read-only bean, using the same bean and interfaces classes for each deployment. For example, the `PersonCMPBean` component discussed earlier in this chapter can be deployed in a read-mostly pattern by modifying the descriptor files to declare two separate EJB components that utilize the same bean, local interface, and home interface classes. Because we are deploying the same bean class twice, both deployments must define the same CMP fields, finders, and home/select methods for the EJB compilation process to work properly. The companion Web site provides example descriptors showing how to deploy the `PersonCMPBean` component twice in this fashion.

Clients that wish to access the read-only version of the bean look up the home interface using the JNDI name used for that deployment, `PersonCMPROHomeLocal`, whereas clients that require the standard read-write version of the bean use the JNDI name `PersonCMPHomeLocal`. In both cases, the home interface obtained by the lookup will implement the same interface, `PersonCMPHomeLocal`, and will define the same set of finder methods. The bean reference returned by either `home` interface will implement the same local interface, `PersonCMPLocal`, eliminating the need for client code to reflect which type of entity bean is being used. It therefore becomes much easier to add the read-mostly pattern to an application later if the single-bean-class approach is used because the existing code can continue to use the same local interface.

BEST PRACTICE The single-bean-class technique allows the configuration of the read-mostly pattern with a minimum of impact on client code and is preferred over the creation of multiple bean classes to implement the pattern.

One downside of the single-bean-class technique is the fact that the read-only bean still contains set methods, and the single shared local interface for the bean also makes these methods available to clients. If a client should modify the bean data using a reference to the read-only bean, the change will be reflected in the cached bean data on the current server, but not saved to the database or propagated to other servers in the cluster. The next time the read-only bean is invalidated, the bean data will be reread from the database and the errant change will disappear. Be careful, therefore, to perform no set operations on read-only bean references when using the single-bean-class technique.

WARNING Clients must be careful to perform set operations on standard bean references, rather than read-only bean references, to avoid losing changes.

BMP entity beans can avoid this problem by modifying the set methods in the shared bean class to assert that they are not being called on an instance of the bean deployed using read-only concurrency, using code similar to the following:

```
if (entityContext.getEJBHome() instanceof CachingHome) {
    throw new EJBException("Attempt to call set on ReadOnly bean!");
}
```

The container for CMP entity beans generates set methods automatically, so this safety code cannot be added directly to these methods. You might consider creating separate set methods that perform this check and call the internal set methods, placing only the safe versions of the methods in the local interface for the bean, as one reasonable solution.

NOTE Nothing in the read-mostly pattern dictates that the two beans must have the same attributes, methods, or even that they must read from the same database table. The read-only bean, for example, might have only a subset of the attributes or might include different methods for returning value objects or collections of bean attributes.

Remember that the container does not attempt to copy data from the standard bean to the read-only bean during invalidation; it simply marks the read-only bean invalid and relies on a database read to refresh the cached data. Any standard CMP entity bean can define an `invalidation-target` **element referencing any read-only entity bean in the same EJB archive.**

The standard entity bean in the read-mostly pattern may use any of the other concurrency strategies available in WebLogic Server: exclusive, database, or optimistic. The standard bean may also employ the caching-between-transactions feature, in some cases, to further reduce the number of database reads required when clients employ the standard entity bean.

Relationships and the Read-Mostly Pattern

A number of problems occur when you use read-only entity beans in CMP-managed relationships.

First, you can't mix relationships between standard beans and read-only beans in the application. Relationships between CMP entity beans are declared in the `ejb-jar.xml` descriptor file using `relationship-role-source` elements referring to specific EJB components by name:

```
<relationships>
 <ejb-relation>
   <ejb-relationship-role>
     ...
     <relationship-role-source>
       <ejb-name>AddressCMPEJB</ejb-name>
     </relationship-role-source>
     ...
```

Note that the relationships are defined using the EJB names, not their local interfaces, so it is not possible to declare a relationship with both the standard and the read-only version of the other bean. Each relationship must be declared to use one version or the other, so typically the entire graph of related beans will exist in an all-standard form and in an all-read-only form. The single-bean-class technique described previously does not help with this problem. Although the underlying beans are the same in both cases, they are deployed twice using different EJB names, requiring duplicate graphs of related beans.

A second problem is that the read-mostly invalidation scheme does not produce reliable invalidation of bidirectional relationships. For example, an update to the standard `PersonCMP` bean removing a particular `Address` from its `addresses` relationship collection would cause the related read-only `PersonCMPRO` bean to become invalidated, but there is no facility for automatically invalidating the related `AddressCMPRO` bean to ensure that the now-defunct relationship is not traversed in the other direction.

Of course, you can still use read-only beans with relationships if you are not using the read-mostly pattern and do not require cluster-wide invalidation. The choice really depends on your application's requirements.

BEST PRACTICE Based on the inherent limitations when declaring relationships involving read-only beans and a minor invalidation problem, we don't recommend that you use read-only beans when relationships are present between beans. Standard beans using cache between transactions are preferable in this situation in most cases.

The bottom line on the read-mostly pattern is that it still has some value in cases where programmatic invalidation of cached data is important, a feature supported only by read-only beans, but in general it has been superceded by the optimistic concurrency and cache-between-transactions approach for most applications.

Combined Caching Support

WebLogic Server supports the creation of combined, or shared, caches for use by multiple entity beans in place of the standard per-bean cache. All entity beans configured to use a particular combined cache will share the space in the combined cache and be subject to passivation or removal using the same rules. The combined cache eliminates the need to determine an appropriate size for each per-bean cache and may result in more efficient use of overall system memory.

The standard per-bean cache was configured in `weblogic-ejb-jar.xml` using the `entity-cache` element:

```
<weblogic-enterprise-bean>
  <ejb-name>PersonCMPEJB</ejb-name>
  <entity-descriptor>
    <entity-cache>
      <max-beans-in-cache>1000</max-beans-in-cache>
      <concurrency-strategy>Optimistic</concurrency-strategy>
    </entity-cache>
    ...
```

```
  </entity-descriptor>
  ...
</weblogic-enterprise-bean>
```

In this configuration, the `PersonCMPEJB` bean will be cached in a unique cache containing a maximum of 1,000 bean instances and will use the optimistic concurrency strategy. Other beans in the application that have similar descriptor elements would likewise be cached in their own per-bean caches.

To use a combined cache, the `entity-cache` element is replaced with an `entity-cache-ref` element referencing the name of the combined cache and specifying the bean's concurrency strategy:

```
<entity-descriptor>
  <entity-cache-ref>
    <entity-cache-name>BigCache</entity-cache-name>
    <concurrency-strategy>Optimistic</concurrency-strategy>
  </entity-cache-ref>
  ...
</entity-descriptor>
```

The combined cache is configured using the `weblogic-application.xml` descriptor in the `META-INF` directory of the enterprise application archive (`.ear`) file or exploded structure. The `weblogic-application.xml` file shown in Listing 6.7 defines a single large cache for use by entity beans in the application referencing this cache rather than defining a per-bean cache.

```
<?xml version="1.0"  encoding="UTF-8"?>

<!DOCTYPE weblogic-application PUBLIC
 "-//BEA Systems, Inc.//DTD WebLogic Application 8.1.0//EN"
 "http://www.bea.com/servers/wls810/dtd/weblogic-application_2_0.dtd">

<weblogic-application>
  <ejb>
    <entity-cache>
      <entity-cache-name>BigCache</entity-cache-name>
      <max-beans-in-cache>50000</max-beans-in-cache>
      <read-timeout-seconds>600</read-timeout-seconds>
      <caching-strategy>MultiVersion</caching-strategy>
    </entity-cache>
  </ejb>
</weblogic-application>
```

Listing 6.7 weblogic-application.xml defining a combined cache.

Detailed descriptions of the XML elements in `weblogic-ejb-jar.xml` and `weblogic-application.xml` are available in the online documentation at http://edocs.bea.com/wls/docs81/ejb/reference.html and http://edocs.bea.com/wls/docs81/programming/app_xml.html, respectively. Some key capabilities and rules include the following:

- The combined cache may be configured using a maximum number of bean instances or by limiting the approximate size of the cache. Note that the size option requires that each bean define its average size using the `estimated-bean-size` tag to estimate the total size of the cache for the purposes of cache management. Beans that do not define their size are assumed to consume 100 bytes of memory for this calculation.
- The combined cache may be configured using the exclusive caching strategy, equivalent to the exclusive concurrency strategy on a per-bean cache, or the multiversion caching strategy, which does not lock bean instances. Beans declaring the exclusive concurrency strategy may only use a combined cache using exclusive, but all other bean strategies may be hosted in a multiversion combined cache.
- Multiple combined caches may be defined providing that their names are unique.

Combined caching represents a significant improvement in both flexibility and ease of configuration. No longer must you estimate the appropriate cache size on a per-bean basis or resign yourself to oversizing most per-bean caches and wasting memory.

BEST PRACTICE Consider using combined caches for most beans, configuring the size of the combined caches to accommodate expected instance requirements. Use separate bean caches for selected high-use or resource-intensive beans to better control the use of cache space.

Specific beans can still be configured with per-bean caches, as before, and all beans of a certain type might be placed in a single combined cache (a `ReadOnlyCache`, for example). Note that read-only beans sharing a single combined cache will have the same `read-timeout-seconds` value because the value is defined in the combined cache and is not configurable on a per-bean basis in the `entity-cache-ref` element.

Sizing entity-bean caches will be discussed in Chapter 12 as part of performance tuning and management.

Tuning Strategies

This section will describe some entity-bean tuning strategies available in WebLogic Server to improve query and database-read operations.

Loading Beans During Finder Operations

One of the classic problems with entity beans involves the $n + 1$ query problem. Fetching and displaying the contents of n beans normally requires one SQL query to fetch the list of primary keys and then n additional single-row SQL statements to fetch the bean data. Setting `finders-load-bean` to `true` can dramatically improve the performance of finder methods that return multiple beans because WebLogic Server will optimize the finder to fetch all of the bean data during a single SQL statement.

Normal finders-load-bean Behavior

The following client code uses a simple finder method on the `PersonCMP` entity bean to retrieve and display people having a particular last name:

```
Collection people = home.findByLastName("Sm%");
Iterator i = people.iterator();
while (i.hasNext()) {
    PersonCMPLocal person = (PersonCMPLocal) i.next();
    out.print("ID: " + person.getId() + " Name: " +
              person.getSalutation() + " " + person.getFirstName() +
              " " + person.getLastName() + "<br>");
}
```

Using a standard CMP entity bean with optimistic concurrency and `finders-load-bean` set to `false`, inspection of the calls made by the EJB container reveals that the following four SQL statements are required to fetch and display the three matching people in the database:

```
... : Finder produced statement string
SELECT WL0.ID  FROM PERSON WL0  WHERE ( (WL0.LASTNAME LIKE ?  ) )
... __WL_loadGroup0 for pk=102
... execute Query: SELECT WL0.FIRSTNAME, WL0.ID, WL0.LASTNAME,
      WL0.MIDDLENAME, WL0.SALUTATION  FROM PERSON WL0  WHERE WL0.ID = ?
... __WL_loadGroup0 for pk=105
... execute Query: SELECT WL0.FIRSTNAME, WL0.ID, WL0.LASTNAME,
      WL0.MIDDLENAME, WL0.SALUTATION  FROM PERSON WL0  WHERE WL0.ID = ?
... __WL_loadGroup0 for pk=106
... execute Query: SELECT WL0.FIRSTNAME, WL0.ID, WL0.LASTNAME,
      WL0.MIDDLENAME, WL0.SALUTATION  FROM PERSON WL0  WHERE WL0.ID = ?
```

The same code executed on a standard optimistic bean with `finders-load-bean` set to `true` results in a single SQL statement:

```
... : Finder produced statement string
SELECT WL0.ID, WL0.FIRSTNAME, WL0.LASTNAME, WL0.MIDDLENAME,
WL0.SALUTATION
FROM PERSON WL0  WHERE ( (WL0.LASTNAME LIKE ?  ) )
```

The result set returned by this query is used by WebLogic Server to preinstantiate and preload all of the beans returned by the finder with data at the time of the finder operation. The beans will be placed in the entity bean cache in the normal manner, and subsequent method invocations using the bean references returned by the finder will use the cached version of the bean. Unless cache between transactions is enabled for this bean, the cached beans are valid only in the context of the transaction used to execute the finder method. The finder and all subsequent bean-method invocations should therefore be in a single transaction to take full advantage of `finders-load-bean=true`.

Generally speaking, it is best to leave the `finders-load-bean` parameter set to the default value of `true`. Preloading retrieved beans avoids the $n + 1$ query problem and provides better performance and scalability in most circumstances. The only exceptions are cases in which the resulting collection will be used in some manner not requiring a complete iteration and inspection of bean data. Examples might include displaying only the first few matching beans, performing the finder in one transaction but accessing the bean data in a different transaction, or passing the collection to a relationship management method on a bean. The `finders-load-bean` value is defined for the entity bean as a whole, unfortunately, so there is no way to specify the setting differently for specific finders.

BEST PRACTICE **Use the default `finders-load-bean` value of `true` for most applications to eliminate the $n + 1$ query problem and improve system performance.**

The internal operation of finders using `finders-load-bean=true` becomes more complex when you consider the many options for caching and concurrency strategy in combination with `finders-load-bean`. We'll discuss a few of the more common combinations.

finders-load-bean with Read-Only Beans

Entity beans using the read-only concurrency strategy are cached for long periods of time to avoid repeated database reads and improve performance. Finder methods used to retrieve read-only bean references or collections of bean references are affected by the `finders-load-bean` parameter according to Table 6.7.

One interesting side-effect of the behavior with read-only beans is that the use of a `findAll()` finder method with `finders-load-bean` set to `true` will essentially fetch and refresh all cached read-only beans immediately with a single SQL statement. The `CachingHome.invalidate()` method of invalidation simply marks the beans invalid and defers the retrieval of new data until each bean is used again by a client, potentially requiring many individual queries. Remember, however, that the `invalidate()` method invalidates beans in all EJB containers in a cluster, but using finders would not affect other servers in the cluster.

Table 6.7 Finder Behavior for Cached Read-Only Beans

FINDER TYPE	FINDERS-LOAD-BEAN=TRUE	FINDERS-LOAD-BEAN=FALSE
Find by primary key	The cached bean reference is returned without performing the SQL statement.	The cached bean reference is returned without performing the SQL statement.
All other finders	The full SQL `select` statement is performed for all finders, and all bean instances are refreshed with fetched data. The query is performed regardless of cached instances.	The key-only SQL `select` statement is performed for all finders, and references are returned to the caller. Calls to cached beans avoid subsequent database read operations.

BEST PRACTICE Consider using finder methods with read-only beans to force the refresh of all matching beans in the cache immediately as a complement for normal invalidation.

finders-load-bean with Cache between Transactions

The cache-between-transactions feature caches bean instances in the entity bean cache and makes them available for subsequent client requests, reducing the number of database read operations and improving performance. Finder methods used to retrieve bean references or collections of bean references for optimistic or exclusive concurrency beans using the cache-between-transactions feature are affected by the `finders-load-bean` parameter, according to Table 6.8.

Choosing the right setting for `finders-load-bean` was easy for beans not employing caching: Always use `true`. It is not quite as clear-cut for beans using cache between transactions, however, because non-primary-key finders always reread all data for cached beans if `finders-load-bean` is `true`. Preloading bean data during the finder will be more efficient than going back to the database for each bean if the matching beans are not yet in the cache, but subsequent finders would be faster without `finders-load-bean` set to `true` because the beans are already in the cache. The right setting therefore depends on the number of times the same cached beans might be accessed through the finder: If the same beans are accessed many times, leaving `finders-load-bean` set to `false` may give you better performance.

BEST PRACTICE Favor setting `finders-load-bean` to `true` even with cache between transactions, but consider setting it to `false` to reduce SQL activity if the same beans are accessed many times through non-primary-key finder queries.

Table 6.8 Finder Behavior for Cached Beans Using Cache between Transactions

FINDER TYPE	FINDERS-LOAD-BEAN=TRUE	FINDERS-LOAD-BEAN=FALSE
Find by primary key	The cached bean reference is returned without performing the SQL statement.	The key-only SQL `select` statement is performed to validate the key in database. A cached bean reference is returned.
All other finders	The full SQL `select` statement is performed for all finders, and all bean instances are refreshed with fetched data. The query is performed regardless of cached instances.	The key-only SQL `select` statement is performed for all finders, and references are returned to the caller. Calls to cached beans avoid subsequent database read operations.

Updating Database after Each Method Invocation

The normal bean life cycle, described earlier in this chapter, includes a database write operation as part of the final transaction completion. Delaying these updates until the end of the transaction makes sense in most cases. In certain circumstances, however, you may need to modify the default behavior and have changes written to the database after every method invocation. This behavior is controlled by the `delay-updates-until-end-of-tx` element in the `weblogic-ejb-jar.xml` descriptor file:

```
<entity-descriptor>
  <persistence>
    <delay-updates-until-end-of-tx>false</delay-updates-until-end-of-tx>
  </persistence>
</entity-descriptor>
```

Setting this parameter to `false` will cause changes to be written to the database after every method invocation. Depending on the type of entity bean, CMP or BMP, and the specific implementation of `ejbStore()`, this may or may not cause a SQL update statement to be executed against the database if no changes in the bean are sensed by the relevant code. If a SQL statement is sent to the database, it will still remain uncommitted until the end of the transaction.

The default value, `true`, is suitable for most applications. Setting it to `false` can help with finders and other queries performed during the transaction that are not properly reflecting modified beans. For example, a JDBC query occurring after a change to bean data, but within the same transaction, will not reflect the bean changes unless this flag is set to `false`. If finder methods are the only queries for which you need this behavior, then you should use the `include-updates` functionality instead of setting `delay-updates-until-end-of-tx` to `false`. The next section discusses the `include-updates` functionality for EJB finder queries.

BEST PRACTICE **Leave `delay-updates-until-end-of-tx` with the default value of `true` unless specific application needs warrant the change.**

Including Updates in Finder Queries

Finder queries are executed using SQL statements sent to the database in the context of the current transaction. Because the default behavior of entity beans is to delay database writes until the end of the current transaction, queries performed in the transaction will typically not reflect updates to bean data made earlier in the transaction. For example, an application may perform the following steps:

1. Start a transaction.
2. Find Person bean #102 by primary key, and update its last name from "Anderson" to "Smith" using `setLastName("Smith")` on the bean reference.

3. Perform a `findByLastName("Sm%")` finder query, where the finder is defined using a `LIKE` comparison, and then display the contents of each bean matching the criteria.

4. End the transaction.

If the `include-updates` element in the `findByLastName()` query is set to `false`, the output in Step 3 will not include bean #102 because the updates to the bean have not been flushed to the database prior to executing the query. Setting `include-updates` to `true` in the finder definition causes all beans with unwritten changes in the current transaction to be flushed to the database, without committing the transaction, prior to executing the finder query. Step 3 would then include bean #102 in the output because it now matches the criteria.

Note that the default value of `include-updates` was `false` in previous versions of Weblogic Server, but it is now `true` in WebLogic Server 8.1 for beans using the database and exclusive concurrency strategies. The default remains `false` in optimistic concurrency. This change was made in order to comply with the J2EE licensing model. This means that the default behavior starting in WebLogic Server 8.1 is to flush unwritten changes to the database prior to executing finder queries for beans using database and exclusive concurrency strategies. While this represents the J2EE-specified behavior, it adds overhead for applications that do not require this functionality. If your application does not require this behavior, set the `includes-update` parameters explicitly to `false` to improve performance.

WARNING **J2EE licensing restrictions have caused the WebLogic Server 8.1 default setting for** `includes-update` **to change from** `false` **to** `true` **for database and exclusive concurrency strategies. If your application doesn't depend on this behavior, setting the value back to** `false` **can improve performance. The default remains** `false` **in optimistic concurrency.**

The `include-updates` element is set in the WebLogic-specific CMP descriptor, `weblogic-cmp-rdbms-jar.xml`, using a finder definition that matches the definition in the standard `ejb-jar.xml` file. The `findByLastName()` finder is defined in `ejb-jar.xml` using a `query` element:

```
<query>
  <query-method>
    <method-name>findByLastName</method-name>
    <method-params>
      <method-param>java.lang.String</method-param>
    </method-params>
  </query-method>
  <ejb-ql>
    SELECT OBJECT(o) FROM PersonCMPEJB o WHERE o.lastName LIKE ?1
  </ejb-ql>
</query>
```

The WebLogic-specific file contains a matching `weblogic-query` element:

```
<weblogic-query>
  <query-method>
    <method-name>findByLastName</method-name>
    <method-params>
      <method-param>java.lang.String</method-param>
    </method-params>
  </query-method>
  <include-updates>false</include-updates>
</weblogic-query>
```

The `include-updates` behavior is not the default for optimistic concurrency, even in WebLogic Server 8.1, because `include-updates` tends to defeat some of the benefits of optimistic concurrency—namely, not holding locks on database rows during a transaction. When updates are flushed to the database before a finder call, update locks are held in the database. Worse yet, the finder queries must be run as part of the global transaction to be able to see uncommitted updates, and this causes read locks to be acquired for many databases.

WebLogic Server 8.1 currently allows `include-updates` to be `true` with optimistic concurrency for only one database type, Oracle, because Oracle does not hold read locks and is less likely to defeat the benefits of optimistic concurrency. The database type must be set at the bottom of the `weblogic-cmp-rdbms-jar.xml` descriptor file:

```
<weblogic-rdbms-jar>
  ...
  <database-type>ORACLE</database-type>
</weblogic-rdbms-jar>
```

Batching Database Operations

WebLogic Server 8.1 provides automatic support for *batching* database operations involving CMP entity beans. This feature delays all database operations until the end of the enclosing transaction and uses the batch update capability of the JDBC driver to perform many SQL operations with a single call to the database. Batching is enabled using the `enable-batch-operations` element in the `weblogic-cmp-rdbms-jar.xml` descriptor file:

```
<weblogic-rdbms-jar>
  <weblogic-rdbms-bean>
    <ejb-name>AddressCMPEJB</ejb-name>
    ...
  </weblogic-rdbms-bean>
  <enable-batch-operations>
    True
  </enable-batch-operations>
</weblogic-rdbms-jar>
```

Note that the `enable-batch-operations` element is defined once for the entire set of beans, rather than on a per-bean basis. The default value is `True`, so by default WebLogic Server will attempt to batch operations at the end of the transaction.

There are several restrictions related to batching:

- The JDBC driver must support the `addBatch()` and `executeBatch()` methods. WebLogic Server will disable batching and log an error message if the driver used for CMP operations does not support batching.
- Certain types of automatic key generation, a topic discussed later in this chapter, are not compatible with batching. Attempting to use the `SQLSERVER` technique for key generation will disable batching.
- The total number of entity beans involved in the transaction, and therefore the batched database operation, must not exceed the maximum cache size specified by the `max-beans-in-cache` element.
- Entity beans containing `OracleClob` and `OracleBlob` data types will not be processed using batched database operations.

One final complication involves the proper ordering of all database operations performed in the batch update. Your beans may have many relationships and dependencies, and these dependencies are likely to be implemented in the database as foreign-key constraints. The database operations must be performed in the proper order to avoid constraint-violation errors. WebLogic Server 8.1 implements a dependency-checking algorithm that uses CMR information in the entity beans to determine the proper order of operations. This feature is enabled by default, but it may be disabled using the `order-database-operations` element in `weblogic-cmp-rdbms-jar.xml`.

BEST PRACTICE Batching database operations can provide a significant benefit when many beans are involved in the transaction. Use automatic batching in your applications to eliminate unnecessary database calls and improve performance.

Controlling Timing of Database Inserts

New CMP entity beans are created using one of the `create()` methods defined on the bean's home interface. During the creation process, the EJB container calls the matching `ejbCreate()` and `ejbPostCreate()` methods on the bean class to allow the bean to initialize attributes and relationships using the parameters supplied on the `create()` invocation.

At some point in the creation process, the bean must be inserted in the database. The batching capability outlined in the previous section treats these insert operations like any other SQL operation and postpones them to the end of the transaction, if possible. If batching is disabled, via the `enable-batch-operations` element, or is not possible for one of the reasons described in the previous section, WebLogic Server provides an alternative technique for controlling the timing of this insert operation. The timing can be set on a per-bean basis using the `delay-database-insert-until` element in the `weblogic-cmp-rdbms-jar.xml` descriptor file:

```
<weblogic-rdbms-bean>
  <ejb-name>AddressCMPEJB</ejb-name>
  ...
  <delay-database-insert-until>
    ejbPostCreate
  </delay-database-insert-until>
</weblogic-rdbms-bean>
```

The valid options in WebLogic Server 8.1 are `ejbCreate` and `ejbPostCreate`, with a default of `ejbPostCreate`. Previous versions also permitted a value of `commit`, but this option has been eliminated in version 8.1 in favor of the new batching support configured through the `enable-batch-operations` element.

Generally speaking, there is little reason to modify the default behavior of database insert operations by disabling batching and using the `delay-database-insert-until` element. Delaying inserts until the end of the transaction and using batch operations provide the best performance. It also avoids unneeded database operations when new beans are created and modified in the same transaction. For example, the following code creates a bean and then updates a CMP field in the same transaction:

```
PersonCMPLocal person = home.create(pk, "Mr.", "Joe", "", "Smith");
person.setAge(40);
...
```

If database inserts take place after `ejbCreate()` or `ejbPostCreate()` in this example, a subsequent `UPDATE` statement will be required at the end of the transaction to update the age value in the database before committing the transaction.

In addition, performing the `INSERT` operation after `ejbCreate()`, rather than after `ejbPostCreate()`, may be impossible due to the following limitations:

- The database is often configured to disallow null values in foreign key columns. In this case, database `INSERT` statements will not succeed until the CMR field in the bean has been set to a valid bean.
- It is not possible to set CMR fields in the `ejbCreate()` method because the primary key of the new bean may not be available at that point in the process.

BEST PRACTICE **Allow the normal database batching logic to control the timing of database inserts unless there is a strong rationale for disabling batching and controlling inserts on a per-bean basis.**

Controlling Lazy Retrieval Using Field Groups

The data contained in a CMP entity bean is generally retrieved from the database using a *lazy-retrieval* approach that performs the SQL `SELECT` statement for some or all bean data when a client requests a data element using a get method. Note that the change to defining only abstract get and set methods in bean classes in EJB 2.0 makes this behavior possible and is a key reason for the vast improvement in CMP entity beans in the 2.0 specification.

In the simplest lazy-retrieval case, a client obtaining and calling methods on a bean reference would cause the bean data to be loaded during the first get invocation:

```
PersonCMPLocal person = home.findByPrimaryKey(pk);
String s = person.getFirstName(); // container fetches bean data here
```

Note that this simple lazy-retrieval example is not typical, given default parameters in your descriptor files. If `finders-load-bean` is `true`, the default setting, finders will load bean data during the finder operation and there will be no need to retrieve the data later when get methods are called by the client. Obviously, if a noncached bean reference is obtained in one transaction and used later in a different transaction, the lazy retrieval scenario would be operative during the second transaction to refetch the bean data in response to get methods.

WebLogic Server allows tuning of lazy-retrieval functionality through the definition of *field groups* containing one or more bean attributes and container-managed relationship fields. Field groups serve two important roles in the control of lazy retrieval:

- Requests for any data in the field group cause the whole group to be loaded from the database with a single SQL statement.
- Field groups may be specified to control the specific data loaded during finder methods when `finders-load-bean` is set to `true`.

Using Field Groups to Tune Data Retrieval

The first role allows retrieval of attributes to be tuned for different types of client requests. For example, there may be a small number of fields in the entity bean used frequently in client requests, with the remaining set of fields used only rarely. By placing these two sets of fields in different field groups, the rarely used fields will be loaded from the database only when a field in that set is actually accessed by a client.

Field groups are defined in the `weblogic-cmp-rdbms-jar.xml` descriptor file in the `weblogic-rdbms-bean` section:

```
<weblogic-rdbms-bean>
  <ejb-name>PersonCMPEJB</ejb-name>
  <data-source-name>MasteringDataSource</data-source-name>
  <table-map>
    <table-name>PERSON</table-name>
    <field-map>
      <cmp-field>id</cmp-field>
      <dbms-column>ID</dbms-column>
    </field-map>
    ...
    <verify-columns>Modified</verify-columns>
  </table-map>
  <field-group>
```

```
    <group-name>summary</group-name>
    <cmp-field>id</cmp-field>
    <cmp-field>lastName</cmp-field>
  </field-group>
  <field-group>
    <group-name>everything</group-name>
    <cmp-field>id</cmp-field>
    <cmp-field>salutation</cmp-field>
    <cmp-field>firstName</cmp-field>
    <cmp-field>middleName</cmp-field>
    <cmp-field>lastName</cmp-field>
  </field-group>
</weblogic-rdbms-bean>
```

In this case we've defined a `summary` group, containing the primary key field and last name of the person, and an `everything` group, containing all `cmp` fields. Note that `lastName` appears in both groups, a perfectly valid configuration. If a client invokes `getLastName()` on an empty bean instance, WebLogic Server will use the first field group containing the attribute and load all fields in that group.

Note that improper use of field groups can actually increase the number of SQL statements required to populate a bean. If a client called `getLastName()` first and then `getFirstName()`, for example, the bean data would be retrieved in two separate SQL statements.

BEST PRACTICE Plan your field groups carefully, according to usage patterns and the normal order of attribute requests by clients. Avoid field groups and usage patterns that require two or more SQL statements to fetch bean data both for performance and data-consistency reasons.

Also recognize one danger inherent in the use of field groups: Because the bean data might be fetched in multiple queries it is possible to have a bean in memory that represents data from different points in time, potentially representing inconsistent state. If another transaction made changes to the bean between the first and second fetches you make, for example, your copy of the bean might contain some data that reflects the update and some that does not. Optimistic concurrency will avoid corruption of the database itself, but your display or business logic might show inconsistent data.

WARNING Using field groups to support partial loading of a bean's data can cause the bean to have inconsistent data loaded, with each group loaded at different points in time. Use caution when defining field groups to make sure that all interdependent fields are in the same group.

Using Field Groups to Tune finders-load-bean

Finder methods provide clients with bean references matching the query parameters provided by the client. If a bean is configured with `finders-load-bean` set to `true`, the default value, finder methods will fetch all data necessary to populate the bean instance in the finder query itself. We discussed this feature earlier and stressed its importance in eliminating the $n + 1$ query problem when using CMP entity beans.

Field groups can be used to tune these finder queries to fetch a subset of bean attributes rather than all attributes, potentially improving performance dramatically for large beans or large result sets. In the limiting case, you could define an `idonly` field group, containing only the primary key attribute, and use that group for certain finder queries to defeat the all-or-nothing nature of `finders-load-bean`. In practice, however, you will probably define a `summary` field group, as shown in the previous example, and configure certain finder methods to use this field group in the `weblogic-query` override section in `weblogic-cmp-rdbms-jar.xml`:

```
<weblogic-rdbms-bean>
  ...
  <weblogic-query>
    <query-method>
      <method-name>findByLastName</method-name>
      <method-params>
        <method-param>java.lang.String</method-param>
      </method-params>
    </query-method>
    <group-name>summary</group-name>
  </weblogic-query>
</weblogic-rdbms-bean>
```

Calls to `findByLastName()` now cause the container to execute a shortened version of the finder query, which fetches only the fields in the `summary` field group:

```
... : Finder produced statement string
SELECT WL0.ID, WL0.LASTNAME  FROM PERSON WL0
    WHERE ( (WL0.LASTNAME LIKE ?  ) )
```

Using field groups to tune finder queries represents a powerful technique for improving performance and reducing the memory footprint required to cache beans loaded via `finders-load-bean`. You can employ this technique without introducing the double-query problem described in the previous section by ensuring that the first field group for the bean includes all fields. This will effectively disable the use of field groups for normal data retrieval caused by get methods, but finder methods that specify other field groups can tune their queries as needed.

BEST PRACTICE **Use field groups to tune finder queries for large beans or large result sets to avoid the *n* + 1 query problem without fetching unnecessary data.**

The default field group, appropriately named `default`, contains all normal data attributes and any CMR fields mapped to foreign keys in the bean's database table. You may redefine the `default` field group to contain a subset of the bean attributes to change the default behavior of finders when `finders-load-bean` is `true`.

Relationship Caching with CMP Entity Beans

The `finders-load-bean` feature improves the performance of CMP entity beans by fetching all of the bean data during the finder SQL `SELECT` statement, thereby avoiding the $n + 1$ query problem for most simple beans. If the beans being fetched include container-managed relationship fields, however, the related beans will not be fetched during the initial finder query. Subsequent access of the CMR field will require individual SQL statements to fetch the related bean data, producing a variation of the $n + 1$ query problem if all relationships are traversed.

WebLogic Server provides a mechanism, *relationship caching,* capable of prefetching related entity beans during the initial finder query in much the same way bean data for simple beans was prefetched by `finders-load-bean`. When relationship caching is enabled for a specific finder method, WebLogic Server will use an outer join in the generated SQL `SELECT` statement to fetch the primary bean data and related bean data in a single query. As you'll see in a moment, options exist to control which relationships in the primary bean are included in this outer join and which fields in the related beans are prefetched by the query.

An example will help explain this feature. The `PersonCMPEJB` bean has a one-to-many relationship with the `AddressCMPEJB` bean, as we've described in previous sections. We've added a new finder method to the `Person` bean, `findByLastNameWithAddress()`, by modifying the `ejb-jar.xml` file:

```
<query>
  <query-method>
    <method-name>findByLastNameWithAddress</method-name>
    <method-params>
      <method-param>java.lang.String</method-param>
    </method-params>
  </query-method>
  <ejb-ql>
    SELECT OBJECT(o) FROM PersonCMPEJB o WHERE o.lastName LIKE ?1
  </ejb-ql>
</query>
```

So far this query is identical to the `findByLastName` query discussed earlier. We could have simply used that query for this example, but it seems reasonable to indicate the presence of relationship caching by the choice of finder name, so we've chosen to call it `findByLastNameWithAddress`.

Recalling that the `cmr` field relating a `Person` to its `Address` beans was called `addresses`, we now declare a particular `relationship-caching` element in the `Person` section of `weblogic-cmp-rdbms-jar.xml` defining the relationship we want to prefetch in the finder and any specific field group to load in the related bean:

```
<weblogic-rdbms-jar>
  <weblogic-rdbms-bean>
    <ejb-name>PersonCMPEJB</ejb-name>
    ...
    <relationship-caching>
```

```
    <caching-name>withaddress</caching-name>
      <caching-element>
        <cmr-field>addresses</cmr-field>
        <!-- can specify field group within Address -->
        <!-- <group-name>summary</group-name> -->
      </caching-element>
  </relationship-caching>
```

The descriptor shown here does not specify a particular field group name in the Address bean, so all fields in the related Address beans will be included in the query.

Next, we override the definition of findByLastNameWithAddress in this descriptor to specify both the field group to fetch for the Person bean and the name of the relationship-caching element that specifies the related beans and groups to include in the query:

```
<weblogic-query>
  <query-method>
    <method-name>findByLastNameWithAddress</method-name>
    <method-params>
      <method-param>java.lang.String</method-param>
    </method-params>
  </query-method>
  <group-name>everything</group-name> <!-- group in Person -->
  <caching-name>withaddress</caching-name>
</weblogic-query>
```

Note that omitting the field group for the Person bean is perfectly acceptable, thereby causing the query to include the default field group or all fields if no default group is defined. The everything field group is included in this example only to illustrate the ability to combine both types of elements in a single finder definition.

Finally, because the prefetching technique uses an outer join, WebLogic Server must generate the finder query using a database-specific syntax for this outer join. A final element in weblogic-cmp-rdbms-jar.xml defines the specific database technology:

```
  <!-- This element required for relationship caching -->
  <!-- Valid: DB2 INFORMIX ORACLE SQL_SERVER SYBASE POINTBASE -->
  <database-type>ORACLE</database-type>
</weblogic-rdbms-jar>
```

That's it! When a client invokes the findByLastNameWithAddress() method, the EJB container will execute a database-specific query similar to the following:

```
SELECT WL0.ID, WL0.FIRSTNAME, WL0.LASTNAME, WL0.MIDDLENAME,
WL0.SALUTATION, WL1.ID, WL1.CITY, WL1.POSTAL_CODE, WL1.STATE,
WL1.STREET, WL1.PERSON_ID FROM PERSON WL0, ADDRESS WL1
    WHERE ( (WL0.LASTNAME LIKE ?  ) )  AND WL1.PERSON_ID (+) = WL0.ID
```

As indicated by this listing, the query joins the PERSON and ADDRESS table using an outer join between the PERSON_ID foreign key in ADDRESS and the ID primary key in PERSON to automatically fetch all addresses for each Person bean matching the driving criteria. Note that Oracle-specific outer-join syntax was employed in this case. After fetching this Cartesian set of rows, the container parses through the results and constructs the individual Person and Address beans, establishes their relationship fields, and caches the beans in their appropriate entity-bean caches.

Viola! In one query you've populated the cache with an entire graph of Person beans and related Address beans. A few nuances worth mentioning are these:

- Make sure finders-load-bean is set to true, the default value, for the parent bean of the relationship. If this parameter is false, the finder methods are not responsible for loading bean data or relationships.
- You may place multiple caching-element definitions in a single relationship-caching element, thereby specifying multiple relationships to traverse and prefetch during the finder query. Be careful that the query doesn't become a monster Cartesian product of all related bean data.
- You may also nest caching-element definitions to prefetch children of the related beans. See the online documentation for an example of this. Be careful here as well to avoid huge Cartesian sets.
- Because the result set includes duplicate rows caused by the outer join, it is not possible for WebLogic Server to distinguish between a duplicate related bean caused by the join and a true duplicate related bean in the relationship. WebLogic Server assumes the duplicates are artifacts of the join and removes them, meaning that CMR relationships will always appear to contain sets of distinct beans. Don't use this feature if you allow duplicate related beans in the relationship.
- Relationship caching does not work with many-to-many relationships.
- Relationship caching may also be used on ejbSelect() methods that return entity beans.

BEST PRACTICE Use relationship caching to create alternate finders that automatically fetch related beans. Consider naming these finders in a manner that indicates the presence of prefetching behavior to avoid their use by clients not requiring the related beans.

Additional CMP Features

A number of additional CMP-related features are available in WebLogic Server related to primary key generation, mapping to multiple tables, EJB-QL extensions, dynamic queries, and cascading deletes.

Automatic Primary Key Generation

WebLogic Server provides a mechanism to generate a numeric primary key for CMP entity beans automatically. Automatic key generation eliminates the need to set the primary key in the `ejbCreate()` method and removes the key from the parameter list for `create()`, `ejbCreate()`, and `ejbPostCreate()`.

For example, the `PersonCMPBean` class defined in Listing 6.1 included the primary key in the `ejbCreate()` and `ejbPostCreate()` methods:

```
public java.lang.Integer ejbCreate(Integer pId, String pSalutation,
                                   String pFirstName,
                                   String pMiddleName,
                                   String pLastName)
{
    LOG.info("ejbCreate()");
    setId(pId);
    setSalutation(pSalutation);
    setFirstName(pFirstName);
    setMiddleName(pMiddleName);
    setLastName(pLastName);
    return null;
}
```

A version using automatic key generation, however, eliminates this parameter and the `setId()` invocation:

```
public java.lang.Integer ejbCreate(String pSalutation,
                                   String pFirstName,
                                   String pMiddleName,
                                   String pLastName)
{
    LOG.info("ejbCreate()");
    setSalutation(pSalutation);
    setFirstName(pFirstName);
    setMiddleName(pMiddleName);
    setLastName(pLastName);
    return null;
}
```

Clients no longer provide the key value when calling `create()` on the home interface:

```
PersonCMPLocal person = home.create("Mr.", "John", "", "Smith");
```

Automatic key generation is configured on a per-bean basis by including an `automatic-key-generation` section in the `weblogic-cmp-rdbms-jar.xml` descriptor using one of three different techniques: named sequence table, Oracle sequence, or SQL*Server identity column.

The *named sequence table* technique is the most portable approach. The descriptor elements identify a table in the database to use for automatic key generation:

```
<automatic-key-generation>
  <generator-type>NAMED_SEQUENCE_TABLE</generator-type>
  <generator-name>PERSON_SEQ_TBL</generator-name>
  <key-cache-size>100</key-cache-size>
</automatic-key-generation>
```

The specified table must contain a single numeric column, `SEQUENCE`, and a single row containing the next primary-key value to be assigned for any bean using this table. Note that multiple beans may use the same table.

The `key-cache-size` element defines the number of primary keys to cache in each EJB container. When the server boots, or whenever this in-memory cache of keys is exhausted, the container will access the named sequence table, retrieve the next key value, and increment the database value by the cache size. Caching keys is important for good performance, but it results in wasted key values whenever servers are shut down with unused keys in their cache.

BEST PRACTICE **Using a reasonable** `key-cache-size` **is very important in reducing the number of database requests when using the named-sequence-table technique. A value of 10 should be considered a minimum, and a value of 100 or more should be used for production systems.**

The *Oracle-sequence* technique uses an Oracle sequence to provide the generated key values:

```
<automatic-key-generation>
  <generator-type>ORACLE</generator-type>
  <generator-name>PERSON_SEQ</generator-name>
  <key-cache-size>10</key-cache-size>
</automatic-key-generation>
```

Again, multiple beans can employ the same sequence if desired, and the `key-cache-size` will be used to cache key values in each container. If keys are cached in the container, the Oracle sequence must be created with the `INCREMENT BY` option set to the same value:

```
CREATE SEQUENCE PERSON_SEQ START WITH 200 INCREMENT BY 10;
```

Failure to follow this rule will cause the container to use key values from the internal cache that are higher than the next value stored in the sequence. This causes duplicate key exceptions once the container exhausts the cached key values and queries the sequence for the next valid value.

BEST PRACTICE **Use a reasonable** `key-cache-size` **with the Oracle-sequence technique, and ensure that the cache size in WebLogic equals the** `INCREMENT BY` **value used in Oracle.**

Finally, the *SQL*Server-identity-column* technique utilizes an identity column in the database schema to assign the primary key automatically when the row is inserted in the database:

```
<automatic-key-generation>
  <generator-type>SQLSERVER</generator-type>
</automatic-key-generation>
```

During the database insert, SQL*Server assigns the next primary key value to the database row and WebLogic Server retrieves this key value and places it in the bean instance. Client code may retrieve the assigned key value immediately after the `create()` invocation using the appropriate get method:

```
PersonCMPLocal person = home.create("Mr.", "Gregory", "A.", "Nyberg");
Integer pk = person.getId();
```

This assumes that database inserts have not been delayed until commit, in which case the key will not be available until the transaction commits.

BEST PRACTICE When using automatic key generation with Oracle or SQL*Server, favor the database-specific key-generation technique over the named-sequence table to optimize performance.

EJB CMP Multiple-Table Mapping Support

Multiple-table mapping allows a single CMP entity bean to map its attributes and relationship foreign keys to multiple database tables. Mapping is configured in the `weblogic-cmp-rdbms-jar.xml` using appropriate `table-map` and `field-map` elements:

```
<weblogic-rdbms-bean>
  <ejb-name>PersonCMPEJB</ejb-name>
  <data-source-name>MasteringDataSource</data-source-name>
  <table-map>
    <table-name>PERSON</table-name>
    <field-map>
      <cmp-field>id</cmp-field>
      <dbms-column>ID</dbms-column>
    </field-map>
    ...
  </table-map>
  <table-map>
    <table-name>PERSONEXTRA</table-name>
    <field-map>
      <cmp-field>id</cmp-field>
      <dbms-column>ID</dbms-column>
    </field-map>
    <field-map>
```

```
        <cmp-field>height</cmp-field>
        <dbms-column>HEIGHT</dbms-column>
      </field-map>
      <field-map>
        <cmp-field>weight</cmp-field>
        <dbms-column>WEIGHT</dbms-column>
      </field-map>
    </table-map>
  </weblogic-rdbms-bean>
```

In this example, we've mapped two additional bean attributes, `height` and `weight`, to database columns in a new `PERSONEXTRA` table. WebLogic Server requires that both tables have the same number and type of primary key columns, although the `dbms-column` names can differ in each table.

When the EJB container retrieves the `Person` bean, it will execute a single SQL statement joining the mapped tables to retrieve all attributes:

```
... : Finder produced statement string
SELECT WL0.ID, WL0.FIRSTNAME, WL1.HEIGHT, WL0.LASTNAME, WL0.MIDDLENAME,
    WL0.SALUTATION, WL1.WEIGHT  FROM PERSON WL0, PERSONEXTRA WL1
    WHERE ( (WL0.ID = ?) ) AND WL0.ID = WL1.ID
```

Updates are stored using a separate SQL statement for each mapped table.

BEST PRACTICE Mapping CMP beans to multiple tables provides a clean, declarative solution. Consider creating a composite entity bean and mapping it to multiple tables as an alternative to one-to-one relationships in your design.

Additional configuration is required for CMP entity beans containing CMR fields if the beans are mapped to multiple tables and one of the tables contains the foreign key implementing the container-managed relationship. In the simple case shown here, the `Person` bean participates in a one-to-many relationship with `Address` beans, but the foreign key is not part of the `PERSON` table, so no additional configuration is required. If the `Address` bean was mapped to multiple tables, however, the simple relationship-mapping section in `weblogic-cmp-rdbms-jar.xml` would have to be modified to indicate the location of the foreign-key column.

See the WebLogic Server documentation at http://edocs.bea.com/wls/docs81/ejb/cmp_advanced.html for more information on mapping relationships with multiple tables.

WebLogic EJB-QL Enhancements

One of the limitations of EJB 2.0 is the lack of support for important SQL modifiers and capabilities in the standard EJB Query Language specification. WebLogic Server extends the functionality of EJB-QL to include a number of additional features and enhancements, including the following:

- `DISTINCT` and `ORDERBY` capabilities

- Aggregate functions such as COUNT, AVG, SUM, MIN, and MAX
- Subqueries, including correlated and uncorrelated subqueries
- Queries that return ResultSet objects containing the selected columns (ejbSelect only)
- SELECT hints for Oracle RDBMS queries

Although a complete discussion of all of these extensions and features is beyond the scope of this book, a simple example using the findByLastName() finder method will help you understand the configuration steps involved.

As discussed earlier, finder and ejbSelect queries must first be declared in the standard ejb-jar.xml descriptor file:

```
<query>
  <query-method>
    <method-name>findByLastName</method-name>
    <method-params>
      <method-param>java.lang.String</method-param>
    </method-params>
  </query-method>
  <ejb-ql>
    SELECT OBJECT(o) FROM PersonCMPEJB o WHERE o.lastName LIKE ?1
  </ejb-ql>
</query>
```

To order the results returned by the finder by lastName and firstName, override the definition of the query in weblogic-cmp-rdbms-jar.xml to include the ORDERBY clause in the weblogic-ql contents:

```
<weblogic-query>
  <query-method>
    <method-name>findByLastName</method-name>
    <method-params>
      <method-param>java.lang.String</method-param>
    </method-params>
  </query-method>
  <weblogic-ql>
     SELECT OBJECT(o) FROM PersonCMPEJB o WHERE o.lastName LIKE ?1
           ORDERBY o.lastName, o.firstName
  </weblogic-ql>
</weblogic-query>
```

The collection returned by the findByLastName() finder method will now be ordered by the desired columns. Many of the WebLogic Server EJB-QL enhancements operate this way: The query is declared in ejb-jar.xml and then redefined in weblogic-cmp-rdbms-jar.xml to include the desired aggregate functions, subqueries, or other features. See the WebLogic Server documentation at http://edocs.bea.com/wls/docs81/ejb/cmp_basic.html for additional examples and information.

BEST PRACTICE **WebLogic Server EJB-QL enhancements provide extremely useful extensions to the basic EJB-QL query language. Use these extensions to reduce manual result set manipulation performed in the EJB container (sorting items, eliminating duplicates, producing averages, and so on).**

Dynamic Query Support

Queries used for CMP finder and `ejbSelect` methods are normally declared and defined in the EJB descriptor files. Although this technique provides a standard, declarative mechanism, it suffers from the requirement to redeploy the entire EJB archive file to modify a query, and it lacks flexibility for certain types of queries. For example, it is impossible to create queries with a variable number of parameters in the `WHERE` clause or a dynamic set of values in an `IN` operator using the standard EJB-QL syntax.

WebLogic Server provides a mechanism for programmatically defining and executing queries in application code to address the limitations of declarative queries. This *Dynamic Query Support*, added to WebLogic Server in version 7.0, provides a special-purpose `Query` object used to define and execute dynamic queries in the context of the EJB container and the desired transaction. Using dynamic queries requires a few straightforward changes to your application.

First, enable dynamic queries for a given CMP entity bean home interface using the `enable-dynamic-queries` element in the `weblogic-ejb-jar.xml` descriptor for the entity bean:

```
<enable-dynamic-queries>True</enable-dynamic-queries>
```

Next, obtain a reference to the home interface, and cast it to the `QueryHome` or `QueryLocalHome` interface as appropriate:

```
PersonCMPHomeLocal home = (PersonCMPHomeLocal)ctx.lookup("...");
QueryLocalHome qhome = (QueryLocalHome)home;
```

The `QueryHome` and `QueryLocalHome` interfaces define two methods: `createQuery()` to create a `Query` helper object and `nativeQuery(String)` to return the SQL statement generated for a specific dynamic query. Use the `createQuery()` method to obtain a reference to a `Query` object:

```
Query myQuery = qhome.createQuery();
```

The `Query` interface defines a number of configuration methods for setting transaction policy, maximum result set size, and whether CMP updates should be flushed before the query is executed. See the WebLogic Server documentation for more information on these methods. The `Query` interface also defines methods for defining and executing finder and `ejbSelect` queries:

```
public java.sql.ResultSet execute(String)
public java.sql.ResultSet execute(String, java.util.Properties)
public java.util.Collection find(String)
public java.util.Collection find(String, java.util.Properties)
```

Use the simple versions of the `execute()` or `find()` method to perform the desired query:

```
Collection people = myQuery.find(
    "SELECT OBJECT(o) FROM PersonCMPEJB o WHERE o.lastName = 'Smith'");
```

This query will be executed using the `DataSource` defined for the entity bean and a collection of entity-bean references will be returned in the same manner as a normal finder method. The dynamic-query processing will be affected by the value of `finders-load-bean` and other parameters in the same manner as well. Note that the current version of WebLogic Server does not support parameters or bound variables in the query, so all parameters must be placed in the string, as shown in the example.

The alternate versions of `execute()` and `find()` allow you to specify configuration parameters during the query execution:

```
Properties p = new Properties();
p.setProperty("GROUP_NAME", "fieldgroup");
p.setProperty("INCLUDE_UPDATES", "true");
Collection people =
    myQuery.find("SELECT OBJECT(o) FROM PersonCMPEJB o WHERE " +
                 "o.lastName = 'Smith'", p);
```

Note that the query string supplied to these methods follows the EJB-QL syntax rather than actual SQL syntax. Attribute names are used rather than column names, relationships are traversed using EJB-QL syntax rather than manual joins, and so on. Use the `nativeQuery()` method on the `QueryHome` interface to view the actual SQL generated by the container for a given query string.

BEST PRACTICE **Use dynamic queries for finder and `ejbSelect` queries that are difficult or impossible to implement in standard declarative EJB-QL.**

Cascade Delete Support

Cascade delete refers to the automatic deletion of dependent children objects and data whenever parent objects are deleted from the persistent store. WebLogic Server supports two different versions of the cascading delete functionality: container-driven and database-driven cascade deletion.

In the container-driven version, the EJB container is responsible for deleting child objects when the parent object is removed using the `remove()` method, either on the bean or the bean's home object. To configure container-driven cascade delete, include the cascade-delete element in the child object's ejb-relationship-role element in ejb-jar.xml:

```
<relationships>
  <ejb-relation>
    <ejb-relation-name>Person-Addresses</ejb-relation-name>
    <ejb-relationship-role>
      <ejb-relationship-role-name>
        Many-Addresses-Have-One-Person
      </ejb-relationship-role-name>
      <multiplicity>many</multiplicity>
      <cascade-delete/>
      <relationship-role-source>
        <ejb-name>AddressCMPEJB</ejb-name>
      </relationship-role-source>
      <cmr-field>
        <cmr-field-name>person</cmr-field-name>
      </cmr-field>
    </ejb-relationship-role>
    ...
  </ejb-relation>
```

cascade-delete is configured on the child object, not the parent, and the multiplicity on the parent side of the relationship must be equal to 1.

When the parent object is removed, the container will automatically retrieve a collection of all related children objects, issue individual SQL statements to delete these children, and eliminate the children from the entity-bean cache if cache-between-transactions is true. Recursion is possible, meaning that child objects can have their own collections of dependent children configured for cascade delete as well, and the container will traverse all appropriate collections and perform individual SQL statements for all objects requiring deletion. Container-driven cascade-delete operations can be relatively costly to perform if the collections are large or if there are many levels of dependent objects to traverse.

An alternative approach, database-driven cascade deletion, makes use of the automatic cascading delete capability of most RDBMS systems by configuring the database to perform the operation behind the scenes. This technique is configured by first including the cascade-delete element in ejb-jar.xml for all dependent children, as in the container-driven version, but then by adding a WebLogic Server-specific db-cascade-delete element in the weblogic-cmp-rdbms-jar.xml file as well:

```
<weblogic-rdbms-relation>
  <relation-name>Person-Addresses</relation-name>
  <weblogic-relationship-role>
    <relationship-role-name>
      Many-Addresses-Have-One-Person
    </relationship-role-name>
    <relationship-role-map>
      <column-map>
```

```
          <foreign-key-column>PERSON_ID</foreign-key-column>
          <key-column>ID</key-column>
        </column-map>
      </relationship-role-map>
      <db-cascade-delete/>
    </weblogic-relationship-role>
  </weblogic-rdbms-relation>
```

When the parent object is removed, the container will traverse relationships and invalidate all appropriate dependent children in the entity bean cache, but it will not issue individual SQL statements to delete the underlying database information. The database must be configured with cascading delete enabled in the foreign-key constraints connecting parent and child tables for this technique to operate properly.

BEST PRACTICE Use database-driven cascade delete for most applications to improve performance. Container-driven cascade delete may be suitable for applications with a small number of child objects that require manual deletion.

Checking for Bean Existence

When using clusters, or employing concurrency strategies other than exclusive concurrency, it is possible to call methods on an entity bean that has been removed from the database by a different transaction. Normally this condition will be caught during the load operation in response to a get method invocation, or at commit time when the container attempts to update the bean's data in the database. WebLogic Server also provides a mechanism to check the existence of a CMP bean at the conclusion of every business method for added safety. Note that once a bean's data has been loaded from the database, no additional checks are made during that transaction. Enable this per-method check using the `check-exists-on-method` element in the `weblogic-cmp-rdbms-jar.xml` file:

```
<weblogic-rdbms-bean>
  <ejb-name>PersonCMPEJB</ejb-name>
  ...
  <check-exists-on-method>true</check-exists-on-method>
</weblogic-rdbms-bean>
```

In previous versions of WebLogic Server, the default value for `check-exists-on-method` was `false`, meaning that no additional method-level checks for existence took place by default. This setting now defaults to `true` in WebLogic Server 8.1, again due to J2EE 1.3 licensing requirements. Consider setting `check-exists-on-method` to `false` in all beans to avoid unnecessary overhead in business methods.

WARNING J2EE licensing restrictions have caused the WebLogic Server 8.1 default setting for `check-exists-on-method` to change from `false` to `true`. If your application doesn't require existence checks after every business method, setting the value back to `false` will improve performance.

Message-Driven Bean Features

Message-driven bean (MDB) components provide a bridge between JMS and EJB components by listening on JMS destinations and invoking EJB components. A number of WebLogic-specific features are available to improve the reliability and performance of MDB components:

- The initial and maximum number of MDB instances can be controlled using the `inital-beans-in-free-pool` and `max-beans-in-free-pool` parameters in `weblogic-ejb-jar.xml`. Limiting the number of instances provides a mechanism to throttle the processing of incoming JMS messages to be consistent with the number of JDBC connections or other resources and the priority of JMS requests versus other synchronous requests. Limiting the pool to a single bean allows you to guarantee strict ordered processing of messages, as opposed to just ordered delivery, which always occurs. See Chapter 9 for more information about this topic and the additional configuration steps necessary to guarantee ordered redelivery of messages in the event of errors.
- The MDB component may be configured to run as a particular principal, or user, using the `run-as` element in `ejb-jar.xml` combined with a `run-as-principal` element in `weblogic-ejb-jar.xml`. This principal will be used for all invocations of EJB components made in the MDB's `onMessage()` message-processing method.
- WebLogic Server supports the inclusion of the message delivery in the container-managed transaction started during the invocation of `onMessage()` if the transaction attribute is `Required` in the `ejb-jar.xml` descriptor. MDB components may also use bean-managed transactions started in `onMessage()` and propagated to all EJB components invoked in the transaction, although the message delivery itself is then outside the scope of the bean-managed transaction.
- WebLogic Server supports the clustering of JMS destinations and the migration of MDB components from failed servers to operational servers using administrative functions. MDB components may also be deployed across all servers in a cluster to provide high levels of performance and availability.
- WebLogic Server permits MDB components to be deployed against third-party JMS providers while retaining proper container-managed transactional behaviors.

Chapter 9 will discuss WebLogic Server JMS and MDB features and best practices.

Chapter Review

This chapter began with a review of key EJB concepts and terminology and a discussion of the EJB life cycle in the WebLogic Server EJB container. Each of the EJB component types was identified, and a few simple examples were presented in preparation for the subsequent discussions.

The bulk of the chapter was dedicated to presenting WebLogic Server-specific features and capabilities related to EJB components. Many of these features are relatively new in the WebLogic Server product and require careful configuration to achieve the desired performance or reliability benefits. The discussion of each feature was accompanied by a best practice indicating its usefulness for typical EJB applications and highlighting any limitations or configuration recommendations.

How should you design your EJB application? Which WebLogic Server-specific configuration options should you employ to improve performance? In the vernacular of the J2EE architect, it depends. It depends on your specific requirements for performance, concurrency control, remote-interface availability, and many other issues. It is impossible to provide a single, overriding recommendation for EJB design or configuration. It's up to you to decide.

To help you make these important decisions for your project, the next chapter includes a discussion of the key application drivers, the selection of a business-tier architecture, and the appropriate configuration options for the example EJB application, *bigrez.com*.

CHAPTER

7

Building an Example EJB Application

In this chapter, we will walk through the design and construction of the business tier of the *bigrez.com* example application, highlighting key concepts and best practices. While it is not meant as a basic tutorial for constructing EJB components or the business tier of J2EE applications, it will discuss some options available to simplify related construction tasks.

This chapter is organized like Chapters 2 through 4, with the discussion proceeding from requirements to architecture and then to implementation:

- We identify a set of business-tier requirements to guide the architecture selection process.
- We identify and examine candidate architectures in light of the requirements to gauge their relative value for our application.
- We identify and discuss techniques for constructing EJB components.
- We examine selected business-tier components required for the *bigrez.com* application to highlight implementation details and best practices.

Ready? We'll start with the requirements.

Business-Tier Requirements

As we stated in Chapter 2, always identify requirements before choosing a design. Before selecting the Struts-based presentation-tier architecture, we spent a fair amount of time identifying the many presentation-tier requirements present in Web applications. Key requirements such as error handling and form redisplay led us to the choice of a robust servlet-centric presentation-tier framework rather than a simpler JSP-centric approach. We'll now follow the same strategy and identify key business-tier requirements that drive our choice of architecture to ensure that we make the right decision.

As in Chapter 2, when we talk about business-tier requirements in this section we mean the general requirements of a business-tier architecture, rather than the specific requirements of a given application. Although the specific application requirements can matter in the architecture selection, there are many common business-tier requirements that should be considered in the decision process as a starting point.

We'll walk through the business tier from the business logic requirements through to the database access requirements and identify key requirements that will be useful in evaluating candidate business-tier architectures.

Business Logic Requirements

The first set of business-tier requirements is derived from the business logic requirements for the application. Most applications have specific business logic requirements based on the required application behaviors and functions. Unlike the common requirements for data access or object-relational mapping, however, it is difficult to generalize and identify business logic requirements that are common to all applications. We will simply identify a few common business logic requirements and include them in our analysis as a starting point.

Process Encapsulation

The first common requirement is the need to encapsulate complex or multistep processes in the business-tier components and to make them available to other tiers through a simple, straightforward interface. The user of the business-tier component should be insulated from the implementation details. In a distributed, transactional environment, this encapsulation also provides performance benefits by eliminating the need for multiple distributed requests from the user to the service.

The session façade pattern is a typical solution for this requirement. As illustrated in Figure 7.1, the session façade pattern uses a stateless session bean component to encapsulate all of the business logic, loading and storing of entity beans, and other activity required to process a particular request. Without the façade, the client component might be required to begin and manage the transaction, make multiple calls to session beans, entity beans, and other business-tier components, and trap and handle all business exceptions. Clearly this is not the optimal solution.

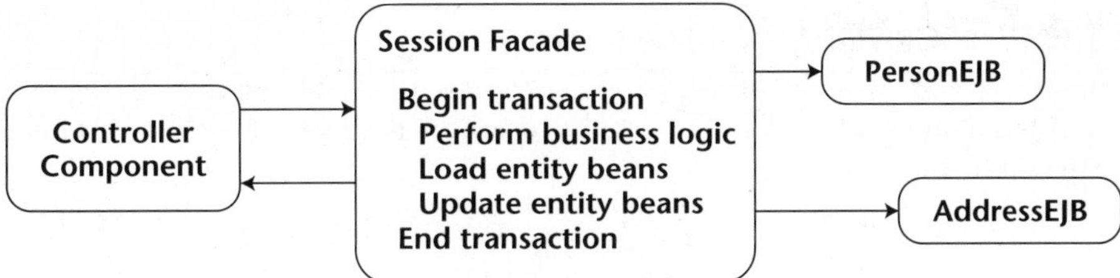

Figure 7.1 Session façade encapsulates complex business logic.

The business-tier architecture must therefore provide a mechanism for encapsulating complex business logic and providing a straightforward interface for client and controller components.

Validation

The second common requirement is for business-tier validation of objects and their data elements. As discussed in Chapter 2, the data values submitted by a Web application user are often validated both on the page itself, via JavaScript, and in a presentation-tier component such as the form bean or controller class. Many applications consider this level of validation sufficient and allow the business-tier components to perform operations on client-provided data without repeating the validation checks.

Other applications have more rigorous requirements, however, and must include validation checks on all data sent to the business-tier components. The need for business-tier validation may not be present in the original application, but it can occur once the component is reused in a subsequent application. For example, a component intended for use with a Web application having validation checks in the presentation tier might eventually be reused by a different application that does not include presentation-tier validation.

The business-tier architecture should provide a mechanism for validating objects and data and returning validation errors in much the same way the controller components provided this functionality in the presentation tier.

Object-Relational Mapping Requirements

Moving farther into the business tier toward the database, the next set of requirements defines the mechanisms for mapping objects to the relational database technology. These object-relational (O-R) mapping requirements define the functions necessary to translate between object technology and relational database representations of the data.

Mapping Simple Classes

The simplest form of object-relational mapping is the simple one-to-one mapping of a business object to a database table. Some of the characteristics of this type of mapping include the following:

- The attributes in the business object are all scalars, strings, or other simple data types.
- Each attribute maps to a single column in the database table.

The object-relational mapping techniques must allow for a straightforward mapping of business objects to tables, including support for basic create, read, update, and delete (CRUD) operations.

It is possible to design a database where a single business object is spread across multiple tables. Inserting the business object creates a row in both tables, removing the object deletes the corresponding row in each table, and modifying the object updates both rows as well. The O-R mapping techniques must allow for objects that span tables in a database, possibly across multiple databases.

Mapping Simple Aggregation

The term *aggregation* refers to ownership, or parent-child, relationships, in which the child cannot exist without the parent. Typically there is a one-to-many relationship between the parent and the child table. If it was a one-to-one relationship, you could simply fold the child data back in to the parent table in most cases.

A good example is the person and address example from Chapter 6. Each person can be related to zero or more addresses, but every address must be associated with a single person. There is a dependent, one-to-many relationship between these tables. The O-R mapping technique must provide a mechanism for identifying children for a particular parent, normally through the use of a foreign key, and must also provide methods for accessing and manipulating children.

Some basic rules apply in aggregation:

- Deleting the parent is dependent on having no remaining children in the database. This is normally enforced by the referential integrity (RI) constraints in the database. Automatic deletion of children during a parent delete is possible, but it must occur before the parent is deleted.
- Inserting child rows also depends on the existence of the parent row for the RI constraints to allow the insert.
- Updating the parent primary key becomes a pain, requiring a multistep process of copying the parent row, changing the children to reference the new parent row, and then deleting the original parent row. This operation is costly and should be avoided by using immutable keys for primary key identifiers if at all possible.

Note that aggregation looks different in memory than it does in a database. In memory, objects are normally linked via memory pointers or references in an *object graph*.

The object-relational mapping technique must provide a mechanism for both creating the interconnected series of objects in memory when reading parent and child tables and writing out the interconnected objects to the proper database tables when making changes.

Ideally, the O-R mapping technique should be capable of the following:

- Automatically creating the object graph during a fetch operation, linking business objects to their children, and prefetching some or all of the graph during the initial database operation
- Automatically walking through all of the parent, child, and grandchild relationships in the object graph and performing the necessary and appropriate CRUD operations on the objects to save any changes

One final topic related to aggregation and relationships in general: You often want to defer the fetching of child objects until the time they are actually required. In many cases, the parent may be all that is required to perform a calculation or present some business data to the user, and it is a waste of resources to fully populate the object graph with all child objects. This technique of waiting to fetch children is sometimes referred to as *lazy instantiation*.

Note that with this lazy instantiation technique, you also need a mechanism to determine whether child objects have been fetched. Parent objects often have a child-fetched flag for each child object or list.

The O-R mapping technique should therefore allow the following:

- Fetching a parent object plus all of its children and grandchildren. This is called a *deep* or full fetch of the entire object graph starting with the parent object.
- Fetching only the parent without fetching any children, often called a *shallow* fetch.
- Fetching some or all of the children objects of the parent without refetching the parent itself as part of a lazy instantiation technique, often called a *children-only* fetch, which can itself be deep or shallow.

Projection Objects and Queries

You may often want to use objects that contain arbitrary subsets of data from one or more tables. One good example of such a *projection* object is a query result object that contains a subset of data from a table needed for the presentation of search results.

For example, the actual `Person` table might have 20 or more columns, so a result list containing many full `Person` business objects would represent a large amount of memory, network bandwidth, and so on. If the user interface needs to display only the first and last name, a specialized projection object could be defined that contains only those two attributes from the `Person` table plus the table primary key. The O-R mapping technique must allow fetching a list of these projection objects from the table using SQL statements that fetch only the required fields.

It is also valuable to create projection objects that span multiple tables, again containing only the attributes required for the specific requirement being satisfied. A highly normalized database will require multitable projection objects for best query performance. The query that fetches the multitable projection object should perform the join using the database rather than trying to fetch objects for each table in to memory and joining them by hand. The O-R mapping technique should allow for projection objects that define a subset of columns from one or more tables.

Mapping Associations/Relationships

Associations are more general forms of relationships between objects than the pure dependent form of association, aggregation. One common form of association is the many-to-many relationship between two tables that are not dependent on each other. For example, in Figure 7.2, the relationship between students at a school and the courses offered at the school is contained in a separate relationship table, `Enrollment`.

Clearly students can exist without courses, and courses can exist without students, so the two entity tables are not related to each other directly via aggregation. The `Enrollment` relationship table exists to indicate that a particular student is taking the specific course and can also include additional information related directly to this relationship. In this example, the student's grade in the specific course would be stored in the `Enrollment` table, not in the `Student` or `Course` table.

A complete discussion of O-R mapping techniques appropriate for general relationships of this sort is beyond the scope of this chapter. Solutions generally fall into one of two categories:

Direct mapping of relationships. Business objects implement relationships directly through internal pointers and lists of pointers to related objects. In this solution, `Student` and `Course` business objects contain lists of pointers to intermediate `Enrollment` objects according to the relationships stored in the enrollment table, and Enrollment objects maintain pointers to both types of objects. This technique is illustrated in Figure 7.3.

Simplified mapping of relationships. Specialized projection objects are used to present simplified views of the relationships and related business objects. In this solution, a student object would contain a list of `CourseEnrollment` projection objects with the required elements from both the `Enrollment` table and related `Course` table, a technique illustrated in Figure 7.4.

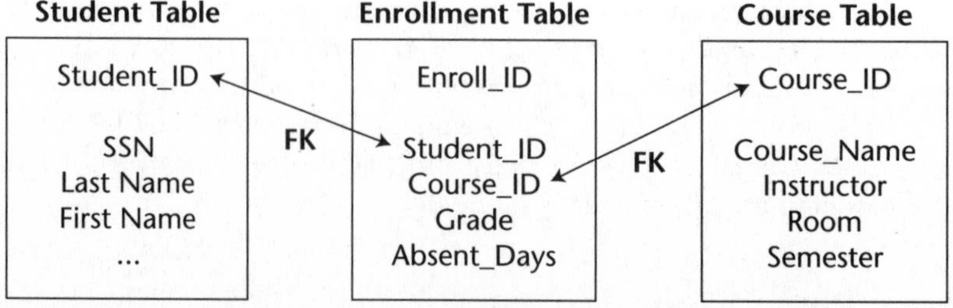

Figure 7.2 The relationship table implements a many-to-many association.

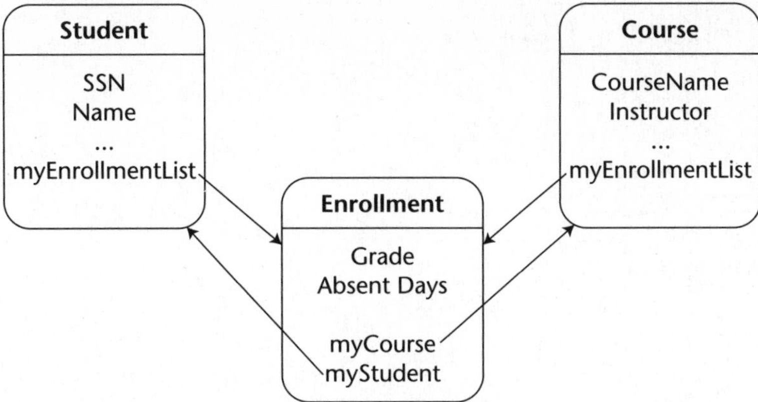

Figure 7.3 Business objects can implement relationships directly.

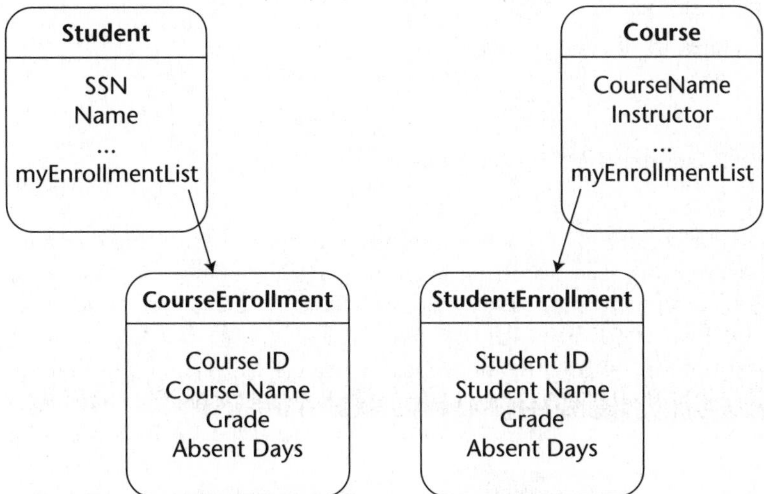

Figure 7.4 Projection objects are used to manage relationships.

Both techniques have advantages and disadvantages. The appropriate technique depends on your specific business requirements and the importance of simplifying the object graph. In either case, the chosen business-tier architecture must support flexible, efficient, and safe techniques for modeling and managing complex relationships.

Mapping Inheritance

Java is an object-oriented language, and one of the strengths of object-oriented technology is the concept of inheritance. Inheritance can be difficult to implement in an object-relational mapping environment, however, because normal database systems do not provide a native technique for inheriting and extending tables.

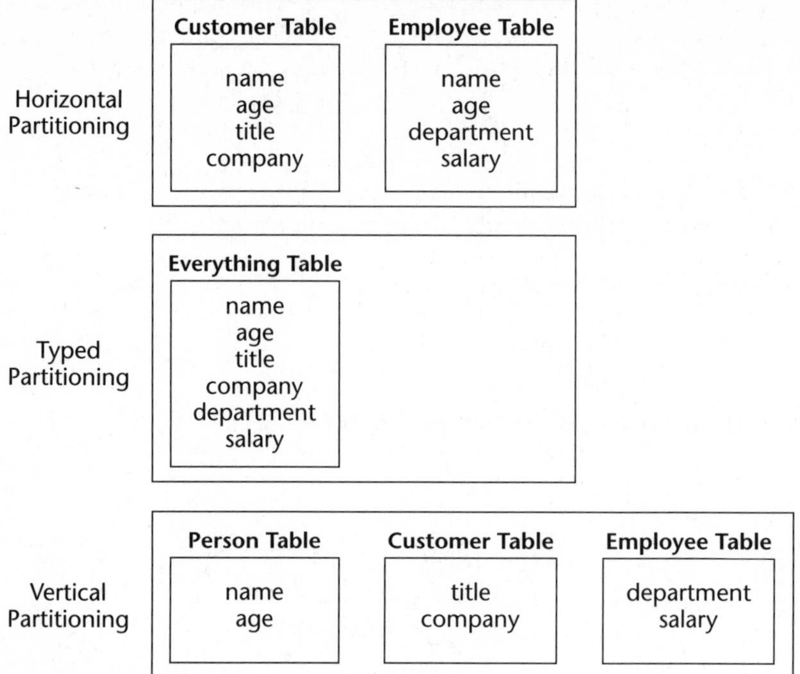

Figure 7.5 Options for O-R mapping of inheritance.

Three primary techniques are available for mapping inheritance to a set of database tables: horizontal partitioning, typed partitioning, and vertical partitioning. Figure 7.5 depicts these three techniques for a simple example containing a single base class, `Person`, and two subclasses, `Employee` and `Customer`.

In horizontal partitioning, only concrete subclass objects are mapped to tables. These tables include all of the base class and subclass attributes. This approach may improve performance because only one table needs to be accessed for instances of a given concrete class.

In typed partitioning, all classes in an inheritance tree are mapped to a single table containing all attributes required for all subclass objects. A type column is used to distinguish which type of object is stored in each row of the table, and many type-specific columns in the table will be empty for a given object.

Finally, in vertical partitioning, every class in the inheritance tree maps to a table in the database. Fetching data for a concrete subclass involves a join operation between the base table and the concrete subclass table.

All three techniques for mapping inheritance in the database are viable, but there are clear advantages and disadvantages present in some of them. Designing the database to match the object inheritance tree exactly, represented in the vertical partitioning technique, can dramatically affect performance and complicate the data access services by requiring joins during all CRUD operations. On the other hand, the placement of all attributes for all object types in a single table, the typed partitioning technique, sacrifices a great deal of flexibility and maintainability to achieve fast and simple queries and CRUD operations. The horizontal partitioning scheme often represents the best compromise between flexibility and performance, and it can also be implemented easily with a variety of O-R mapping technologies including CMP entity beans.

BEST PRACTICE Horizontal partitioning provides the simplest and most efficient method for modeling inheritance in a relational database.

All of the object-relational mapping requirements discussed in this section are important in real-world applications containing large, complex object models. Simple architectures may have no problem implementing the business logic and simple object-relational mapping requirements discussed in this section, but they often break down when they encounter more complex requirements in the object model such as nested aggregation or multiple sets of associated objects. Don't adopt an architecture that will not support the long-term needs in these areas.

Data Access Requirements

The business tier must provide basic data access services to support the object-relational mapping and business logic requirements outlined previously. Although this is not a complete list, most applications require at least the following set of data access services and functions:

- Basic create, read, update, and delete operations at an object level to meet basic object persistence requirements
- Support for more complex object-relational requirements, such as the lazy instantiation of children and persisting associations between objects
- Flexible mechanisms for performing queries against tables to retrieve single business objects, arrays of business objects, and arrays of projection or custom query objects
- Creation of custom SQL statements to perform complex logic without resorting to fetching objects and performing logic in business-tier components
- Standardized mechanisms for handling large result sets and limiting returned results
- Standardized mechanisms for handling and reporting data-related errors
- Efficient bulk insert, update, and delete mechanisms to avoid reading and updating multiple objects one at a time
- Concurrency control to eliminate the loss of data in the event of multiple simultaneous update transactions

Other Business-Tier Requirements

Finally, many applications have additional business-tier requirements in the following areas:

- Creation of detailed audit trails of business-tier service requests, data access, data manipulation, and other activity. The audit tracks who, what, when, and even why these activities were performed.
- Robust logging and instrumentation capability. It is used to troubleshoot system problems during system development and to provide usage profiling information during production operation.
- High levels of performance and scalability. These are normally expressed as overall system requirements, of course, but the business-tier architecture plays a large role in ensuring good performance. The architecture must represent sound design principles and leverage all of the clustering, caching, and performance-related features of the application server hosting the components.
- Security implemented in all tiers and services in the architecture. Requiring authentication and authorization at each business-tier interface provides a higher level of security than simply authenticating at the Web application level and allowing services to be called with impunity.

Review of Business-Tier Requirements

Table 7.1 summarizes all of the requirements outlined in this section and provides the set of criteria we'll use to evaluate candidate business-tier architectures for the *bigrez.com* application.

Table 7.1 Summary of Business-Tier Requirements

REQUIREMENT	DESCRIPTION
Process encapsulation	Straightforward technique available to encapsulate complex or multistep business processes
Validation	Ability to perform business-tier validation
Simple O-R mapping	Basic create, read, update, and delete operations on simple objects that map one-to-one with tables
Objects spanning tables	Basic CRUD operations on objects representing data from multiple tables
Aggregation (read operations)	Ability to perform deep fetching of parents and children, shallow fetching with lazy instantiation, and fetching of only children to support the lazy-fetching process

Table 7.1 *(continued)*

REQUIREMENT	DESCRIPTION
Aggregation (other operations)	Ability to automatically walk through an object graph and perform correct CRUD operations on each object according to its status
Projection objects	Ability to fetch objects containing subsets of columns from one or more tables
Associations	Ability to map relationships and perform all required CRUD operations on complex object graphs
Inheritance	Ability to map inheritance in object model to the database
Basic data access operations	CRUD operations, queries, persisting associations
Advanced data access operations	Limiting result sets, performing dynamic queries, supporting queries across multiple tables, projection objects, bulk operations, and concurrency controls
Audit, logging, and instrumentation	Techniques available to log, audit, and instrument business-tier activity at the method level
Security	Deep security providing authentication/ authorization throughout business-tier architecture

Business-Tier Architecture Options

Chapter 3 introduced the *bigrez.com* example application and described the Web application architecture chosen for the presentation tier. The next step in the construction is the selection of a business-tier architecture based on the general business-tier requirements outlined in the previous sections and our particular application requirements for *bigrez.com*.

We'll examine three candidate business-tier architectures in this chapter:

- Stateless services using JDBC to perform SQL operations
- Stateless services using entity beans for persistence operations
- Combination of stateless services, entity beans, and direct interaction

Clearly there are many more candidates that might be considered, including Java Data Objects (JDO), the use of third-party object-relational mapping tools, such as CocoBase or TopLink and others. A complete survey of all possible architectures is beyond the scope of this book. Use the discussion in this chapter to aid you in choosing the right architecture for your application by applying a similar selection process that considers your particular business-tier requirements and limitations.

Stateless Services with JDBC

The first candidate business-tier architecture uses stateless services to encapsulate all business logic, a pass-by-value technique to accept and return business objects, and simple JDBC functionality to implement persistence. Figure 7.6 illustrates this architecture for a simple application containing a single service and business object. Services can be implemented as either stateless session beans or simple Java classes if the security, transaction, and pooling features of EJB technology are not required.

As shown in the figure, each business-tier request is implemented as a separate method on the service. Process encapsulation is achieved by creating coarse-grained methods on the service that encapsulate multistep processes. All of the object-relational mapping requirements and data access requirements are implemented with custom Java code and SQL statements. You can develop methods to find business objects by any number of criteria, and a general find method accepting the actual `WHERE` clause for the SQL statement is also possible.

The primary advantage of this architecture is its flexibility. All the business-tier requirements can be met with this architecture, although some require a large amount of custom coding. Table 7.2 presents a list of the business-tier requirements and describes the capabilities and limitations of this simple service- and JDBC-based architecture in each area.

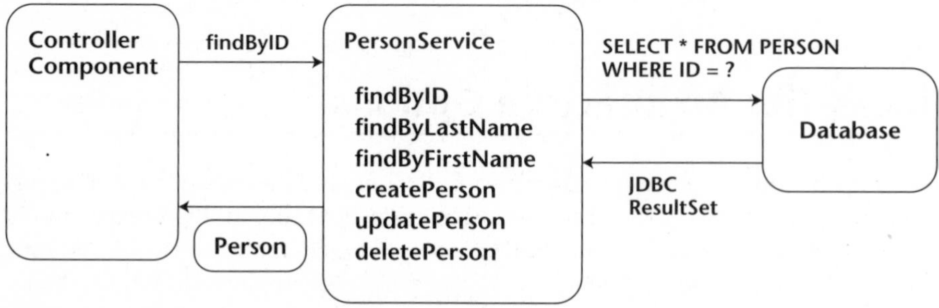

Figure 7.6 Stateless service JDBC architecture.

Table 7.2 Stateless Service JDBC Architecture Requirements Analysis

REQUIREMENT	HOW DOES ARCHITECTURE MEET REQUIREMENT
Process encapsulation	The use of stateless session beans or services provides a natural boundary for process encapsulation. Transaction control and propagation are normally handled in custom code.
Validation	Validation can be performed by business-tier components using data in value objects.
Simple O-R mapping	The SQL statements required for basic CRUD operations are coded in some component in the business tier and executed by business-tier components when necessary. JDBC results must be translated to value objects in code.
Objects spanning tables	The SQL statements can span multiple tables.
Aggregation (read operations)	Business-tier components must implement aggregation behavior in code. SQL statements can be designed to fetch shallow or deep. Value object graphs must be constructed from JDBC results.
Aggregation (other operations)	Business-tier components must implement all desired behavior for walking through the object graph and performing the proper SQL statements. The value object graph must be translated to variables in SQL statements by business-tier code.
Projection objects	The SQL statements can limit columns returned and span multiple tables. JDBC results must be translated to value objects in code.
Associations	Business-tier components must implement all desired behavior for walking through the object graph and performing the proper SQL statements. The value object graph must be translated to variables in SQL statements by business-tier code.
Inheritance	The SQL statements can implement any of the inheritance techniques described in this chapter. Value objects can inherit and share attributes.
Basic data access operations	All data access is performed using SQL statements executed through a JDBC connection.
Advanced data access operations	The SQL statement can implement any advanced feature available in JDBC and meet all of these requirements. A substantial amount of custom code will be required for most features.

(continued)

Table 7.2 *(continued)*

REQUIREMENT	HOW DOES ARCHITECTURE MEET REQUIREMENT
Audit, logging, and instrumentation	The use of stateless session beans provides a natural audit and logging point. All SQL statements can be executed through a common service or helper, providing additional logging and instrumentation opportunities.
Security	Security is limited to method-level security on the stateless session bean methods.

This architecture continues to be a very common and useful choice for many applications. You can essentially do anything in this architecture because you control, and are responsible for writing, everything in the service. You can optimize business logic and SQL queries for performance, making this architecture a good choice for high-volume OLTP applications. Recognize, however, that with this control and flexibility comes additional complexity: You must code everything yourself, including all O-R mapping and advanced data-access operations.

Note that there are many possible variations of the basic architecture. The SQL statements required for persisting objects can be defined in additional data access tiers, factory components, or in the objects themselves. JDBC `RowSet` objects can replace value objects as the mechanism for passing data between components. In all cases, however, persistence is accomplished through direct JDBC statements at some level in the architecture.

BEST PRACTICE **Consider a service- and JDBC-based architecture when the ability to optimize performance and control all business and persistence operations is more important than the added complexity.**

Our *bigrez.com* application needs to perform well and contains a relatively simple object graph, so we could very well build it using an architecture such as this without too much difficulty. Let's move on to the next candidate and see if it represents an improvement.

Stateless Services with Entity Bean Persistence

The second candidate architecture resembles the first choice in some respects. It also uses stateless services, but it replaces the JDBC-based data access logic with an entity bean layer modeling the business objects. As shown in Figure 7.7, the stateless service acts as a session façade encapsulating both business logic and the basic persistence operations for business objects.

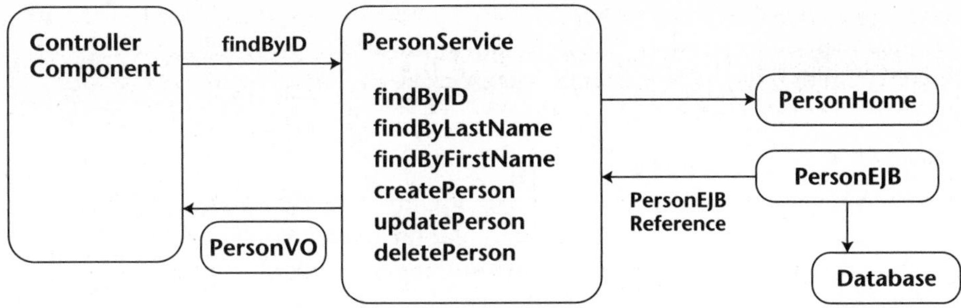

Figure 7.7 Stateless service entity-bean architecture.

Each business-tier request is implemented as a separate method on the service, meeting the process encapsulation, validation, and other business-tier requirements in the same manner as the last architecture. We've simply swapped out the JDBC-based persistence layer and replaced it with entity beans. The entity beans are responsible for all data access services and for meeting some, if not all, of the object-relational mapping requirements. The entity beans can be either bean-managed persistence (BMP) beans or container-managed persistence (CMP) beans, although CMP beans are favored in this role. Using BMP entity beans behind a stateless service requires hand-creation of JDBC code in the bean callback methods, as discussed in Chapter 6, and provides little or no opportunity to optimize the persistence logic. Using CMP beans eliminates the hand-coding of persistence logic and provides access to all of the persistence optimization capabilities of the WebLogic Server EJB container.

Note that the client or controller component requesting the business service is not allowed to communicate directly with the entity bean in this architecture, nor can entity beans be passed to services or be returned by them. A separate value object is normally used to contain the data in the related entity bean for use in communicating with the service. These value objects almost invariably contain a mirror image of the attributes in the entity bean, but they are defined to be *serializable* to enable passing by value via remote (RMI) invocations. The stateless service is normally responsible for copying data back and forth between value objects and the related entity beans in addition to performing any business logic contained in the service itself.

Table 7.3 presents a list of the business-tier requirements and describes the capabilities and limitations of this service and entity bean architecture in each area. We're assuming the use of container-managed persistence in the entity beans in this analysis to maximize the benefits of entity beans.

Clearly one big advantage of this architecture is the built-in separation between controller components and entity bean components provided by the stateless service. There are at least four resulting benefits:

Encapsulation. The callers use only the specified service-level interfaces, allowing business logic and persistence operations in the service to change without breaking client code.

Remotable. It is easy to modify interfaces defined at the service level to support remote method invocation. This provides additional deployment flexibility and may aid in the creation of separate Web services that invoke business services.

Single entry point. Transaction and security controls can be set in the service alone.

Separate value objects. Value objects can be simple mirrors of entity bean data or specialized structures useful to the presentation layer, possibly containing data from multiple beans or formatting data in some convenient manner.

Table 7.3 Stateless Service Entity Bean Architecture Requirements Analysis

REQUIREMENT	HOW DOES ARCHITECTURE MEET REQUIREMENT
Process encapsulation	The use of stateless session beans provides a natural boundary for process encapsulation. Transaction control and propagation are normally handled by the EJB container automatically.
Validation	Validation can be performed by business-tier components using data in value objects or in the entity beans themselves.
Simple O-R mapping	CMP entity bean functionality is used for simple mapping.
Objects spanning tables	CMP multiple table spanning capability is employed.
Aggregation (read operations)	CMP relationship modeling provides aggregation mapping and desired behavior. WebLogic Server field groups and relationship caching are employed to control the depth of fetches. Value object graphs must be constructed from fetched entity beans.
Aggregation (other operations)	Business-tier components must implement all desired behavior for walking through the value object graph and performing the proper entity bean operations. Data in the value object graph must be translated to set methods on CMP beans by business-tier code.
Projection objects	It is difficult to provide flexible projection capability and multitable queries with CMP entity beans. New WebLogic Server finder and `ejbSelect` features may help.

Table 7.3 *(continued)*

REQUIREMENT	HOW DOES ARCHITECTURE MEET REQUIREMENT
Associations	Business-tier components must implement all desired behavior for walking through the value object graph and performing the proper entity bean operations. The data in the value object graph must be translated to set methods on CMP beans by business-tier code.
Inheritance	It is difficult to implement inheritance in CMP entity beans because of a lack of inherited CMP behaviors. Inheritance through aggregation is possible using container-managed relationships by creating unidirectional, one-to-one associations with base classes.
Basic data access operations	Substantially all data access is performed by CMP entity beans and related finders and `ejbSelect` methods.
Advanced data access operations	The ability to implement advanced data access operations is limited to the support present in the EJB container. WebLogic Server includes support for most of the advanced operations listed in the requirements.
Audit, logging, and instrumentation	The use of stateless session beans provides a natural audit and logging point. There is limited ability to log or instrument container-managed persistence operations.
Security	Security can be implemented at the method level on services and on each entity bean at the class or method level using standard J2EE security models. WebLogic Server adds additional policy-based security features.

This architecture is very popular and useful for applications of all sizes. The CMP entity bean technology in EJB 2.0 is leveraged to provide automatically generated persistence services rivaling the best handwritten JDBC code, and the stateless services provide the encapsulation and other benefits required for a robust business-tier architecture. With the big improvements in CMP entity beans in EJB 2.0 and the new WebLogic Server-specific caching and optimization features, it is hard to beat this architecture for most J2EE applications.

BEST PRACTICE **The combination of stateless services and CMP entity beans is a very strong candidate for most J2EE applications. Consider this architecture for more complex applications requiring maximum deployment flexibility.**

This architecture is not perfect, however. There are some subtle, but significant, drawbacks inherent in the conversion from value objects to entity beans in the services. As indicated in Table 7.3, the handling of aggregations and associations can be significantly more complex when all relationships must be represented in the value object graph for the purposes of communication with the services.

As a simple example of this drawback, consider the case of a parent-child relationship between two objects and the logic required in the services to maintain these objects and their relationships. You would need methods on the stateless service to perform at least the following set of services:

- Fetching one or more parent objects using supplied criteria, and returning the parent objects plus children objects for each parent if desired by the client. The service would fetch the parent entity beans, walk through the list creating the parent value objects, optionally iterate on the children relationship fields to fetch each child entity bean, create a value object for each child, and place it in the object graph.
- Fetching one or more child objects using supplied criteria, including the parent object for each child if desired by the client. The service would fetch the child entity beans, walk through the list creating each child value object, optionally traverse the relationship to the parent entity bean, create a value object for the parent, and place it in the graph.
- Updating a parent object, including the update of any attached children objects. The service must determine the proper insert, update, or delete operation to perform for each child value object in the graph. Child value objects would require a status flag set by the client, or separate lists of child objects would have to be supplied by the client representing each desired type of operation. The service would fetch and update the parent entity bean using the data in the parent value object, then fetch and process each child object according to the required operation.

The difficulty in using value objects only intensifies when many-to-many relationships and other complex associations are modeled in the entity beans. The simple copying of value objects to entity beans becomes a nightmare very quickly if the object graph becomes large and complex. Remember that making multiple calls to the service to process portions of the object graph may not be a viable solution if you have strict requirements for transactional consistency. To ensure consistency, the service must begin and end the transaction in a single method call, so all of the required value objects, relationships, and required CRUD operations must be represented by the parameters and data structures passed to the service in that single method invocation.

Despite this limitation, the service and entity bean architecture remains a very strong candidate for many J2EE applications, including our *bigrez.com* example application. We could stop here and simply build the application using this architecture, and no one would be likely to argue with the decision. We want to examine one additional candidate, however, and see if there is some way to eliminate the minor drawbacks of this architecture and truly leverage the built-in persistence services defined in the CMP entity beans.

Stateless Services, Entity Beans, and Direct Interaction

The final candidate architecture builds on the previous service and entity bean architecture by combining the use of stateless services, entity bean persistence, and the direct interaction of client and presentation-tier controller components with the entity bean components when performing certain operations. The goal is to reduce or eliminate the need for value objects and eliminate the creation of methods in the service that mirror the basic persistence and relationship-handling methods already present in the entity beans themselves.

For example, the simple fetch operation depicted in Figure 7.8 is performed by the controller component directly using the home interface for the entity bean. This request returns a reference to the entity bean, and the controller component interrogates the bean directly for its data using get methods on the bean's local interface.

As described in Chapter 3, all access to the entity bean must be done in a transaction started by the controller component to avoid multiple loads from the database in a noncached environment. Clearly, the controller component should also be collocated in the same instance of WebLogic Server to avoid remote communication with the entity bean as the individual get methods are called on the bean to retrieve its contents. These two drawbacks represent the largest arguments against the use of direct interaction, and they are not minor drawbacks, but let's examine what we gain in this architecture before we jump to any conclusions.

Recognize that this architecture does not eliminate stateless services completely. Business logic and multiple-step processes are still placed in stateless services to provide process encapsulation and other benefits described previously. Even when employing a service in this way, however, the use of value objects for parameters and return types is discouraged in favor of entity bean references. Figure 7.8 does not include a service because in the case of the `PersonService` depicted in Figures 7.6 and 7.7, there were no methods defined on the service that could not be performed directly using home-interface finder methods or direct interaction with the entity bean.

Table 7.4 presents a list of the business-tier requirements and describes the capabilities and limitations of this combined service, entity bean, and direct interaction architecture in each area.

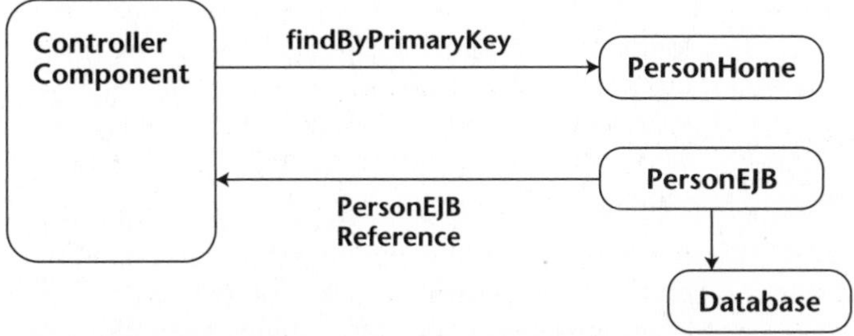

Figure 7.8 Direct interaction eliminates value objects.

Table 7.4 Combined Architecture Requirements Analysis

REQUIREMENT	HOW DOES ARCHITECTURE MEET REQUIREMENT
Process encapsulation	The use of stateless session beans provides a natural boundary for process encapsulation. The EJB container normally handles transaction control and propagation automatically.
Validation	Validation can be performed by business-tier components using data in the entity beans or in the entity beans themselves.
Simple O-R mapping	CMP entity bean functionality is used for simple mapping.
Objects spanning tables	CMP multiple-table spanning capability is employed.
Aggregation (read operations)	CMP relationship modeling provides aggregation mapping and desired behavior. WebLogic Server field groups and relationship caching are employed to control the depth of fetches. Collections of parent bean references are returned to the caller. WebLogic Server automatically provides lazy fetching logic as the caller traverses relationships.
Aggregation (other operations)	Modifications made to any child beans or relationships are automatically persisted at the end of the transaction by WebLogic Server CMP facilities. No business-tier logic is required to identify the required operations or walk value object graphs.
Projection objects	It is difficult to provide flexible projection capability and multitable queries with CMP entity beans. New WebLogic Server finder and `ejbSelect` features may help.
Associations	Modifications made to any relationships are automatically persisted at the end of the transaction by WebLogic Server CMP facilities. No business-tier logic is required to identify the required operations or walk value object graphs.
Inheritance	It is difficult to implement inheritance in CMP entity beans because of a lack of inherited CMP behaviors. Inheritance through aggregation is possible using container-managed relationships by creating unidirectional, one-to-one associations with base classes.

Table 7.4 *(continued)*

REQUIREMENT	HOW DOES ARCHITECTURE MEET REQUIREMENT
Basic data access operations	Substantially all data access is performed by CMP entity beans and related finders and `ejbSelect` methods.
Advanced data access operations	The ability to implement advanced data-access operations is limited to the support present in the EJB container. WebLogic Server includes support for most of the advanced operations listed in the requirements.
Audit, logging, and instrumentation	The use of stateless session beans provides a natural audit and logging point. There is limited ability to log or instrument container-managed persistence operations.
Security	Security can be implemented at the method level on service and on each entity bean at the class or method level using standard J2EE security models. WebLogic Server adds more policy-based security features.

This table is very similar to Table 7.3 because the architectures are, in fact, very similar. The primary benefit of direct interaction with entity beans is in the aggregation and association object-relational mapping requirements. There is no value object graph to walk or complex business logic to code in order to determine the proper set of entity beans to enlist in the transaction and the proper set of operations to perform. Whatever changes were made to the entity beans through their own attribute and relationship set methods will be persisted by the CMP facilities at the end of the transaction. That, in a nutshell, is the benefit we are after.

What about the four advantages listed in the previous section? Let's review them and see how direct interaction stacks up:

Encapsulation. Callers continue to be separated from business and persistence operations using interfaces, although in this architecture these interfaces are located in services, home interfaces, and bean interfaces. You can also encapsulate all operations in services as long as entity bean references are returned instead of value objects.

Remotable. Entity bean home interfaces, bean interfaces, and services that return entity bean references are not remotable through simple declarative techniques. Web applications and EJB components must be collocated in the same enterprise application, and separate interfaces supporting remote invocation and pass-by-value semantics must be created if required.

Single entry point. Transaction and security controls must be set in the service and in all entity beans accessed by controllers or other client code.

Separate value objects. Specialized value objects are still possible, if desired, although the direct interaction approach avoids the use of value objects for normal operations. Entity beans can easily be extended to include methods that return formatted data or simulate flattened projection objects.

Did we gain enough benefit in the use of direct interaction to offset the drawbacks? We've eliminated value objects and their constant copying and creation, dramatically simplified the services layer by eliminating all methods related to persistence and object-relational mapping, and leveraged all of the lazy-instantiation and caching features in WebLogic Server to the fullest extent. Not too shabby.

Obviously, the appropriateness of this architecture depends largely on the complexity of the object model and the related benefits provided by the direct interaction approach. Recognize that EJB 2.0 introduced many of the new features being leveraged by this architecture, so it is not surprising that the industry has not examined direct interaction as a viable alternative to value objects prior to EJB 2.0. Now that relationships are handled very efficiently in the entity beans themselves, however, it deserves some attention.

BEST PRACTICE **Consider the use of direct interaction with entity beans in applications that can leverage local interfaces and the improved aggregation and association handling afforded by this architecture.**

Chosen Architecture for bigrez.com

We've chosen to implement the *bigrez.com* application using a combination of stateless services, value objects, and direct interaction with entity bean components. We'll introduce a handful of stateless session beans and use them to encapsulate complex or multistep business processes, but we will allow controller components to interact directly with the entity beans for most queries, data retrieval, and data update operations.

As shown in Figure 7.9, the *bigrez.com* application requires a fair number of business objects and relationships to model the business domain. Implementing all of the business-tier requirements for this object model using only stateless services and value objects would be possible, of course, but the chosen design allows us to explore the benefits of direct interaction for a realistic object model to gain additional insight.

We've introduced three stateless session beans (`InventorySessionBean`, `OfferSessionBean`, and `ReservationSessionBean`) and implemented eight CMP entity beans representing the primary business objects in the object model. There are also a variety of helper classes, utility classes, base classes, and a handful of value objects. The value objects are used to encapsulate data for communication with the session beans in certain operations.

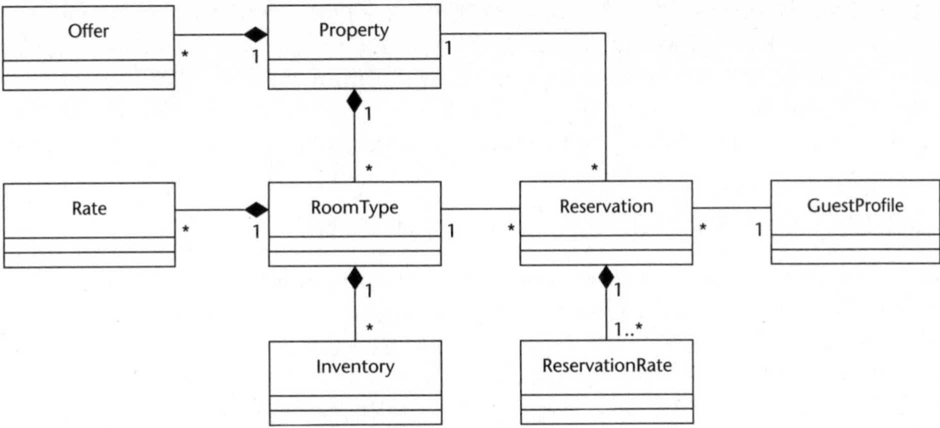

Figure 7.9 Object model for bigrez.com application.

One thing you might note about the components in this application is the lack of administration-related business-tier components. All of the property-related data can be edited through the administration Web site, as discussed in Chapter 4, but very few business-tier components are required to support this functionality. This is a direct result of the choice of direct interaction with entity beans for the majority of persistence behaviors. Most administration Web components do not require stateless session beans and other business-tier components to find, create, read, update, or delete business objects or their relationships because these operations are performed directly through the entity bean interfaces.

The remainder of this chapter will walk through the construction of a number of these business-tier components to highlight choices made, techniques used, and best practices that can be applied to your development efforts.

EJB Construction Options

Once you have chosen your business-tier architecture and identified the EJB components required for your application, it is time to construct the components. What is the best way to build EJB components? Ask any 10 J2EE programmers and you're likely to get 10 different answers.

It is both a strength and a weakness of J2EE that many different techniques and tools are available for the construction, configuration, and packaging of EJB components. Some integrated development environments, for example, provide a rich GUI-based set of tools for defining, building, and deploying EJB components. Other tools such as XDoclet and EJBGen are file-based and provide techniques more suitable for command-line build processes. Some tools are very expensive, while others are free or included in WebLogic Server product. The trick is to find a tool or technique that fits in your budget and supports your specific project needs.

A complete discussion of all tools available in the J2EE community is beyond the scope of this book and would, in any case, be rendered quickly out of date by advances in the capability and EJB-version support of each tool or product. We'll concentrate instead on three candidate techniques for building EJB components in WebLogic Server that support many of the EJB 2.0 and WebLogic Server-specific features and capabilities.

Manual Construction and Configuration

The first option, manual construction and configuration, simply refers to the manual creation and editing of all Java source files and XML descriptor files required for the EJB components in your project. Table 7.5 represents the minimum set of files and descriptors for a simple J2EE application containing two entity beans, `PersonBean` and `AddressBean`, and a single stateless session bean, `PersonSessionBean`.

Although Table 7.5 illustrates the typical requirement of at least three to five Java source files for each EJB component, it does not tell the whole story. The three descriptor files, `ejb-jar.xml`, `weblogic-ejb-jar.xml`, and `weblogic-cmp-rdbms-jar.xml`, grow substantially with each additional EJB component, and they represent a significant development and maintenance effort. Even with a good XML editor, the proper construction of descriptor files can become quite tedious and error-prone for typical applications. The manual creation of descriptors becomes all but impossible when complex container-managed relationships exist between EJB components in the application.

Table 7.5 Required Files for Simple EJB Application

SOURCE FILE	DESCRIPTION
`PersonBean.java`	Person entity bean class file
`PersonLocal.java`	Person local interface file
`PersonHomeLocal.java`	Person home local interface file
`AddressBean.java`	Address entity bean class file
`AddressLocal.java`	Address local interface file
`AddressHomeLocal.java`	Address home local interface file
`PersonSessionBean.java`	Person session bean class file
`PersonSessionLocal.java`	Person session local interface file
`PersonSessionRemote.java`	Person session remote interface file
`PersonSessionHomeLocal.java`	Person session home local interface file
`PersonSessionHomeRemote.java`	Person session home remote interface file
`ejb-jar.xml`	Standard EJB descriptor file
`weblogic-ejb-jar.xml`	WebLogic EJB descriptor file
`weblogic-cmp-rdbms-jar.xml`	WebLogic CMP EJB descriptor file

BEST PRACTICE Manual construction techniques may be suitable during the learning process to emphasize all of the required files, formats, and descriptor elements. Avoid manual construction for production applications if a suitable tool is available.

The next two sections discuss tools provided by WebLogic Server to improve the EJB construction process.

Using WebLogic Builder Utility

The WebLogic Server installation provides a utility called WebLogic Builder that provides a GUI-based technique for constructing the descriptor files for a set of EJB components. The developer is still responsible for creating all Java source files for each EJB component, but the three XML descriptor files listed in Table 7.5 are then created using the WebLogic Builder utility.

To use WebLogic Builder, construct the required Java source files by hand and compile them to a `build` directory or other staging area. Run WebLogic Builder from the Start menu in Windows or by starting the utility from the command line using the `startWLBuilder` script. The utility will create an initial set of descriptors by interrogating the EJB class files in the staging area, and then it will allow you to modify all descriptor information in the utility itself, avoiding hand-editing of the descriptor files.

Once the configuration is complete, use the `Save` menu option to write the generated descriptor elements to the `build/META-INF` directory for subsequent compilation and packaging. The main menu also provides the option to view the current descriptors as XML, although editing the XML directly to make desired changes is not allowed. Changes made to descriptor files between executions of WebLogic Builder will be picked up and reflected in the configuration display as long as the features present in the descriptors are supported by the utility. See the online documentation at http://edocs.bea.com/wls/docs81/wlbuilder/index.html for details on supported and unsupported elements in descriptors.

Finally, WebLogic Builder provides a mechanism for executing the EJB compiler to package the resulting EJB components and the ability to deploy the components to a running instance of WebLogic Server.

WebLogic Builder obviously represents an improvement over creating descriptor elements manually, especially for developers just coming up to speed with EJB and WebLogic Server-specific features. Unfortunately, the need to hand-code all Java source files for the EJB components and the difficulty inherent in keeping generated files in synch with source files as changes are made limit its usefulness.

BEST PRACTICE Consider using WebLogic Builder during the learning process to see how advanced EJB and WebLogic Server features are implemented in the descriptors.

The descriptor generation utility embedded in the WebLogic Builder code is available from the command line as a stand-alone utility as well. Create a jar file containing the compiled EJB classes, or compile them to a specific build directory structure, and use the following command:

```
java weblogic.marathon.ddinit.EJBInit <jar file or build directory>
```

Using the WebLogic EJBGen Utility

The final construction technique we'll examine in this text is the EJBGen utility packaged with WebLogic Server. The EJBGen utility generates selected EJB component source files and all required descriptor files using only the EJB bean class file. In other words, you write one Java source file per EJB component, and EJBGen creates everything else. The simple example represented in Table 7.5 now requires the manual construction of only three source files: `PersonBean.java`, `AddressBean.java`, and `PersonSessionBean.java`.

How can any tool accurately create all of the local, home, and remote interface files, standard descriptor elements, WebLogic Server-specific descriptor elements, CMP mapping information, primary key classes, and other files for an EJB component from the bean class file alone? The answer is that it can't, of course, without some help. In the case of EJBGen, this help is provided by the developer in the form of specially formatted Javadoc tags placed in the bean class file to control the creation of all of the supporting files and descriptors.

The EJBGen Javadoc tags come in two basic forms: class-level tags and method-level tags.

Class-Level EJBGen Tags

Class-level tags are used to configure attributes of the EJB component at the class level. Examples include the local or remote JNDI name, pool and caching information, finder methods, and the presence of relationships with other beans. Class-level tags are placed at the top of the bean class in the normal class-level Javadoc location, as shown in this simple example for the `PersonSessionBean` stateless session bean component:

```
package mastering.weblogic.ch07.example1.ejb;

import javax.ejb.*;
import javax.naming.*;

/**
 * @ejbgen:session
 *    ejb-name = PersonSessionEJB
 *    default-transaction = Required
 *    max-beans-in-free-pool = 500
 *
 * @ejbgen:jndi-name
 *    local = PersonSessionHomeLocal
 *    remote = PersonSessionHomeRemote
 *
```

```
 */
public class PersonSessionBean
    extends mastering.weblogic.ch07.example1.ejb.base.BaseSession
{
...
}
```

Entity beans use class-level tags to define database resources, table names, finders, and container-managed relationships in a similar manner:

```
package mastering.weblogic.ch07.example1.ejb;

import java.util.Collection;
import javax.ejb.EntityContext;
import javax.ejb.EJBException;
import javax.ejb.FinderException;

/**
 * @ejbgen:entity
 *   ejb-name = PersonEJB
 *   default-transaction = Required
 *   prim-key-class = java.lang.Integer
 *   data-source-name = MasteringDataSource
 *   table-name = PERSON
 *   max-beans-in-cache = 1000
 *
 * @ejbgen:jndi-name
 *   local = PersonHomeLocal
 *
 * @ejbgen:finder
 *   signature="Collection findByLastName(java.lang.String lastname)"
 *   ejb-ql =
 *     "SELECT OBJECT(o) FROM PersonEJB as o WHERE o.lastName LIKE ?1"
 *
 * @ejbgen:finder
 *   signature="Collection findByFirstName(java.lang.String firstname)"
 *   ejb-ql =
 *     "SELECT OBJECT(o) FROM PersonEJB as o WHERE o.firstName LIKE ?1"
 *
 * @ejbgen:relation
 *   name = Person-Addresses
 *   target-ejb = AddressEJB
 *   multiplicity = one
 *   cmr-field = addresses
 *
 */
public abstract class PersonBean
    extends mastering.weblogic.ch07.example1.ejb.base.BaseEntity
{
...
}
```

See the online documentation at http://edocs.bea.com/wls/docs81/ejb/EJB_tools.html for a complete list of class-level EJBGen tags. Most tag names follow the naming convention of their respective descriptor elements.

Tag values may be hard-coded in the tags, as shown in the earlier code listings, or may be placed in properties files with placeholders in the source files. For example, the `max-beans-in-cache` value could be defined using the placeholder `cachesize`:

```
* @ejbgen:entity
*    ejb-name = PersonEJB
*    ...
*    max-beans-in-cache = ${cachesize}
```

`cachesize` would then be defined in a properties file:

```
#
# Example ejbgen property file
#

cachesize = 1000
```

Include `-propertyFile ejbgen.properties` in the command line used to invoke EJBGen to enable this feature.

BEST PRACTICE **Use parameter substitution throughout class-level EJBGen tags to provide an easy way to change common settings and names without touching the source files.**

Method-Level EJBGen Tags

Method-level tags are used to configure descriptor elements and interface classes at the individual method level. The most common method-level tags control the presence of a bean method in one or more of the EJB interface classes and the mapping of CMP fields to database columns.

For example, a stateless session bean must declare which methods defined in the bean class should be published to the remote and local interfaces for the bean. In our simple example there is only one method, `sayHello()`, and we've configured EJB-Gen to place this method on both the local and remote interfaces:

```
/**
 * @ejbgen:local-method
 * @ejbgen:remote-method
 */
public void sayHello() throws EJBException
{
    LOG.info("Hello from PersonSessionBean!");
}
```

The EJBGen utility will now include a declaration for this method in the generated interface files PersonSessionLocal.java and PersonSessionRemote.java.

Entity beans using container-managed persistence (CMP) define both the interface information and the mapping from bean attributes to database columns with method-level tags:

```
/**
 * @ejbgen:cmp-field column = FIRSTNAME
 * @ejbgen:local-method
 */
public abstract String getFirstName();
/** @ejbgen:local-method */
public abstract void setFirstName(String pFirstName);
```

Both getFirstName() and setFirstName() will be included in the generated interface file PersonLocal.java, and appropriate elements will be created to map the firstName attribute to the FIRSTNAME column in the database table defined at the class level.

CMP entity beans with container-managed relationships identify the abstract get and set methods associated with the relationships:

```
/**
 * @ejbgen:cmr-field
 * @ejbgen:local-method
 */
public abstract java.util.Collection getAddresses();
/** @ejbgen:local-method */
public abstract void setAddresses(java.util.Collection addresses);
```

These simple method-level tags, combined with the ejbgen:relation class-level tags in both components, provide enough information for EJBGen to create all of the required descriptor code in ejb-jar.xml and weblogic-cmp-rdbms-jar.xml automatically to define the relationship for the CMP process.

Invoking the EJBGen Utility

The EJBGen utility is a *Doclet* intended for use with the Javadoc processor built in to the Java development environment. To invoke EJBGen from the command line, run javadoc with the following parameters:

```
javadoc
  -docletpath ejbgen.jar
  -doclet weblogic.tools.ejbgen.EJBGen
  <source file or directory>
```

There are many additional command-line parameters for controlling the location of generated files, naming conventions for generated Java classes, and many other features. See the online documentation for a complete list.

One important command-line parameter required in the current release of EJBGen is the version-control parameter, normally `-wls7` or `-wls81`. This parameter forces the creation of WebLogic Server-specific descriptor files using the correct WebLogic Server schemas, thereby allowing all of the new caching and concurrency features.

The example command line assumes that `ejbgen.jar` is located in the current directory. Because the EJBGen utility is included in the standard `weblogic.jar` archive in `/server/lib`, the `-docletpath` could point to that archive file rather than a stand-alone copy of `ejbgen.jar`:

```
javadoc -docletpath %WL_HOME%\server\lib\weblogic.jar ...
```

Because the tool is constantly undergoing revision and improvements, the EJBGen version packaged with WebLogic Server may not be sufficient for your particular requirements. Cedric Beust, one of the WebLogic Server engineers and the creator of the EJBGen utility, makes the latest version available at his Web site, http://www.beust.com/ejbgen, and this version may be downloaded and used in place of the version in `weblogic.jar`. There is also an active mailing list for EJBGen. Now that EJBGen is an officially supported part of WebLogic Server 8.1, however, we expect that the included version will be kept up to date as new versions of the product are released. WebLogic Workshop 8.1 also fully supports EJBGen-based EJB development in that environment.

The EJBGen utility may also be invoked from within Ant build scripts using either `javadoc` tasks or `exec` tasks with appropriate command-line arguments. The downloadable example code for *bigrez.com* includes a `build.xml` file with an `ejbgen` task to create all of the EJB components for the example.

If it is not already obvious, let's make it clear: EJBGen is a very powerful, useful utility that provides a tremendous amount of functionality and flexibility. We'll use it extensively on *bigrez.com*, and we highly recommend it for your WebLogic Server EJB development efforts.

BEST PRACTICE The EJBGen utility provides a very powerful technique for building EJB applications and should be considered by every new EJB development effort.

Construction of Business-Tier Components

The *bigrez.com* business tier contains a fair number of entity beans, three stateless session beans, and a single message-driven bean. This section will examine each of these types of beans and highlight key aspects of their design and construction.

Construction of Entity Beans

The top-level parent bean in the property-related set of entity beans is the `PropertyBean` component. This bean contains basic property information as well as container-managed relationships to all of the room, rate, offer, and reservation beans associated with the property. Please download the `PropertyBean.java` bean class file from http://www.wiley.com/compbooks/masteringweblogic and examine it before proceeding.

There are a number of sections to note in this class file. First, the class-level EJBGen tags at the top of the file specify required class-level information for the EJB descriptor files, including the name of the JDBC `DataSource`, the table name, automatic key-generation information, and the JNDI name to use for the local home interface:

```
/**
 * @ejbgen:entity
 *   ejb-name = PropertyEJB
 *   prim-key-class = java.lang.Integer
 *   data-source-name = BigRezDataSource
 *   table-name = PROPERTY
 *   default-transaction = Required
 *
 * @ejbgen:jndi-name
 *   local = PropertyHomeLocal
 *
 * @ejbgen:automatic-key-generation
 *   type = NAMED_SEQUENCE_TABLE
 *   name = COMMON_SEQUENCE
 *   cache-size = 1
```

Note that we've chosen to hard-code this information directly in the tag attributes rather than use a properties file for substitutions in order to keep the example simple and readable. The substitution capability, discussed previously in this chapter, is very powerful and should be used in your applications.

The next section of the bean class file defines a set of finder methods and their underlying EJB-QL definitions using `ejbgen:finder` tags:

```
 * @ejbgen:finder
 *   signature = "Collection findAll()"
 *   ejb-ql = "SELECT OBJECT(o) FROM PropertyEJB as o"
 *
 * @ejbgen:finder
 *   signature = "Collection findByCity(java.lang.String city)"
 *   ejb-ql = "SELECT OBJECT(o) FROM PropertyEJB o WHERE o.city = ?1"
...
```

These tags cause EJBGen to create appropriate method declarations in the home interface file and `ejb-ql` entries in the `ejb-jar.xml` descriptor file for each finder method. Services, clients, and controller objects can execute these finder methods to retrieve collections matching `PersonBean` references using the home interface:

```
String city = ...;
PropertyHomeLocal propertyhome =
    (PropertyHomeLocal)Locator.getHome("PropertyHomeLocal");
Collection props = propertyhome.findByCity(city);
```

The `Locator` class, described in detail in Chapter 5, is a simple utility class used by *bigrez.com* to encapsulate the JNDI lookup process for home interfaces and entity bean instances. The class implements a variety of the EJBHomeFactory design pattern by caching home references and providing a reflection-based technique for looking up entity beans by primary key with a single method invocation. Examine the `Locator.java` file in the downloadable example code to see how these functions are implemented if you are curious.

The next section of `PropertyBean.java` completes the class-level EJBGen tags by defining the relationships between the `Property` and other beans in the application:

```
 * @ejbgen:relation
 *   name = Property-Reservations
 *   target-ejb = ReservationEJB
 *   multiplicity = one
 *   cmr-field = reservations
 *
 * @ejbgen:relation
 *   name = Property-RoomTypes
 *   target-ejb = RoomTypeEJB
 *   multiplicity = one
 *   cmr-field = roomTypes
 *
 * @ejbgen:relation
 *   name = Property-Offers
 *   target-ejb = OfferEJB
 *   multiplicity = one
 *   cmr-field = offers
 *
 */
```

Each relationship is named, and the target EJB component, source-side multiplicity, and container-managed relationship (CMR) field name are specified to complete the definition. Recognize that the multiplicity specified in this tag is the `Property` multiplicity rather than the target EJB's multiplicity. Each target bean class file will have a corresponding `ejbgen:relation` tag with the same relationship name and appropriate attributes defining that end of the relationship. For example, the one-to-many, bidirectional relationship between `Property` and `RoomType` requires a corresponding `ejbgen:relation` tag on the `RoomTypeBean` class file:

```
 * @ejbgen:relation
 *   name = Property-RoomTypes
 *   target-ejb = PropertyEJB
 *   multiplicity = many
 *   cmr-field = property
 *   fk-column = PROPERTY_ID
 *   cascade-delete = true
```

This tag in `RoomTypeBean` also specifies the foreign-key column name because the relationship is defined in the database using a parent foreign key in the child table, in this case PROPERTY_ID. The cascade-delete attribute is also set in this child class file, activating the container-based cascade-delete logic discussed in Chapter 6.

Continuing in the PropertyBean class file, the next section defines the class as a subclass of our simple base class, BaseEntity, and provides the required ejbCreate() and ejbPostCreate() methods. As discussed in Chapter 6, attributes are normally set in ejbCreate() and relationships are set in ejbPostCreate(), a practice we've followed in this class.

Following these create-related methods is a series of get and set methods for each of the container-managed attributes in the class. Each set of methods is prefixed by the appropriate EJBGen tags to declare the desired interface on which to place the methods, whether the attribute is part of the primary key, and what database column the attribute maps to in the persistent store. For example, consider the section for the description attribute:

```
/**
 * @ejbgen:cmp-field column = DESCRIPTION
 * @ejbgen:local-method
 */
public abstract String getDescription();
/** @ejbgen:local-method */
public abstract void setDescription(String description);
```

This specifies that both getDescription() and setDescription() should be placed in the EJB's local interface, and it defines the column in the database table to be DESCRIPTION.

After the get and set methods for the simple container-managed attributes come the methods for accessing and modifying the CMR fields:

```
/**
 * @ejbgen:cmr-field
 * @ejbgen:local-method
 */
public abstract Collection getReservations();
/** @ejbgen:local-method */
public abstract void setReservations(Collection reservations);

/**
 * @ejbgen:cmr-field
 * @ejbgen:local-method
 */
public abstract Collection getRoomTypes();
/** @ejbgen:local-method */
public abstract void setRoomTypes(Collection roomtypes);

...
```

Because the ejbgen:relation tag at the top of the class file declared a cmr-field attribute for each relation, there must be a corresponding get and set method for each one. As before, the EJBGen tags in front of each method define the interface on which to place the get or set method—in this case, the EJB's local interface.

The bean class also includes special methods useful for returning the contents of relationships in a new, normal collection object rather than returning the internal container-managed collection directly to the caller. These methods are declared to return a `Collection` and are placed on the local interface for the bean:

```
/**
 * @ejbgen:local-method
 */
public Collection getRoomTypesReadOnly()
{
    return makeReadOnlyList(getRoomTypes());
}
```

The `makeReadOnlyList()` method, defined in `BaseEntity.java`, simply iterates through the relationship collection and creates a normal `ArrayList` collection containing the references:

```
protected Collection makeReadOnlyList(Collection cmrlist)
{
    Collection rolist = new ArrayList();
    Iterator i = cmrlist.iterator();
    while (i.hasNext()) {
        rolist.add(i.next());
    }
    return rolist;
}
```

A technique similar to this will be employed in some beans to create and return a sorted collection of bean references from a container-managed relationship. Unless these relationship collections are sorted in memory, the results will be returned in a nondeterministic manner based on the database access path for the underlying query.

Finally, two `ejbHome` methods are defined to fetch lists of valid state codes and city names as a crude but effective way to fill the associated drop-lists in the property search page. These methods use a custom `SQLHelper` utility class to execute simple SQL statements and return collections of strings.

That's all there is to the `PropertyBean` class file. The EJBGen utility uses this file to create the `PropertyLocal` interface class, the `PropertyHomeLocal` home interface class, and all of the `ejb-jar.xml`, `weblogic-ejb-jar.xml`, and `weblogic-cmp-rdbms-jar.xml` descriptor elements related to this bean. All of the other entity beans are constructed in the same manner and use many of the same tags and techniques.

The downloadable example code includes full listings of all entity beans in the *bigrez.com* example application. Many additional examples of relationships and other entity bean features are contained in these bean files, but space does not permit us to cover them in detail.

Construction of Session Beans

The *bigrez.com* application uses a combination of entity beans and stateless session beans to implement the business tier. In this section, we will examine some of the key stateless session beans used to encapsulate complex business logic. Because we are using direct interaction between the controller components and the entity beans for most query, data retrieval, and data update logic, these stateless session beans do not include create, read, update, and delete methods.

There are three stateless session beans, or services, in the *bigrez.com* application. The first is the `InventorySessionBean`, a service encapsulating logic for reading and updating inventory information. The methods in this service are used by the administration Web site to view and manage inventory. Most of these methods accept or return collections of `Inventory` entity bean references, consistent with the direct interaction approach.

The second service is the `OfferSessionBean`, a stateless session bean encapsulating the business logic for reading and ordering the targeted offers displayed to the user depending on their current search criteria or property selection. The main method in this service, `getOffersForDisplay()`, returns a collection of local references to `OfferBean` objects rather than a set of value objects. The caller then iterates through this collection and retrieves the offer information from each entity bean directly.

The third service is the `ReservationSessionBean`, a stateless session bean encapsulating complex business logic associated with rate and availability search functions and the creation of the final reservation object at the end of the process. Like the other session beans, the methods on `ReservationSessionBean` interact with entity bean home interfaces to perform the desired business logic, accepting and returning local references in many cases.

Please examine these session beans in the downloadable example code. A fair amount of complex business logic is encapsulated in these beans, a clear argument for the use of stateless session beans in these particular cases. Logic this complex does not belong in presentation-tier components. Space does not permit a complete walk-through of the code, but the following list presents key techniques and highlights for the `ReservationSessionBean`:

- EJBGen tags at the top of the bean class file are used to define JNDI names and class-level descriptor information. Method-level EJBGen tags are used to indicate which methods should appear on local and remote interfaces.
- The `calculateRates()` method has a `RoomType` entity bean reference as a parameter, along with simple `Date` parameters, and returns a collection of `ReservationRateInfo` value objects. Because we are requiring collocation of the Web application and EJB components in a single `.ear` file, there is no reason to avoid passing entity beans as parameters in service methods.
- The `createReservation()` method, on the other hand, uses a `ReservationInfo` value object as the input parameter, and it constructs and returns a `Reservation` entity bean to the caller as the result of the method. Again, the choice of parameters and return types is made freely, without requiring value objects due to deployment limitations.

- The `createReservation()` method encapsulates a very complex series of steps required to update inventory, create the reservation record in the database, and post a message to an outbound email JMS queue. A variety of entity beans are fetched, created, and updated in this process, demonstrating the ability to perform this activity without resorting to JDBC SQL statements or other techniques.

As long and complex as the `ReservationSessionBean` and the other two session beans are, they represent the bulk of all business-tier coding required for the *bigrez.com* example application. The 600 or so lines of code in these three services represent only business logic with no data access or other services. All persistence services and object-relational mapping are performed by the container-managed entity beans themselves. Implementing the pure session façade approach with value objects would require hundreds, if not thousands, of lines of code in the services to implement all of the query, data retrieval, data manipulation, and object-relational mapping functions required for the simple *bigrez.com* object graph. Direct interaction results in significantly smaller session beans, as evidenced by this example.

Construction of Message-Driven Beans

The *bigrez.com* application includes a simple message-driven bean, `EmailProcessorBean`, used to create outbound emails to customers containing reservation information. Class-level `ejbgen` tags are used to define the required EJB parameters for the bean:

```
/**
 * @ejbgen:message-driven
 *   ejb-name = EmailProcessorEJB
 *   destination-jndi-name = BigRezEmailQueue
 *   destination-type = javax.jms.Queue
 *   initial-beans-in-free-pool = 5
 *   max-beans-in-free-pool = 10
 *   acknowledge-mode = auto-acknowledge
 *   transaction-type = Container
 *
 * @ejbgen:resource-ref
 *   name = jms/BigRezEmailSession
 *   jndi-name = BigRezEmailSession
 *   type = javax.mail.Session
 *   auth = Container
 */
```

The `onMessage()` method simply retrieves the email content in the JMS `MapMessage` and creates the outbound email using standard JavaMail interfaces:

```
public void onMessage(javax.jms.Message message)
{
    try {
        LOG.info("EmailProcessorBean::onMessage() called..");
```

```
            MapMessage emailMsg = (MapMessage)message;
            String emailFrom = "reservations@bigrez.com";
            String emailTo = emailMsg.getString("TO");
            String emailSubject = emailMsg.getString("SUBJECT");
            String emailContent = emailMsg.getString("CONTENT");
            LOG.info("Preparing email for "+emailTo+
                     " with subject "+emailSubject);
            javax.mail.Session session = (javax.mail.Session)
                jndiContext.lookup("java:comp/env/jms/BigRezEmailSession");
            javax.mail.Message msg = new MimeMessage(session);
            msg.setFrom(new InternetAddress(emailFrom));
            msg.setRecipient(javax.mail.Message.RecipientType.TO,
                             new InternetAddress(emailTo));
            msg.setSubject(emailSubject);
            msg.setSentDate(new Date());
            msg.setContent(emailContent, "text/plain");
            Transport.send(msg);
            LOG.info("onMessage complete");
        }
        catch (JMSException e) {
            LOG.error("JMSException sending email confirmation", e);
            ejbContext.setRollbackOnly();
        }
        catch (NamingException e) {
            LOG.error("NamingException sending email confirmation", e);
            ejbContext.setRollbackOnly();
        }
        catch (MessagingException e) {
            LOG.error("MessagingException sending email confirmation", e);
            ejbContext.setRollbackOnly();
        }
    }
```

We've now completed our discussion of the design and construction of the *bigrez.com* business tier. Noticeably absent from this section is any mention of the EJB-related deployment descriptors. Because we are using EJBGen we never create or hand-edit these descriptors. Good riddance!

Chapter Review

This chapter examined the process for selecting a business-tier architecture and constructing the business-tier components for the *bigrez.com* example application. Important business-tier requirements were identified, candidate architectures were outlined and mapped against the requirements, and a specific architecture was chosen for the example application. The chosen architecture combined the encapsulation benefits of a stateless service-based architecture with direct manipulation of container-managed entity beans to eliminate significant design and coding complexity in the services.

Three possible EJB construction techniques were then examined and the EJBGen tool selected for our effort. The required entity bean and stateless session bean components for the *bigrez.com* application were identified, and key components were examined in detail to illustrate the use of EJBGen to construct interface files and deployment descriptors.

In the next chapter, we'll discuss packaging and deploying this application using WebLogic Server-specific tools and techniques.

CHAPTER

8

Packaging and Deploying WebLogic EJB Applications

This chapter discusses the steps required to package and deploy WebLogic Server EJB applications. Consistent with the intermediate to advanced nature of this book, we assume that you have some knowledge of the J2EE specification and the required elements in a well-structured EJB application. We also assume that you have a basic level of experience with the Ant build tool provided by the Apache Software Foundation.

Figure 8.1 presents the basic process for creating EJB archive files and the options available for packaging and deploying EJB applications using WebLogic Server. This chapter discusses each of these steps, compares the packaging and deployment options available, identifies best practices, and walks through the packaging and deployment of the *bigrez.com* application.

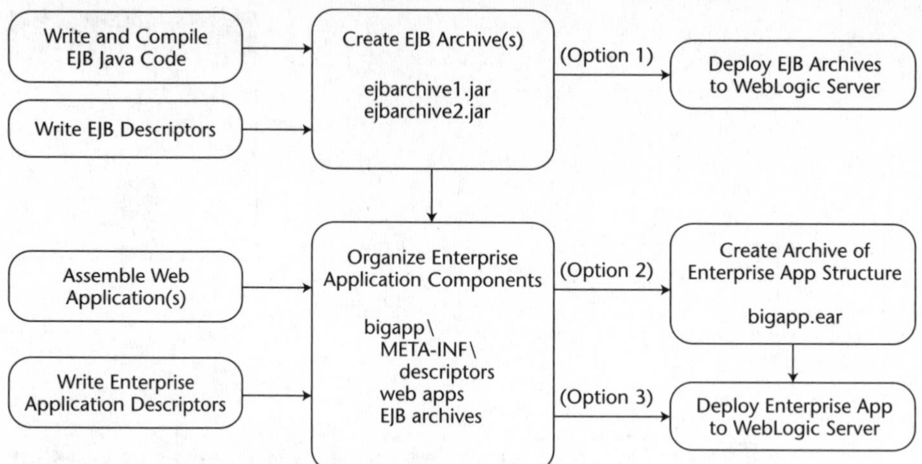

Figure 8.1 Basic packaging and deployment process.

Creating an EJB Archive File

The first step, creating an EJB archive file, is well documented in other EJB references and should be familiar to you. To review the process: EJB components are developed as separate Java source files defining the implementation, interfaces, and home interfaces. As shown in Figure 8.2, these individual files must be compiled using the standard Java compiler, combined with XML descriptors defining key bean attributes and behaviors, and processed through the WebLogic Server EJB compiler to create the archive file.

This book is not intended to be a primer, introduction, or reference for general EJB topics, so we will not spend time reviewing the details of the standard EJB descriptor files or the EJB compilation process. If you are unfamiliar with the basics of EJB, we suggest you consult one of the EJB references listed at the beginning of Chapter 6.

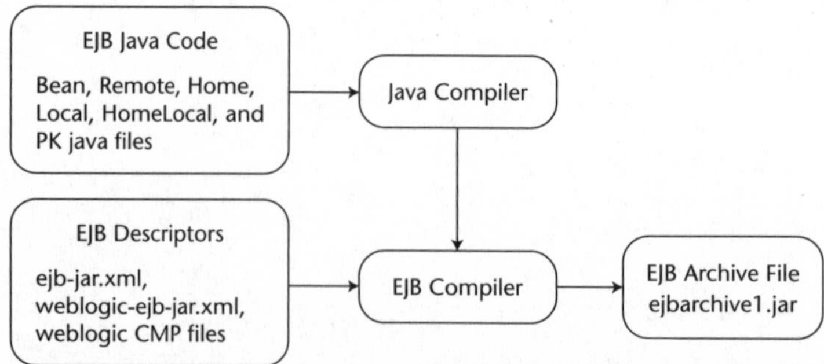

Figure 8.2 EJB archive created using Java and EJB compilers.

Let's pause for a moment and discuss the directory structure used in the working area for *bigrez.com*. It will be much easier to follow the build process if you understand the directories and related property definitions in the `build.xml` file.

Figure 8.3 presents the important directories in the work area for the application. These directories are defined in key properties in the `build.xml` file:

```
<project basedir="." default="all" name="Mastering WebLogic">
...
<property name="src" value="${basedir}/src"/>
<property name="build" value="${basedir}/build"/>
<property name="dd" value="${basedir}/dd"/>
<property name="srcjava" value="${src}/java"/>
<property name="webuser" value="${src}/web-user"/>
<property name="webadmin" value="${src}/web-admin"/>
```

Note that we have chosen to consolidate all Java code in a single source code hierarchy beginning with `src/java`, rather than adopting a split directory approach in which source code is segregated into separate areas for EJB classes, support classes (value objects, utility classes, and so on), and Web application classes. In a split directory approach, all Web application classes for the `user` site would be located in a directory structure beneath the Web application itself, perhaps in `src/web-user/WEB-INF/src/com/bigrez/...`, and the `admin` site's classes would be in a similar location in `src/web-admin`. EJB classes would be in a separate hierarchy such as `src/ejb/com/bigrez/ejb/...`, and value objects would be in yet another location. A split directory approach simplifies some of the EJB compilation and packaging steps by providing a clearly defined directory structure for inclusion in the EJB archive. The consolidated approach keeps things simple in terms of source-code organization, although it does require some additional work up front to create the proper build scripts. Either option will work; we've chosen the consolidated approach for *bigrez.com* to be more in line with typical organization strategies.

Figure 8.4 presents a high-level view of the main targets in the *bigrez.com* build script and their dependencies. Use this figure as a reference as we walk through various portions of the script throughout this chapter.

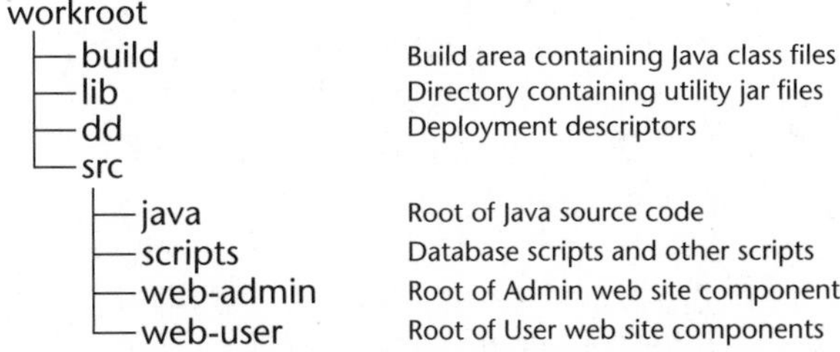

Figure 8.3 Summary of work directory structure.

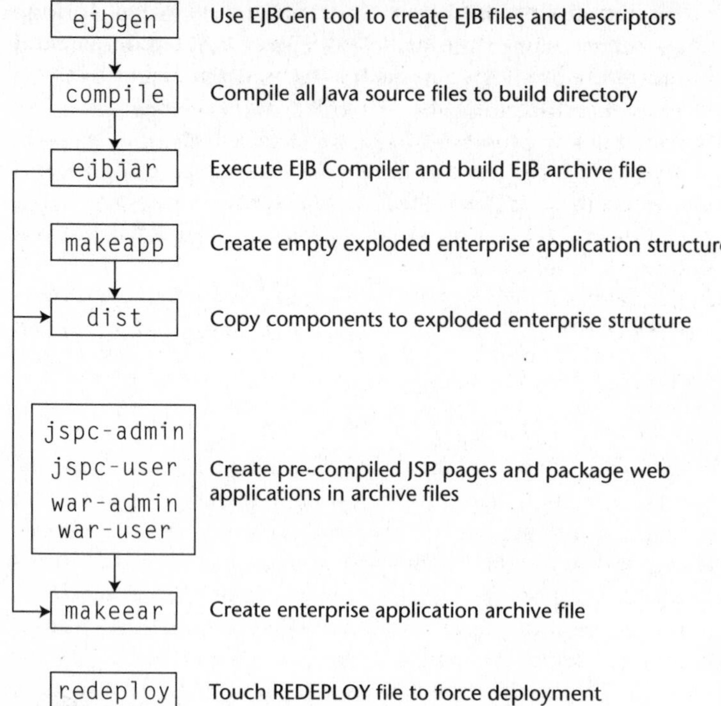

Figure 8.4 BigRez.com primary build file targets.

Creating EJB Source Code and Descriptor Files

The first step in the creation of an EJB archive file is the creation of Java source files and appropriate EJB descriptors for the EJB components. We assume you are familiar with the basics of this process.

WebLogic Server supplements the standard EJB descriptor file, `ejb-jar.xml`, with two WebLogic-specific descriptor files required to supply all necessary configuration information for the EJB components:

- The `weblogic-ejb-jar.xml` descriptor defines configuration parameters related to pooling, caching, JNDI names, the mapping of logical references in `ejb-jar.xml` to actual resources and beans, and various miscellaneous features.
- The `weblogic-cmp-rdbms-jar.xml` descriptor defines container-managed persistence (CMP) parameters for entity beans. It maps beans to database tables, defines the storage mechanism for container-manager relationships, modifies standard finder and `ejbSelect` methods to employ WebLogic Server-specific features and optimizations, and configures many of the new WebLogic Server caching and optimization capabilities.

A complete discussion of these descriptor files and their contents is beyond the scope of this book. The WebLogic Server online documentation is your best reference source for this information. Note that Chapter 6 also presented examples of many WebLogic Server-specific EJB features along with the corresponding descriptor elements.

The good news is that you may never have to learn the details of these descriptors, or the `ejb-jar.xml` descriptor for that matter, because tools such as EJBGen create these files for you. As described in Chapter 7, EJBGen uses Javadoc tags placed in the bean class file to generate all related Java files and descriptor files. Figure 8.5 illustrates the EJB archive-creation process using EJBGen.

The *bigrez.com* application uses EJBGen in all EJB components, eliminating all hand-editing of the EJB descriptor files. The Ant build script includes a target to execute EJBGen and build the Java and descriptor files:

```
<property name="ejbgen.jar.filename"
          value="${WEBLOGIC_HOME}/server/lib/weblogic.jar"/>
<property name="ejbgen.class.path"
          value="${WEBLOGIC_HOME}/server/lib/weblogic.jar;
                 ${basedir}/lib/log4j.jar;${build}"/>
...
<target name="ejbgen">
  <delete>
    <fileset dir="${srcjava}/com/bigrez/ejb"
             includes="*Local.java, *Remote.java"/>
  </delete>
  <exec dir="${srcjava}" executable="javadoc">
    <arg line="-classpath ${ejbgen.class.path}
               -docletpath ${ejbgen.jar.filename}
               -doclet weblogic.tools.ejbgen.EJBGen -wls81
               -noValueClasses -remoteSuffix Remote
               -remoteHomeSuffix HomeRemote
               -localSuffix Local -localHomeSuffix HomeLocal
               -sourcepath ${srcjava}"/>
    <arg value="com.bigrez.ejb"/>
  </exec>
  <move todir="${dd}">
    <fileset dir="${srcjava}" includes="*-jar.xml"/>
  </move>
</target>
```

The EJBGen process executes in the `/src/java` directory (defined by the `srcjava` property) and will examine and process all files located in the `com.bigrez.ejb` package. We were careful to place only EJB class files in this package to avoid EJBGen errors. The generated Java code and descriptors will be created in the `/src/java` directory structure by `ejbgen`, and the final `move` task places the descriptors in the `/dd` directory in preparation for the next step in the process.

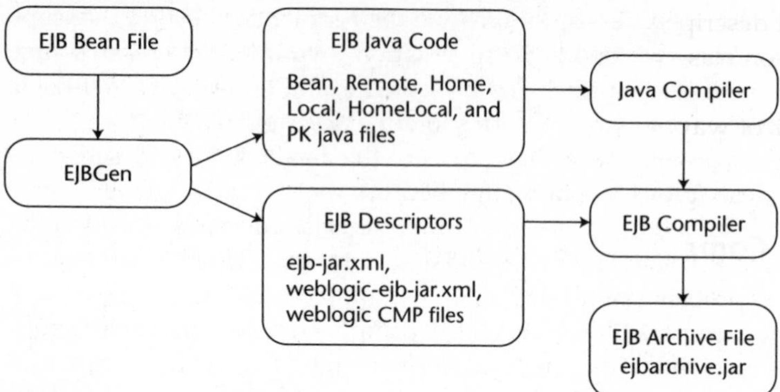

Figure 8.5 EJB archive creation process using EJBGen.

Compiling EJB Components

After you have all of the required EJB source files and descriptors, the source files must be compiled using the standard Java compiler in preparation for the EJB compilation step. The `build.xml` file for *bigrez.com* defines a classpath for compilation and a `compile` target to perform the call to the Java compiler:

```
<!-- Set up the development classpath -->
<path id="dev.classpath">
  <pathelement location="${JAVA_HOME}/lib/tools.jar"/>
  <pathelement location="${WEBLOGIC_HOME}/server/lib/weblogic.jar"/>
  <pathelement location="./lib/struts.jar"/>
  <pathelement location="./lib/log4j.jar"/>
  <pathelement location="./lib/junit.jar"/>
  <pathelement location="./lib/httpunit.jar"/>
  <pathelement location="${build}"/>
</path>
...
<target name="compile">
  <javac classpathref="dev.classpath" destdir="${build}"
         srcdir="${srcjava}">
    <include name="com/**/*.java"/>
  </javac>
</target>
```

All Java classes are compiled to the `build` directory, a staging area for the construction of the EJB archive file and for the classes intended for inclusion in one or more deployed Web applications.

Executing the EJB Compiler

Once the EJB source files are compiled to Java classes the EJB compiler is invoked to combine the classes and descriptors and create the EJB archive. The EJB compiler validates the files and descriptors, creates the required stubs, skeletons, proxies, and concrete implementation classes, and produces a single `.jar` archive file containing everything.

There are a number of ways to invoke the EJB compiler and integrate this step in your build process.

Invoking the EJB Compiler Directly

The EJB compiler may be invoked directly as a command-line utility by first creating a `.jar` archive containing all of the descriptors and compiled Java classes and then using a command similar to the following:

```
java weblogic.ejbc build.jar ejbarchive.jar
```

The `ejbarchive.jar` file will contain all of the `weblogic.ejbc`-generated container classes along with the original classes and descriptors. Note that the classpath must include files such as `weblogic.jar` either through the `CLASSPATH` environment variable or by using the `-classpath` option in the command line.

This command-line technique can be difficult to integrate in your overall build script. You must manually assemble the `build.jar` file by creating and populating a temporary directory and invoking the `jar` utility prior to executing the `weblogic.ejbc` command using a `java` task.

Using the WebLogic Application Compiler

WebLogic Server 8.1 deprecates the `weblogic.ejbc` utility and replaces it with `weblogic.appc`, a new utility combining the capabilities of `weblogic.ejbc` and `weblogic.jspc`, the JSP compiler, in a single program. The new `weblogic.appc` utility provides the same ability to process a prepackaged `.jar` file to create a complete EJB archive, if desired, but adds the ability to process Web application archive (`.war`) and complete enterprise application archive (`.ear`) files as well. In addition, `weblogic.appc` can operate on an exploded version of any of the supported file types, providing one useful technique for avoiding unnecessary `jar` steps during the build process. The exploded directory structure must mirror the contents of the associated archive file for proper operation.

The `weblogic.appc` utility may be invoked through a normal java task:

```
<java classname="weblogic.appc" fork="yes"
      failonerror="yes" classpathref="ejbjar.classpath">
  <arg value="${myejbdirectory}"/>
</java>
```

The new `wlappc` Ant task provided in WebLogic Server 8.1 may also be used to invoke the utility:

```
<wlappc source="${myejbdirectory}"
        classpathref="ejbjar.classpath" verbose="true" />
```

To use the `wlappc` task, you need to first define it:

```
<taskdef name="wlappc" classname="weblogic.ant.taskdefs.j2ee.Appc"/>
```

To operate as an EJB compiler, the `weblogic.appc` utility requires a directory structure or archive file populated with the correct EJB classes and deployment descriptors. We have two choices in *bigrez.com*: copy everything required for EJB compilation to a separate staging area before invoking `weblogic.appc` or use the `build` directory as the staging area for EJB compilation. The first option is very common and simple enough to implement, requiring only a temporary directory and appropriate `copy` tasks prior to invoking the EJB compiler. The second option is more promising because it avoids the creation of a temporary directory and makes better use of the in-place compilation capabilities of `weblogic.appc`.

To execute the EJB compiler using the `build` directory as the staging area, the `build` directory must contain the deployment descriptors for the EJB archive. The `ejbjar` target therefore copies the descriptors from the `dd` directory, preserving timestamps, before invoking the `weblogic.appc` utility using the `wlappc` Ant task:

```
<target name="ejbjar" depends="compile">
  <mkdir dir="${build}/META-INF"/>
  <copy todir="${build}/META-INF" preservelastmodified="true">
    <fileset dir="${dd}" includes="*-jar.xml"/>
  </copy>
  <wlappc source="${build}"
          classpathref="ejbjar.classpath" verbose="true" />
```

The `weblogic.appc` utility will create all of the necessary container classes in the `build` directory, leaving it ready for packaging as an archive file. Subsequent calls to `weblogic.appc` may not require a full recompilation of the entire set of EJB classes. It depends on the components and files that have changed since the last invocation. This can be very important on projects with many EJB components.

Because we are using consolidation of all source code in one directory structure, the `build` directory also contains Web application classes that must be omitted from the EJB archive. To accomplish this selectivity, the `jar` task in the `ejbjar` target explicitly defines the files to include in the archive:

```
  <jar destfile="${ejb.jar.filename}">
    <fileset dir="${build}" includes="com/bigrez/ejb/**/*.class,
                                      com/bigrez/utils/**/*.class,
                                      com/bigrez/val/**/*.class,
                                      META-INF/*-jar.xml"
    />
    <manifest>
      <attribute name="Class-Path" value="lib/log4j.jar"/>
    </manifest>
  </jar>
</target>
```

Note that the `jar` task also creates a manifest `Class-Path` entry referencing a required logging utility archive file, `log4j.jar`. This `Class-Path` entry in the manifest causes the container to load additional utility classes in the top-level application classloader, making them available to EJB components and Web components. We'll discuss this manifest `Class-Path` technique, along with a new alternative technique using the `APP-INF/lib` and `APP-INF/classes` directories, in a later section when we describe the packaging of enterprise applications.

Properties required by the `ejbjar` target are defined earlier in the build.xml file:

```
<property name="ejb.jar.filename" value="bigrezejb.jar" />
...
<path id="ejbjar.classpath">
  <pathelement location="${JAVA_HOME}/lib/tools.jar"/>
  <pathelement location="${WEBLOGIC_HOME}/server/lib/weblogic.jar"/>
  <pathelement location="./lib/log4j.jar"/>
  <pathelement location="${build}"/>
</path>
```

The EJB archive file is now ready for deployment. It contains all of the EJB class files, supporting value-object and utility classes, descriptors, and `weblogic.appc`-created container classes for the EJB components defined in the archive.

BEST PRACTICE The `weblogic.appc` compiler is the recommended approach for EJB compilation in WebLogic Server 8.1. The `wlappc` Ant task provides a convenient mechanism for integrating this step in your build script.

Using the ejbjar Optional Ant Task

One alternative option for invoking the EJB compiler involves the use of an optional task that comes with Ant, `ejbjar`, to create the EJB archive and perform the compilation:

```
<target name="ejbjar" depends="compile">
  <ejbjar srcdir="${build}"
          descriptordir="${dd}"
          basejarname="${ejb.jar.basename}">
    <include name="ejb-jar.xml"/>
    <classpath refid="ejbjar.classpath" />
    <weblogic destdir="${basedir}" rebuild="false"/>
    <support dir="${build}">
      <include name="**/ejb/**/*.class"/>
      <include name="**/utils/**/*.class"/>
      <include name="**/val/**/*.class"/>
    </support>
  </ejbjar>
  <jar destfile="${ejb.jar.filename}" update="true">
    <manifest>
      <attribute name="Class-Path" value="lib/log4j.jar"/>
    </manifest>
  </jar>
</target>
```

The attributes of the `ejbjar` task define the location of the compiled classes and EJB descriptors and the name to use for the EJB archive file. The `ejbjar` task also makes it easy to specify the additional support classes (value objects, utility classes, etc.) to be placed in the EJB archive using `support` elements. The `rebuild` attribute is also useful; setting it to `false` causes `ejbjar` to skip a full recompilation of all container classes whenever possible.

Note that the `ejbjar.classpath` definition includes the `build` directory, making all compiled Java classes available during the `weblogic.ejbc` processing step in the `ejbjar` task. The presence of the EJB classes in the classpath causes a few warnings similar to the following during the `weblogic.ejbc` process:

```
[ejbc] <Apr 6, 2003 5:53:38 PM CDT> <Warning> <EJB> <BEA-010054>
<EJB Deployment: ReservationSessionEJB has a class com.bigrez.ejb.
ReservationSessionBean that is in the classpath. This class should
only be located in the ejb-jar file.>
```

These warnings can be safely ignored, and they can be suppressed in WebLogic Server 8.1 by including a `disable-warning` element in the `weblogic-ejb-jar.xml` file:

```
<disable-warning>BEA-010054</disable-warning>
```

The final step in the overall `ejbjar` target involves updating the generated `bigrezejb.jar` archive file to include the `Class-Path` manifest entry described in the previous section. The EJB archive file is now complete and ready for deployment.

BEST PRACTICE **Consider using the** `ejbjar` **optional Ant task with earlier versions of WebLogic Server in place of a direct invocation of** `weblogic.ejbc`**. The built-in** `support` **element is a useful way to package supporting classes in the EJB archive.**

We've considered three approaches for creating the EJB archive file: direct invocation of the EJB compiler, the use of `weblogic.appc` through a `java` task or the new `wlappc` task, and the `ejbjar` optional Ant task. The build process for *bigrez.com* uses the `wlappc` task because it provides the best integration with the build process and utilizes the new standard mechanism for EJB compilation in WebLogic Server 8.1, `weblogic.appc`.

At this point in the build process the EJB archive file is located in our work root directory awaiting deployment. Choosing the final destination for this file is the subject of the next section.

Packaging Enterprise Applications

There are a number of ways to package and deploy EJB archives and Web application components for your application. As indicated in Figure 8.1 earlier in this chapter, the three primary options are these:

1. Deploying the EJB archives directly to the server as independent applications. Web application components are deployed alongside the EJB archive file as independent applications, and they access the EJB components using remote interfaces.
2. Deploying the EJB archives in an enterprise application archive (`.ear`) file containing all EJB archives, Web application archives, and enterprise application descriptor files.
3. Deploying the EJB archives in an exploded enterprise application directory structure containing all EJB archives, Web application archives, and enterprise-application descriptor files.

The first option, direct deployment of EJB archives and Web applications, is depicted in Figure 8.6. Each EJB archive and Web application is deployed as an independent J2EE application in WebLogic Server using one of the standard deployment techniques (discussed later in this chapter).

This technique is not recommended for the following reasons:

- The applications are loaded with separate, independent application classloaders (see Figure 8.7). Because each application classloader is independent, classes loaded by one application classloader are not visible to other application classloaders. This means that in order for your Web applications to invoke one of your EJBs, the Web applications must include client `.jar` files containing client-related EJB classes (typically remote interfaces, home interfaces, primary key classes, and any classes used as arguments or return types to any methods in the public interfaces) to communicate with the EJB components. As the number of Web applications and EJB archives increases, the management of these client `.jar` files becomes tedious and error prone.
- All communication between applications loaded by independent application classloaders must use remote interfaces and `Serializable` objects to prevent `ClassCastException` errors because each application has its own versions of the shared classes.
- Applications are difficult to manage as a single unit because they are not, in fact, a single application in the view of the server. For example, controlling the order of deployment during server startup is difficult in this technique, and many of the application staging and deployment features present in the latest version of WebLogic Server will be unable to process multiple applications as a single deployment unit.
- There is no way to combine entity-bean caches or configure application-wide resources in this technique because these features are available only when enterprise applications are employed for deployment.

Note that all classloaders used for the separate applications are children of the Java system classloader. The classes in the system classloader are defined by the `CLASSPATH` used for the server process itself during startup. Any components in a child classloader may reference classes present in parent classloaders, meaning that your EJB and Web applications can use classes loaded by the system classloader.

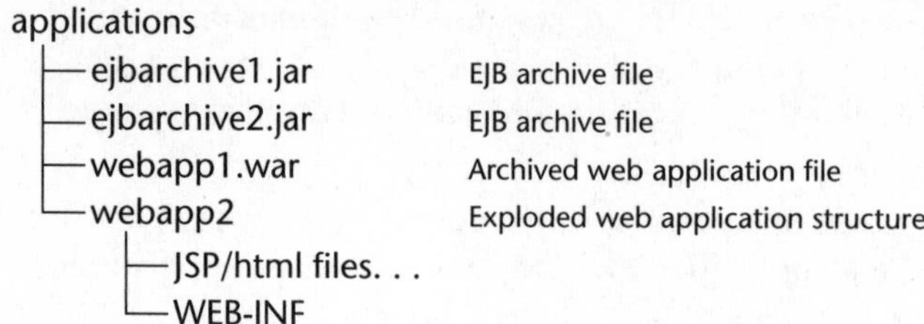

Figure 8.6 EJBs and Web apps deployed as separate applications.

One alternative to placing client `.jar` files for each EJB archive in each Web application might appear to be the placement of such files in the system classpath, making the client classes available to all child classloaders and therefore to all of your application components. Don't fall into this trap! There are two very good reasons to avoid this system classloader shortcut:

- Placing application-related classes in the system classpath prevents a complete redeployment of your application because classes loaded by the system classloader cannot be removed and reloaded.
- Classes in the parent classloader cannot reference classes in children classloaders. If any class in the system classloader attempts to use a class found only in the EJB archive or Web application `lib` or `classes` directory, you will get a `NoClassDefFoundError` exception. If you solve this problem by moving more and more classes to the system classpath, pretty soon you'll find that every class in your application winds up in the system classloader and all hope for hot redeployment is gone.

We recommend that only classes required for system-wide components be present in the system classpath and therefore loaded by the Java system classloader. Examples include classes in JDBC driver `.jar` files, the `weblogic.jar` file, and the Java `tools.jar` file. Even classes such as logging utilities and frameworks used by your application do not belong in the system classpath. There is a better location for such libraries in an enterprise application. We'll cover this topic in detail later in this chapter.

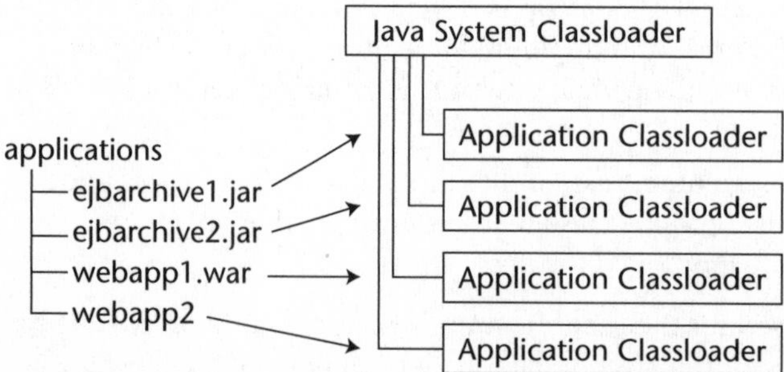

Figure 8.7 Separate classloader used for each application.

BEST PRACTICE **Place only system classes, such as JDBC drivers and WebLogic classes, in the system classpath. Don't place client `.jar` files or any other application-specific classes in the system classpath or you will likely encounter `NoClassDefFoundError` problems.**

Although it might be tempting to deploy your application as separate independent archives for small applications or for larger applications in the early stages of development, we recommend that you avoid this technique for all applications containing EJB archive files. Once you get in the habit of using remote interfaces and copying client `.jar` files to Web applications, it may be difficult to migrate to the better techniques discussed later.

BEST PRACTICE **Avoid deploying EJB archives and Web applications as separate, independent applications in WebLogic Server.**

Enterprise Application Directory Structure

The other two options for EJB deployment involve creating an enterprise application containing all of the EJB archives and Web application components. The options differ only in the final packaging step: Should the enterprise application be deployed as an exploded directory or as a single enterprise archive (`.ear`) file? We'll address that question last and begin by reviewing the contents of an enterprise application and examining the enterprise-application descriptor files that allow us to configure the application components.

Figure 8.8 presents the standard directory structure and contents of an enterprise application. The key difference from the previous EJB deployment option is the `bigapp` enterprise application root directory. This directory contains all of the individual application components and represents a single directory in the `applications` directory for the server. The server treats everything in the `bigapp` directory as a single J2EE application, eliminating many of the problems associated with the previous deployment option.

The EJB archives and Web application components are placed at the root level of the enterprise application directory structure along with a required `META-INF` directory and any other directories required by your application. We recommend creating a `lib` directory to contain utility archive files loaded using the manifest `Class-Path` technique discussed later in this chapter. Note that WebLogic Server 8.1 adds support for a special set of directories in the enterprise application, `APP-INF/lib` and `APP-INF/classes`, which WebLogic Server automatically examines and loads in the top-level application classloader without requiring manifest `Class-Path` entries.

A critical difference in this deployment option relates to the structure of the classloaders used to load an enterprise application containing both EJB archives and Web components. In the first option each archive and Web application was loaded as a separate application in a separate classloader descended directly from the Java system classloader (see Figure 8.7). When EJB archives and Web applications are placed in an enterprise application structure, however, WebLogic Server uses the classloader structure depicted in Figure 8.9.

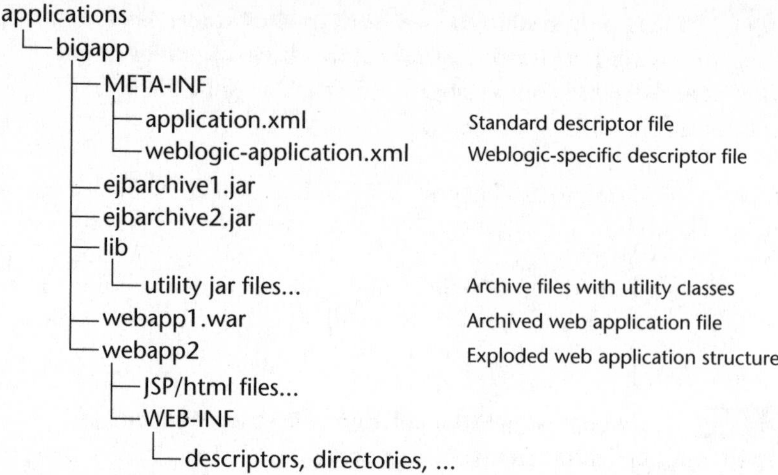

Figure 8.8 Standard enterprise application directory structure.

All EJB archives, along with utility classes referenced in an EJB archive file's manifest `Class-Path` entry or located in the `APP-INF` directory structure, are loaded by a single top-level application classloader, thereby permitting local interfaces and pass-by-reference semantics between components in these EJB archives. More importantly, the Web application classloaders are *children* of the application classloader rather than *siblings* of it. Recall that a child classloader is able to reference all classes loaded by its parent classloader, so the Web application components also have full access to the classes in the EJB archives. This child-sees-parent visibility has two important ramifications:

- Web applications may use local EJB interfaces and pass-by-reference semantics with EJB components located in the same enterprise application. There is no need to use remote interfaces or `Serializable` parameters and return types, although their use is not precluded in this option.
- There is no need for the Web applications to include client `.jar` files because they have full visibility to these classes by virtue of the parent application classloader.

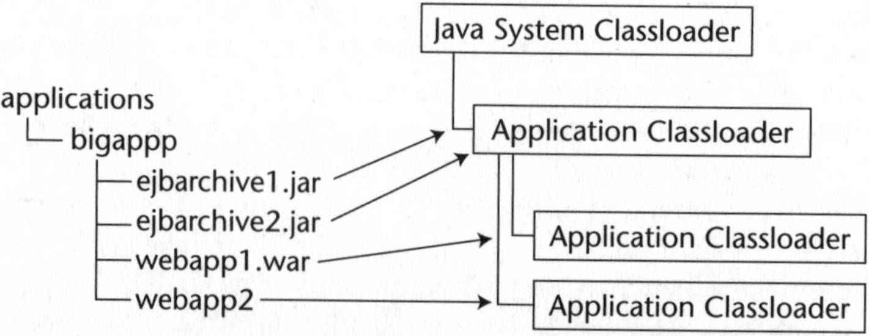

Figure 8.9 Classloader hierarchy in enterprise application.

Figure 8.10 presents the enterprise application directory structure for the *bigrez.com* example application. *Bigrez.com* relies on parent-child classloader visibility and the ability of Web application components such as JSP pages and `Action` controller classes to communicate directly with EJB components using local interfaces and pass-by-reference semantics. It also relies on the accessibility of container-managed relationship fields in Web application components, a technique that works only with local interfaces. In other words, the direct interaction approach is not possible unless components are located in a single enterprise application. For more information about WebLogic Server classloaders, please see the WebLogic Server documentation at http://edocs.bea.com/wls/docs81/programming/classloading.html.

Note that Figure 8.10 represents the structure of an enterprise application containing exploded Web applications. Just as the enterprise application itself can be archived or exploded, the Web applications in it can be archived or exploded. Generally, it makes sense to leave the Web applications exploded if the enterprise application itself is exploded and to use archived Web applications within archived enterprise applications. Leaving Web applications exploded in development also has advantages when making changes to JSP and HTML files in the Web application. As described in Chapter 5, changes to these display components can be deployed to the exploded application without requiring a complete redeployment of the Web application.

Assembling all of these components in their correct location in the enterprise application is covered later in the chapter, along with a walkthrough of the build scripts that perform this activity in the *bigrez.com* application. Before moving on to these packaging topics, however, we first need to complete our discussion of the enterprise-application structure itself by describing the contents of the `META-INF` and `lib` directories.

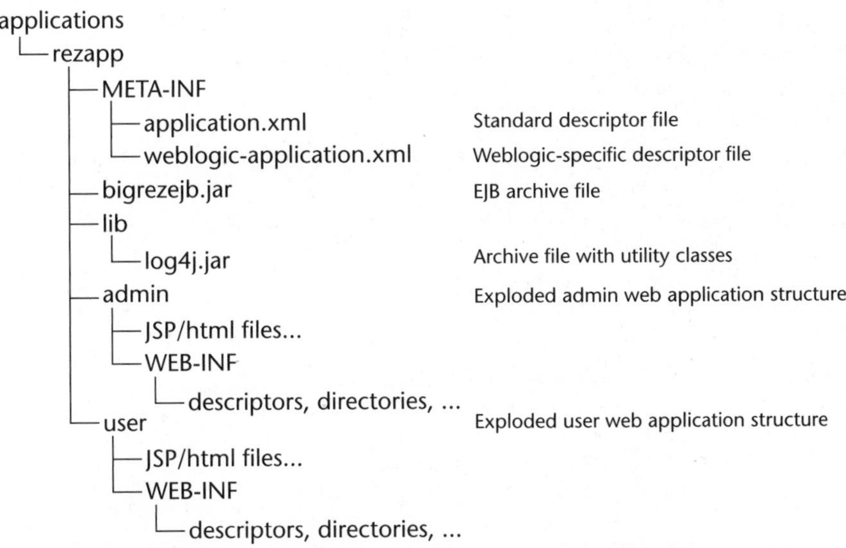

Figure 8.10 BigRez.com enterprise application directory structure.

Enterprise Application Descriptor Files

The META-INF directory in the enterprise application directory structure contains two descriptor files used to control the deployment of the components and resources in the enterprise application. The first descriptor file is application.xml, a standard file required by the J2EE specification. The second file, weblogic-application.xml, is a WebLogic Server-specific descriptor file used to configure shared caches and resources common to all components in the enterprise application. We'll examine the contents of these descriptors and walk through the *bigrez.com* versions to understand their use and highlight best practices.

Standard application.xml Descriptor File

The application.xml descriptor file is defined by the J2EE specification and is used by WebLogic Server to control basic configuration and deployment of the application. Table 8.1 outlines the high-level sections of the application.xml file and lists the key elements used in each section.

The *bigrez.com* version of application.xml, presented in Listing 8.1, includes module definitions for the EJB archive file and the two Web applications.

```
<!DOCTYPE application PUBLIC
 '-//Sun Microsystems, Inc.//DTD J2EE Application 1.2//EN'
 'http://java.sun.com/j2ee/dtds/application_1_2.dtd'>

<application>
  <display-name>Mastering WebLogic Example Application</display-name>
  <description>Mastering WebLogic Example Application</description>
  <module>
    <web>
      <web-uri>user</web-uri>
      <context-root></context-root>
    </web>
  </module>
  <module>
    <web>
      <web-uri>admin</web-uri>
      <context-root>admin</context-root>
    </web>
  </module>
  <module><ejb>bigrezejb.jar</ejb></module>
</application>
```

Listing 8.1 BigRez.com application.xml descriptor file.

Table 8.1 Sections of the application.xml Descriptor File

APPLICATION.XML SECTION	PURPOSE AND KEY TOP-LEVEL XML ELEMENTS
Deployment attributes	Defines graphics and descriptions used by deployment and management tools. `<icon>, <display-name>, <description>`
Module definitions	Defines the location of each module (application) contained in the enterprise application. `<module>, <connector>, <ejb>, <web>`
Security information	Defines application-wide security roles available for all modules. `<security-role>`

The module definitions in this version of `application.xml` refer to the exploded Web application directory structures `user` and `admin`, consistent with the directory structure in Figure 8.9. If the Web applications were archived in the enterprise application, the two `web-uri` elements would reference the Web application archive (`.war`) files:

```
<module>
  <web>
    <web-uri>user.war</web-uri>
    <context-root></context-root>
  </web>
</module>
<module>
  <web>
    <web-uri>admin.war</web-uri>
    <context-root>admin</context-root>
  </web>
</module>
```

The *bigrez.com* application uses archived Web applications in the archived enterprise application, so a version of `application.xml` with these changes is used when creating the final archive file. We'll discuss this process later in the chapter.

Note that both versions of `application.xml` specify an empty context root for the `user` Web application, making it available using URLs that do not specify a context. WebLogic Server 8.1 eliminates the concept of a *default* Web application configured through the WebLogic Console. You must now specify an empty `context-root` for one, and only one, Web application on the server to make it the default Web application.

BEST PRACTICE **Use an empty `context-root` element in the `application.xml` file to specify the server's default Web application.**

weblogic-application.xml Descriptor File

The `weblogic-application.xml` descriptor file is a WebLogic-specific file used to configure resources and control WebLogic Server-specific features at the enterprise application level. This file is optional. Table 8.2 outlines the high-level sections of the `weblogic-application.xml` file and lists the key elements used in each section.

See the online documentation at http://edocs.bea.com/wls/docs81/programming/app_xml.html and DTD definition for complete information on this descriptor file and its elements.

Table 8.2 Sections of the weblogic-application.xml Descriptor File

WEBLOGIC-APPLICATION.XML SECTION	PURPOSE AND KEY TOP-LEVEL XML ELEMENTS
EJB configuration	Defines application-wide EJB caches and MDB startup policies. `<ejb>`, `<entity-cache>`, `<start-mdbs-with-application>`
XML configuration	Defines XML parsing, document building, and transformation factories for use in this application. Also defines entity-mapping information. `<xml>`, `<parser-factory>`, `<entity-mapping>`
JDBC configuration	Defines JDBC connection pools and `DataSource` resources visible in this application. `<jdbc-connection-pool>`, `<data-source-name>`, `<connection-factory>`, `<pool-params>`, `<driver-params>`, `<acl-name>`
Container behavior	Defines various parameters affecting container behaviors. `<application-param>`
Security information	Defines the security realm required by this application. `<realm-name>`
Classloader hierarchy	Defines the organization of classloaders for the application modules. `<classloader-structure>`, `<module-ref>`
Listener, startup, and shutdown configuration	Defines customer listeners, startup classes, and shutdown classes. `<listener>`, `<startup>`, `<shutdown>`

The *bigrez.com* weblogic-application.xml file, presented in Listing 8.2, defines an application-wide entity-bean cache called MultiVersionCache with a maximum size of 5,000 beans. As described in Chapter 6, the MultiVersionCache cache is used for all entity beans having no explicit per-bean cache or reference to a named application-wide cache.

```
<!DOCTYPE weblogic-application PUBLIC
 '-//BEA Systems, Inc.//DTD WebLogic Application 8.1.0//EN'
 'http://www.bea.com/servers/wls810/dtd/weblogic-application_2_0.dtd'>

<weblogic-application>
  <ejb>
    <entity-cache>
      <!-- Define the size of the default cache for beans -->
      <entity-cache-name>MultiVersionCache</entity-cache-name>
      <max-beans-in-cache>5000</max-beans-in-cache>
      <caching-strategy>MultiVersion</caching-strategy>
    </entity-cache>
  </ejb>
</weblogic-application>
```

Listing 8.2 BigRez.com weblogic-application.xml descriptor file.

The *bigrez.com* application uses JDBC connection pools and JDBC DataSource resources to support the CMP entity beans. Although these resources can be configured in the weblogic-application.xml file, we decided to configure them in the WebLogic Server domain itself using the WebLogic Console.

Depending on the requirements of your application, there may be good reasons to configure JDBC connection pools and related resources in the weblogic-application .xml file rather than through the WebLogic Console. By configuring them in weblogic-application.xml, the enterprise application is more self-contained, in theory, requiring less configuration work through the administration console.

Although the ability to configure JDBC-related resources in the application is useful, there are likely to be additional resources required by your application that are not currently available through the weblogic-application.xml file. Examples include JMS resources (servers, stores, connection factories, destinations) and JavaMail Session objects. In addition, the facilities to monitor and manage JDBC resources at the domain level are more powerful and complete.

We recommend that you configure JDBC resources in the domain using the WebLogic Console to be consistent with all other resources and to provide easier management for the WebLogic Server administrator.

BEST PRACTICE **Create JDBC resources in the WebLogic Server domain using the WebLogic Console rather than employing the** weblogic-application.xml **technique.**

That's it for the enterprise application descriptor files. The final topic to cover in the enterprise application directory structure, the `lib` directory, is the subject of the next section.

Packaging Utility Archives in Enterprise Applications

Many enterprise applications make use of prepackaged libraries of classes containing third-party utilities, client classes for external EJB components, or other collections of classes not compiled or packaged by the application build process. These *utility archives* must be loaded by the proper classloader in the server to make their classes visible to the appropriate application components.

Web applications provide a built-in mechanism to load utility archives in the same classloader as the Web application itself: the `/WEB-INF/lib` directory. Any `.jar` file placed in that directory will automatically be loaded by the Web application classloader, and its classes will be available to the Web application components. Recognize that because the Web application classloader is a child of the application classloader (see Figure 8.8) the EJB components will not be able to reference the classes loaded in the Web application classloader.

Prior to WebLogic Server 8.1 there was no corresponding automatic behavior available with EJB archive files. There was no `lib` directory in the EJB archive or magic location in the enterprise-application directory structure that caused the server to load utility archives automatically in the same way that `WEB-INF/lib` operates in a Web application.

WebLogic Server 8.1 added support for two new directories, `APP-INF/lib` and `APP-INF/classes`, located at the root level of an enterprise application. These directories provide the same type of automatic classloading behavior for enterprise applications that the `WEB-INF/lib` and `WEB-INF/classes` directories provide for Web applications. If you are using WebLogic Server 8.1, simply place utility archives and classes in these new directories in the enterprise application structure and you're done. If you are using an earlier version of WebLogic Server or want to use the J2EE-defined technique that does not rely on this WebLogic Server-specific behavior, read on.

BEST PRACTICE **When using WebLogic Server 8.1, make use of the new** `APP-INF/lib` **and** `APP-INF/classes` **directories in the enterprise-application directory structure to simplify the packaging of utility classes and libraries.**

Note that individual classes contained in a properly constructed EJB archive file are automatically loaded by the application classloader, a feature we use in *bigrez.com* to load support and value-object classes in the application classloader to make them available to all components in the enterprise application. You can use this trick in other ways as well, perhaps by creating a separate EJB archive file containing any arbitrary collection of classes along with a single, dummy EJB component. As long as the EJB is constructed properly, the application classloader will load everything in the file. This trick isn't useful with utility archives, however, because packaging the utility `.jar` file inside the EJB archive does not cause it to be loaded during deployment.

Two basic techniques are used to make utility archives available to the entire enterprise application without making use of APP-INF/lib: using the system classpath and using the manifest Class-Path technique.

Utility archives placed on the Java system classpath (by including them in the CLASSPATH used during server startup) are visible to all classes in the system classloader and all children classloaders. This technique works for the most part, but, as discussed earlier, we do not recommend putting any nonsystem classes in the system classpath. That leaves us with the manifest Class-Path technique for loading utility archives. Fortunately, this technique is pretty easy to implement despite its complex-sounding name.

Basically, the J2EE specification provides a mechanism to identify classes required by an EJB archive using the MANIFEST.MF file embedded in the EJB archive itself. This mechanism is configured by placing Class-Path entries in the manifest file listing the .jar files required by this EJB archive. The server is responsible for loading these archives in the same classloader used for the EJB components themselves. Once you configure the manifest to include the utility archive files in Class-Path entries, the problem is solved.

This same mechanism allows you to tell the application server about dependencies between different EJB jar files that you might package together inside your enterprise application. Without this mechanism, the application server might try to load the EJB jar files in the wrong order, causing the enterprise application to fail to deploy.

The enterprise application directory structure presented back in Figure 8.7 included a lib directory as the proper location for utility archive files. Recognize that the use of lib is simply a good naming practice to differentiate utility .jar files from EJB archive files located at the root of the enterprise application. It is not a J2EE requirement. To load utility archive files located in the lib directory we modify the MANIFEST.MF file in the EJB archive to include a line similar to the following:

```
Class-Path: lib/utility1.jar lib/utility2.jar
```

The directory portion of a filename in the Class-Path entry is relative to the location of the EJB archive, so we prefix all of the archives with the lib directory. The classloader configuration for a typical enterprise application using this manifest Class-Path technique is depicted in Figure 8.11.

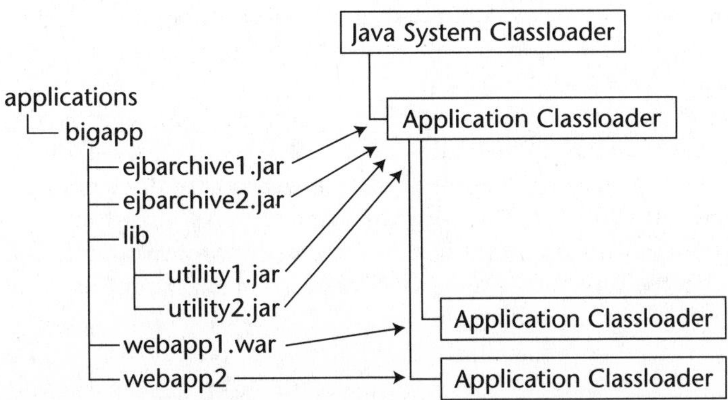

Figure 8.11 Application classloader used for utility archives.

You should specify Class-Path entries in each EJB archive in the application, including entries that define dependencies on other EJB archives. This practice ensures that the server will load the utility archives and EJB archives in the proper order and avoids ClassNotFoundError problems.

Lines in manifest files are limited to 72 characters, so be careful to limit the number of archive files on a single line. Multiple Class-Path lines are allowed, and long lines may be continued by starting the next line in the manifest with a single space.

The *bigrez.com* application requires a Class-Path entry in the file referencing a single utility archive, log4j.jar:

```
Class-Path: lib/log4j.jar
```

The ejbjar target in the build process used a jar task that included this entry in the EJB archive file using a nested manifest element in the jar task:

```
<jar destfile="${ejb.jar.filename}" ... >
  <manifest>
    <attribute name="Class-Path" value="lib/log4j.jar"/>
  </manifest>
</jar>
```

The log4j.jar archive file must be located in the lib directory in the enterprise application, a configuration depicted in Figure 8.9 earlier in this chapter.

Now that we've discussed the structure and contents of an enterprise application, it is time to examine techniques for constructing enterprise applications using Ant-based build processes. We'll cover the creation of both exploded enterprise applications, suitable for development and unit test environments, and archived enterprise applications, suitable for promotion to test and production environments.

Creating an Exploded Enterprise Application

The structure of an exploded enterprise application was discussed earlier in this chapter. As shown in Figures 8.8 and 8.10, exploded enterprise applications are basically directory structures that mirror the structure and content of an enterprise application archive file. They contain EJB archives, descriptors, utility archive files, and exploded or archived Web applications. Creating the exploded application consists of creating the proper directory structure and then copying all application components to the correct locations in the structure.

The directory structure can be created by hand in the applications directory in the WebLogic Server domain if you prefer the manual approach. Be sure to create all of the required directories because the copy task in Ant will not create required directories on the fly. Although you can create the directory structure by hand, we recommend an automated approach using the Ant build script to avoid errors and better control the process.

For example, in *bigrez.com* the directory structure is created using mkdir Ant tasks in a makeapp target in the build.xml script:

```
<property name="domain.dir" value="${DOMAIN_HOME}/${DOMAIN}"/>
<property name="applications" value="${domain.dir}/applications"/>
<property name="deploy.dir" value="${applications}/${APPLICATION}"/>
<property name="webapp.user.dir" value="${deploy.dir}/user"/>
<property name="webapp.admin.dir" value="${deploy.dir}/admin"/>
...
<target name="makeapp">
  <!-- make exploded application structure -->
  <mkdir dir="${deploy.dir}"/>
  <mkdir dir="${deploy.dir}/META-INF"/>
  <mkdir dir="${deploy.dir}/lib"/>
  <mkdir dir="${webapp.user.dir}"/>
  <mkdir dir="${webapp.user.dir}/WEB-INF"/>
  <mkdir dir="${webapp.user.dir}/WEB-INF/classes"/>
  ...
</target>
```

The properties DOMAIN_HOME, DOMAIN, and APPLICATION are defined in a build.properties file:

```
DOMAIN_HOME=c:/mastering/user_projects
DOMAIN=bigrezdomain
APPLICATION=rezapp
```

The makeapp target simply creates the empty enterprise application directory structure. With this technique you can change the location of the application or rebuild it from scratch in a completely automated fashion.

Moving all of the compiled and assembled components to the application structure is the responsibility of the dist target in the build.xml script, a portion of which is shown here:

```
<target name="dist" depends="makeapp, ejbjar">

  <!-- Copy all of the webapplication files to the proper webapps -->
  <copy todir="${webapp.user.dir}" preservelastmodified="true">
    <fileset dir="${webuser}" includes="**/*.*"/>
  </copy>
  <copy todir="${webapp.admin.dir}" preservelastmodified="true">
    <fileset dir="${webadmin}" includes="**/*.*"/>
  </copy>

  <!-- Copy the user webapp classes to the user/WEB-INF/classes -->
  <copy todir="${webapp.user.dir}/WEB-INF/classes">
    <fileset dir="${build}" includes="**/ui/**/*.class,
            **/form/**/*.class" excludes="**/admin/**/*.class" />
  </copy>

  <!-- Copy the admin webapp classes to the admin/WEB-INF/classes -->
  <copy todir="${webapp.admin.dir}/WEB-INF/classes">
    <fileset dir="${build}" includes="**/ui/**/*.class,
```

```
                **/form/**/*.class" excludes="**/user/**/*.class" />
    </copy>

    <!-- Copy the EJB jar file  -->
    <copy file="${ejb.jar.filename}" todir="${deploy.dir}" />

    ... copy utility archives, application-level descriptors, etc.

  </target>
```

Note that all required files, descriptors, and libraries are present in the work area for the application and are copied to the enterprise application structure using this target. There is no hand-copying of files to the application area or hand-creating or -editing of the files in the enterprise application. It is a much better practice to build the enterprise application using an Ant build script and files in the work area for the application. This technique allows the rapid recreation of the application at any time and keeps all required files in one place for the purposes of source code control and project organization.

BEST PRACTICE **Use the Ant build script to create and populate exploded enterprise applications rather than hand-creating directory structures and hand-copying files to their proper locations.**

Once the `dist` task has completed, the exploded enterprise application is ready to deploy.

Creating an Enterprise Application Archive File

Enterprise application archive (`.ear`) files are simply archived versions of exploded enterprise application directory structures. Although it is possible to create an `.ear` file manually by invoking the `jar` utility, we recommend including a target in your Ant build script to create the archive file using the EJB archives and Web application components built in the work area.

The *bigrez.com* application includes a `makeear` target responsible for assembling the final `.ear` file using the proper application components. Because the `.ear` file is intended for promotion to test and production environments it must be a production-ready archive. By this we mean that the `.ear` file contains the following:

- Precompiled JSP pages in each Web application
- Archived Web applications rather than exploded Web applications
- All required libraries in the `lib` directory and the proper manifest `Class-Path` entries in the EJB archive to use them
- Descriptor files consistent with production resource requirements

The first two requirements are met by individual Ant targets in the build script responsible for precompiling the JSP pages and archiving the Web applications. The last two requirements are met by the makeear target itself. As indicated in Figure 8.12, the makeear target is dependent on the jspc- and war-related targets and performs the final archive step once both admin and user Web application components are ready.

We walked through the jspc-admin, jspc-user, war-admin, and war-user targets in Chapter 5, so we will not repeat that discussion here. The products of these targets are admin.war and user.war Web application archive files in the work root directory ready for inclusion in the .ear file.

The makeear target is responsible for assembling all of the components and creating the final .ear file. Normally this would require only a simple jar task with the appropriate files included from the work directory structure. Two wrinkles complicate matters slightly:

- Archived admin.war and user.war files are used in the enterprise application archive rather than exploded Web applications. The .ear must therefore include an application.xml descriptor file that properly declares the Web applications as .war files.
- The archive is intended for production, so it may require different parameters in the WebLogic-specific weblogic-application.xml descriptor file than were used in development.

The *bigrez.com* application meets these requirements by using separate application.xml and weblogic-application.xml descriptor files stored in the dd/ear directory. The makeear target simply uses these descriptors, rather than the ones intended for exploded deployment, in the ear task that assembles the enterprise archive file:

```
<target name="makeear"
        depends="ejbjar, jspc-admin, jspc-user, war-admin, war-user">
  <!-- Create .ear enterprise-application archive file -->
  <ear destfile="${basedir}/bigrez.ear"
       appxml="${dd}/ear/application.xml">
    <metainf dir="${dd}/ear" includes="weblogic-application.xml"/>
    <fileset dir="${basedir}"
             includes="${ejb.jar.filename},
                       admin.war, user.war, lib/log4j.jar"/>
  </ear>
</target>
```

The end result of this target is a single enterprise application archive file, bigrez.ear, containing the files depicted in Figure 8.13.

The bigrez.ear file is now complete and ready for deployment. We'll discuss deployment in a development environment in the next section, and Chapter 11 will cover the deployment of *bigrez.com* in a production environment.

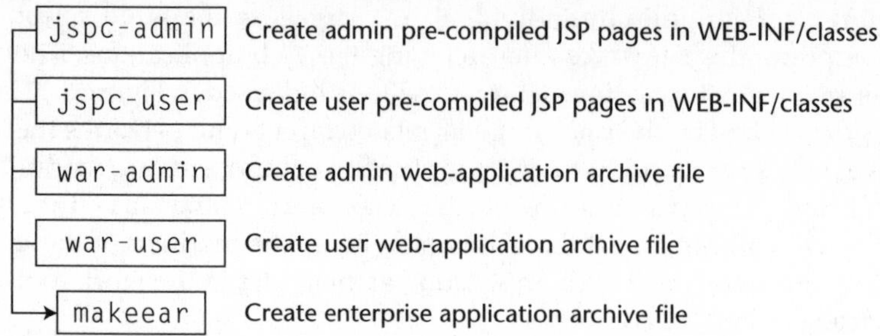

Figure 8.12 Enterprise archive created by the makeear target.

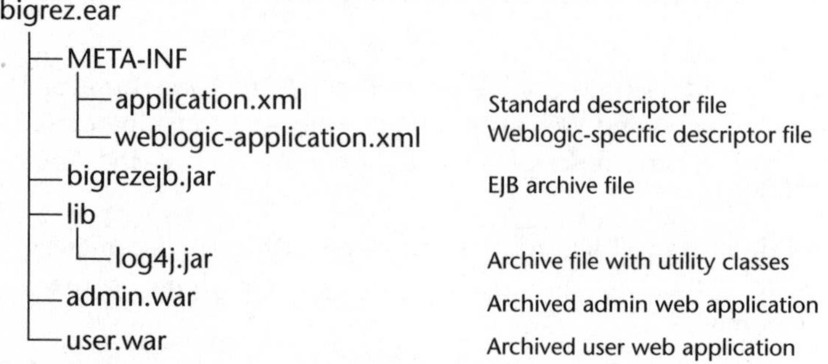

Figure 8.13 bigrez.ear contains all required components.

Deploying EJB Applications

There are three basic ways to deploy an EJB application, or any other J2EE application, in a WebLogic Server environment:

- Automatic deployment
- WebLogic deployer utility or Ant tTask
- WebLogic Console deployment

These three methods were examined in the context of deploying Web applications in Chapter 5. Most of the same rules, best practices, and limitations discussed in that chapter apply to their use with EJB and enterprise applications. In this section, we'll briefly discuss preparing the environment for deployment and then walk through the deployment process for the *bigrez.com* enterprise application using two of the methods, automatic deployment and WebLogic Console deployment. See Chapter 5 for a discussion of the WebLogic Deployer Utility and `wldeploy` Ant task.

Creating Required Services

Before attempting to deploy an EJB application or enterprise application, you should configure the required services (JDBC connections, JMS resources, etc.) in the server environment. Although some applications may deploy properly without the required services, applications with container-managed persistence (CMP) entity beans, message-driven beans (MDBs), or startup components requiring services will not deploy.

When a CMP entity bean component is deployed, for example, WebLogic Server tests that the JDBC `DataSource` defined in the bean descriptor file is available and that the underlying database contains the table and column information defined in the CMP bean. This test is repeated for each CMP bean in the EJB archive file. All beans must pass the test, or none of them will be deployed successfully.

When an MDB component is deployed, the server will attempt to connect the MDB to the JMS destination defined in its descriptor file. If the JMS destination is not available the server will display an error message in the log and attempt to reconnect to the destination periodically until it is available. This will not stop the MDB from deploying, although it will not operate properly until the JMS resource is created.

As a general rule, you should configure the required services and resources before attempting to deploy the application.

BEST PRACTICE **Create and configure all required services and resources before attempting to deploy the application.**

The *bigrez.com* application uses a JDBC `DataSource` in the CMP entity beans, a JMS queue in the `ReservationSessionBean` stateless session bean and `EmailProcessingBean` MDB component, and a JavaMail `Session` object in the `EmailProcessingBean`. All of these services and their underlying resources should be configured before deploying the application.

Creating services and resources in a single-server development environment is fairly easy. The WebLogic Console provides straightforward screens for creating resources in the current domain. Rather than walk through each screen in detail we will simply list the required resources for *bigrez.com* and provide specific configuration information as a reference.

The JDBC resources required by *bigrez.com* in the development environment are the following:

- A JDBC connection pool named `BigRezPool` connected to the development database. The specific driver class name, URL, properties, and password obviously depend on your database. The new JDBC Connection Pool Wizard will help you select the proper values. See the WebLogic Server online documentation at http://edocs.bea.com/wls/docs81/ConsoleHelp/jdbc_connection_pools.html or your database documentation for more information. This pool must be targeted to the current server and should have `Maximum Capacity` set to at least four connections.
- A JDBC `DataSource` that `Honors Global Transactions` named `BigRezDataSource` using the `BigRezPool` as its underlying connection pool. This `DataSource` should use the JNDI name `BigRezDataSource` and must be targeted to the current server as well.

The JMS resources required are the following:

- A JMS FileStore called JMSFileStore configured to use the ./jmsstore directory to persist JMS messages. Create an empty jmsstore directory below the domain root directory (the directory containing the config.xml file) to hold the JMS message files.
- A JMS ConnectionFactory called BigRezEmailConnectionFactory using the default values for all message, transaction, and flow-control parameters. The default values are sufficient for development and unit test purposes. Chapters 9 and 11 will discuss best practices and provide configuration parameters suitable for a production environment. Don't forget to target this resource to the server.
- A JMS Server called JMSServer configured to use the JMSFileStore and targeted to the server. All other configurations parameters can be left with default values.
- A JMS Queue called BigRezEmailQueue in the JMSServer configured to use the JNDI name BigRezEmailQueue. Target the queue to the current server. It is also a good idea to set the Redelivery Limit to a reasonable number (3–5) rather than leaving it at the default value of -1. The default value allows unlimited redeliveries of the message in the case of errors in the component processing the message. All other parameters can use default values.

The final resource required by *bigrez.com* is a JavaMail Session resource used to send outgoing email. The name and JNDI name should be BigRezEmailSession, and the properties should be similar to the following with the placeholder information replaced with valid smtp information:

```
mail.smtp.user=nyberg
mail.transport.protocol=smtp
mail.smtp.host=mail.mymail.com
mail.smtp.password=something
```

Target this resource to the current server, and you are done configuring resources for *bigrez.com*.

The domain is now ready for the deployment of the *bigrez.com* enterprise application using either the exploded directory structure or the single archive file. We'll discuss the two recommended approaches for deployment in the next two sections.

Automatic Deployment

Because we discussed automatic deployement at some length in Chapter 5 we will simply review the technique here and present the steps required to deploy the *bigrez.com* application.

First, ensure that automatic deployment is enabled by setting the PRODUCTION _MODE variable in the server boot script to the value false. The administration server will now scan the applications directory in the domain for new (or modified) application archives and exploded directory structures during each boot process and periodically during server operation.

Next, copy the `bigrez.ear` archive file or the entire `rezapp` exploded application structure to the `applications` directory in the domain. The server can be running, if desired, although with exploded applications it is usually best to copy the structure with the server stopped to avoid the race condition discussed in Chapter 5.

Note that the `makeapp` and `dist` targets in the `build.xml` script served to deploy the exploded application to the local domain by creating the exploded directory structure and copying all of the required files to the proper locations in that structure. In other words, we designed the Ant scripts to employ automatic deployment on the developer's workstation whenever we issue the `dist` target.

Automatic redeployment of the application occurs whenever the `bigrez.ear` file is overwritten or the `META-INF/REDEPLOY` file is touched and its timestamp changes. These rules were discussed at length in Chapter 5. The `build.xml` file includes a useful target, `redeploy`, which touches the `REDEPLOY` file and causes a redeployment in a running server:

```
<target name="redeploy">
  <touch file="${deploy.dir}/META-INF/REDEPLOY"/>
</target>
```

Automatic deployment is a very useful technique for deploying exploded and archived enterprise applications in a single-server development or test environment. The ability to redeploy the application without rebooting the server or accessing the WebLogic Console is very useful during development. As Chapter 11 will discuss, however, automatic deployment can be problematic in production environments with multiple servers and should be avoided in these environments.

BEST PRACTICE Use automatic deployment on developer workstations and other single-server environments to eliminate manual deployment steps and provide quick redeployment of modified applications. Avoid its use in production and multiple server environments.

WebLogic Console Deployment

Chapter 5 also walked through the process of deploying a simple Web application using the WebLogic Console. Deploying an enterprise application to a single server environment is very similar to deploying a Web application. The process involves the following steps:

1. Start the WebLogic Server instance in production mode by including `PRODUCTION_MODE=true` in the `startWebLogic` script.
2. Copy the exploded archive file or `.ear` file to the `applications` directory or any other desired directory.
3. Deploy the application using the administration console.

As in Chapter 5, the first two steps are self-explanatory. Using production mode disables the automatic deployment of archives and directory structures placed in the `applications` directory, allowing you to control this deployment manually through the console. The application may be placed in the `applications` directory, as in the automatic deployment case, or it may be placed in any desired directory on the server. We suggest a directory such as `myapps` in the domain directory structure to avoid confusion.

The remaining steps to deploy an enterprise application follow the same general process outlined in Chapter 5 for a Web application:

1. Start the server and open the WebLogic Console.
2. Open the list of current applications deployed in the server using the `Applications` link on the left side of the screen.
3. Click the `Deploy a new Application` link on the right side. Use the supplied screens to navigate to the location of your new application, and select the application archive file or root directory to be deployed.
4. Continue the process by targeting the new application to your server, giving it a name, and clicking the `Deploy` button to deploy the application.
5. Use the standard application tabs and screens to modify the deployment information if required.

The application is now deployed and ready for users.

As long as automatic deployment remains disabled via `PRODUCTION_MODE=true`, changes to the enterprise archive file or `REDEPLOY` file will not be sensed by the server and no redeployment will occur automatically. Use the WebLogic Console to redeploy a modified application by selecting the application using the link on the left side of the screen and employing the deployment features provided on the right (see Figure 8.14). The application may also be undeployed using this screen, a function that eliminates the application components from the server but does not remove the file or directory structure from the disk.

Deploying applications using the WebLogic Console is appropriate for complex test and production environments requiring better control of the process than provided by automatic deployment. It is not required for single-server environments in which the automatic approach properly deploys the application.

BEST PRACTICE **Manual deployment of applications using the WebLogic Console is more appropriate for complex test and production environments involving multiple servers and clustering.**

We didn't cover the WebLogic Deployer Utility or `wldeploy` Ant task in this section, but that does not mean they are inappropriate as deployment techniques. As stated in Chapter 5, these tools provide a viable alternative for deploying and redeploying applications in WebLogic Server. Choose the option that best meets your needs.

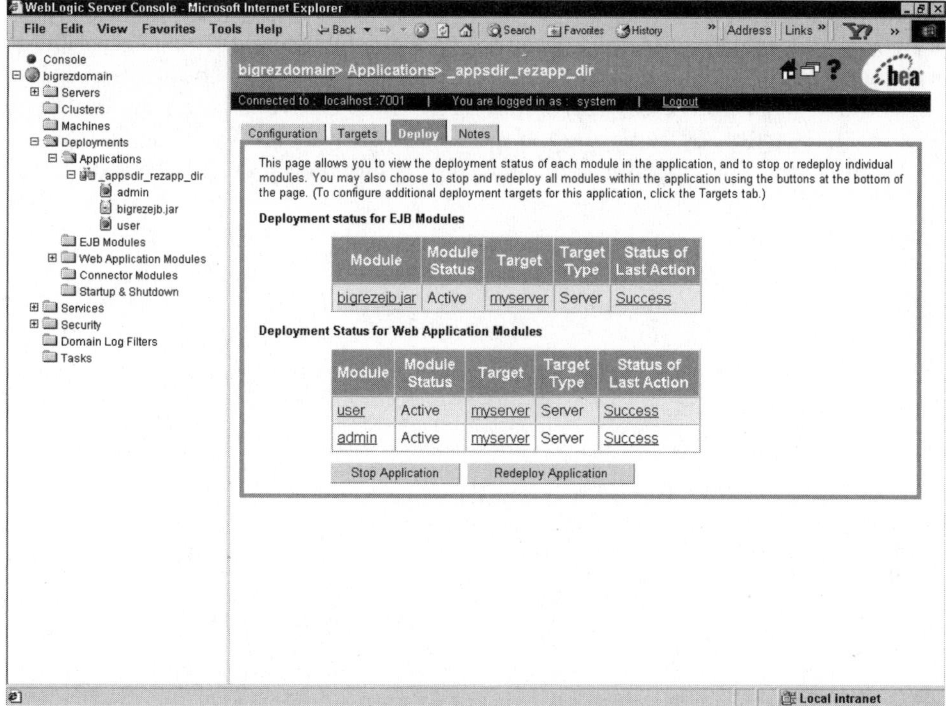

Figure 8.14 Use WebLogic Console to redeploy applications.

Chapter Review

This chapter discussed the steps required to package and deploy an EJB or enterprise application to the WebLogic Server environment.

The first section reviewed the structure and contents of an EJB archive file and discussed the steps required to compile and build the EJB archive using Ant-based build scripts.

The second section discussed the proper way to package your application using an enterprise application structure. We reviewed the structure and contents of an enterprise application including the application descriptor files and the manifest `Class-Path` technique for packaging utility archives. Both exploded and archived enterprise application structures were presented and built for *bigrez.com* using Ant-based build scripts.

The final section presented the steps necessary to deploy your enterprise application using two standard deployment techniques and discussed the importance of preparing the environment before deployment.

The *bigrez.com* application is now complete and ready for deployment in production, a task we tackle in Chapter 11. The next two chapters continue our discussion of development-related techniques by examining best practices and WebLogic Server features in the areas of JMS messaging and security. Chapter 15 completes discussion of development practices by exploring the use of Web services in WebLogic Server and then creating and deploying Web services for key reservation processes in *bigrez.com*.

Using WebLogic JMS

The Java Message Service (JMS) specification defines a standard set of interfaces for accessing messaging systems. WebLogic Server provides an enterprise-class messaging system that completely supports the JMS APIs. In addition, WebLogic Server goes the extra mile to make it easy to use other JMS-accessible messaging systems transparently from your J2EE applications. In this chapter, we begin by giving you a brief review of some key JMS concepts. Next, we jump into a detailed discussion of how the WebLogic JMS provider works. Then, we spend some time talking about WebLogic JMS design considerations. We follow that with a brief discussion of WebLogic JMS programming. Finally, we finish up this chapter with a brief discussion on using external JMS providers with WebLogic Server.

Like the rest of this book, this chapter is not intended as an introduction to either JMS or WebLogic Server's JMS implementation. If you are unfamiliar with the basics of JMS, we suggest that you study the book *Java Message Service* by Richard Monson-Haefel and David Chappell (O'Reilly, 2000) for a complete treatment of JMS. For more information on WebLogic JMS, please refer to the WebLogic Server JMS documentation at http://edocs.bea.com/wls/docs81/jms/index.html.

JMS Key Concepts

In this section, we will give you a brief review of key JMS concepts. We begin by discussing the messaging models that JMS supports. Next, we spend the bulk of this section reviewing the JMS API, which will be important for our discussions in the following sections. We end the chapter with a brief discussion of the next version of the JMS specification.

Understanding the Messaging Models

JMS supports two distinct messaging models: *point-to-point* and *publish-and-subscribe*. With point-to-point messaging, the message *producer*, also known as the *sender*, creates a message and sends it to a destination known as a *queue*. Messages sent to queues can be *persistent* or *non-persistent*. Persistent messages sent to a queue will survive server shutdowns and failures. When a message arrives at a queue, the JMS provider places the message in the queue in the order in which it was received. Each message is held in the queue until one of the following events occurs:

- A message consumer successfully processes the message.
- The message time-to-live expires.
- If the message is non-persistent, the server on which the queue resides shuts down or fails.
- The queue is deleted.

Message *consumers*, also known as *receivers*, process messages placed in a queue. Each message will be processed by only a single receiver. By default, JMS delivers messages in first-in-first-out (FIFO) order. If multiple receivers are concurrently processing messages from a single queue, the JMS provider makes sure that each message goes to only one receiver.

With the publish-and-subscribe model, the message producer creates a message and sends it to a destination known as a *topic*. Messages sent to topics can be persistent or non-persistent. Messages sent, or *published*, to a topic are delivered only to the active consumers, also known as *subscribers*, which have registered their interest, or *subscribed*, to messages sent to the topic. Subscriptions can be either *durable* or *nondurable*. When a consumer subscribes to the topic, that subscriber will receive messages sent only during the lifetime of that subscription. For durable subscriptions, the JMS provider will save a message until one of the following events occurs:

- All durable subscribers successfully process the message.
- The message time-to-live expires.
- If the message is non-persistent, the server on which the topic resides shuts down or fails.
- The topic is deleted.

For nondurable subscriptions, the JMS provider delivers each message only to the currently connected subscribers.

Reviewing the JMS 1.0.2b API

In this section, we briefly review the primary objects associated with the JMS 1.0.2b APIs. This review is intended to make it easier for you to differentiate between what the JMS specification provides and what WebLogic JMS provides. As we hope will become clear, JMS is just an interface to messaging systems that defines some of the expected behavior of the underlying messaging provider. The JMS specification stops well short of defining everything you need to build enterprise-class messaging applications using J2EE.

Connection Factories

In JMS, you use a connection factory to create connections. Applications look up connection factories in JNDI. You can think of connection factories as a set of templates used by an administrator to define common attributes about connections. Connection factories come in two primary flavors, `javax.jms.QueueConnectionFactory` and `javax.jms.TopicConnectionFactory`, which you use to create either point-to-point or publish-and-subscribe connections. JMS also provides XA versions of these connection factories for use in distributed transactions. To get a connection factory, an application uses code similar to the following:

```
InitialContext ctx = new InitialContext(connectionProperties);
QueueConnectionFactory queueConnectionFactory =
    (QueueConnectionFactory)ctx.lookup("MyConnectionFactory");
```

Connections

A JMS connection conceptually represents a physical connection to the underlying messaging system. Each JMS application will require a JMS connection in order to communicate with the JMS provider. For multithreaded applications, the specification guarantees JMS connections to be thread-safe and does not provide any specification-related reason to require more than one JMS connection to a particular JMS provider. Of course, you may find reasons for needing multiple JMS connections when working with a specific provider.

There are two types of JMS connections: `javax.jms.QueueConnection` and `javax.jms.TopicConnection`. Applications use the connection object to authenticate themselves to the provider, to create sessions, to obtain meta data about the provider, and to register for callbacks when JMS detects there is a problem with the connection. To create a connection, just invoke the appropriate method on the connection factory:

```
QueueConnection queueConnection =
    queueConnectionFactory.createQueueConnection();
```

Destinations

Destinations represent the intermediate location that producers and consumers use to exchange messages. JMS applications typically look up a destination from JNDI and use it to create a producer or consumer tied to that destination. JMS also provides methods on the session objects for obtaining references to existing destinations using a provider-specific naming syntax. Like JMS connections, destinations are thread-safe. Destinations come in two primary flavors: `javax.jms.Queue` and `javax.jms.Topic`. To get a destination, an application uses code similar to this:

```
InitialContext ctx = new InitialContext(connectionProperties);
Queue queue = (Queue)ctx.lookup("MyQueue");
```

JMS also provides a mechanism for creating temporary destinations that are specific to the JMS connection on which they are created. These temporary destinations are often used to specify a response destination in the `JMSReplyTo` message header to tell the receiver where to send the response to that particular message.

Sessions

Sessions represent a single-threaded context for producing and consuming messages and are not thread-safe. If an application wants to share a session across multiple threads, it is the application's responsibility to synchronize access to the session. Applications use sessions as factories for creating different types of objects: message producers and consumers, temporary destinations, references to existing destinations, and messages. In addition, sessions provide a mechanism for defining transaction boundaries, serializing the consumption of messages, and limiting the scope of message acknowledgment. Again, sessions come in two primary flavors: `javax.jms.QueueSession` and `javax.jms.TopicSession`. XA versions of these sessions also exist.

When a JMS message consumer finishes processing a message or set of messages, it needs to notify the JMS provider that it may delete the message(s). JMS provides two mutually exclusive ways to do this: *message acknowledgment* and *transacted sessions*. Message acknowledgment simply involves sending the JMS provider a message that tells it the messages are no longer needed. JMS sessions offer three distinct acknowledgment modes that can be used with nontransacted sessions. The message acknowledgment modes are as follows:

AUTO_ACKNOWLEDGE. Messages are automatically acknowledged by the underlying provider after the consumption of each message—for example, when the `onMessage()` method of the `javax.jms.MessageListener` returns successfully. While this is the easiest form of message acknowledgment, it is generally the most inefficient because it acknowledges only a single message at a time. With `AUTO_ACKNOWLEDGE` mode, there is a small window during which it is possible for the last message received, but not yet acknowledged, to be redelivered in the event of a failure.

DUPS_OK_ACKNOWLEDGE. This is similar to AUTO_ACKNOWLEDGE mode except that the underlying provider can acknowledge the messages in a lazy fashion, making it more efficient. As the name indicates, this lazy acknowledgment can result in the application receiving duplicate messages. This is generally the most efficient form of acknowledgment because it minimizes the work done by the session to eliminate duplicate messages and allows the provider to optimize acknowledgments. This mode exposes the application to the possibility of receiving sets of duplicate messages.

CLIENT_ACKNOWLEDGE. Messages are acknowledged only when the client explicitly calls the `acknowledge()` method on a message. Calling `acknowledge()` acknowledges all consumed messages on the current session, not just the message on which it is invoked. The efficiency of this mode and the application's exposure to duplicate messages depend on the application's acknowledgment strategy. We will talk more about acknowledgment strategies later.

Transacted sessions allow you to define units of work that apply only to messages sent or received in the scope of the JMS session. In contrast to nontransacted sessions that use JTA transactions, transacted sessions do not include any other external resources such as EJBs, databases accessed via JDBC, or enterprise information systems accessed through J2EE Connector Architecture (J2EE CA) adapters. Message acknowledgment is handled automatically when transacted sessions either commit or roll back their units of work.

When creating sessions, applications must specify the transaction and message acknowledgment modes. The transaction mode defines whether you want to use a transacted session; message acknowledgment mode defines which of the acknowledgment modes you want to use for nontransacted sessions. To create a nontransacted session that uses AUTO_ACKNOWLEDGE mode, an application would use code similar to this:

```
QueueSession queueSession =
queueConnection.createQueueSession(false, Session.AUTO_ACKNOWLEDGE);
```

JMS also supports the use of XA transactions with providers that implement the XA versions of the JMS objects. Many large enterprise applications that use JMS will probably also use XA transactions. As is the case with transacted session, message acknowledgment is handled automatically at transaction commit or rollback. When using XA transactions, make sure to create the session with the *transacted* argument (the first argument) set to `false` and any message acknowledgment mode you like because the message acknowledgment mode will be ignored when a transaction context is present.

Message Producers and Consumers

Message producers allow an application to send a message to a destination. Producers also have characteristics that affect messages sent through them. These characteristics include things such as whether to use persistent delivery, the priority of the message, and the message's time-to-live. JMS defines two types of message producers: `javax.jms.QueueSender` and `javax.jms.TopicPublisher`. The code to create a message producer looks like this:

```
QueueSender queueSender = queueSession.createSender(queue);
```

The two types of message consumers are `javax.jms.QueueReceiver` and `javax.jms.TopicSubscriber`. Message consumers provide the context by which an application can receive messages from a particular destination. By specifying a message selector, consumers can limit the messages they receive to only the subset of messages in which they have an interest. Message consumers can receive messages synchronously by explicitly calling the consumer's `receive()` method or asynchronously by registering a callback object that implements the `javax.jms.MessageListener` interface using the consumer's `setMessageListener()` method:

```
QueueReceiver queueReceiver = queueSession.createReceiver(queue);
queueReceiver.setMessageListener(new MyMessageListener());
queueConnection.start();
```

Notice that we are calling the connection's `start()` method to tell the connection we are ready to start receiving messages. JMS requires that you explicitly start a connection before any messages can be received.

Durable Subscribers

When subscribing to a topic, you can create either a durable or nondurable subscription. Nondurable subscriptions are valid only from the time that you create them until the time you either unsubscribe or otherwise disconnect from the messaging system. This means that any failure that disconnects the application will automatically terminate the subscription. When you resubscribe, any messages sent between the time that you were disconnected and you resubscribed will not be available—even if the message's delivery mode is persistent. In many situations, this is the desired behavior; if it is not, then you need to use a durable subscription.

With durable subscriptions, the subscriber provides a unique identifier to identify the subscription. Once the subscription is accepted, the messaging system will try to deliver all messages it receives to the durable subscriber. If the subscriber disconnects without unsubscribing, the JMS provider will buffer all of the messages the subscriber has not seen until the subscriber returns. If the delivery mode is non-persistent, the messages are buffered in memory and thus subject to message loss during failures.

Asynchronous Consumers and Transactions

JMS supports two types of transactions: transacted sessions and JTA transactions. With transacted sessions, the transaction includes only the JMS resources associated with the transacted JMS session. JTA transactions are truly global transactions that can include JMS, EJB, JDBC, and J2EE CA resources.

JMS also supports asynchronous message consumers. These asynchronous message consumers can use transacted sessions to define JMS-only units of work. They cannot, however, generally support JTA transactions that include the asynchronous delivery of the message. The reasons for this are somewhat complex. When registering an asynchronous `MessageListener`, JMS does not provide a mechanism to tell the JMS provider to start a JTA transaction before delivering the message. Because the JMS provider does not start the transaction before it delivers the message, the only other way that we could include the message delivery in the JTA transaction would be if JMS supported a callback mechanism to tell it that a previously delivered, but unacknowledged message should be considered part of an existing JTA transaction (started by the `MessageListener` after the message was delivered).

The story gets worse when you consider the EJB 2.0 specification's requirements for supporting JTA transactional delivery of messages to message-driven EJBs. There are two primary strategies for addressing this issue. The first strategy is for the JMS provider to provide a nonstandard API that can be used to associate a previously delivered, but unacknowledged message with a JTA transaction. While this works fine for applications that use the same vendor for both the EJB and JMS providers, it clearly does not work when mixing vendors unless the vendors can agree on the nonstandard API and semantics. The other strategy is to simulate asynchronous delivery using synchronous delivery under the covers. As we will see later, WebLogic Server supports both of these strategies to make it possible to integrate J2EE applications with any JMS provider that supports XA transactions.

Message Selectors

Sometimes a consumer is interested in only a subset of the messages delivered to a destination. JMS provides a standard filtering facility for message consumers, known as *message selectors*. Message selectors use a syntax similar to a `SQL WHERE` clause to create expressions that JMS will evaluate against message headers and/or properties. You can specify a selector when you create a message consumer:

```
QueueReceiver queueReceiver =
    queueSession.createReceiver(queue, "JMSPriority > 5");
queueReceiver.setMessageListener(new MyMessageListener());
queueConnection.start();
```

This selector ensures that messages will be delivered to this consumer only if the value of the `JMSPriority` header is greater than 5.

Message selectors are static. You cannot change them without first closing the current consumer and creating a new one. Changing a durable subscription's selector ends the subscription; all unconsumed messages for that subscription are deleted and the subscription is recreated, as required by the JMS specification.

As you can imagine, the use of selectors adds overhead to message delivery that will affect the performance and scalability of the application. Where possible, it is often better to split a destination into multiple destinations and eliminate the need for message selectors. We will discuss message selector design and performance implications in more detail later.

Messages

Messages form the foundation of any JMS application. Applications use messages to carry data associated with a particular event. As shown in Figure 9.1, JMS divides messages into three logical parts: headers, properties, and the body.

Message headers specify certain characteristics of a message potentially of interest to applications. For most JMS headers, the JMS provider is responsible for setting the values of these characteristics. `JMSReplyTo` and `JMSCorrelationID` are two notable exceptions often used by applications to implement a request/reply pattern of message exchange.

Message properties allow applications to define additional characteristics about a message. The JMS specification reserves all property names that begin with `JMSX`. Typically, message properties are most useful for applications that need to apply message selectors to application-specific data.

The message body contains the payload of the message. What type of information a message contains depends on the type of message the application chooses to use. JMS defines five different types of message objects, all of which derive from `javax.jms.Message`:

TextMessage. Applications use this message type to send simple text strings or more complex, text-based data structures like XML messages.

BytesMessage. Applications use this message type to send a raw array of bytes. Typically, you would use this to retain an application's native data format.

ObjectMessage. Applications use this message type to send a serialized Java object.

StreamMessage. Applications use this message type to send an ordered stream of Java primitive types or the object versions of these primitive types, such as `java.lang.Integer` or `java.lang.Double`.

MapMessage. Applications use this message type to send an unordered set of name-value pairs. All names must be unique, and the values must be Java primitive types or the object versions of these primitive types.

To create a message and send it to a destination, use code like that shown here:

```
TextMessage message = queueSession.createTextMessage("message body");
queueSender.send(message);
```

Upcoming JMS 1.1 Changes

J2EE 1.3 currently includes the JMS Specification 1.0.2b as a mandatory component for any J2EE 1.3-compatible application server. With the introduction of J2EE 1.4, JMS 1.1 will replace the older 1.0.2b specification. Before we move on, we want you to understand the changes coming in JMS 1.1.

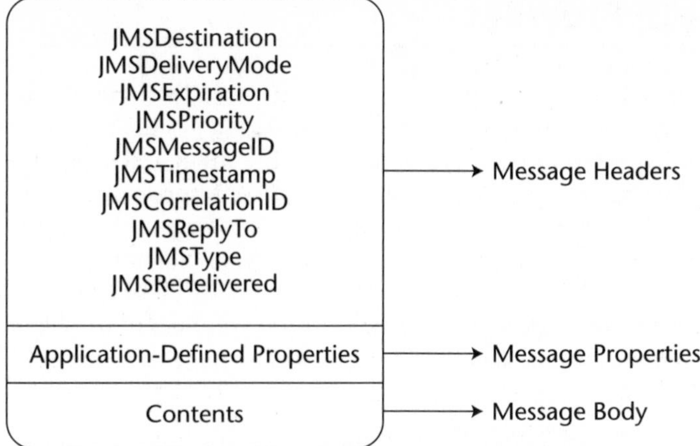

Figure 9.1 The anatomy of a JMS message.

As we have seen, JMS 1.0.2b forces an application developer to make a strong distinction between the two messaging models during development. Once a developer selects a particular model, it is difficult to switch to a different model because the underlying APIs for each messaging model are very different. Moreover, the two messaging models cannot interoperate within the same JMS transaction context, as defined by transacted sessions. For example, in order to receive messages from a queue and publish messages to a topic, an application must create two sessions, a `QueueSession` for the receiver and a `TopicSession` for the publisher. JMS defines the transacted session's transaction scope to be that of the session, and because the receiver and publisher were forced to use two different sessions, the work could not be completed in the context of a single transaction. Of course, this deficiency can be overcome by using JTA transactions if they are available for the chosen JMS provider. We will discuss both transacted sessions and JTA transactions in more detail a little later in this chapter.

JMS 1.1 addresses these problems by defining a unified API for both messaging models. The unified API simplifies the client-programming model, and applications can use the same interfaces regardless of the messaging model used. Additional methods have also been added to support the ability to include point-to-point and publish-and-subscribe messaging in the same transaction. Fortunately, the JMS 1.1 specification is completely backward compatible with JMS 1.0.2b so that existing JMS applications will continue to work without modification.

Although we will not spend additional time discussing JMS 1.1, we wanted to point it out for a specific reason. WebLogic Server provides a unified JMS implementation that can support both the 1.0.2b and 1.1 versions of the JMS specification. Because of J2EE licensing restrictions imposed by Sun Microsystems, the JMS 1.1 specification is not yet officially supported by WebLogic Server. If you download the JMS 1.1 `JAR` file from Sun's Web site at http://java.sun.com/products/jms/docs.html and put it at the front of your WebLogic Server instance's classpath, you will be able to use the JMS 1.1 APIs. This works for both WebLogic Server 7.0 and 8.1.

The WebLogic JMS Provider

In this section, we will take a detailed look at the WebLogic JMS provider implementation. As you will see, WebLogic JMS not only provides a messaging system that fully implements the JMS specification but also provides other configuration and programming options that go well beyond what JMS defines to provide enterprise-class messaging features. We will not attempt to provide comprehensive coverage of WebLogic JMS, but will instead focus our discussions on the details that we feel are most important for designing and building robust messaging applications with WebLogic JMS. For more comprehensive coverage of JMS, we refer you to the WebLogic JMS documentation at http://edocs.bea.com/wls/docs81/jms/index.html.

Understanding WebLogic JMS Servers

WebLogic JMS introduces the *JMS server*. A JMS server defines a set of JMS destinations and any associated persistent store that reside on a single WebLogic Server instance. A WebLogic Server instance can host zero or more JMS servers and can serve as a migration target for zero or more JMS servers. All destination names must be unique across every JMS server in a WebLogic Server instance. If you are deploying a JMS server into a clustered server, the destination names must be unique across every JMS server deployed to any member of the cluster.

When you are using WebLogic Clustering, a JMS server represents the unit of migration when failing over a set of destinations from one WebLogic Server instance to another. By associating destinations with a JMS server, WebLogic JMS makes it easier to migrate a set of destinations from one WebLogic Server instance to another. We will talk more about JMS server migration in the next section.

Clustering WebLogic JMS

WebLogic JMS clustering is built on top of the basic WebLogic Server clustering mechanisms. It provides a JMS application with the features you would expect from a clustered messaging infrastructure. In this section, we will take a closer look at WebLogic JMS clustering, which will include discussions on the following features of clustering:

- *Location transparency* provides the application with a uniform view of the messaging system by hiding the physical locations of JMS objects.
- *Connection routing, load balancing,* and *failover* provide the application with a single, logical connection into the messaging system.
- *Distributed destinations* provide a single, logical destination distributed across multiple servers in the cluster to support both load balancing and high availability.
- *JMS server migration* allows you to migrate a set of destinations to another server in the event of server failure or maintenance outage.

Location Transparency

WebLogic JMS registers managed objects such as connection factories and destinations in JNDI. Because WebLogic Server provides JNDI replication across a cluster, an application can simply look up the objects by their JNDI name, regardless of which servers in the cluster are hosting the objects. For example, applications can access a JMS destination without knowing which WebLogic Server instance hosts the JMS server that holds the destination. In the same way, you can create a JMS connection and session without having to worry about what servers are in the cluster or where the destinations you are using reside.

Connection Routing, Load Balancing, and Failover

When deployed to a cluster, WebLogic JMS connection factories provide transparent access to all JMS servers in the cluster. This means that any JMS connection you create using one of these factories will have access to every JMS destination across the cluster. How this works depends on where the application is located in relation to the WebLogic Server cluster.

For client applications not running in a WebLogic Server instance, WebLogic JMS defaults to using a simple round-robin algorithm to distribute connection requests across all running servers in the cluster on which the connection factory is deployed. The algorithm's state, however, is tied to each client's copy of the connection factory. Because most clients create only one connection with their connection factory, the overall load distribution will be relatively uniform because the load-balancing algorithm is initialized by randomly selecting the initial server. Connection factories provide failover by routing connection requests around failed servers.

Once the client creates a connection, WebLogic JMS routes all JMS operations over that same connection to any WebLogic Server in the cluster. This enables WebLogic JMS clusters to support a large number of concurrent clients but does expose the client to failures if the server to which it is connected fails. To handle this problem gracefully, clients must use the standard JMS mechanism to register an object that implements that `javax.jms.ExceptionListener` interface with the connection by calling the `setExceptionListener()` method. To recover from a failed connection, you will need to use the connection factory to create a new connection and any other objects that were associated with the failed connection object.

Another interesting failure scenario occurs when the JMS connection is still operational but the WebLogic Server instance on which a particular JMS destination resides fails. For example, the client's JMS connection is talking with `server1`, but it is asynchronously consuming messages from a destination on `server2`. If the client is asynchronously consuming messages using one of the failed destinations, then you need some way to notify the client application that the `MessageConsumer` is no longer valid. Unfortunately, the JMS specification does not specify how to handle such problems.

WebLogic JMS provides an extension that allows you to register objects that implement the `javax.jms.ExceptionListener` interface on a JMS session. To use this extension, the application needs to cast the session to a `weblogic.jms.extensions.WLSession` type in order to invoke the `setExceptionListener()` method:

```
WLSession wlSession = (WLSession)queueSession;
wlSession.setExceptionListener(new MyExceptionListener());
```

Whenever the destination failure scenario happens, the exception listeners will receive a callback with a `weblogic.jms.extensions.ConsumerClosedException` event for any affected consumers. At this point, the JMS consumers for destinations not on the failed server are okay, the JMS session is okay, and the JMS connection is okay. If the application has received but not acknowledged any messages from the failed server, though, the application cannot acknowledge these messages. Unfortunately, this means that the only thing left to do is to call the session's `recover()` method. Invoking this method will recover all unacknowledged messages for the entire session, which may cause all of the recovered messages to be redelivered—even for consumers that did not fail. To mitigate this scenario, as well as to maximize concurrency, you should use one session per message consumer.

BEST PRACTICE Client applications consuming messages asynchronously should register exception listeners on their JMS sessions using the `weblogic.jms.extensions.WLSession` extension. Because recovering from this state requires invoking the `recover()` method on the session, you should use a separate session for each consumer to minimize the impact of the failure of a destination's server.

For server-side applications, WebLogic JMS avoids extra network traffic by processing connection requests locally wherever possible. If the connection factory is not deployed locally, then the server-side application will connect to one of the servers where the connection factory exists. In most applications, it is very desirable to distribute the load across all servers in a cluster. There are multiple ways to achieve this. In almost all situations, it is best to distribute the load as it enters the cluster and keep all processing of a particular message within the local server to which the message was delivered. Therefore, we recommend deploying your applications and JMS resources homogeneously across the cluster. Because any particular destination must reside on only one server in the cluster, we need to use distributed destinations to accomplish this homogenous distribution.

BEST PRACTICE For JMS applications that use all servers in the cluster, deploy your connection factories to all servers in the cluster. For applications that use only a subset of the cluster for JMS, deploy the connection factories on the WebLogic Server instances where the JMS servers reside. Following this rule will help eliminate unnecessary routing of JMS requests through servers with no JMS server deployed.

Distributed Destinations

Distributed destinations give WebLogic JMS the ability to make JMS destinations highly available and load balanced. To create a distributed destination, simply map multiple member JMS destinations to a single, logical, distributed JMS destination. JMS applications use distributed destinations just like any other JMS destination. How WebLogic JMS routes application requests to the underlying member JMS destinations depends on many different factors, such as where the application resides (in a remote client or in a server), what the application is doing (sending messages or receiving messages), what type of destination is used (queue or topic), and how many consumers there are.

WebLogic JMS load balances message producers to a distributed destination on a request-by-request basis. This means that, all other things being equal, the messages produced by a client will be evenly distributed across the member destinations of the distributed destination. For message consumers, WebLogic JMS load balances them at creation time, thereby pinning each consumer to a member destination. WebLogic JMS also looks at several other factors when load balancing producers and consumers, such as the number of consumers for a member destination, the location of the member destinations, the availability of a persistent store (if the message delivery mode is persistent), and the current transaction context. Any of these other factors can cause WebLogic JMS to alter its default load-balancing policy for a particular message or destination. We will spend the rest of this section explaining how WebLogic JMS routes application requests that use distributed destinations.

One important thing to note: WebLogic JMS is a robust, enterprise-level messaging system. As such, many different configuration options can lead to many different situations that alter the behavior of message routing. For example, if a message producer is sending a persistent message to a distributed destination where not all member destinations have an associated persistent store, WebLogic JMS will do its best to route the message to a destination with a persistent store. There are so many of these types of situations and rules that we cannot possibly cover all of them here. In general, we highly recommend that you deploy distributed destinations homogeneously across the cluster using similar configurations for each participating JMS server and its associated destinations. Therefore, we will focus on describing the behavior of distributed destinations when deployed in homogenous configurations. For more complete information, please refer to the WebLogic Server documentation at http://edocs.bea.com/wls/docs81/jms/implement.html.

BEST PRACTICE **When you are deploying distributed destinations, always use similar settings for every JMS server and member destination in the cluster.**

Producing Messages to a Distributed Queue

Figure 9.2 illustrates the producer's perspective of distributed queue operation using the default load-balancing configuration. There are three WebLogic Server instances running in a cluster, each hosting a member destination (`Queue1`, `Queue2`, and `Queue3`) of the distributed queue, `DistributedQueue`. Each message sent by the producer is load balanced across the member destinations. Because this is a point-to-point messaging model, only one consumer will receive each message.

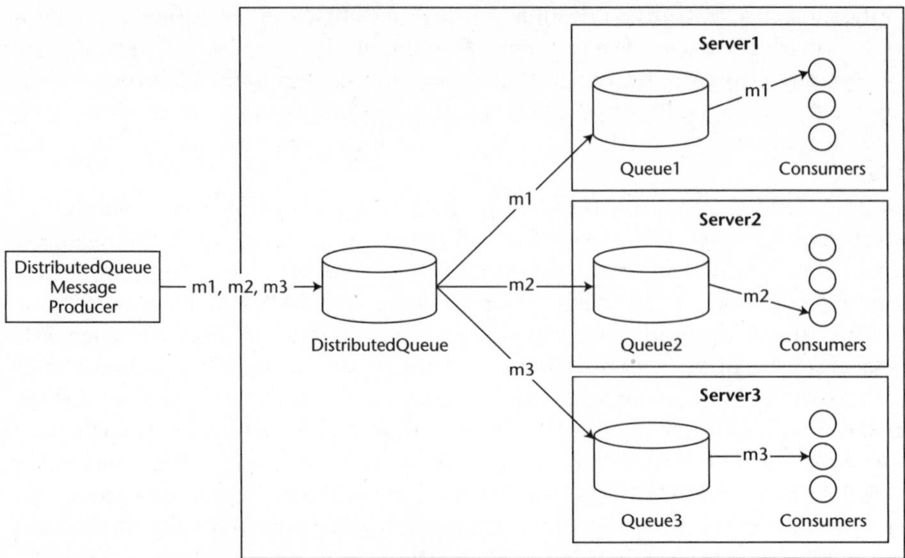

Figure 9.2 Sending messages to a distributed queue.

When a producer sends messages to a distributed queue, WebLogic JMS first determines how to load balance the `send()` requests. You can control this with the connection factory's `Load Balancing Enabled` checkbox, which is enabled by default, and the distributed destination's `Load Balancing Policy`, which is round-robin by default. If load balancing is enabled, WebLogic JMS load balances each producer on every `send()` call using the algorithm specified by the load-balancing policy. If it is disabled, WebLogic JMS load balances only each producer's first call to `send()`; all subsequent messages from a particular producer will be sent to the same member destination.

WebLogic JMS uses several other heuristics that override the default load-balancing behavior; the heuristics are applied in this order:

- *Persistent store availability* means that WebLogic JMS will prefer destinations whose underlying JMS server has a persistent store for delivering persistent messages.
- *Transaction affinity* means that WebLogic JMS will try to send all messages associated with a particular transaction context to the same JMS server to minimize the number of JMS servers involved in the transaction.
- *Server affinity* means that WebLogic JMS will try to use a destination in the local process. WebLogic JMS will use member destinations in the WebLogic Server instance in which the producer/consumer is running or to which the producer/consumer's JMS connection is connected. Although this is the default behavior, you can disable this behavior by deselecting the connection factory's `Server Affinity Enabled` checkbox.

- *Zero consumer queues* means that WebLogic JMS will do its best to avoid sending messages to member queues with zero consumers, unless all member queues have zero consumers. Because of the transient nature of some message consumers, it is still possible for messages to end up on queues with zero consumers.

Figure 9.2 portrays a conceptual view of how a distributed queue works. In reality, all routing to a member queue occurs inside a WebLogic Server process. Each producer has a JMS connection attached to one WebLogic Server in the cluster. By default, server affinity causes WebLogic JMS to attempt to send the messages from a particular producer to a member destination on the server to which the producer's JMS connection is attached. The message may be routed to a different destination if server affinity is disabled, there is no local member destination, or one of the other heuristics takes precedence.

TIP By default, server affinity causes message producers sending messages to a distributed queue always to send to the member queue in the JMS server to which the producer is connected. To enable a producer to load balance messages across member destinations, disable server affinity on the connection factory the producer is using. Of course, this load balancing will still be subject to other heuristics that might skew the distribution of messages.

Another important feature of distributed queues is message forwarding. The zero consumer queues heuristic will try to prevent routing point-to-point messages to a member destination with no consumers if there are other member destinations with consumers. It is still possible, though, for messages to end up on a queue with no consumers if, for example, a consumer exits after the message is sent but before it is received. WebLogic JMS provides a forwarding mechanism by which messages can be forwarded from a member queue with no consumers to a member queue with consumers after a specified amount of time. The distributed queue's `Forward Delay` attribute controls the number of seconds WebLogic JMS will wait before trying to forward the messages. By default, the value is set to –1, which means that forwarding is disabled.

Consuming Messages from a Distributed Queue

When an application creates a message consumer for a distributed queue, WebLogic JMS associates the consumer with one of the member destinations of the distributed queue. From that point on, the consumer is pinned to that member destination. Figure 9.3 illustrates the operation of a distributed queue from the consumer's perspective. In this figure, the three `DistributedQueue` consumers have each been associated with one of the member destinations. Each consumer will be eligible to receive only messages routed to his or her respective member destinations.

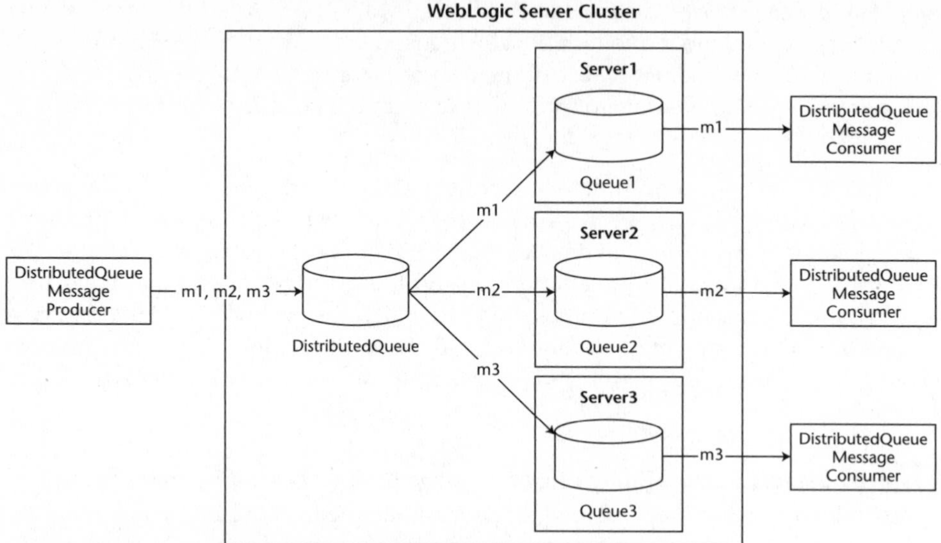

Figure 9.3 Consuming messages from a distributed queue.

When consumers are created, WebLogic JMS associates the consumer with a member destination by load-balancing the consumers across the available member destinations. Although this load balancing is done only once for each consumer, the mechanisms are very similar to those used for load balancing messages sent to a distributed queue. All other things being equal, WebLogic JMS will use the distributed destination's load-balancing policy to distribute the consumers across all member destinations. Just as before, WebLogic JMS uses heuristic optimizations that will override the default load-balancing mechanism. If server affinity is enabled, WebLogic JMS will try to associate the consumer with a local member destination, as described previously. WebLogic JMS will also try to associate new consumers with member destinations that currently have zero consumers, unless server affinity prevents this.

When a WebLogic Server hosting a member of a distributed queue fails, all unconsumed persistent messages remain on the failed server's queue. These messages will not be available until either the WebLogic Server instance is restarted or the JMS server containing the member queue is migrated to another WebLogic Server instance. We will talk more about JMS server migration later in this section. If the messages are nonpersistent, all of the unconsumed messages will be lost.

WebLogic JMS distributed queue consumers are essentially the same as nondistributed queue consumers once the association between the consumer and the member destination has been established. If the WebLogic Server hosting the member queue fails, WebLogic JMS throws a `javax.jms.JMSException` to all synchronous consumers. For asynchronous consumers, the behavior varies depending on whether the server hosting the destination is also the one to which the consumer's JMS connection is attached. If the server is the one to which the JMS connection is attached, the connection's `ExceptionListener` is notified and the application will have to recreate the JMS connection and all of its associated objects (sessions, consumers, producers, etc.). The more interesting case occurs when the consumer is using one server for the JMS connection and another server for the destination. As we discussed in the "Connection Routing, Load Balancing, and Failover" section, you can register an `ExceptionListener` with the WebLogic JMS session to receive notification when the destination's server fails but the connection's server does not. Make sure you understand the caveats to this approach, which we have already discussed.

Producing Messages to a Distributed Topic

Figure 9.4 illustrates the operation of a distributed topic from the producer's perspective. As in the previous example, there are three WebLogic Server instances running in a cluster, each hosting a member destination (`Topic1`, `Topic2`, and `Topic3`) of the distributed topic, `DistributedTopic`. When a producer sends messages to a distributed topic, WebLogic JMS sends a copy of the message to every available member topic that has at least one consumer. Because all member topics in Figure 9.4 have at least one consumer, every message is sent to the three member topics. If the three consumers attached to `Topic3` were to unsubscribe from `DistributedTopic`, any future messages would be sent only to `Topic1` and `Topic2` until a new consumer was assigned to `Topic3`.

If you publish messages directly to a topic that is associated with a distributed topic, WebLogic JMS will replicate the messages to every member of the distributed topic, just as it would if you had published the messages to the distributed topic itself. This means that any topic associated with a distributed topic will distribute messages just as the distributed topic does.

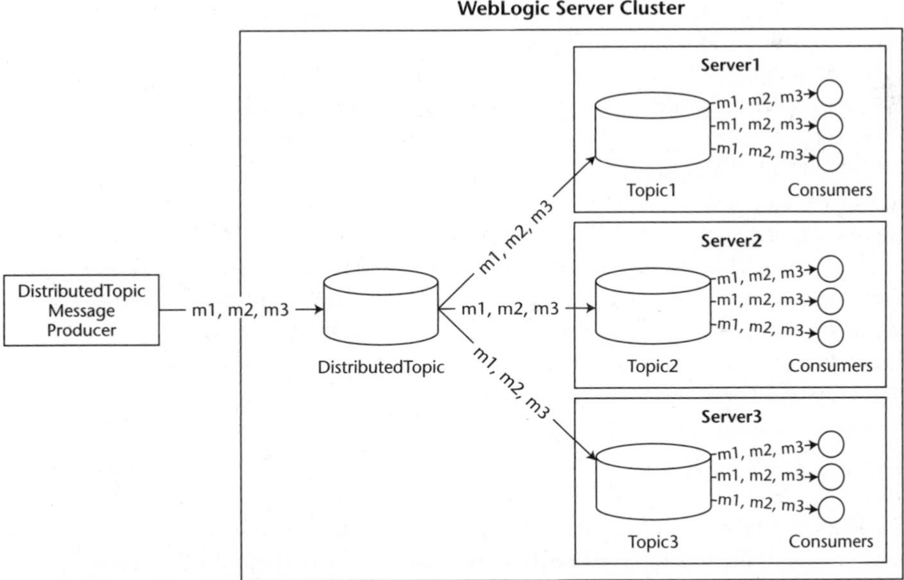

Figure 9.4 Publishing messages to a distributed topic.

As we discuss later in the "Persistent Stores" section, persistent messages sent to a distributed topic are not actually persisted unless there are one or more durable subscribers. If one or more of the distributed topic's member topics is unavailable, then WebLogic JMS will save the persistent messages and forward them once the member topic becomes available. This means that any durable subscribers for member topics will eventually receive messages once their member topics become available and they are able to reconnect. On the other hand, messages sent to distributed topics with no durable subscribers are delivered only to the active set of subscribers at the time the message is published. We will talk more about durable subscribers and message persistence later.

Consuming Messages from a Distributed Topic

Distributed topic consumers are similar to distributed queue consumers; WebLogic JMS associates them with a member destination at the time they are created. WebLogic JMS uses the same load-balancing mechanisms and optimization heuristics for distributed topic consumers that it uses for distributed queue consumers. The same error-handling mechanisms that we discussed for distributed queue consumers also apply to distributed topic consumers. There are two important differences in how consumers work with distributed topics that we need to mention.

First, any durable subscriptions must be made with a distributed topic's member destinations. WebLogic JMS does not currently support creating a durable subscription with a distributed topic directly. This is really unfortunate because while it does not prevent you from building an application that leverages distributed topics with durable subscribers, it does make it more difficult (because you have to build knowledge of the member topics into the application) and potentially less efficient (you won't be able to leverage server affinity because you have no way of knowing with which server your JMS connection is associated).

Second, message-driven bean (MDB) deployments are treated as a single consumer per member topic. This means that regardless of how many MDB instances are in the pool on each server, messages will be sent to a single MDB instance for each member topic. If you stop to think about it, this is desirable because the whole idea of deploying an MDB is to create one virtual consumer per deployment. You probably do not want each message sent to the topic to be processed by multiple MDB instances in the same server. Where this becomes less clear is when you think about deploying an MDB to a cluster using a distributed destination. In some cases, you might actually want each message processed in each server; in others, it might be desirable to process each message once across the entire cluster. Currently, WebLogic JMS supports only sending each message to all servers hosting the MDB.

Migrating JMS Servers

WebLogic Server provides a migration framework that allows for an orderly migration of services from one WebLogic Server instance to another instance in the same cluster. You can use the WebLogic Console, the `weblogic.Admin` program, or a JMX program to perform the actual migration. Currently, you are responsible for deciding when to migrate a service. WebLogic JMS supports a migration framework that simplifies the migration of a JMS server from one instance of WebLogic Server to another instance of WebLogic Server in the same cluster, if properly configured.

Migrating a JMS server from one WebLogic Server instance to another is simple provided that the target server has access to all of the JMS server's resources used by the source server. If a persistent store is involved, the persistent store will need to be available on the target server. If the source server failed with transactions in flight, you will also need to migrate the JTA service, and its associated transaction log files, so that these in-flight transactions can be recovered. A complete discussion of the configuration and use of the WebLogic Server migration framework to perform JMS server migration can be found in Chapter 11.

BEST PRACTICE **If you need to be able to move a JMS destination to another server to handle failover, always use the migration framework rather than trying to do it yourself.**

Configuring WebLogic JMS

Now that you understand the high-level overview of WebLogic JMS clustering, let's take a more detailed look at the many different configuration options that can affect your JMS applications. We will cover only a subset of the functionality, and we recommend that you consult the WebLogic JMS documentation for more information.

Connection Factories

A JMS connection factory can be thought of as a template defining common connection attributes. Once you create connection factories using the WebLogic Console, the connection factories are bound into JNDI when WebLogic Server starts up. Each connection factory can be deployed on multiple WebLogic Server instances or clusters. An application accesses JMS by looking up a connection factory and using the connection factory to create a connection. Once the connection is established, all predefined connection factory attributes are applied to the connection.

Let's look at a few of the more important connection factory attributes. A complete discussion of individual attributes is outside the scope of this chapter, and you should consult the WebLogic JMS documentation if you're interested. Using the WebLogic Console, navigate to the `Services->JMS->Connection Factories` folder in the left-hand navigation bar and create a new connection factory. The following list explains some of the settings on the connection factory's `General Configuration` tab:

Default Message Delivery Attributes. These settings include `Priority`, `Time to Live`, `Time to Deliver`, `Delivery Mode`, and `Redelivery Delay`. Values set here are used for messages for which these attributes are not explicitly set in the application or not overridden by other configuration parameters.

Messages Maximum. This parameter is not a true message quota, as the name might lead you to believe. For a normal JMS session, this value indicates the maximum numbers of outstanding messages (that is, messages that have not yet been processed by the consumer's business logic) that a consumer is willing to buffer locally. If a consumer falls behind to the point where it has too many outstanding messages, WebLogic JMS will buffer the messages at the server until the client starts to catch up. If the session is a WebLogic JMS multicast session, the server will not buffer the overflowed messages and will instead discard them based on the policy specified by the `Overrun Policy` attribute.

Acknowledge Policy. This setting applies only to message consumers that use the `CLIENT_ACKNOWLEDGE` acknowledgment mode. In previous versions of the JMS specification, the exact semantics of the `acknowledge()` method were not well defined. WebLogic JMS chose to implement the `acknowledge()` method so that it acknowledged all messages up to and including the current message being acknowledged. With the release of the JMS 1.0.2b specification, Sun clarified the behavior to state that the `acknowledge()` method should acknowledge all messages received by the associated JMS session—even those received after the message currently being acknowledged. A value of `ACKNOWLEDGE_PREVIOUS` in the `Acknowledge Policy` retains the old WebLogic JMS behavior while `ACKNOWLEDGE_ALL` yields the JMS 1.0.2b behavior.

Load Balancing Enabled. This setting indicates whether to load balance the messages sent to a distributed destination on a per-call basis. If checked (the default), associated producers' messages are load balanced across the member destinations on every call to `QueueSender.send()` or `TopicPublisher.publish()`. Otherwise, the load balancing occurs only on the first invocation, and all future invocations will go to the same member destination, unless a failure occurs. This attribute has no effect on the consumers and applies only to *pinned* producers created through this connection factory. A pinned producer sets its destination when it is created and cannot change it afterward.

Server Affinity Enabled. This checkbox controls how WebLogic JMS load balances consumers or producers running inside a WebLogic Server instance across a distributed destination. If enabled, WebLogic JMS prefers to associate consumers and producers with member destinations located in the same server process. If disabled, WebLogic JMS load balances them across all member destinations in the distributed destination just as it would if the consumers and producers were running in a remote client process.

BEST PRACTICE Most applications should use the default values for Server Affinity Enabled and Load Balancing Enabled, which are true for both settings.

We will discuss the connection factory's `Transactions Configuration` and `Flow Control Configuration` tabs later in this chapter. Like most configuration objects in WebLogic Server, connection factories must be targeted to one or more WebLogic Server instances to make them accessible to applications.

WebLogic JMS defines one connection factory, `weblogic.jms.ConnectionFactory`, which is enabled by default. WebLogic Server 8.1 also adds another new XA connection factory, `weblogic.jms.XAConnectionFactory`, which is also enabled by default. You can disable them by deselecting the `Enable Default JMS Connection Factories` checkbox in the server's `JMS Services` tab of the WebLogic Console. Note that this also disables the `javax.jms.QueueConnectionFactory` and `javax.jms.TopicConnectionFactory` connection factories that are deprecated but still available to support backward compatibility with WebLogic Server 5.1. Because the default connection factory settings cannot be changed, we recommend that you always define application-specific connection factories. When choosing JNDI names for user-defined connection factories (or, for that matter, anything else), avoid using JNDI names in the `javax.*` and `weblogic.*` namespaces.

BEST PRACTICE Always define application-specific JMS connection factories and disable the default JMS connection factories. Avoid using JNDI names in the `javax.*` or `weblogic.*` namespaces.

Templates

Templates provide an efficient way to define multiple destinations with similar attribute settings. By predefining a template, you can very quickly create a set of destinations with similar characteristics. Changing a value in a template changes the behavior for all destinations using that template. Each destination can override any template-defined attribute by setting the value for the attribute explicitly on the destination itself. Using JMS templates is completely optional for applications that use predefined destinations. Any application wishing to use temporary destinations, though, is required to assign a `Temporary Template` to the WebLogic JMS server(s) involved.

BEST PRACTICE Use JMS templates to create and maintain multiple destinations with similar characteristics.

Destination Keys

By default, WebLogic JMS destinations use first-in-first-out (FIFO) ordering. Simply put, the next message to be processed by a consumer will be the message that has been waiting in the destination the longest. WebLogic JMS also gives you the ability to use message headers or property values to sort messages in either ascending or descending order. To do this, you need to define one or more *destination keys* and associate these keys with a JMS destination, either directly or through the use of a template. Any destination can have zero or more destination keys that control the ordering of messages in the destination. By creating a descending order destination key on the `JMSMessageID` message header, we can configure a destination to use last-in-first-out (LIFO) ordering.

It is important to note that using sorting orders other than FIFO or LIFO increases the overhead of sending a message. WebLogic JMS will have to scan some portion of the messages in a destination to determine where to place the incoming message. While this is not a big deal for destinations with a small backlog of messages, it can be a huge performance penalty for destinations containing a large backlog of messages. Therefore, we recommend avoiding sorted destinations unless the price of not sorting the destination (for example, in increased application complexity) is higher than the cost of the potential performance degradation.

In most cases, the default FIFO sort order works best and will always give the best performance. You can change the sorting order to LIFO using the `JMSMessageID` without any significant performance penalty. Sorting destinations by any other property can cause significant performance degradation on the producer and/or the consumer. The amount of performance degradation will depend on the number of undelivered messages stored in the destination at any point in time.

BEST PRACTICE FIFO or LIFO sort orders provide the best performance. Any other sorting order can cause significant performance degradation that will be proportional to the number of undelivered messages stored in the destination.

Time-to-Deliver Extension

WebLogic JMS provides a *time-to-deliver* extension, which allows sending messages that will not be delivered until some time in the future. This extension can be a very useful feature for implementing certain types of application functionality. To use it, simply set the producer's time to deliver before sending the message, as shown here. This will cause the producer to set the WebLogic JMS-specific `JMSDeliveryTime` header when the message is sent. Note that you must cast the standard JMS producer to a WebLogic JMS-specific type in order to use this extension:

```
// Send the message one minute from now...
long timeToDeliver = System.currentTimeMillis() + (60 * 1000);
weblogic.jms.extensions.WLMessageProducer producer =
    (WLMessageProducer)queueSender;
producer.setTimeToDeliver(timeToDeliver);
queueSender.send(message);
```

One important point to note: the JMS provider sets most JMS message header fields. This means that regardless of what values are set using the JMS `Message` interface, the JMS producer will overwrite them. We mention this here because the `weblogic.jms.extensions.WLMessage` interface provides a `setJMSDeliveryTime()` method. Trying to use this mechanism to set the `JMSDeliveryTime` header will have no effect because the message producer will overwrite this header field value when it sends the message.

WARNING The `setJMSDeliveryTime()` method in the `weblogic.jms.extensions.WLMessage` interface is like most of the other setter methods on the `javax.jms.Message` interface. Setting a value on `WLMessage` has no effect because the producer overwrites it when a message is sent.

Persistent Stores

WebLogic JMS uses persistent stores for two different purposes. When WebLogic JMS determines that a message should be persistent, it uses the `Message Store` associated with the destination's JMS server to store the entire message. By default, WebLogic JMS keeps all messages in memory for faster access—even persistent messages that it has already written to secondary storage. If the backlog of messages is small, this can significantly improve performance without consuming significant amounts of memory. Of course, as the backlog of messages gets larger, the memory demands can cause the JVM to run out of memory. WebLogic JMS uses the `Paging Store` to page the body of the message out of memory to save memory. Message headers and properties remain in memory for faster access. As we will see in the "Delivery Overrides, Destination Quotas, and Flow Control" section, we can use quotas and thresholds to help control the amount of memory consumed.

Configuring Message Stores

WebLogic JMS supports two types of persistent stores for saving JMS messages: JDBC and file-based persistent stores. The choice of a particular store type has no effect on the application code. As their name suggests, JDBC persistent stores save messages in database tables, while the file stores save messages in files. To use a persistent store, create a message store and assign it to a JMS server. Each JMS server must have its own backing JDBC or file store. In order to migrate a JMS server with an associated message store, the message store must be accessible via the same path on the target WebLogic Server. The path is either the JDBC connection pool name or the directory where the file resides.

JDBC-based stores may share the same physical database schema, but each must have its own uniquely named set of tables. The JDBC store uses two tables whose base names are `JMSStore` and `JMSState`. By using the `Prefix Name` parameter, you can prepend values to these base names to create unique names per store. By knowing the table-naming syntax for your database, you can force the tables to be in different schemas; for example, specifying a `Prefix Name` of `bigrez.JMS_Store1_` will cause the JDBC store to create tables in the `bigrez` schema with the names `JMS_Store1_JMSStore` and `JMS_Store1_JMSState`. Failure to specify unique table names for multiple stores sharing the same database can result in message corruption or loss.

WARNING Multiple JMS servers cannot share the same persistent store. For JDBC-based stores, you must specify a unique `Prefix Name` value for every store that uses the same underlying database connection pool (and, thus, the same database schema). Failure to do so can result in message corruption or message loss.

In the case of file stores, multiple JMS servers can share the same directory. WebLogic JMS will automatically create unique names of the form `<JMSFileStore-Name>######.DAT`, where `######` is a unique number. Let's compare and contrast the two types of stores.

File stores generally perform better than JDBC stores. By default, writing to a file store is a synchronous operation. WebLogic JMS provides three `Synchronous Write Policy` settings for controlling how messages are written to the store:

- `Cache-Flush` is the default policy that forces all messages to be flushed from the operating system cache to disk before the completion of a transaction, or a JMS operation in the nontransactional case. The `Cache-Flush` policy is reliable and scales well as the number of simultaneous users increases.
- `Direct-Write` bypasses the operating system cache and forces all messages to be written to disk. WebLogic JMS supports only the `Direct-Write` policy on Solaris, HP-UX, and Windows operating systems. If this policy is set on an unsupported platform, the file store automatically uses the `Cache-Flush` policy instead. This policy's reliability and performance depend on operating system and hardware support of on-disk caches.
- `Disabled` allows for maximum performance, but because messages may remain in operating system caches, it exposes the application to message loss and duplicate messages.

When using the `Direct-Write` policy, the performance and scalability are significantly reduced without the use of an on-disk cache. Unfortunately, the use of an on-disk cache can expose the application to message loss or duplication in the event of a power failure unless the on-disk cache is reliable. Many high-end storage devices that offer on-disk caches also provide a battery backup to prevent the loss of data during a power failure.

To add to the complexity of this setting, Windows provides an OS option to enable write caching on the disk; this is enabled by default. The problem is that some versions of Windows do not send the correct synchronization commands to tell the disk to synchronize the cache (for more information, please refer to http://support.microsoft.com/default.aspx?scid=kb%3Ben-us%3B281672). You can disable write caching with most disk drives using the Windows Device Manager entry for the disk in question; the `Write Cache Enabled` checkbox is located on the `Disk Properties` tab.

Solaris does not support the use of on-disk caches when using `Direct-Write`. This means that all disk writes go directly to disk and will not take advantage of any reliable on-disk caches. If your storage device uses a reliable on-disk cache, you should test with both `Direct-Write` and `Cache-Flush` to see which one is actually faster for your particular device.

BEST PRACTICE `Cache-Flush` **is generally the safest policy. If your hardware and OS support using reliable on-disk caches with** `Direct-Write`**, you may be able to improve performance significantly by switching to** `Direct-Write`**. Remember, using on-disk caches without battery backup can cause data loss or corruption should a power failure occur.**

One final word of caution: Some third-party JMS providers set their default write policy to the equivalent of WebLogic JMS's `Disabled` policy, which allows the operating system to buffer all file writes without flushing them to disk. While this is great for performance, it can cause data loss and corruption in the event of a power failure. Before you try to compare performance numbers for persistent messages with WebLogic JMS, make sure you understand the write policy configuration for each JMS provider.

WARNING Some third-party JMS providers default to the equivalent of WebLogic JMS's `Disabled` policy, so make sure you check before trying to compare performance numbers with those of WebLogic JMS.

Because file stores are often collocated with the JMS server, writing to a file store may generate less network traffic. File store availability, however, is subject to hardware failures so it is often desirable to place file stores on shared disks or storage area networks (SANs). Do not use NFS to share access to a file store; any attempt to do so may result in message loss, corruption, and/or duplicate messages. Because of these issues, JDBC stores may provide an easier solution for addressing the failover issues since the database typically resides on a separate machine from the application servers.

WebLogic JMS never attempts to reduce the size of a file store. The file store grows as needed to hold all unconsumed messages up to the quota limits configured for the JMS server or its individual destinations. Although the entire file store can be reused to store new messages, the amount of disk space that the store consumes will never shrink even when the file store has no messages in it.

WARNING WebLogic JMS will never shrink the size of a file store, though it will reclaim the space inside the file for future use.

Finally, a file store can be thought of as a database. For JMS applications that process large number of persistent messages, you should configure disk access just as you would when setting up high-performance database servers. Isolate file stores on separate disks. When using multiple file stores, you may need to put each store on a separate disk, or even disk controller. Using advanced, on-disk caching technology can provide large performance improvements without sacrificing the integrity of the message store. If the messages are important enough to store to disk, then they are probably too important to lose due to hardware failure. Consider using a SAN, a multiported disk, and/or disk mirroring technology to make the file store highly available.

Setting Up Paging Stores

A WebLogic JMS server can also move in-memory messages out of the server's memory to secondary storage to prevent trying to hold too many messages in memory; this is known as paging. When a message that has been paged out of memory is needed, the server moves it back into memory. This paging behavior is completely transparent to the JMS application. Of course, reading and writing messages to disk will have a significant performance impact, but this is much better than filling up all of the server's available memory.

By default, WebLogic JMS keeps all messages in memory for faster access—even persistent messages. This can cause problems as the number and size of the persistent messages in the destination grow. You must enable paging to tell WebLogic JMS that it is okay to page messages out of memory.

TIP **Paging is important for both persistent and non-persistent messages.**

To give WebLogic JMS the ability to page messages, configure each JMS server with a *Paging Store*. A paging store is nothing more than a message store being used for paging messages. Like message stores, each JMS server must have its own paging store. WebLogic Server 8.1 will automatically create a paging store for you if you enable paging but forget to configure a paging store. Of course, you probably want to configure the paging store explicitly so that you can control the location of the store, which might be on a RAID disk array to increase performance for high-volume systems.

WebLogic JMS does not allow the same message store to be used for both message persistence and message paging. For persistent messages, WebLogic Server actually does not use the paging store to page the messages because they already exist in the message store; however, you still need to enable paging for persistent messages. One important thing to note is that even though the paging process writes nonpersistent messages to secondary storage as needed, these messages will not survive server restarts or system crashes. Because of this, there is no need to worry about high availability of a paging store, and we always recommend using a file-based paging store to maximize performance.

BEST PRACTICE **Always enable paging for your JMS server. Failure to do so can result in a WebLogic Server instance running out of memory if the message consumers are not able to keep up with the producers. For production systems, we recommend explicitly configuring a paging store rather than relying on WebLogic Server 8.1 to do it for you so that you can control the location of the file store.**

Understanding When Messages Are Persisted

On the surface, message persistence seems straightforward, and for point-to-point messaging it is. Point-to-point message producers can specify a message's delivery mode, which determines whether the message is persistent. For WebLogic JMS, the producer's desired delivery mode can be overridden by several JMS configuration options. In the end, the message will either be persistent or non-persistent based on the application's request and the WebLogic JMS configuration. The section on overrides, quotas, and flow control provides more information on how to control message delivery characteristics such as persistence.

For publish-and-subscribe messaging, the message's delivery mode and WebLogic JMS configuration do affect the persistence or nonpersistence decision. WebLogic JMS also considers the number and type of subscribers to the topic. If a topic has one or more durable subscribers, messages will be retained until all durable subscribers have received a copy of the message. If the delivery mode for the message is non-persistent, WebLogic JMS retains the messages by buffering them in memory (or paging them out to the paging store, if configured); persistent messages are written to the message store. If there are no durable subscribers currently subscribed, WebLogic JMS will not persist the message because there is no need to retain the message because the JMS specification requires only that the currently active subscribers receive the message.

The durable subscription itself is persisted to ensure that it survives server restarts or system crashes, as required by the JMS specification. Because of this, WebLogic JMS requires that a persistent message store be configured on any WebLogic JMS server that hosts topics that will have durable subscribers, even if all of the messages are non-persistent. WebLogic JMS will throw a `javax.jms.JMSException` if an application attempts to create durable subscribers on a topic that is hosted by a WebLogic JMS server with no message store.

Delivery Overrides, Destination Quotas, and Flow Control

As we discussed previously, you can override default delivery attributes for messages either programmatically in the application or administratively using the WebLogic Console. In this section we will take a look at how to use delivery overrides. We will then examine different WebLogic JMS throttling features such as quotas, paging, and flow control.

Overriding Message Delivery Characteristics

Message delivery attributes include `Priority`, `Time to Live`, `Time To Deliver`, `Delivery Mode`, and `Redelivery Delay`. As we saw earlier, default values for these can be set in the connection factory; however, the application can override these values by setting them explicitly in the code. In addition, the WebLogic JMS destination configuration can override both the connection factory and the application-specified values. You can specify destination configuration overrides either directly in the destination's settings or indirectly in the destination's template settings. Any settings in the destination override the setting in the destination's template.

Let's look at an example to make sure that you understand how this works. In our example, we list the different ways to configure the `Delivery Mode` for a message being sent to a particular destination in ascending order of precedence. Each subsequent method will override all of the previously mentioned methods so that the last one that is applicable will define the actual `Delivery Mode` for the message:

1. The connection factory specifies the `Default Delivery Mode`, which defaults to persistent.
2. The application may override the `Delivery Mode` by explicitly setting it in the application code prior to sending the message. For example,

   ```
   queueSender.setDeliveryMode(deliveryMode);
   queueSender.send(message);
   ```

   where `deliveryMode` can be set to one of the following constants:

```
javax.jms.DeliveryMode.PERSISTENT
javax.jms.DeliveryMode.NON_PERSISTENT
```

3. The destination's template can override the `Delivery Mode` by setting it to `Persistent`, `Non-Persistent`, or `No-Delivery`, where `No-Delivery` is the default and simply means that the template does not override the values specified by the application and/or the connection factory.
4. The destination can override the `Delivery Mode` by setting it to `Persistent`, `Non-Persistent`, or `No-Delivery`, where `No-Delivery` is the default and simply means that the destination does not override the values specified by the template, the application, and/or the connection factory.
5. The JMS server can implicitly override a `Delivery Mode` value of `Persistent` by not configuring a `Store`, which will force all messages delivered to destinations associated with the JMS server to be non-persistent. If the JMS server has a store configured, this simply implies that the JMS server is not overriding the `Delivery Mode`.

WARNING If an application invokes the `setJMSDeliveryMode(deliveryMode)` or `setJMSPriority(priority)` methods from the `javax.jms.Message` interface, WebLogic JMS will override these values, as the JMS specification designates that these methods are strictly for use by JMS providers. You must set the delivery mode or priority using the appropriate producer method calls for them to take effect.

Understanding Quotas and Thresholds

WebLogic JMS provides mechanisms for establishing quotas either on individual JMS destinations or on the entire JMS server. These quotas control the maximum amount of data that can be stored, either in a message store or in memory. Without quotas in place, producers can continue to produce messages until their messages consume all available space in the persistent store or all available memory in the JMS server. When the quota is reached, WebLogic Server 8.1 JMS producers will wait until space becomes available up to the user defined time-out period. If the quota condition does not subside before the timeout period, producers get a `javax.jms.ResourceAllocationException`. It is up to the application how to handle this condition.

The connection factory's `SendTimeout` attribute controls the maximum number of milliseconds a producer will block when waiting for space. You can disable blocking sends by setting this value to 0. An application may choose to override this setting by changing the value on the producer:

```
weblogic.jms.extensions.WLMessageProducer producer =
    (WLMessageProducer)queueSender;
producer.setSendTimeout(sendTimeoutMillis);
queueSender.send(message);
```

You should be very careful about using blocking sends with message producers running inside a WebLogic Server instance. These will cause server execute threads to block and could bring the entire server to a grinding halt and possibly deadlock the server for the amount of blocking time. In most cases, application message producers running inside the server should either disable blocking sends or set their values very small to prevent thread starvation. Also, be careful about retrying sends indefinitely inside the server for similar reasons.

WARNING Blocking sends are a convenient way to shield applications from temporary quota limits. Care needs to be given, though, when the producers are running inside a WebLogic Server so as not to block execute threads that are needed to consume messages and clear the quota limit condition. To disable blocking sends, set the `SendTimeout` **to 0.**

The `BlockingSendPolicy` attribute of the JMS server defines the expected behavior when multiple senders are competing for space on the same JMS server. The valid values are as follows:

FIFO. This value indicates that all send requests are to be processed in the order in which they were received. When the quota condition subsides, requests for space are considered in the order in which they were made.

Preemptive. This value indicates that any send operation can preempt other blocking send operations if space is available. That is, if there is sufficient space for the current request, that space is used even if there are other requests waiting for space. This can result in the starvation of larger requests. If sufficient space is not available for the request, the request is queued up behind other existing requests.

WebLogic JMS also supports message paging and flow control to help limit the amount of memory consumed by unconsumed messages and prevent applications from ever reaching the quota, respectively. Message paging allows WebLogic JMS to page messages out of memory to the associated paging store once the high threshold is reached. This will help prevent unconsumed messages from using too much of the server's available memory but will slow down the overall throughput of messages because they now must be written to disk. Once the consumers catch up, WebLogic JMS will suspend message paging until the threshold is reached again. WebLogic JMS uses a low threshold value to determine when consumers have caught up.

Flow control allows WebLogic JMS to slow down the rate at which message producers are sending messages in an attempt to allow consumers to catch up. As with message paging, WebLogic JMS will begin flow control once the high threshold is reached and will suspend flow control once the low threshold is reached.

Both flow control and message paging require defining the quota and the thresholds. Message paging also requires creating a message store dedicated to message paging and associating it with the JMS server. Message paging is disabled by default. By default, flow control is enabled on all connection factories but will never be used unless the appropriate quotas and thresholds are configured. We will talk more about flow control configuration in the "Understanding Flow Control" section later in this chapter.

To configure quotas and thresholds, use the `Thresholds & Quotas Configuration` tab of the JMS server, JMS template, or JMS destination. Quotas and thresholds can be set in terms of the number of bytes or messages, as shown in Figure 9.5. Let's discuss the meaning of these parameters in the context of a JMS server.

`Bytes Maximum` and `Messages Maximum` specify the quota of the associated JMS server. These parameters indicate the maximum number of bytes or messages that may be stored in the JMS server. `Bytes Maximum` and `Messages Maximum` must be greater than or equal to the corresponding threshold parameters. This means you cannot use message paging or flow control without quotas.

BEST PRACTICE Always use quotas to prevent the server from consuming all available space storing unconsumed messages.

`Bytes Threshold High` and `Messages Threshold High` specify the upper threshold that WebLogic JMS uses to determine when to start paging and flow control. When the number of bytes or messages exceeds the upper threshold, WebLogic JMS will log a warning message and take action to try to prevent reaching the quota. If the JMS server has paging enabled, WebLogic JMS will begin paging to the configured paging store. If flow control is enabled, WebLogic JMS will start limiting the producers' message flows.

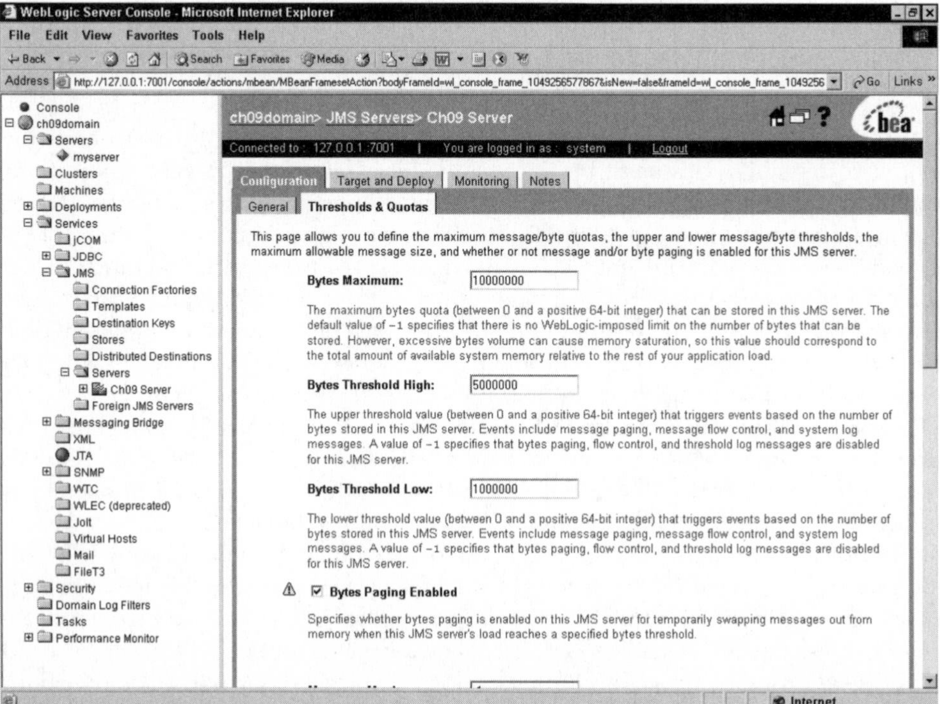

Figure 9.5 Configuring a JMS server's thresholds and quotas.

`Bytes Threshold Low` and `Message Threshold Low` specify the lower threshold that WebLogic JMS uses to determine when to stop paging and flow control. When the number of bytes or messages drops below the lower threshold, WebLogic JMS triggers events indicating that the threshold condition is cleared. When this happens, WebLogic JMS logs a message, stops any paging that was occurring, and disarms any flow control that was occurring and instructs all of the flow-controlled producers to begin increasing their message flow rates.

You can also configure quotas and thresholds for individual JMS destinations or templates. The attributes are similar to those of the JMS server and have similar meanings with the exception of the `Bytes Paging Enabled` and `Messages Paging Enabled` parameters. When configuring paging on a destination or template, the values specified complement those set at the JMS server level. By setting a value to `default`, you are telling WebLogic JMS to use the values from the JMS server.

Because the quotas and thresholds can be set at the JMS server level and at the individual destination level, the values specified at the server level can limit the effective settings of the individual destinations. Let's look at an example to make sure you understand the implications of this. Imagine that you have a JMS server that hosts two destinations, `Queue1` and `Queue2`. If you set the `Bytes Maximum` for the server to be 50,000 and the `Bytes Maximum` for each destination to 30,000, then you may run into a situation where the overall quota of the server limits the quota of the individual destination. If `Queue1` currently contains 25,000 bytes of messages, then the effective quota for `Queue2` at that point is 25,000 bytes instead of the 30,000 bytes specified by the `Bytes Maximum` parameter for `Queue2` because of the JMS server's 50,000 byte quota.

WARNING JMS server quota and threshold parameters apply across all destinations in a JMS server and may limit those specified for each destination.

Enabling Message Paging

Message paging is a mechanism that allows WebLogic JMS to remove message data from memory and write it to a persistent message store configured for paging. By using paging, WebLogic JMS can prevent unconsumed messages from using up all of the WebLogic Server's available memory. Paging allows a WebLogic JMS server to hold more messages without increasing the heap size of the JVM. When WebLogic JMS is paging, it writes message bodies to the JMS server's paging store. Message headers and properties are never paged out of memory.

You should always enable paging as a preventive mechanism. Most non-persistent messaging applications, however, choose to use non-persistent messages for speed. Because paging will significantly reduce the performance of your messaging application, you should tune your application configuration to try to prevent paging from ever occurring. Remember, a healthy messaging system requires consumers to keep up with producers.

Persistent messages do not actually use the paging store because they already exist in the message store, and non-persistent messages that have been paged out of memory do not survive server restarts or crashes. Therefore, you do not need to worry about high availability for messages stored in a paging store. Because file-based stores are generally much faster than the equivalent JDBC-based stores, we strongly recommend using file-based stores for paging.

BEST PRACTICE **Always enable paging and use a file-based paging store as a precaution, but tune your application to avoid paging for best performance.**

Understanding Flow Control

WebLogic JMS starts using flow control only if you enable it on the producer's connection factory and the JMS server or destination exceeds the configured upper threshold. Once WebLogic JMS starts controlling the flow of messages to a particular server or destination, it will continue to do so until the number of unconsumed bytes or messages drops below the configured lower threshold. At that point, WebLogic JMS will tell the producers to start increasing their flow of messages gradually until message rates are no longer being throttled.

You have already seen how to configure the threshold values for a JMS server and destination. The attributes that control the tuning of the flow control algorithm are set via a producer's connection factory. When you create a connection factory, flow control is enabled by default and the flow control tuning parameters are given some default values, as shown in Figure 9.6. Of course, you can change the default values as necessary. Let's spend some time looking at the flow control algorithm and how these tuning parameters affect its behavior.

WebLogic JMS engages the flow control algorithm when an upper threshold is reached. At that point, WebLogic JMS will limit the flow rate of all producers by setting their maximum allowable flow rate to that specified by their connection factory's `Flow Maximum` parameter. Unless the lower threshold is reached first, WebLogic JMS will continue to slow down producers over time until all producers are at their minimum flow rate, as specified by the connection factory's `Flow Minimum` parameter. The rate at which WebLogic JMS slows down producers is controlled by the `Flow Interval` and `Flow Steps` parameters. `Flow Interval` defines the time interval over which a producer is slowed from its maximum rate to its minimum rate. `Flow Steps` is the number of incremental steps WebLogic JMS uses in the slow-down process.

Once the maximum allowable flow rate reaches the `Flow Minimum` value, WebLogic JMS will maintain the producers' flow rates until the JMS server or destination backlog reaches the lower threshold. At that point, WebLogic JMS will linearly increase the producers' maximum allowable flow rates `Flow Steps` times over the `Flow Interval` period, with the final step disengaging flow control completely.

As with paging, flow control should be used as a preventive measure. Flow control is no substitute for proper application design and tuning so that consumers can keep up with producers. Because flow control effectively slows down the sending thread, care should be given when using flow control on producers running inside the WebLogic Server. We discuss this more in the next section where we will go into more detail about how to design JMS applications properly with WebLogic Server.

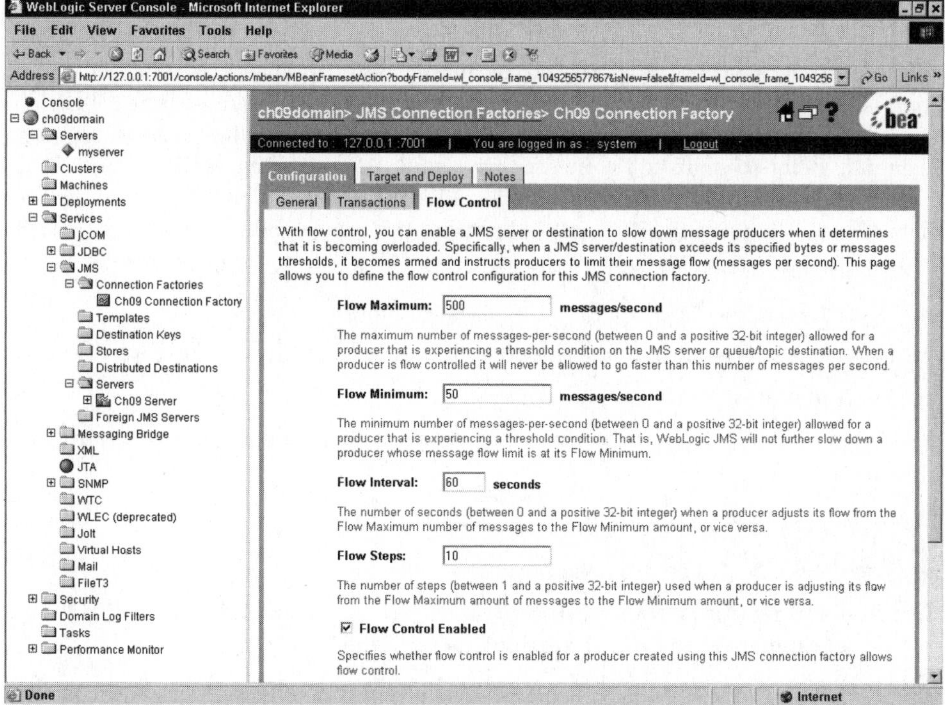

Figure 9.6 Configuring the flow control parameters.

BEST PRACTICE Always use flow control as a preventive measure for producers that run outside the WebLogic Server process. Be careful using flow control inside the server because it will cause server threads to slow down.

WebLogic JMS Application Design

In the previous section, we looked at the different throttling mechanisms WebLogic JMS provides to help offset temporary spikes in message production. In general, you need to design your messaging applications so that the consumers can keep up with the producers over long periods of time. If messaging applications tend to produce more messages than they can consume, eventually the application will fall so far behind that it runs into physical resource constraints such as running out of memory or disk space. In this section, we will discuss some design considerations for messaging applications.

Choosing a Destination Type

When designing a JMS application, a commonly asked question is whether to use queues or topics. Trying to think in terms of destination type often leads to confusion. Instead, you should think about what type of messaging your application requires. In general, point-to-point style messaging should use queues while publish-and-subscribe style messaging should use topics. Of course, there is no hard and fast rule, and it is possible to use either type of destination with most applications if you are willing to do enough work. When using queues, some things to remember are

- Each message will be processed by one consumer.
- Messages will remain on the queue until they are consumed or expire.
- Persistent messages are always persisted.
- Using message selectors becomes expensive as the number of messages in the queue gets large.

When using topics, some things to remember are

- Each message can be processed by every consumer.
- Unless using durable subscriptions, messages will be processed only if at least one consumer is listening at the time the message is sent.
- Persistent messages are persisted only when durable subscriptions exist.
- Using message selectors with topics becomes expensive as the number of consumers gets large.

BEST PRACTICE Choose your destination type based on the type of messaging. Point-to-point messaging implies queues, and publish-and-subscribe messaging implies topics.

Locating Destinations

In WebLogic JMS, a destination physically resides on a single server. JMS provides two ways for an application to obtain a reference to a destination. You can look up the destination in JNDI and cast it to the appropriate destination type, `Queue` or `Topic`, or use the `QueueSession.createQueue(destinationName)` or `TopicSession.createTopic(destinationName)` methods to locate an existing queue or topic. These create methods require an application to pass destination names using a vendor-specific syntax. For WebLogic JMS, the syntax is `jms-server-name/jms-destination-name`; for example, to obtain a reference to a destination named `queue1` that resides in the JMS server named `JMSServer1`, you would use a destination name of `JMSServer1/queue1`. When referring to a distributed destination, the JMS server name and forward slash should be omitted because a distributed destination spans JMS servers. We will talk more about distributed destinations later.

Given that the `createQueue()` and `createTopic()` methods require specifying the WebLogic JMS server name, we feel that these methods are of limited value because we generally want to hide the location of the destination from the application. Any advantages that might be gained by using these methods rather than JNDI are likely to be offset by requiring the application to understand what JMS server the destination lives in. As a result, we recommend using JNDI to obtain references to JMS destinations. JNDI lookups, though, are relatively expensive so applications should attempt to look up JMS destinations once and cache them for reuse throughout the life of the application.

BEST PRACTICE **Use JNDI to locate destinations. Caching and sharing JMS destinations throughout the application will help to minimize the impact of the JNDI lookup overhead.**

Choosing the Appropriate Message Type

Choosing a message type is the second design choice you face when designing JMS applications. `TextMessage` is one of the more commonly used message types simply because of the type of data typically exchanged. As the popularity of XML increases, `TextMessage` popularity increases because the JMS specification does not explicitly define a message type for exchanging XML documents. Unfortunately, serializing a string is more CPU intensive than serializing other Java primitive types. Using strings as the message payload often implies that the receiver must parse the message in order to extract the data encoded in the string. WebLogic JMS also provides an `XMLMessage` type. The primary advantage of the `XMLMessage` type is the built-in support for running `XPATH`-style message selectors on the body of the message.

Let's take a minute to talk more about XML messages. Exchanging XML messages via JMS makes it easy to think about solving many age-old application integration problems. While JMS uses Java and Java already provides a platform-independent way of exchanging data, not all messaging applications are written in Java. Fortunately, many popular legacy messaging systems, such as IBM's WebSphere MQ, offer a JMS API in addition to their other language bindings. BEA is also providing a C API to WebLogic JMS as alpha code on its developer's Web site at http://dev2dev.bea.com/resourcelibrary/utilitiestools/environment.jsp. We hope that this will become a supported part of the product in the future. This solves the message exchange part of the problem.

XML solves the data exchange part of the problem by providing a portable, language-neutral format with which to represent structured data. As a result, it is not surprising to see many JMS applications using XML messages as their payload. Of course, the portability and flexibility of XML do not come without a cost. Not only are XML messages generally sent using `TextMessage` objects, which makes their serialization more costly, but they also generally require parsing the data in order to convert it into language object representations that the application can manipulate more easily. All of this requires that the receivers to do more work just to be able to get the message into a form where it can be processed.

This is not to say that you should avoid XML messages completely. XML is the format of choice for messages that cross application and/or organizational boundaries. When talking about applications here, we define an application as a program or set of programs that are designed, built, tested, and more importantly, deployed together as a single unit. What we want to caution you on is using XML message formats everywhere—even within the boundaries of a single application—just to be using XML. Use XML where it makes sense, and use other binary representations where XML is not required.

BEST PRACTICE **Use XML messages for inter-application messaging and binary messages for intra-application messaging.**

When choosing the message type for an application, there are several things you should consider. A well-defined message should have just enough information for the receiver to process it. You should consider how often the application will need to send the message and whether the message needs to be persistent. Message size can have a considerable impact on network bandwidth, memory requirements, and disk I/O. Keep messages as small as possible without removing information needed to be able to process the message efficiently.

Once you decide on the information to pass, use the simplest message type that can do the job. If possible, use a message format that is directly usable by the receiver, such as a `MapMessage` or `ObjectMessage`. If you need to pass a string message, converting it to a byte array and sending it using a `BytesMessage` may perform better than sending it as a string in a `TextMessage`, especially for large strings.

If you have only a few primitive types to send in a message, try using a `MapMessage` instead of an `ObjectMessage` for better performance. As the number of fields gets larger, however, the mapping code itself can add complexity. You might find that the performance benefit is outweighed by the additional maintenance burden. `MapMessage` also provides some extensibility in the sense that you can add new name-value pairs without breaking existing consumers. When you are using an `ObjectMessage`, passing objects that implement `Externalizable` rather than `Serializable` can improve the marshalling performance, at the added cost of requiring you to provide implementations of the `readExternal()` and `writeExternal()` methods.

We should caution you about the implications of using an `ObjectMessage` to pass data across application boundaries. `ObjectMessage` uses Java serialization, which relies on the sender and the receiver having the same exact versions of the class available. This can lead to tightly coupled producers and consumers—even though you are using asynchronous messaging for communication. It might be possible to escape some of this coupling by using `Externalizable` objects, but this just means that your externalization code has to deal with object versioning.

BEST PRACTICE **Use the simplest and smallest message type that is directly usable by the receiving application. Favor `MapMessage` when sending collections of primitive data types, and avoid `ObjectMessage` to reduce coupling between disparate systems.**

Compressing Large Messages

XML messages tend to be larger than their binary counterparts. As you can imagine, larger messages will require more network bandwidth, more memory, and more importantly, more storage space and disk I/O to persist. If the messages are infrequent, this may not be an issue, but as the message frequency increases, the overhead will compound and start affecting the overall health of your messaging system. One way to reduce this impact is to compress large messages that carry strings as their payload. Compressed XML messages may actually provide a more compact representation of the data than any binary format.

The `java.util.zip` package provides everything you need to support message compression and decompression. The performance impact of message compression, however, is not clear-cut and needs to be evaluated on a case-by-case basis. When considering the use of compression, there are a number of things to weigh. First, are your messages big enough to warrant compression? Small messages do not generally compress very well so using compression can, in some cases, actually increase the size of your message.

Second, will the extra overhead of compressing and decompressing every message prevent your applications from meeting your performance and scalability requirements? Compressing messages can be thought of as a crude form of throttling because the compression step will slow down your message producers. Of course, this isn't necessarily a good thing because your consumers will also have to decompress the message before processing it.

Finally, will compression significantly reduce your application's network and memory resource requirements? If the producers and consumers are not running inside the same server as the destination, compressing the messages can reduce the network transfer time for messages. It can also reduce the memory requirements for your WebLogic JMS server. If the messages are persistent, it can also reduce the amount of disk I/O for saving and retrieving the messages. When the persistent store type is JDBC, it can reduce the network traffic between the WebLogic Server and the database. If the producers, consumers, and JMS server are all running inside the same WebLogic Server instance, many of these benefits may be outweighed by the additional CPU and memory overhead of compression and decompression.

BEST PRACTICE The decision on whether to use compression is something that needs to be carefully considered. If the producers, consumers, and destinations are collocated inside a WebLogic Server instance, it is generally better not to use compression.

Selecting a Message Acknowledgment Strategy

WebLogic JMS retains each message until the consumer acknowledges that it has received the message. Only at this point can WebLogic JMS remove the message from the server. Committing a transaction is one way for an application to acknowledge a message has been received. If transactions are not being used, an application uses message acknowledgments to acknowledge that a message, or set of messages, has been received. Message acknowledgments and transactions are mutually exclusive. If you specify both transactions and acknowledgments, WebLogic JMS will use transactions and ignore the acknowledgment mode.

Your application's message acknowledgment strategy can have a significant impact on performance and scalability. WebLogic JMS defaults to using `AUTO_ACKNOWLEDGE` mode. This means that WebLogic JMS will automatically acknowledge each message after the receiver processes it successfully. Using `AUTO_ACKNOWLEDGE` mode can reduce the chance of duplicate messages; however, it comes at a cost because the receiver's run time must send an acknowledgment message to the JMS server after each message to tell the server to remove the message.

If your application can tolerate duplicate messages, JMS defines the `DUPS_OK_ACKNOWLEDGE` mode to allow the receiver's run time to acknowledge the messages lazily. WebLogic Server 8.1 does not currently do anything special for `DUPS_OK_ACKNOWLEDGE` mode; this mode behaves exactly like `AUTO_ACKNOWLEDGE` mode. Another technique that gives you a little more control is using `CLIENT_ACKNOWLEDGE` mode to explicitly acknowledge groups of messages rather than each message individually. While message duplication is still possible, it typically occurs only because of a failure where your receiver has already processed some messages but had not acknowledged them. You could imagine building a strategy that tries to detect duplicate messages when starting up and/or recovering from a failure condition.

For stand-alone, nondurable subscribers, WebLogic JMS caches local copies of the message in the client JVM to optimize network overhead. Because this caching strategy also includes message acknowledgment optimizations, these subscribers really will not benefit from using the aforementioned `CLIENT_ACKNOWLEDGE` strategy; `AUTO_ACKNOWLEDGE` should perform equally well.

In addition to the standard JMS message acknowledgment modes, WebLogic JMS provides two additional acknowledgment modes through the `weblogic.jms.WLSession` interface:

NO_ACKNOWLEDGE. This mode tells WebLogic JMS not to worry about message acknowledgments and simply provide a best-effort delivery of messages. In this mode, WebLogic JMS will immediately delete messages after they have been delivered, which can lead to both lost and duplicate messages. Applications that want to maximize performance and scalability and can tolerate both lost and duplicate messages should use this acknowledgment mode.

MULTICAST_NO_ACKNOWLEDGE. This mode tells WebLogic JMS to use IP multicast to deliver messages to consumers. As the name implies, this mode has similar semantics to the `NO_ACKNOWLEDGE` mode.

We will talk more about using multicast sessions later in this section.

BEST PRACTICE Applications that explicitly acknowledge sets of messages will generally be faster and more scalable than those that acknowledge each message individually to minimize the possibility of receiving duplicate messages.

Designing Message Selectors

As we discussed earlier in the "JMS Key Concepts" section, message selectors allow consumers to further specify the set of messages they want to receive. Consumers specify a logical statement using an `SQL WHERE` clause-like syntax that the JMS provider evaluates against each message's headers and/or properties to determine whether the consumer should receive the message. WebLogic JMS adds another type of selector for use with the WebLogic JMS `XMLMessage` type. With this message type, you can specify `XPATH` expressions that evaluate against the XML body of the message.

In WebLogic JMS, all selector evaluation and filtering takes place on the JMS server, with the exception of multicast subscribers, which we will discuss later. For topics, WebLogic JMS evaluates each subscriber's message selector against every message published to the topic to determine whether to deliver the message to the subscriber.

For queues, the evaluation process is more complex. A message is always delivered to a queue, and WebLogic JMS will evaluate the message against each receiver's message selector until it finds a match. If no consumer's message selector matches the message, the message will remain in the queue. When a new consumer associates itself with the queue, WebLogic JMS will have to evaluate its message selector against each message in the queue. Because of this, message selectors generally perform better with topics than with queues. As with any such general statement, your mileage may vary depending on the exact circumstances in your application.

It is often better to split a destination into multiple destinations and eliminate the need for message selectors. For example, imagine an application that sends messages to the `trade` queue. If the application's consumers that use message selectors to select only `buy` or `sell` orders, we can split the `trade` queue into `buy` and `sell` queues and eliminate the need for a message selector. When a producer sends a *buy* message, it sends the message directly to the `buy` queue, and only `buy` consumers need to listen to that queue. Partitioning application in this way has other advantages besides performance. With this architecture, you can monitor each message type individually in each queue, and if performance does become an issue down the road, you can even separate the queues onto separate servers.

BEST PRACTICE Always evaluate the advantages and disadvantages of partitioning your application before deciding to use message selectors. Favor splitting destinations over the use of message selectors when there is a clear separation of message types.

Of course, there will be situations when using a message selector is unavoidable. In these situations, there are several things to keep in mind when designing your message selector strategy. First, what fields does your selector need to reference? Message header fields such as `JMSMessageID`, `JMSTimestamp`, `JMSRedelivered`, `JMSCorrelationID`, `JMSType`, `JMSPriority`, `JMSExpiration`, and `JMSDeliveryTime` and application-defined message properties are the fastest to access. Examining an `XMLMessage` message body adds a significant amount of overhead and, therefore, will be much slower.

Suppose that, in the previous example, the producer sends a message in XML format like the one shown here:

```
<order type="buy">
   <symbol>beas</symbol>
   <quantity>5000</quantity>
</order>
```

The consumers can use an XPATH message selector like this:

```
"JMS_BEA_SELECT('xpath','/Order/attribute::type') = 'buy'"
```

These XPATH message selectors are the most expensive expressions to evaluate because they involve parsing at least some portion of the XML document. Of course, XPATH selectors are convenient to use, but you should realize that they are expensive and plan your use of them accordingly.

Second, what type of operators do you need to use? In general, you should strive to keep selectors as simple as possible. Avoid complex operators such as `like`, `in`, or `between` in favor of primitive operators such as =, >, or <. The more complex the selector is, the slower its evaluation will be. In general, an XPATH expression will be the most expensive because it has to scan the XML body of the message looking for the element or attribute value to compare.

BEST PRACTICE **Keep message selectors as simple as possible. Try to avoid more complex operators such as** `like`**,** `in`**, or** `between`**.**

Third, what data type do you need to use for the selector? Where possible, avoid the use of strings in message properties, especially if they are large. Strings are more expensive to serialize and more expensive to compare than other primitive types. In our previous example, if we decided to use message selectors to distinguish between `buy` and `sell` messages, we would be better off performance-wise defining the message property as an integer (for example, 1 = buy, 2 = sell) rather than using the strings `buy` or `sell`.

WebLogic Server 7.0 SP2 and 8.1 introduce the concept of *indexed selectors* for applications that need to use strings to differentiate messages. With an indexed selector, an application uses message property names, rather than the value of a particular message property, to distinguish the messages. For example, the application would set the `buy` message property to any value on all `buy` messages and the `sell` message property to any value on all `sell` messages. Consumers only interested in `sell` messages would use the expression `sell IS NOT NULL` for its message selector. Since the message property names are indexed, it is generally faster to use an indexed selector than it is to use the strings `buy` and `sell` as the value for the `trade_type` message property.

TIP **String data types are typically the slowest, most expensive types to compare. Using other primitive data types will generally improve the efficiency of your application. If your application needs to use strings to differentiate messages, use indexed selectors to improve the performance of the message selectors.**

Fourth, when using compound selectors, which elements are most efficient to process and which elements are most selective? If a selector involves both message header fields and message property fields, place the message header field to the left of the expression. It is less expensive to use the expression `JMSPriority > 5 AND (trade_type == 'buy')` than it is to use the expression `(trade_type == 'buy') AND JMSPriority > 5`. When a selector involves multiple evaluation criteria one field is much more selective than the other, it may make sense to put this one first to reduce the number of evaluations necessary to rule out a particular message. For example, if you had a selector that did something like `(trade_type == 'buy') AND (trade_num-shares > 100000)`, it would make more sense to reverse the order because presumably there are many more buy orders than there are orders that involve more than 100,000 shares. Selector evaluation is always left-to-right, except where parentheses explicitly preclude it.

TIP With compound selectors, order matters. WebLogic JMS will short-circuit message selector evaluation once it determines the message does not match. Design your selectors to take advantage of this default left-to-right evaluation order.

Finally, what type of messaging do you need to use? We certainly do not recommend that you choose the messaging model based on whether you need to use message selectors. You should know, though, that message selectors generally tend to be faster and more predicable with topics than with queues. Of course, this is not always the case. When using message selectors with queues, the performance will be very dependent on the consumers keeping up with the producers and with quick matching of a message to a consumer. In cases where the queue is typically empty and it is easy to find a match between a message and a consumer, queues will actually outperform topics. The problem is that when something happens to make the consumers not keep up, the performance of message selectors with queues will degrade much faster than with topics.

One last thing to mention before moving on to other design considerations is the interaction between message selectors and paging. WebLogic JMS maintains messages in memory whenever possible. Whenever paging is necessary, only the message body is paged out of memory. This means that WebLogic JMS can evaluate most selectors even if the message body itself is paged out. The exception to this would be `XPATH` selectors. Because WebLogic JMS evaluates the selectors on topics at the time the message is published, this is only a big concern for `XPATH` selectors used in conjunction with queues.

Choosing a Message Expiration Strategy

By default, JMS messages never expire. When your application is sending messages to queues or topics with durable subscribers, WebLogic JMS must retain the message until it is consumed. This is fine in most point-to-point messaging applications because consumers are constantly consuming messages. Any message sent to a queue will typically be consumed in a relatively short period of time. If the queue consumers get disconnected, they will typically reconnect as soon as possible and start processing any messages that might have built up in the queue.

For durable subscribers to a topic, this is not necessarily true. The messaging system is forced to retain any message that has not been consumed by a durable subscriber, regardless of whether that durable subscriber will ever return. In this case, WebLogic JMS is at the mercy of the durable subscriber to unsubscribe when he or she no longer wishes to receive the messages. If the durable subscriber logic is flawed in such a way that the subscribers do not unsubscribe properly, then the messaging system will start to fill up with messages that may never be delivered. As you can imagine, this calls for real caution in your use of durable subscribers. Fortunately, there is another way to help deal with this problem.

Conventional wisdom suggests that the time-sensitive messages should be sent only to nondurable subscribers, and that is true for the most part. There are situations when a producer may wish to publish time-sensitive messages even when a subscriber is not connected. For example, an employee portal application may wish to publish messages to a topic that represents all employee mailboxes. If each employee uses his or her login id as the durable subscription's client id, the employees can receive published messages every time they log in. Imagine that you want to send 401(k) enrollment information to all your employees. The problem is that the JMS server must retain the message until every employee reads the message, which may never happen. Because the message is really irrelevant after the enrollment period ends, it is better to set an expiration time on the message so that WebLogic JMS can discard the message when it becomes unimportant—even if some employees never read it.

Message expiration can be set at the connection factory level or via any of the other override mechanisms discussed earlier. Using the `Time To Live` attribute or by explicitly calling the `setTimeToLive()` method on the `QueueSender` or `TopicPublisher`, you can specify the number of milliseconds the WebLogic JMS should retain an undelivered message after it is sent.

BEST PRACTICE For messages that become irrelevant after a certain time, set the `Time To Live` attribute or call `setTimeToLive()` on the producer to avoid message buildup.

Active Expiration

Prior to WebLogic Server 8.1, WebLogic JMS used a lazy message expiration policy. This means that it would remove expired messages from the system only when it happened to discover them in its normal course of processing messages. If a destination was idle, it was possible for expired messages to accumulate and continue to consume system resources. This meant that, under certain conditions, it was possible for a new message to be rejected because of quota restrictions even though the destination or JMS server contained expired messages that, if removed, would have cleared the quota condition and allowed for the delivery of the message.

WebLogic Server 8.1 adds support for active message expiration, in addition to the lazy message expiration scheme. Active message expiration works by having each JMS server periodically scan all destinations for expired messages. The JMS server's `Expiration Scan Interval` property controls the frequency of the scans. If a message expires at time `t`, the maximum length of time that the message will be retained is `t + ExpirationScanInterval + s`, where `s` is the time it takes to scan all message expiration times in the JMS server at the next scan interval. Some messages may be removed almost immediately, by lazy message expiration. Other messages may not be removed until the full amount of `ExpirationScanInterval + s` seconds has elapsed. Setting `ExpirationScanInterval` to 0 disables active message expiration. Even with active expiration disabled, messages will still expire and be removed during normal message processing by the lazy message expiration mechanism.

WARNING **Setting `ExpirationScanInterval` to a very large value effectively disables active scanning for expired messages. Of course, expired messages will still be removed during normal message processing by the lazy expiration mechanism.**

Expiration Policies

Prior to WebLogic Server 8.1, WebLogic JMS simply discarded all expired messages it found. Although this is still the default behavior, WebLogic Server 8.1 supports the concept of an *Expiration Policy* on a destination. Expiration policies allow you to define the action that WebLogic JMS should take when it finds an expired message. Configure the `Expiration Policy` using the JMS template or destination's `Expiration Policy Configuration` tab in the WebLogic Console. The valid values are as follows:

(none). Same as the `Discard` policy, WebLogic JMS removes expired messages from the destination.

Discard. WebLogic JMS removes expired messages from the destination.

Log. WebLogic JMS removes the expired messages from the destination and writes an entry to the server log file indicating that the messages have been removed. The `Expiration Logging Policy` defines the actual information that is logged.

Redirect. WebLogic JMS moves the expired messages from their current destination to that destination's configured `Error Destination`, if defined.

WARNING **You cannot use the `Redirect` policy when there is no valid error destination defined for the destination. Similarly, you cannot remove the error destination for a destination that is using the `Redirect` policy.**

By setting the `Expiration Policy` to `Log`, you are telling WebLogic JMS to write a log entry for every expired message it removes. Using the `Expiration Logging Policy` attribute, you can tell WebLogic JMS what information to log. WebLogic JMS will always write the JMSMessageID header; by default, this is the only information logged. You can add message headers or properties to the list by explicitly listing their names using a comma to separate the entries. WebLogic JMS also provides two wildcard values, `%header%` and `%properties%`, that will write all message headers or all message properties to the log, respectively.

NOTE **When the** `Expiration Policy` **is set to** `Log`**, WebLogic JMS always writes the** `JMSMessageID` **field to the log. If you forget to set the** `Expiration Logging Policy`**, then the log entry will contain only the message's** `JMSMessageID` **value.**

Handling Poison Messages

At some point, most messaging applications encounter situations where they are unable to process a message successfully. There are multiple reasons that this might occur; for example, the message could contain bad data, or the business logic might require access to a back-end system that is temporarily unavailable. In these situations, the message consumer cannot successfully process the message and needs to do something with that message so that it can move on to do other useful work, if possible. For example, a message-driven bean (MDB) using transactional delivery might call `setRollbackOnly()` on its `MessageDrivenContext` object to prevent the transaction from committing, thus forcing the JMS provider to requeue message.

Of course, the problem with our example is that the JMS provider will simply try to redeliver the message at some point in the future. If the redelivery occurs and the application is still unable to process the message, the application can end up in a deadly cycle of trying to process a *poison* message. When designing your messaging application, you need to understand in what situations your application might encounter poison messages and come up with strategies that make sense to reduce the burden on the underlying messaging system.

If your application accepts messages from another application, you might want to plan for unexpected or invalid message formats or data. While you could use WebLogic JMS's support for *dead-letter queues* to handle this situation, it really doesn't solve the problem. In this case, the problem is not a system-level problem with the actual delivery of the message, but an application-level problem with the expected contents of the message. As a result, asking the messaging system to try to redeliver the message is a waste of resources because the application will never be able to process the message. Furthermore, the offending message producer might continue to try to resend this message or, worse, all messages with this invalid message format or data. In this situation, you almost always want the application to reject the message, possibly by notifying the sending application that the message was rejected because of a bad message format or bad data. This means that you need the receiving application to divert the poison message to an error-handling process that will notify the sender of the problem rather than rejecting the message and forcing the messaging system to try to redeliver it.

BEST PRACTICE Use application-level error handling rather than redelivery and error destinations to handle errors in message content, including invalid formats and bad data.

Another common situation that occurs in the message processing application is that a back-end system becomes temporarily unavailable. Because the receiving application may require access to this back-end system to be able to process the incoming messages, the application must somehow delay the processing of the messages until the back-end system becomes available. Ideally, you could somehow detect that the back-end system is unavailable and simply tell the application to stop trying to consume any messages until further notice. Unfortunately, today this means writing your application to support this. For example, an application using MDBs to consume the messages would need to stop or undeploy the MDB to prevent it from continually trying to consume the messages and restart or redeploy it only once the back-end system becomes available. For cases where you expect, or at least want to plan for, long periods of back-end system unavailability, you should carefully consider using a mechanism for stopping and restarting the consumption of messages. If your back-end systems are highly available and you never expect more than transient periods of unavailability, then you might want to rely on the JMS provider's ability to redeliver the message at some point in the future. WebLogic JMS supports this through the use of `Redelivery Delay`, `Redelivery Limit`, and `Error Destinations`.

TIP For receiving applications that require access to external systems that are known to be unavailable occasionally, you will want to use a mechanism to stop and restart your message consumers when the system becomes unavailable.

Redelivery Delay

`Redelivery Delay` instructs WebLogic JMS to defer the redelivery of messages for a specified amount of time. Messages with a redelivery delay do not prevent other messages behind the delayed message from being delivered and can alter message ordering. You can set the `Default Redelivery Delay` on your WebLogic JMS connection factory. From there, you can explicitly override the `Redelivery Delay` on the session by using the WebLogic JMS extensions:

```
((WLSession)queueSession).setRedeliveryDelay(redeliveryDelayMilliseconds);
```

You can also administratively override both the connection factory and session settings by setting the `Redelivery Delay Override` on a template or destination.

Redelivery Limit and Error Destination

`Redelivery Limit` controls the number of times that WebLogic JMS will attempt to deliver a message before declaring it undeliverable. When a message is determined to be undeliverable, WebLogic JMS will move the message from its current destination to the `Error Destination` associated with the current destination. This `Error Destination` feature is sometimes known as a *dead-letter queue*. If an `Error Destination` is not configured, WebLogic JMS will silently delete the messages.

If the `Error Destination` has reached its quota, WebLogic JMS will drop the message and log an error message once every five minutes until the quota problem is resolved. For non-persistent messages, this means that the message is discarded; for persistent messages, the message will remain in the persistent store and will reappear in the original destination the next time the server starts.

Message producers can set the redelivery limit for messages they produce using the WebLogic JMS `WLMessageProducer` extension:

```
((WLMessageProducer)queueSender).setRedeliveryLimit(3);
```

If you pass -1 as the argument to `setRedeliveryLimit()`, it means that there is no limit unless it is overridden by the destination. Both the `Redelivery Limit` and `Error Destination` are configurable on a JMS template or destination. Setting the `Redelivery Limit` on a template or destination overrides any setting passed in from the producer; a value of -1 specifies that there is no override. An `Error Destination` can be a queue or a topic but must physically reside in the same JMS server as the associated destination.

When using error destinations, it is very important to incorporate the processing of messages from this destination in your application. One of the biggest challenges in doing this can be determining why the message was not successfully processed and what your application needs to do with it. We highly recommend that you do not let the error queue be used to handle application-level message content errors. If you can handle these errors through a separate process, then you should be able to treat all messages in the error destination as messages that could not be processed due to transient failures. One way of processing them would simply be to resend them to their original destination once you know that the transient failure has subsided. If you are using an `Expiration Policy` of `Redirect`, you may also have to look at message expiration times to segregate the messages to retry from those that expired. This isn't a big deal because it is easy to accomplish. Trying to segregate application-level errors from transient system-level errors placed onto the error queue is much more difficult.

WARNING Trying to separate messages on an error queue that got there because of both application-level errors and system-level errors can be very difficult, if not impossible. Designing your application to use a separate application-level destination for application errors will make processing messages in an error destination much simpler.

Ordered Redelivery

To add to this complication, some systems depend on the order of the messages. While the JMS specification requires that consumers receive messages in the order they were received by the JMS provider, it does not define the ordering requirements for message redelivery. WebLogic JMS can support ordered redelivery of messages but only when the consumer configuration meets certain constraints.

First, ordered redelivery requires that the destination have only one consumer. While this seems like a huge limitation at first, we will show you in the next section why this is necessary even for truly ordered delivery. Next, the destination sort order must be set such that the message will be placed at the top of the ordering. For example, sorting on message priority might cause a message to be placed behind a higher-priority message that just arrived. Finally, message selectors will cause the ordered redelivery to be applicable only to the current message and any other messages that match the selector.

TIP **Ordered redelivery of messages requires you to use only one consumer for the destination. Destinations with custom sort orders and consumers using message selectors can affect and/or prevent ordered redelivery.**

Recall from our earlier discussion that, for asynchronous consumers, messages are pipelined and the `MessagesMaximum` attribute of the connection factory controls this pipeline size. This creates a problem when a message is redelivered. In the previous versions of WebLogic Server, setting `MessagesMaximum` to 1 does not solve the problem because, in reality, it means two messages are outstanding, one in possession of the consumer and another in flight. If the consumer rolls back the first message, that message will be redelivered only after the in-flight message. This causes us to lose the desired message ordering.

WebLogic Server 8.1 redefines the behavior of the `MessagesMaximum` attribute, and a value of 1 now means that there will be no in-flight messages. Therefore, you must also create an application-specific connection factory and set its `MessagesMaximum` value to 1 to achieve ordered redelivery.

WARNING **You must set your application's connection factory's** `MessagesMaximum` **attribute to 1 to get ordered redelivery of messages. In previous versions of WebLogic Server, even this did not guarantee that the message redelivery will maintain message order even if there is only one asynchronous consumer.**

For more details on these constraints, please refer to the WebLogic JMS documentation at http://edocs.bea.com/wls/docs81/jms/implement.html. We will talk more about message ordering issues in the next section.

Handling Message Ordering Issues

Many applications require processing of messages in the order in which they were received. The problem is that the only way to guarantee that messages are processed in order is to have a single consumer processing one message at a time. For example, imagine that you have to send three messages to a queue in the following order: `message1`, `message2`, and `message3`. If you have two consumers, `consumer1` and `consumer2`, processing messages concurrently from that queue, WebLogic JMS will pick up `message1` and hand it to `consumer1` and then pick up `message2` and hand it to `consumer2`. From a WebLogic JMS perspective, it has delivered the messages in order; from an application perspective, the messages may or may not be processed in order, depending on the thread or process scheduling between the two consumers. It is a race condition at this point. As such, it is entirely possible for `consumer2` to get more resources than `consumer1` and complete the processing of `message2` before `consumer1` completes the processing of `message1`. Furthermore, it is also possible for `consumer2` to go back to WebLogic JMS to get `message3` and complete the processing of `message3` before `consumer1` ever finishes with `message1`. In short, as soon as you start parallel processing, message ordering across the threads or processes can no longer be guaranteed.

Clearly, you need a way to maintain ordering without creating a bottleneck in your application that can process only one message at a time. Unfortunately, there are no easy answers to this problem, and any messaging vendor that claims to have solved the problem is probably talking about a different problem. The typical way to handle message ordering issues is to try to define sets of messages that require ordering only within the set and parallelize the processing by assigning different sets of messages to different threads/processes. WebLogic JMS supports ordered messaging for destinations that have a single consumer. It is up to you, as the application architect, to determine your application's ordering requirements and your options for addressing them.

WARNING **Strict ordered processing of a set of messages is possible only if there is one consumer. Make sure you truly understand the application's ordering requirements so that you can explore your options for partitioning the messages to achieve parallelism while still maintaining order where it counts.**

Using Transactions

Transactions are used when multiple operations need to be treated as single atomic unit. As discussed earlier, the JMS specification introduces the concept of a transacted session to allow multiple JMS operations to be performed within the scope of a transaction. If your transactions involve multiple JMS operations only within a single session, you should use transacted sessions. For transactions that involve multiple JMS sessions and other resources, you can make your JMS session *JTA-aware* by enabling XA transaction support on your connection factory. Using the WebLogic Console, simply check the `XA Connection Factory Enabled` checkbox on the `Transactions`

`Configuration` tab. This will make WebLogic JMS return a connection factory that implements the `javax.jms.XAConnectionFactory` interface whenever you look up the connection factory from JNDI.

If your transaction involves multiple resources, the WebLogic JTA transaction manager detects this and switches automatically to the two-phase commit (2PC) protocol. WebLogic JMS implements its own XA resource manager and therefore can participate in a 2PC transaction without requiring support from the underlying storage manager (for example, the JDBC driver for JDBC-based message stores). One side effect of this is that transactions that involve JMS and any other database resource—even if JMS is using the same database as its message store—will always involve a 2PC transaction. Another side effect of this is that any JMS JDBC-based message stores cannot use XA JDBC drivers. You must use the non-XA version of the driver for accessing the message store; WebLogic JMS will handle the global transactions commit or rollback on the underlying database.

NOTE Do not use an XA JDBC driver to create JMS JDBC stores even when the store would participate in global transactions.

For any other database work done by other components as part of the transaction, you need to be using a JTA-aware `DataSource` that refers to a JDBC connection pool set up with an XA-compliant JDBC driver. A JTA-aware `DataSource` means one that has the `Honors Global Transactions` attribute selected; in previous versions of WebLogic Server, this was known as a `TxDataSource`. It is possible for WebLogic JTA to involve one non-XA resource in a global transaction. For a `DataSource` that refers to a JDBC connection pool that is not using an XA-compliant driver, you can use the `Emulate Two-Phase Commit for Non-XA Driver` option. WebLogic JTA uses a variation of the last-agent commit algorithm where the non-XA resource is committed only after all of the XA resources have responded that they are prepared to commit. If the non-XA resource fails, WebLogic JTA tells the XA resources to roll back; otherwise, it tells them to commit. While this algorithm is the best that can be done with non-XA resources in a global transaction, it is always better not to involve non-XA resources in global transactions in order to minimize the risk of failures.

If you are going to be using global transactions that involve JMS, the most important thing to keep in mind is that WebLogic JTA will optimize global transaction coordination for collocated resources. Some of the ways that you can collocate resources are as follows:

- If your transactions involve JMS and one or more EJBs, deploy all of your EJBs and JMS destinations on the same WebLogic Server instances. If you are using distributed destinations, deploy all of the EJBs to every server that hosts a member destination.
- If your transactions involve JMS and JDBC resources, deploy your JDBC connection pools, JTA-aware `DataSource` objects, and JMS destinations on the same WebLogic Server instances. Again, for distributed destinations this means deploying them to every server that hosts a member destination.

- If your transactions involve multiple JMS destinations, deploy all of the destinations on the same WebLogic Server instance. For applications accessing multiple distributed destinations, make sure to collocate the members of each distributed destination on the same WebLogic Server instances. It is even more efficient if you can deploy them in the same JMS servers.

Before moving on, it is worth noting that a transacted session performs better than JTA-aware sessions when using a stand-alone client application. JTA-aware sessions have to manage resources on both the client and the server hosting the JMS connection. Transacted sessions use a transaction delegation model where the transaction scope is restricted to the JMS server. Transacted sessions are well suited for batching send and receive requests from stand-alone clients running in their own JVM. JTA-aware sessions are well suited for server-side applications, which typically access other J2EE components within the same global transaction context.

Using Multicast Sessions

Multicast sessions are a WebLogic JMS extension that can improve performance dramatically, especially when your application needs to send individual messages to a large number of subscribers. When using IP multicast to transmit messages, the underlying network needs to carry only one copy of the message regardless of the number of subscribers. Because of the inherent unreliable nature of the UDP protocol on which IP multicast is based, WebLogic JMS cannot guarantee delivery of messages sent using multicast sessions. Network congestion plays a big role in the quality of service. Clearly, applications that cannot tolerate message loss should not consider the use of multicast sessions.

Multicast also requires a tightly controlled network environment. Most routers and firewalls are not configured to allow multicast traffic to pass through them. While it is possible to configure them, this implies that your subscribers and WebLogic JMS servers are all connected by a network that you can control. Multicast messages use a *time-to-live* (TTL) concept that routers use to control the propagation of multicast messages. Each router that forwards a multicast packet decrements the packet's TTL; once the TTL reaches zero, the packet will no longer be forwarded between network segments. Multicast uses a special class of IP addresses, known as *Class D addresses*, which range from 224.0.0.0 to 239.255.255.255. Typically, addresses in the 224.0.0.x range are reserved for multicast routing.

WebLogic JMS supports only multicast sessions for topics. This makes sense because the benefit of multicast is seen only when the same message is sent to large numbers of consumers. To use multicast sessions, you need to configure the multicast information for your topics. When using multicast, we highly recommend that you select unique multicast address and port combinations for each topic that will be using multicast for message delivery. Doing this will help segregate the traffic for a particular topic and will reduce the chances of message loss.

BEST PRACTICE Always select unique multicast address and port number combinations for each topic that will use multicast message delivery. Never use the same multicast address and port number used by your WebLogic clusters.

Once the topics are properly configured, you need to create a JMS session that uses the WebLogic JMS-specific MULTICAST_NO_ACKNOWLEDGE acknowledgment mode, as shown here. Note that multicast sessions cannot use transacted sessions or JTA transactions. Use the following code to create a multicast session:

```
TopicSession topicSession = topicConnection.createTopicSession(false,
                                   WLSession.MULTICAST_NO_ACKNOWLEDGE);
```

Next, we create the TopicSubscriber as we normally would, as shown here. This call will fail if the topic is not configured to support multicast. Also note that multicast consumers cannot be durable subscribers.

```
TopicSubscriber topicSubscriber = topicSession.createSubscriber(topic);
```

Finally, we need to register our MessageListener and start the connection, if it is not already started. Multicast sessions must use asynchronous delivery via the MessageListener:

```
topicSubscriber.setMessageListener(new MyMessageListener());
topicConnection.start();
```

For multicast sessions, WebLogic JMS tracks the message sequence. A sequence gap occurs when messages are lost or received out of order. When WebLogic JMS detects a sequence gap, it will deliver a weblogic.jms.extensions.SequenceGapException to the multicast session's ExceptionListener, if one is registered.

TIP If your application cares about sequence gaps when using multicast delivery, you can register an ExceptionListener **with the WebLogic JMS session to be notified when sequence gaps occur.**

Handling Request/Reply Style Message Exchange

JMS is all about sending and receiving messages. Whenever an application sends a message to another application, it is not uncommon for the sending application to require a response message after its original message is processed. This pattern is so common that JMS explicitly supports the pattern in several ways.

First, JMS supports that concept of a temporary destination, and the JMS messages headers include a JMSReplyTo field for passing a reference to a *reply-to* destination as part of a message. While there is nothing that requires the reply-to destination to be a temporary one, this is a common pattern that clients use to prevent having to use message selectors to find their response among responses for other clients. An example of how you might use this is the following:

```
Queue responseQueue = queueSession.createTemporaryQueue();
QueueReceiver queueReceiver =
queueSession.createReceiver(responseQueue);
queueReceiver.setMessageListener(new MyMessageListener());
```

```
textMessage.setText("My Request Message");
textMessage.setJMSReplyTo(responseQueue);
queueSender.send(textMessage);
responseQueue.delete();
```

Now, let's look at the consumer of the request message. In the consumer, we simply get the `JMSReplyTo` destination from the request message, generate our response message, and send the response message to the destination:

```
Queue replyQueue = (Queue)requestMessage.getJMSReplyTo();
queueSender.send(replyQueue, replyMessage);
```

In this example, our request producer is using the `MessageListener` to asynchronously receive the response that will be sent to the temporary destination. This is the recommended way of accomplishing the request/response pattern. Of course, applications sometimes want to block until the response comes back. You could achieve this using the synchronous `receive()` method:

```
Queue responseQueue = queueSession.createTemporaryQueue();
QueueReceiver queueReceiver =
queueSession.createReceiver(responseQueue);
textMessage.setText("My Request Message");
textMessage.setJMSReplyTo(responseQueue);
queueSender.send(textMessage);
Message responseMessage = queueReceiver.receive();
responseQueue.delete();
```

Here, we used the *no-args* `receive()` method that blocks until a message arrives. There is also a version that accepts a time-out value, after which the method will return control to the application even if no message has arrived. Finally, there is a `receiveNoWait()` method that does not block and will return `null` if no message is waiting.

WARNING Use the `receive(long timeout)` or `receiveNoWait()` methods inside server applications that need to receive a response message synchronously from another application. Even in stand-alone JMS client applications, think twice before using the *no-args* `receive()` method, which can cause the application to block for an uncontrolled length of time.

Notice that, in both cases, we call the `delete()` method on the temporary destination when we are through with it. Applications should try to reuse temporary destinations rather than continually creating and deleting them, wherever possible. WebLogic Server will automatically delete temporary destinations when the JMS connection is closed.

The JMS specification authors must have thought that this pattern was so common that they created an easier way to accomplish the same thing by using a *Requestor* object. The code shown here demonstrates how to accomplish the same synchronous request/response pattern using a temporary queue.

```
QueueRequestor queueRequestor =
new QueueRequestor(queueSession, requestQueue);
textMessage.setText("My Request Message");
Message responseMessage = queueRequestor.request(textMessage);
```

The `QueueRequestor` and `TopicRequestor` utility classes automatically create the temporary destination and block waiting for the response. Be forewarned that these classes do not allow you to perform nonblocking or blocking with a time-out request. You must use nontransacted sessions with these classes. As with all temporary destinations, the messages sent to them are non-persistent because temporary destinations, by definition, do not survive application restarts or failures.

BEST PRACTICE When using request/response style messaging in a WebLogic Server, be very careful about calling blocking methods to receive the response. If you must call `receive()`, always use a relatively short time-out to prevent tying up WebLogic Server execute threads for extended periods of time. Wherever possible, use the asynchronous `MessageListener` to wait for the reply.

The other major approach for supporting request/reply messaging is through the use of a *correlation ID*. Correlation IDs provide you with the ability to assign a unique identifier to a message and its reply. JMS doesn't do anything with these correlation IDs; it is up to the application to use them to correlate requests with replies. By using correlation IDs, you have much more freedom about where and when you send the reply. Using correlation IDs can be useful even when used in conjunction with temporary destinations to help applications that can have multiple outstanding messages at any point in time.

To use correlation IDs, the first thing you need to decide on is what unique identifier you are going to use to correlate the messages. The JMS provider creates a unique identifier for every JMS message that it stores in the `JMSMessageID` header. As a result, using the `JMSMessageID` as the correlation ID is a common practice. JMS messages also contain a `JMSCorrelationID` header that applications can use to set the correlation ID for a particular message.

When using this scheme, the producer sending the message needs to call only the `getJMSMessageID()` method on the `Message` *after* the message is sent. It is important to wait until after the message is sent because WebLogic JMS does not actually set the message's `JMSMessageID` header until the message is sent. The producer doesn't actually need to set the `JMSCorrelationID` field in the request message because the consumer is going to associate the `JMSMessageID` of the request message with the `JMSCorrelationID` of the reply message:

```
replyMessage.setJMSCorrelationID(requestMessage.getJMSMessageID());
```

Of course, there is nothing preventing you from using your own correlation ID scheme. Simply set the correlation ID in the original request message, and have the consumer read the incoming request message's correlation ID using the `getJMSCorrelationID()` method and then set it on the outgoing reply message.

The last thing we need to discuss as it relates to correlation IDs is the use of a shared reply queue across all requests. A very common pattern we see occurs where you have a synchronous client, such as a Web application responding to a request from a browser, needing to call a back-end system that is accessible only via a messaging system. Usually, the synchronous client wants to send a message and wait for the response. The client, however, will typically only wait so long and then give up on the response, possibly even resending the original request. This causes a problem if our back-end system is slow but still working in that the shared reply queue may end up with reply messages that have already been abandoned by the requestor. Fortunately, there are several things that we can do to handle this problem.

First, we can use message expiration on the reply messages to prevent them from accumulating. For that matter, we might want to use expiration times on the request messages to try to prevent the back end from receiving messages that the client has given up on. Finally, you could just use temporary destinations that the client deletes when giving up on the reply. This will also give your back-end system some indication that the client has left when it gets an error trying to send the response to the temporary destination that no longer exists. Of course, none of these solutions really solves all of the application-level problems associated with this type of scenario, but at least they help keep the messaging system healthy. The preferred approach to dealing with this type of scenario is to try to separate the synchronous client request into two parts, one to submit the request and another to look for the response.

WebLogic JMS Programming

In this section, we are going to look at how to use WebLogic JMS in your application. We start out by talking about the WebLogic JMS resource pooling and how to leverage that support with Web applications and EJBs. This is a new feature added in WebLogic Server 8.1. Next, we discuss how to use WebLogic Server's message-driven bean support to consume JMS messages from server-side applications. We finish up this section with a discussion of strategies for integrating foreign JMS providers into WebLogic Server applications.

Using WebLogic JMS with Servlets and EJBs

Using WebLogic JMS from within your server-side application is as simple as using it from within stand-alone client applications. By making use of the J2EE-defined mechanisms for referencing JMS objects through deployment descriptor resource reference mappings, WebLogic JMS now transparently substitutes the real JMS objects for wrappers that pool JMS resources like connections and sessions. This is new in WebLogic Server 8.1 and also works with foreign JMS providers. To use this, you simply add a `resource-ref` into your standard J2EE deployment (that is, `web.xml` or `ejb-jar.xml`):

```
<resource-ref>
  <res-ref-name>jms/BigRezEmailConnectionFactory</res-ref-name>
```

```
    <res-type>javax.jms.QueueConnectionFactory</res-type>
    <res-auth>Container</res-auth>
    <res-sharing-scope>Shareable</res-sharing-scope>
</resource-ref>
```

Then, you add a matching `resource-description` entry in our WebLogic Server-specific deployment descriptor (that is, `weblogic.xml` or `weblogic-ejb-jar.xml`):

```
<resource-description>
    <res-ref-name>jms/BigRezEmailConnectionFactory</res-ref-name>
    <jndi-name>BigRezEmailConnectionFactory</jndi-name>
</resource-description>
```

Finally, you simply look up the connection factory and write standard JMS code, as shown in this excerpt from the ReservationSessionBean in our bigrez.com example:

```
QueueConnectionFactory factory = (QueueConnectionFactory)
    jndiCtx.lookup("java:comp/env/jms/BigRezEmailConnectionFactory");
Queue queue = (Queue)
    jndiCtx.lookup("java:comp/env/jms/BigRezEmailQueue");
QueueConnection connection = null;
try {
    connection = factory.createQueueConnection();
    ...
}
catch (JMSException jmse) {
    ...
}
finally {
    if (connection != null) {
        try { connection.close(); } catch (JMSException ignore) { }
    }
}
```

Notice that we are closing our connection at the end of each use inside the finally block. This is critical when using pooled resources and is just like what you would do when using JDBC connection pools. In our example, we are looking up the connection factory and queue each time. You could cache the results of these two lookups if you choose, though the overhead for a local JNDI lookup should be small. Do not try to cache any of the intermediate objects like the connection, session, or sender. WebLogic JMS is already pooling these objects so it is important to release them back to the pool when you have finished using them.

BEST PRACTICE From your server-side applications, take advantage of JMS resource pooling by binding your JMS connection factory into your component-local JNDI tree. Always close your connection objects at the end of each use to allow WebLogic JMS to release these pooled objects back into the pool.

If you use JMS within XA transaction, you do not need to reference the XA versions of the JMS objects when using the WebLogic JMS pooling mechanism. The wrapper object is smart enough to detect the presence of a JTA transaction and will automatically use the XA capabilities of the JMS provider to enlist it in the XA transaction. If the underlying JMS provider does not support XA, then you will need to suspend the JTA transaction either by telling the container that the EJB does not support transactions or by using the JTA APIs. We will talk more about integrating with foreign JMS providers in the last section of this chapter.

If you happen to be using an older version of WebLogic Server, then you will not have the benefits of the new JMS resource pooling and you may need to come up with a caching strategy to cache the connections, sessions, and producers because you will be working with the actual JMS objects, rather than a pooling wrapper.

BEST PRACTICE When working with older versions of WebLogic Server, you should consider caching the JMS connection, session, and producer objects to improve performance. WebLogic Server 8.1 takes care of the caching through the new JMS resource-pooling facilities.

One other thing to be aware of is that these new wrapper objects now enforce some J2EE restrictions on these pooled objects that were never enforced when working with the real JMS objects. These restrictions basically prevent you from calling certain JMS methods that require asynchronous delivery and thus require a thread to be created. For example, you are not allowed to associate a `MessageListener` with a consumer. What this means is that the only way to asynchronously consume messages from a J2EE application is to use either a message-driven bean or a server session pool. Because both of these mechanisms are using pooled objects that are not specific to a particular client or request, the main thing that you lose through this is the ability to create a `MessageListener` that contains state about the specific client or request. This simply means that any state that you require the asynchronous listener to have must be passed through or accessible using the contents of the message. For more information on the methods that are not allowed, see the "J2EE Compliance" section of http://edocs.bea.com/wls/docs81/jms/j2ee_components.html.

WARNING WebLogic JMS resource pooling now enforces the restrictions laid out for server-side applications in Section 6.7 of the J2EE 1.3 specification. This means that existing server-side applications that use the asynchronous `MessageListener` pattern will no longer work properly if resource pooling is in use.

Consuming Asynchronous Messages on the Server

When building server-side applications that asynchronously consume JMS messages, you have two primary options for how to do this: message-driven beans (MDBs) and server session pools. While WebLogic Server supports both mechanisms, there are few reasons left for using server session pools now that message-driven beans have arrived. As a result, we will focus our discussion on MDBs. For more information on using WebLogic JMS support for server session pools, please refer to the WebLogic JMS documentation at http://edocs.bea.com/wls/docs81/jms/implement.html.

Message-Driven Beans

Our coverage of MDBs is not intended to be exhaustive. If you want to learn more about MDBs, please refer to the WebLogic Server documentation at http://edocs.bea.com/wls/docs81/ejb/message_beans.html.

Understanding Concurrency

Like stateless session beans, the WebLogic Server EJB container pools message-driven bean instances in memory. You can control the size of the pool using the `initial-beans-in-free-pool` and `max-beans-in-free-pool` parameters found in the `weblogic-ejb-jar.xml` deployment descriptor. When messages arrive at the associated destination, the EJB container tries to find a bean in the free pool to handle the message. If no instance is available, the container will create a new instance if the size of the pool is currently less than `max-beans-in-free-pool`. If the pool is already at its maximum size, the message will remain in the destination until a bean in the pool becomes available. Of course, the maximum amount of parallelism, and therefore the maximum number of beans the EJB container will ever create, is also controlled by the maximum number of threads available for use by the MDB instances. Unlike stateless session beans, the maximum number of available threads varies depending on how the MDB is deployed.

When you deploy an MDB, the WebLogic EJB container associates it with an execute queue and its associated execute threads. By default, all MDBs are associated with the default execute queue, now known as the `weblogic.kernel.Default` queue. When MDBs are using the default queue, WebLogic Server determines the maximum number of threads used by all MDBs associated with the default execute queue using the following formula. This limit is imposed to prevent deadlocks between the MDBs and other components that share the default execute queue.

$$MaximumNumberOfMDBThreads = \left(\frac{SizeOfDefaultExecuteQueueThreadPool}{2}\right) + 1$$

A recent addition to WebLogic Server is the ability to control the execute queue MDBs use through the use of the `dispatch-policy` element in the `weblogic-ejb-jar.xml` deployment descriptor. When you associate MDBs with an application-defined execute queue, then WebLogic Server will allow the MDBs to use up to the number of threads in the execute queue's thread pool. What this means is that you can dedicate a thread pool for the exclusive use of one or more MDBs. We strongly recommend that you take advantage of this as it will give you more control over the concurrency and allow you to partition your MDB message processing from other nonmessage-related activities.

BEST PRACTICE Always deploy your message-driven beans to a dedicated execute queue.

When you deploy an MDB to listen for messages on a queue, WebLogic Server uses one JMS session and consumer per bean instance in the pool. This allows for parallel processing of queued messages. In contrast, WebLogic Server uses one JMS session and consumer per pool for MDBs listening for messages on topics. Although this means that the EJB container receives one message at a time, it actually dispatches the messages to the bean instances in parallel.

Using Transactions

MDBs provide a declarative mechanism to tell the EJB container to start a transaction before delivering a message to them. As we discussed earlier, JMS does not generically support the concept of transactional delivery of asynchronously received messages. For JMS providers whose session objects implement the `weblogic.jms.extensions.MDBTransaction` interface, WebLogic Server will support truly asynchronous transactional delivery by receiving the message using the `CLIENT_ACKNOWLEDGE` mode, start a JTA transaction, and then use this callback interface to associate the message delivery with the JTA transaction. Obviously, this interface is specific to WebLogic Server, but at least one other third-party JMS vendor implements this interface. For JMS providers that do not implement this interface, WebLogic Server uses a synchronous mechanism under the covers in order to support transactional delivery of JMS messages to MDBs.

MDBs support both container-managed and bean-managed transactions. You can control the transactional semantics for your MDBs through the `ejb-jar.xml` deployment descriptor, just as you do for any other type of EJB. When using container-managed transactions, WebLogic Server will automatically start a JTA transaction before invoking to MDB's `onMesssage()` method so that the incoming message delivery is part of the JTA transaction. If you want to force the container to roll back the transaction, you should call the `setRollbackOnly()` method on the `MessageDrivenContext` object. In general, you should avoid throwing a `RuntimeException` like `EJBException` from the `onMessage()` method. While this will cause the container to roll back the transaction, it also forces the container to remove the MDB instance from the pool, as required by the EJB specification. Of course, the container is free to create another instance should it need to do so.

BEST PRACTICE Avoid throwing a `RuntimeException`, such as `EJBException` from an MDB's `onMessage()` method to roll back transactions. If an MDB does throw a `RuntimeException`, the EJB specification required the container to remove the instance that threw the exception from memory. Calling `setRollbackOnly()` works just as well and does not force the container to remove the instance from memory.

To deploy an MDB that uses container-managed transactions, the MDB must use an XA connection factory. If the referenced connection factory does not support XA, WebLogic Server will not deploy the MDB.

TIP MDBs that use container-managed transactions must use XA connection factories.

MDBs also support bean-managed transactions. When using bean-managed transactions, the incoming message delivery cannot be included as part of the transaction. In the `onMessage()` method, the WebLogic EJB container gives you access to the JTA `UserTransaction` object through the `MessageDrivenContext` so that your application can begin, commit, and roll back transactions as necessary. In all cases, you must end your transaction before the `onMessage()` method returns. Once the `onMessage()` method returns, the EJB container will acknowledge the message. To prevent this message acknowledgment from occurring, you must throw a `RuntimeException` *after* ending the transaction.

You have several choices for controlling the type of message acknowledgment that the container uses. By setting the acknowledge-mode element in the `ejb-jar.xml` deployment descriptor, you can control the acknowledgment mode for any MDB that is *not* using a container-managed transaction. When container-managed transactions are being used, this attribute is ignored. By default, the container uses `AUTO_ACKNOWLEDGE` mode when container-managed transactions are not in use (or the transaction type is set to `NotSupported`). You can also choose to use `DUPS_OK_ACKNOWLEDGE` or one of the WebLogic JMS-specific modes, `NO_ACKNOWLEDGE` or `MULTICAST_NO_ACKNOWLEDGE`. An MDB is prohibited from using client acknowledgment by the EJB specification.

Dealing with Durable Subscriptions

MDBs can also use durable subscriptions; however, there is a problem with deploying a message-driven bean that uses durable subscriptions to a cluster that warrants discussion. To create an MDB with a durable subscription, you are required to specify the connection factory that sets the durable subscription's client identifier in the MDB deployment descriptor. WebLogic JMS supports clustering through the process of defining a JMS server in each WebLogic Server instance in the cluster. When you target an MDB to a cluster, WebLogic Server deploys a copy of the MDB in each JMS server. Because each copy of the MDB deployed to the individual servers is treated as a separate deployment, this causes a problem because, as far as WebLogic JMS is concerned, you have just deployed multiple durable subscriptions that are using the same client identifier.

What this means is that you need to make sure that each server's MDB is using a unique client identifier. WebLogic Server lets you set the client identifier for an MDB's durable subscription in two ways: using the `jms-client-id` element in the `weblogic-ejb-jar.xml` deployment descriptor or using the `Client ID` attribute on the connection factory's `General Configuration` tab in the WebLogic Console. This is where the trouble begins.

Because each server in the cluster must use a unique client ID for their individual MDB deployment, you need some way of making your MDB application use either a different deployment descriptor for each server or a different connection factory. To set the client ID explicitly in the deployment descriptor, you would need to create one MDB deployment unit per WebLogic Server instance. Of course, most applications do not deploy MDBs separately from the rest of the application so this means that you end up creating separate application deployment units (for example, separate EAR files) for every server in the cluster just to handle this shortcoming.

To use the connection factory to solve the problem, you need each server to use a different connection factory. The problem is that the JNDI name to use to locate the connection factory is specified using the `connection-factory-jndi-name element` in the `weblogic-ejb-jar.xml` deployment descriptor. The only way to make this work currently without having to create separate application deployment units for each server is to create a separate connection factory for each server and have them all use the same JNDI name. While this works, it does prevent you from migrating one JMS server to another WebLogic Server instance that already has a JMS server deployed because of the JNDI naming conflict when both servers need to deploy two different connection factories with the same JNDI name.

In addition, don't forget that WebLogic JMS does not support creating durable subscriptions to a distributed topic. As we discussed previously, you need to create the durable subscriptions directly against the distributed topic's member destinations. Again, this creates a problem for a clustered deployment of MDBs because the durable subscriber's target topic must be identified in the MDB's `ejb-jar.xml` deployment descriptor. Because each member topic must have a unique JNDI name, this also forces you to create a separate MDB deployment unit for each member destination. We expect that both of these shortcomings will be addressed in a future release.

WARNING Avoid using durable subscriptions with message-driven beans in WebLogic Server. Due to limitations in the implementation, you will need to create a separate copy of the MDB for each server in the cluster. Because MDBs are usually packaged with the rest of the application, this will mean that you will need to create a separate copy of your application for every server in the cluster or separate the MDB into its own application. Moving the MDBs into a separate application has performance implications because the calls from the MDBs to other EJBs can no longer take advantage of `enable-call-by-reference` **and EJB local interface optimizations.**

Application Design Considerations

When designing your MDB-based application, there are several things to keep in mind. First, it is generally better to use a delegation model to keep the business logic inside the `onMessage()` method to a minimum. By delegating the actual message processing to another component, you can turn the MDB into a controller that does nothing more than dispatch messages to the right business component. This promotes modular design and component reusability.

Remember that an MDB instance can process only one message at a time. This creates a problem if the business logic takes a relatively long time to process a message. As we have mentioned several times throughout this chapter, a well-designed messaging application requires consumers to be able to keep up with producers over long periods of time. If your message processing takes a long time, you need to make sure that you have enough concurrency to handle the incoming message volume.

When deploying MDBs, it is always better to deploy them to the same WebLogic Server instance that hosts the destination whenever possible. When deploying to a cluster where the MDBs and the JMS destinations are both hosted in the same cluster, you should make sure that the MDBs are listening only on destinations in the same server instance. Remember that by default with distributed destinations, WebLogic Server always uses server affinity to help enforce this pattern. In addition, when deploying MDBs that listen to JMS destinations in the same cluster, WebLogic Server starts the MDB instances only on servers that contain the actual destination, or a member destination in the case of distributed destinations. Of course, all of the other considerations we discussed previously in the "WebLogic JMS Application Design" section apply to MDBs as well.

External JMS Providers

Sometimes, you may need to use another messaging system to be able to access a legacy application. Many of the legacy messaging systems in use today are starting to provide JMS APIs that make this job easier. The J2EE 1.3 specification does not really define exactly how J2EE applications deployed using one vendor's application server should be able to integrate with JMS providers from another vendor. For example, the EJB 2.0 specification does not define how the MDBs should support interaction with a foreign JMS provider. Fortunately, WebLogic Server provides seamless integration with foreign JMS providers.

In general, there are two strategies for integrating your J2EE applications deployed in WebLogic Server with external JMS providers: direct and indirect integration. These external JMS providers might be another vendor's JMS product or just another WebLogic Server instance that hosts the JMS destinations. With direct integration, the application interacts directly with the external JMS destinations from the application code or the MDB's deployment descriptors. This method has the advantage of being the most efficient but exposes the J2EE application to the availability of the external provider.

Indirect integration uses a *store-and-forward* model where the application produces messages to and/or consumes messages from local JMS destinations. A *message bridge* is responsible for moving messages between the local and external destinations. Because all availability and reconnection issues are handled by the bridge, the application itself never has to worry about the external JMS provider.

In this section, we will start by looking briefly at the capabilities of the WebLogic JMS Messaging Bridge. We follow that with a discussion of MDB support for foreign JMS providers. Next, we discuss the new *foreign JMS provider* support. We end this section with a brief discussion of the trade-offs of the different approaches.

Understanding the Messaging Bridge

WebLogic Server provides a built-in message bridge that you can configure using the WebLogic Console to move messages between any two JMS destinations. The WebLogic Server Messaging Bridge provides several qualities of service (QoS) that control the message delivery: `Exactly-once`, `Atmost-once`, and `Duplicates-okay`. `Exactly-once` delivery means just that; the message will be delivered from the sending destination to the receiving destination using XA transactions so that the receiver gets exactly one copy of each message. `Atmost-once` delivery uses a best-effort delivery mode to make sure that the receiving destination receives only a single copy of the message or does not receive it at all. With the `Duplicates-okay` delivery mode, the bridge acknowledges receiving the message from the source destination only after writing it to the target destination. Because this is done outside the scope of a transaction, failures after writing the message to the target and before acknowledging the source can result in duplicate messages being delivered but should never result in a message being lost. This type of delivery is better known as *at-least-once* delivery.

The bridge uses J2EE CA adapters to connect to the different messaging systems, though the adapters it can use are currently limited to the following built-in set of adapters:

jms-xa-adp.rar. The bridge uses this adapter to communicate with any XA-compliant JMS provider to provide `Exactly-once` delivery.

jms-notran-adp.rar. The bridge uses this adapter to communicate with any JMS provider to provide either `Atmost-once` or `Duplicates-okay` delivery.

jms-notran-adp51.rar. This adapter provides interoperability with WebLogic Server 5.1's JMS implementation. As the name suggests, it does not support transactional delivery so it supports only the `Atmost-once` and `Duplicates-okay` delivery modes.

You must create an instance of the bridge for each source and target destination pair and deploy it to a WebLogic Server instance. Before you can do this, you need first to deploy the appropriate adapters that the bridge will need, based on the messaging systems and QoS being used. The WebLogic Server Messaging Bridge provides many different configuration options that we will not spend time on here. For a complete discussion of the bridge, please refer to the WebLogic Server documentation at http://edocs.bea.com/wls/docs81/ConsoleHelp/messaging_bridge.html.

BEST PRACTICE Use the WebLogic Server Messaging Bridge to store and forward messages between different JMS providers.

Using Message-Driven Beans

MDBs use JNDI to retrieve connection factories and destinations. You can use MDBs in WebLogic Server to work with any JMS provider that supports and implements the JMS and JNDI specifications. When configuring an MDB to use a remote JMS provider, you must provide the JNDI information needed to look up the remote connection factory and destination using the `weblogic-ejb-jar.xml` deployment descriptor. This information includes the values of the JNDI `Context.INITIAL_CONTEXT_FACTORY` and `Context.PROVIDER_URL` parameters that WebLogic should use to create the `InitialContext`, as well as the JNDI names of the connection factory and destination.

WebLogic Server also supports using container-managed transactions with foreign JMS providers to provide transactional delivery of messages to the MDBs. Make sure that the connection factory the MDB deployment descriptors references is an instance of `javax.jms.XAConnectionFactory` so that WebLogic Server will fully support the transactional settings of the MDB and provide for transaction coordination between the external provider and any other resources your business logic might involve in the transaction.

Mapping External JMS Objects to WebLogic JNDI

WebLogic Server 8.1 introduces the ability to create a sort of *symbolic link* between a JMS connection factory and destination in an external JNDI provider and a binding in your local WebLogic Server's JNDI tree. This makes it easier for your applications, or the Messaging Bridge configuration, to abstract itself away from the external JNDI provider's configuration details. To use this facility, you start by using the WebLogic Console to create a `Foreign JMS Server` entry for each of your external JMS providers. This entry contains the information about how to connect to the external JMS provider's JNDI provider. Once the `Foreign JMS Server` entry exists, you can configure any number of links between external connection factories and destinations for that server and local JNDI bindings. For more information about using this feature, see http://edocs.bea.com/wls/docs81/ConsoleHelp/jms_config.html.

Though this new feature allows you to map foreign JMS provider's JNDI objects in the local WebLogic Server's JNDI tree easily, it does come with a price. To avoid the synchronization problems associated with caching remote objects locally, WebLogic Server automatically does a remote JNDI lookup every time your application looks up these local bindings. This approach is highly desirable because some JMS providers' connection factory and destination objects are invalid once the JMS provider is restarted. This also means that a JNDI lookup of one of these objects is not any cheaper than looking it up directly from the remote location.

BEST PRACTICE **Use the new `Foreign JMS Server` capabilities to isolate the rest of your application configuration away from the external JMS provider's configuration by making the objects visible from the local JNDI tree.**

Choosing an Integration Strategy

When your application is consuming messages from an external JMS provider, consider using the direct integration approach with MDBs rather than the indirect bridging approach. MDBs deployed in WebLogic Server can support the same qualities of service supported by the bridge. MDBs support exactly-once delivery through the use of XA transactions. By using either `AUTO_ACKNOWLEDGE` or `DUPS_OK_ACKNOWLEDGE` modes, you can get at-least-once delivery. The trade-offs between the two acknowledgment modes are really about reducing the chances for duplicate messages versus improving performance. By using the WebLogic JMS-specific modes of `NO_ACKNOWLEDGE` or `MULTICAST_NO_ACKNOWLEDGE`, you can achieve at-most-once delivery of your messages. MDBs also support automatic reconnection to the external provider should the connection fail, such as when the external JMS provider is restarted. You can tune the polling interval with which the MDBs will try to reconnect by using the `jms-polling-interval-seconds` element in the `weblogic-ejb-jar.xml` deployment descriptor. The default value is to try to reconnect once every 10 seconds.

WebLogic Server provides a configurable mechanism to pause MDB message consumption after some number of consecutive errors when using transactions with foreign JMS providers that do not implement the `weblogic.jms.extensions.MDBTransaction` interface. By default, WebLogic Server MDBs will pause their message processing for 5 seconds when the MDB deployment encounters 10 consecutive errors. An error is defined by either the MDB calling `setRollbackOnly()` or throwing a `RuntimeException`, such as `EJBException`, from the `onMessage()` method. You can tune the number of consecutive errors and sleep time by setting the following Java system properties at the server startup:

weblogic.ejb20.MaxMDBErrors. This property controls the number of consecutive errors before processing of a message-driven bean will pause. Each message-driven bean deployment has an independent counter, which is reset every time a message is successfully processed.

weblogic.ejb20.MDBErrorSleepTime. This property specifies the number of seconds a message-driven bean's processing will pause after encountering `weblogic.ejb20.MaxMDBErrors` consecutive errors.

This feature could be very useful in solving the more general problem of how to suspend message processing when the system is temporarily unable to process messages, such as when the back-end database is down. We hope that future versions of WebLogic Server will use this or some similar mechanism to help you address the more general problem. We would also expect to see this feature promoted into the WebLogic Console and made configurable per destination or MDB rather than at the entire server level.

To debug connection problems with message-driven beans using an external provider, try setting the `weblogic.ejb.jms.connect.verbose` and `weblogic.ejb.jms.connect.debug` Java system properties to true on the server command line (in older version, these properties were named `weblogic.ejb20.jms.connect.verbose` and `weblogic.ejb20.jms.connect.debug`). As with all of these undocumented properties, these properties are subject to change without notice.

For applications that are sending messages to a foreign provider, using the messaging bridge is typically a better option unless the application is waiting on a response to be able to continue processing. For example, a Web application that is using request/reply style messaging to an external back-end system in order to be able to send a Web page back to the client's browser would not be a good candidate for the messaging bridge. Of course, we could argue that this isn't the best design, as we did earlier in the chapter, but we hope that the example gets our point across. Using the bridge allows the application to complete requests by writing the message to a local JMS queue. This means that the application will continue to function properly even when the remote system is down. The bridge handles all of the reconnect logic to deal with the external JMS provider being unavailable for a period of time.

Chapter Review

We covered a lot of ground in this chapter. We started off by reviewing some key concepts of JMS. We spent quite a bit of time talking about the WebLogic JMS provider, covering how it works and what features it provides. After that, we discussed things to consider when designing WebLogic JMS applications. Next, we talked briefly about WebLogic JMS programming and how to best use WebLogic JMS from within J2EE applications. This discussion included the new server-side JMS resource pooling and a discussion of message-driven beans. We finished up the chapter with a discussion of how to integrate WebLogic Server applications with external JMS providers using either the direct or indirect approach to integration. In the next chapter, we will talk in detail about WebLogic Server security.

CHAPTER

10

Using WebLogic Security

In this chapter, we discuss the new WebLogic Server Security Service. If you are unfamiliar with general security concepts or J2EE security features, you should consult the WebLogic Server documentation at http://edocs.bea.com/wls/docs81/security.html for more information.

We begin with an overview of WebLogic Server security, so that you understand the big picture of how clients interact with WebLogic Server and it, in turn, interacts with the security service. Next, we dive into the details of the WebLogic Security Framework and the security providers that are available to the security service. We will follow that with a brief discussion of how to use external security stores with WebLogic Server. Next, we will show you how to set up WebLogic Server to use Secure Socket Layer/Transport Layer Security (SSL/TLS). From there, we will move into a discussion of client-side programming to the WebLogic Server Security Service. This includes a detailed discussion of how to set up and use two-way SSL between different types of Java clients and WebLogic Server. Then, we briefly discuss how to manage application security using J2EE security features. We end the chapter with a discussion of managing application security using WebLogic Security features.

In this chapter, the term server will refer to one instance of a WebLogic Server or multiple instances of WebLogic Server acting as a cluster. We will treat the cluster of servers as one logical entity. Throughout the chapter, we refer to several examples when discussing certain features. As with the other chapters, these examples are available on our companion Web site at http://www.wiley.com/compbooks/mastering weblogic.

WebLogic Security Overview

Let's start our discussion of WebLogic Server security by looking at the different types of clients and how they can be used to access a WebLogic Server application. WebLogic Server supports many different types of clients and protocols that can be used to access the server, as shown in Figure 10.1. As far as security is concerned, two primary types of clients will be calling into the server.

The first type is typically a browser or a Web Services client that either calls directly into the server or accesses the server via an intermediate Web server running one of the WebLogic Web server plug-ins. Java or non-Java applications that make standard HTTP requests would also fall into this category. These clients generally authenticate themselves to the WebLogic Server using one of the standard HTTP authentication mechanisms: basic authentication or certificate-based authentication using two-way SSL.

The second type is the application client that typically calls directly into the server using a distributed object-based protocol like T3, IIOP, or JRMP. These clients generally authenticate themselves using the security mechanisms associated with the particular protocol or programming model, such as the Java Authentication and Authorization Service (JAAS) or the Common Secure Interoperability Version 2 (CSIv2) in the case of CORBA clients. Although HTTP tunneling of these protocols can allow these clients to communicate also through an intermediate Web server, authentication still uses the same mechanisms that it would if the protocols were not being tunneled.

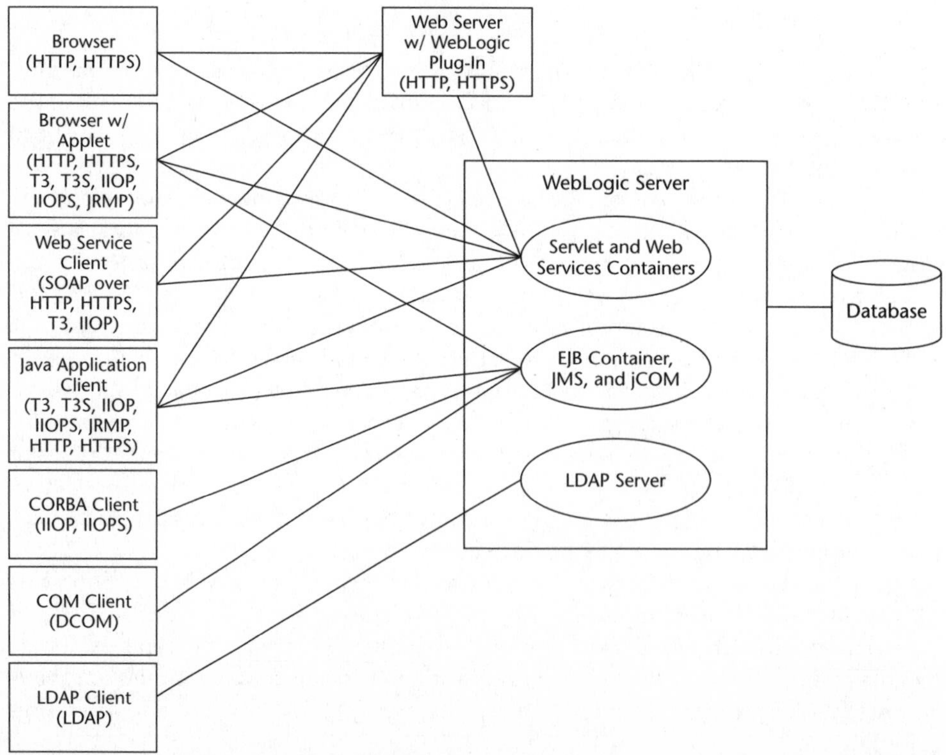

Figure 10.1 Client connectivity options.

With either type of client, the calls could be routed through one or more firewalls. We will talk about suggested firewall layouts later on in Chapter 14.

As these clients make calls into the various business applications on the server, these applications use the WebLogic Server Security Service to authenticate users, authorize their access to application functionality, audit security decisions, and perform other security-related tasks. This can include the J2EE security features as well as specialized WebLogic Server security features. When the WebLogic Server Security Service is called, it makes calls into the WebLogic Security Framework for security decisions. The WebLogic Security Framework defines a rich set of service provider interfaces (SPIs) that are called when security decisions must be made. Through these provider interfaces, the framework calls into one or more security providers that are configured for the server. Figure 10.2 shows the architecture and where each component fits into the big picture.

If you are familiar with the older security realm interfaces in earlier releases of WebLogic Server, you can see right away that this security framework is much more comprehensive. The new framework provides backward compatibility with the older realm interfaces by running the security framework in compatibility mode. Compatibility mode, however, does not support any of the new features provided by the new security service. Therefore, you must make the decision either to continue to use the old security realms in compatibility mode or to switch to use the security framework. Throughout the rest of this chapter, we will assume that you're running the new security framework using the default security providers that ship with WebLogic Server.

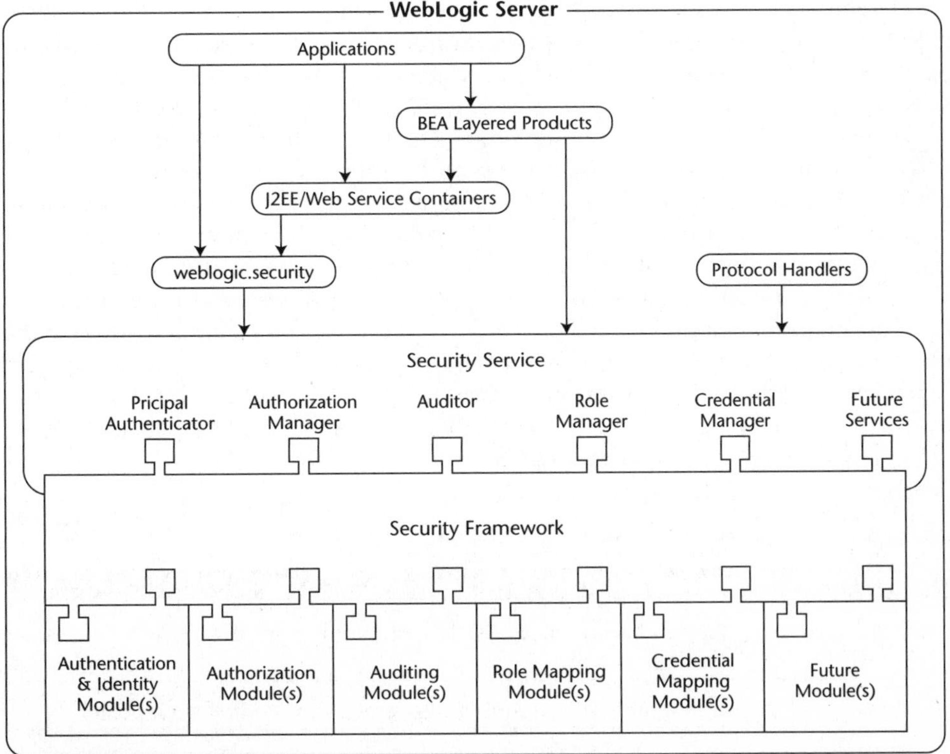

Figure 10.2 WebLogic Server security architecture.

WebLogic Security Framework

This section will discuss the WebLogic Security Framework in detail, with particular emphasis on the out-of-the-box functionality. As you may have noticed in Figure 10.1, WebLogic Server ships with an embedded LDAP server. This server is used by the default security providers to store security-related information. Our first topic in this section is the embedded LDAP server. Next, we present an overview of the default security providers. Because these providers are fairly complex, we will cover only some of the more important features. For more detailed information, please refer to the WebLogic Server Security documentation at http://edocs.bea.com/wls/docs81/security.html. We will finish up this section with a discussion of how to use the Realm Adapter to run some of the pre-WebLogic Server 7.0 security realms in compatibility mode.

Embedded LDAP Server

WebLogic Server's default security providers use an embedded LDAP server to persist all security-related data. This data is stored locally on each server and includes all of the user, group, role, access control policy, and credential information. For each domain, the admin server acts as the master LDAP server and replicates new information to the managed servers' LDAP servers once every 30 seconds. Each LDAP server does automatic backups of the entire LDAP directory tree once a day. You can configure the time that the backup task kicks off with the `Backup Hour` and `Backup Minute` parameters found on the `Security` folder's `Embedded LDAP Configuration` tab in the WebLogic Console. All backup files are compressed and stored with the LDAP server's data files; the maximum number of backup files the server will keep is also configurable through the same `Embedded LDAP` page in the console.

Whenever a WebLogic Server is started, it places all of its internal files in a server instance-specific directory. By default, the server's directory is located in the directory it was started from and has the same name as the server instance (for example, `user_projects/mydomain/myserver`). Inside this server directory is an `ldap` subdirectory where you will find the LDAP server's files. Table 10.1 shows the full directory structure and description of the embedded LDAP server directory contents. If you ever encounter a problem where a managed server won't start and you suspect that its LDAP data may be corrupt, you can either try to use one of the backup zip files from the backup directory to revert the contents of the `ldapfiles` directory or simply remove the entire `ldap` directory and let it be recreated when the managed server starts up and connects to the admin server.

Table 10.1 Embedded LDAP Server Directory Structure and Usage

DIRECTORY	INFORMATION STORED
`backup`	Zipped backup files created once a day from the `ldapfiles` directory
`conf`	Configuration files that are generated on the first server start

Table 10.1 *(continued)*

DIRECTORY	INFORMATION STORED
ldapfiles	LDAP server data files
log	LDAP server log files
replicadata	Managed server replicated data

Within the ldapfiles directory, you will find seven data files. EmbeddedL-DAP .tran, EmbeddedLDAP.trpos, and EmbeddedLDAP.twpos are the transaction tracking files. If there is ever an internal problem with the embedded LDAP server these files may be deleted without loss of data. EmbeddedLDAP.data is the main data file where all the users, groups, roles, and policies are stored. EmbeddedLDAP .delete contains information about deleted entries, and EmbeddedLDAP.index is the index of data files. Finally, the EmbeddedLDAP.lok file is used to ensure access consistency to the LDAP information. In some cases, a WebLogic Server might shut down without allowing the embedded LDAP server to unlock the data. If this happens, the server will go into a loop, waiting for the file to be removed and printing out a warning message:

```
<Apr 1, 2003 11:18:28 PM CST> <Warning> <EmbeddedLDAP>
<BEA-171520> <Could not obtain an exclusive lock for directory:
.\myserver\ldap\ldapfiles. Waiting for 10 seconds and then
retrying in case existing WebLogic Server is still shutting
down.>
```

Typically, deleting the EmbeddedLDAP.lok file will resolve this issue.

WebLogic Server stores the default security providers' default configuration information in a set of files with the ldift extension. Most of these files are located in the $WL_HOME/server/lib directory, though you will also see a couple of these ldift files in your WebLogic Server domain's root directory. WebLogic Server runs these ldift files through a preprocessor to convert them into standard LDAP ldif files that can then be fed directly into the embedded LDAP server.

The embedded LDAP server listens on the normal WebLogic Server listen port. Because the WebLogic Server installation program automatically generates a random, unique password for the LDAP server, this does not pose any significant security threat. You should avoid changing this password unless you absolutely need to because the generated password is typically harder to crack than ones you might normally choose. If you need to access the embedded LDAP server using standard LDAP mechanisms, you will need to change the security credential. You can change the embedded LDAP server's credential through the same Embedded LDAP console page we previously discussed. Once you have set this credential to a known value, you can use any LDAP tool to access the server's LDAP directory by setting the Base DN to the pattern dc=<your_domain_name>, the username to cn=Admin, and the password to the value used to set the credential through the WebLogic Console.

The embedded LDAP server uses replication between the administration server and any managed servers. This replication uses the server's SSL port, if it is enabled. Therefore, if you are concerned about the security of your LDAP replication data flowing between the administration server and any managed server, you should configure and enable SSL on all servers in the domain. We will talk about how to enable and configure SSL a little later.

BEST PRACTICE If the network connecting the WebLogic Servers in your domain is not trusted, make sure you enable SSL on each server in the domain so that WebLogic Server may use SSL for all LDAP replication between the Admin server and all managed servers.

Default Security Providers

WebLogic Server ships with default providers that plug into the security framework. In this section, we will begin by looking at the default providers in more detail. We will briefly look at how to set up new providers and discuss when you might want to do that. Finally, we end this section with a look at how to manage these default providers using the JMX capabilities of WebLogic Server.

Let's start by looking at the different types of security providers. Table 10.2 shows the different types of providers and explains their functionality. To see the security providers running in your server, use the WebLogic Console to navigate to the `Security->Realms->myrealm->Providers` folder in the left navigation bar.

Table 10.2 Security Provider Types and Features

PROVIDER TYPE	FEATURES
Authentication	The default security provider allows for username-and-password-based, direct-to-server certificate-based, and HTTPS certificate-based authentication. The authentication provider gives the server a JAAS configuration that points at a specific JAAS `LoginModule`.
Identity Assertion	This security provider maps an outside authentication token to a username. This allows for things like perimeter authentication. It is part of the authentication provider.
Authorization	This security provider decides whether an authenticated `Subject` may access a set of resources given a certain application context.

Table 10.2 *(continued)*

PROVIDER TYPE	FEATURES
Adjudication	When multiple authorization providers are configured, this provider tallies the decisions and decides on the final verdict of authorization. It is unnecessary if there is only one authorization provider.
Audit	This security provider collects and stores the security logs.
Role Mapper	After a `Subject` is authenticated, as it tries to access resources, the Role Mapper decides what roles apply to the `Subject` and stores them in the `Subject` object.
Credential Mapper	This security provider supplies the credentials for legacy systems to an authenticated `Subject` when needed.

Figure 10.3 describes the typical call flow to those security providers.

WebLogic Server loads the default security providers from two Java archive files in the `server/lib/mbeantypes` directory, `wlSecurityProviders.jar` and `wlManagement.jar`. These files contain not only the default security provider implementation classes but also their JMX configuration MBeans. When loading the security providers, WebLogic Server does not load these files from the classpath, but rather dynamically loads them using an internal class loader.

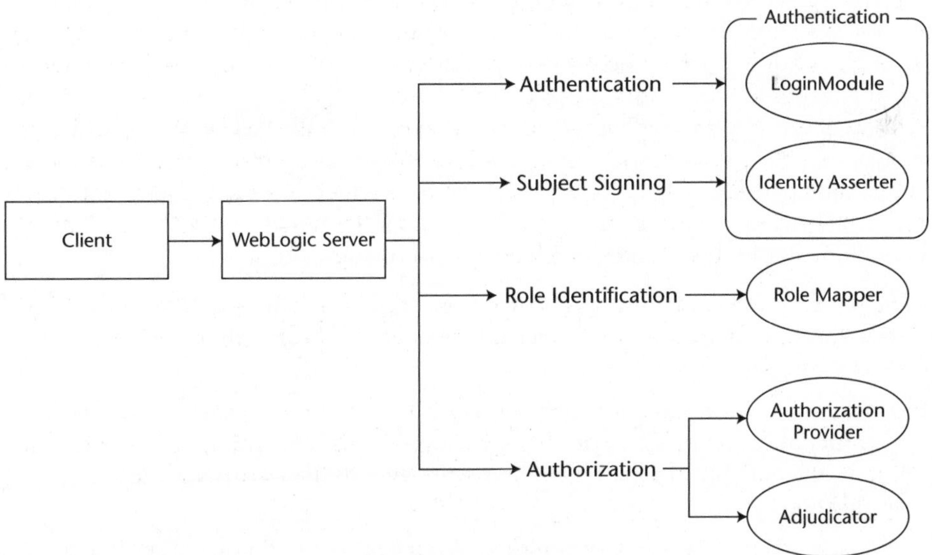

Figure 10.3 Authentication and authorization call flow.

Authentication

In addition to the preconfigured providers, WebLogic Server comes with several built-in, configurable authentication providers. At the time of writing, these options primarily include support for external LDAP servers; these include support for iPlanet (and SunOne), ActiveDirectory, OpenLDAP, and Novell LDAP Servers. If you want to use an external LDAP server as your sole authentication provider, you must map WebLogic Server's `Admin` role to at least one group or user. By default, this `Admin` role maps to the `Administrators` group, so simply defining an `Administrators` group in your external LDAP tree is sufficient.

Also included in the list of built-in providers is the `RealmAdapter`, which can be used to plug in an old WebLogic Security Realm built against the old security realm SPIs. We will discuss the `RealmAdapter` in more detail in the compatibility mode overview at the end of this section. If you are familiar with the built-in authentication of earlier versions of WebLogic Server, you will notice that some previously supported providers are not currently supported. These include native Windows domain authentication, native UNIX PAM authentication, and database-based authentication. Currently, the only way to use these providers is either by using the old security realms in the compatibility mode or by writing your own authentication provider. The new `MedRec` example that ships with WebLogic Server 8.1 provides an example of how to build a new, custom authentication provider that uses a database for its security store.

WebLogic Server's security framework fully supports the Java Authentication and Authorization Service (JAAS) specification. JAAS specifies that all authentication is to be routed through a `LoginModule` interface. `LoginModules` can be stacked together to form a pluggable framework. WebLogic Server's security framework supports multiple authentication providers in exactly the same way, thus allowing for multiple, pluggable providers. Each authentication provider supports one `LoginModule`; therefore, using multiple `LoginModules` requires using multiple authentication providers. Each authentication provider has a configuration option called a *control flag*. This control flag allows the provider to specify how its authentication results affect the overall authentication process. These control flag options, which are the same as the JAAS `LoginModule` configurations that we will discuss in the *Writing Java Clients That Use JAAS* section later in this chapter, can have the following values:

`Required.` The authentication provider is required to succeed. If it succeeds or fails, the authentication process continues to proceed through the list of configured providers.

`Requisite.` The authentication provider is required to succeed. If it succeeds, the authentication process continues through the list of configured providers. If it fails, the authentication process immediately fails and returns control to the application.

`Sufficient.` The authentication provider is not required to succeed. If it does succeed, the authentication process succeeds and control immediately returns to the application. If it fails, the authentication process continues down the list of configured providers.

`Optional.` The authentication provider is not required to succeed. If it succeeds or fails, the authentication process continues down the list of configured providers.

When you create a new authentication provider, you should use a less strict control flag while in development. The primary reason is that a value of `Required` or `Requisite` will cause the authentication to fail if the new provider fails. Because the server must authenticate the administrative user used to start the server, a misconfigured provider using one of these strict control flags will prevent the server from starting. If the control flag is set to either `Sufficient` or `Optional`, the server will show you the error information about the incorrectly configured provider but will start, thus allowing you to use the WebLogic Console to modify the configuration. Once you verify that everything is working in the new provider, set the control flag to the desired value.

BEST PRACTICE Set the control flag for all authentication providers to `OPTIONAL` before applying any changes to prevent a configuration error from causing the server not to boot.

The WebLogic Console now sets the default value for the `Control Flag` attribute to `OPTIONAL`. You should be aware, though, that the default value in the underlying MBean is still `REQUIRED`. This means that if you create the MBean by hand, through hand-editing of the `config.xml` or writing JMX programs, you need to explicitly set the `Control Flag` attribute or it will automatically be set to `REQUIRED`. Because most people use the WebLogic Console, this should not be a problem.

If you find yourself in a situation where your server will not boot because of a security realm configuration issue, you can recover a WebLogic Server 7.0 server by deleting the `userConfig` subdirectory found in the domain's root directory and starting the security provider configuration process over from scratch. Starting in WebLogic Server 8.1, you can simply edit the provider's `config.xml` entry to change the `ControlFlag` setting:

```
<weblogic.security.providers.
    authentication.OpenLDAPAuthenticator
    ControlFlag="OPTIONAL" Realm="Security:Name=myrealm"
    Name="Security:Name=myrealmOpenLDAPAuthenticator" />
```

Of course, you can also restore the `config.xml` from one of the backups that WebLogic Server automatically makes.

When using an external LDAP authentication provider, you might want WebLogic Server to continue to serve any unprotected information even when it cannot get authentication information from the external LDAP server, such as when the LDAP server is unavailable. To accomplish this, you must make certain the server's boot identity is defined in the embedded LDAP server, so it can be used whether or not the external LDAP server is operational. You can use the WebLogic Console to set connection and search result time-out values on the external LDAP authentication provider. This will ensure that the server does not hang when attempting to authenticate against the external LDAP server. Following these steps will allow you to boot and serve up unprotected information with the WebLogic Server even when your external LDAP server is unavailable.

BEST PRACTICE When using an external LDAP provider, it is a good idea to store the server's boot identity in the embedded LDAP server. By doing this and setting time-outs on the external LDAP authentication provider, you can continue to boot and serve up unprotected information with WebLogic Server when the external LDAP server is unavailable.

Before we move on to talk about identity assertion, we should talk about what to do if you forget your administrative password and cannot boot the server. Please note that the following procedure works only for the default authenticator using the embedded LDAP server and only if you have not modified the global `Admin` role, which by default is granted to the `Administrators` group. For our example, we will assume that your server name is `myserver`. To reset the password, follow these steps:

1. Using the command line, change the directory to your WebLogic Server domain's root directory and run your `setEnv` script to set up your `PATH` and `CLASSPATH`.
2. Create a new initialization file for the default authenticator by creating a new `DefaultAuthenticatorInit.ldift` file in the current directory:

   ```
   java weblogic.security.utils.AdminAccount <tempadmin>

       <temppassword> ./
   ```
3. Remove the initialized status file `DefaultAuthenticatormyrealmInit.initialized` from the `myserver/ldap/` subdirectory.
4. Restart the server, and enter the `<tempadmin>` username and `<temppassword>` password supplied in step 2.

Identity Assertion

Identity asserters take an outside identity token, validate it, and map it to a valid WebLogic Server user. The default identity assertion provider, known as the `DefaultIdentityAsserter`, can validate WebLogic Security tokens, X.509 certificates, and IIOP CSIv2 tokens. By default, the `DefaultIdentityAsserter` is enabled only to support WebLogic Security tokens; use the WebLogic Console to enable support for the other supported token types. This default identity assertion provider does its work via a `UserNameMapper` interface, which maps either an X.509 certificate array or an X.501 distinguished name to a username. Using the WebLogic Console, you can enable and configure the `Default User Name Mapper` that comes with the server to extract the username automatically from most fields in an X.509 certificate. You can also write your own username mapper implementation class by implementing the `weblogic.security.providers.authentication.UserNameMapper` interface and configuring the `DefaultIdentityAsserter` to use it.

Of course, you can also write a custom identity assertion provider to support other types of tokens, such as Kerberos or SAML tokens.

Probably the two most common reasons to change the default configuration of the `DefaultIdentityAsserter` are to support authentication via client certificates from a two-way SSL connection or to support certificate validation for WebLogic Server's Web Services Security implementation. To enable identity assertion for X.509 certificates, first you need to add `X.509` to the list of chosen types at the bottom of the `General` tab. Next, you need to enable and configure the `Default User Name Mapper`, currently found on the `DefaultIdentityAsserter`'s `Details` tab in the WebLogic Console.

The `Default User Name Mapper Attribute Type` allows you to choose which field in the distinguished name (DN) of the `Subject` of the X.509 certificate to use to obtain the username. If the field being used contains more than the username, the `Default User Name Mapper Attribute Delimiter` can be used to truncate the extraneous information. For example, if you select the `E` value for the attribute type, you may need to strip off the domain name information from the email address. If the email address was `bauersc@bigrez.com` and the WebLogic Server username was `bauersc`, setting the delimiter to `@` would allow the username mapper to map the email address field in the certificate to the correct WebLogic Server username properly.

It is important not to remove the `DefaultIdentityAsserter` because it handles the authentication context interoperability with prior versions of the WebLogic Server. It does this work via the `AuthenticatedUser` token in the `Chosen Types` box.

WARNING **The** `AuthenticatedUser` **token type supported by the** `DefaultIdentityAsserter` **plays a critical role in supporting authentication interoperability with earlier versions of WebLogic Server. Removing the** `DefaultIdentityAsserter` **will cause your domain to be unable to exchange authentication tokens with earlier versions of WebLogic Server.**

Before we leave the topic of identity assertion, we need to talk about cross-domain trust. When a WebLogic Server authenticates a user, it digitally signs the authentication context using its domain's *shared secret* credential. Any server with the same shared secret can accept the authentication context and participate in single sign-on (SSO) across J2EE applications deployed in different WebLogic Server instances, clusters, or domains.

In older versions of WebLogic Server, this *shared secret* credential was the `system` user's password. Starting with WebLogic Server 7.0, this *shared secret* credential is an automatically generated, domain-wide value, which is very random and almost certainly better than any password you might use. So, change this credential only if you absolutely must.

To enable two WebLogic domains to interoperate, you must set their *shared secret* credential to be the same value. You can set this value using the `Security` folder's `Advanced Configuration` tab to disable generated credentials and specify the actual credential to use. For interoperating with pre-WebLogic Server 7.0 releases, you will need to set the credential to the value of the `system` user's password for the older server.

Authorization and Adjudication

WebLogic Server's security framework supports the use of one or more authorization providers to make authorization decisions about whether a particular subject (authenticated user) may have access to a particular resource. When using multiple providers, it is possible that some providers may permit access while others either abstain or deny access. This is where the adjudicator comes in. An adjudicator looks at all of the responses from the different authorization providers and decides whether access is granted or denied.

When making authorization calls into the WebLogic Security Service, the server passes information about the identity of the caller, the resource being accessed, and other contextual information about the call to an `AccessDecision` object. The `AccessDecision` object will use this information to make its authorization decision. For example, when a caller tries to access a protected method of an EJB, an `AccessDecision` object could get access to the parameters that were used to call the method for which it is being asked to make an authorization decision. Having this additional contextual information about the request allows the `AccessDecision` object to make access decisions using arbitrarily complex security policies. Of course, the complexity of the authorization decisions depends on what type of contextual information the server provides for a given type of resource. We expect that the amount of information available to the authorization provider will expand over time to include just about anything that the provider could possibly want.

This contextual information is passed using objects that implement the `weblogic.security.service.ContextHandler` interface. A `ContextHandler` is essentially a list of name-value pairs. WebLogic Server's default authorization provider uses the information in the `ContextHandler` to decide whether a given subject may have access to a given resource. We hope that you will not need to write your own authorization provider because the default provider supports fairly complex policy statements. If you do, we encourage you to look at the "Developing Security Providers for WebLogic Server" documentation at http://edocs.bea.com/wls/docs81/dvspisec/index.html and the sample providers on the BEA developer's Web site at http://dev2dev.bea.com/direct/SampleSecurityProviders.zip for more information.

TIP If you need to extend or implement your own security providers, some very good example providers are available on the BEA developer Web site at http://dev2dev.bea.com/direct/SampleSecurityProviders.zip. These are source code examples of everything it takes to write a set of providers, and we highly recommend them.

Unless you develop your own authorization provider, you may never need to use the adjudication provider. Even if you add a second authorization provider, the default adjudication provider can be configured to resolve almost any conflict.

Auditing

WebLogic Server's default audit provider simply sends security events to the `DefaultAuditRecorder.log` file in the domain's root directory. By default, this audit provider is disabled, so you will need to use the WebLogic Console to enable it. You could write your own audit provider to send security logs to a specialized, non-repudiation data store. To do this, your provider must implement the `weblogic.security.spi.AuditChannel` interface, which receives a `weblogic.security.spi.AuditEvent` whenever an audit message occurs.

Role Mapping and Credential Mapping

The default role mapper provider handles all the global and application-scoped role definitions, as described later in the "Working with Roles and Policies" section. This default provider also reads the role definitions from the deployment descriptors, by default. If multiple role mapper providers are specified, the resulting sets of roles returned from the providers are *intersected* to determine the set of applicable roles.

The credential mapper provider supplies credentials for legacy systems and EIS systems. It takes the arguments of the current authenticated subject, the legacy resource type, and the type of credential requested. The default credential mapper provider will most likely be sufficient for all your needs.

Similar to the `ignore roles and policies from DD` option discussed later in the "Working with Roles and Policies" section, there is a provider-specific flag to do the same thing. The authorization, role mapper, and credential mapper providers each have individual flags on their MBeans to adjust whether that specific provider will accept configuration information from the deployment descriptors. This requires extreme caution, and it should be left to the default value in most cases. Read the "Working with Roles and Policies" section for more information before changing these values on the providers themselves.

Managing Security Provider Configuration

WebLogic Server uses JMX MBeans to hold all of the security providers' configuration data. When a new server is first configured, it will read the default security configuration information from `$WL_HOME/server/lib/SecurityDefaultConfig.xml` the first time is started. While all other server configuration MBeans are persisted to the `config.xml` file, WebLogic Server 7.0 persists the default security providers' configuration MBeans into the `userConfig` subdirectory, under the domain's root directory. This configuration information contains only the information necessary to tell the booting server which security providers to use and the provider-specific configuration information of those providers. All security data is kept in either the embedded LDAP server or the provider's external data store. This duality of configuration persistence forms is obviously confusing. WebLogic Server 8.1 eliminates this duality, as you will see in a moment.

In addition, persisting the data in binary form makes it difficult to see the changes you make to the security providers outside of the WebLogic Console. It's also hard to stage servers without more insight into this binary data. You can convert this binary security configuration information into XML using the `WebLogicMBeanDumper` utility. For example, running the following command from the domain's root directory will dump all security MBeans into a new file called `out.xml`.

```
java weblogic.management.commo.WebLogicMBeanDumper
    -name Security:* out.xml
```

Fortunately, WebLogic Server 8.1 moves the security provider MBean configuration data into the `config.xml` along with the rest of the server configuration MBean data; however, this does not rule out the possibility that third party security providers may still use this alternate binary persistence form. As a result, it is important to check with any third-party provider vendors you might be using to see where they persist their configuration data.

Most of WebLogic Server's default security providers have import and export facilities in the WebLogic Console. Currently, the most notable exception is the authentication provider, which has only an import facility. These facilities can be useful when trying to move from a development to a production environment, or to any other staged server setup. Although these facilities allow for more granular staging of the specific providers, it is probably much easier to simply copy the security MBeans and then copy the entire embedded LDAP tree and the `SerializedSystemIni.dat` file (which contains the server's encryption key and salt) to the new server.

You can gain programmatic access to the security providers through the WebLogic Security MBeans in the `weblogic.management.security` package. The following example, `PasswordChanger`, shows how to modify a user's password programmatically using the `weblogic.management.security.authentication.UserPasswordEditor` interface. A complete source code version of this program can be found on this book's companion Web site (http://www.wiley.com/compbooks/masteringweblogic).

```
public void changePassword(MBeanHome adminServerHome,
                           String username, String oldPassword,
                           String newPassword)
    throws InvalidParameterException, NotFoundException
{
    DomainMBean domain = adminServerHome.getActiveDomain();
    SecurityConfigurationMBean security =
        domain.getSecurityConfiguration();
    RealmMBean realm = security.findDefaultRealm();
    AuthenticationProviderMBean [] providers =
        realm.getAuthenticationProviders();

    for (int i = 0; i < providers.length; i++) {
        if (providers[i] instanceof UserPasswordEditorMBean) {
            UserPasswordEditorMBean editor =
                (UserPasswordEditorMBean)providers[i];
            editor.changeUserPassword(username,
```

```
                                        oldPassword, newPassword);
                System.out.println("Password for user " + username +
                                   " changed to " + newPassword +
                                   " in provider " +
                                   providers[i].toString());
            }
        }
    }
```

By looking through the Javadocs for these MBean interfaces, you can see how to manipulate both the default security providers and any third-party security providers that are capable of management. These methods are available only to programs running with the `Admin` role. We will talk more about the `Admin` role and the other default roles later in this chapter.

So far, all our discussions have assumed that you are using the default realm, called `myrealm`. As you can easily see from the WebLogic Console, it is possible to create and configure an entirely separate realm. A domain may run with only one active realm at a time. You can choose the active realm for a domain using the `Default Realm` attribute in the `Security` folder's `General Configuration` tab. Be aware that switching active realms can be dangerous. For example, if the new realm doesn't define any users in the `Administrators` group, the new server configuration cannot be managed by anyone and must be reverted.

We recommend testing the realm to verify its configuration before trying to switch realms. In WebLogic Server 8.1, you can test a realm using the realm's `Testing` tab in the WebLogic Console. Rather than trying to describe everything you need to do to back out from a bad realm configuration, we recommend that in addition to testing your realm you make a backup of the entire domain directory tree just before activating the new realm. This way, you can revert by simply restoring the entire domain directory and restarting the server.

Before we go on to talk about the `RealmAdapter`, we should tell you that the security framework has some undocumented debugging flags that will allow you to see what is happening with particular providers. You need to add these flags directly to your server's `ServerDebug` element in the `config.xml` file:

```
<ServerDebug Name="myserver"
    DebugSecurityAtn="true"
    DebugEmbeddedLDAP="true"
    DebugSecurityAtz="true"
    DebugSecurityRoleMap="true"
    DebugSecurityAdjudicator="true"
    DebugSecurityAuditor="true"
/>
```

As with any manual changes to `config.xml`, always make sure that the admin server is shut down and that you make a backup copy of the `config.xml` in case you get into trouble while trying to edit it.

TIP Use the `ServerDebug` flags to help debug security provider issues.

Using Compatibility Mode with the RealmAdapter

If you take a typical WebLogic Server 6.x config.xml and use it to start a WebLogic Server 7.0 or newer server, the server will automatically convert the config.xml over to the new security framework. This conversion process, however, will create a Compatibility Realm, using the RealmAdapter to run in compatibility mode. Using the automatic conversion capability is a very elegant way to get started with newer versions of WebLogic Server using your old 6.x security realm. Make sure that you use a copy of the 6.x config.xml file because this process does not create a backup of the original config.xml file. Because the filerealm.properties file contains a keyed and salted hash of the passwords, you will need to copy the SerializedSystemIni.dat file, along with the config.xml and filerealm.properties files.

This conversion process will set up realm adapters for all the pertinent security providers. It will allow you to continue using the various features of the WebLogic Server 6.1 security model. For example, the LDAPRealm (v1 and v2), the NTRealm, the RDBMSRealm, and the UnixRealm are supported through this model. If the WebLogic Server 6.x config.xml file contains references to CertAuthenticator, you must manually add another authentication provider to use it. Simply go to Security-> Realms->CompatibilityRealm->Providers->Authentication Providers-> RealmAdapterAuthenticator's General tab and add X.509 to the list of Chosen Types. If you happen to be using WebLogic Server 7.0, accomplishing this is a little less obvious. You need to add a new line in the Active Types text box that simply says X.509. Once you apply the changes and restart the server, the RealmAdapter will be active and will use the CertAuthenticator to map X.509 certificates to a WebLogic Server user.

Using External Security Stores

WebLogic Server can also use external security stores for storing security data. In this section, we will look at a few of the most common external stores used with WebLogic Server. We focus primarily on using these external stores for authentication data because that is by far the most common usage, since most authorization is still done using J2EE deployment descriptor security, third-party application security products, or custom code in the application. As we will see later in the *Setting Up WebLogic Application Security* section, WebLogic Server is now offering its own application security functionality to provide parametric, policy-based authorization that can be configured outside of the application code or deployment descriptors. We expect that upcoming versions of WebLogic Server will continue to build in more functionality over time.

Managing External LDAP Authentication

LDAP servers have become the de facto standard for managing corporate user information. Current versions of WebLogic Server support using both its embedded LDAP server as well as several of the more popular commercial LDAP servers on the market today. Supporting different LDAP servers generally means that WebLogic Server has built-in knowledge of the default schemas used by these servers and can make them easy to configure. Just because WebLogic Server does not support a particular LDAP server out of the box, it does not mean you cannot use it. Typically, it is possible to make it work; you just need to customize the authentication provider configuration to match the LDAP schema and server information.

The new security framework has a series of built-in LDAP authentication providers. These options include support for iPlanet (and SunOne), ActiveDirectory, OpenLDAP, and Novell LDAP Servers. Each authentication provider is specialized for the default or standard schemas used by that LDAP server. You can easily create and configure them via the console.

In some cases, the default or standard schema that is configurable via the console may not give you enough fine-grained control over the LDAP queries. If you find yourself in this situation, you may need to write your own custom authentication provider or use one of the older *LDAPRealm* implementations.

Two versions of the LDAPRealm were written for the old security realm APIs. The first version of the LDAPRealm (`LDAPRealmv1`) uses Sun's LDAP-JNDI plug-in, whereas the second version (`LDAPRealmv2`) uses the Mozilla LDAP Java library. If your LDAP schema is complex enough to have led you to look at one of the older LDAPRealms to handle it, then it is very likely that `LDAPRealmv1` may not be versatile enough for your needs.

`LDAPRealmv2` is more versatile than `LDAPRealmv1`, but it is also more complex. The `LDAPRealmv2` is configured as a custom realm, in the realm adapter's authentication provider, using `weblogic.security.ldaprealmv2.LDAPRealm` as the realm class. One important limitation of the older LDAPRealms is that the new security framework's LDAP authentication providers will follow referrals and handle dynamic groups, whereas the older LDAPRealms will not.

NOTE While the older `LDAPRealmv2` realm gives you much more granular control, it will not follow referrals or handle dynamic groups. If either of these is important, you will need to use one of the new LDAP providers.

The realm adapter `LDAPRealmv2` configuration for the typical LDAP server is this:

```
user.dn.1=ou=people, o=engin, dc=bigrez, dc=com;
user.dn.2=ou=Security, ou=Groups, o=engin, dc=bigrez, dc=com;
user.filter=(&(cn=%u)(objectclass=person))

group.dn.1=ou=groups, o=engin, dc=bigrez, dc=com;
group.dn.2=ou=Security, ou=People, o=engin, dc=bigrez, dc=com;
group.filter.1=(&(cn=%g)(objectclass=groupofnames));
group.filter.2=(&(cn=%g)(objectclass=group));

membership.filter=(&(member=%M)(objectclass=groupofnames));
membership.search=true;
```

For the ActiveDirectory LDAP server, the typical configuration is this:

```
user.dn=cn=Users, DC=dcName, DC=bigrez, DC=com
user.scope=subtree
```

```
group.dn=cn=Users, DC=dcName, DC=bigrez, DC=com
group.filter=(&(cn=%g)(objectclass=group))
membership.filter=(&(member=%M)(objectclass=group))
```

ActiveDirectory has some interesting differences that we need to mention. If the `sAMAccountName` is different from the DN, you should use this:

```
user.filter=(&(sAMAccountName=%u)(objectclass=user)
            (objectcategory=person))
membership.search=true
```

If the `sAMAccountName` is the same as the CN portion of the DN, you need to use this:

```
user.filter=(&(CN=%u)(objectclass=user)(objectcategory=person))
membership.search=false
```

If you disable a user in Active Directory, WebLogic Server will still successfully authenticate that user by default. In order to get WebLogic Server to recognize that the user's account has been disabled, you need to modify the `user.filter`. To return only the accounts that do not have the `UF_ACCOUNTDISABLE` bit set, use this:

```
user.filter=(&(sAMAccountName=%u)
           (&(objectclass=user)(objectcategory=person)
             (!(userAccountControl:1.2.840.113556.1.4.803:=2))
            ))
```

Using the WebLogic Console, you can map the preceding configuration information to the new LDAP providers by simply providing the information in the appropriate fields. As we mentioned before, just because your LDAP server vendor is not listed, it does not mean you cannot use it with WebLogic Server. Consulting your LDAP administrator and finding the best match to your schema is the best way to create a specialized LDAP authentication provider.

You can configure your LDAP provider to one or more `user.dn` entries, as shown in the ActiveDirectory and typical LDAP server configurations, respectively. Another important option that we have illustrated in the typical LDAP configuration is the use of a single filter for all `user.dn` entries, but specific filters for each `group.dn`. Using this, you can point the WebLogic Server at very specific spots in the LDAP directory tree. The more specific the tree is, the smaller the search will be, which means better performance.

In a typical LDAP schema, a group will list the DN of only the users that are its members. WebLogic Server needs to determine the user's ID. Most of the time, this user ID is part of the `User` object's DN, so WebLogic Server can determine the user ID by simply looking at the DN of the users in the `Group` object. However, if the user ID is not part of the `User` object's DN and can be found only in an attribute of the `User` object itself, a secondary search using the `User` object's DN to locate the `User` object and retrieve the appropriate attribute will be required. You can use the `membership.search` property to configure this secondary search. This property exists in

WebLogic Server 8.1 and was added in WebLogic Server 6.1 Service Pack 4 and WebLogic Server 7.0 Service Pack 2.

For most applications, it will be very important to optimize the performance of your LDAP-based authentication and group membership queries. You should try to tune your WebLogic Server LDAP configuration filters to be as specific as possible. Another critical step in enhancing your performance is to have your LDAP server index all of the attributes that you will use as search keys in your LDAPRealm search filters. Failing to index these attributes will typically cause performance problems as the number of objects in your LDAP server grows because the LDAP server is forced to perform linear searches. In earlier versions of WebLogic Server, a `CachingRealm` was provided to cache the authentication and group membership information. Starting in WebLogic Server 7.0, each LDAP connection caches its own LDAP searches and results. The only drawback to this new approach is that caching is per connection, rather than per WebLogic Server, which can result in higher cache miss ratios.

BEST PRACTICE Always tune your WebLogic Server LDAP configuration filters to be as specific as possible. Indexing LDAP attributes that are used as search keys is critical for achieving good performance with LDAP servers that contain more than a handful of objects.

Setting Up UNIX-Based Authentication

WebLogic Server comes with a custom realm, based on the old security realm APIs, that supports authentication via Pluggable Authentication Modules (PAM). Because it was written using the old realm APIs, you must run in compatibility mode to use it with newer versions of WebLogic Server. This realm, known as the *UnixRealm*, uses Java Native Interface (JNI) to make native calls to the local operating system for authentication and group membership information. Therefore, it can be very particular to set up.

The UnixRealm runs only on Solaris and Linux and uses a small native program called `wlauth`. The `wlauth` program must run as root, so you must set it up with the `chown root wlauth` and `chmod +xs wlauth` commands. You also need to set up the PAM configuration file. For Solaris, add these lines to your `/etc/pam.conf` file:

```
wlauth auth required      /usr/lib/security/pam_unix.so.1
wlauth password required  /usr/lib/security/pam_unix.so.1
wlauth account required   /usr/lib/security/pam_unix.so.1
```

For Linux, create a file called `/etc/pam.d/wlauth` and add:

```
#%PAM-1.0
auth required     /lib/security/pam_pwdb.so shadow
account required  /lib/security/pam_pwdb.so
```

If you do not use a shadow password file, remove the word "shadow" from the end of the first line.

Setting Up Windows Domain Authentication

WebLogic Server also comes with a custom realm, based on the old security realm APIs, that supports native Windows domain authentication. This realm, known as the *NTRealm*, is useful with Windows domains that are not set up to use ActiveDirectory. Whenever possible, you should always use ActiveDirectory instead of the NTRealm because it is far less fragile and gives you more granular control.

BEST PRACTICE Wherever possible, use ActiveDirectory authentication instead of native Windows domain authentication for production environments.

The NTRealm is set up with a single argument, the hostname of the primary domain controller—not the domain name. You can run the NTRealm on either the primary domain controller or any member of that domain. You can also run the NTRealm on any machine that is a member of a domain and wants to use a second, mutually trusted, domain for authentication. Doing this requires you to set up an explicit mutual trust relationship between the two domains. What you cannot do is use a stand-alone machine that is not part of a domain to authenticate to a Windows domain.

To run the NTRealm's native library, WebLogic Server will need to run as a specific Windows user that has some specific Windows privileges:

- Act as part of the operating system
- Create a token object
- Replace a process-level token

Note that all versions of Windows require a reboot for any privileges to take effect.

To update the privileges on Windows NT, use the User Manager program, which can be found under the Administrative Tools program group, to do the following steps:

1. Select the `User Rights` menu option from the `Policies` menu. Select the `Show Advanced User Rights` checkbox in the lower-left corner.
2. Grant the previously mentioned privileges to the user who will run the WebLogic Server.
3. Reboot the machine.

To update the privileges on Windows2000 and XP, use the `Local Security Policy` program, which can be found under the `Administrative Tools` program group, to do the following steps. Note that if you do not have an `Administrative Tools` program group, you may need to use the `Taskbar & Start Menu` option under the Windows Start Menu's `Settings` option to make the `Administrative Tools` program group visible:

1. In the left-hand folder view, select the `Local Policies->User Rights Assignment` folder.
2. For each privilege listed previously, add the user that will run WebLogic Server to the list of users with these privileges.
3. Reboot the machine.

Another important configuration concern applies when trying to run WebLogic Server using the NTRealm as a Windows service. The problem is that the native calls the authentication library makes (Net*Enum) are disabled by the `RestrictAnonymous` setting on the primary domain controller. Because the `LocalSystem` user has limited access to network resources, the service will fail to start because the authentication calls made during server startup will fail. To start the WebLogic Server service as a user other than `LocalSystem`, you will need to use the `SRVANY` service to run the `startWebLogic.cmd` script. The `SRVANY` service comes with the Microsoft Windows Resource Kit, which is downloadable from the Microsoft Web site. The only issue with the `SRVANY` service is that it knows only how to start the WebLogic Server instance; the only way to shut down the instance properly will be to use the WebLogic Console or the `weblogic.Admin SHUTDOWN` command.

An excellent troubleshooting tool is built into the NTRealm itself. This tool will perform a complete functional sweep of the NTRealm configuration and will tell you immediately whether your configuration will work. To invoke this tool, use the following syntax, where the username and password are for the user that will be running WebLogic Server:

```
java weblogic.security.ntrealm.NTRealm <username> <password> <hostname>
```

The hostname is optional, as the native library can determine the domain to which your machine belongs. The first line of output will tell you if the authentication succeeded, as shown here for username `bauersc`.

`auth?bauersc.` This means authentication worked for user `bauersc`.

`auth?null.` This means it did not authenticate properly.

The remaining output of the unit test utility will enumerate all the users and groups available to it.

Custom Authentication Providers

In addition to using built-in external authentication providers, you can also write your own. There are several source code examples that you can use to get started. As we mentioned previously, the BEA developer's Web site contains an example authentication provider (http://dev2dev.bea.com/direct/SampleSecurityProviders.zip). Another source code example that you can use as a starting point for developing a realm for the old security realm APIs is the *RDBMSRealm*, which shipped with previous versions of the server in the `samples/examples/security/rdbmsrealm` directory. Of course, we strongly encourage you to write any custom providers to the new security framework to give your application access to all of the new features and improvements in the new WebLogic Security Service.

At this point, we need to warn you about trying to use these examples as your production providers. These two source code examples are meant to help you understand how to build your own custom providers—they are not designed to be production-ready implementations. At a minimum, you should make certain performance and fault-tolerance enhancements before trying to use them in a production environment.

WARNING The example security providers are meant as learning tools to help you understand how to interface with the WebLogic Server security service. These examples lack performance optimizations and fault-tolerance features required in any production-ready security provider.

Setting Up SSL/TLS

WebLogic Server supports secure communications with clients and other servers using either Secure Sockets Layer (SSL) or Transport Layer Security (TLS) connections. We assume that everyone is familiar with SSL; for those not familiar with TLS, all you really need to know is that TLS is essentially the next generation of SSL and that WebLogic Server currently supports TLS version 1.0. For the remainder of this book, we will not bother to make the distinction between SSL and TLS and will simply refer to both as SSL. Should we need to differentiate between the two, we will make it a point to say so explicitly.

In this section, we begin by giving you a brief review of SSL technology. Next, we talk about how to obtain X.509 certificates, private keys, and the CA certificates needed to configure SSL. We end this section with a detailed walkthrough of how to configure WebLogic Server to use SSL.

Reviewing SSL Technology

SSL supports two different connection modes or types. The two types are commonly called one-way and two-way SSL. *One-way SSL* allows the SSL client to uniquely verify that the SSL server is, in fact, who it claims to be. *Two-way SSL* extends one-way SSL by allowing the SSL server to uniquely verify that the client is who it claims to be.

These verifications are accomplished through the use of public/private key technology. This technology uses a set of two related keys known as a public key and a private key for encryption and signing purposes. Anything encrypted using the public key can be decrypted only using the private key, and vice versa. As the names suggest, the owner of the private key keeps this key locked away where only the owner has access to it and gives its public key to everyone who might need it. In almost all cases, private key files are additionally encrypted with a passphrase that must be supplied to get the actual private key as an additional safety check against unauthorized use. The standard way of distributing public keys is to use X.509 certificates that contain information about the certificate's owner and public key.

X.509 certificates are issued by different authorities that digitally sign the certificates with their private key to allow verification (through the use of their public key) that they did, in fact, issue the certificate and that it has not been tampered with. In some cases, the signing authority's certificate might have been signed by another authority and so on. This brings about the notion of a certificate chain where the top of the chain is known as the root certificate authority (CA) whose certificate is always self-signed.

When you get the CA's certificate, that certificate will generally contain the entire certificate chain back to the root CA. This root CA and/or certificate chain is used by the receiver of the original certificate to determine whether he or she trusts that the certificate is legitimate.

Public/private key technology supports different encryption strengths by supporting keys of different lengths. Up until recently, U.S. software companies were strictly regulated against exporting encryption technology above a certain strength. This gave rise to the labeling of the encryption strengths as either *export* or *domestic*. Currently, with the proper paperwork, software companies can legally export domestic-strength encryption to most other countries. WebLogic Server supports both domestic- and export-strength encryption. At the time of writing, you still need a special license key to enable the server to use domestic-strength encryption technology. We expect that this may change by the time you are reading this book.

With one-way SSL, the SSL client uses the server's certificate (actually, the public key contained in the certificate) to encrypt data that can be decrypted only with the server's private key. This is why it is critical for the server to keep its private key safe and its passphrase a secret. With two-way SSL, the SSL server uses that client's certificate to encrypt data that can be decrypted only with the client's private key. The SSL server may use the client's certificate to uniquely identify and authenticate the client in the application layer. In order for the client to trust the certificate provided by the server, it must verify the signing chain of the server's certificate. If the client trusts the server's certificate authority, it can verify the server's certificate and prove that it is real and has not been tampered with. This verification requires the client to have the CA's certificate for the server available locally, as a notion of which certificates the client will *trust*.

In the case of two-way SSL, the server must use the exact same mechanisms to verify the client's certificate. The server requires the client's root CA's certificate locally for two-way SSL. See Table 10.3 for this listing of required data on either side. Notice the concepts of *identity* and *trust* for both the SSL server and the SSL client. The identity is the certificate and private key. The trust is the certificate authority.

Table 10.3 Required SSL Configuration Data

SSL MODE	CLIENT	SERVER
One-way SSL	Copy of server root CA certificate	Server root CA certificate and chain Server certificate Server private key
Two-way SSL	Copy of server root CA certificate Client root CA certificate and chain Client certificate Client private key	Server root CA and chain Server certificate Server private key Copy of client root CA certificate

Obtaining X.509 Certificates

Now that you understand what you need, we can walk through the process of generating a new certificate and private key for the server. WebLogic Server provides two utilities you can use to generate a new certificate and private key, or you can use the `keytool` program that comes with the Java 2 SDK. If you want to generate certificates and private keys quickly for demonstration or development purposes, then you can use the `utils.CertGen` utility. We will use `utils.CertGen` in the "Configuring Two-Way SSL" section, so we won't spend any time on it here.

If you need certificates for a production server, you will probably want to get your certificates signed by a well-known certificate authority (CA) or use a public key infrastructure (PKI) product. This means that in addition to generating the certificate and the private key, you will need to generate a *Certificate Signing Request* (CSR) that can be submitted to a certificate authority. If you have done this with a previous version of WebLogic Server, you are probably already familiar with the `Certificate Request Generator Servlet`. As of WebLogic Server 8.1, this servlet has been deprecated. To use this servlet, you will need to deploy the `certificate.war` web application to your server and log in as a user with the `Admin` role get access to the application. Since its deprecation in WebLogic Server 8.1, the `certificate.war` file that used to be deployed by default to all servers is now located the `$WL_HOME/server/lib` directory. For more information about the `Certificate Request Generator Servlet`, please refer to the WebLogic Server documentation at http://edocs.bea.com/wls/docs81/secmanage/ssl.html.

Going forward, BEA recommends using the `keytool` program that comes with Java 2 SDK. The `keytool` program can be tedious and unforgiving, so we will walk you through the certificate-generation process step by step. First, you need to generate your self-signed certificate and private key:

```
keytool -v -genkey -alias server_cert -keyalg RSA -keysize 1024
        -dname "CN=www.bigrez.com,OU=Operations,
                O=BigRez.com,L=Dallas,S=Texas,C=US"
        -keypass secret_key_passphrase
        -keystore server_keystore.jks
        -storepass secret_store_password
```

This command generates a self-signed certificate and private key, whose passphrase is `secret_key_passphrase`, using a 1024-bit RSA algorithm and stores them in the key store file `server_keystore.jks`, whose password is `secret_store_password`, under the alias `server_cert`. Pay special attention to the key size and CN element of the distinguished name. The hostname you enter for the CN here *must* be the same as the hostname your SSL clients will use to connect to your SSL server.

WARNING Set the CN field to the hostname that your SSL clients will ultimately use to reach your server. Failure to do this will result in a certificate that your SSL client may reject because the hostname does not match the IP address the client is using to reach the server.

You should set the key size to the highest value your WebLogic Server license will allow. At the time of writing, WebLogic Server supports 512-, 1024-, and 2048-bit key-lengths; anything over 512-bit key lengths currently requires a domestic-strength SSL license key. We expect that this information may change, so please check the WebLogic Server documentation for more information.

WARNING Key lengths of less than 1024 bits are generally considered too weak. If SSL is important enough to use in your environment, we recommend obtaining a domestic-strength license from BEA.

The next step is to generate a certificate signing request:

```
keytool -certreq -v -alias server_cert
        -file www_bigrez_com-request.pem
        -keypass secret_key_passphrase
        -storepass secret_store_password
        -keystore server_keystore.jks
```

The result of this command will be a text file called `www_bigrez_com-request.pem` containing our certificate signing request.

Once we have the CSR, we can go to our certificate authority and request a signed certificate. Several different, well-known certificate authorities will sell you a signed certificate. Some CAs will allow you to use a CSR to get a temporary trial server certificate in about 15 minutes. These can be very useful for development and testing efforts prior to production. VeriSign will give you a 14-day trial certificate when you submit your CSR at https://digitalid.verisign.com/server/trial/trialStep2.htm. You can get VeriSign's signing chain of certificates for that temporary trial certificate at http://www.verisign.com/server/trial/faq/. Baltimore Technologies will also provide a 30-day trial certificate at http://www.baltimore.com/servercert/ssltrial.asp.

Depending on your CA, you might get your signed certificate and/or the CA's certificate in one of several different formats. Privacy-Enhanced Mail (PEM) format is the most common and is just a text file containing special beginning and ending delimiters with the certificate information Base64-encoded in between. Look at the `www_bigrez_com-request.pem` file in the downloadable example code to see what a PEM-formatted certificate looks like. Distinguished Encoding Rules (DER) is the other common format, which is a binary format.

Some certificate authorities might give you a certificate file with a `.cer` file extension. This is a Microsoft file extension for certificates and can contain either a binary-encoded (DER format) or a Base64-encoded (PEM format) certificate. Some tools may check the file extensions and refuse to recognize the `.cer` file as a valid certificate. If this happens, open up the file in a text editor to see if the file is Base64-encoded or binary. If it is Base64-encoded, rename the file using a `.pem` extension; if the file is binary, use a `.der` extension.

Should you ever need to convert between PEM and DER formats, WebLogic Server provides two utility programs, `utils.der2pem` and `utils.pem2der`, that will convert between PEM and DER formats. See http://edocs.bea.com/wls/docs81/toolstable/ToolsTable.html for more information on these utilities.

Once you have your signed certificate and the CA's certificate chain available in either PEM or DER format, you will need to import your signed certificate into the key store. Because the `keytool` program will not allow you to import a certificate for which it cannot verify the certificate's signing chain, you need to import the CA's certificate chain as a trusted CA certificate before importing the signed certificate:

```
keytool -import -v -noprompt trustcacerts -alias cacert
        -file getcacert.der -keystore server_keystore.jks
        -storepass secret_store_password
```

Now you are ready to import the signed certificate that will replace the self-signed certificate you created earlier:

```
keytool -import -v -alias server_cert
        -file www_bigrez_com-cert.pem
        -keystore server_keystore.jks
        -keypass secret_key_passphrase
        -storepass secret_store_password
```

At this point, you have a key store that contains the server's signed certificate, the server's private key, and the trusted CA certificate, which should include the entire certificate chain. All you need to do now is to configure the server and provide the client with the trusted CA certificate, if the client doesn't already have it.

Configuring One-Way SSL

You finished all of the hard configuration work in the last section; now we'll help you set up the server to use your key store. All you need to do is to edit the server's configuration using the server's `Keystores & SSL Configuration` tab in the WebLogic Console. First, change the key store information by selecting the `Change` link in the `Keystore Configuration` heading at the top of this page. Because you are going to supply a new certificate but use the Java 2 SDK-supplied key store, select the `Custom Identity and Standard Java Trust` option for the `Keystore` attribute.

Now, you simply fill in the file name, key store type, and key store password for the `Custom Identity Keystore` and the password for your standard Java key store. The standard Java key store is always found at `$JAVA_HOME/jre/lib/security/cacerts` and has a default key store password of `changeit`. You can change the password of this key store using the `keytool -storepasswd` command; however, we recommend that you do not modify this file. If you are not comfortable with having this trust key store with this well-known password, we recommend copying this key store to another location, resetting the password, and switching to use a custom trust key store. This makes it easier to upgrade your WebLogic Server software without running the risk of losing your customized trust key store.

BEST PRACTICE Never modify the standard Java trust key store directly. If you want to use it as a starting point and customize it, make a copy of it into someplace that is associated with your application configuration and modify the copy.

The downloadable example places the identity key store file in the domain's root directory. You can place the file anywhere you want but remember that this file must be protected so we recommend keeping it close to the rest of your server's configuration files. Any relative path that you enter for the key store file name is relative to the domain's root directory. The key store type is `JKS` (short for Java key store), and the value of the `Key Store Pass Phrase` attribute is simply the key store's password you used when creating the key store—`secret_store_password` in our example.

Next, we need to provide information that allows the server to retrieve the private key from the key store, which includes the private key's alias in the key store and its passphrase. The private key alias you should use in this example is the alias for the server's certificate: `server_cert`. Once this is finished, simply restart the server for your changes to take effect. Don't forget to enable the SSL Listen Port.

Finally, you need to make the server's CA certificate chain available to the client. If you are using real certificates from well-known authorities, your client will probably already have the certificate chain in its trusted CA certificates store. If not, you will need to make the CA's certificate chain available to the client.

For browser-based clients, the browser will simply prompt the user to ask whether he or she wants to trust this certificate, as well as giving the user an option to install it. You can also proactively install the trusted CA certificate chain on the client. For Internet Explorer, you need to install the trusted CA certificate chain in the operating system. Please talk to your Windows administrator or refer to the MSDN article on how to manage end-user certificates at http://www.microsoft.com/technet/prodtechnol/windows2000serv/howto/enducert.asp. For Netscape or other browsers, please refer to the browser documentation.

For Java-based clients, you can either add the new certificates to the Java 2 SDK's `$JAVA_HOME/jre/lib/security/cacerts` key store or create a new client trust key store. If you create a new client trust key store, you need to tell your Java client to use it. Depending on whether you are using WebLogic SSL or JSSE, you do this by setting the Java system property `weblogic.security.SSL.trustedCAKeyStore` or `javax.net.ssl.trustStore` to point at your new trust key store file before any SSL connection is made. We will talk more about how to do this in the *Writing Java Clients That Use SSL* section later in this chapter.

Configuring Two-Way SSL

Now that you have seen how to configure the server for one-way SSL, getting to two-way SSL is pretty simple. In this section, you will use the `utils.CertGen` utility that comes with WebLogic Server to generate client certificates. Remember that `utils.CertGen` is not intended for use in production environments. You could just as easily use the same keytool-based process used to generate certificates for the server to generate the client certificates. Our primary motivation for using `utils.CertGen` here is to show you how you can use it to generate certificates for demonstrations or development environments without incurring the cost of buying real certificates for every demo/development machine.

First, let's generate the client certificate, private key, and key store. `utils.CertGen` is a simple utility that can be used to generate export- or domestic-strength certificates (512- or 1024-bit key lengths, respectively). The syntax of the command is as follows:

```
java utils.CertGen <key_passphrase> <cert_file_name>
                   <key_file_name> [export|domestic] [hostname]
```

In this example, we want to generate a domestic-strength certificate for a machine called bauersc.bigrez.com so that we can run the following command on any machine. The output of this command is four files containing the certificate and the primary key in both PEM and DER formats:

```
java utils.CertGen client_key_passphrase bauersc_bigrez_com-cert
     bauersc_bigrez_com-key domestic bauersc.bigrez.com
```

You can find the CA certificate used to sign all certificates generated by utils.CertGen at $WL_HOME/server/lib/CertGenCA.der.

You will need to make the client's CA certificate available to the server. Because your server is currently configured for one-way SSL and using the standard Java Trust key store, you either need to add the client CA cert to the standard Java key store or create a new server trust key store. Recall that we don't recommend modifying the standard Java trust key store. We recommend copying the standard Java trust key store because it already contains most of the root CA certificates you will need. If your application is an internal application, you may want to start with a new key store and add only the CA certificates approved for use within your organization.

TIP For sites using two-way SSL with external clients, starting with the standard Java trust key store will ensure that most clients will be able to connect using their existing certificates.

Start by copying the standard Java trust key store to a file called server_trust_keystore.jks in the domain's root directory and changing its password:

```
keytool -storepasswd -new secret_trust_password
        -keystore server_trust_keystore.jks -storepass changeit
```

Then, import the client's CA certificate, just as you did before, using the keytool -import -trustecacerts command:

```
keytool -import -v -noprompt -trustcacerts -alias cacert3
        -file %WL_HOME%\server\lib\CertGenCA.der
        -keystore server_trust_keystore.jks
        -storepass secret_trust_password
```

Now, you need to reconfigure the server to use this new trust key store. Simply go back to the server's Keystores & SSL Configuration tab in the WebLogic Console and select the Change link in the Keystore Configuration heading. Now, select the Custom Identity and Custom Trust option for the Keystores attribute. Next, set the trust key store name, type, and passphrase to the appropriate values (server_trust_keystore.jks, JKS, and secret_trust_password, respectively). You can leave everything else unchanged and finish applying the changes. Before restarting the server, let's go ahead and make the other SSL changes to enable two-way SSL.

Back on the `Keystores & SSL Configuration` tab, scroll down to the bottom of the page and select the `Show` link in the `Advanced Options` heading. There are two settings of interest to our current discussion. First, you need to change the `Two Way Client Cert Behavior` attribute that tells the server how to handle client certificates. Setting it to a value of `Client Certs Requested But Not Enforced` will turn on two-way SSL, but the SSL connection process will continue even if the client does not provide a certificate. If you want to require two-way SSL, then set the value to `Client Certs Requested And Enforced`. We will use the last setting because we want to verify that two-way SSL is working properly.

The other attribute of interest is `Hostname Verification`, which controls the behavior that the server uses when validating a certificate sent to it. This applies when the server is acting as a client to another SSL server. By default, this is set to the value `BEA Hostname Verifier`, which tells the server to use the internal implementation for verifying that the hostname in the certificate matches the destination from which the certificate originated. In some cases, you might want to change this setting to `None` to allow the use of certificates that do not match while in development. Never use this setting in a production environment. In extreme circumstances, you might need to provide your own implementation of the hostname verifier. You can do this by setting the value to `Custom Hostname Verifier` and setting the `Custom Hostname Verifier` attribute to the fully qualified class name of a class that implements the `weblogic.security.SSL.HostnameVerifier` interface.

It is also possible to disable all hostname verification completely in any WebLogic SSL client or server by setting the Java system property `weblogic.security.SSL.ignoreHostnameVerification` to `true`. Of course, another way to do this would be to provide your own hostname verifier class that always returns true. Either way, this is extremely dangerous because it disables all verification that the certificate being used is actually from the other process supplying it. It can be useful, though, in a development or demonstration environment when you simply want to use the demonstration certificates that come with WebLogic Server. Do not forget to re-enable hostname verification when migrating your configuration to a production environment.

BEST PRACTICE Disabling hostname verification can make things simpler in a development or demonstration environment; always re-enable hostname verification for your production environments.

If you are using browser-based clients, you will need to install the client certificates used by the browsers. Of course, these client-side, brower-based certificates will likely be user-specific certificates, so make sure to install them appropriately. If you intend to use two-way SSL as an application authentication mechanism, make sure that each user's certificate contains his or her WebLogic Server username somewhere in the distinguished name. We will talk more about application authentication after we discuss configuring Java clients.

For Java clients, you need to create identity and trust key stores for the client to use. Again, these key stores can be the same or different key stores. In this example, you will use two separate key stores to help you understand what needs to go in each key store. The identity key store needs to contain the client's certificate and private key. To create this client key store, you will use another WebLogic Server-provided utility called `utils.ImportPrivateKey`, whose syntax is as follows:

```
java utils.ImportPrivateKey <keystore_file> <keystore_password>
     <certificate_alias_to_use> <private_key_passphrase>
     <certificate_file> <private_key_file> [<keystore_type>]
```

If the `keytool` program provided an easy way to import an existing private key from a file, you would not need this `utils.ImportPrivateKey` utility. Because it doesn't, use the following command to create your identity key store and import your existing certificate and primary key:

```
java utils.ImportPrimaryKey client_keystore.jks
     client_store_password client_cert client_key_passphrase
     bauersc_bigrez_com-cert.pem bauersc_bigrez_com-key.pem
```

Notice that by using the `utils.ImportPrivateKey` utility you did not have to import the CA certificate chain first.

Next, you need to create your trust key store. Because Java client programs are not typically talking with a large number of servers controlled by different organizations, we have chosen to create a new trust key store rather than starting with the one included with the Java 2 SDK. You will place both the client's and the server's CA certificate chain in the trust key store. Once again, you can use the `keytool` program to create the new store and import both certificate chains:

```
keytool -import -v -noprompt -trustcacerts -alias client_cacert
        -file %WL_HOME%\server\lib\CertGenCA.der
        -keystore trust_store_keystore.jks
        -storepass _trust_store_password

keytool -import -v -noprompt -trustcacerts -alias server_cacert
        -file getcacert.der -keystore trust_store_keystore.jks
        -storepass _trust_store_password
```

Finally, you just need to get your Java client programs to use these new key stores. You can use the Java system property `weblogic.security.SSL.trustedCAKeyStore` to tell your client which trust key store to use. As you will see later in the *Writing Java Clients That Use SSL* section, the identity key store to use is referenced directly from within the client-side Java code.

The last thing we need to discuss is how to use two-way SSL as an application authentication mechanism. To use client certificates to authenticate your client users, you need to configure the server to support this. If you want to require users to be authenticated without prompting them for a username and password, make sure that you set the `Two Way Client Cert Behavior` attribute to `Client Certs Requested And Enforced`. Otherwise, WebLogic Server will treat any client that does not present a certificate as a one-way SSL client, and accessing a protected resource will cause them to be prompted for a username and password. Next, you need to create WebLogic Server users for mapping to client certificates. We will talk more about user management in the *Setting Up WebLogic Application Security* section later in this chapter. Finally, you need to configure the `DefaultIdentityAsserter` to support X.509 token types and set up the username mapper to extract the mapping information from the certificate and return the username, as previously discussed in the "Identity Assertion" section.

In this example, because the CN of our `utils.CertGen`-created client certificates contains the fully qualified hostname, you should set the `Default User Name Mapper` to extract the user information from the CN field and use the "`.`" character as the delimiter to map the hostname `bauersc.bigrez.com` properly to the WebLogic Server user `bauersc`. Once you have everything configured correctly, you should be able to use normal J2EE and/or WebLogic Server security mechanisms with your users without requiring them to log in or supply a password.

Debugging SSL Problems

Debugging problems with SSL configurations can be a frustrating task because most of the real work happens during the initial SSL handshake, before the server application code is ever invoked. Fortunately, WebLogic Server has some debugging flags that cause the server to print out very detailed information during the handshake. Without this sort of information, it is almost impossible for you (or BEA technical support) to debug the problem. To turn on this debugging output, you must use the Java command-line options to set both the `ssl.debug` and `weblogic.StdoutDebugEnable` Java system properties to `true` for the WebLogic Server, the Java-based application client, or both. This will cause the debugging information to be written to `stdout`.

Be aware that in some previous versions of WebLogic Server, Java-based WebLogic Server application clients using SSL cannot have the Sun's Java Secure Sockets Extension (JSSE) implementation in their classpath. Because the Java 2 SDK 1.4.x ships this implementation in the `$JAVA_HOME/jre/lib/jsse.jar` file, this can often be a problem. If this is, in fact, a problem with your particular situation, moving this file to a directory outside of the classpath will resolve the problem. WebLogic Server 8.1 clients do not suffer from this limitation. Please check the release notes for the WebLogic Server version you are using to see if this could be related to your problem.

TIP When having SSL problems, first check the release notes for any known problems that may apply to your particular configuration. Turning on the SSL debugging flags can make debugging SSL configuration problems much simpler.

Writing Security-Aware Java Clients

In this section, we will show you how to write security-aware Java clients that interact with WebLogic Server. The focus will be primarily around authentication and the use of SSL. First, we talk about how your Java application client can use JAAS to authenticate to WebLogic Server. Then, we show you how to set up an SSL connection between your application client and WebLogic Server. In Chapter 15, we show you how to write security-aware Web Services clients that use both SSL and Web Services Security to encrypt the message itself.

Writing Java Clients That Use JAAS

Before we jump into the details of how to use JAAS with your WebLogic Server Java client application, let's briefly look at the theory behind it. JAAS provides a standard way to authenticate specific users and authorize those users for specific sets of code and resources.

JAAS authentication is designed to be a pluggable framework that removes authentication methods and decisions from business logic entirely. This framework allows for a new method of authentication to be added to an application to either replace or augment the current authentication modules without requiring the application code to change. We will spend the bulk of this section looking at how JAAS authentication works.

JAAS authorization is built using the existing Java 2 Security model, which uses a security policy to restrict the rights of executing code. JAAS extends this model by allowing the policy to be defined for specific users and groups. Typically and by default, this policy is defined in a text file that uses a special syntax; this file is `java.policy`. Through this mechanism, JAAS allows the Java run time to restrict access based on where the code came from, who the code might be digitally signed by, and what authenticated principal the code is running on behalf of. The granularity of restriction is still limited to the same low-level, system resources of the Java run time. For example, you could restrict access to reading and/or writing specific Java system properties, files, or network ports. JAAS authorization does not address the problems associated with protecting a server's application-level resources such as an EJB method or JMS queue. Such access control restrictions are left to the application server itself and do not use JAAS.

You can turn on JAAS authorization by adding the following two Java command-line options to set the required Java system properties:

```
-Djava.security.manager -Djava.security.policy=weblogic.policy
```

The `RecordingSecurityManager` is a useful utility when dealing with some of the policy requirements your application will need, plus dealing with the policy file syntax. This utility runs during development time as a replacement for the Java run time's default Security Manager and records the permissions your application will require. It can be found in the `Alpha Code` section for WebLogic Server on the BEA developer's Web site at http://dev2dev.bea.com/.

JAAS authorization might be useful to restrict the Java run-time permissions for untrusted code running on your server. Most production environments, though, typically are not running untrusted code on the server, so using JAAS authorization to control access on your application server is probably not worth pursuing. A typical J2EE environment has at least minimal audits of the business applications and code running on the server. The only real-world situation where the extra performance hit of using JAAS authorization might be useful would be for application service providers (ASPs). JAAS authorization makes sense only if you host applications that you don't directly control or have the ability to audit. In most cases, the benefits do not justify the run-time performance overhead.

BEST PRACTICE JAAS authorization only addresses authorization only for low-level system resources or capabilities like reading or writing to a file or creating a new class loader. All application-level resources are left as an exercise for the application server and/or application security vendors. Most production server environments are not typically running untrusted code, and the performance overhead of JAAS authorization can be substantial. Therefore, we do not recommend JAAS authorization for most application authorization needs.

JAAS authentication occurs in a few basic steps. A JAAS client application begins the authentication process by instantiating a `LoginContext` object with the client type and a new custom `CallbackHandler`, as shown in the following code fragment:

```
CallbackHandler callback =
    new MasteringWebLogicCallbackHandler(username, password, url));
LoginContext loginContext =
    new LoginContext("MasteringWebLogic", callback);
```

In this case, the client type is `MasteringWebLogic` and the custom `CallbackHandler` is the `MasteringWeblogicCallbackHandler`.

When this client code executes, the `LoginContext` looks up its configuration to determine the required authentication types, or `LoginModules`, to be used in performing the authentication. While JAAS supports a pluggable configuration model, the Java run time ships only with the file-based implementation, so the configuration typically comes from a file. The `LoginContext` matches the client type with the `LoginModule` and its associated flags. In our example, the configuration information is stored in the `masteringweblogic.config` file, whose contents are as follows:

```
MasteringWebLogic {
   weblogic.security.auth.login.UsernamePasswordLoginModule
             required debug=false;
};
```

When the `LoginContext` reads this file, it finds the entry for its client type, `MasteringWebLogic`, and determines that the correct `LoginModule` to use is `weblogic.security.auth.login.UsernamePasswordLoginModule`, whose control flag is set to `Required` and debug flag is set to `false`. This control flag value has the exact same semantics as we previously discussed when covering `Login Module` settings in the "Authentication" section.

So, the next question that should come to mind is how does the `LoginContext` know where to find its configuration? Java provides two mechanisms for telling the `LoginContext` where to find its configuration information. One way to specify the location of the JAAS login configuration is through the Java system property `java.security.auth.login.config`, which can be set to point to the configuration file the Java program should use. If this system property is not set, the Java run time will search through the list of entries like the one shown next in the

$JAVA_HOME/jre/lib/security/java.security file looking for a configuration file that contains an entry that matches our client type:

```
login.config.url.1=file:/c:/book/ch10_examples/masteringweblogic.policy
```

The next step in the application is to call the LoginContext's login() method, which starts the whole authentication process. The LoginModules are called with the original CallbackHandler. A basic LoginModule might simply use the CallbackHandler to prompt for a username and password on the command line. More complex ones might require an X.509 certificate, a Kerberos token, or even some biometric information. Each new authentication method requires a new LoginModule, and possibly a new CallbackHandler to deal with any new Callback types the LoginModule might need. Each LoginModule uses the CallbackHandler to decide whether to authenticate this subject.

In our example, we use a MasteringWebLogicCallbackHandler to hold the username and password. We chose this approach so that you could see the inner workings of the CallbackHandler. In this case, it would be just as easy to use the WebLogic Server's built-in weblogic.security.SimpleCallbackHandler or weblogic.security.URLCallbackHandler. The SimpleCallbackHandler supports only prompting for the username and password; the URLCallback Handler supports prompting for the username, password, and server URL.

Upon success, LoginModules associate various Principals with the newly created Subject. If the LoginContext is successful, the application can then retrieve the Subject from it. This new Subject has a list of Principal objects that represent the identity of the currently authenticated user. To invoke business logic, you must create a class that implements PriviledgedAction and contains the business logic, and you must pass it to the WebLogic Security subsystem along with the newly created Subject:

```
loginContext.login();
Subject subject = loginContext.getSubject();
JAASExampleAction clientAction = new JAASExampleAction(url);
Security.runAs(subject, clientAction);
```

You should notice right away that the business logic is now encapsulated inside a PriviledgedAction object, which is just a wrapper of a Runnable. We pass the PriviledgedAction object to the WebLogic Security subsystem, along with the authenticated Subject, to be run. This is different from standard JAAS, which uses the Subject itself to run the PriviledgedAction. Although covering the rationale for this is beyond the scope of this book, suffice it to say that there are problems with losing the user identity when combining the JAAS-specified Subject.doAs() with AccessController.doPriviledged(). Because J2EE requires the use of AccessController.doPriviledged() in certain conditions, WebLogic Server provides a Security.runAs() method that is similar in spirit to Subject.doAs() and works with all of your JAAS code, but does not suffer from the user identity problem.

Another important point is that the LoginModule being used by the client is not the same as the one being used by the WebLogic Server Security Service on the server.

The client-side `LoginModule` calls to the server to try to authenticate the client. As a result of this request, the server will call into the Security Framework, which will end up invoking the server-side `LoginModule`(s) to make the actual authentication decision. Your application client should either use the WebLogic Server-provided `LoginModule`, called the `UsernamePasswordLoginModule`, or provide its own custom `LoginModule`. If you use a custom `LoginModule`, always call `weblogic.security.auth.Authenticate.authenticate()` from within its login method, as shown here:

```
Subject subject = new Subject();
weblogic.jndi.Environment env = new weblogic.jndi.Environment();
env.setProviderUrl(url);
env.setSecurityPrincipal(username);
env.setSecurityCredentials(password);
weblogic.security.auth.Authenticate.authenticate(env, subject);
```

The basic idea here is that the client application running the custom `LoginModule` must contact the server to allow the server to do the authentication. As a part of this server-side authentication process, the server will populate and digitally sign the `Subject` before returning. You can place any `Serializable` object in the `Environment` to act as the credential instead of a password as long as the server's configured authentication provider knows how to use it to authenticate the user. This `authenticate()` method is only for authentication to a remote server. To authenticate to the server from code running inside that server, you need to use the `weblogic.security .service.Authenticate.login()` method.

BEST PRACTICE **Use only the** `weblogic.security.auth.Authenticate.authenticate()` **method to authenticate to a remote server process. Always use the** `weblogic.security.services.Authenticate.login()` **method for code running inside the server to which you want to authenticate.**

Writing Java Clients That Use SSL

When writing a Java client that uses SSL, there are three main types of application clients to consider: RMI clients, programmatic HTTP clients, and Web Services clients. We discuss RMI clients and HTTP clients in this section, but we defer the discussion of Web Services clients to Chapter 15. We end this section with a discussion of application authentication, hostname verification, and trust managers.

RMI Clients

The first type of client to discuss is an RMI client using SSL. For one-way SSL, it is as simple as specifying an SSL protocol and port in the `PROVIDER_URL` that you use to create the JNDI `InitialContext` object:

```
Hashtable ht = new Hashtable();
ht.put(Context.INITIAL_CONTEXT_FACTORY,
       "weblogic.jndi.WLInitialContextFactory");
ht.put(Context.PROVIDER_URL, "t3s://localhost:7002");
InitialContext ctx = new InitialContext(ht);
```

Making a two-way SSL connection from a stand-alone client is a little bit more work. When running inside the server, there is no need to supply the credentials because the server will automatically provide them for any outgoing SSL connection in which the remote SSL server requests the credentials. In the stand-alone client case, you simply need to get the certificate chain and private key from the key store and pass it into the `InitialContext` constructor:

```
weblogic.jndi.Environment env = new weblogic.jndi.Environment();
env.setProviderUrl(url);
env.loadLocalIdentity(certificateChain, privateKey);
Initial Context ctx = env.getInitialContext();
```

Another example available for downloading shows how to accomplish the same thing using the new thin RMI client that also supports using a key store but does it by using JSSE under the covers. This example will work only if the client is using the new thin client jar file, `wlclient.jar`, and not running inside a WebLogic Server. As mentioned previously, you don't need to worry about outgoing SSL connections from the WebLogic Server as long as you have the server configured with the proper information to find its certificate and private key.

JSSE uses the `KeyManagerFactory` to handle all interaction with the `KeyStore`. It queries the `KeyStore` to determine which certificate and private key to use when asked to provide credentials. One important thing to point out is that `KeyStore Manager` uses the same password for accessing every key in the key store. This means that you should set your key store password and all of the private key passphrases to be the same. Given this, you should always try to use one identity key store per client certificate to protect the integrity of the private key.

WARNING **When using JSSE's `KeyManagerFactory`, you must use the same password for the key store password and the passphrase for all private keys in the key store. We strongly recommend that you do not store more than one user's certificate in each identity key store to prevent compromising the integrity of the private keys.**

When using JSSE, you can either configure a `TrustManagerFactory` to use your trust key store or tell the default `TrustManagerFactory` which trust key store to use by setting the Java system property `javax.net.ssl.trustStore`. To have the `TrustManagerFactory` verify the integrity of the data it retrieves from the key store, specify the key store password using the `javax.net.ssl.trustStorePassword` Java system property. You simply need to package up the `KeyManagerFactory` and the `TrustManager` in an `SSLContext` object and supply it to the first `Initial Context` creation:

```
import javax.net.ssl.KeyManagerFactory;
import javax.net.ssl.SSLContext;
import javax.net.ssl.TrustManagerFactory;

...

KeyManagerFactory kmf =
    KeyManagerFactory.getInstance("SunX509", "SunJSSE");
kmf.init(identityKeyStore, keyStorePassword);
TrustManagerFactory tmf =
    TrustManagerFactory.getInstance("SunX509", "SunJSSE");
tmf.init(trustKeyStore);

SSLContext sslCtx = SSLContext.getInstance("SSL");
sslCtx.init(kmf.getKeyManagers(), tmf.getTrustManagers(), null);
Hashtable props = new Hashtable();
props.put(Context.INITIAL_CONTEXT_FACTORY,
         "weblogic.jndi.WLInitialContextFactory");
props.put(Context.PROVIDER_URL, "iiops://127.0.0.1:7002");
props.put(Context.SECURITY_CREDENTIALS, sslCtx);
InitialContext ctx = new InitialContext(props);
```

Programmatic HTTP Clients

The next type of client is a Java application client making HTTP requests over SSL using `URLConnection` objects. You might wonder how common it is to need a Java client that makes HTTP requests. The answer is that while it may not be very common for a true client application, it is a relatively common thing to do when writing server-side code that may need to call out to some other site to get information.

When writing these types of clients, there are two main ways of establishing the SSL connection: WebLogic SSL APIs or JSSE APIs. First, let's look at using the WebLogic SSL APIs. For one-way SSL (or two-way SSL from inside the server) you simply create your `HttpsURLConnection` object:

```
URL url = new URL("https", hostname, sslPortNumber, page);
weblogic.net.http.HttpsURLConnection sslConn =
    new weblogic.net.http.HttpsURLConnection(url);
sslConn.connect();
```

If you want to make a two-way SSL connection from outside the server, you need to do a little bit more work. You need to get the X.509 certificate chain and the private key and use these to store the client's identity in WebLogic Server's version of the `SSLContext`. Then, you get the WebLogic Server `SSLSocketFactory` from the `SSLContext` and use it to call `setSSLSocketFactory()` on the `weblogic.het.http.HttpsURLConnection` object before you call `connect()`. The downloadable examples contain a complete working example, the highlights of which are shown here.

```
import weblogic.net.http.HttpsURLConnection;
import weblogic.security.SSL.SSLContext;
import weblogic.security.SSL.SSLSocketFactory;

...

SSLContext ctx = SSLContext.getInstance("https");
ctx.loadLocalIdentity(certChain, privateKey);
SSLSocketFactory sslSocketFactory = ctx.getSocketFactoryJSSE();

URL url = new URL("https", hostName, sslPortNumber, page);
HttpsURLConnection sslConn = new HttpsURLConnection(url);
sslConn.setSSLSocketFactory(sslSocketFactory);
sslConn.connect();
```

For JSSE clients making a one-way SSL connection, it is simply a matter of changing the type of `HttpsURLConnection` object:

```
URL jsseUrl = new URL("https", hostname, sslPortNumber, page);
javax.net.ssl.HttpsURLConnection sslConn =
    (javax.net.ssl.HttpsURLConnection)url.openConnection();
sslConn.connect();
```

For a two-way SSL connection, it is almost the same as we saw with the RMI thin client except that you use the JSSE `SSLContext` object to get a JSSE `SSLSocket Factory` and use it to call `setSSLSocketFactory()` on the `javax.net.ssl .HttpsURLConnection` object before you call `connect()`, as highlighted here. See the downloadable examples on the companion Web site for a complete working example:

```
import javax.net.ssl.HttpsURLConnection;
import javax.net.ssl.KeyManagerFactory;
import javax.net.ssl.SSLContext;
import javax.net.ssl.SSLSocketFactory;
import javax.net.ssl.TrustManagerFactory;

...

KeyManagerFactory kmf =
    KeyManagerFactory.getInstance("SunX509", "SunJSSE");
kmf.init(identityKeyStore, args[1].toCharArray());
TrustManagerFactory tmf =
    TrustManagerFactory.getInstance("SunX509", "SunJSSE");
tmf.init(trustKeyStore);

SSLContext ctx = SSLContext.getInstance("SSL");
ctx.init(kmf.getKeyManagers(), tmf.getTrustManagers(), null);
SSLSocketFactory sslSocketFactory = ctx.getSocketFactory();

URL url = new URL("https", serverName, sslPortNumber, page);
```

```
HttpsURLConnection sslConn =
    (HttpsURLConnection)url.openConnection();
sslConn.setSSLSocketFactory(sslSocketFactory);
sslConn.connect();
```

Web Services Clients

The last type of SSL client we need to discuss is a Web Services client. Because you may be new to Web Services, we have decided to delay this discussion to Chapter 15, where we will cover both connection- and data-level security. Before we leave the topic of SSL, we need to discuss a few miscellaneous options related to SSL: application authentication, hostname verification, and trust managers.

Application Authentication

You can use two-way SSL to authenticate a client to your WebLogic Server application. To do this, you simply need to map the client certificate presented to the server to a WebLogic Server username. You can do this using the identity assertion capabilities of the WebLogic Server Security Framework, as discussed earlier in the "Identity Assertion" section. All of the two-way SSL examples we just discussed use this capability to allow the server-side application to determine the username. Once the WebLogic Server identity is established, you can use any standard J2EE or WebLogic Server authorization capabilities to restrict access to protected resources.

Hostname Verification

Both WebLogic Server and JSSE try to verify that the certificate a remote process presents matches its hostname. They do this by invoking a default set of rules to try to match the common name (CN) field of the X.509 certificate's distinguished name (DN) to the host from which it came. If they are unable to do that, they will invoke the registered hostname verifier class to verify that the certificate is, in fact, from the host. In most situations, the hostname verification process will not need the hostname verifier. By default, both WebLogic Server and JSSE are configured to fail all verification calls that need to call the hostname verifier. This means that if your certificates are failing the default verification rules, you will need to get new certificates or provide your own implementation of the `weblogic.security.ssl.HostnameVerifierJSSE` or `javax.net.ssl.HostnameVerifier` interface, depending on which SSL implementation you are using.

There are three ways to register your custom hostname verifier class with WebLogic SSL. You can call the `setHostnameVerifierJSSE()` method on either the WebLogic `HttpsURLConnection` or `SSLContext` objects. If your code is running in the server, you can use the `Advanced Options` section of the server's `Keystores & SSL` tab in the WebLogic Console. Finally, you can use the Java system property `weblogic.security.SSL.HostnameVerifierJSSE` to point to the fully qualified class name of your hostname verifier class.

Trust Managers

Our last topic is the `TrustManager` interface. A `TrustManager` is a secondary means of verifying the certification chain supplied by the other party participating in the SSL handshake. It is a simple interface that is called only if the default certification chain verification failed. A common example of this occurs when an SSL client connects to an SSL server that has a single expired certificate somewhere in its certificate signing chain and the expired certificate has been replaced with a new certificate, next to it in the chain. Using the new certificate in the server certificate chain and simply ignoring the expired certificate will verify correctly. The problem is that standard SSL certificate verification will not accept a certificate chain like this. It is considered untrusted, and the SSL handshake will fail.

If the SSL client has been set up with a `TrustManager`, the client's `TrustManager` will be called with the unverified server certificate chain. The `TrustManager` can then decide whether to allow the certificate chain verification and thus the SSL handshake to continue. Use of a `TrustManager` is not required if the default SSL certificate chain verification is all that is needed. Both WebLogic SSL and JSSE support registering a custom `TrustManager`. With WebLogic SSL, you need to provide an implementation of the `weblogic.security.SSL.TrustManagerJSSE` interface and register it with the `weblogic.security.SSL.SSLContext` object. For JSSE, you need to create and register your own `javax.net.ssl.TrustManagerFactory` or implement the `javax.net.ssl.X509TrustManager` interface directly. Both of these are then used in conjunction with the `javax.net.ssl.SSLContext` object's `init()` method.

Managing Application Security

In this section, we present a brief overview of the setup, management, and administration of the WebLogic Server application security features. We start with a brief review of the J2EE standard security settings in various deployment descriptors. Next, we will show you how to set up roles and access control policies using the built-in WebLogic Security providers' capabilities. We finish by talking about the different ways to specify the username and password needed to boot the WebLogic Server.

Setting Up J2EE Application Security

In this section, you will learn how to use J2EE security mechanisms to set up authentication requirements, configure access control policies, and define role mappings for Web applications, Enterprise JavaBeans (EJB), resource adapters, and enterprise applications. We will cover Web Services security in Chapter 15 after we have covered WebLogic Server's Web Services container in more detail.

With most J2EE components types, WebLogic Server uses a two-level process for mapping roles defined in the J2EE standard deployment descriptors to actual WebLogic users or groups in the WebLogic Server-specific deployment descriptor. This mechanism allows you to use standard role names in your application and then map them to physical users or groups at deployment time.

Securing Web Applications

When setting up Web application security, the first decision you need to make is the type of HTTP authentication mechanism to use. In the following `web.xml` deployment descriptor, we define the desired HTTP authentication mechanism in the `auth-method` element, within the `login-config` element:

```
<login-config>
  <auth-method>FORM</auth-method>
  <form-login-config>
    <form-login-page>/login.jsp</form-login-page>
    <form-error-page>/login_error.jsp</form-error-page>
  </form-login-config>
  <realm-name>BigRez Realm</realm-name>
</login-config>
```

This tells the Web container that the Web application will be using form-based authentication. Three different types of authentication are supported:

BASIC. Using this method causes the Web browser to pop up the HTTP authentication dialog box requesting a username and password. To define basic authentication in your Web application, simply replace `FORM` with `BASIC` in the `auth-method` element and eliminate the entire `form-login-config` element. The `realm-name` tag is used only with `BASIC` authentication to specify the authentication realm displayed in the browser's pop-up authentication dialog box. It is completely cosmetic and has no other purpose at this time.

FORM. When using form-based authentication, the browser is redirected to the configured HTML login form, as defined in the `<form-login-page>` element, whenever the user tries to access a protected URL. Once authentication succeeds and authorization is granted, the Web container automatically redirects the browser to the originally requested HTTP resource, complete with its original HTTP headers. If this authentication fails, the browser will be redirected to the HTTP resource defined in the `<form-error-page>` element. When using form-based authentication, your form must use the `j_username` and `j_password` form element names to identify the username and password attributes to the container. The form's action attribute must be set to `j_security_check`, as shown here. These form element and action names are required by the Java Servlet specification:

```
<form method="POST" action="j_security_check">
  <input type="text" name="j_username">
  <input type="password" name="j_password">
  <input type="submit" name="Login">
</form>
```

CLIENT-CERT. If you are using two-way SSL between the browser and the server, you can choose client certificate-based authentication. This option requires not only two-way SSL connections but also the use of an appropriate identity asserter to map the certificate to a WebLogic Server username, as we discussed at length in earlier sections of this chapter. To specify client certificate-based authentication, simply replace `FORM` with `CLIENT-CERT` in the `auth-method` element. When using this type of authentication, the `form-login-config` and `realm-name` elements may be omitted.

It is important to remember that with any of these authentication options, the container will not authenticate the user until the browser tries to access a protected URL. While this seems intuitive with either basic or form-based authentication, it also applies to client certificate-based authentication. This means that even though the SSL handshake is complete and the client certificate is available to the server, WebLogic Server will not invoke the identity asserter until you try to access a protected resource.

Because the security realm is defined at the domain level, all Web applications on the server use the same authentication realm. By default, WebLogic Server uses the same cookie name (`JSESSIONID`) for all Web applications on the server. That way, no matter what type of authentication method is used in a particular Web application, an authenticated user will have single sign-on to all other Web applications in the WebLogic Server. You can modify this behavior by changing the cookie path or cookie name for specific Web applications. The following extract from the `weblogic.xml` deployment descriptor shows how to modify the cookie name. To modify the cookie path instead, simply change the `param-name` element from `CookieName` to `CookiePath`:

```
<session-descriptor>
  <session-param>
    <param-name>CookieName</param-name>
    <param-value>ApplicationSpecificCookieName</param-value>
  </session-param>
</session-descriptor>
```

Now that you have set up the authentication mechanism, you are ready to set up the access control policies and roles for the Web application. The policies themselves are specified exclusively in the `web.xml` deployment descriptor within the `security-constraint` element, as shown here:

```
<security-constraint>
  <web-resource-collection>
    <web-resource-name>SecureArea</web-resource-name>
    <description>Our Secure Area</description>
    <url-pattern>/secure/*</url-pattern>
    <http-method>POST</http-method>
    <http-method>GET</http-method>
  </web-resource-collection>
  <auth-constraint>
    <description>Constraints for secure area</description>
    <role-name>manager</role-name>
```

```
      <role-name>security-admin</role-name>
    </auth-constraint>
    <user-data-constraint>
      <description>SSL is not required</description>
      <transport-guarantee>NONE</transport-guarantee>
    </user-data-constraint>
  </security-constraint>
```

As the bold highlighting shows, all HTTP POST and GET requests for any URL matching the pattern /secure/* relative to the root context of this Web application will be protected. It's typical to *always* define both GET and POST here, unless there are some very special circumstances in your particular Web application. We have restricted access to these resources so that only users in the role manager or security-admin can access them, but we are not requiring the use of SSL transport for access. Setting the transport-guarantee to CONFIDENTIAL would further restrict access to only those users in one of the specified roles who are using SSL to access the page.

BEST PRACTICE When restricting resources always protect against both HTTP GET and POST unless your application has special requirements that do not allow them. Even if your application uses only one method to access the resource, protecting against both methods will prevent unintended access by determined users.

Now, you need to declare the roles used in the auth-constraint elements, using the security-role elements:

```
<security-role>
  <description>the managers role</description>
  <role-name>manager</role-name>
</security-role>
<security-role>
  <description>the security-admin role</description>
  <role-name>security-admin</role-name>
</security-role>
```

If we stopped here, WebLogic Server would try to map these roles to principals, either users or groups, with the same name, as defined in the active security realm's authentication provider. In most cases, you don't actually want this so you need to define the mapping from these roles to actual principals defined in the WebLogic Security realm.

To map these roles to principals in the underlying security realm, you use the security-role-assignment element in the weblogic.xml deployment descriptor. As our example here shows, we are mapping the manager role to the Administrators group and the security-admin role to three unique users: paulb, rpatrick, and billjg.

```
<security-role-assignment>
  <role-name>manager</role-name>
  <principal-name>Administrators</principal-name>
</security-role-assignment>
<security-role-assignment>
  <role-name>security-admin</role-name>
  <principal-name>paulb</principal-name>
  <principal-name>rpatrick</principal-name>
  <principal-name>billjg</principal-name>
</security-role-assignment>
```

We should point out that changing these role mappings in the weblogic.xml deployment descriptor requires that you redeploy the application for the changes to take effect. In most cases, you will want to map roles to groups defined in the underlying realm so that you can dynamically change who has access to your protected resources by simply changing the group membership in the underlying security realm.

BEST PRACTICE **Always explicitly specify the mapping of your deployment descriptor roles to principals in the underlying security realm. In most cases, you will want to map these roles to groups, rather than users, to allow you to dynamically change who has access to protected resources without redeploying the application.**

Web applications also support the ability to run the application always as a specific principal, regardless of any authentication that may have occurred. This is an alternative to the authentication and protection mechanisms already discussed. To configure your Web application to run as a specific principal, you first need to specify the role using the run-as element in the web.xml deployment descriptor, as shown here. This declaration will tell the container to run the Web application always as the AppAdmin role.

```
<run-as>AppAdmin</run-as>
```

Next, we want to specify the mapping of the role to a specific principal in the underlying security realm. The best way to do this is to use the run-as-role-assignment element in the weblogic.xml deployment descriptor, as shown here:

```
<run-as-role-assignment>
  <role-name>AppAdmin</role-name>
  <run-as-principal-name>lauren</run-as-principal-name>
</run-as-role-assignment>
```

This mapping applies for the entire Web application. If the run-as-role-assignment is not defined for a given role, the container will choose the first principal name defined for that role in the security-role-assignment stanza.

It is also possible to scope the run-as configuration to a specific servlet in the Web application. This servlet-scoped run-as-principal-name configuration overrides the more general one specified using the run-as-role-assignment stanza. In this example, we will always run the SampleServletName servlet as the user hugh in the underlying realm:

```
<servlet-descriptor>
  <servlet-name>SampleServletName</servlet-name>
  <run-as-principal-name>hugh</run-as-principal-name>
  ...
</servlet-descriptor>
```

If needed, you can use programmatic security checking in the business logic of your Web applications. While we will not bother to go through all of the servlet security-related APIs, one interesting method to point out is the isUserInRole() method:

```
boolean isUserInManagerRole = request.isUserInRole("manager")
```

Using this method, you can test whether the current user should get certain types of options or data. By defining this role and mapping it to one or more principals in the Web application deployment descriptors, the application code can do fine-grained security checks without sacrificing the level of indirection that role mapping gives you. The bigrez.com application used this technique to control the list of properties displayed to a user based on his or her role.

Just to be complete, there is another way to restrict what a Web application can do by using JAAS authorization policies. As discussed previously, JAAS authorization typically uses a policy file to store its authorization policies. This policy file specifies a set of Java run-time permissions based on where the code originated. Because that file doesn't know where the deployed Web application will exist on the server's filesystem, the CodeBase cannot be statically defined. As a result, you cannot define a JAAS authorization policy for Web applications in the server-wide weblogic.policy file. To get around this limitation, WebLogic Server allows you to define a JAAS authorization policy for a Web application in the weblogic.xml deployment descriptor. This example shows how to restrict the Web application's java.net.SocketPermission to allow it to connect only to the BEA Web site:

```
<security-permission>
  <description> Connect permission to BEA Web site</description>
  <security-permission-spec>
    grant {
        permission java.net.SocketPermission
                   "www.bea.com:80", "connect"
    };
  </security-permission-spec>
<security-permission>
```

As we alluded to earlier, most applications running on a server can be audited by other means to make sure that they are not doing something they shouldn't. The run-time overhead of JAAS authorization is high so we recommend very careful consideration and performance testing before going too far down this path.

WARNING **JAAS authorization provides very fine-grained, system-level control of Java run-time resources. This system-level control comes at a high price in run-time overhead. Always prototype and performance test any application making use of JAAS authorization before committing to that approach.**

Managing EJB Security

To set up an access control policy in an EJB, you use the `security-role` and `method-permission` elements of the `ejb-jar.xml` deployment descriptor. In the following example, we restrict access to the `AdvertiseProduct` EJB's `getResults()` method to users in either the `manager` or `ejb-admin` roles:

```
<assembly-descriptor>
  <security-role>
    <role-name>manager</role-name>
    <role-name>ejb-admin</role-name>
  </security-role>
  <method-permission>
    <role-name>manager</role-name>
    <role-name>ejb-admin</role-name>
    <method>
      <ejb-name>AdvertiseProduct</ejb-name>
      <method-name>getResults</method-name>
    </method>
  </method-permission>
        ...
</assembly-descriptor>
```

EJBs also support the concept of role mapping. Similar to Web applications, the application server-specific deployment descriptor, `weblogic-ejb-jar.xml`, contains the actual mapping data. The following example maps the `manager` role to both the `Administrators` group and the user `paulb`. Additionally, you can use the `externally-defined` element to force a role to be defined in the Role Mapper security provider; this `externally-defined` tag replaces the old `global-role` tag:

```
<security-role-assignment>
  <role-name>manager</role-name>
  <principal-name>Administrators</principal-name>
  <principal-name>paulb</principal-name>
</security-role-assignment>
<security-role-assignment>
  <role-name>ejb-admin</role-name>
  <externally-defined/>
</security-role-assignment>
```

As you might expect, EJBs also support the ability to run as a specific principal. Similar to Web applications, we start by specifying the `run-as` role in the `ejb-jar.xml`, as shown in the following example where we set the `run-as` role to `EJBAppAdmin`:

```
<security-identity>
  <run-as>EJBAppAdmin</run-as>
</security-identity>
```

Now, we map the specified `run-as` role to a specific principal using the `run-as-role-assignment` tag in the `weblogic-ejb-jar.xml` deployment descriptor. Here, we map the `EJBAppAdmin` role to the user `bob`:

```
<weblogic-ejb-jar>
  ...
  <run-as-role-assignment>
    <role-name>EJBAppAdmin</role-name>
    <run-as-principal-name>bob</run-as-principal-name>
  </run-as-role-assignment>
</weblogic-ejb-jar>
```

We can also scope the `run-as` configuration to a specific EJB within the jar file, as shown in the code that follows, where we map the `run-as` role to the user `jason` for the `BandEJB`. As before, this EJB-scoped `run-as-principal-name` configuration overrides the more general one. If there is no `run-as-principal-name` element specified in either place, the container will match the `run-as` role to the first principal listed in the normal role mapping elements:

```
<weblogic-enterprise-bean>
  <ejb-name>BandEJB</ejb-name>
  ...
  <run-as-principal-name>jason</run-as-principal-name>
</weblogic-enterprise-bean>
```

You can use programmatic security checking in the business logic of an EJB. This can allow for business logic with very specific requirements to test whether the current user should get certain types of information. To get the currently authenticated user, use the `getCallerPrincipal()` method:

```
Principal currentUser = ejbContext.getCallerPrincipal();
```

To check whether the currently authenticated user has a specific role, use the `isCallerInRole()` method:

```
boolean isUserInRole = ejbContext.isCallerInRole("manager");
```

WebLogic EJBs also support using JAAS authorization policies in the `weblogic-ejb-jar.xml` deployment descriptor to restrict the system-level resources an EJB can use. To do this, you use the `security-permission` element, whose syntax is exactly the same as that of the `security-permission` element in the `weblogic.xml` deployment descriptor entry. For the same reasons, we caution you against trying to use JAAS authorization without first proving to yourself that the benefits are worth the costs.

Securing J2EE CA Resource Adapters

J2EE Connector Architecture (J2EE CA) resource adapters store their security configuration in the `ra.xml` and `weblogic-ra.xml` deployment descriptors. Using the `weblogic-ra.xml`, you can define the mapping between the authenticated application server user and the username and password to use to connect to the underlying resource:

```
<security-principal-map>
  <map-entry>
    <initiating-principal>WLSuser</initiating-principal>
    <resource-principal>
      <resource-username>EISuser</resource-username>
      <resource-password>EISpasswd</resource-password>
    </resource-principal>
  </map-entry>
</security-principal-map>
```

It is important to note that this mapping has been deprecated in favor of the WebLogic Security framework's Credential Mapper, which supports dynamic changes and persists the mapping information to a more secure data store.

BEST PRACTICE Use the Credential Mapper to map WebLogic security principals to the username and password to use to connect to the underlying resource.

Securing Enterprise Applications

One problem with defining roles in the Web application and EJB components is that you may need to define them in multiple places. Enterprise applications can define roles that apply to all of their containing components in their `application.xml` deployment descriptor. This allows application-scoped role definitions using the same techniques as Web applications and EJBs.

For enterprise applications, `weblogic-application.xml` is the WebLogic Server-specific deployment descriptor used to define application-scoped configuration information. The descriptor offers little in terms of security configuration. It does not currently allow you to define any role mappings. This means that you would have to map any roles defined in the `application.xml` to the underlying principals using the individual Web application and EJB deployment descriptors or using the global Role Mapper provided in the security framework.

Although the `weblogic-application.xml` deployment descriptor provides a `realm-name` element that is said to allow you to specify the security realm that the application should use, this parameter has no real use except as a way of preventing an application from trying to start if the wrong domain-wide security realm is active.

Setting Up WebLogic Application Security

This section begins with a very brief discussion of how to create and manage WebLogic Server users and groups because every application that uses application-level security will need to do this. Next, we will talk about roles, both application-scoped and global. From there, we will explain setting up access control on specific server resources and then forming a set of policies. We will end this section with a brief explanation of how to set up single sign-on across WebLogic Server domains.

Managing Users and Groups

If you are using the default configuration—which uses WebLogic embedded LDAP Server as the security store—then you can manage users and groups using the WebLogic Console. By navigating to the `Security->Realms->myrealm` folder in the left navigation bar, you will see entries for `Users`, `Groups`, and `Roles`. Selecting `Users` or `Groups` displays pages that allow you to add, delete, modify, and view different users or groups in the domain. Each user and group must be uniquely identifiable in a WebLogic Server domain. Because users and groups are identified only by their names and a WebLogic Server Principal can refer to either a group or user, every user and group must have a unique name.

In previous versions of WebLogic Server, there were a default set of users and groups that are no longer present in newer versions of the server. Three such built-in users and groups warrant further discussion: the `guest` and `system` users and the `everyone` group.

The `guest` user was used to represent any unauthenticated user; its default password was `guest`. By changing the `guest` user's password to something else, you could effectively disable anonymous access to the server. Unfortunately, there was a loophole that still allowed you to create a new JNDI `InitialContext` without supplying a username and password unless you had explicitly protected the JNDI tree with an access control list (ACL). This allowed effective anonymous access, even though the `guest` user was turned off.

Fortunately, the introduction of the new security service, which first appeared in WebLogic Server 7.0, fixed this problem. The `guest` user no longer exists, and any unauthenticated access to the server runs as user `<anonymous>`, which the authorization providers can check for. If you really need to use the `guest` user scheme, you can re-enable it by setting the `weblogic.security.anonymousUserName` Java system property to `guest` on the command line.

If you are familiar with older versions of WebLogic Server, you will remember the `everyone` group that was used in ACLs to allow access to any user in the domain. This built-in group no longer exists in the new security service and has been replaced by the `Anonymous` role.

Finally, older versions of WebLogic Server had the notion of the `system` user. This user was the administrator for the entire domain, but its username could not be changed from `system`. Starting in WebLogic Server 7.0, this administrative user has been redefined through the use of the `Admin` role, which by default is granted only to members of the `Administrators` group. As part of this change, administrative functions have been subdivided into several functional categories and assigned to global roles, which we'll discuss in the next section.

Before moving on, we should mention WebLogic Server's User Lockout feature. By default, a user has five attempts to enter the correct password before being locked out of the server. You can adjust the user lock-out characteristics using the `Security->Realms->myrealm` folder's `User Lockout` tab. Anyone with the `Admin` role can unlock the user prior to the time-out. To unlock a locked-out user, use the WebLogic Console to navigate to the appropriate server in the left-hand navigation bar and then choose the server's `Security Monitoring` tab. Enter the username in the `Unlock User` field, and press the `Apply` button.

Working with Roles and Policies

There are two types of roles, *global* roles and *scoped* roles. Scoped roles are specific to a particular application component like an EJB or Web application, an entire enterprise application, or a specific resource like a JDBC connection pool. As we discussed in the "Setting Up J2EE Application Security" section, J2EE deployment descriptor roles are scoped roles unless specified as externally defined. WebLogic Server uses these scoped roles only when making access control decisions about the target object that defines the role's scope. This is different from a *global* role, which applies to access control decisions anywhere in the server, regardless of the application or resource.

Using the WebLogic Console, we can define both global and scoped roles. Going back to the `Security->Realms->myrealm` folder where we previously looked at the `Users` and `Groups` folders, we can also see the default set of global roles, as well as the default groups used to map them. Because this data is associated with the default security providers, it is stored only in the embedded LDAP server. Table 10.4 explains the default roles and group mappings.

Table 10.4 Default Roles and Groups

DEFAULT GLOBAL ROLES	ACCESS POLICY	DEFAULT GROUPS
Admin	All access to the console. This means deploying applications, startup and shutdown classes, Web Services, and J2EE connectors. It can also modify server configuration and edit deployment descriptors.	Administrators

Table 10.4 *(continued)*

DEFAULT GLOBAL ROLES	ACCESS POLICY	DEFAULT GROUPS
Deployer	May deploy applications, startup and shutdown classes, Web Services, and J2EE connectors. It may view the server configuration.	Deployers
Operator	Start, stop, and resume servers. It may view the server configuration.	Operators
Monitor	View the server configuration.	Monitors
Anonymous	Similar to the old `everyone` group, this role implies all users, authenticated or not.	Everyone
No Matching Role	Any authenticated user.	Users

Each default administrative role has a mapping to a specific default group. If a user is a member of that group, they are in the matching role. As you can see, the default role names are all singular while the default group names are plural. This is done solely to make it easier to differentiate which names are roles and which names are groups.

BEST PRACTICE **Keeping role names singular and group names plural will help make security discussions involving roles and groups less confusing.**

Take a look at one of the default global role definitions. This can be found under the `Conditions` tab of a specific global role's page in the WebLogic Console. Currently, there are only three options for expressing the definition of a role: a username, a group name, or the time of day. You can modify the order of the qualifying expressions, but all must be true for a user to be considered in a role. You can easily define a new global role in the default security provider via this `Global Roles` page.

We can also use the WebLogic Console to create application- or resource-scoped roles by right-clicking on the application or resource in the left-hand navigation tree and selecting the `Define Role` menu option in the pop-up menu. Using this same pop-up menu, you can define access control policies for the applications and services. In addition to the EJB resources and Web application resources that we've discussed so far, you can define access control policies for many other types of resources in the server including administrative resources, which apply to control of the WebLogic Console, deployment of applications, and other actions. Some of the resources include jCOM resources, EIS resources, JMS resources, JDBC resources, JNDI resources, MBean resources, and Web Services resources, all of which control access to their specific server services.

Access control policy is hierarchical. For example, a policy set on all Web applications will apply to any specific Web applications. To make certain you always know the entire policy for a specific application, there is a section called `Inherited Policy Statement` on the Console's `Policy Definition` page. You can even define a scoped role and policy to a branch of the JNDI tree. Simply use the WebLogic Console to select a server and use either the pop-up menu or the link at the bottom of the server's configuration pages to select `View JNDI tree`. Table 10.5 shows the default security policy for the server.

Now that you know how to define both global and scoped roles and access control policies using both the WebLogic Console and J2EE deployment descriptors, you need to understand the persistence of this information. For deployment descriptors, it's easy to see that the persistence mechanism is the deployment descriptor itself. For the WebLogic Console, roles and policies are stored using the default security provider's store. If you are using a custom provider, you cannot use the WebLogic Console to manage roles and policies.

The new security framework can consume the role definitions in the deployment descriptors and merge them with the globally defined roles in the underlying Role Mapper security provider. There are a few options you can use to explicitly define that merging process. With the default server configuration, WebLogic Server reads the deployment descriptor role and policy information and integrates it into the default security provider's configuration. This makes the information immediately visible in the WebLogic Console. If at this point you use the WebLogic Console to modify the application's role or policy configuration in any way, the WebLogic Security Service will persist this modified information into the default security provider rather than into the deployment descriptors. Regardless of how you define the role, the server will always calculate the role membership at run time, so they are very dynamic.

If you are not careful, the complexity of the merging and storing of role and policy definitions can get you into trouble. We recommend that you come up with a simple plan that specifies where the role mapping and policy information will live and stick to it.

Table 10.5 Default Policy

WEBLOGIC RESOURCE	DEFAULT SECURITY POLICY
Administrative resources	Roles: Admin, Deployer, Operator, Monitor
Server resources	Roles: Admin, Operator
COM resources	Role: jCOMRole
EIS resources	Role: Anonymous
EJB resources	Role: Anonymous
JMS resources	Role: Anonymous
JDBC resources	Role: Anonymous
JNDI resources	Role: Anonymous
MBean resources	Role: Anonymous
Web Service resources	Role: Anonymous

BEST PRACTICE Define a simple set of guidelines for where you will define the roles and policies your application needs and then stick to them to reduce confusion resulting from the WebLogic Server's complex merging policies.

To summarize, you have four different ways to restrict access to Web applications and EJBs:

Use only the J2EE Deployment Descriptors. WebLogic Server reads the roles and policies information from the deployment descriptor at deployment time and uses it throughout the life of the application. Using this option, you define users and groups using the WebLogic Console but define the roles, policies, and the mapping of roles to principals using J2EE deployment descriptors. If you need to modify the access control information at run time, this is typically done by modifying the group membership to one or more groups that are mapped to the relevant roles in the deployment descriptors. In WebLogic Server 8.1, the default configuration checks roles and policies only for Web applications and EJBs that have these configured via deployment descriptors.

Use only the WebLogic Console. In this case, the server maintains all of the access control information based on the information you enter using the WebLogic Console. To prevent accidentally picking up any deployment descriptor information that might be present, you need to change the default setting on the realm. To do this for WebLogic Server 8.1, go to the `Security->Realms->myrealm` folder and set the `Check Roles and Policies for` attribute to `All Web applications and EJBs` and the `On Future Redeployments` attribute to `ignore roles and policies from DD` prior to deploying any applications.

Seed the roles and access control policies with values from the deployment descriptors and then use the WebLogic Console to modify it from that point forward. To set this up, you need to set the `Check Roles and Policies for` attribute to `All Web applications and EJBs` and the `On Future Redeployments` attribute to `initialize roles and policies from DD` before deploying the application and then reset `On Future Redeployments` to `ignore roles and policies from DD` *after* deploying the application. Unless you reset this switch before redeployment, the data will get reinitialized every time you redeploy the application. From this point on, you will use the WebLogic Console to modify roles or access policies.

Configure the policies in the deployment descriptors but configure the role-to-principal mapping in the console. With this fourth option, you use the `ejb-jar.xml` or `web.xml` to set up the access control policy for specific roles but use the `weblogic-ejb-jar.xml` or `weblogic.xml` to specify that the roles map to a global role using the `<externally-defined/>` element rather than a formal principal mapping. With this option, you do the role mappings *only* with the WebLogic Console.

While it is easy to define scoped roles and policies with the WebLogic Console, it is currently hard to manage such roles and policies. While the scoped roles are now visible through the console, there is currently no way for you to view the policies after initially defining them.

BEST PRACTICE Until WebLogic Server provides better management capabilities for these console-defined scoped roles and policies, use J2EE deployment descriptors for access control policies.

Be aware that in WebLogic Server 7.0 and 8.1, none of these console-defined roles or policies will ever be used unless you set the `weblogic.security.fullyDelegateAuthorization` Java system property to `true` on the Java command line.

WARNING In WebLogic Server 7.0 and 8.1, you must set the Java system property `weblogic.security.fullyDelegatedAuthorization` **to** `true` **on the command line in order to use WebLogic Console-defined roles or policies.**

Booting WebLogic Server

When you start a WebLogic Server, it needs a username and password for a user in the `Admin` role. Because this username and password will authenticate a user in the `Admin` role, it is vital to keep this information as secret as possible. There are several different ways to make the username and password available to the server for booting.

The first way, and the most simple way, is to specify nothing on the command line. This will cause the server to prompt for a username and password in the shell. This may be acceptable for development purposes, but it has an obvious drawback for production systems where you do not want to rely on human intervention to start the server. You can also provide the username and password through Java system properties specified either as command-line arguments, as shown here, or programmatically using a Java program that wraps the call to `weblogic.Server.main()`:

```
java -Dweblogic.management.username=bauersc
     -Dweblogic.management.password=password ... weblogic.Server
```

Of course, this is not an elegant solution for a production system either because the command-line arguments may be seen by users having access to the operating system—for example, by using the UNIX `ps` command to list the processes running on the machine.

The preferred way to provide the username and password is to use the `boot.properties` file, stored in the domain's root directory. This file contains the boot identity in an encrypted form. Both the username and password are encrypted with the Triple DES algorithm. If you set the `weblogic.system.StoreBootIdentity` Java system property to true, the server will use the supplied boot information to create the file for you. The easiest way to create the file, however, is simply to create a two-line text file that looks like the one shown here for a server using the `system` username with a password of `insecure`:

```
username=system
password=insecure
```

In WebLogic Server 8.1, the WebLogic Configuration Wizard will automatically create this file for you when creating a new domain that uses development mode. We will talk more about development mode in the next chapter.

After creating this file manually, simply start the server once and it will encrypt the values of the username and password. If you want to rename the file to something less obvious, you can use the `weblogic.system.BootIdentityFile` Java system property to specify the name of the `boot.properties` file. Finally, you can tell the server to delete the file after it uses it. You might use this in conjunction with a shell script that copies the file from a secure location to the local directory just prior to starting the server. Setting the `weblogic.system.RemoveBootIdentity` Java system property to `true` will tell the server to delete the file:

```
java -Dweblogic.system.RemoveBootIdentity=true ...
```

BEST PRACTICE **Use the `boot.properties` file mechanism to specify the server's boot identity on startup.**

Chapter Review

In this chapter, we covered a large amount of information related to the WebLogic Server security features. We started with an overview of the WebLogic Security Service. From there, we went on to discuss the WebLogic Security Framework and its built-in providers. We touched on how to use external authentication providers with WebLogic Server and followed that with a detailed discussion of how to configure SSL/TLS support. After that, we talked about how to write different types of Java application clients that use SSL. We finished the chapter off with a discussion of managing application security, starting with the use of J2EE deployment descriptors to define access policies, discussing the use of WebLogic Security access control policies, and finishing with a brief discussion about server boot identity security. In the next chapter, we will concentrate on WebLogic Server administration and management.

Administering and Deploying Applications in WebLogic Server

In this chapter, we will discuss the finer points of WebLogic Server administration. If you are unfamiliar with WebLogic Server administration, you should consult the WebLogic Server documentation at http://edocs.bea.com/wls/docs81/admin.html for more information. We begin by reviewing the key WebLogic Server architectural concepts. The purpose of this discussion is to give you a big-picture understanding of how the WebLogic Server product works. Next, we discuss WebLogic Server administration concepts. Finally, we end the chapter by discussing WebLogic Server configuration, management, and monitoring.

WebLogic Architecture Key Concepts

In this section, we will review some of the key concepts associated with the WebLogic Server deployment architecture. Before jumping into the details, we need to define a few terms that will be used throughout the rest of this chapter. In this chapter, the terms *server* and *instance* are used to describe a Java Virtual Machine process that is running the WebLogic Server software program. We will use the term *machine* to describe a computer with its own CPU, memory, and secondary storage that is running its own copy of the operating system software. Even though it is often possible to partition large computers into several logical, smaller computers, we will not make a distinction between multiple machines that, through logical partitioning, are part of the same chassis and those that are not. Now, we are ready to review the WebLogic Server deployment architecture.

Domain Architecture

A *WebLogic Server instance* is the process responsible for receiving incoming requests from the user, dispatching those requests to the appropriate J2EE application component(s), and returning responses to the user. This server instance provides the J2EE containers necessary to deploy any J2EE-based application and handles all of the resource management for the application. We will talk more about the internal architecture of the server in the next section.

A *WebLogic Server cluster* is a loosely coupled grouping of WebLogic Server instances that provide a cluster-wide naming service, load distribution, and some fault tolerance to hosted application(s). WebLogic Server dynamically determines the membership of the cluster using heartbeat messages that are periodically sent via IP multicast. Through these multicast messages, each cluster member maintains its own cluster membership list. In a similar fashion, every server in the cluster maintains a complete copy of the cluster-wide JNDI namespace. WebLogic Server uses a reliable IP multicast-based protocol to propagate all changes to the JNDI namespace on any particular server to the other cluster members. This loosely coupled clustering architecture allows each server to function independently of any other WebLogic Server process.

Using the ability to define a machine in your WebLogic Server domain, you can tell WebLogic Server which servers run on which machines. The in-memory replication feature of WebLogic Server clustering uses this knowledge to locate the secondary copy of a particular object so that the primary and secondary copies of an object reside on different machines, whenever possible. The administration server also relies on this machine configuration information to determine how to contact a particular WebLogic Server instance's node manager. We will talk more about clustering, in-memory replication, and the node manager later.

A *WebLogic Server domain* is an administrative grouping of servers and/or clusters. You configure, manage, and monitor the domain from a central location; this central location is the *administration* (or *admin*, for short) *server*. The admin server is just a WebLogic Server instance that runs some special administrative applications. Through these applications, the admin server maintains a repository of configuration information for the domain, acts as a centralized application deployment server, and provides a browser-based administrative console application that the administrator uses to configure, manage, and monitor all aspects of the domain. A *managed server* is the term for any other server in the domain other than the admin server. On startup, a managed server contacts the admin server to obtain its configuration information and applications to deploy. WebLogic Server optimizes this transfer of information to include only information that has changed since the managed server was shut down. Once the managed server is running, it no longer depends on the admin server to be able to process client requests. As you will see later in this chapter, the admin server introduces a centralized location for configuration, management, and monitoring but does not significantly compromise the benefits of the loosely coupled cluster architecture.

The *node manager* is an optional daemon process that runs on each machine where managed servers may be run. WebLogic Server 6.1 uses the node manager only to allow administrators to start servers on remote machines from the WebLogic Console. As we shall discuss later, the node manager's role now includes server monitoring and automatic restart capabilities.

Figure 11.1 shows how all the pieces fit together. In this example, we have the admin server for the `mydomain` domain running on machine `m1`. This admin server manages the configuration information for two different clusters, `abc` and `mycluster`, and one stand-alone server, `X`. Each machine has a node manager running on it; the configuration information would also specify which servers are running on each machine.

WebLogic Server Architecture

A high-level understanding of the server's internal architecture is important to understanding how to design, build, deploy, and debug applications that will run on WebLogic Server. While many things have changed since the early versions of Tengah (the name of the server before the BEA acquisition), the fundamental message processing architecture remains relatively unchanged. As shown in Figure 11.2, the core components of the server are the *listen threads*, the *socket muxer*, and the *execute queue* with its associated *execute threads*. When the server process starts up, it binds to one or more ports and assigns a thread to each port to listen for connection requests. Once the server accepts the connection request and establishes the connection, the server hands off control of the connection to the socket muxer, which waits for incoming requests. At a high level, the socket muxer detects an incoming request, reads the request off of the socket, and places the request along with any associated security or transaction context onto the appropriate execute queue (typically, the default execute queue). Once a request appears on the execute queue, an idle execute thread takes the request off of the queue, assumes the identity of the user who submitted the request, executes the request, returns the response to the caller, and goes back to wait for the next request.

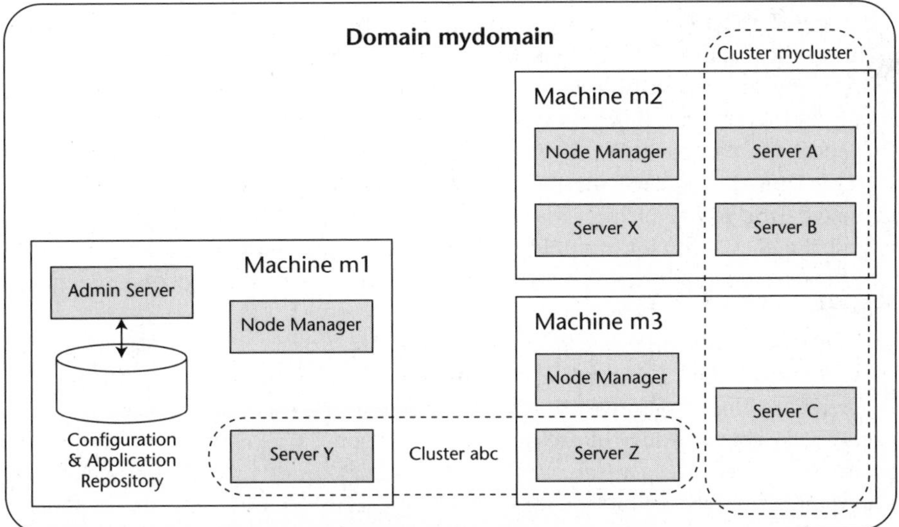

Figure 11.1 WebLogic Server domain architecture.

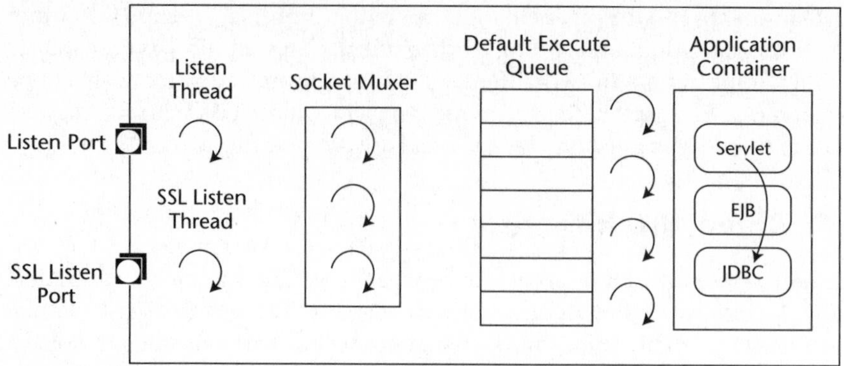

Figure 11.2 WebLogic Server internal architecture.

Execute Queues and Execute Threads

Once an execute thread invokes the target component of the request, that execute thread will, under most circumstances, process the entire request. Figure 11.2 depicts this fact by showing a single execute thread spanning the servlet, EJB, and JDBC components in the application container. The call to the servlet, its call to a method on an EJB, and the EJB's use of JDBC to query a database will all occur within the same execute thread. During the execution of a request, the execute thread will be unavailable to process any other requests until the request processing code completes successfully or throws an exception. This is an extremely important point to recognize.

If the application code blocks the execute thread for an extended period of time, the server will not be able to use that thread to process other requests coming into the execute queue. While WebLogic Server does some basic sanity checks during the execution of any request (for example, checking the transaction time-out before dispatching an EJB method invocation), it is generally not possible for the server to tell the execute thread to abort the processing of a request. If the application gets into a state where every execute thread is blocked for an extended period of time, the server will become nonresponsive (for requests targeted to that execute queue). Although the listen threads and the socket muxer are able to accept new requests from clients and place them into the execute queue, no execute threads will be available to process the request and return the response to the client.

When these long-running requests cause the execute threads to block, the incoming requests will start to back up in the execute queue. Even if the condition causing the execute threads to block goes away, it is very likely that the execute queue will end up with a relatively large number of messages. This not only will cause degradations in response time but also may cause users to cancel their requests (by pressing the stop button on their browsers) and to resubmit them. Typically, this will only make the situation worse because WebLogic Server currently processes every message on the execute queue in first-in-first-out order. In certain conditions (for example, reading HTTP POST data associated with a Web application request), WebLogic Server will detect that the client is no longer waiting on the response and will short-circuit the request processing. Other conditions, though, may cause WebLogic Server to process the request even if the client is no longer waiting for the response.

In WebLogic Server 7.0, BEA introduced the ability to grow the number of execute threads associated with an execute queue. Several configuration parameters control this growth. To view a server's execute queue configuration parameters using the WebLogic Console, right-click on the server in the left-hand navigation bar and select the `View Execute Queues` menu item. On the resulting screen, select the link for the execute queue of interest (such as `weblogic.kernel.Default`, which is the new name of the default queue) to display the execute queue's `Configuration` tab. Let's talk briefly about the meaning of some of these configuration parameters. For more information on how to optimize the execute queue configuration, please refer to Chapter 12.

BEST PRACTICE Always do proper capacity planning and server tuning to choose the optimal number of execute threads. Avoid using the server's ability to grow the number of execute threads to handle normal peaks in application load.

The `Queue Length` parameter controls the maximum number of requests that the execute queue can hold. If the execute queue fills up, WebLogic Server will reject any requests bound for that queue until space becomes available. Whenever the server rejects a request, it writes error messages to the log file indicating that the execute queue is full. The `Thread Count` determines the number of execute threads that the server creates at startup. If the number of requests on a queue reaches the `Queue Length Threshold Percent` of the `Queue Length`, the server will create additional execute threads equal to the number in the `Threads Increase` setting to try to alleviate the queue backup. If, at some point after this initial allocation of more execute threads, the queue length drops below the `Queue Length Threshold Percent` full and later reaches the threshold again, the server again tries to spawn more threads. The server will continue to operate in this fashion up until it reaches the maximum number of threads, as specified by the `Threads Maximum` parameter. If the queue length never drops below the threshold, the server will not allocate any more execute threads even if the current number of threads is less than the `Threads Maximum` limit. Currently, WebLogic Server never tries to shrink the number of threads in the execute queue.

BEST PRACTICE Do not allow the execute queue to get so long that the response time for new requests would be longer than most clients are willing to wait. Spawning new threads to try to catch up when most requests coming into the execute queue will never have their responses returned to the client will help only if you have enough excess CPU capacity to take advantage of the extra threads.

WebLogic Server checks for stuck threads. Stuck threads are threads that have been processing a particular request for more than the `Stuck Thread Max Time`. The server checks for stuck threads periodically; the `Stuck Thread Timer Interval` parameter controls the frequency of this check. If the server determines that all of the execute threads for a particular queue are stuck, it will allocate more threads (according to the `Threads Increase` parameter), log an emergency message that this has happened, and set the health state of the server to a critical level (we will talk more about server health checks and states later). In a similar fashion to the queue length threshold percent protection mechanism, the server will continue to increase the number of threads if the problem continues to propagate to the newly created threads until it reaches the `Threads Maximum` limit.

In WebLogic Server 7.0, these parameters are tunable through the server's `Tuning Configuration` tab. At the time of writing, these parameters are not surfaced in the WebLogic Server 8.1 Console. We expect that this may change by the time you read this so please consult the WebLogic Server documentation at http://edocs.bea.com/wls/docs81/perform/WLSTuning.html for more information.

BEST PRACTICE **Do not set the** `Stuck Thread Max Time` **and** `Stuck Thread Time Interval` **too low so that normal requests during peak processing times will be mistaken for stuck threads. Be sure, though, to set them low enough to allow the server to take corrective action before it is too late. For many applications, values on the order of 60 to 120 seconds will be sufficient.**

WebLogic Server provides the ability to create user-defined execute queues. Through this mechanism, you can limit the resources a server is using to process different types of requests. Because each execute queue has its own configurable pool of execute threads, you can limit the number of threads concurrently processing requests associated with the particular execute queue. At the same time, you can also guarantee that a certain number of threads will always be available to process the requests for a given execute queue. To some extent, this allows certain types of requests to have priority by keeping those requests from going to the default execute queue and waiting behind every other request for processing.

The ability to define new execute queues also helps to eliminate certain deadlock situations. For example, if all of the execute threads in one server are blocked waiting on responses from another server while the other server's execute threads are all blocked waiting on responses from the first server, a cross-server deadlock situation can occur. Configuring a separate execute queue for these server-to-server requests prevents the deadlock. We will discuss this in detail in the *WebLogic Server Clustering Architecture* section.

BEST PRACTICE **Create user-defined execute queues to partition application components and provide a dedicated amount of resources to a particular component or to eliminate potential cross-server deadlock situations.**

Defining a new execute queue is easy. Use the `View Execute Queues` menu item on the server's pop-up menu and select the link entitled `Configure a new Execute Queue`.

Once you have created the new execute queue, you need to configure the dispatch policy for your application's J2EE components to map them to the new queue. It is important to understand that the selection of an execute queue happens in the socket muxer. This means that once an execute thread begins executing a request, a call to another component will always take place on the same execute thread, regardless of the target component's dispatch policy.

To configure a servlet or JSP to use a user-defined execute queue, use the `wl-dispatch-policy` initialization parameter to specify the name of the execute queue in the Web application's `web.xml` deployment descriptor:

```
<servlet>
  <servlet-name>HighPriorityServlet</servlet-name>
  <jsp-file>high_priority.jsp</jsp-file>
  <init-param>
    <param-name>wl-dispatch-policy</param-name>
    <param-value>MyPriorityQueue</param-value>
  </init-param>
</servlet>
```

To map the entire Web application to a user-defined execute queue, use the `wl-dispatch-policy` element in the `weblogic.xml` deployment descriptor:

```
<weblogic-web-app>
  ...
  <wl-dispatch-policy>MyPriorityQueue</wl-dispatch-policy>
  ...
</weblogic-web-app>
```

To map an EJB to a user-defined execute queue, use the `dispatch-policy` element in the `weblogic-ejb-jar.xml` file:

```
<weblogic-enterprise-bean>
  <ejb-name>HighPrioritySessionEJB<ejb-name>
  ...
  <dispatch-policy>MyPriorityQueue</dispatch-policy>
</weblogic-enterprise-bean>
```

In addition to partitioning requests using separate execute queues, you can augment these prioritization capabilities by setting the priorities of an execute queue's threads. By reducing the thread priority for a particular execute queue, you can give a lower priority to this queue's requests and help ensure that requests bound for other queues get preferential treatment by the JVM/OS thread scheduler. Conversely, increasing the thread priority can help ensure that the server will process an execute queue's requests before requests in other queues with lower thread priorities. This is useful for processing time-critical requests. You must be careful, however, when adjusting thread priorities. Lowering an execute queue's thread priority below the default value of 5 may affect the server's ability to keep up with requests coming into this queue and could ultimately cause the queue to overflow. Raising the thread priority too high not only can prevent the server from being able to keep up with requests being targeted to other execute queues but also can impact the ability of the server to manage its resources effectively and respond to administrative control. Another point to keep in mind is that if a lower-priority thread yields to a higher priority thread while holding a shared (and exclusive) resource, the high-priority thread will end up waiting for the lower-priority thread to release the resource. This condition, known as *priority inversion*, can cause thread priority settings to be ineffective. Careful consideration, capacity planning, and rigorous load testing should always accompany any plans to change execute thread priorities.

We strongly discourage changing the priorities of any of WebLogic Server's built-in execute queues, including the default execute queue. Typically, it is best to avoid using priorities unless load testing of the application demonstrates the need to do so. Even then, we recommend adjusting thread priorities only for execute queues that expect a small volume of messages, and only adjusting the priority of a single queue either up or down (or in the worse case, one of each). Adjust the thread priority up or down by only one or two. Never use a value of 9 or 10 because WebLogic Server uses these levels to keep high-priority tasks running behind the scenes.

WARNING Think twice before changing the thread priority of execute threads for any execute queue because this can affect the server's ability to process requests in a timely manner. Priority inversion can occur if components running in threads with different priorities depend on exclusive access to a shared resource. Always load test the application for an extended period of time after making any thread priority adjustments to make sure that the server's ability to process requests has not been compromised.

Socket Muxer

The socket muxer manages the server's existing socket connections. The first thing it does is determine which sockets have incoming requests waiting to be processed. Then, it reads just enough of the data to determine the protocol, packages the socket up into a protocol-specific data structure, and dispatches the socket to the appropriate run-time layer. In this run-time layer, the socket muxer thread reads the entire request off the socket, sets up any required context information, determines which execute queue to use, and places the request onto the execute queue.

WebLogic Server has two versions of the socket muxer, an all-Java version that currently has to poll each socket to determine whether a request is waiting and a version that uses a small native library leveraging the more efficient operating system call to make that determination. The `Enable Native IO` checkbox on the server's `Tuning Configuration` tab tells the server which version to use; this is on by default on most platforms. It is important to remember that in order to use native I/O, you must make sure that the native library is in the server's shared library path. The default scripts that come with the server set this up for you. If the server fails to load the native library, it will throw a `java.lang.UnsatisfiedLinkException` and then load the all-Java version, so you need to pay close attention to the server output and log file to make sure that you are, in fact, using the native version.

With a small number of concurrent connections, the all-Java version tends to be faster; this is probably due to the huge overhead associated with making JNI method calls compared to making Java method calls. As the number of concurrent socket connections grows, however, the native I/O muxer quickly becomes more efficient. We recommend using the native I/O muxer in most production environments if it is available on the target platform.

BEST PRACTICE Always enable native I/O, if available, and check for errors at startup to make sure it is being initialized properly.

WebLogic Server 8.1 also has a new socket muxer based on the non-blocking I/O (NIO) capabilities of the Java 2 SDK 1.4. This new muxer will eventually replace the native muxer because the operating system calls used by the native muxer are now being surfaced in Java. At the time of writing, the new NIO muxer is not officially supported by BEA and does not support SSL. We expect both of these to change, so check the WebLogic Server documentation for more information. To enable the NIO muxer, set the Java system property `weblogic.MuxerClass` to `weblogic.socket.NIOSocketMuxer` on the Java command line. One advantage of the NIO muxer is that it also works on the WebLogic Server client run time, unlike the native I/O muxer. Remember, however, never to use an unsupported feature in a production environment.

The Java socket muxer steals threads from the default execute queue's thread pool. The `Socket Readers` parameter controls the maximum number of threads the Java socket muxer can steal as a percentage of the total number in the queue. By default, the `Socket Readers` parameter is set to 33, meaning that the Socket Muxer can take up to 33 percent of the total number of execute threads from the default execute queue. For example, if the default execute queue has 15 threads, we may have only 10 threads processing requests and 5 threads reading incoming requests off the sockets. The `Socket Readers` parameter is also configurable using the server's `Tuning Configuration` tab.

In previous versions of WebLogic Server, the native I/O version of the socket muxer used a fixed number of threads from the default execute queue's thread pool. On Windows, it used two times the number of CPUs; on Unix platforms, it always used three threads. Starting in WebLogic Server 8.1, the native I/O and NIO muxers use their own execute thread pool (associated with the `weblogic.socket.Muxer` queue) and now use $n + 1$ threads by default, where n is the number of CPUs.

It is possible to increase the number of socket muxer threads. For the all-Java version, increase the `Socket Readers` parameter or increase the number of execute threads associated with the default execute queue. WebLogic Server uses Java system properties to control the number of threads used by the native I/O version. WebLogic Server 8.1 uses the `weblogic.SocketReaders` Java system property to control the number of socket reader threads for both the native I/O and NIO muxers. Previous versions of the server used the `weblogic.NTSocketReaders` and `weblogic.PosixSocketReaders` Java system properties to control the number of socket reader threads stolen from the default execute queue on Windows and Unix, respectively. In our experience, the only reason we have ever changed the number of socket reader threads was to allow Java application clients to be more responsive when talking to a large cluster of servers, and even then, the change was made only on the Java application client and not on the server. Recent changes in the client run time have made even this unnecessary.

Listen Ports and Listen Threads

By default, WebLogic Server starts up listening on two ports. The plain-text listen port accepts connections for HTTP, T3, IIOP, COM, and LDAP protocols. The SSL listen port accepts connections for HTTPS, T3S, and IIOPS protocols. Each port has a listen thread associated with it. This thread simply waits for connection requests, accepts the connection, hands the connection off to the socket muxer, and goes back to listen for the next connection request.

WebLogic Server also has the concept of an *administration* (*admin*, for short) *port*, allowing administration requests to the server to be directed to a separate port and associated listen thread. When using the admin port, WebLogic Server will reject all administrative requests that arrive at any listen port other than the admin port. Use of the admin port also requires all administrative requests to use SSL.

In addition to the default network configuration (also known as the default *channel*) described already, WebLogic Server gives the administrator more flexibility and control over the server's network configuration. While the server still requires at least one enabled port on this default channel, it gives us the ability to turn off the default channel's plain-text listen port, something that was impossible in previous versions. We will talk more about these more advanced network configuration capabilities in the *Network Channels* section.

Application Container

The *application container* is simply the mechanism in which the server deploys applications. WebLogic Server requires that all application components be packaged as some type of J2EE application component. This packaging has multiple benefits that we discuss in other portions of this book, but the main implication that affects administration is the ability to perform what is known as *hot deployment*. Using hot deployment, we can deploy, redeploy, or undeploy an application while the server is running without affecting other applications or requiring a server restart.

To support unloading an application and achieving hot deployment, WebLogic Server relies on Java's ability to define custom classloaders. The reason for using custom classloaders is simple: Java does not provide any mechanism to unload or reload classes loaded by its default classloader, known in the WebLogic Server documentation as the *system classloader* (the one that uses the `CLASSPATH` environment variable for its search path). The system classloader simply loads the class from disk the first time it encounters a need for that class and then never looks at the class file on disk again. This means that once the system classloader loads a class, it will never pick up any changes to that class. Restarting the JVM is the only way to reload a class with the system classloader. Fortunately, Java does provide the ability to define and use custom classloaders. WebLogic Server deploys J2EE applications using custom classloaders so that you can unload or reload an application without restarting the server. See the discussion in

Chapter 8 or the WebLogic Server documentation at http://edocs.bea.com/wls/docs81/programming/classloading.html for more information.

In this section, we have discussed the primary architectural features of WebLogic Server. A thorough understanding of these features will go a long way toward helping application architects, developers, and administrators make good decisions about application design, development, debugging, configuration, management, and monitoring. Many problems with WebLogic Server applications can be explained in terms of the concepts discussed in this section, so always keep these concepts in mind when looking for the root cause of a problem. We'll now take an in-depth look at the WebLogic Server clustering architecture.

WebLogic Server Clustering Architecture

WebLogic Server clustering provides load balancing and failover capabilities to J2EE-based applications. Through its clustering mechanisms, WebLogic Server loosely couples together a set of server processes, distributed across one or more machines, so that they can share the responsibilities of processing requests for the applications deployed to the cluster. Exactly what facilities WebLogic Server clustering provides to an application depends on whether the application is Web-based or RMI-based. Before we get into the details of the application-level facilities provided, let's look under the hood to see how WebLogic Server clustering works.

As previously mentioned, WebLogic Server clustering provides a loose coupling of the servers in the cluster. Each server in the cluster is independent and does not rely on any other server for any fundamental operations. Even if contact with every other server is lost, each server will continue to run and be able to process the requests it receives. Each server in the cluster maintains its own list of other servers in the cluster through periodic heartbeat messages. Every 10 seconds, each server sends a heartbeat message to the other servers in the cluster to let them know it is still alive. Heartbeat messages are sent using IP multicast technology built into the JVM, making this mechanism efficient and scalable as the number of servers in the cluster gets large. Each server receives these heartbeat messages from other servers and uses them to maintain its current cluster membership list. If a server misses receiving three heartbeat messages in a row from any other server, it takes that server out of its membership list until it receives another heartbeat message from that server. This heartbeat technology allows servers to be dynamically added and dropped from the cluster with no impact on the existing servers' configurations.

WebLogic Server also provides a cluster-wide JNDI namespace. Again, each server maintains its own view of the cluster-wide JNDI namespace, and any changes to the cluster-wide JNDI namespace on one server are propagated to the other servers via a reliable IP multicast-based protocol. This allows applications to have a global view of the cluster-wide JNDI namespace from any server in the cluster. Recognize that this JNDI replication is designed for service advertisement across the cluster, and not for replicating or sharing non-RMI-based objects across the cluster. Any object bound into the cluster-wide JNDI tree is always associated with the server that did the binding. If that server goes down, all JNDI references to the object will be removed from every server in the cluster. Of course, this is what you want for RMI-based references, but probably not what you would expect or want for cluster-wide sharing of objects.

Clustering for Web Applications

For Web applications, WebLogic Server clustering provides persistence mechanisms for `HttpSession` objects. Through these persistence mechanisms, Web applications that make use of `HttpSession` objects to store temporary state information can transparently fail over when a server in the cluster fails. Configuring the persistence mechanisms involves making changes to the Web application's `weblogic.xml` deployment descriptor.

The most popular form of session persistence is in-memory replication. WebLogic Server uses a primary-secondary replication scheme in this form of persistence. The primary copy of the `HttpSession` object will be created by whichever server happens to be processing the user's first request requiring access to the `HttpSession`. At the end of that request, and before the response is returned to the user, the server will create a secondary copy of the `HttpSession` on another server in the cluster, encode the location of the primary and secondary copies of the `HttpSession` in the session ID, and add a cookie that contains the session ID to the response (the server can use URL rewriting if cookies are disabled). Typically, the primary server for a particular session will receive all future requests for that session. If the primary server fails, the first request following the failure will be routed to another server in the cluster. When the server receives a request for which it is not the primary, it will become the new primary server and make sure that another server in the cluster is holding the secondary.

Three burning questions may occur to you at this point:

- How is the routing accomplished?
- How does WebLogic Server determine where to place the secondary copy of a session?
- How does WebLogic Server detect changes to the primary copy and transmit them to the secondary?

Session-Based Routing

WebLogic supports two different mechanisms for accomplishing the routing of HTTP requests. The first routing mechanism uses a Web server plug-in to proxy requests from a Web server to the WebLogic Server cluster. While Chapter 14 discusses deployment models in more detail, Figure 11.3 shows a common deployment model for this architecture. Web server plug-ins are available for Netscape/iPlanet, Microsoft IIS, and Apache Web servers and for WebLogic Server itself.

When the plug-in receives a request from the Web server, the plug-in looks for a session ID associated with the request. If a request does not contain a session ID, the plug-in uses a round-robin load-balancing algorithm to determine the server to which the request should be sent. When a request does contain a session ID, the plug-in uses information encoded in the session ID to determine the location of both the primary and secondary copies of the particular session. Whenever possible, the plug-in will route the request to the server that contains the primary copy of the session. If the server holding the primary copy is down, the plug-in tries to send the request to the server holding the secondary copy. When the server with the secondary copy receives the request, it will promote the secondary copy to the primary copy, create a new secondary copy, create a new session ID, and return the new session ID along with the response.

If both the primary and secondary servers are down (or have been restarted), the plug-in will treat the request as if it did not contain a session ID and route it to any server in the cluster that is available. This is an inherent feature of the in-memory replication model and is not a shortcoming of the plug-in. WebLogic Server replicates only session data as the result of a request for that session. Given that WebLogic Server does not attempt to keep cluster-wide session-to-server mapping information (presumably for performance and scalability reasons), the only way to locate a session is by the information contained in the session ID that is passed back to the browser.

The plug-in also supports transparent retry logic so that if it fails to deliver a request successfully to a WebLogic Server instance, it can resend the request to a different server in the cluster. If the plug-in determines that the server never received the request, it will always try to resend the request to another server in the cluster. In cases where the plug-in successfully sent the request to the server, but never received a response, you can configure the plug-in either to retry the request (the default) or to return an error to the caller. The two plug-in configuration parameters that control this behavior are `Idempotent` and `HungServerRecoverSecs`.

If the `Idempotent` parameter is set to `true` (which is the default value), the plug-in will retry any request for which it does not receive a response within the `HungServerRecoverSecs` time-out interval. The default time-out value is 300 seconds; the accepted range of values is 10 to 600 seconds. When using the `Idempotent` feature, applications must be able to handle duplicate requests properly because the server may have already processed the message (or may process the message later if the server's execute queue is backed up). For applications that are unable to handle duplicate requests, set the `Idempotent` parameter to `false`. For the Netscape/iPlanet and Apache Web servers, these parameters can be set differently for different URLs and MIME types.

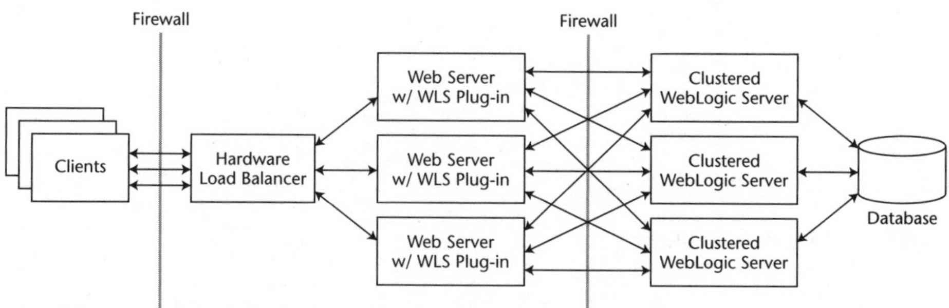

Figure 11.3 Web server proxy-based deployment model.

The second routing mechanism uses a hardware load balancer that routes directly to the cluster. Figure 11.4 shows a common deployment model for this architecture. Because the hardware load balancers generally do not understand the contents of the WebLogic Server session ID, WebLogic Server had to introduce a mechanism by which requests not directed to the server holding the primary copy of the session can be promoted to the primary. When a server receives a request with a session ID for which it does not hold the primary copy of the session, it will look at the location information in the session ID to determine the location of the session copies. If both the primary and secondary servers still exist, the server will call out to the primary server to tell it to send back a copy of the session and to give up its rights as the primary for this session. If only the secondary exists, the server will call out to the secondary server to tell it to send back a copy of the session, and it will then become the new primary for this session. While this mechanism is general enough to work with all hardware load-balancing schemes, the overhead of copying the session between servers will dramatically compromise both the performance and the scalability of the cluster. Fortunately, most hardware load balancers on the market today support one or more sticky load-balancing algorithms.

Using a sticky load-balancing algorithm, the load balancer remembers where it sent the last request for the particular user's session and always tries to route all subsequent requests from that session to the same server. The only time the load balancer will route the request to a different server is in the event of a failure of the primary server. When this happens, the load balancer will remember the new location and route all subsequent requests there until another failure happens. Clearly this mechanism is highly desirable because it will prevent moving the session between servers except when the primary server fails. In fact, this proxy-less deployment model using a hardware load balancer and a good sticky load-balancing algorithm has several advantages over the Web server proxy-based model. We will discuss this deployment model and its advantages and disadvantages in more detail in Chapter 14.

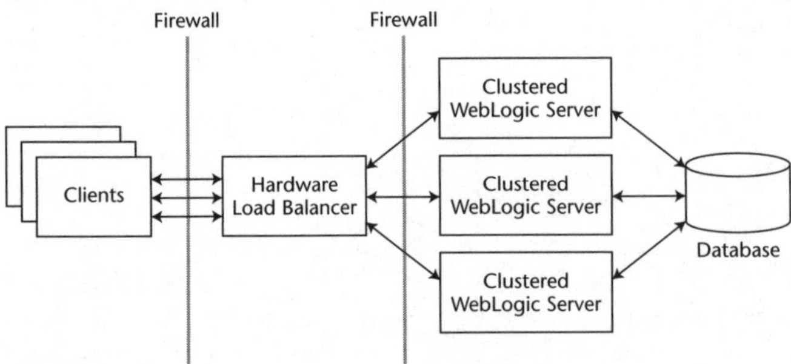

Figure 11.4 Proxy-less deployment model.

Secondary Selection

WebLogic Server uses two mechanisms to help select the secondary server for in-memory replication: machine definition and replication group definition. If we choose not to use either of these mechanisms, WebLogic Server uses a simple ring algorithm to select the secondary server (for example, server 1 has primaries that are replicated to server 2, server 2 has primaries that are replicated to server 3, and server 3 has primaries that are replicated to server 1). This works fine as long as all server instances are running on separate hardware and there are no special circumstances that require more deterministic selection.

By defining machines and assigning server instances to machines, you can tell WebLogic Server which server instances live on which machines. If the machine information is available, the secondary selection algorithm will use this information to ensure that the primary and secondary copies are on two different machines, if possible. In addition, you can use replication groups to gain even more control over the secondary selection process. By grouping servers into replication groups, you can tell WebLogic Server that a particular replication group should use another replication group as its preferred secondary replication group. If replication groups are in use, the secondary selection algorithm changes to the following sequence:

1. Is there a server in the preferred secondary replication group that is located on another machine?
2. Is there a server in the preferred secondary replication group that is located on the same machine?
3. Is there a server in any other replication group that is located on another machine?
4. Is there a server in any other replication group that is located on the same machine?

While specifying machines and replication groups is completely optional, we recommend specifying the machine information in all environments given the fact that some of the node manager configuration information is set at the machine level. Replication groups, on the other hand, are something that you should use only if you have a specific purpose in mind because, by default, WebLogic Server will make every effort to replicate objects across machines even without the use of replication groups.

BEST PRACTICE Always specify the machine information for servers in a cluster when using in-memory replication. Define replication groups only if you need more control over the secondary selection process.

Change Detection and Propagation

The server detects changes to the `HttpSession` objects by trapping all calls to the methods used to modify the objects bound into the session. WebLogic Server simply sets hooks in the `setAttribute()` and `removeAttribute()` methods to detect attribute modification during the course of processing a request. At the end of the request processing, but before returning the response to the user, the server will synchronously update the secondary copy of the session (or the persistence store) by propagating only the changes. This implementation has a couple of implications.

First, objects that already exist in the session from a previous request will need to be rebound into the session if we make changes to them during the current request processing. This is somewhat unnatural to most Java programmers. When writing a servlet or JSP to access a previously created object stored in the session, the `HttpSession.getAttribute()` method returns a reference to the existing object. Because the session obviously already has a reference to the object, it seems like an unnecessary step to reset the attribute with the same object's reference, but it is critical because this is how WebLogic Server identifies the modified attributes. We feel that the trade-off of having to invoke `setAttribute()` explicitly every time you modify an existing object is better than the alternative. Without the signal provided by `setAttribute()`, the server would incur more overhead during session persistence, perhaps by copying the entire object every time or using before and after images to determine what, if anything, has changed in the session.

WARNING **WebLogic Server will persist the changes to the** `HttpSession` **object only when using session persistence. The server detects changes to the** `HttpSession` **objects by trapping calls to the** `setAttribute()` **and** `removeAttribute()` **methods. This means that any objects previously bound into the session before the beginning of the current request must be rebound into the session by calling** `setAttribute()` **if they are modified. Failure to do so will result in changes not being persisted.**

Second, the server propagates changes to objects bound into `HttpSession` at the `HttpSession` attribute level. This means that the server propagates any change to an attribute by serializing the entire object associated with the attribute and sending it to the secondary server (or the persistent store), regardless of the magnitude of the change to the object (or even if there is no change at all) whenever you call the `setAttribute()` method for that object. This means that the size and granularity of the objects bound into the `HttpSession` will directly affect performance and scalability. We will revisit this discussion in Chapter 12.

Clustering for RMI-Based Applications

In RMI-based applications (which include EJB applications), the client uses a stub to invoke a method on the remote, server-side object. In standard,non-clustered RMI, this stub contains a single reference to the server process where the server-side object resides. WebLogic Server clustering introduces the concept of a *replica-aware stub* (also referred to as a *cluster-aware stub*)—a stub that contains references to all servers in the cluster that have a replica of the particular object. The stub load-balances method invocations on the stub by distributing the requests across servers in the cluster based on the load-balancing algorithm in use. By default, WebLogic Server uses a round-robin algorithm, but it also supports a couple of other load-balancing algorithms as well as an extensible mechanism, known as *call router* objects, whereby programmers can supply their own load-balancing logic. Unfortunately, the current interface for this extensible load-balancing mechanism does not provide access to the dynamic cluster list contained in the stub. This makes the mechanism of limited value because without this, there is no dynamic way for the call router object to know which servers are in the cluster and supporting replicas of the target object—at least, not without having the call router make calls to the Java Management Extensions (JMX) APIs in the server to determine this information.

BEST PRACTICE **Use one of the built-in load-balancing algorithms rather than trying to use call routers due to their limitation of not having access to the dynamic cluster list maintained by the stubs.**

It is important to note that the load-balancing state is per stub instance. What this means is that each time the caller gets a new stub (for example, via a JNDI lookup, calling a `Home` interface method on an EJB home object, etc.), the first invocation on the stub will randomly pick a server in the list to use to process the first request. All subsequent requests on that same stub will apply the chosen load-balancing algorithm. For example, if the stub's replica list has servers `s1`, `s2`, and `s3` in it and you are using the default load-balancing algorithm, if the first request is sent to `s2`, the next requests will go to `s3`, `s1`, `s2`, and so on. If, however, the client gets a new stub for every request, the load distribution will be somewhat random based on the fact that each stub instance selects a random starting point in the list to begin applying its algorithm. Keep this point in mind when trying any tests of WebLogic Server clustering to observe the load-balancing behavior.

If a server fails, the stub provides retry logic under certain conditions. Much like the previous discussion concerning the proxy plug-in, the stub will always retry requests that it knows never reached the server. The stub, though, will not try to resend failed requests that may have reached the server unless specifically told to do so. One important thing to remember is that if the stub and the target are collocated, no load balancing will be done because it is almost always more efficient to invoke the local replica of the object than it is to call out to another replica on another server.

RMI programmers have a great deal of control and flexibility when configuring the replica-aware stub behavior. For example, the `-methodsAreIdempotent` switch to WebLogic's RMI compiler (`weblogic.rmic`) allows the programmer to tell the stub that the object's methods have been written in such a way that it is safe to retry failed requests whose state is unknown. While this particular option is also surfaced in the deployment descriptor for stateless session beans, the RMI compiler has other options available. Fortunately, most of the important options are available to EJB programmers, and in many cases, the WebLogic Server default settings are often good enough for configuring EJB clustering. Because most J2EE developers are using the EJB programming model instead of the lower-level RMI programming model, we will spend the rest of our time talking specifically about EJB clustering.

WebLogic Server provides a very robust clustering model for EJBs. By default, all EJB home objects, stateless session beans, and entity beans use cluster-aware stubs when they are running in a clustered environment. This means that even if your programmers are not developing in a clustered environment, their deployed beans will generally become cluster-aware once they are put into a cluster. Stateful session beans can also use in-memory replication, much like that previously described for `HttpSession` objects. The load-balancing and failover behavior of the stubs varies depending on the types of objects in question.

All EJB home objects and stateless session beans use load-balancing stubs by default. Whether the stubs should be cluster-aware and what load-balancing algorithm they should use are configurable on a per-bean basis in the `weblogic-ejb-jar.xml` deployment descriptor. EJB home stubs for stateless session beans are always set to use idempotent behavior; all other types of EJB home stubs are not. By default, stateless session beans are not set to be idempotent, but they can be configured to use idempotent behavior by setting a flag in the deployment descriptor. All EJB methods (home and remote interface methods) can be configured to be idempotent using the `idempotent-methods` element in the `weblogic-ejb-jar.xml` deployment descriptor:

```
<weblogic-ejb-jar>
  ...
  <idempotent-methods>
    <method>
      <ejb-name>TellerEJB</ejb-name>
      <method-intf>Remote</method-intf>
      <method-name>checkBalance</method-name>
      <method-params>
        <method-param>java.lang.String</method-param>
      </method-params>
    </method>
  </idempotent-methods>
  ...
</weblogic-ejb-jar>
```

By default, stateful session bean instances exist only on the server on which they were created. They can be configured to use in-memory replication, just like the `HttpSession` object, using the `weblogic-ejb-jar.xml` deployment descriptor, a topic discussed in Chapter 6. If a stateful session bean is using replication, the stub will be aware of both the primary and secondary copy of the bean but will always route the calls to the primary copy of the bean except in the case of failure. Unlike `HttpSession` replication, stateful session beans do not require (or support) a routing layer because the stub handles all the routing. Therefore, stateful session bean replication does not use the machinery that redirects a misdirected request in the case of the `HttpSession` object requests. The change detection mechanism for stateful session beans uses a serialized before and after image to determine the changes that need to be sent to the secondary at the end of the transaction (or method call for non-transactional invocations) because there are no methods by which the server can detect changes to the bean's internal state.

By default, entity beans use stubs that are cluster-aware; however, entity bean stubs use a sticky routing algorithm to route requests to the cluster. The primary reasons for doing this are to improve the caching capabilities of the server and to reduce transaction propagation across servers in the cluster to improve performance.

In this section, we discussed the details of the WebLogic clustering architecture and the application facilities it provides. A thorough understanding of the architecture will help application programmers make good decisions on application design to maximize the benefits of clustering. Administrators should also understand the architecture and its implications when determining production deployment configurations. The next section talks about the admin server and its critical role for the application administrator.

Admin Server

WebLogic Server uses the admin server to configure, manage, and monitor the servers in a domain. The admin server is simply a WebLogic Server with two internally deployed applications that provide administrative capabilities for the entire domain (`wl_management_internal2.war` and `console.war`). All servers internally deploy an administrative application (`wl_management_internal1.war`) that allows the admin server to send administrative information to them.

The admin server maintains an XML repository of configuration information in the `config.xml` file. This file contains information about every server, every cluster, every application, and every service deployed in the domain. Although you can edit the `config.xml` file by hand, we strongly recommend that you use the WebLogic Console to change configuration information.

The typical application deployment model also uses the admin server as the application repository. Under this model, you only need to place the J2EE application package(s) physically on the admin server. You can use the WebLogic Server administration tools to deploy the applications to any server or cluster in the domain. At startup, the managed servers contact the admin server to determine their configuration and download any changes that may exist. In addition, you can deploy applications to a managed server that is already running because the admin server will push the applications out to the managed server and deploy it into the server.

One word of caution: the admin server has a feature known as *auto-deployment* that is enabled by default. With this feature, the server watches the `applications` directory for changes and automatically deploys new or changed applications that it finds there. As discussed in Chapter 5, this feature is useful during development, when the developers are using a single server as both the admin server and the application deployment server. There are several issues with this feature that make it undesirable for any environment other than a single-server development environment, however. Before discussing the issues with auto-deployment mode, recognize that disabling auto-deployment mode does not disable hot deployment or redeployment of applications. It only forces the administrator to tell the server when to hot deploy the application via one of the WebLogic Server administration tools (for example, the WebLogic Console).

The first issue with auto-deployment mode is that the admin server will try to deploy a new application only to the admin server. Although this is okay for development on a single server, it is almost never the desired behavior in multi-server environments. The second issue is that, in certain cases (probably due to bugs), auto-deployment will cause the admin server to become confused about which applications are new and which already exist. This can cause the admin server to attempt to deploy an existing application a second time as if it were new. This leads to several potential problems, the least of which is having multiple copies of the same application running. More typically, this prevents the second copy of the application from deploying and can corrupt the first copy so that the server boots up without any copies of the application running. During this process, the admin server is saving what it believes to be the new application's configuration information to the `config.xml` file. This will very likely cause the `config.xml` file to have multiple entries for the same application. To recover from this state, you will need to use the WebLogic Console to remove unwanted copies of the application or edit the `config.xml` file by hand. If you choose to edit the `config.xml` file by hand, make sure that the admin server is not running before you try to edit the file.

Fortunately, it is very easy to disable auto-deployment by setting the `weblogic.ProductionModeEnabled` system property to true. The server startup scripts created by the WebLogic Configuration Wizard (to be discussed later in this chapter) have an environment variable called `PRODUCTION_MODE` that controls this feature; set it to `true` to disable auto-deployment mode.

BEST PRACTICE Disable auto-deployment mode for any multiserver environment. Applications can still be hot deployed using the WebLogic administration tools such as the WebLogic Console even with auto-deployment mode disabled.

In case of an admin server crash, the admin server retains information about all of the running managed servers in the `running-managed-servers.xml` file. By default, the admin server will read this file and try to contact any managed servers that were previously running. Setting the `weblogic.management.discover` system property to `false` in the startup script will disable this feature; however, there is usually no reason to disable this feature.

BEST PRACTICE Always use the default discovery mode so that the admin server will reconnect with any managed servers already running.

WebLogic Server now uses a two-phase deployment model. In phase 1, the admin server stages the application by distributing the new application code to each of the target servers and having each server prepare the application for deployment. Once all target servers complete phase 1, the admin server tells each target server to activate the application in phase 2. If any failures occur, the admin server rolls back the activation of the application, giving you the chance to fix the problem without leaving the application running on some servers but not on others.

As described previously, managed servers typically contact the admin server when they boot to gather their configuration and application information. If the admin server is unavailable, the managed servers will not start. *Managed server independence* (MSI) allows a managed server to start up using a cached copy of the configuration information and applications when the admin server is not available. When the admin server restarts, it will discover the managed servers, as previously discussed. When this happens, any managed server running in managed server independence mode will leave this mode and register itself with the admin server for future updates to their configuration.

To use this capability, the managed server must have access to the configuration file (`config.xml`) and the `SerializedSystemIni.dat` file. To achieve this, you can place the files on a shared disk, copy them from the admin server, or have the admin server replicate the files periodically. Currently, the replication period is every five minutes. To use the replication service, go to the server's `Tuning Configuration` tab in the WebLogic Console, select the `Show` link in the `Advanced Options` heading, and enable the `MSI File Replication Enabled` checkbox. By default, managed servers use managed server independence but do not use MSI file replication. All production environments should use managed server independence. Whether they should use MSI file replication depends on the requirements, the frequency of updates to the domain configuration, and personal preference.

BEST PRACTICE Production environments should always use managed server independence. If you frequently update your production deployment configuration while the system is running, make sure you have a mechanism in place to replicate changes in the `config.xml` file to the managed servers. MSI file replication is one easy way to implement this mechanism.

WebLogic Server supports a flexible deployment model that is configurable via the server's `Deployment Configuration` tab in the WebLogic Console. The `Staging Mode` parameter controls the deployment model. In the default model known as `stage`, you place the applications on the admin server, and it pushes the applications out to the managed servers' staging directories as part of phase 1 of the two-phase deployment process. By default, the admin server uses the `nostage` mode. In `nostage` mode, WebLogic Server assumes that the files are in the server's deployment directory (typically, the `applications` directory) and deploys them from there. In the `external_stage` mode the admin server does not push out the files to the managed servers' staging directories. Instead, it assumes that some other process (for example, a content management system) handles this and the managed servers simply prepare and deploy the applications from the staging directories. In either `nostage` or `external_stage` mode, you are responsible for making sure that the files are in sync across all of the managed servers.

Node Manager

The node manager provides a mechanism allowing you to start and force the shutdown of WebLogic Server instances from the WebLogic Console. The admin server depends on the machine definitions for each managed server to know which node manager to contact for a specific server. By running the node manager as a daemon process started at machine boot time, the admin server is able to tell the node manager on a remote machine to start or kill a particular WebLogic Server instance. In addition, the node manager monitors the health of the servers for which it is responsible and can restart failed servers. This makes the node manager a critical part of any production deployment. By default, WebLogic Server instances allow the node manager to restart them should the JVM process terminate (either because the process dies or because the machine reboots). The node manager can monitor and restart only those servers that it starts. To disable the restart capability of a particular server, uncheck the `Auto Restart Enabled` checkbox on the server's `Health Monitoring Configuration` tab. Several additional parameters affect the behavior of this restart capability.

The `Max Starts within Interval` parameter tells the node manager the maximum number of times it can automatically restart the server within a specified time interval; the `Restart Interval` parameter value specifies the time interval. `Restart Delay Seconds` tells the node manager to wait for a period of time before attempting to restart the server. This parameter comes in handy in cases where the underlying operating system does not immediately release TCP listen ports for reuse—a condition that prevents the server from re-establishing its listen ports upon restart.

WebLogic Server instances monitor their health status by monitoring the status of their critical subsystems. We discuss this in more detail in the "WebLogic Administration Key Concepts" section. The node manager periodically checks the health status of its servers. If any server is in the failed state, the node manager can kill and restart it. To enable the restart of servers in the failed state, use the `Auto Kill If Failed` checkbox. The `Health Check Interval` controls the frequency with which the server checks its own health as well as the frequency with which the node manager queries the server for its health status. If one of the node manager queries takes longer than the time specified by the `Health Check Timeout` parameter, the node manager will consider the server as being failed and will kill and restart it. Remember that the node manager monitors the health of only those servers that it starts.

In this section, we have discussed the important architectural features of the WebLogic Server architecture. This should give you a good fundamental understanding of how the product works and how the pieces fit together. Next, we will examine in more detail some important administrative concepts that you will need to understand before jumping into our discussion of how to administer a WebLogic Server domain.

WebLogic Administration Key Concepts

In the previous section, we discussed the core components of the WebLogic Server architecture. Now, we are ready to talk in more detail about some administrative concepts before jumping into the details of WebLogic Server administration. We begin the discussion by talking about the server life cycle. From there, we proceed to talk in more detail about server self-health monitoring, and we finish up with a discussion of network channels.

Server States

WebLogic Server formally defines the server life cycle. In previous versions of WebLogic Server, the server was basically either running or not. This caused two problems for WebLogic Server administrators. First, starting the server involved one long-running step. Depending on the number of applications in use and the required preparation work the server would perform to prepare the applications and services for use, the server could take a very long time to start up to a point where it could start accepting client requests. Second, there was no way to guarantee that the server would process all in-flight requests before shutting down. Other, less obvious problems also existed because the server did not rigorously define the boot order of its subsystems.

Figure 11.5 shows the full server life cycle state transition diagram. The four primary states are *shutdown*, *standby*, *running*, and *failed*. A server is in the shutdown state when the JVM process for that server does not exist. When a server first starts up, it initializes itself to a point where it deploys the applications and listens on the administration port, but not on its external listen ports. In standby mode, the server tries to keep its claim on shared resources to a minimum. This allows the server to act as a hot standby in conjunction with a high availability (HA) framework.

In order for a server to exist in standby mode (rather than just passing through this state on the way to the shutdown or running states), you must enable the domain-wide administration port. The reason for this is simple: if the standby state does not claim the listen port resources, the only way to tell the server to change from the standby state is if it is listening for administrative commands on its administration port.

When gracefully shutting down a server, the server passes through standby mode but continues to shut down. There is currently no way to go from running to standby without stopping and restarting the server. When a server is told to shut down gracefully, the server will stop accepting new requests and will continue processing in-flight requests until all requests in its execute queues are complete. Once the server has reached a quiescent state, it will transition itself into the standby mode briefly before continuing to shut itself down. Forcing a server to shut down will not allow any in-flight requests to complete and will cause any in-flight requests to fail.

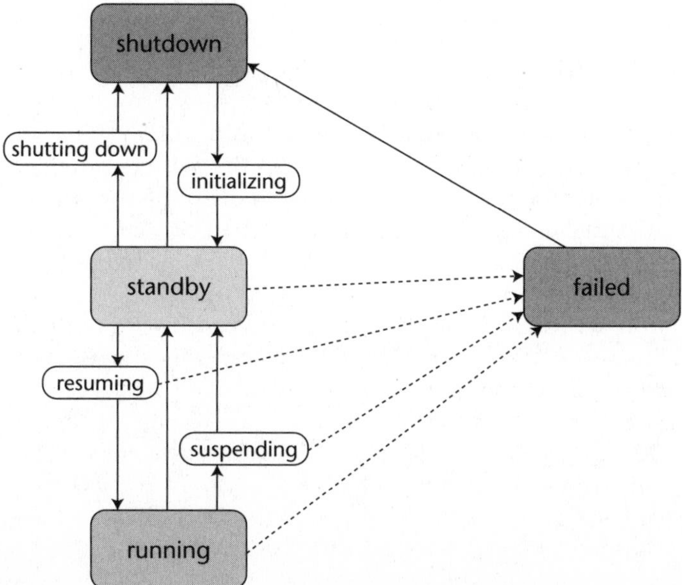

Figure 11.5 Server life cycle state transition diagram.

Once an initializing server reaches the standby state on its way to starting up, it is possible for the server subsystems to fail. If enough of the critical subsystems fail, the server will transition itself into the failed state. At this point, the server process is running, but it is not capable of doing any useful work. Fortunately, the node manager is now capable of monitoring the health of the server and can restart servers whose state is failed. For more detailed information on each of the states, please see the WebLogic Server documentation at http://edocs.bea.com/wls/docs81/adminguide/overview_lifecycle.html.

Server Self-Health Monitoring

WebLogic Server subsystems are responsible for monitoring their own status. The criteria each subsystem uses to determine its health status is specific to the particular subsystem. For example, the core server subsystem monitors the health of the default and user-defined execute queue thread pools. At startup, each subsystem registers itself with the server and specifies whether it is critical to the overall server's operation. Currently, the list of critical subsystems is not configurable and includes systems like RMI, JTA, and core.

The server monitors the health state of each registered subsystem and uses this information to determine the overall health of the server. Currently, the server periodically polls each subsystem to ask for its current health state. The frequency with which the server polls is controlled by the `Health Check Interval` parameter on the server's `Health Monitoring Configuration` tab. Although the WebLogic Console does not currently display the health of the server's subsystems, it is available programmatically through the JMX MBean APIs. If any of the server's critical subsystems fail, the server changes its state to failed.

Network Channels

Older versions of WebLogic Server did not support many network configuration options. Server instances could listen on one plain-text port and one SSL port. The IP address or DNS name had to be the same across both ports. As a result, the network configuration options available were limited by what the operating system provided naturally for a single TCP port environment. For example, by not specifying a listen address, the server could receive requests sent to the specified port on that machine, regardless of the IP address used to get there. This worked well for supporting machines with a single network interface card (NIC) and one or more IP addresses. Unfortunately, this method broke down if you tried to use machines with multiple NICs operating on different networks. The server was still able to receive the requests, but it could not always determine the correct IP address to embed in the response data to facilitate the next request reaching the right destination. More recent versions of WebLogic Server support defining additional listen ports (and an associated listen thread) through something called a *network channel*. WebLogic Server 8.1 allows you to define as many network channels as you want. Use the server's `Channels Protocols` tab in the WebLogic Console to manage a server's network channels.

A network channel is a conceptual combination of a `Listen Address`, `Listen Port`, and `Protocol` that must be unique within a server. Network channels can share the same address and port number provided that their protocols are different. When this happens, WebLogic Server combines these channels and creates a single listen thread and port that accepts all of the protocols with that address and port number combination. The choice of protocols includes t3, IIOP, COM, HTTP, t3s, IIOPS, HTTPS, or admin. The admin protocol is simply a network channel that accepts only administrative requests and requires the use of SSL.

Network channels also support network address translation (NAT) firewalls directly by providing the ability to specify the `External Listen Address` and `External Listen Port` attributes that WebLogic Server should use when communicating with clients through this channel. In addition, each network channel has its own TCP-related configuration parameters that you will find under the `Advanced Options` areas of the channel's `Configuration` tab in the WebLogic Console.

By providing the ability to define new network channels, WebLogic Server goes a long way toward helping you support the more complex networking requirements often found in production environments. Using network channels is completely optional, however. By default, the server still supports the old model of a single plain-text listen port, a single SSL listen port, and an optional domain-wide administration port. This default model is sometimes called the *default channel*; the domain-wide administration port is known as the *administrative channel*. WebLogic Server does not currently allow the default channel to be completely disabled. The good news, though, is that it is now possible to disable the plain-text listen port on this default channel if the SSL listen port is enabled. If you enable the domain-wide administration port, you must use it or another admin channel instead of the default channel ports for all administrative tasks; however, its use is completely optional.

We have barely scratched the surface of network administration using network channels. Further reading is available on the BEA Web site at http://edocs.bea.com/wls/docs81/adminguide/network.html. In the next section, we will show an example of using network channels in a WebLogic Server cluster configuration.

In the next three sections, we will show the highlights of how to configure, administer, and monitor a WebLogic Server domain and discuss some of the important things to consider. This coverage is intended to provide insights into best practices in WebLogic Server domain configuration, administration, and monitoring, rather than a comprehensive, step-by-step coverage of all of the possible options. For more comprehensive coverage of WebLogic Server administration, please refer to one of the WebLogic Server Administration books available or the WebLogic Server documentation at http://edocs.bea.com/wls/docs81/admin.html.

Configuring a WebLogic Server Domain

Determining the best configuration for a particular set of applications requires careful analysis of the applications' resource requirements, service-level agreements, corporate policies, network policies, security policies, and so on. Some of the best practices for choosing production system deployment architectures are covered in Chapter 14 and therefore will not be covered here. This section will focus on configuring a typical deployment architecture for a Web-based application that also has some Java application and Web Services clients. Where appropriate, we will discuss the available deployment architectures and the things to consider when choosing among the alternatives. The primary purpose of this section, though, is to discuss WebLogic Server domain configuration.

The first thing to do when preparing to configure a WebLogic Server domain is to determine what applications we will need to deploy in the domain. Although there are many things to consider when making this decision, probably one of the most important criteria is whether the same person or group within the organization will be administering all of the applications. The reality is that a WebLogic Server domain is just a logical grouping of WebLogic Server instances, clusters, or both that are controlled through a single administration server. While it is certainly possible to share a WebLogic Server domain among different sets of administrators, it is typically better for corporate harmony not to do so. Other questions to consider are these:

- Do the applications need to interact with one another?
- Do the applications share a common security model?
- Do the applications need to share critical, but limited resources (for example, connections to legacy system)?

In this section, the example will focus on deploying a single application that has multiple client interfaces. Because there are no other applications to consider, we will create a new domain. The example uses our *bigrez.com* hotel reservation system that supports Internet bookings via a Web browser-based interface, customer service agent bookings using a Java client application, and Web services-based bookings from global reservation systems bookings via a virtual private network (VPN). While this example certainly won't cover every possible configuration issue, it does attempt to provide a broad overview of common issues you might encounter while configuring a WebLogic Server domain.

Figure 11.6 shows the deployment architecture we chose for this example. The Web browser-based Internet requests come in through a firewall to a hardware load-balancing device that distributes the requests across the Apache Web servers. Using the WebLogic Server Apache plug-in, the Apache Web servers proxy requests through a network address-translating firewall to the cluster of WebLogic Server instances. Global reservation systems come into the network through a VPN server. From there, we route the requests through a hardware load balancer and a network address translating firewall before they finally arrive at our cluster. Because customer service agents use computers connected to the company's internal network, their EJB-based application accesses the servers directly through a network address-translating firewall. The WebLogic Server administrator can also use the WebLogic Console from inside the data center or from any computer connected to the company's internal network through that same network address-translating firewall.

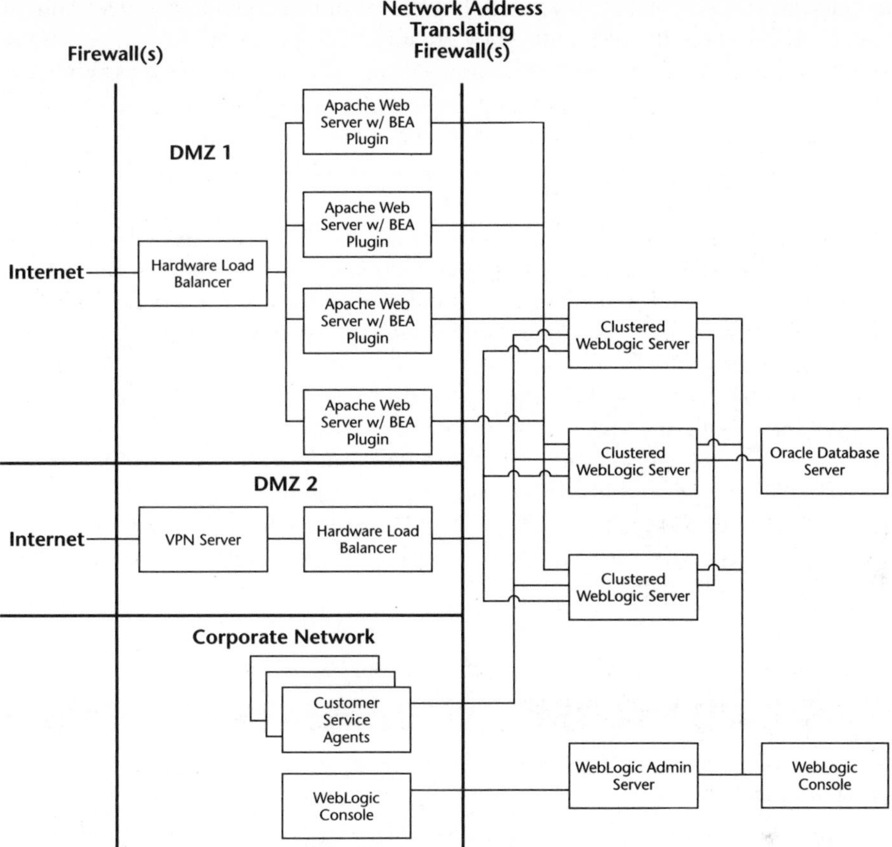

Figure 11.6 bigrez.com deployment architecture.

Our configuration assumes that all of the Apache Web server and WebLogic Server instances are running on separate machines. The machines running WebLogic Server have (at least) three separate NICs, one for customers coming in through Apache, one for the global reservation systems coming in through the VPN server, and one for corporate users. For the purposes of our example, we really do not care which network the database server is on as long as there is connectivity to that network from the application servers.

In Figure 11.6, the admin server and the cluster of managed servers are all communicating with each other on the same network as the end users. At the time of writing, limitations in the WebLogic Server network channel support require this design. We will go into the details of why we chose this configuration later, but we suspect that these limitations may be addressed by the time you read this book. We will use the administrative channel for server administration. We will configure an additional admin network channel that our WebLogic Server administrators can use to access the admin server from the corporate network. Having an administration port accessible from the corporate network may or may not be acceptable in your environment. We believe that this is an acceptable risk given that the administrators may need access to the system at all hours of the night and they already have secure remote access to the corporate network but not to the data center. Now, let's start walking through the process of setting up this configuration and deploying our application.

Setting Up a New Domain

The first step in creating a new domain is to set up and configure the admin server. After installing the WebLogic Server software on the machine where the admin server will reside, you need to create the files that define the admin server. WebLogic Server provides a Configuration Wizard to help create the initial directory structure and configuration files.

On Windows platforms, the WebLogic Configuration Wizard is available through the Windows Start Menu; the `$WL_HOME/common/bin` directory contains the `config` scripts for Windows and Unix. Table 11.1 shows the Configuration Wizard parameter values used to create the example admin server configuration files. Note that these values are in the WebLogic Server 8.1 Configuration Wizard's order of presentation at the time of writing; the order, names, and pages may change depending on the version of WebLogic Server you are using.

Table 11.1 Example Admin Server Configuration Wizard Values

NAME	VALUE
Create a Configuration or Add to an Existing Configuration	Create a new WebLogic Configuration
Configuration Template	Basic WebLogic Server Domain
Choose Express or Custom Configuration	Custom
Administration Server Configuration:	
Name	AdminServer
Listen Address	192.168.1.20
Listen Port	7001
SSL Listen Port	7002
SSL Enabled	No (unchecked)
Multiple Servers, Clusters, Machine Options	Yes
Managed Server(s) Configuration:	
Name	Server1
Listen Address	192.168.1.21
Listen Port	7001
SSL Listen Port	7002
SSL Enabled	No (unchecked)

Table 11.1 *(continued)*

NAME	VALUE
Name	Server2
Listen Address	192.168.1.22
Listen Port	7001
SSL Listen Port	7002
SSL Enabled	No (unchecked)
Name	Server3
Listen Address	192.168.1.23
Listen Port	7001
SSL Listen Port	7002
SSL Enabled	No (unchecked)
Cluster Configuration:	
Cluster Name	BigRezCluster
Cluster Multicast Address	237.168.1.20
Cluster Multicast Port	7777
Cluster Address	
Servers to Cluster Assignments	Server1, Server2, and Server3 to BigRezCluster
Machine Configuration:	Unix Machine
Name	Machine1
Post Bind GID Enabled	No (unchecked)
Post Bind GID	
Post Bind UID Enabled	No (unchecked)
Post Bind UID	
Node Manager Listen Address	192.168.1.21
Node Manager Listen Port	5555
Name	Machine2
Post Bind GID Enabled	No (unchecked)
Post Bind GID	
Post Bind UID Enabled	No (unchecked)
Post Bind UID	
Node Manager Listen Address	192.168.1.22
Node Manager Listen Port	5555
Name	Machine3
Post Bind GID Enabled	No (unchecked)
Post Bind GID	
Post Bind UID Enabled	No (unchecked)
Post Bind UID	
Node Manager Listen Address	192.168.1.23
Node Manager Listen Port	5555

(continued)

Table 11.1 *(continued)*

NAME	VALUE
Servers to Machine Assignments:	
Server1	Machine1
Server2	Machine2
Server3	Machine3
Database (JDBC) Options	Skip
Messaging (JMS) Options	Skip
Advanced Security Options	Yes
User:	
Name	system
Password	insecure
Description	WLS admin user
Name	BIGREZADMIN
Password	password
Description	bigrez.com admin user
Name	BIGREZMPLS
Password	password
Description	BigRez Inn MPLS administrator
Name	BIGREZDUL
Password	password
Description	BigRez Inn Duluth administrator
Name	DEWDROP1
Password	password
Description	DewDrop Inn Downtown administrator
Group:	
Name	BigRezAdministrators
Description	Can use bigrez.com admin app to administer all hotels
Name	HotelAdministrators
Description	Can use bigrez.com admin app to administer their hotel
Assign Users to Groups	
system	Administrators
BIGREZADMIN	BigRezAdministrators
BIGREZMPLS	HotelAdministrators
BIGREZDUL	HotelAdministrators
DEWDROP1	HotelAdministrators

Table 11.1 *(continued)*

NAME	VALUE
Assign Groups to Groups	No action required
Assign Users and Groups to Global Roles	No action required
Windows Options: Create Start Menu Install Administrative Server as Service	 Yes No (you can add this later, if desired)
Build Start Menu Entries: Shortcut Link Name Program Argument Working Directory	 Start bigrez.com Admin Server startWebLogic.cmd
WebLogic Configuration Environment: WebLogic Configuration Startup Mode Java SDK Selection	 Production Mode JRockit SDK
Create WebLogic Configuration: Configuration Location Configuration Name	 C:\mastering\ch11_examples\deploy\AdminServer\user_projects bigrezdomain

Now that the admin server setup is complete, it is time to install the WebLogic Server software and create the configuration files for the managed servers. At the time of writing, the WebLogic Server 8.1 Configuration Wizard did not support an option for creating new directory structures for managed servers. While it is possible to use the Configuration Wizard to create a new domain directory and modify the files manually, it is easier to copy the files needed from the `bigrezdomain` directory from the admin server to the managed servers. The primary files of importance for the managed servers are the `SerializedSystemIni.dat` file and the `setEnv` and `startManagedWebLogic` scripts. If you are using a different platform for the managed servers and the admin server, you may need to edit the scripts. For example, we chose to use the JRockit JVM for the admin server so if the managed servers ran on a platform that does not support JRockit, you would need to edit the scripts to refer to the correct JVM for that platform. Once this process is complete, the next step involves starting the admin server and configuring the domain to match our desired deployment environment.

To make it easy to start the admin server, the Configuration Wizard creates `startWebLogic` shell script files in the admin servers' root directory (for example, `C:\mastering\ch11_examples\deploy\AdminServer\user_projects\bigrezdomain`). Because our admin server will run on a machine using a version of the Microsoft Windows operating system, the relevant shell script file is `startWebLogic.cmd`. Before starting the admin server, we want to configure the script so that you don't have to type in the username and password of the administrative users every time the script is run. The start script provides the WLS_USER and WLS_PW variables for specifying the administrative username and password so that the server doesn't prompt for them at boot time. This is handy, but now there is a better solution that does not leave the administrative username and password stored in clear text on the file system. Recent versions of WebLogic Server now support specifying the administrator's username and password in a boot identity file that the server will read on startup. To create the boot identity file, use a text editor to create a two-line boot.properties file like the one shown here in the server's root directory:

```
# Initial contents of the boot.properties file
username=system
password=insecure
```

The next time you start the server it will find the boot.properties file and encrypt the username and password property values.

Now, start the admin server and bring up the WebLogic Console using your favorite browser. At this stage, we are not ready to go through the network address translating firewall to the admin server's administration port (because it has not yet been configured). Therefore, we need to run the console from a machine inside the data center firewalls that can point directly at the admin server's plain-text listen port (for example, http://192.168.1.20:7001/console). The first thing to do is to enable the domain-wide administration port (that is, the admin channel). Because the administration port requires SSL, the admin server's SSL settings need to be configured properly (actually, all of the managed servers' SSL settings can be configured at this point as well). Rather than our covering SSL configuration again here, refer to Chapter 10 for more information on how to do this. Once the SSL configuration is complete, configure the admin channel settings using the domain's General Configuration tab. Once you restart the admin server, the WebLogic Console will need to use the administration port (for example, https://192.168.1.20:9002/console).

Before moving on to configuring the individual servers, you should configure the domain logging characteristics. Use the domain's Logging Configuration tab to change the File Name attribute to .\logs\bigrezdomain.log, the Rotation Type attribute to By Time, and the Limit Number of Retained Log Files checkbox to checked. Don't forget to create the logs subdirectory in the admin server's root directory. These changes cause the admin server to place the domain log file in its logs subdirectory, rotate the domain log file every day at midnight, and retain only one week's worth of log files. While in practice the domain log file does not typically grow very quickly unless you configure server log message propagation, it is still a good idea to use log rotation to prevent having to stop the server to remove a large log file that is filling up the file system. In the next section, we will enable log rotation for other log files that are more likely to grow very large in a short period of time.

BEST PRACTICE Always enable log rotation for the domain log file to prevent having to restart the admin server should the log file grow too large.

Configuring Servers

Configuring a WebLogic Server instance is an important part of any WebLogic Server administrator's job. Out of the box, the server comes with a default configuration that will allow you to start it without any additional configuration. While this default configuration is convenient and contributes much to the ease of use of the product, WebLogic Server has a large number of configuration parameters available to tune the server's behavior for almost any environment. Rather than attempting to cover all of the options, we will focus on those parameters that typically require changes from the default values to satisfy production environment requirements. Fortunately, the reservation system example provides us with enough complexity to be able to present these configuration changes in the context of a real-world example.

The first task is to make sure that we properly configure the default network channel. Because the admin server and the managed servers will not be using their default channel SSL listen port, we did not enable the SSL ports of any of the servers when creating the configuration. Check to make sure that the default SSL ports are disabled on the server's `General Configuration` tab. The `Advanced Options` portion of the `General Configuration` tab provides the `Local Administration Port Override` attribute that allows you to override the domain-wide administration port number for a server. We will not need to do this for our example.

The next item on our list is to configure some of the denial-of-service-related parameters that we discuss more in Chapter 14. Because our customer-facing Web application never posts more than a few kilobytes of data, we want to limit both the maximum amount of time to receive an entire request's data and the maximum allowable size of a request. Using the `HTTP Protocols` tab for each managed server, leave the `Post Timeout` set to the default of 30 seconds and set the `Max Post Size` to 100,000 bytes for all three managed servers. Because the application's `Max Post Size` is limited to 100,000 bytes, limiting the total HTTP message size to 200,000 bytes should provide more than enough space to allow all valid HTTP requests to reach the application. Set the `HTTP Max Message Size` for each managed server to 200,000 bytes. You should also set the `HTTP Message Timeout` to 60 seconds. You can find these attributes under the `Advanced Options` section of the `HTTP Protocols` tab.

Several parameters on the server's `Tuning Connections` tab are important. `Accept Backlog` controls the length of the underlying TCP/IP listen queue. See Chapter 12 for more information on tuning the length of the listen queue. For now, it is sufficient to understand that this parameter will limit the number of concurrent connection requests to the server. While the default value of 50 is sufficient for most purposes, you may need to increase this value for servers processing many concurrent HTTP requests to prevent clients from getting "connection refused" errors.

`Login Timeout` is the amount of time the server allows for a newly established connection to start sending request data. In high-volume Web sites, it may be necessary to increase this parameter to 10 seconds or so to prevent clients from receiving login timed-out errors. Do not set this parameter too high, though, as this could make the server more vulnerable to a denial-of-service attack. For our example, the `SSL Login Timeout` for the default channel is not important (because the SSL ports are disabled), but this parameter serves a similar purpose for SSL connections.

The Maximum Open Sockets parameter controls the number of sockets the server can have open at any time. As with the Accept Backlog parameter, this parameter provides a mechanism to set a limit that the operating system also controls. A typical use for this parameter would be to limit the number of connections to a server to a number lower than the limit imposed by the operating system. This is the recommended way of throttling requests into the server to prevent overloading the server with so many concurrent requests that the response time for processing a request cannot meet service-level agreements. For this example, we will increase the Accept Backlog to 100, the Login Timeout to 10,000 milliseconds (10 seconds), and the number of socket connections to 1,000.

Before moving on to configure logging, enable MSI File Replication for the managed servers using Advanced Options section of the Tuning Configuration tab. This will tell the admin server to periodically replicate the configuration files used by the managed servers to start up in stand-alone mode when the admin server is not available. To speed up the compilation of run-time-generated Java code (such as when we access a JSP page for the first time), we will configure the server to use the Jikes open source Java compiler (see www.ibm.com/developerworks/oss/jikes/), which is many times faster than the default javac compiler supplied with the Java 2 Software Development Kit (J2SDK). To do this, use the servers' General Configuration tab to set the Java Compiler attribute to the full path to Jikes (for example, /usr/local/bin/jikes).

Because our customer-facing Web site is using Apache Web servers to proxy requests to our cluster through a NAT firewall, you need to configure the servers to know about their external addresses that the plug-in must use to reach them from outside the firewall. We do this by using the External Listen Address attribute available in the Advanced Options section of the server's General Configuration tab. In the example, the firewall maps all IP addresses in the 192.168.1.xxx subnet to the 10.168.1.xxx subnet in DMZ 1. Therefore, we will set the External Listen Address parameters for each managed server to the values shown in Table 11.2.

Before leaving this area, you should set the WebLogic Plug-in Enabled attribute for each managed server. This causes WebLogic Server to return the value of the WL-Proxy-Client-IP HTTP header when the application calls the getRemoteAddr() method on an HttpServletRequest object. By doing this, the application is able to obtain the client information reliably for requests being routed through one of WebLogic Server's Web server plug-ins.

Table 11.2 Managed Servers' External Listen Address Attribute Values

SERVER NAME	EXTERNAL LISTEN ADDRESS
Server1	10.168.1.21
Server2	10.168.1.22
Server3	10.168.1.23

Our next task is to configure server logging. Using the servers' `Server Logging` tabs, specify the location and name of each server's log file. This tab also controls how verbose the server output to the console window (that is, stdout) should be. For the example, the default log file names and stdout settings will suffice. We will use the servers' `Server Logging` tabs to configure server log rotation. As with the domain log, we will set up server log rotation for all four servers to rotate once a day at midnight and to limit the number of old log files to keep only the log files for the past week. To do this, set the `Rotation Type` to `By Time` and check the `Limit Number of Retained Log Files` checkbox.

BEST PRACTICE Always configure the server and HTTP access logs to use rotation. This will prevent the need to stop the server to remove large log files.

Now, we need to configure HTTP logging for all four of the servers. Using the `HTTP Logging` tab, you can control the format, location, buffering, and rotation of the HTTP access log. The first decision you need to make is whether to use common or extended logging format. Because we want to gather statistical information about site usage, we are going to choose extended logging for the managed servers. The HTTP access log files grow proportionally to the number of requests. This means that the log file sizes can vary greatly depending on the amount of traffic to our Web site. Because we hope that our Web site will be very popular, we will choose rotation by log file size rather than by time. While this decision will make it harder to pinpoint a particular day's entries, it will guarantee that you don't end up with a very large log file that could fill up the available disk space, leaving you with no other recourse than to stop and restart the server. Set the `Format` to `extended` and the `Maximum Log File Size` to 10,000 kilobytes.

WARNING HTTP access log files grow proportionally to the number of requests. If you do not configure log rotation properly, the access log file can grow to a very large size and potentially fill up the disk, causing the application and the operating system to stop working. Once this condition is reached, the only way to remove the log file is to stop and restart the application server.

By default, WebLogic Server buffers all writes to the HTTP access log to improve performance. The `Log Buffer Size` and `Flush Every` attributes control this behavior. `Log Buffer Size` controls the size at which WebLogic Server will flush its internal, in-memory buffer for HTTP access log entries and write them to disk. `Flush Every` controls the frequency with which the server checks the log buffer to see if it is larger than `Log Buffer Size`; if it is, the server will flush the buffer and write the buffered entries to the access log file. For high-volume Web sites, access log file buffering can improve performance dramatically at the risk of losing a few entries if the server were to crash. For most systems, this trade-off is acceptable.

At this point, we are ready to move on to configuring our system for clustering. We have not attempted to cover every possible server option. Some additional parameters will be covered in the upcoming sections, while others are covered elsewhere in the book. For a complete discussion of all possible configuration options, refer to the online documentation at http://edocs.bea.com/wls/docs81/admin.html.

Configuring the Cluster

The first thing you need to do when setting up a cluster is choose a multicast address and multicast port number. Older versions of WebLogic Server used the plain-text listen port number as the UDP port for sending multicast messages to a WebLogic Server cluster. This meant that in order for every server in the cluster to communicate via multicast, the plain-text listen port for every server in the cluster had to be the same. Because multiple processes cannot bind to the same IP address and TCP port number combination, every server in the cluster had to have its own unique IP address. Starting with WebLogic Server 7.0, each cluster has its own `Multicast Port` attribute to specify the UDP port to use for multicast traffic, rather than relying on all servers in the cluster having the same plain-text listen port. This gives you more flexibility when setting up clusters.

When choosing a multicast address and port, it is important to make sure that no other programs on your network are using the same multicast address and multicast port number combination. Although more recent versions of WebLogic Server allow different clusters to share the same multicast address and port number, it is much more efficient, from a server processing standpoint, if they do not. Every server in a cluster must use the same multicast address and multicast port number. Multicast addresses can range from 224.0.0.1 to 244.255.255.255. The general recommendation is to avoid the 224.0.0.x range of addresses as these are typically reserved for multicast routing. Because the WebLogic Configuration Wizard has already set this up using the parameters listed in Table 11.1, you don't need to do anything with the configuration.

WARNING Do not try to add the admin server to the cluster. The admin server is not clusterable. We will discuss admin server failover later in this chapter.

Next, we need to create definitions for the machines on which the managed servers are running. Telling WebLogic Server which servers run on which machines serves two important purposes. First, it lets WebLogic Server be smart about the location of in-memory replicated objects so that it tries to keep copies of the same object on different machines. Because our configuration is currently running only one WebLogic Server instance per machine, this particular aspect is not important in our example. Second, it lets the admin server know which node manager to talk to when starting or stopping a particular managed server. Because the Configuration Wizard already created the machines and associated the servers with the machines according to the parameters shown in Table 11.1, you don't need to do anything else.

If we were configuring our system for disaster recovery, we might decide to spread our cluster across two data centers, provided that both data centers were relatively close together and connected by one or more high-speed network links. This type of configuration can support both data centers actively processing requests and allow for failover between data centers. Of course, WebLogic Server clustering does not handle all of the issues involved with setting up this type of environment, such as data replication of back-end systems; however, it can support replicating objects between data centers. To accomplish transparent failover of in-memory replicated objects, you need some way to tell WebLogic Server to store the replicated objects' primary and secondary copies in different data centers. Replication groups give you this type of control over how WebLogic Server selects the location of the secondary server.

In our example, we are not considering disaster recovery and do not have any need to control the secondary-server selection process. Therefore, we will not set up any replication groups. We discuss disaster recovery considerations and options in more detail in Chapter 14. At this point, we are ready to move on and discuss configuring network channels.

Configuring Network Channels

Our application uses three distinct networks to segment different types of user traffic. Using network channels, you can control the network resources, protocols, and tuning parameters of each network independently. The customer Web site is using the default channel that you have already configured. So, we need to configure two additional channels: the global reservation systems (GRS) channel and the internal customer service agents (CSA) channel. To create a network channel, you need to specify the name, default listen ports, cluster address, and protocol that the channel will support.

In this example, the GRS channel will support only the HTTP protocol because all requests on this channel should be Web service requests over HTTP. The internal network listen addresses used by each server will be in the 206.168.1.x subnet, so the GRS channel for `Server1`, `Server2`, and `Server3` uses a `Listen Address` of 206.168.1.21, 206.168.1.22, and 206.168.1.23, respectively. Because we are using a NAT firewall, we need to set the `External Listen Address` attributes to 10.12.1.21, 10.12.1.22, and 10.12.1.23, respectively. We will use an `External Listen Port` value of 80.

Next, you will want to tune the settings of the GRS channel using the channel's `Advanced Options` section. You should make sure that the `Accept Backlog`, `Login Timeout`, `Complete Message Timeout`, and `Idle Connection Timeout` attributes are set to reasonable values. Because server-to-server communication may use network channels and multiple channels may be available, WebLogic Server uses the `Channel Weight` setting to define the preferred channel(s) between two servers. The `Outgoing Enabled` checkbox allows us to disable the initiation of server-to-server communication over a particular channel. Because *bigrez.com* will not use the GRS channel for server-to-server communication (all server-to-server communication will use the default channel), you should leave the `Outgoing Enabled` checkbox unchecked. Because the GRS channel is not used for EJB communication, the `Cluster Address` setting is not important. You should, however, adjust the `Maximum Message Size` to a reasonable value based on the application's needs. Because our GRS channel is transmitting Simple Object Access Protocol (SOAP) messages over HTTP, you will need to allow larger HTTP messages than we previously did in the default channel for the customer Web site. After consulting with our application architects, we know that no SOAP message from our GRS partners will ever be larger than 750 KB, so you should set the maximum message size to 1,000,000 bytes.

At this point, we are ready to set up the CSA channel that our internal customer service agents will use. Because the Java client application uses RMI to talk with the cluster, the CSA channel will need to support only the `t3` protocol.

Now that we understand what needs to be done to support our CSA channel, go ahead and set up the network channel to support only the `t3` protocol and deploy it to the cluster. Use the information in Table 11.3 to configure the CSA channel for each managed server. Use the default value for all other parameters.

The last step is to set up an additional network channel for the admin server that only supports the admin protocol. This allows our administrators to access the WebLogic Console from anywhere inside the corporate network. To do this, simply create a network channel for the admin server by setting the `Name` to `Internal Admin Channel`, the `Protocol` to `admin`, the `Listen Address` to `192.168.1.20`, the `Listen Port` to `443`, the `External Listen Address` to `10.11.1.20`, and the `External Listen Port` to `443`.

At this point, our network channel configuration is complete and we are ready to move on to the node manager. The configuration of the node manager is relatively simple. Unfortunately, debugging problems with the node manager can be tricky. In the next section, we will try to point out all of the things to be aware of in order to avoid such problems as well as try to describe the debugging process.

Table 11.3 CSA Network Channel Configuration Parameter Values

NAME	VALUE
Name	CSA Channel
Protocol	t3
Listen Address	209.168.1.21 for Server1
209.168.1.22 for Server2	
209.168.1.23 for Server3	
Listen Port	7001
External Listen Address	10.11.1.21 for Server1
10.11.1.22 for Server2	
10.11.1.23 for Server3	
External Listen Port	7001
Cluster Address	10.11.1.21,10.11.1.22,10.11.1.23
HTTP Enabled for This Protocol	No (unchecked)
Maximum Message Size	100,000

Setting Up the Node Manager

The node manager is a daemon process that provides remote server start capabilities to the WebLogic Console, monitors the health of its servers, and allows for automatic restart of failed servers. As such, we recommend installing and configuring the node manager on all machines where managed servers will run. Typically, we recommend installing the node manager so that it starts up when the machine boots. On Windows, this means installing it as a Windows service. On Unix, it generally means writing a boot script to run the node manager start script as the correct user with the correct environment. Because the managed servers in our example all run in a Unix environment, we will focus primarily on installing and configuring the node manager on a Unix-based operating system. We will try to point out places where the process is significantly different under Windows. For more complete information, please refer to the WebLogic Server online documentation at http://edocs.bea.com/wls/docs81/adminguide/nodemgr.html.

The first thing you need to do is determine the location from which the node manager will run. Because the default location for the node manager is under the `$WL_HOME/common/nodemanager` directory, we recommend creating a separate directory outside the WebLogic Server software install directory to run the node manager. We will choose to create a directory called `/mastering/ch11_examples/deploy/Machine#/NodeManager`, where # is either 1, 2, or 3, on each of the three machines where managed servers will run. Now, copy the `$WL_HOME/server/bin/startNodeManager.sh` file (`startNodeManager.cmd` on Windows machines) to the newly created `NodeManager` directory. Edit your copy of the `startNodeManager` script to set the `NODEMGR_HOME` environment variable to the script's current directory.

The `startNodeManager` script takes two arguments: the listen address and the listen port. We could have created three scripts to invoke the `startNodeManager` script with proper arguments for each machine. The node manager also looks for a property file called `nodemanager.properties` in the `NODEMGR_HOME` directory for configuration information. If this file doesn't exist, the node manager creates it the first time it is started. By adding the following lines to each node manager's property file, you do not need to create three separate scripts. The `nodemanager.properties` file for `Machine1` looks like this:

```
PropertiesVersion=8.1
ListenPort=5555
ListenAddress=192.168.1.21
```

The admin server uses two-way SSL to communicate with the node manager. In a real production environment, you should always configure SSL using real certificates tied to each machine and configure the node manager to use its machine's certificates and private keys. Rather than our repeating the discussion of SSL configuration here, please refer to Chapter 10. Once you have SSL configured, you can use the `nodemanager.properties` file to point the node manager to the identity and trust key stores. For our example, you simply add the following lines to specify the node manager's SSL configuration:

```
KeyStores=CustomIdentityAndCustomTrust
CustomIdentityKeyStoreFileName=ServerKeyStore.jks
CustomIdentityKeyStorePassPhrase=server_keystore_passwd
CustomIdentityAlias=server_key
CustomIdentityPrivateKeyPassPhrase=server_key_passwd
CustomTrustKeyStoreFileName=ServerTrustStore.jks
CustomTrustKeyStorePassPhrase=server_truststore_passwd
```

The first time you start the node manager it will replace the clear-text passwords in the property file with Triple DES encrypted versions.

BEST PRACTICE Always obtain, install, and configure server-specific SSL certificates and enable SSL hostname verification for node managers running in a production environment. Failing to do so can compromise the security of your applications.

The node manager uses a trusted hosts file to determine the set of machines from which it is allowed to accept requests to start or stop servers. By default, the node manager uses the `nodemanager.hosts` file located in the `NODEMGR_HOME` directory. At a minimum, you need to add the admin server's `Listen Address` to the hosts file (192.168.1.20 in our example). Please note that if you choose to use a DNS name in the hosts file, you need to enable reverse DNS lookup on the node manager. To do this, set the `ReverseDnsEnabled` property to `true` by either defining it as a Java system property on the command line or by adding it to the `nodemanager.properties` file. Remember to account for any admin server migration support in your environment. We will discuss strategies for admin server migration in the "Managing WebLogic Server Applications" section.

BEST PRACTICE Unless DNS names play a critical role in your admin server migration strategy, use only IP addresses in the node manager's trusted host file and leave reverse DNS lookup disabled. By not using DNS names and reverse lookup, you eliminate the need for the node manager to talk with your DNS server and remove another potential point of failure.

Next, you need to configure the node manager settings in the WebLogic Console. These settings are split between settings that apply to the node manager on a specific machine and those that contain information the node manager needs to start each individual server on the machine. Using the WebLogic Console, navigate to the machine settings for `Machine1` and select the `Node Manager Configuration` tab. You should see that the Configuration Wizard already set the `Listen Address` to 192.168.1.21 and the `Listen Port` to 5555. If not, set these values appropriately for each of the three machines.

The next step is to set the server-specific settings. Using the `Remote Start Configuration` tab of each of the managed servers, you must tell the node manager enough information to start the server with the proper configuration. Although the managed servers will inherit the environment of the node manager, we find it is best to configure all of the managed server's remote start attributes explicitly. While most of the remote start attributes are self-explanatory, we will take a minute to review them because debugging problems with starting servers via the node manager can be frustrating. The server's remote start attributes are as follows:

`Java Home.` The full path to the JDK installation directory on the node manager's machine that will be used to start the server. This parameter must be set such that appending `/bin` to the value of this parameter will give the server the fully qualified directory path to the Java Virtual Machine executable. Typically, this would be set to something like `c:\bea\jdk141_02` or `/opt/bea/jdk141_02` depending on the operating system and where you installed the WebLogic Server software.

`BEA Home.` The full path to the BEA software installation directory on the node manager's machine. Typically, this would be set to something like `c:\bea` or `/opt/bea` depending on the operating system and where you installed the WebLogic Server software.

`Root Directory.` The full path to the domain's root directory on the node manager's machine. The value of this parameter will affect the location of all relative directory and file names. For example, if the root directory is set to `/mastering/ch11_examples/deployment/Machine1/user_projects/bigrezdomain` and the server's log file is set to `./Server1//Server1.log`, the server's log file will be `/mastering/ch11_examples/deployment/Machine1/user_projects/bigrezdomain/Server1/Server1.log`. Typically, this would be set to something that includes the WebLogic Server domain name, such as `/mastering/ch11_examples/deployment/Machine1/user_projects/bigrezdomain`.

`Classpath.` The complete Java classpath that WebLogic Server requires to start your applications. In most cases, the only things that need to be in the classpath are the JRE's `tools.jar`, the WebLogic Server's `weblogic.jar`, and any JDBC driver's classes or `.jar` files. You should always question developers who require application classes in the server's classpath because this will prevent hot redeployment of these classes with the application.

`Arguments.` The JVM arguments to use to start the managed server on the node manager machine. Typical things to set here are the Java HotSpot Compiler options (for example, `-server`), the JVM heap size (for example, `-Xms32m -Xmx200m`), garbage collection tuning parameters, and any Java system properties required by WebLogic Server and/or your applications.

`Security Policy File.` The fully qualified name to the Java 2 security policy file to use to start the managed server on the node manager's machine. Typically, it is sufficient to use WebLogic Server's default policy file (for example, `/opt/bea/weblogic81/server/lib/weblogic.policy`).

`Username.` The administrative user name to use to start and stop the server and perform other administrative operations. In our examples, we use the username `system` as the administrative user because historically this has been the WebLogic Server default.

Password. The password of the administrative user that corresponds to the supplied Username parameter's value. In our examples, we use the password insecure just to stress that the password you select for the administrative user(s) will directly affect the security of your WebLogic Server applications.

BEST PRACTICE Explicitly configure all remote start attributes for a managed server rather than relying on the node manager's environment for a managed server's configuration.

After doing the configuration work just described for each of the three machine's node managers, you are ready to start the node managers on the three machines by running the startNodeManager scripts on each machine. When you first start the node manager on a particular machine, the node manager creates a directory structure for its log files; the top-level directory is called NodeManagerLogs, and it is created in the NODEMGR_HOME directory. If you look inside this directory, you will find a single directory (unless you have used this Node Manager before) called NodeManager Internal. This is where the node manager writes its log file and other information that it needs to persist. If you look inside this directory, there are three files: MonitoredProcessList, NodeManagerProperties, and a file whose name is of the form nm_<machine_name>_<date_started>-<time_started>.log, where <machine_name> is the hostname of the machine, <date_started> is the numeric date in MM_DD_YYYY format, and <time_started> is the 24-hour clock time in HH_MM_SS format. This last file is the node manager's log file. You should look through this file to make sure that the node manager started up properly and that there were no warnings or errors. This file becomes extremely important when running the node manager as a Unix daemon process (or a Windows service) where the stdout and stderr output streams are not visible.

Once the node managers start, you can use each server's Start/Stop Control tab to start the managed servers. Because the server runs in the background, you must use log files to troubleshoot any problems with the server configuration. Fortunately, the node manager captures the stdout and stderr output streams and writes them to disk. The node manager creates these files underneath the NodeManagerLogs directory. If you look inside this directory again, there will be a new directory with a name of the form *<domain name>*_*<server_name>* (for example, bigrezdomain_Server1). Inside this directory will be four files: nodemanager.config, *<server name>*_error .log, *<server name>*_output.log, and *<server name>*_pid. The *<server name>*_ output.log and *<server name>*_error.log files are the stdout and stderr output streams of the server, respectively. These files allow you to determine why the server failed to start, and they can be invaluable if the server fails before it begins writing to its own log file.

In addition, the admin server creates separate log files for logging any communication with a node manager. The admin server creates these log files under the Node ManagerClientLogs directory in the admin server's root directory. These client log files can help debug configuration errors related to communication between the admin server and the node manager, perhaps something as simple as accidentally specifying the wrong node manager listen address or port.

WebLogic Server currently requires that the node manager start all servers that it monitors. Currently, only the admin server can tell the node manager to start or stop a server. This creates a problem for managed servers using managed server independence (MSI) mode. MSI mode allows you to start a managed server with a cached copy of its configuration when the admin server is unavailable. Because there is no way to tell the node manager to start a managed server without the admin server, any managed servers started in MSI mode will not be monitored by the node manager. This means that, while WebLogic Server can automatically switch a server from MSI mode to normal mode when the admin server comes back up, any server started in MSI mode will eventually have to be restarted once the admin server becomes available if you want the node manager to monitor the server's health. We expect that this limitation will be addressed in a future release.

Operating System Configuration

Configuring the operating system is an important part of setting up any WebLogic Server deployment. RMI-based applications feature long-lived connections between the clients and the servers, while HTTP-based applications feature short-lived connections. Because operating systems represent each connection as a file descriptor, the number of available file descriptors effectively controls the number of client connections. To conserve resources, many operating systems have a default configuration that supports only a relatively small number of file descriptors per process. While this is fine for many types of applications, it can prove to be a limiting factor with large, server-based applications. Fortunately, most operating systems allow the system administrator to tune the maximum number of file descriptors per process.

In addition to the actual number of file descriptors a process can allocate, processes that open and close a lot of short-lived connections are vulnerable to another related operating system implementation detail. Without going into the details of the TCP/IP protocol, the problem is that the operating system must keep information about a closed TCP socket connection for some period of time. During this period of time, the operating system still considers the file descriptor for this connection to be active and therefore counts it in the process's total number of file descriptors. As you might imagine, applications that open and close a lot of connections in a relatively short period of time (for example, HTTP-based applications) can quickly consume many more file descriptors than you would normally expect given the number of concurrent connections. Fortunately, the period of time that the operating system holds on to these closed connection file descriptors is tunable in most operating systems. While the name of this parameter varies across operating systems, it is generically known as the *TCP time wait interval.*

From this short discussion of some fundamental operating system concepts and how they affect server-based applications, we hope that it is clear why it is critical to verify the operating system configuration before deploying a production application. While the details of all possible tuning parameters and operating systems are well beyond the scope of this book, we will talk more about operating system tuning in Chapter 12. We highly recommend consulting the WebLogic Server supported platforms documentation at http://edocs.bea.com/wls/certifications/certifications/index.html for more detailed recommendations on tuning any particular operating system.

Java Virtual Machine Configuration

Java Virtual Machine (JVM) tuning is another important configuration task for a WebLogic Server administrator. Choosing the right JVM, selecting the right JIT or HotSpot compiler options, selecting the appropriate heap size settings, and tuning the garbage collector are critical to the performance, scalability, and reliability of WebLogic Server-based applications. Although an in-depth discussion of the options is beyond the scope of this chapter, we recommend reading through the "Java Virtual Machine Tuning" section of Chapter 12, reviewing the recommendations on the BEA and JVM vendors' Web sites, and talking with other experienced developers and administrators on the BEA public newsgroups (see http://www.bea.com/support/newsgroup.shtml for more information).

Web Server Plug-in Configuration

The final topic in this section is configuring the WebLogic Server Web server plug-ins to proxy requests to a WebLogic Server instance or cluster (see Figure 11.3). WebLogic Server supports Web server proxy configurations with several different third-party Web servers (that is, Netscape/iPlanet, Microsoft, and Apache) as well as from another instance of WebLogic Server itself. For the three third-party Web servers, the proxy support uses a Web server plug-in, written to the native extension API of the Web server (for example, ISAPI for Microsoft's Internet Information Server), to proxy requests to WebLogic Server. A built-in servlet class, `weblogic.servlet.proxy.HttpClusterServlet`, provides the functionality when using WebLogic Server as the proxy. While a full discussion of all of the configuration options across all of the different supported Web servers is beyond the scope of this book, we will cover some of the important points in the context of the Apache Web Server plug-in configuration. Although the configuration details for each plug-in vary, the general concepts are similar across all Web server plug-ins. We believe that the discussion will still be useful even when not using Apache. For more complete and detailed coverage of Web server plug-in configurations, please see the WebLogic Server documentation on the BEA Web site at http://edocs.bea.com/wls/docs81/plugins/index.html.

In this example, we use the Apache Web server, so we will focus on the details of configuring the Apache plug-in. Some knowledge of Apache is useful when configuring the plug-in, but we will try our best to cover the trickier aspects of plug-in configuration without assuming too much prerequisite knowledge. For more complete information about the Apache Web server, or to download a copy of the software, please see the Apache Web server Web site at http://httpd.apache.org.

The first step in configuring any plug-in is to install the WebLogic Server plug-in's native libraries and tell the Web server to load them. For Apache, this means copying the appropriate shared library to a directory that Apache can find and adding the `LoadModule` directive to the Apache configuration file. Before you do anything, you need to verify WebLogic Server plug-in support for your version of Apache and verify that your version of Apache includes support for Dynamic Shared Objects. Please refer to the WebLogic Server documentation at http://edocs.bea.com/wls/certifications/certifications/overview.html for more information on the versions of Apache that WebLogic Server currently supports. To determine whether your version of Apache supports Dynamic Shared Objects, you need to run the server with the -l option. Change directories to the $APACHE_HOME/bin directory and run the Apache -l command (or the httpd -l command for Apache 1.3); the output should look similar to the following snippet and must include mod_so.c. If it does not, please refer to the WebLogic Server Apache plug-in documentation (http://edocs.bea.com/wls/docs81/plugins/apache.html) or the Apache Web server documentation (http://httpd.apache.org/docs-2.0/) for procedures for enabling this support.

```
> Apache -l
Compiled in modules:
  core.c
  mod_win32.c
  mpm_winnt.c
  http_core.c
  mod_so.c
```

Next, you need to locate the plug-in shared library for the operating system on which Apache is running. The operating system specific subdirectories under the $WL_HOME/server/lib directory contain the different plug-in shared libraries (under Windows, the plug-in will be in $WL_HOME/server/bin). The name of the plug-in varies depending on the version of Apache it supports and the operating system, but it always begins with mod_wl and ends with a shared library extension (for example, so, sl, or dll). Please consult the WebLogic Server Apache plug-in documentation for the correct shared library name for a particular platform and version of Apache.

Our example will use Apache 2.0.44 running under Windows 2000. Copy the mod_wl_20.so file from the $WL_HOME/server/bin directory to the $APACHE_HOME/modules directory, which, in our case, is c:\apache\Apache2\modules. Locate the httpd.conf file (in the $APACHE_HOME/conf directory) and add the following line at the end of the file:

```
LoadModule weblogic_module modules/mod_wl_20.so
```

At this point, it is a good idea to save these changes and try to restart the server. Run the following command to restart the server (replace "restart" with "start" if the server is not already running):

```
> Apache -k restart
```

To proceed further, you need more information about the application. The example reservation system application will use the Apache Web server only for customer self-service bookings. Although we won't be exploring the details of the application until the next section, we will assume that you know from your development staff that you want to redirect all requests to your Web site to your WebLogic Server cluster. To do this, you use the Location directive in conjunction with the SetHandler directive to tell Apache that all requests whose URLs match a particular pattern should be handled by the WebLogic Server plug-in. Add the following lines to the end of the httpd.conf to accomplish this:

```
<Location />
   SetHandler weblogic-handler
</Location>
```

Of course, this means that Apache will delegate every request to the WebLogic Server plug-in. In many cases, you may not actually want this. The plug-in also supports proxying requests by MIME type through the use of the `IfModule` directive in conjunction with the `MatchExpression` directive. Because our use of Apache is simple, you won't need to do this, so we suggest reviewing the WebLogic Server Apache plug-in documentation for more information on how to set this up.

At this point, you have configured Apache to send all requests that begin with `/user` and `/admin` to the plug-in, but how does the plug-in know what to do with the requests once they arrive? You need to tell the plug-in where to send the requests that it receives. To do this, use either the `WebLogicHost` and `WebLogicPort` directives or the `WebLogicCluster` directive, depending on whether you are forwarding to a single server instance or a cluster. We are forwarding requests to the cluster, so you must use the `WebLogicCluster` directive. Before you do this, however, you need to remember that we are using a NAT firewall between Apache and the WebLogic cluster. Therefore, we need to use the external IP addresses of the firewall instead of the actual (internal) IP addresses so that the plug-in can reach the servers. Let's modify the Location directive to add the `WebLogicCluster` directive with the external IP addresses and port number of our cluster.

```
<Location /user>
   SetHandler weblogic-handler
   WebLogicCluster 10.168.1.21:7001,10.168.1.22:7001,10.168.1.23:7001
</Location>
<Location /admin>
   SetHandler weblogic-handler
   WebLogicCluster 10.168.1.21:7001,10.168.1.22:7001,10.168.1.23:7001
</Location>
```

This completes the basic setup of the Apache plug-in for our simple application. The WebLogic Server plug-ins offer a wide variety of possible configurations and parameters to modify a plug-in's behavior. While the WebLogic Server documentation covers these in great detail, we will cover a few of the most commonly used parameters. The first set of parameters is as follows:

`PathTrim`. This parameter tells the plug-in to strip off a leading portion of the requested URL before forwarding the request to WebLogic Server.

`PathPrepend`. This parameter tells the plug-in to add to the leading portion of the requested URL before forwarding the request to WebLogic Server.

`DefaultFileName`. This parameter tells the plug-in what the default file name should be for URLs that end with `/`.

The parameters should be self-explanatory, but let's look at an example. Imagine that the request coming from the browser is for http://www.bea.com/wls/. If our

`PathTrim` is set to `/wls`, our `DefaultFileName` is set to `index.html`, and our `PathPrepend` is set to `/weblogic`, the plug-in will apply the following steps, in order, to transform the URL before sending it on to WebLogic Server.

1. The plug-in applies the `PathTrim` value to convert the relative URL from `/wls/` to `/`.
2. The plug-in applies the `DefaultFileName` value to convert the relative URL from `/` to `/index.html`.
3. The plug-in applies the `PathPrepend` value to convert the relative URL from `/index.html` to `/weblogic/index.html`.

Therefore, the plug-in transforms the original URL request of `/wls/` to `/weblogic/index.html` before sending the request to WebLogic Server. While these parameters can be useful, they also can cause unexpected problems you need to watch out for.

The plug-in's `PathTrim` and `PathPrepend` operations are unidirectional. This means that while the plug-in will intercept all requests and remove or add the specified values, it will not parse the HTML responses created by WebLogic Server to fix up any of the embedded URLs by reversing the trimming or prepending process. The browser will therefore see URLs representing the values returned by WebLogic Server rather than the values expected by the plug-in. While these parameters are useful for making a set of pages appear available at a different URL, the application must modify any navigational links within the pages to fit the new URL scheme. This behavior catches many administrators (and programmers) by surprise because you might expect any URL changes at the plug-in level to be completely transparent to the application—they are not.

The `DefaultFileName` value must match the Web application deployment descriptors' welcome file values. The plug-in uses this parameter to append to any URLs that end with `/`. Therefore, the administrator needs to make sure that the value set for `DefaultFileName` is the same as the welcome file setting the `web.xml` deployment descriptor(s) to which the `Location` parameter is forwarding (because the `Location` directive value might imply forwarding to multiple Web applications).

WARNING `PathTrim` **and** `PathPrepend` **do not modify navigational URLs embedded in the HTML returned to the browser. As a result, the application must be able to modify these navigational URLs to match the values created by these two parameters.** `DefaultFileName` **must match the value of the welcome file for all Web applications to which it applies.**

The plug-in uses the next set of parameters to determine its behavior in the case of response time degradations or failures:

`ConnectTimeoutSecs.` The total amount of time the plug-in waits for a connection to be established with a server. If the plug-in is unsuccessful, it returns an HTTP 503 (Service Unavailable) response code to the browser. The default value is 10 seconds.

ConnectRetrySecs. The amount of time the plug-in sleeps between connection requests to a server (or other servers in a cluster). Although the plug-in will always try to connect at least twice, the result of dividing the ConnectTimeoutSecs by the ConnectRetrySecs will determine the total number of connection requests before the plug-in gives up. The default value is 2 seconds.

HungServerRecoverSecs. The amount of time the plug-in will wait for a response from WebLogic Server. If the plug-in submits a request and the server does not respond within a certain time period, the plug-in will declare the server as dead and fail over to another server, if appropriate (see the following Idempotent parameter). The default value is 300 seconds.

Idempotent. Whether the plug-in should try to resend a request for which it did not receive a response within HungServerRecoverSecs. The default value is ON (which means the plug-in will retry).

ErrorPage. The absolute or relative URL to the page to display when the plug-in is unable to forward a request to WebLogic.

The plug-in's default values for ConnectTimeoutSecs and ConnectRetrySecs are usually sufficient for most situations. The appropriate value of Idempotent depends on the semantics of the application. When a request fails in such a way that the plug-in is unsure whether the server received the request, it is only safe for the plug-in to resend the request if the application is idempotent. Essentially, this means that the application state should be the same no matter if the server processes the request in question only once or multiple times. HungServerRecoverSecs controls the maximum amount of time for a server to process a request. If the time exceeds this, the plug-in will retry the request (if Idempotent is ON) or return an error to the user (if Idempotent is OFF or there are no more servers to accept the request). The ErrorPage simply tells the plug-in what to send back to the browser if it is unable to forward a request to WebLogic Server.

The last set of parameters controls the debugging features of the plug-in.

Debug. The value of this parameter controls how much logging information about requests and response the plug-in writes to the log file. By default, Debug is set to OFF so that no logging occurs.

WLLogFile. This parameter specifies the name and location of the log file (see the Debug parameter). If logging is on, the default log file location is either c:\temp\wlproxy.log or /tmp/wlproxy.log, depending on the platform.

DebugConfigInfo. This parameter controls access to the plug-in's configuration information by supplying the __WebLogicBridgeConfig query parameter on any URL the plug-in receives. By default, this feature is set to OFF.

The WebLogic Server plug-ins support many levels of logging to help debug problems with proxied requests. The valid values for the Debug parameter are

OFF. The plug-in doesn't log any information.

ON. The plug-in logs only informational and error messages.

HFC. The plug-in logs HTTP headers sent from the client to the plug-in.

HTW. The plug-in logs HTTP headers sent from the plug-in to WebLogic Server.

HFW. The plug-in logs HTTP headers sent from WebLogic Server back to the plug-in.

HTC. The plug-in logs HTTP headers sent from the plug-in back to the client.

ALL. The plug-in logs all of the information listed in the other settings.

The `Debug` parameter also supports combining any of the four individual HTTP header logging values by using a comma-separated list. Of course, turning logging on in a production situation may result in huge log files, so you need to keep this in mind. The `WLLogFile` parameter simply controls the name and location of the plug-in's log file if logging is enabled.

The `DebugConfigInfo` parameter offers a quick way of determining the configuration of the plug-in via a browser. By setting the parameter to `ON` and sending a URL to the plug-in containing the `__WebLogicBridgeConfig` query parameter, the plug-in will send back its current configuration information. For example, turn `DebugConfigInfo` on for your configuration by modifying the `Location` directive entry to look like this one:

```
<Location /user>
   SetHandler weblogic-handler
   WebLogicCluster 10.168.1.21:7001,10.168.1.22:7001,10.168.1.23:7001
   DebugConfigInfo ON
</Location>
```

Now, restart the Apache server. Enter http://www.bigrez.com/user?__WebLogicBridgeConfig in the browser to ask the plug-in for the configuration information. The return page should look something like the screen shown in Figure 11.7.

At this point, we have finished with the general configuration of the *bigrez.com* production environment. Even though the complexity of the example may seem a little overwhelming, rest assured that most production environments do not require this much configuration complexity. In fact, the simpler you can make the production environment, the better. The whole purpose of choosing such a complex environment was to demonstrate the flexibility of WebLogic Server for supporting almost any imaginable configuration requirement. Now, we are ready to move on to demonstrate how to take an application from your developers and deploy and manage it in a WebLogic Server environment.

Configuring Applications for WebLogic Server

Application developers typically set up their development environment to make it easy to go through the frequent compile, deploy, and test cycles of iterative development rapidly. This often means that when you are ready to promote an application into a more controlled environment, you may want to do some reorganizing and repackaging to make the production deployment environment simpler.

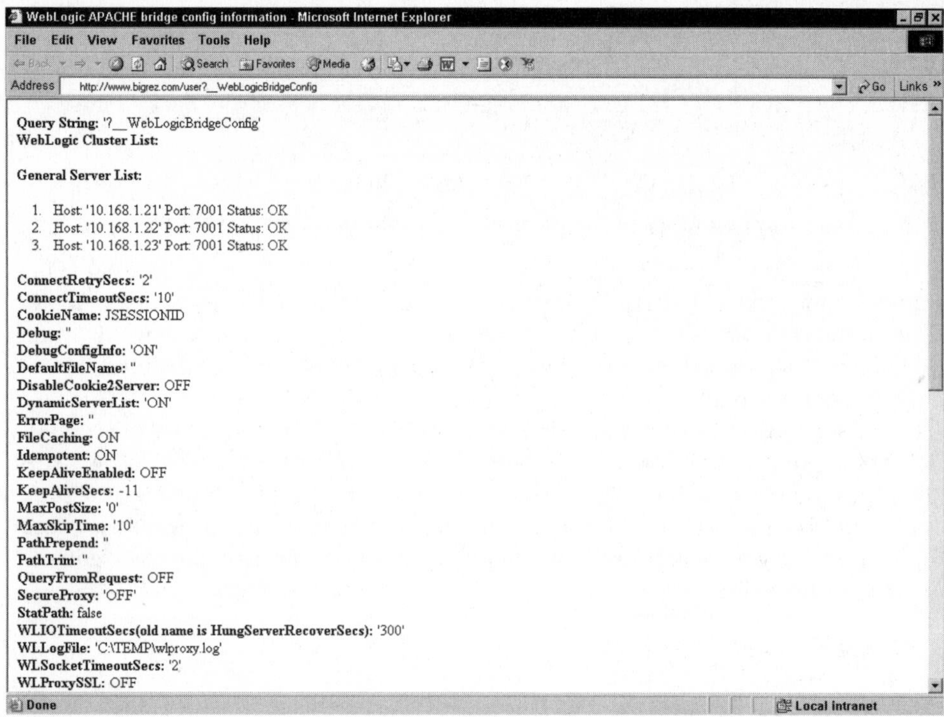

Figure 11.7 Viewing plug-in configuration data.

In Chapter 8, we discussed how to package the *bigrez.com* enterprise application into a self-contained enterprise application archive (EAR) file. While many administrators may not be responsible for application packaging, an understanding of J2EE application packaging will help you identify certain types of problems that may occur. Rather than covering application packaging again here, we suggest that you review the discussion in Chapter 8.

Configuring Database Resources

Most applications depend on databases to read and write pertinent application data. As a result, configuring database resources will be a common task of most WebLogic Server administrators. WebLogic Server provides a database connection pooling framework that provides applications with an efficient, standards-based mechanism for accessing databases without requiring them to optimize connection usage to improve performance. This framework also provides some critical, behind-the-scenes functionality to make sure that Java Transaction API (JTA) transactions have proper database transaction semantics. If your application uses JTA (as most EJB applications do), you must use this framework. Failure to do so can cause data consistency problems in event of rollbacks or failures. In this section, we will attempt to cover the important points of setting up a database connection pool and the associated `DataSource` objects that provide the application with standards-based access to the connection pooling facilities.

BEST PRACTICE Always use WebLogic Server's JDBC connection pooling rather than some other pooling mechanism. In addition to providing a robust pooling framework, JDBC connection pooling provides some critical, yet hidden transactional semantics to ensure that JTA transactions have the correct transactional semantics without any additional work on the part of the developer. Failure to use this may cause data integrity issues for applications that depend on JTA transactions involving database access.

Configuring JDBC Connection Pools

WebLogic Server supports making connections to any database management system for which a JDBC 2.0-compliant driver is available. JDBC drivers are available from a number of sources, including the database vendors, application server vendors, and other third-party companies. Unfortunately, the quality, features, and performance characteristics of JDBC drivers vary from driver to driver, and sometimes from release to release of the same driver. All other things being equal (which, in our experience, is usually not the case), we recommend using Type 4 drivers over Type 2 JDBC drivers because they do not depend on loading native libraries into the application server (bugs or improper use of native libraries can cause the JVM to crash). Typically, you will want to work with your development team to determine which JDBC driver works best for your application.

Once you know which JDBC driver to use, you will need to know a few things about the driver and a few things about the database to which you are connecting. Because the purpose of this discussion is to demonstrate how to configure WebLogic Server JDBC connection pools, we are going to choose a database and a JDBC driver and show the details of how to create a database connection pool. For more specific information on a particular JDBC driver configuration, please refer to the JDBC driver documentation and the WebLogic Server documentation.

For our example, we will use an Oracle database and the Oracle Thin JDBC Driver, a Type 4 driver available directly from Oracle. WebLogic Server includes a copy of the driver in the `$WL_HOME/server/lib` directory that it automatically loads with the server. If you were to choose the Oracle OCI (Type 2) Driver or the WebLogic jDriver for Oracle, you would have to install and configure the Oracle Client libraries and include them in the shared library path of the WebLogic Server.

The first thing we want to do is to get the right version of the driver available to the server. As mentioned earlier, WebLogic Server ships with a version of the Oracle Thin Driver `ojdbc14.jar` jar file. Although WebLogic Server tries to include the newest version of the driver, bug fixes and enhancements for this driver may mean that you may want to download a newer version from Oracle. Access to the drivers is currently available from http://technet.oracle.com/software/tech/java/sqlj_jdbc/content.html, though access to the drivers requires that you register with the Oracle Technology Network.

Once the required files exist on each machine where WebLogic Server instances will connect to the database, you need to make sure that each server's classpath is set to include references to these files before the reference to the WebLogic Server classes (for example, `weblogic.jar`). Because WebLogic Server 8.1 includes the latest Oracle 9.2

Thin Driver, we will use the included driver. If you want to use a different driver, you must modify the servers' `Classpath` attributes in their `Remote Start Configuration` tab (and restart the server if it is already running).

If you use a Type 2 driver, you either have to modify the node manager start scripts to put the shared libraries in its shared library search path or add an argument to the `Arguments` entry in the server's Remote `Start Configuration` tab to define the `java.library.path` system property with the correct shared library search path. Unfortunately, both of these mechanisms are problematic. The node manager start script modification works fine, but it assumes that all servers started by the node manager on a particular machine have the same shared library search path. In many situations, this might be okay, but it can be problematic if different servers are using different software versions of these native libraries (for example, different versions of the Oracle Client or different versions of WebLogic Server, in the case of the WebLogic jDriver). We prefer to use the `java.library.path` system property instead because it is server-specific rather than machine-specific. The only real issue with this mechanism is that you must remember to list all of the directories that need to be in the search path, including the ones that WebLogic Server scripts tend to set for you behind the scenes (for example, the platform-specific directories under the `$WL_HOME/server/lib` subdirectory on Unix or `$WL_HOME/server/bin` on Windows).

Now that the server has the necessary class files in the correct place in the classpath, we are ready to move on to setting up the connection pool. In previous versions of WebLogic Server, you needed to gather the following information before creating a connection pool:

Driver Class Name. The fully qualified name of the class that implements the `java.sql.Driver` interface. Your JDBC driver documentation should provide this information.

Driver URL Format. The format for the URL that tells the driver how to locate the correct database. Your JDBC driver documentation should provide information on the expected format. Depending on the information required, you may need some additional information from your database administrator (DBA).

Driver Properties. Properties that allow you to pass in driver-specific information. Every driver has a core set of information that it needs to connect to the database. Some of this information may be contained in the URL, while other information may have to be passed via properties. Please refer to the JDBC driver documentation for more specific information on what is required.

Database username/password. Required for connection pools. Connection pools are a set of connections that are functionally equivalent and shared by the application to process requests from all users. Therefore, you will need a database username and password with sufficient permissions to execute all the database work an application requires.

WebLogic Server 8.1 provides a JDBC Configuration Wizard in the WebLogic Console that allows you to pick from a list of known drivers and fill in the appropriate information. For our example, we just need to know the following information:

- Database Type: Oracle.
- Database Driver: Oracle's Driver (Thin) Versions: 8.1.7, 9.0.1, 9.2.0.
- Database Name: The Oracle SID (for example, ORCL).
- Host Name: The hostname or IP address of the server where the database is running (for example, 192.168.1.24).
- Port: The port where the Oracle Server is listening (for example, 1521).
- Database User Name: The database user to connect as (for example, bigrez).
- Database Password: The database user's password (for example, password).
- Properties: Any extra database-specific properties you need to set (none for this example).

Using this information, the WebLogic Console will guide you through the process of creating, testing, and deploying the JDBC connection pool to the cluster.

Once the pool is deployed, use the pool's Connections Configuration tab to set information about the connections in the pool. On this tab, three main parameters control the number of database connections in the pool: Initial Capacity, Maximum Capacity, and Capacity Increment. As you might expect, Initial Capacity defines the initial number of connections, Maximum Capacity defines the maximum number of connections, and Capacity Increment defines the number of connections by which to grow the pool when WebLogic Server determines it needs to increase the size of the pool.

BEST PRACTICE Whenever possible, try to size database connection pools properly so that they never need to grow the number of connections. Trying to grow the number of connections during a peak load situation can aggravate the situation because database connection creation is expensive.

If the application makes use of JDBC PreparedStatement objects, WebLogic Server can transparently cache these objects and dramatically improve the performance of the queries whose PreparedStatement object is in the cache. The Statement Cache Size parameter controls the size of the cache for each connection in the pool (because JDBC prepared statements are scoped to an individual connection). By default, WebLogic Server 8.1 uses a least-recently-used (LRU) caching algorithm to make room for new statements. Previous versions of WebLogic Server supported only the FIXED cache that simply fills each connection's cache with the first *n* prepared statements it encounters while using that connection, where *n* is the size of the cache. There may be memory, database resource, or other issues associated with the use of this feature. See the "Usage Restrictions for the Statement Cache" section of the WebLogic Console help page at http://edocs.bea.com/wls/docs81/ConsoleHelp/jdbc_connection_pools.html for more details on the potential issues with this feature.

BEST PRACTICE Make use of Prepared Statement caching if the application can tolerate the restrictions.

Under the `Advanced Options` section of the `Connections Configuration` tab, there are quite a few options that allow you to tailor the way the pool behaves. While we will not attempt to cover every option, we will discuss several of the more important options. For more complete information, see the WebLogic Server documentation at http://edocs.bea.com/wls/docs81/ConsoleHelp/jdbc_connection_pools.html.

The `Allow Shrinking` attribute will cause WebLogic Server to reclaim any dynamically created connections that are no longer in use after a certain amount of time. It will never try to shrink the pool below the value in `Initial Capacity`, however. The `Shrink Frequency` parameter defines the frequency (in seconds) with which WebLogic Server will scan the pool looking for unused connections to reclaim.

WebLogic Server also provides a mechanism to have the server periodically test unused connections from the pool to make sure that they are still valid. The `Test Frequency` attribute defines the frequency (in seconds) with which the server tests the unused connections. To determine the validity of a connection, WebLogic Server issues a query on the connection. The `Test Table Name` parameter allows the administrator to control the validation query. By default, the query is `SELECT count(*) FROM` <*Test Table Name*>. Most database systems can optimize this query to avoid a table scan, but it is still a good idea to use a table with no rows just in case. For Oracle, we recommend using the `DUAL` table for maximum performance. WebLogic Server also allows you to use the `Test Table Name` attribute to specify a different validation query. If `Test Table Name` begins with the characters `SQL`, WebLogic Server interprets everything that follows these characters as the literal query to execute.

The `Test Reserved Connections` checkbox enables validating connections as they are requested from the pool by the application. In the same way, `Test Released Connections` validates connections being released before they are placed back into the pool. Because the tests are done synchronously as part of the application's request to get a connection or to release it (by calling the `Connection.close()` method), using either of these two options will add some overhead to the application. Using `Test Reserved Connections` makes your application more resilient to network glitches that may close existing database connections. We do not see any reason to ever use `Test Released Connections` because, even if you make sure that the connection is good before returning it to the pool, there is no guarantee that it will still be good the next time it is needed.

BEST PRACTICE If you can afford the overhead of testing connections as part of normal request processing, always use `Test Reserved Connections` **to make the application more resilient. Make sure to use an empty table (or** `DUAL` **if using Oracle) as the** `Test Table Name`**.**

`Connection Reserve Timeout` specifies the maximum amount of time an application request to get a connection from the pool is allowed to block. By default, WebLogic Server 8.1 sets this to 10 seconds. The `Maximum Waiting for Connection` attribute limits the number of threads that can block waiting for a connection from the pool; by default, this is set to `java.lang.Integer.MAX_VALUE`. While this functionality helps applications deal with unexpected loads, never use this as a substitute for properly sizing connection pools. Any threads that have to block to get a connection are slowing down your application request processing.

Set the BigRezPool values according to those shown in Table 11.4. Any values not specified should be left at the default values.

Configuring JDBC DataSources

Now that you have a connection pool, you need to define one (or more) `DataSource` objects that allow your application developers to access the connection pool using standard J2EE mechanisms. WebLogic Server supports configuring `DataSource` objects through the WebLogic Console. These `DataSource` objects can either *honor global transactions* or not. In previous versions of WebLogic Server, a `DataSource` that honors global transactions was known as a `TxDataSource`. Unfortunately, many people do not understand the differences between the two.

Table 11.4 BigRezPool Connection Pool Configuration Parameters

NAME	VALUE
Database Type	Oracle
Database Driver	Oracle Driver (Thin) Versions: 8.1.7, 9.0.1, 9.2.0
Name	BigRezPool
Database Name	ORCL
Host Name	192.168.1.24
Port	1521
Database User Name	bigrez
Password	password
Targets	BigRezCluster (All servers in the cluster)
Initial Capacity	60
Maximum Capacity	60
Capacity Increment	0
Statement Cache Type	LRU
Statement Cache Size	100
Allow Shrinking	No (unchecked)
Test Frequency	300
Test Reserved Connections	Yes (checked)

The primary difference is that DataSources that honor global transactions are JTA transaction-aware. Realize that JTA transactions do not necessarily mean XA transactions and two-phase commits (2PC). JTA transactions also allow two independently written components that modify the same database to participate in a transaction without having to know about each other. Non-XA database transactions require the use of a single database connection to provide the proper transactional semantics. If you choose not to use the Honor Global Transactions option, you need to write your application components in such a way that they get a database connection from the pool at the start of every transaction and pass that connection around to every component that participates in the transaction. This is clearly not desirable and not even possible with certain types of components (for example, container-managed entity beans).

A DataSource that honors global transactions will make sure that your components participating in a JTA transaction get the proper transactional semantics whether they are using JTA transactions or not. When not using XA transactions, the DataSource accomplishes this by associating a database connection with a JTA transaction context. Every time a component asks for a database connection using the DataSource that honors global transactions, WebLogic Server will check to see if the current transaction already has a database connection, and if so, it will always hand back the same underlying database connection. This allows non-XA transactions to maintain the proper database semantic guarantees without having to worry about what database connection to use and what the transactional boundaries are for the application.

What this means is that every application that uses JTA transactions, which includes most EJB applications and many JMS applications, must use DataSource objects that honor global transactions to access their respective database connection pools. Failure to do so will expose the application to database consistency problems during JTA transaction rollback or failures. DataSource objects that do not honor global transactions will ignore any JTA transaction context. Therefore, unless your application is intentionally trying to do database work outside the scope of a transaction, you must use the Honors Global Transactions option. When in doubt, always use the Honors Global Transactions option.

BEST PRACTICE When defining DataSource **objects for a connection pool, you almost always want to use the** Honors Global Transactions **option even if you are not using XA transactions. By honoring global transactions, WebLogic Server keeps any JTA transactional semantics in sync with the underlying database transaction semantics. When in doubt, always use the** Honors Global Transactions **option.**

Let's define the DataSource for the BigRezPool. Using the WebLogic Console, you simply specify the Name, JNDI Name, and Pool Name for the DataSource. Make sure to leave the Honors Global Transactions checkbox enabled. Before selecting the JNDI name, you should check with the developers to determine what JNDI name they are using to look up the DataSource object in the application.

Typically, the code will use a logical name specific to the J2EE component (for example, a session EJB might use the logical name java:comp/env/jdbc/BigRezDataSource), and the component's deployment descriptor will map this logical name to the actual name that you should specify in the WebLogic Console. For example, the `ejb-jar.xml` deployment descriptor for one of our session EJBs declares the logical name the code is using by the following entry:

```
<resource-ref>
  <res-ref-name>jdbc/BigRezDataSource</res-ref-name>
  <res-type>javax.sql.DataSource</res-type>
  <res-auth>Container</res-auth>
</resource-ref>
```

Notice that the `java:comp/env/` prefix in the code tells WebLogic Server that the name is logical, so you don't see it here.

Then, this logical name is mapped to the actual name with the following entry in the session EJB's `weblogic-ejb-jar.xml` deployment descriptor:

```
<reference-descriptor>
  <resource-description>
    <res-ref-name>jdbc/BigRezDataSource</res-ref-name>
    <jndi-name>BigRezDataSource</jndi-name>
  </resource-description>
</reference-descriptor>
```

This means that our application is expecting to find the `DataSource` it needs by using the JNDI name of `BigRezDataSource`. The nice part about this is that you can easily change the JNDI name of the `DataSource` objects without having to change the actual application code. Unfortunately, not all J2EE application developers take advantage of this feature, so your application may be using the actual JNDI names in the code.

So, this means that the application is expecting the `JNDI Name` for our `BigRezDataSource` to be `BigRezDataSource`. Set this value in the WebLogic Console window used to create the `DataSource`.

BEST PRACTICE **Encourage developers to use logical JNDI names in their code and leverage the EJB or Web application deployment descriptors to map these logical names to the actual names configured in WebLogic Server.**

Configuring XA Support

Although we haven't talked about configuring JMS yet, our developers have just informed us that they are adding a persistent JMS queue to the application and need to use XA transactions for operations that involve both the JMS queue and our Oracle database. This means that we need to change our database resources to support using Oracle's XA interface. Fortunately, making these changes to an existing configuration is easy.

To support true XA transactions, we need to use an XA-enabled JDBC driver. Because the Oracle Thin Driver supports XA, we simply change the `Driver Classname` attribute from `oracle.jdbc.driver.OracleDriver` to `oracle.jdbc.xa.client.OracleXADataSource`. When you restart the managed servers, the log file will now have an entry like the one shown here that lets you know that the pool is now using XA connections:

```
####<Apr 11, 2003 12:21:12 PM CDT> <Info> <JDBC> <machine1> <Server1>
 <main> <<WLS Kernel>> <> <BEA-001072> <Connection for XA pool
 "BigRezPool" created.>
```

Before we move on, we should mention a couple of additional features surrounding XA and JDBC. The first is the `Supports Local Transaction` option in the `Advanced Options` section of the connection pool's `Connections Configuration` tab. This option lets the administrator tell WebLogic Server whether the XA Driver supports updates without a global transaction context. The proper setting for this will vary by database vendor (for example, Oracle does not support local transactions, but Sybase does). Because the Oracle Thin Driver does not support this, no configuration changes are necessary.

WebLogic Server also allows non-XA resources to participate in XA transactions. Before we go any further, this does not mean that WebLogic Server can turn a non-XA resource into an XA resource. What this means is that WebLogic Server will fake a two-phase commit with a non-XA resource in a manner that attempts to maintain the transactional integrity. To enable this option, use the `Emulate Two-Phase Commit for non-XA Driver` option in the `Advanced Options` section of the `DataSource` object's `Configuration` tab.

WebLogic Server allows only one such non-XA resource per transaction. WebLogic Server 8.1 uses a *last commit* algorithm that minimizes the exposure to heuristic failures introduced by using the non-XA resource. This algorithm starts by preparing the XA resources. If the XA resources all prepare successfully, the transaction coordinator then tries to commit the non-XA resource. If the commit succeeds, the coordinator tells the XA resources to commit; if the non-XA resource fails to commit, the coordinator tells the XA resources to roll back.

Configuring JMS Resources

Many applications use some sort of messaging. Common uses for messaging involve asynchronous communication with other applications, store-and-forward situations where the external system may not always be available, and even situations where you want to avoid the overhead of performing a particular operation synchronously as part of processing a user request (for example, sending an email confirmation). The Java Message Service (JMS) is the J2EE standard API for interacting with messaging systems. WebLogic Server provides a robust, high-performance messaging system that fully supports the JMS specification. In addition, WebLogic JMS also supports plugging in external, third-party messaging systems via their JMS APIs to support things like message-driven beans (MDBs) listening directly to externally provided destinations for messages. For more information about WebLogic JMS, please see Chapter 9 and the WebLogic Server documentation at http://edocs.bea.com/wls/docs81/jms/index.html.

Our example application uses three JMS queues. The global reservation systems' Web services interface uses two queues—an incoming queue to buffer requests from the external system and an outgoing queue to buffer responses to the external system. Internet customer bookings use a queue to buffer email confirmations of interactions with the *bigrez.com* site. In this section, we will walk through the steps for configuring the JMS services needed for a production deployment of the *bigrez.com* application. We assume that you have read Chapter 9, and therefore we do not spend much time describing particular JMS objects or features here.

Creating JMS Servers and Stores

The first thing we need to do is set up the JMS servers. A JMS server is an administrative grouping of JMS destinations that run on the same WebLogic Server instance and share a set of common characteristics. One WebLogic Server instance can support multiple JMS servers. In the event of failure or maintenance, we can migrate JMS servers from one WebLogic Server instance to another. As part of this migration, we may need to migrate the JTA service to recover any incomplete transactions involving the JMS server's persistent store, depending on whether we are using JTA transactions with persistent messages for any of the JMS server's underlying destinations.

Before we create our JMS Servers, we need to determine if we need a JMS persistent store and, if so, what type of store to use. WebLogic JMS supports two types of JMS Stores: file-based and JDBC-based. For the file-based store, JMS messages are persisted to disk. The JDBC-based store writes the messages to a database using a WebLogic Server connection pool. In general, the file-based store is much faster than JDBC-based stores. WebLogic JMS provides an XA Resource interface to allow the file store to participate in XA transactions. Because the file store is disk-based, migration support for a JMS Server using a file store depends on the file store being accessible from another machine.

Applications that choose to use persistent messages generally do so because they cannot afford to lose any messages. Both the file- and JDBC-based stores give the application the persistence that they need. If a WebLogic Server (or the machine on which it is running) goes down, the messages will remain in the JMS store until either the server is restarted or the JMS server is migrated to another machine. The need for migration varies with the application. For some applications, it may be sufficient to wait until the failed server restarts to process the messages in the failed server's JMS store; other applications may be time-sensitive and require the ability to process the messages in the failed server's store.

BEST PRACTICE Don't automatically assume that your JMS-based applications require support for JMS server migration. Migration is typically important for persistent messages sent to a queue where the processing of those messages is time-critical.

If you need to migrate JMS servers that are using file-based message stores, you need to invest in multi-ported disks, a SAN, or other highly available disk-sharing technology. Never use NFS for this purpose because NFS generally cannot provide the transactional guarantees that JMS requires for disk writes. For simplicity, we will use a JDBC-based store to demonstrate JMS migration capabilities without requiring costly disk-sharing technology. Realize that we are making a trade-off here because a JDBC-based store is generally slower than a file store.

BEST PRACTICE High-volume, performance-critical applications should use the JMS file store rather than the JDBC-based store. If migration is required, use a multi-ported disk array or SAN-based solution for making the file store available across servers. Never use NFS to share a file store in a production system.

Before creating the JDBC-based store, you need to set up a JDBC connection pool for the store. Because WebLogic JMS implements the XA Resource interface to allow the file store to participate in XA transactions, the JDBC-based store must use a non-XA connection to the underlying database. So, let's go back and create a non-XA connection pool for our JDBC store using the properties shown in Table 11.5.

Use the WebLogic Console to create the JDBC-based stores. You need a separate store for each server in the cluster. Table 11.6 shows the values to use for creating the store for `Server1`. Create similar stores for `Server2` and `Server3`.

Table 11.5 JMS JDBC-Based Store Connection Pool Configuration Parameters

NAME	VALUE
Database Type	Oracle
Database Driver	Oracle Driver (Thin) Versions: 8.1.7, 9.0.1, 9.2.0
Name	JMS Store Pool
Database Name	ORCL
Host Name	192.168.1.24
Port	1521
Database User Name	bigrez
Password	password
Targets	BigRezCluster (All servers in the cluster)
Initial Capacity	1
Maximum Capacity	3
Capacity Increment	1
Statement Cache Type	LRU
Statement Cache Size	10

Table 11.6 Server1's JDBC-Based JMS Store Configuration Parameters

NAME	VALUE
Name	JMS JDBC Store1
Connection Pool	JMS Store Pool
Prefix Name	JMS_Store1_

Finally, you are ready to create the JMS servers. Create three JMS servers with the names `JMS Server1`, `JMS Server2`, and `JMS Server3` using the persistent stores `JMS JDBC Store1`, `JMS JDBC Store2`, and `JMS JDBC Store3`, and target them to `Server1`, `Server2`, and `Server3`, respectively. Notice that each JMS server can be targeted only to one server instance.

Creating Distributed JMS Destinations

Each JMS server will contain one or more JMS destinations and will live on a particular server instance. Because our application uses three distributed JMS destinations and does not need to refer to the individual member destinations explicitly, you can move directly to creating the distributed destinations. WebLogic Server can create the individual member destinations for you automatically.

We will use `GRS Request Queue`, `GRS Response Queue`, and `BigRez Email Queue` as the names of our distributed queues. We also need to specify their JNDI names. Like the JDBC `DataSource` earlier, we want to decouple the JNDI names that our application uses to look up the JMS queues from their actual JNDI names. This is just as easy to accomplish using similar deployment descriptor mechanisms. For example, our `ejb-jar.xml` deployment descriptor should have a reference like the one shown here to declare that the application is using the logical JNDI name `java:comp/env/jms/BigRezEmailQueue` to look up the queue:

```
<resource-ref>
    <res-ref-name>jms/BigRezEmailQueue</res-ref-name>
    <res-type>javax.jms.Queue</res-type>
    <res-auth>Container</res-auth>
</resource-ref>
```

A corresponding entry in the `weblogic-ejb-jar.xml` deployment descriptor will map this logical JNDI name to the actual JNDI name.

```
<reference-descriptor>
    <resource-description>
        <res-ref-name>jms/BigRezEmailQueue</res-ref-name>
        <jndi-name>BigRezEmailQueue</jndi-name>
    </resource-description>
</reference-descriptor>
```

This means that the application is expecting us to use the JNDI name `BigRezE-mailQueue` when registering this queue. The other two queues use similarly constructed JNDI names.

Distributed queues must also specify a `Load Balancing Policy` and a `Forward Delay`. The `Load Balancing Policy` describes the way in which WebLogic JMS distributes incoming messages across the distributed queue's member queues, all other things being equal. Remember that WebLogic JMS uses sophisticated algorithms to optimize processing of messages so that the load balancing policy applies only when every queue has similar run-time characteristics. `Forward Delay` specifies the number of seconds WebLogic JMS will wait before attempting to forward messages from one member queue to another if the queue in question has no active consumers. For our example, we will use round-robin load balancing and a `Forward Delay` of –1, which disables forwarding of messages. Because all of our queues are using MDBs as consumers, we do not expect ever to have a member queue available without any consumers for any extended period of time.

Once the distributed queue exists, you need to configure it and have WebLogic Server automatically deploy the underlying member queues to the cluster. Using the `Thresholds & Quotas Configuration` tab, you can set limits on the size of the queue as well as thresholds at which WebLogic JMS will begin paging or controlling the producer's message flow rates.

In the *bigrez.com* application, external clients never send messages directly to any of the JMS queues. For these queues, the application produces the messages that go into the queues so under no circumstances do we want to slow down the message producers (our application) by enabling flow control. So, what does this all mean to you as the WebLogic Server administrator trying to configure the JMS destinations?

It means that the primary goal of setting the thresholds and quotas is to limit the amount of memory consumed rather than controlling the flow. To control the flow of messages into the system through the `GRS Request Queue`, you should use connection throttling to limit the number of concurrent connections to a particular server rather than trying to throttle requests once they have reached the server. Unfortunately, there is currently no way to limit the number of connections through a particular network channel so you would have to try to limit the number of connections at the server level, or maybe use network hardware in front of the server. We expect BEA will add this type of support in a future release.

Because all we want to do is prevent the JMS messages from filling up the server's memory, you need to determine how many messages of each type you will permit in memory before you want WebLogic JMS to start paging the messages out of memory. Remember, even persistent messages stay in memory for speed so paging is important even for persistent messages. You don't need to create a separate paging store for persistent messages, though, because the messages are already written to the message store.

After thorough analysis of our message sizes, JVM heap sizes, and application characteristics, we have decided to limit the maximum number of each type of message in a single server to 50,000 before paging starts. We can support many more messages when using message paging but we want to avoid message paging because it adds significant overhead and will hurt performance. We will also limit the maximum number of bytes of memory consumed by each type of message to 50 MBs before paging starts. As a result, we use the values shown in Table 11.7 for setting the thresholds and quotas.

Table 11.7 Distributed Destination Threshold and Quotas Configuration Parameters

NAME	VALUE
Bytes Maximum	500,000,000
Bytes Threshold High	50,000,000
Bytes Threshold Low	25,000,000
Bytes Paging Enabled	Yes (checked)
Messages Maximum	500,000
Messages Threshold High	50,000
Messages Threshold Low	25,000
Maximum Message Size	1,000,000
Message Paging Enabled	Yes (checked)

Now, you need to assign member queues to each distributed queue. If the member queues already exist, you need to use the distributed queue's `Members Configuration` tab to add member queues from one or more JMS servers. Because we chose not to create the individual queues manually, you will use the `Auto Deploy` tab's wizard to step you through the process of automatically creating the member queues. Simply tell the wizard that you want to target the `BigRezCluster`, create members on `Server1`, `Server2`, and `Server3`, and use `JMS Server1`, `JMS Server2`, and `JMS Server3`; the wizard does the rest. Once you complete this process, the `Members Configuration` tab will show you the results of this process.

Configuring Member Destinations

While the Auto Deploy Wizard saves a lot of tedious configuration, distributed destinations do not expose all of the underlying options for configuring a JMS destination. For a production system, you may want to tweak the settings on your individual member destinations a bit. JMS queues have many different configuration options that are important in different situations. We are not going to attempt to cover all of them here; Chapter 9 covers these options in great detail. For any additional information, please refer to the WebLogic Server documentation at http://edocs.bea.com/wls/docs81/ConsoleHelp/jms_config.html.

The first thing you should do is to set the `Enable Store` parameter on each member queue's `General Configuration` tab. Because we want to make sure that all of the messages are persistent, which requires each JMS server to have a persistent store, you should set `Enable Store` to `true` so that the WebLogic JMS server will fail to boot if the persistent store does not exist. This is simply a way to double-check that the system configuration is correct and prevent starting the application if it is not.

One important thing to note is that if you look at a particular member queue's `Thresholds & Quotas Configuration` tab, you will not see the values entered in the distributed destination used to create this queue. The reason is that the distributed destination's auto-deploy process created a JMS template that the member queues automatically inherit the values from if not overridden on the destination itself.

Next, you want to override the delivery mode by setting the `Delivery Mode Override` to persistent. While you could use the member queues' `Overrides Configuration` tab, it is easier to set the override on the JMS templates' `Override Configuration` tab. Again, this is simply a sanity check to make sure that our application is not trying to send non-persistent messages to these destinations. On this same tab, you should set the `Time To Live Override` for the two GRS-related templates. Given that we know that the client time-out for receiving a particular request is 15 seconds, there is no point to store a message in these queues for longer than 15 seconds. Set the value to 15000 because the value is set in milliseconds. By specifying this here rather than in the application, it is simpler to change should the clients decide to change their time-out value.

Finally, we need to set the redelivery characteristics of our member queues. For the email-related member queues, the only reason the application should fail to deliver the message is if the email server is down (because other conditions like invalid email addresses are handled in the business logic). From past experience, we know that it normally takes 3 minutes for us to detect that the email server is down and restart it. Because the timeliness of these email messages is not critical, we will set the `Redelivery Delay Override` to 180000 milliseconds (3 minutes) and the `Redelivery Limit` to 80 using the `BigRez Email Queue` template.

For the GRS-related queues, the application cannot afford any significant delay in redelivery, and there is no reason to retry for too long because the client times out in 15 seconds. Therefore, we set the `Redelivery Delay Override` to 1000 milliseconds and the `Redelivery Limit` to 15 using the GRS-related templates. By specifying a `Redelivery Limit` but not specifying the `Error Destination`, you are telling WebLogic JMS to discard the message after the set number of failed redelivery attempts. If you set the `Error Destination`, WebLogic JMS will move the message onto the `Error Destination`.

BEST PRACTICE **Tune thresholds and quotas, overrides, and redelivery to explicitly control the behavior of JMS destinations. Leaving the behavior up to the clients can make it difficult to change configurations as requirements change and can expose the application's behavior to configuration mistakes.**

Creating JMS Connection Factories

At this point, we are ready to set up the JMS connection factories. A JMS connection factory is the object through which JMS applications obtain a JMS connection. Configuring a JMS connection factory allows the administrator to customize the behavior of all JMS clients that use the connection factory without requiring code changes. We will configure three JMS connection factory objects, one for each distributed destination. As with JMS destinations, the JNDI names required during configuration should be entirely dependent on the EJB or Web application deployment descriptors.

Creating a JMS connection factory requires specifying a large number of configuration parameters. For many of these parameters, you will simply use the default values and skip over detailed explanations of what they do. Refer to Chapter 9 or the WebLogic JMS documentation at http://edocs.bea.com/wls/docs81/messaging.html

for more information. The parameters of interest in this discussion are `Default Time To Live`, `Default Delivery Mode`, and `Default Redelivery Delay`. For each distributed queue, create a connection factory for use with each queue, and set the values according to those shown in Table 11.8.

Next, you need to configure the transactional semantics of the JMS Connection Factories. Using the `Transactions Configuration` tab, you should set the `Transaction Timeout` to 60 seconds for the email-related connection factory and 15 seconds for the GRS-related connection factories. Unlike the time-out values on the previous tab, which were specified in milliseconds, the `Transaction Timeout` is specified in seconds. This tab also lets you enable the use of XA connection factories. Because we are using XA transactions with all three queues, you must check the `XA Connection Factory Enabled` checkbox for all three connection factories.

Configuring JMS Migration Support

The last step of configuring JMS is to configure the ability to migrate our JMS Servers from one WebLogic Server instance to another. This means we have to go back and configure migration in several places. Because we are using XA transactions with our JMS destinations, we will also need to make sure that the JTA transaction logs are available via a highly available, shared disk. It might seem odd that we have waited until now to talk about migration, but the reality is that many WebLogic Server-based applications do not require migration. JMS applications that use persistent queuing may need to be able to migrate the JMS Server (and JTA service, if applicable) to another server so as to be able to process the persistent messages in a timely fashion.

To configure WebLogic Server to support migration, you start by configuring the backup servers for each WebLogic Server instance. For our example, we are going to allow each server to use any other server in the cluster as a potential migration target. Use each server's `JMS Migration Config. Control` tab to add all servers to the `Chosen` list of possible migration destinations. Do the same thing for each server's JTA service using the `JTA Migration Config. Control` tab. Now, go back to each JMS server and use the `Target And Deploy` tab to retarget each JMS server to the migratable version of each WebLogic Server instance. For example, `JMS Server1` should now be targeted at `Server1 (migratable)`.

At this point, the configuration of our application's JMS resources is complete. We only have to configure our JavaMail session for our email confirmation service, set up and tune our application-specific execute queues, and deploy our application.

Table 11.8 JMS Connection Factory Configuration Parameters

CONNECTION FACTORY NAME	DEFAULT TIME TO LIVE	DEFAULT DELIVERY MODE	DEFAULT REDELIVERY DELAY
BigRez Email Connection Factory	0	Persistent	180000
GRS Request Connection Factory	15000	Persistent	1000
GRS Response Connection Factory	15000	Persistent	1000

Configuring JavaMail Sessions

The *bigrez.com* application uses the JavaMail API to send email confirmations to our customers via a mail server. To make that process more transparent to the application, WebLogic Server provides the ability to define JavaMail sessions that applications can look up from JNDI and use without having to understand where the mail server lives, how to authenticate, what protocols to use, and so on. For our example, we will use a mail server on our network, `mail.bigrez.com`. Go to the `Services->Mail` folder in the WebLogic Console's left-hand navigation bar and create a new mail session with the name `BigRez Email Session`. As with our other resources, the JNDI name that applications use to locate this session will be a logical name. The EJB or Web application deployment descriptor will map the logical name to the actual name that the session will use. Use the JNDI name `BigRezEmailSession` to create the mail session. The `Properties` attribute is simply the JavaMail properties to use when creating the session:

```
mail.transport.protocol=smtp
mail.smtp.host=mail.bigrez.com
mail.smtp.user=bigrez
mail.smtp.password=password
```

After creating the Mail Session, don't forget to target it to all servers in the `BigRez-Cluster`.

Configuring Execute Queues and Threads

For our application, you are going to use one application-specific execute queue to guarantee a certain number of resources (that is, threads) are always available to process requests from our internal reservation agents. To accomplish this, you need to define another execute queue on each server in the cluster. Create an execute queue named `CSA Execute Queue` with 10 threads in each server. To make use of this execute queue, you need to use the `dispatch-policy` element of the `weblogic-ejb-jar.xml` deployment descriptor to specify that the EJB requests should use the `CSA Execute Queue`.

In addition, you should adjust the number of execute threads in the default queue to 50. Notice that the total number of execute threads in each server is the same as the number of database connections in the JDBC connection pool, `BigRezPool`. This is not just a coincidence. Because the application spends most of its time in the database, you want to make sure that every execute thread can get a database connection from the pool without having to wait. We will talk more about optimizing the number of database connections and execute threads later. Now, let's deploy the application.

Deploying Applications

Deploying the application is easy. As long as the EAR file is accessible from either the admin server machine or the machine from which you are running the WebLogic Console, you can do everything from the browser. Using the WebLogic Console, open the

Deployments->Applications folder in the left-hand navigation bar. After selecting the Deploy a new Application link, select the upload your file(s) link embedded in the help text, upload the bigrez.ear file, and deploy it to all servers in the BigRezCluster. Don't forget to start the cluster before trying to deploy the application.

In addition to the WebLogic Console, WebLogic Server provides a rich set of command-line accessible administrative functionality. The first tool we will look at is the command-line deployment tool, weblogic.Deployer. The weblogic.Deployer program allows an administrator to deploy, undeploy, and get the status of deployed applications. While we will not attempt to cover all of the possible options with weblogic.Deployer, we will cover some basic features. For more information, please see the WebLogic Server documentation at http://edocs.bea.com/wls/docs81/deployment/tools.html.

The first task we want to accomplish is making the deployment tool talk to the administration port of the admin server. Remember that by enabling this administration port, the plain-text port can no longer be used to perform administrative functions, and all communication with the admin server requires SSL communication. To accomplish this, you must define the Java system property weblogic.security.SSL.trustedCAKeyStore to tell the deployer tool where to find your trusted CA key store (see Chapter 10 for more information). If you are using the demo certificates that came with WebLogic Server, you also need to set the Java system property weblogic.security.SSL.ignoreHostnameVerification to true to tell the deployer tool to ignore the hostname in the server's certificate. In our example, the first portion of every command you invoke using the deployer tool will look like the following line:

```
java -Dweblogic.security.SSL.trustedCAKeyStore=ClientTrustStore.jks
```

When using the deployer tool, we also need to specify the URL to use to contact the admin server, a username with sufficient privileges to invoke the command, and the user's password. If you use the system account, that means that every time you invoke the deployer tool, the command line will always begin with the following contents:

```
java -Dweblogic.security.SSL.trustedCAKeyStore=ClientTrustStore.jks
     weblogic.Deployer -adminurl https://192.168.1.20:9002
                       -username system -password insecure
```

Of course, you also need to make sure that the PATH and CLASSPATH environment variables are set properly so that you find the JVM and the weblogic.Deployer class. To make this simpler, let's create the following script file called weblogicDeployer.cmd in the Chapter 11 example directory (for example, c:\mastering\ch11_examples):

```
@SETLOCAL
@call setEnv.cmd
java -Dweblogic.security.SSL.trustedCAKeyStore=ClientTrustStore.jks
weblogic.Deployer -adminurl https://192.168.1.20:9002 -username system
-password insecure %*
@ENDLOCAL
```

This script will allow us to run the deployer tool with a command of the form `weblogicDeployer` *<args>**. For example, let's run the new script using the Deployer's `list` command to see what applications are deployed in our cluster:

```
> weblogicDeployer -targets BigRezCluster -list

#TaskID Action    Status  Target          Type    Application  Source
0       Activate  Success BigRezCluster   Cluster bigrez       ...
```

Using the deployer, you can also deploy new applications and undeploy running applications. For example, let's say that you just received a new copy of the `bigrez.ear` file from your developers and want to deploy the new version into the `BigRezCluster` that is already running an older version. You need to run the following commands to undeploy the old version.

```
> weblogicDeployer -targets BigRezCluster -name bigrez
                   -unprepare bigrez.ear

Operation started, waiting for notifications...
...............
#TaskID Action    Status  Target          Type    Application  Source
1       Unprepare Success BigRezCluster   Cluster bigrez       null
```

Now, run the following command to deploy the new version.

```
> weblogicDeployer -source c:\temp\bigrez.ear -targets BigRezCluster
                   -name bigrez -activate

Operation started, waiting for notifications...
........................
#TaskID Action    Status  Target          Type    Application  Source
0       Activate Success  BigRezCluster   Cluster bigrez       ...
```

You now have at least two ways to deploy an application: the WebLogic Console and the `weblogic.Deployer` program. We favor the deployer program because it lends itself to scripting common actions and provides a rich set of deployment options.

During our discussions of WebLogic Server configuration issues and options, we have covered a lot of ground. We hit many of the high points that we feel are likely to be relevant to the largest percentage of applications. However, we haven't covered everything. Our hope is that we provided enough information to give you a good head start on what you need to become an effective WebLogic Server administrator. From this point on, we will turn our focus to discussing how to monitor and manage WebLogic Server applications to keep them running optimally and how to handle different types of failure conditions.

Monitoring WebLogic Server Applications

Before we discuss how to manage applications, we are going to cover some techniques for monitoring WebLogic Server applications. Fortunately, WebLogic Server provides numerous tools and techniques for monitoring different aspects of a distributed application. This section starts off by introducing another command-line administration tool, `weblogic.Admin`. Next, we look into areas of the WebLogic Console that allow you to monitor the run-time behavior of the server and your applications. We will spend a little time discussing the Java Management Extensions (JMX) APIs, which provide programmatic access to most configuration capabilities as well as run-time monitoring. We finish off the section by briefly touching on the SNMP capabilities of WebLogic Server.

Using the Command-Line Administration Tool

WebLogic Server offers access to most administrative functionality through a command-line administration tool called `weblogic.Admin`. Through this tool, you can do almost everything from basic sanity checks for things like version information, connectivity, and latency, to issuing JMX commands to alter the configuration of a server. Although we will discuss this tool in multiple places throughout the rest of this chapter, we will not attempt to cover every possible option exhaustively. For more information, see the WebLogic Server documentation at http://edocs.bea.com/wls/docs81/admin_ref/cli.html.

As with the deployer tool, the admin tool requires that the same Java system parameters be defined to support using the SSL protocol to communicate with the administration port on the admin server. In addition, the admin tool requires certain command-line options for every command. Therefore, we will create another script called `weblogicAdmin.cmd` to automate the process of invoking this program. Once again, we will place this script in the Chapter 11 examples directory (`c:\mastering\ch11_examples`):

```
@SETLOCAL
@call setEnv.cmd
@if "%URL%" == "" set URL=t3s://192.168.1.20:9002
@java -Dweblogic.security.SSL.trustedCAKeyStore=ClientTrustStore.jks
weblogic.Admin -url %URL% -username system -password insecure %*
@ENDLOCAL
```

Unlike the deployer tool, some commands in the admin tool support talking directly to the managed servers through their admin port. For example, you can use the admin tool to check the WebLogic Server software version information for `Server1` using the following commands:

```
> set URL=t3s://192.168.1.21:9002
> weblogicAdmin VERSION
WebLogic Server 8.1  Thu Mar 20 23:06:05 PST 2003 246620
WebLogic XMLX Module 8.1  Thu Mar 20 23:06:05 PST 2003 246620
```

Now, let's look at some of the monitoring capabilities of the admin tool. We have already seen how to get the WebLogic Server software version information from a specific server. We can also look at the licenses for the server using the LICENSES command. Like the VERSION command, the LICENSES command takes no additional arguments and returns the license information for the server to which we send the command. The GETSTATE command displays the status of a particular server, either by asking the server itself or by asking the admin server, as shown here:

```
> set URL=

> weblogicAdmin GETSTATE Server3
Current state of "Server3" : RUNNING
```

To verify that a server is accepting connections and processing requests, we can use the PING command. This command connects to the targeted server, sends one or more requests to the server, waits for the server to respond to each request, and measures the round-trip time. These ping requests go through the same mechanism as other requests in that they get placed onto the default execute queue and an execute thread picks up the request and returns the response to the caller. Using the optional arguments of the PING command that specify the number of requests and the size of each request (in bytes), you can use this tool to measure server response time to these empty ping requests, as shown here:

```
> set URL= t3s://192.168.1.21:9001
> weblogicAdmin PING 1000 10000
Sending 1,000 pings of 10,000 bytes.
  RTT = ~6309 milliseconds, or ~6 milliseconds/packet
```

The results indicate that the total round-trip time (RTT) was about 6.3 seconds, so, on average, the server is processing these empty ping requests in about 6 milliseconds. By looking at the latency of processing these empty requests, you can determine if the server itself is being overloaded during periods of slower-than-normal system response time. This tool is an extremely important diagnostic tool because it enables you to see if, and how quickly, the server is processing requests in the default execute queue.

The LIST command allows you to list all of the objects bound into a particular location in the JNDI tree. Simply specify the JNDI context name, and the LIST command will print a textual representation of all subcontexts and objects, and their names, as shown here:.

```
> weblogicAdmin LIST javax/transaction
Setting credentials
Contents of javax/transaction
  UserTransaction:
weblogic.transaction.internal.ClientTransactionManagerImpl
  TransactionManager:
weblogic.transaction.internal.ClientTransactionManagerImpl
```

The SERVERLOG command allows you to look at portions of a server's log file. To use this command, you need to point directly at the server in question and specify the start and end times of the entries in which you are interested using the YYYY/MM/DD HH:MM format, as shown here:

```
>weblogicAdmin SERVERLOG "2003/04/12 11:00" "2003/04/12 13:00"
BEA-000213  Apr 12, 2003 12:59:56 PM CDT  Info   WebLogicServer
    Adding address: 192.168.1.20 to licensed client list
BEA-000360  Apr 12, 2003 12:59:21 PM CDT  Notice WebLogicServer
    Server started in RUNNING mode
...
```

Notice that the entries are displayed in reverse chronological order. At the time of writing, the SERVERLOG command displays a maximum of 500 entries and does not provides an option to change this setting. This may change by the time you read this, so check the WebLogic Server command-line interface documentation at http://edocs.bea.com/wls/docs81/admin_ref/cli.html for more information.

The last monitoring command we will discuss is the THREAD_DUMP command. In certain situations, the server may slow down or even become unresponsive. Another important debugging tactic is looking at the call stacks of the server's threads to determine exactly what they are doing. Although there are other ways to generate a thread dump, the admin tool command is a simple one that does not require operating system-specific knowledge. In certain situations (for example, running the server via the node manager on a Windows platform), this command may be the only way to get a thread dump. Much like the VERSION, LICENSES, PING, and SERVERLOG commands, the target server must receive the THREAD_DUMP command directly. The results of the thread dump are written to the stderr output stream of the server.

We will come back to the admin tool in later sections. For now, let's move on to the WebLogic Console to look at some of its monitoring capabilities.

Monitoring with the WebLogic Console

Most of our use of the WebLogic Console so far has focused on configuration. The WebLogic Console also offers a rich set of monitoring capabilities. In this section, we will highlight some of these capabilities that provide insight into the behavior of the application, as well as WebLogic Server. Covering all of the monitoring capabilities of the WebLogic Console in detail is beyond the scope of this book. Please refer to the WebLogic documentation at http://edocs.bea.com/wls/docs81/ConsoleHelp/index.html for more information.

Let's start by discussing the most basic, yet one of the most important, monitoring features of the WebLogic Console. When running a WebLogic Server application, you often need a glimpse inside the server to get a feel for how well it is running. Use the server's Performance Monitoring tab to get a look at the request throughput, execute queue backlog, and the JVM heap usage. Looking at Figure 11.8, you see that the request throughput is averaging around 240 requests per second in this example display.

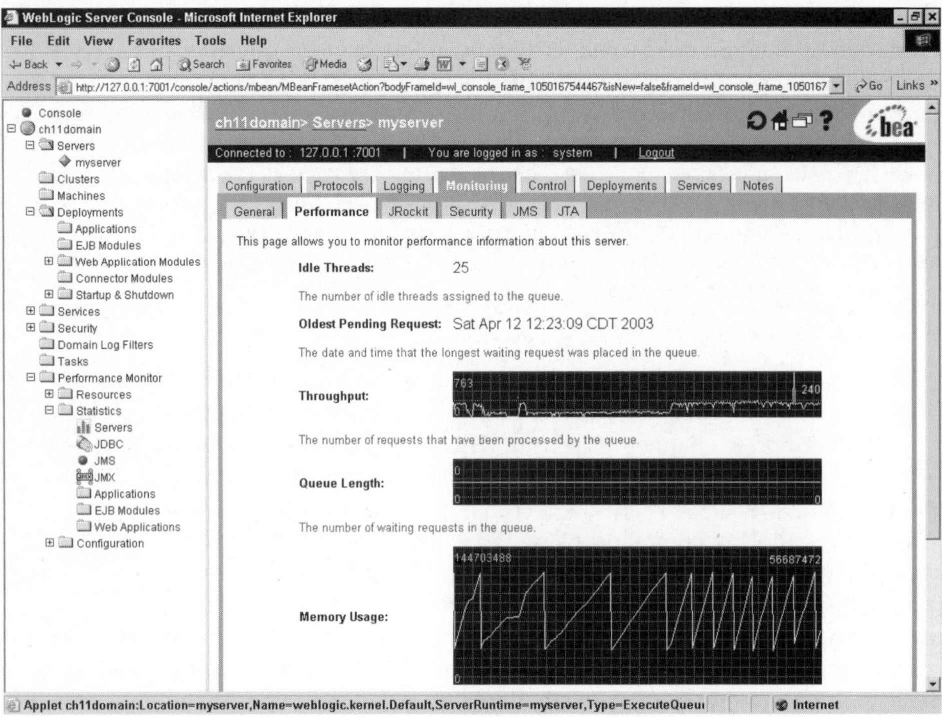

Figure 11.8 Monitoring server performance.

The execute queue length is zero, which means that we never have more concurrent requests waiting than we have available execute threads to process them. Although this is the optimal situation, it will not always be achievable for actual production systems. The bottom graph shows frequent spikes in memory usage. In this case, the heap size is probably too small, or the garbage collector needs tuning, or both, to try to minimize the frequency of the peaks of high heap usage. See the discussion of JVM tuning in Chapter 12 for more information on how to minimize this behavior.

At the time of writing, these graphical execute queue monitoring capabilities are only for each server's default execute queue. You can also get snapshots of the current statistics for all execute queues by selecting the `Monitor all Active Queues` link on the server's `General Monitoring` tab.

Much more run-time information about a server is available through the WebLogic Console. The `Cluster Monitoring` gives information about the membership of the cluster, replicated primary and secondary objects on each server, and multicast heartbeat message statistics. Using the `Security Monitoring` tab, you can view the statistics for failed logins, users that are locked out due to too many authentication failures, and other related information. The `JTA Monitoring` tab gives you access to transaction statistics and allows you to monitor the particular transactions and view in-flight transactions. At the bottom of all of these monitoring tab pages are links to view the server's log file and its JNDI tree. If you are using the JRockit JVM to run the server, the server's `JRockit Monitoring` tab gives you a view into the JVM performance and garbage collection statistics.

Next, let's look at monitoring JDBC connection pools. Under a connection pool's `Monitoring` tab, the WebLogic Console provides a configurable view of each database connection pool's run-time statistics. Three particular parameters are especially important in diagnosing the health of your WebLogic Server application: `Connections High`, `Wait Seconds High`, and `Waiters High`. These parameters are not shown by default, but you can add them by using the `Customize this view` link.

`Connections High` tells you the maximum number of connections reached in the pool at any time since the server started. By comparing this number with your pool's `Initial Capacity` and `Maximum Capacity` settings, you can determine if the pool is sized properly for the application load the server has experienced. When all the connections in a pool are in use and the pool size is at its maximum value, a thread requesting a connection from the pool will have to wait until one becomes available or until it times out. The `Waiters High` value tells you the maximum number of threads that were waiting (at any particular point in time) to get a database connection from the pool because there were no connections available. `Wait Seconds High` tells you the longest time a thread had to wait to get a connection. If you are using a non-negative value for `Connection Reserve Timeout`, realize that `Wait Seconds High` will never exceed this value. If your database connection pool shows non-zero values for `Waiters High` or `Wait Seconds High`, you should consider increasing the size of your database connection pool.

WebLogic Server pools EJB instances. The `weblogic-ejb-jar.xml` deployment descriptor controls the size of the pool. Because stateless session bean instances do not have any client-specific conversational state, the server assigns each request to a bean instance only for the duration of the method call. Idle instances reside in a pool. Because the EJB specification prohibits two threads from using the same bean instance at the same time, the container must synchronize access to each bean instance. This means that if the maximum number of beans in the pool is too small, the container must block calling threads until a bean instance becomes available. Obviously, this situation is undesirable because it will impact performance. The EJB application's `Stateless EJBs Monitoring` tab provides you with statistics concerning the pool. The `Pool Waiter Total Count` tells you the cumulative number of times a thread had to wait for a bean instance because none was available. `Pool Timeout Total Count` tells you the number of threads that have timed out waiting for a bean instance. Fortunately for stateless session beans, the default value of the `max-beans-in-free-pool` deployment descriptor element that controls the pool size is the maximum integer value so this problem will occur only if the value is explicitly set too small.

For stateful session beans, the server does not pool idle instances, but it does maintain a cache of recently used bean instances. As this cache starts to fill up, WebLogic Server will passivate bean instances to make room for other instances by writing the bean's state to disk, as discussed in Chapter 6. The next time a request comes in for a passivated bean, the container must read the bean's state in from disk before dispatching the request to the bean. As you might imagine, this can have a significant impact on performance. By default, the `max-beans-in-cache` deployment descriptor element that controls the cache size is set to 1,000 instances. Whenever the container must activate or passivate a bean instance, it updates internal statistics that can be seen using the EJB application's `Stateful EJBs Monitoring` tab. For stateful session beans, you should keep an eye on the `Activation Count`. The container passivates bean instances when appropriate, but the cost of reactivating these beans can slow down your application tremendously. If the `Activation Count` for a particular bean is high, you should consider increasing the size of the cache.

Entity beans have both a free pool and a cache. The container uses the free pool of bean instances to invoke finder methods, home methods, create methods, and the cache to hold in-use or recently used instances. While the container never passivates an entity bean's state to disk (because its state already exists in the underlying database), it does remove bean instances from the cache whenever it needs space for other instances. Entity beans have several configuration options that can affect both the optimum size and importance of the cache, such as the concurrency strategy and the `cache-between-transactions` deployment descriptor setting. Rather than cover the details here, please refer to the discussion of these topics in Chapter 6 and the WebLogic Server documentation at http://edocs.bea.com/wls/docs81/ejb/EJB_environment.html.

The EJB application's `Entity EJBs Monitoring` tab allows you to monitor the statistics necessary to help you determine the optimum pool and cache sizes. The `Pool Waiter Total Count` and `Pool Timeout Total Count` numbers work just as they do for stateless session beans. The `Cache Miss Ratio` tells you how frequently the application went to access an entity bean that was not in the cache. For entity beans that use the exclusive concurrency strategy, the `Lock Mgr. Waiter Total Count` and `Lock Mgr. Timeout Total Count` allow you to see just how much contention the application is experiencing for instances of a particular bean.

WebLogic JMS also supports monitoring through the WebLogic Console. The JMS server's monitoring tab links to monitor JMS servers, destinations, and session pools. Two of the most important statistics to look at for JMS servers and destinations are the `Bytes Threshold Time` and `Messages Threshold Time`. These values will tell you how much time the JMS server or destination has spent controlling flow and/or paging because the upper threshold was crossed. For more information about JMS monitoring, see Chapter 9 and the WebLogic Server documentation at http://edocs.bea.com/wls/docs81/ConsoleHelp/jms_monitor.html.

WebLogic Server 8.1 Service Pack 1 adds more monitoring capabilities to the WebLogic Console, which you will find in the `Performance Monitoring` folder. This new functionality allows you to monitor the machine, JVM, server, and applications all through the WebLogic Console. As shown in Figure 11.9, this new feature also allows you to view performance information about your application components and classes. At the time of writing, this feature is still evolving so we will not spend any more time covering its use. Please refer to the WebLogic Server documentation for more information.

At this point, we have touched on the most important monitoring features of the WebLogic Console. These features provide a quick insight into the operation of your application so that you can determine if configuration changes may help to improve performance or reduce resource consumption. Now, we are ready to move on to talk about WebLogic Server's JMX support.

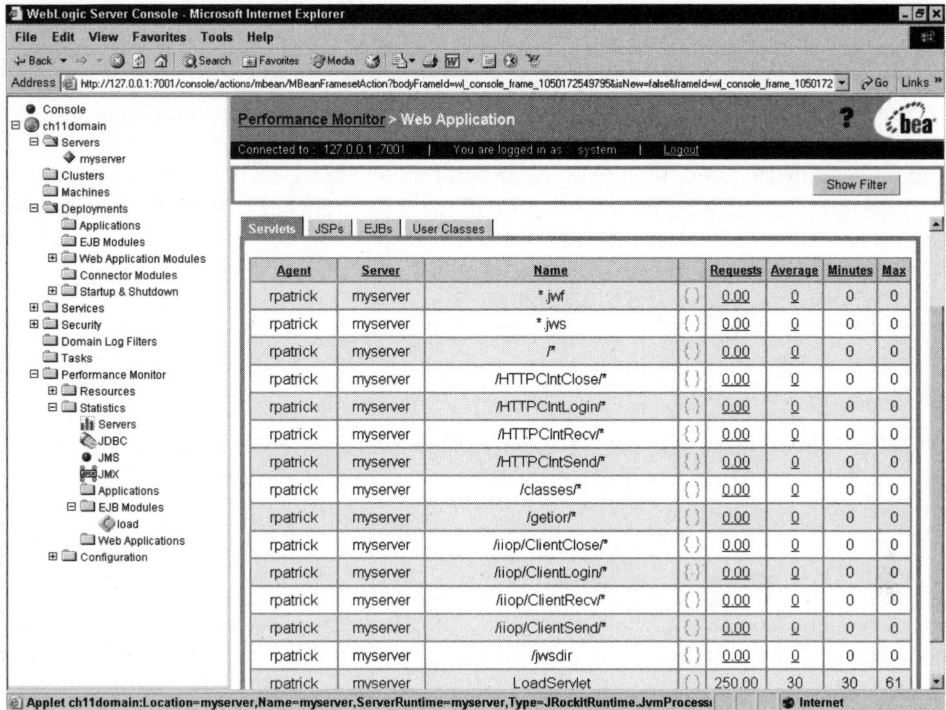

Figure 11.9 Monitoring execute queue statistics.

Programmatic Monitoring with JMX

WebLogic Server implements the Java Management Extensions (JMX) specification and provides JMX-based services to manage server and application resources. While the WebLogic Console can be thought of as a user interface to JMX, the real power of JMX is the ability to programmatically manage resources through either a Java program or from a script using one of the available administrative tools that support JMX. A complete discussion of JMX and JMX programming is beyond the scope of this book; please refer to the WebLogic Server documentation at http://edocs.bea.com/wls/docs81/jmx/index.html and the JMX documentation at http://java.sun.com/products/JavaManagement/ for more information.

When you are trying to use the JMX interface to access WebLogic Server administrative functionality, the `weblogic.management` packages will be very useful (see http://edocs.bea.com/wls/docs81/javadocs/index.html) as these classes provide strongly typed access to the JMX functionality and thus are easier to use than the loosely typed, pure JMX APIs.

In this section, we will show how to get the execute queue length and calculate the execute queue throughput and percentage of the JVM heap currently in use using WebLogic JMX. To execute JMX commands, you will need to authenticate to the server. While we will not revisit Chapter 10's discussion of JAAS authentication, we will use the WebLogicLoginHelper class from the book's companion Web site to handle the authentication so that we can focus on JMX programming here. In the interest of space, we do not list the entire WebLogicPerformanceMonitor class, but it is available on the companion Web site at http://www.wiley.com/compbooks/masteringweblogic. Let's walk through the important parts of this program that are related to JMX.

The first thing that you need to do once you log in is to look up the MBeanHome for the server you want to monitor. If you wanted to monitor Server1, the code would look like this:

```
import weblogic.management.MBeanHome;
...
MBeanHome home =
    (MBeanHome)ctx.lookup(MBeanHome.JNDI_NAME + "." + serverName);
```

Once you have the correct MBeanHome object, you can use it to obtain the ExecuteQueueRuntimeMBean for the default execute queue and the JVMRuntimeMBean, using the following code:

```
import javax.management.InstanceNotFoundException;
import weblogic.management.runtime.ExecuteQueueRuntimeMBean;
import weblogic.management.runtime.JVMRuntimeMBean;
...
try {
    ExecuteQueueRuntimeMBean executeQueue = (ExecuteQueueRuntimeMBean)
        home.getRuntimeMBean("weblogic.kernel.Default",
                             "ExecuteQueueRuntime");

    JVMRuntimeMBean jvm = (JVMRuntimeMBean)
        home.getRuntimeMBean(serverName, "JVMRuntime");
}
catch (InstanceNotFoundException infe) {
    ...
}
```

Now, use the methods of these two objects to get the attributes that are of interest. For example, the following line of code will provide the length of the execute queue from the ExecuteQueueRuntimeMBean:

```
int executeQueueLength = executeQueue.getPendingRequestCurrentCount();
```

That is really all there is to using JMX to read information. As we will see later, the JMX code to modify configuration information is a little more involved, though it is still relatively simple. You should download the WebLogicPerformanceMonitor example before proceeding.

The WebLogicPerformanceMonitor program takes one argument, the name of the property file where we pass in the relevant information. Once the program reads the information from the property file, it then uses the Java Authentication and Authorization Service APIs (via the WebLogicLoginHelper) to log in and execute the JMX code hidden in the `getPerfStats()` method. `getPerfStats()` first checks the length of the execute queue; if it is nonzero, it calculates the difference between the current time and the oldest request on the queue to estimate how long a request is waiting on the queue before an execute thread picks it up. Next, we determine the total number of processed requests at two different points in time to calculate the instantaneous request throughput. Finally, we get the current JVM heap size as well as the current amount of free heap to calculate the percentage of the heap currently in use.

To run this program, we need to create a property file that looks like the one shown here and pass the name of the property file to the `WebLogicPerformanceMonitor` class as an argument:

```
server_url=t3s://192.168.1.21:9002
server_name=Server1
username=system
password=insecure
```

As always, when using a Java client to talk to WebLogic Server using SSL, you need to add the appropriate Java system property definitions to the command line. In our example, we use the property file name `perfmon.properties` and create a script called `perfmon.cmd`, as shown here:

```
@SETLOCAL

@call setEnv.cmd

@java -Dweblogic.security.SSL.trustedCAKeyStore=ClientTrustStore.jks
      mastering.weblogic.ch11.example2.WebLogicPerformanceMonitor
      perfmon.properties

@ENDLOCAL
```

If you run the `perfmon` script while Server1 is under load, you will get results that look something like the ones shown here:

```
> perfmon
username: system
password: ********
URL: t3s://192.168.1.21:9002
The execute queue length is 0.
The current throughput is 18.25168107588857 requests/second.
The JVM heap is currently 94.75636790320637% full.
```

You can also use the `weblogic.Admin` tool to collect the same information from the server. Using our `weblogicAdmin` script, we can obtain the length of Server1's default execute queue with the following command:

```
> set URL=t3s://192.168.1.21:9002

> weblogicAdmin GET -pretty -mbean
```

```
     "bigrezdomain:Location=Server1,Name=weblogic.kernel.Default,
      ServerRuntime=Server1,Type=ExecuteQueueRuntime"
     -property PendingRequestCurrentCount
---------------------------
MBeanName: "bigrezdomain:Location=Server1,Name=CSAExecuteQueue,
            ServerRuntime=Server1,Type=ExecuteQueueRuntime"
        PendingRequestCurrentCount: 16
```

The most difficult thing in this technique is figuring out the name of the MBean. Fortunately, as long as you know the interface class of the MBean you want, you can specify the type of MBean and the server will return a list of all MBeans of that type along with their names. To determine the appropriate type name, simply remove the MBean suffix from the interface class name. Because the information we want is available via the `weblogic.management.runtime.ExecuteQueueRuntimeMBean` interface, the type name is `ExecuteQueueRuntime`. The following example shows the result of running the `GET` command with the `ExecuteQueueRuntime` type:

```
> weblogicAdmin GET -pretty -type ExecuteQueueRuntime
---------------------------
MBeanName: "bigrezdomain:Location=Server1,Name=weblogic.kernel.Default,
            ServerRuntime=Server1,Type=ExecuteQueueRuntime"
    CachingDisabled: true
    ExecuteThreadCurrentIdleCount: 25
    ExecuteThreads: [Lweblogic.management.runtime.ExecuteThread;@fb6354
    Name: weblogic.kernel.Default
    ObjectName: weblogic.kernel.Default
    Parent: Server1
    PendingRequestCurrentCount: 0
    PendingRequestOldestTime: 1050184873220
    Registered: true
    ServicedRequestTotalCount: 31
    Type: ExecuteQueueRuntime
---------------------------
MBeanName: "bigrezdomain:Location=Server1,Name=weblogic.admin.RMI,
            ServerRuntime=Server,Type=ExecuteQueueRuntime"
    CachingDisabled: true
    ExecuteThreadCurrentIdleCount: 1
    ExecuteThreads: [Lweblogic.management.runtime.ExecuteThread;@e7c5cb
    Name: weblogic.admin.RMI
    ObjectName: weblogic.admin.RMI
    Parent: Server1
    PendingRequestCurrentCount: 0
    PendingRequestOldestTime: 1050184873250
    Registered: true
    ServicedRequestTotalCount: 25
    Type: ExecuteQueueRuntime
...
```

At this point, you have all the information you need to query WebLogic Server to get information via the JMX interface. Of course, the JMX interface also gives us the ability to create new configuration artifacts and to modify existing ones. We will see an example of this in the "Managing WebLogic Server Applications" section.

There are additional options available for integrating with JMX. WebLogic Server 8.1 provides an Ant task called `wlconfig` that provides a simpler scripting interface to JMX; see http://edocs.bea.com/wls/docs81/admin_ref/ant_tasks.html for more information on how to use `wlconfig`. WLShell is a freeware tool that provides an interactive shell environment and batch scripting capabilities for JMX programming with WebLogic Server. See http://www.wlshell.com to download the latest version of WLShell. We'll also take a brief look at these tools in Chapter 13 when we discuss the management of configuration information in the development environment.

Before we move on to management, let's have a quick look at WebLogic Server's SNMP support.

Monitoring via SNMP

WebLogic Server 8.1 supports Simple Network Management Protocol (SNMP) versions 1.0 and 2.0. An SNMP manager contacts the admin server, who acts as the SNMP agent for the entire domain. With proper configuration, the WebLogic SNMP agent can act as a proxy for other SNMP agents on the same machine (for example, an Oracle database agent). While complete coverage of WebLogic SNMP is beyond the scope of this book, we will try to cover the basic information needed to communicate with WebLogic Server using SNMP. For more information, please refer to the WebLogic SNMP Management Guide at http://edocs.bea.com/wls/docs81/snmpman/index.html and the WebLogic SNMP MIB Reference at http://edocs.bea.com/wls/docs81/snmp/index.html.

To use SNMP with WebLogic Server, you need to enable SNMP support using the domain's `SNMP Configuration` tab. Enabling SNMP support is as simple as checking the `Enabled` checkbox, selecting an `SNMP Port`, and restarting the admin server. By default, WebLogic SNMP uses port 161 to receive SNMP requests. The `SNMP Port` allows you to specify what port you want to use for SNMP traffic. Before restarting the server, let's talk about some of the other parameters on this tab.

SNMP uses passwords known as *community names* to authenticate SNMP requests. Because much of the WebLogic SNMP MIB data is available for each server in a domain (for example, the default execute queue length), you need some way for the SNMP manager to tell the WebLogic SNMP agent what data it wants. The way that WebLogic SNMP accounts for this is by piggybacking the server information with the community name. WebLogic Server's SNMP manager needs to send the community name in the form *<community_name>*`@`*<server_name>*. You tell WebLogic SNMP what community name to expect from the SNMP manager via the `Community Prefix` parameter. To get information about the admin server itself, you can either specify the name of the admin server or omit the server name altogether. To get information from the entire domain, replace the server name with the domain name.

The admin server gathers data from the managed servers to respond to SNMP requests. For efficiency, the admin server caches this data for a period of time to prevent excessive communication with the managed servers. `MIB Data Refresh Interval` specifies the minimum amount of time to cache the collected information before refreshing it. `Server Status Check Interval Factor` specifies the number of `MIB Data Refresh Intervals` between the admin server's health checks of the managed servers. The `Debug Level` simply turns on extra debugging output on the admin server to help debug any SNMP problems between the SNMP manager and the WebLogic SNMP agent. Before talking about the last two items in the domain's `SNMP Configuration` tab, let's verify that the SNMP agent is working. To do this, you need to restart the admin server, so please do that now.

WebLogic Server does not provide an SNMP manager. For this purpose, we will use the AdventNet MIB Browser and Trap Viewer that come with the AdventNet SNMP API 4 product (available from http://www.adventnet.com/products/snmp/download.html). The MIB Browser allows us to interact with the WebLogic SNMP agent by sending `SNMP GET` requests to retrieve WebLogic Server configuration and run-time information. This is the same information available through the JMX APIs. WebLogic SNMP does not currently support the `SNMP SET` operation to make changes to the WebLogic Server configuration.

To communicate with the WebLogic SNMP agent, you need to load the WebLogic Server management information base (MIB) data into the MIB Browser. Using the MIB Browser application's `File` menu, select the `Load MIB` menu item, browse to the `$WL_HOME/server/lib` directory, and select the `BEA-WEBLOGIC-MIB.asn1` file. After expanding the `BEA-WEBLOGIC-MIB` folder on the left, you should see a list of WebLogic SNMP MIB tables and attributes similar to those shown in Figure 11.10. Replace the `Community` entry with the string `public@Server1` and perform an `SNMP GET` operation to get the names of the execute queues in Server1, as shown in Figure 11.10.

All of this is interesting, but the main reason to use SNMP is to send unsolicited messages to the SNMP manager whenever something happens. These unsolicited messages are called SNMP *traps*. WebLogic SNMP can generate traps to notify the SNMP manager of certain types of events. WebLogic Server comes with a set of predefined traps for server startup, server shutdown, cold start (admin server startup), and authentication failure. You can also set up three other types of traps: attribute change traps, log message traps, and monitor traps. Before we talk about defining new traps, let's configure the WebLogic SNMP agent and the AdventNet Trap Viewer and verify that we are seeing traps propagate from WebLogic Server to the Trap Viewer.

The first step is to configure the Trap Viewer to listen for traps. Using the MIB Browser's `View` menu, select the `Trap Viewer` menu item. Use the Trap Viewer's `Start` button to tell it to start listening for traps on its default port, port 162, with a `Community` of `public`. Now, you need to configure the WebLogic Server side of things. Under the `Services->SNMP` folder in the left-hand navigation bar, select `Trap Destinations` and create a new trap destination. Then, go back to the domain's `SNMP Configuration` tab and move the new trap destination into the `Chosen` column of the `Targeted Trap Destinations` attribute.

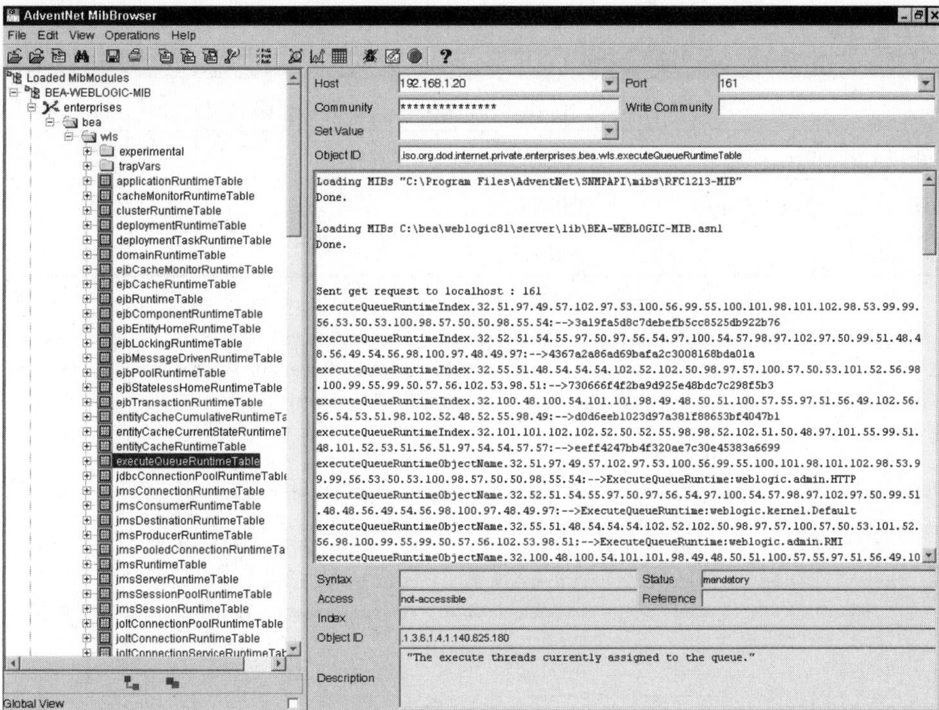

Figure 11.10 Viewing the WebLogic Server MIB.

Now, let's test the trap mechanism by shutting down and restarting Server1. Trap Viewer eventually receives two traps, one for server shutdown and one for server startup. The server shutdown trap has a `Generic Type` of 6 (that is, an enterprise-specific type) and `Specific Type` of 70 (that is, server shutdown). We are now ready to explore the other trap types that WebLogic SNMP supports.

WebLogic SNMP supports defining three types of traps. The first type of trap is an attribute change trap. With this trap, the WebLogic SNMP agent generates a trap whenever a configuration value changes. These traps work directly on the JMX MBeans. To define an attribute change trap, select the `Services->SNMP->Traps->Attribute Changes` folder in the left-hand navigation bar and specify the trap's `Name`, `Attribute MBean Type`, `Attribute MBean Name`, and `Attribute Name`. You must create the new trap before you can select the servers to which the trap applies. Create a trap to notify you if someone changes the `Targets` attribute of the `BigRezPool` using the values shown in Table 11.9. Once you define the trap and restart the admin server, try changing the targets for the `BigRezPool` to exclude `Server3`. Notice that `Server3` is not included in the Enabled Servers list, but you still get the trap because the `JDBCConnectionPool` MBean is a configuration MBean and all configuration is controlled by the admin server.

Table 11.9 BigRezPool Targets Attribute Change Trap Configuration Parameters

NAME	VALUE
Name	BigRezPool Targets Attribute Trap
Attribute MBean Type	JDBCConnectionPool
Attribute MBean Name	BigRezPool
Enabled Servers	AdminServer

A log filter trap generates a trap whenever an entry appears in the WebLogic Server log file matching the filter. Log filters can specify several different parameters by which to filter log messages that should generate a trap. Let's examine a WebLogic Server log file entry.

```
####<Apr 13, 2003 11:22:41 AM CDT> <Info> <JDBC> <machine1> <Server1>
  <ExecuteThread: '22' for queue: 'weblogic.kernel.Default'>
  <<anonymous>> <BEA1-00066F94280AD6ED52CF> <BEA-001156>
  <Stack trace associated with message 001129 follows:
    java.sql.SQLException: Io exception: The Network Adapter could
    not establish the connection
  at
    oracle.jdbc.dbaccess.DBError.throwSqlException
      (Ljava.lang.String;Ljava.lang.String;I)V(DBError.java:134)
  at
    oracle.jdbc.dbaccess.DBError.throwSqlException
      (ILjava.lang.Object;)V(DBError.java:179)
...
```

Each log file entry has the following format.

```
<Date/Time> <Severity Level> <Subsystem> <Machine> <Server> <Thread>
    <User Identity> <Transaction> <Message ID> <Message Text>
```

Imagine that you want to set up a trap every time this message appears (because this message alerts you that the database is no longer reachable). You do this by defining a log filter trap using the settings listed in Table 11.10.

Table 11.10 BigRezDataSource Deployment Log Filter Trap Configuration Parameters

NAME	VALUE
Name	BigRezDataSource Deployment Log Filter Trap
Severity Level	Info
Subsystem Names	JDBC
User Ids	

Table 11.10 *(continued)*

NAME	VALUE
Message Ids	BEA-001156
Message Substring	
Enabled Servers	Server1, Server2, Server3

The last type of trap to discuss is the monitor trap. Monitor traps are used to monitor an attribute value of an MBean; they come in three types: counter, string, and gauge. A counter trap simply generates a trap when a particular attribute value meets or exceeds the threshold value. For example, you might want to define a counter monitor trap to let you know when a server is using all of the connections in the `BigRezPool` JDBC connection pool. To do this, you need to use the `ActiveConnectionsHighCount` attribute of the `JDBCConnectionPoolRuntime` MBean for `BigRezPool` on `Server1`, `Server2`, and `Server3`.

A string monitor trap compares the attribute value against a string and can raise a trap when the string matches or when it differs. A gauge monitor trap will alert you whenever the attribute value meets or exceeds the `Threshold High` value and when it reaches or falls below the `Threshold Low`. If you had a JDBC connection pool where the `Initial Capacity` and `Maximum Capacity` attributes were different, you might want to create a gauge monitor to monitor the maximum and minimum number of connections. By setting the `Threshold Low` value to be one less than the `Initial Capacity`, your gauge monitor trap could monitor the ActiveConnectionsCurrentCount attribute of the `JDBCConnectionPoolRuntime` MBean and alert you whenever the number of active connections are less than the `Initial Capacity` (which might indicate database connectivity problems).

This ends our discussion of WebLogic SNMP. While there are very few built-in traps, the ability to define custom traps makes it possible to define most of the types of traps that you might want. Of course, the real difficulty here is that you must know the JMX APIs, what the possible values of each attribute are, what the expected and abnormal ranges of values are, and so on. We hope that future versions of WebLogic Server will simplify this task so that it does not require so much system-level knowledge of the JMX APIs to be able to define custom traps.

Managing WebLogic Server Applications

We are finally ready to talk about the toughest part of a WebLogic Server administrator's job—how to manage WebLogic Server-based applications. While this coverage is by no means comprehensive, we hope to cover the most common problems encountered while managing WebLogic Server applications. We start off this section by discussing how to manage applications by touching on such topics as application troubleshooting and versioning, and we finish with a discussion of handling failure conditions.

Troubleshooting Application Issues

Application troubleshooting can take many forms. Sometimes, you need to figure out why your application is not performing as fast or scaling as well as someone thinks it should. At other times, the application is not functioning properly and you need to determine the root cause of the problem. In a distributed system, this means that you must consider the entire application environment from the client application and hardware, the network and network devices, the server hardware and operating system, the Web and application servers, the JVMs, the database and other back-end server hardware and software to the application itself. This can be a daunting task, and the possibilities are endless. While we cannot expect to cover all the possible problems or diagnostic approaches, we do hope to describe the use of some of the tools that you have at your disposal to make it easier to narrow down the possible causes of the problem.

When problems arise with a distributed system, people naturally suspect the component(s) of the system for which they have the least knowledge or trust. In many cases, this means that WebLogic Server gets the blame, and it is your job as WebLogic Server administrator to prove the problem lies elsewhere (if, in fact, it does). When you encounter a problem, it is important to get as much information about the symptoms of the problem as possible while trying to recognize that people's biases for what they believe to be the problem may cause them to lead you in the wrong direction. Although it is important to listen to all the evidence, it is also important not to jump to conclusions that are not backed up by the facts.

In almost every situation where you suspect a problem might be related to WebLogic Server, you should use the WebLogic Console to determine the health of the server. The last section discussed many of the WebLogic Console's most important monitoring capabilities. Before doing anything, you should look at the relevant WebLogic Server log files to see if they contain any errors that might indicate the cause of the problem. If the problem at hand is performance-related, looking at the relevant execute queue lengths and throughputs as well as the JVM's heap usage profile should be one of the first pieces of evidence to examine. If the execute queue is empty or no longer than normal (and garbage collection does not appear to be unusually frequent) even though the clients are experiencing a significant degradation in response time, you need to determine whether the problem is with the server or the components in front of or behind the server.

To narrow down the possible causes of a performance problem, it is useful to be able to run your client application and the `weblogic.Admin` tool's `PING` command from various points in your application environment. For example, let's say that your Internet users are complaining of very slow response time. By being able to run a browser on one of the Web server machines, you can determine if the cause of the slowdown is between the users and the Web server or somewhere starting at the Web server and going back into your application and database environment. By again moving the browser to an application server machine, you can isolate or eliminate the Web server and the network environment between as potential causes. If the application is not available, the admin tool's `PING` command can serve a similar purpose.

If you determine through testing that the problem appears to be that WebLogic Server is taking too long to process the requests (even though it is processing `PING` requests very quickly), the next step is to try to determine what is causing the application request processing to be so slow. Create a series of thread dumps over the span of a minute or so and look at the call stacks for the threads over time. This information will help you understand what the execute threads are doing and may tell you where they are spending most of their time. The optimum frequency and duration of the series of thread dumps depends on how long it takes to process an application request. For example, if a request is taking 15 seconds to process once it is picked up by an execute thread, taking thread dumps 60 seconds apart probably won't help you as much as taking them 5 seconds apart so that you can see if the same thread is in the same place in consecutive thread dumps.

Resource contention is a common cause of performance problems and can occur at many levels. Use the WebLogic Console monitoring tools to detect resource contention for things like JDBC connections and EJB instances. For other types of application-specific resource contention, thread dumps may be your only detection mechanism (outside of either a thorough understanding of how the application works or the use of profiling tools). Data access contention inside the database is best detected by database monitoring tools but may sometimes be seen in application thread dumps.

BEST PRACTICE Use a series of properly spaced thread dumps to gain insight into the possible causes of long-running requests.

Garbage collection is another common problem. While modern JVMs have much better garbage collection algorithms than their predecessors, these new garbage collectors can require much more tuning to get optimum, or even reasonable, performance. Most JVMs now have multiple garbage collection algorithms that allow a properly tuned JVM to minimize the number of full garbage collection cycles it runs. Typically, these full garbage collection runs must stop all other activity while the garbage collector scans the heap for unreachable objects, removes unreachable objects, and relocates reachable objects to compact the heap (which packs the reachable objects together so as to maximize the contiguous free memory space within the heap). By looking at the JVM heap usage profile (for example, via the server's Performance Monitoring tab), you can detect how often these full garbage collection scans are occurring.

Whenever the heap usage reaches a certain percentage of capacity, the garbage collector will perform a full GC to reclaim as much free memory as possible. The result is that users will see that requests that are in-flight during a full GC take longer to process. In extreme situations, full GC sweeps can occur multiple times in the life of a single request. Because most server-side Java applications tend to create a lot of transient objects (ones that are used for a very short time and thrown away), it is often possible to reduce the number of full GC sweeps significantly by tuning the garbage collector. For more information about garbage collector tuning, and performance tuning in general, see Chapter 12, the WebLogic documentation at http://edocs.bea.com/wls/docs81/perform/index.html, and your JVM documentation (for example, the WebLogic JRockit documentation at http://edocs.bea.com/wljrockit/docs81/tuning/index.html).

BEST PRACTICE Frequent spikes that indicate high JVM heap usage can have a significant effect on the user's experience. Adjusting the heap size and garbage collection tuning parameters can significantly reduce the frequency of full GC sweeps and improve the user experience.

Versioning Applications

Applications change. Deployment strategies for putting in new versions of already running applications vary. Certain application characteristics can make rolling out new versions of an application messy. The purpose of this section is to point out the issues around application versioning. We will not attempt to propose a solution because there are currently no good solutions that address every possible situation. Choosing the right strategy for an application involves analyzing the application requirements and the sorts of application changes occurring, then trading those off against the pros and cons of the available approaches.

WebLogic Server supports the notion of hot deployment of an application. This means that you can take a new version of an application and push it into a set of running servers without restarting the servers. What it does not currently mean is that you can prevent the redeployment of the new version of the application from affecting the user experience. If there are periods of time when the application is quiescent, rolling out new versions of the application can be as simple as hot deploying the new version, assuming that you have no changes that affect other systems (for example, database schema changes). Many applications, however, do not have a well-defined time when the system is quiescent. Hot redeploying an application when active users are using the site will not only cause the application to be unavailable for a short period of time but may also cause the users to lose transient state data that may exist in the memory. WebLogic Server 8.1 does provide improved support in this area through the retention of `HttpSession` data during a Web application redeployment, potentially allowing relatively transparent application upgrades if no conflicts with previous `HttpSession` data exist.

Things get even more complicated if you have Java application clients communicating via RMI. In many cases, the client application may need to be updated simultaneously with the server. This is nothing new, and it is something that we have seen in the client/server world for years. Even in cases where the client application does not require upgrading, the objects to which the client was talking will disappear. It may also mean that some of the dynamically generated RMI stubs the client is using will no longer be valid and may require the client application to be restarted.

In WebLogic Server's defense, no application server on the market today provides solutions to these fundamental problems. We hope that application server vendors will accept this as a challenge to realize that these issues are fundamental to providing an enterprise-class application server on which to build mission-critical, 24 x 7 applications.

Other versioning strategies exist that work well for certain types of applications. For example, a common solution to the versioning problem for Web applications is to use a parallel cluster to deploy a new version of the application. Hardware load balancers are now sophisticated enough to allow you to redirect new users of the application to the new version while existing users continue to use the old version until they end their current session. Of course, this solution requires a lot of administrative work. We expect future versions of WebLogic Server to simplify this versioning strategy.

Managing Failure Conditions

Failures happen. As an administrator, you want to make your system as resilient as possible. Sometimes it is possible to automate processes so that when a particular type of failure occurs, the system can take steps to recover; other times, it is not. WebLogic Server provides some built-in mechanisms to help make applications fault tolerant and transparently recoverable (for example, clustering, in-memory replication, database connection testing). Currently, though, certain situations require manual intervention from an administrator, or at least require the administrator to provide the logic to automate the process. In general, these situations have sufficiently complex conditions that make it difficult to provide a general-purpose failover mechanism. For example, when a WebLogic Server instance fails, how do you decide whether to migrate the JMS servers and JTA transaction service associated with the server? In many cases, the server may restart faster than the services could be migrated. In this section, we talk about several common failure scenarios and the mechanisms that WebLogic Server provides for recovering from these situations.

Database Failures

A very common scenario is that a database goes down (or is taken down) and restarted, either automatically by a high-availability (HA) framework or by the database administrator. When this happens, the connections in WebLogic Server database connection pools become invalid and the applications trying to use them will begin to fail. As we discussed earlier, WebLogic Server does provide mechanisms to allow the server to eventually recover from the situation without any intervention, although these mechanisms come at the cost of some extra overhead. Depending on the mechanism(s) chosen and the configuration, the application may continue to fail for an extended period of time after the database recovers. Fortunately, WebLogic Server also provides a manual mechanism to tell a server to reset a connection pool.

To reset a database connection pool, you can use the admin tool's `RESET_POOL` command. Using this command, it is possible to provide a script that can reset all of the connection pools associated with a particular database server. Once you have such a script, you need only to have the database administrator or the HA framework run the script whenever the database startup completes (to the point where it is accepting connections). The following example demonstrates manually resetting the `BigRezPool` on `Server1`:

```
> set URL=t3s://192.168.1.21:9002
> weblogicAdmin RESET_POOL BigRezPool
```

The admin tool also provides other commands related to connection pools. Rather than covering them all here, we will refer you to the WebLogic Server documentation at http://edocs.bea.com/wls/docs81/admin_ref/cli.html. The `DISABLE_POOL` and `ENABLE_POOL` commands are ones that might prove useful in certain situations. `DISABLE_POOL` allows you not only to disable all access to the pooled connections but also to destroy all of the existing connections if you choose to do so. For planned database restarts, you might want to disable the pool and destroy the connections before shutting down the database. This might allow your application to trap the exception raised and display an error page indicating that the system is down. Once the database is back up, you can use the `ENABLE_POOL` command to re-enable the connection pool, causing the destroyed connections to be recreated.

Migrating the JTA Service

When machines fail, you need to be able to bring up services on other machines. Migrating the JTA Service can play a critical factor in recovery from a failure scenario. In-flight transactions can hold locks on the underlying resources. If the transaction manager is not available to recover these transactions, resources may hold on to these locks for long periods of time, making it difficult for the application to function properly. JTA Service migration is possible only if the JTA logs are accessible to the server to which the service will migrate. Once you guarantee this, migration is simple, although you must be careful how you share these files. Distributed file systems such as NFS typically do not provide the necessary semantics to guarantee the integrity and content of transaction logs. Typically, this means using some higher-end means of sharing the files, such as a multi-ported disk or storage area network (SAN).

Migrating the JTA Service from one server to another is as simple as using the host server's `JTA Migrate Control` tab to select the target server and cause the migration. You must stop the failing server before you can migrate the JTA service. When you migrate the JTA service, it will not accept any new work and will focus solely on the recovery of incomplete transactions. Once the destination server finishes recovering all of the incomplete transactions, it releases its claim on the migrated JTA service so that the original server can reclaim it once it restarts.

The admin tool also provides JTA service migration capabilities through its `MIGRATE` command. The basic syntax is as follows.

```
MIGRATE [-jta] -migratabletarget [migratable_target_name|server_name]
    -destination [server_name] [-sourcedown] [-destinationdown]
```

For example, migrating the JTA service from `Server1` to `Server2` when `Server1` is already down requires invoking our `weblogicAdmin` script with the following command:

```
> weblogicAdmin MIGRATE -jta -migratabletarget "Server1 (migratable)"
    -destination Server2 -sourcedown
Started attempt to migrate Transaction Recovery service(s) for Server1
to destination server Server2 ..."
Transaction RecoveryMigration succeeded.
Ok
```

Migrating JMS Servers

JMS servers are another important service that must be migratable. Again, any persistent JMS store must be accessible from a shared disk or database. If using JTA transactions with persistent JMS messages, you may need to migrate the JTA service to recover incomplete transactions. We suggest migrating the JMS servers first so that the JMS server's XA resource manager is available for transaction recovery.

Again, you can accomplish migration via the server's `JMS Migrate Control` tab in the WebLogic Console or via the admin tool's `MIGRATE` command, as shown here:

```
> weblogicAdmin MIGRATE -migratabletarget "Server1 (migratable)"
    -destination Server2
Started attempt to migrate  service(s) for Server1 (migratable) to
destination server Server2 ..."
Migration succeeded.
Ok
```

In this example, we migrated the JMS server on `Server1` to `Server2` before we shut down `Server1`.

Of course, once we are ready to let `Server1` resume its duties, we must migrate the JMS server back to `Server1`:

```
> weblogicAdmin MIGRATE -migratabletarget "Server1 (migratable)"
    -destination Server1
Started attempt to migrate  service(s) for Server1 (migratable) to
destination server Server1 ..."
Migration succeeded.
Ok
```

Migrating the Admin Server

The last thing we want to discuss is how to handle admin server availability because the admin server is not currently clusterable. This means that if the admin server goes down, you cannot administer your WebLogic Server domain until you bring it back up. In most cases, you may not be too concerned if the admin server goes down because all you need to do is restart it. What happens if the machine where the admin server runs fails in such a way that you cannot restart the admin server? The answer is simple if you prepare for this unlikely event.

Proper operation of the admin server relies on several configuration files and any application files it controls. Typically, the best thing to do is to store the admin server's directory tree on a shared disk. As long as the configuration and application files are accessible, you can restart the admin server on another machine. It is up to you to make sure that you don't have more than one admin server running at a time. If the new machine can assume the original admin server's `Listen Address` (or if it was not set), you can simply start the admin server on the new machine without any configuration changes. Otherwise, you will need to change the admin server's `Listen Address`. The managed servers will learn about the new admin server when the admin server contacts them on startup. If this is a graceful shutdown and migration, use the WebLogic Console to change the `Listen Address` just before shutting down the admin server. If not, you will need to edit the `config.xml` file by hand to replace the old `Listen Address` with the new one. You also need to make sure that your node managers' trusted hosts files include the DNS name or IP address for the new admin server. Typically, we recommend planning ahead so that everything you need is already in place to make admin server failover as painless as possible.

Chapter Review

We covered a lot of ground in this chapter. We began with a thorough discussion of the WebLogic Server product architecture to give us a good understanding of how the product works. We followed that with a discussion of other administrative concepts, such as server health states and network channels. The rest of the chapter was dedicated to covering WebLogic Server administration including configuration, monitoring, and management of WebLogic Server and WebLogic Server-based applications. We hope that this gives you the basic fundamentals of WebLogic Server administration. These basics should go a long way toward demystifying the complex task of administering J2EE applications running on WebLogic Server. In the next chapter, we will explore WebLogic Server performance optimization.

CHAPTER

12

Optimizing WebLogic Server Performance

This chapter presents best practices for delivering and troubleshooting scalable high-performance systems. It is organized into three major sections:

- *System Performance,* a discussion of core principles and strategies for scalable J2EE systems
- *Performance Best Practices,* a collection of important design patterns and best practices that affect performance and scalability
- *Troubleshooting Performance Problems,* a set of steps and techniques you can use to improve performance and solve scalability issues for your system

This chapter discusses design considerations and best practices we use while delivering scalable systems for numerous BEA customers. Information presented in this chapter represents the experience gathered while designing, prototyping, building, and benchmarking distributed systems over the last eight years. We have had the opportunity to work with very bright architects on many of the largest and most demanding systems deployed using BEA software.

This chapter cannot cover all aspects of J2EE performance, which could be the topic of its own book. We instead provide a number of key best practices and troubleshooting tips to help you achieve your performance goals. If you want more information about performance tuning, then we suggest looking at some of the existing books and Web sites on performance tuning and testing. In our experience, there is no one book that will tell you everything you need to know. To better understand operating system performance tuning, books like *Sun Performance and Tuning: Java and the Internet* by Adrian Cockroft and Richard Pettit (Prentice Hall, 1998) are invaluable. To better understand how to build applications that run in multithreaded Java environments, we recommend *Concurrent Programming in Java: Design Principles and Patterns* by Doug Lea (Addison-Wesley, 1999). To better understand Web application performance testing models, we recommend books like *Capacity Planning for Web Performance: Metrics, Models, and Methods* by Daniel A. Menascé and Virgilio A.F. Almeida (Prentice Hall, 1998). There are also several books available on both J2EE and WebLogic Server performance that may provide some additional insight. We also recommend looking at the WebLogic Server documentation at http://edocs.bea.com/wls/docs81/perform/index.html.

Overview of System Performance

In this section, we discuss the core principles and tuning techniques that underlie many of the performance best practices and troubleshooting tips that we cover later in the chapter. Having a good understanding of the basic operating system, network, JVM, and server resources and tuning options will help you apply these best practices and tips. It is not enough to know what to do; you need to understand why it helps.

Reviewing the Core Principles

Before we get started talking about techniques for achieving *scalability*, we should define the term itself. Scalability generally refers to the ability of an application to meet additional capacity demands without significantly affecting the request processing time. The term is also used to describe the ability to increase the capacity of an application proportional to the hardware resources added. For example, if the maximum capacity of an application running on four CPUs is 200 requests per second with an average of 1-second response time, then you might expect that the capacity for the application running on eight CPUs to be 400 requests per second with the same 1-second response time. This type of linear scalability is typically very difficult to achieve, but scalable applications should be able to approach linear scalability if the application's environment is properly designed. Good scalability in multi-tier architectures requires good end-to-end performance and scalability of each component in each tier of the application.

When designing enterprise-scale applications, you must first understand the application itself and how your users interact with it. You must identify all of the system components and understand their interactions. The application itself is a critical component that affects the scalability of the system. Understanding the distribution of the workload across the various tiers will help you understand the components affected most severely by user activity. Some systems will be database intensive; others will spend a majority of their processing time in the application server. Once you identify these heavily used components, commonly referred to as *application hotspots*, you can use proper scaling techniques to prevent bottlenecks.

This strong understanding of the system itself will also allow you to choose the correct system architecture to meet the demands of the application. Once you choose the system architecture, you can begin to concentrate on the application and apply good performance design practices. There are no silver bullets for choosing the correct system architecture. In our experience, it is best to take an overall system approach to ensure that you cover all facets of the environment in which the application runs. The overall system approach begins with the external environment and continues drilling down into all parts of the system and application. Taking a broad approach and tuning the overall environment ensures that the application will perform well and that system performance can meet all of your requirements.

NOTE WebLogic Server-based application performance depends on many different factors that include the network, operating system, application server, database, and application design and configuration. Many of these factors vary from installation to installation, so you should review all recommendations made in this chapter to determine if they are applicable to your environment.

Before we dive into the lower-level tuning techniques, let's review some system-level approaches for increasing the performance and throughput of your J2EE application.

Use more powerful machines. This technique applies equally well across the Web, application, and database tiers. If a particular tier's processing is CPU-intensive, then using more powerful machines can allow this layer to do the same amount of work in less time and/or to do more work, thereby increasing throughput. Keep in mind that this technique is effective only on CPU-intensive applications. If your system performance is limited by I/O operations, adding processing power will do very little to improve performance or eliminate bottlenecks. Increasing an application's capacity by adding more CPUs to a machine is often referred to as *vertical scaling*.

Use clustering. By distributing the load across multiple Web and/or application servers, you can increase the capacity of your application. Increasing an application's capacity by adding more machines is often referred to as *horizontal scaling*. Horizontal scaling also provides a secondary benefit: increased redundancy at the hardware level to improve the overall system reliability.

Take advantage of network appliances. Today, there are a wide variety of specialized hardware devices that are optimized to perform specific tasks, such as fast and reliable data storage, content caching, load balancing, and SSL termination. These devices operate at various layers within the system architecture and can either offload or significantly reduce the processing work that the software needs to do, and do it in a much more scalable way than can be accomplished with software only. As such, they can dramatically increase the performance and scalability of your applications.

Cache whenever possible. Caching can significantly improve response time and increase the scalability of Web, application, and database servers. Network appliances that cache static content and prevent those requests from ever hitting the Web servers can dramatically improve performance. Most Web servers also offer page caching, which you should use whenever possible. WebLogic Server also offers dynamic content caching through its JSP caching features, a technique discussed in Chapter 1. WebLogic Server 8.1 adds support for RowSets in addition to its various options for entity bean caching; you can use these to cache application data to reduce trips to the database or other back-end systems. Of course, caching application data that changes frequently can often create more problems than it solves. In most cases, we recommend using the database to cache this data. Most database management systems offer a variety of tuning options for optimizing their caching strategies to better suit a particular application; this can significantly reduce the amount of I/O that the database has to do to answer application queries. You should evaluate each of these techniques to determine how best to use caching to improve your application's performance and scalability.

Tuning a WebLogic Server-Based Application

Achieving maximum performance and scalability for your WebLogic Server-based application requires tuning at many different layers within the overall environment. We'll structure our discussion of tuning from the bottom-up, starting with the operating system itself and ending with application-server tuning.

Operating System Tuning

Many J2EE applications have some sort of Web interface through which the users interact. HTTP is a stateless protocol used by browsers to talk to Web and/or application servers. When initiating a request, the browser opens a connection to the server, sends a request, waits for the response, and then closes the connection. Although HTTP keep-alive allows the browser to reuse an existing connection to the server for multiple requests, both the browser and the server will typically close the connection after a fairly short period of inactivity. A typical time-out for one of these connections might be 30 seconds or less. As a result, busy Web applications with hundreds, or even thousands, of concurrent users will open and close a large number of connections between the browser and the Web or application server.

These HTTP connections to the Web or application server are nothing more than operating system-level TCP sockets. All modern operating systems treat sockets as a specialized form of file access and use data structures called file descriptors to track open sockets and files for an operating system process. To control resource usage for processes on the machine, the operating system restricts the number of open file descriptors per process. The default number of file descriptors available for a process depends on the operating system type and its configuration. Without going too far into the gory details of TCP/IP, you should be aware that all TCP connections that have been gracefully closed by an application will go into what is known as the TIME_WAIT state before being discarded by the operating system. The length of time that the socket stays in the TIME_WAIT state is commonly known as the *time wait interval*. While in this TIME_WAIT state, the operating system will maintain the resources allocated for the socket, including its file descriptor. To learn more about the details of this, see *Internetworking with TCP/IP Volume II: Design, Implementation, and Internals* by Douglas A. Comer and David L. Stevens (Prentice Hall, 1998).

As a result of this phenomenon, combined with the fact that HTTP servers end up opening and closing a lot of TCP sockets, busy server processes can fill up the server process's file descriptor table. To deal with this problem, you often need to tune the operating system to allow your application to scale without running into these operating system limits. When tuning the operating system, you should follow your hardware vendor's tuning recommendations, if these exist. Remember to tune the operating system on all machines that exist in the system, especially any Web or application server machines that use the HTTP protocol. On Unix servers, this typically means tuning the number of file descriptors and/or some of the TCP/IP device driver's tuning parameters. On platforms such as HP-UX, it may be necessary to change some of the kernel parameters. When tuning TCP parameters, you should work with your system administrator to determine what modifications your machines require.

Each operating system sets important tuning parameters differently. We will start with a detailed coverage of the Solaris operating system and then briefly discuss the differences on other common Unix operating systems and Windows.

Tuning Solaris

On Solaris, one common problem is that the default value for the time wait interval is too high for high-volume HTTP servers. On most Unix operating systems, you can determine the number of sockets in the TIME_WAIT state using the netstat command:

```
netstat -a | grep TIME_WAIT | wc -l
```

This command will count all of the TCP connections that are in the TIME_WAIT state. As this number approaches the maximum number of file descriptors per process, your application's throughput will suffer dramatic degradations because new connection requests may have to wait for a free space in the application's file descriptor table. To determine the current setting for the time wait interval, use the ndd command shown here:

```
/usr/sbin/ndd /dev/tcp tcp_time_wait_interval
```

Note that prior to Solaris 2.7, this parameter was somewhat erroneously called tcp_close_wait_interval. By default, Solaris sets this parameter to 240,000 milliseconds, or 4 minutes. Our recommendation, which follows the recommendations of both BEA and SUN, is to reduce this setting to 60,000 milliseconds, or 1 minute. You should use the following ndd command to change the tcp_time_wait_interval setting dynamically:

```
/usr/sbin/ndd -set /dev/tcp tcp_time_wait_interval 60000
```

This command will change the setting of the TCP device driver for the entire machine and therefore requires superuser privileges. Be forewarned that this value, and any other values you change with ndd, will reset to the default value when you reboot the machine. To make the changes permanent, you will need to create a boot script.

According to recommendations on Sun's Web site at http://docs.sun.com/db/doc/816-0607/6m735r5fl?a=view, you want the ndd boot script to run between the S69inet and S72inetsvc scripts. This means that you should create the script file in the /etc/init.d directory and create symbolic links to your script from the /etc/rc2.d, /etc/rc1.d, and /etc/rcS.d directories. The link names should begin with either S70 or S71 because the S tells Solaris that this script should run at startup and the numeric value determines the order in which the scripts run.

There are a number of other TCP-related parameters available on Solaris that may yield performance improvements in certain situations. To get a list of all of the names of the TCP device driver parameters, use the following ndd command:

```
ndd /dev/tcp \?
```

The output from this command will also show you which parameters are *read-write* and which ones are *read-only*. Read-only parameters cannot be changed with ndd and must be changed in /etc/system. In addition to the tcp_time_wait_interval parameter, you may also want to consider changing some of the other parameters like tcp_conn_hash_size, tcp_conn_req_max_q, tcp_xmit_hiwat, and tcp_recv_hiwat parameters.

The tcp_conn_hash_size parameter controls the size of a hash table that helps quickly locate the TCP socket's data structure in the kernel. If the size is too small, it will result in long hash chains in each bucket that force the operating system into a linear search for the socket entry of interest, and performance will suffer accordingly. By default, Solaris 8 and 9 set this parameter to 512; we recommend raising the value to 8192 for machines hosting HTTP servers. To set tcp_conn_hash_size, change the /etc/system file, as shown here:

```
set tcp:tcp_conn_hash_size=8192
```

The tcp_conn_req_max_q parameter controls the maximum allowable number of completed connections waiting to return from an accept call (that have completed the three-way TCP connection handshake). You should increase this parameter only if you notice that your system is dropping connections. You can determine the number of drops using the netstat command:

```
netstat -s | grep tcpListenDrop
```

By default, this value is set to 128. If the system is dropping connections, try increasing the value of tcp_conn_req_max_q to 1024.

The tcp_xmit_hiwat and tcp_recv_hiwat parameters control the default size of the *send window* and *receive window* for each TCP connection, respectively. On very fast networks, you should make sure that the values are set to at least 32K. By default, Solaris 8 sets these parameters to 16K and 24K, respectively. Solaris 9 changes the default settings for both parameters to 48K.

BEST PRACTICE Increase the size of key TCP-related parameters to improve system performance and reduce dropped connections.

As we mentioned previously, most operating systems limit the number of open file descriptors a process can have. On Solaris (and most other Unix operating systems), there are actually two file descriptor limits. The first limit is the default limit imposed on each process; this is sometimes called the *soft* limit. The second limit is the maximum number of file descriptors per process that the operating system can support in its current configuration; this is sometimes called the *hard* limit. Use the `ulimit` command to change the soft limit to increase the maximum number of file descriptors for a particular process. You can increase this number only up to the hard limit unless you are the *superuser*, whose username is typically `root`—regardless of any feedback that the `ulimit` command may give you to the contrary. To change the hard limit for processes not running as the `root` user, you need to reconfigure the operating system. On Solaris, this means modifying the `/etc/system` file. The two parameters of interest in the `/etc/system` file are `rlim_fd_cur` and `rlim_fd_max`, which control the soft and hard limits, respectively. You will need to reboot the machine in order for changes to the `/etc/system` file to take effect.

For any machine that will host an HTTP server, we strongly recommend that you increase both the soft and hard limits to 4096 or even 8192. Please make sure to check your operating system documentation and release notes; there are some negative performance implications on some older versions of Solaris if you set these numbers too high. The syntax for adjusting these parameters in the `/etc/system` file is shown here:

```
set rlim_fd_cur=4096
set rlim_fd_max=4096
```

BEST PRACTICE On any machine that hosts an HTTP server, increase the maximum number of file descriptors per process to either 4096 or 8192. On Solaris, this means setting the `rlim_fd_cur` and `rlim_fd_max` parameters in the `/etc/system` file and rebooting the machine.

For more information on tuning the Solaris operating system, please refer to the *Solaris Tunable Parameters Reference Manual*, available on Sun's Web site at http://docs.sun.com/db/doc/816-0607 (Solaris 8) or http://docs.sun.com/db/doc/806-7009 (Solaris 9).

Tuning AIX

On AIX, the `no` command is equivalent to the `ndd` command on Solaris. Running the `no -a` command will display the current values of all network attributes. Issuing the following command will change the time wait interval:

```
no -o tcp_timewait=4
```

This example command sets the tcp_timewait parameter to 4 15-second intervals, or 1 minute. For more information on the no command, see http://publib16.boulder.ibm.com/pseries/en_US/cmds/aixcmds4/no.htm.

When a server listens on a port for connections, TCP creates a queue that it uses to buffer connection requests while waiting for the server to accept the connection. This *listen queue* is a fixed size, and if it fills up, the operating system will reject any new connection requests until there is space available in the queue. AIX controls the maximum length of this listen queue with the somaxconn parameter. By default, AIX sets this to 1024, but on machines with busy HTTP servers, you might want to increase this to 8192. Note that this increases only the maximum allowable length of the listen queue. You will still need to adjust the WebLogic Server instance's Accept Backlog parameter so that WebLogic Server will ask for a longer listen queue, using the server's Tuning Configuration tab in the WebLogic Console. Of course, this particular configuration is also important for other operating systems, including Solaris.

Some other TCP parameters you may need to tune on AIX include tcp_sendspace and tcp_recvspace, which control the socket's sending and receiving buffer sizes, respectively. For more information about tuning AIX, please refer to the AIX Performance Management Guide at http://publib16.boulder.ibm.com/pseries/en_US/aixbman/prftungd/prftungd.htm.

Tuning HP-UX

HP-UX provides the ndd command to use for setting the TCP parameters, just like Solaris (although parameter names are slightly different). To adjust the maximum allowable length of the listen queue to 1024, execute the ndd command shown here:

```
ndd -set /dev/tcp tcp_conn_req_max 1024
```

By default, HP-UX sets the tcp_time_wait_interval to 60000 milliseconds, so you do not typically need to adjust this. HP-UX reads a file in /etc/rc.config.d/nddconf to get customized settings for the TCP parameters at boot time. See this file for further information about how to use it to customize the TCP settings for your machine.

On HP-UX, you may also need to modify some kernel parameters to ensure that WebLogic Server performs optimally. Use the /usr/sbin/sam program to modify kernel parameters. HP-UX limits the maximum number of threads per process. On older versions of HP-UX, this value defaults to 64, a value that large applications can easily exceed. Newer versions of HP-UX set the default value to 256, but you can change this using the max_thread_proc kernel parameter. The maximum number of threads allowed on the system at any point in time is set using the nkthread kernel parameter. Older versions of HP-UX come with a default value of 499 that can be too low on larger multi-CPU machines; newer versions have a default value of 8416. Also remember to adjust the maxfile and maxfile_lim parameters that control the soft and hard limits on the maximum number of file descriptors, if needed. For more information on kernel tuning parameters, see http://docs.hp.com/hpux/onlinedocs/TKP-90203/TKP-90203.html.

Tuning Linux

When tuning Linux operating systems, use either the `sysctl` command or the `/proc` file system. Because the `sysctl` command provides the ability to read from the `/etc/sysctl.conf` file, we generally prefer to use `sysctl` over the `/proc` method. On Linux, the default time wait interval is 120 seconds; you can reset this by changing the value of the `ip_ct_tcp_timeout_time_wait` parameter:

```
sysctl -w ip_ct_tcp_timeout_time_wait=60
```

Linux also limits the maximum number of open files for all users. If this is set too low, your HTTP server process might run out of file descriptors. To change this setting, you can add an entry into the `/etc/sysctl.conf` file and then run `sysctl -p`. The required entry is

```
fs.file-max = 20000
```

Then, if you want to allow your HTTP server process to be able to have 8,192 open file descriptors, you need to edit the `/etc/security/limits.conf` file to add the following entry for your `weblogic` user (assuming that the server is running as user `weblogic`). Remember that this number applies across all processes running as the `weblogic` user. The entry is

```
weblogic hard nofile 8192
```

Finally, you need to use the `ulimit` command to actually make the setting active for the current login session, as shown here:

```
ulimit -n 8192
```

For more information on Linux tuning, please consult you Linux vendor's documentation or check out some of the Linux resources on the Web, such as http://ipsysctl-tutorial.frozentux.net/ipsysctl-tutorial.html, which provides a description of the TCP/IP tuning parameters available on Linux.

Tuning Windows

The concepts behind tuning the Windows operating system are similar to those for tuning other operating systems. Most of the TCP/IP parameter settings are located in the registry under the `HKEY_LOCAL_MACHINE\SYSTEM\CurrentControlSet\Services` folder. To change the maximum length of the TCP listen queue, whose default value is 15, you create a `DWORD` entry called `ListenBackLog` in the `Inetinfo\Parameters` subfolder in your Windows registry. Windows sets the default for the time wait interval to four minutes; the `TcpTimedWaitDelay` parameter in the `Tcpip\Parameters` subfolder allows you to change its value. For more information on tuning Windows, please consult the Microsoft Windows documentation. One excellent paper that discusses the Microsoft TCP/IP implementation in Windows 2000 can be found at http://www.microsoft.com/windows2000/techinfo/howitworks/communications/networkbasics/tcpip_implement.asp.

Network Tuning

Most networks today are very fast and are rarely the direct cause of performance problems in well-designed applications. In our experience, the most frequent network problems come from misconfigured network devices. Whether it is a network interface card in your server, a firewall, a router, or another, more specialized network device such as a load balancer, improper configuration can lead to insidious problems that are very difficult to figure out. This is why it is important to monitor your network when troubleshooting performance problems. Some very simple tests can indicate problems with the network.

First, you can use the `ping` command to generate network traffic between two nodes in your network and look for packet loss. On a high-speed local area network, you should almost never see any packet loss. If you are only seeing performance problems during peak load, make sure to run your ping tests during these times to make sure that the network is still working properly under load. Second, look for send or receive errors on your machine's network interface. You can use the `netstat` command shown here to do this on Solaris:

```
netstat -I /dev/hme0 5
```

This command will generate output every five seconds that shows the statistics for the `hme0` network interface card. Always remember that the first line of output is the cumulative output since the last reboot, so you should generally ignore it. The output of this command will look similar to that shown here. Pay particular attention to the `errs` columns.

```
     input    /dev/h     output              input  (Total)      output
packets errs  packets errs   colls  packets errs   packets errs  colls
0         0   0         0    0      142034  0      40794   242   0
0         0   0         0    0      48        0    6         0   0
0         0   0         0    0      50        0    7         0   0
0         0   0         0    0      48        0    7         0   0
```

Even when the network is properly configured, it is still important to monitor your network performance in both your testing and production environments, concentrating on three areas: packet retransmissions, duplicate packets, and listen drops of packets.

Packet retransmissions occur when the TCP layer is not receiving acknowledgments (ACKs) from the receiver quickly enough, causing TCP to retransmit the packet. If your retransmission rate is 15 percent or higher, this generally indicates a problem with the network. Bad network hardware or a slow or congested route can cause excessive packet retransmission. You should monitor retransmissions using the `netstat -s -P tcp` command to get the `tcpRetransBytes` and `tcpOutDataBytes` statistics. From these numbers, calculate the retransmission percentage using the following formula:

$$PercentRetransmits = \left(\frac{tcpRetransBytes}{tcpOutDataBytes} \right) \times 100$$

If the remote system is retransmitting too quickly, this will cause duplicate packets. Like packet retransmissions, duplicate packets can also indicate a bad network device or a slow or congested route. Using the same `netstat` command we just showed you, get the `tcpInDupBytes` and `tcpInDataBytes` statistics and calculate the duplication percentage using the following formula:

$$PercentDuplicates = \left(\frac{tcpInDupBytes}{tcpInDataBytes}\right) \times 100$$

Listen drops occur when your system has a full listen queue and cannot accept any new connections. To eliminate listen drops, increase the size of the Solaris TCP parameter `tcp_conn_req_max_q` (or its equivalent on your operating system) or add more servers to handle the network load. Use the `netstat -s -P tcp | grep tcpListenDrop` command to measure the frequency of listen drops.

BEST PRACTICE Modern networks are fast enough to avoid performance problems in well-designed systems, but you should monitor key network statistics such as packet retransmissions, duplicate packets, and listen drops to ensure good performance. When troubleshooting performance problems, don't forget to check your network for packet loss or errors.

Java Virtual Machine Tuning

The Java Virtual Machine (JVM) you use to run your WebLogic Server-based application is a key factor in the final server performance. Not all JVMs are created equal—we have seen certain applications perform up to 20 percent better simply by using a different JVM. Performance is nothing without stability, and fast applications do not do your users any good if they are not running. We recommend that you look for stability first and then performance when selecting the JVM on which to run your application server. If more than one JVM is available and supported on your target deployment environment, you should test them head to head to determine which JVM best meets your reliability, performance, and scalability requirements.

Garbage collection is the single most important factor when tuning a JVM for long-running, server-side applications. Improperly tuned garbage collectors and/or applications that create unnecessarily large numbers of objects can significantly affect the efficiency of your application. It is not uncommon to find that garbage collection consumes a significant amount of the overall processing time in a server-side Java application. Proper tuning of the garbage collector can significantly reduce the garbage collector's processing time and, therefore, can significantly improve your application's throughput.

While we spend most of our time in the next sections specifically talking about the Sun JVM, a lot of these concepts are similar in other JVMs, such as BEA's JRockit. Our discussion of JVM tuning will start by reviewing garbage collection. Next, we will walk through key JVM tuning parameters and options for the SUN JVM. We will touch briefly on JRockit toward the end of this section.

Understanding Garbage Collection

Garbage collection (GC) is the technique a JVM uses to free memory occupied by objects that are no longer being used by the application. The Java Language Specification does not require a JVM to have a garbage collector, nor does it specify how a garbage collector should work. Nevertheless, all of the commonly used JVMs have garbage collectors, and most garbage collectors use similar algorithms to manage their memory and perform collection operations.

Just as it is important to understand the workload of your application to tune your overall system properly, it is also important to understand how your JVM performs garbage collection so that you can tune it. Once you have a solid understanding of garbage collection algorithms and implementations, it is possible to tune application and garbage collection behavior to maximize performance. Some garbage collection schemes are more appropriate for applications with specific requirements. For example, near-real-time applications care more about avoiding garbage collection pauses while most OLTP applications care more about overall throughput. Once you have an understanding of the workload of the application and the different garbage collection algorithms your JVM supports, then you can optimize the garbage collector configuration.

In this section, we give you a brief overview of different approaches that JVMs use for garbage collection. For more information on garbage collection algorithms and how they affect JVM performance, we recommend looking at the two very good articles on Sun's Web site: "Improving Java Application Performance and Scalability by Reducing Garbage Collection Times and Sizing Memory" by Nagendra Nagarajayya and Steve Mayer (http://wireless.java.sun.com/midp/articles/garbage) and "Improving Java Application Performance and Scalability by Reducing Garbage Collection Times and Sizing Memory Using JDK 1.4.1 - New Parallel and Concurrent Collectors for Low Pause and Throughput applications" by Nagendra Nagarajayya and Steve Mayer, (http://wireless.java.sun.com/midp/articles/garbagecollection2).

As we discussed previously, the purpose of the garbage collection in a JVM is to clean up objects that are no longer being used. Garbage collectors determine whether an object is eligible for collection by determining whether objects are being referenced by any active objects in the system. The garbage collector must first identify the objects eligible for collection. The two general approaches for this are reference counting and object reference traversal. Reference counting involves storing a count of all of the references to a particular object. This means that the JVM must properly increment and decrement the reference count as the application creates references and as the references go out of scope. When an object's reference count goes to zero, it is eligible for garbage collection.

Although early JVMs used reference counting, most modern JVMs use object reference traversal. Object reference traversal simply starts with a set of root objects and follows every link recursively through the entire object graph to determine the set of *reachable* objects. Any object that is not reachable from at least one of these root objects is garbage collected. During this object traversal stage, the garbage collector must remember which objects are reachable so that it can remove those that are not; this is known as *marking* the object.

The next thing that the garbage collector must do is remove the non-reachable objects. When doing this, some garbage collectors simply scan through the heap, removing the unmarked objects and adding their memory location and size to a list of available memory for the JVM to use in creating new objects; this is commonly referred to as *sweeping*. The problem with this approach is that memory can fragment over time to the point where there are a lot of small segments of memory that are not big enough to use for new objects but yet, when added all together, can make up a significant amount of memory. Therefore, many garbage collectors actually rearrange live objects in memory to *compact* the live objects, making the available heap space contiguous.

In order to do their jobs, garbage collectors usually have to stop all other activity for some portion of the garbage collection process. This *stop-the-world* approach means all application-related work stops while the garbage collector runs. As a result, any in-flight requests will experience an increase in their response time by the amount of time taken by the garbage collector. Other, more sophisticated collectors run either incrementally or truly concurrently to reduce or eliminate the application pauses. Some garbage collectors use a single thread to do their work; others employ multiple threads to increase their efficiency on multi-CPU machines. Let's look at a few of the garbage collectors used by modern JVMs.

Mark-and-sweep collector. This type of collector first traverses the object graph and marks reachable objects. It then scans the heap for unmarked objects and adds their memory to a list of available memory segments. This collector typically uses a single thread to do its work and is a stop-the-world collector.

Mark-and-compact collector. A mark-and-compact collector, sometimes known as a mark-sweep-compact collector, uses the same marking phase as a mark-and-sweep collector. During the second phase, it compacts the heap by copying marked objects to a new area of the heap. These collectors are also stop-the-world collectors.

Copying collector. This type of collector divides the heap into two areas, commonly known as *semi-spaces*. It uses only one semi-space at a time; the JVM creates all new objects in one semi-space. When the garbage collector runs, it copies any reachable objects it finds to the other semi-space as it finds them, thus compacting the heap as it copies live objects. All dead objects are left behind. This algorithm works well for short-lived objects, but the expense of continually copying long-lived objects makes it less efficient. Again, this is a stop-the-world collector.

Incremental collector. Incremental collectors basically divide the heap into multiple areas and collect garbage from only one area at a time. This can create much smaller, though more frequent, pauses in your application. There are numerous approaches defining how the actual collection is handled from traditional mark-and-sweep to algorithms designed explicitly for use with multiple smaller areas like the *train* algorithm. See "Incremental Mature Garbage Collection Using the Train Algorithm" by Jacob Seligmann and Steffen Grarup (http://www.daimi.aau.dk/~beta/Papers/Train/train.html) for more information.

Generational collector. This type of collector divides the heap into two or more areas that it uses to store objects with different lifetimes. The JVM generally creates all new objects in one of these areas. Over time, the objects that continue to exist get tenure and move into another area for longer-lived objects. Generational collectors often use different algorithms for the different areas to optimize performance.

Concurrent collectors. Concurrent collectors run concurrently with the application, typically as one or more background threads. These collectors typically have to stop-the-world at some point to complete certain tasks, but the amount of time they halt all processing is significantly reduced because of their other background work.

Parallel collectors. Parallel collectors typically use one of the traditional algorithms but use multiple threads to parallelize their work on multiprocessor machines. Using multiple threads on multi-CPU machines can dramatically improve the scalability of a Java application on multiprocessor machines.

Tuning the Sun HotSpot 1.4.1 JVM Heap Size

Sun Microsystem's HotSpot JVM uses a generational collector that partitions the heap into three main areas: the new generation area, the old generation area, and the permanent generation area. The JVM creates all new objects in the new generation area. Once an object survives a certain number of garbage collection cycles in the new generation area, it gets promoted, or *tenured*, to the old generation area. The JVM stores `Class` and `Method` objects for the classes it loads in a section of the heap known as the permanent generation area. From a configuration perspective, the permanent generation area in the Sun HotSpot 1.4.1 JVM is a separate area that is not considered part of the heap. Before we go any further, let's look at how to control the size of these areas.

You can use the `-Xms` and `-Xmx` flags to control the initial and maximum size of the entire heap, respectively. For example, the following command sets the initial size of the entire heap to 128 megabytes (MBs) and the maximum size to 256 MBs:

```
java -Xms128m -Xmx256m ...
```

To control the size of the new generation area, you can use the `-XX:NewRatio` flag to set the proportion of the overall heap that is set aside for the new generation area. For example, the following command sets the overall heap size to 128 MBs and sets the new ratio to 3. This means that the ratio of the new area to the old area is 1:3; the new area is one-fourth of the overall heap space, or 32 MBs, and the old area is three-fourths of the overall heap space, or 96 MBs.

```
java -Xms128m -Xmx128m -XX:NewRatio=3 ...
```

The initial and maximum sizes for the new area can be set explicitly using the `-XX:NewSize` and `-XX:MaxNewSize` flags or the new Java 2 SDK 1.4 `-Xmn` flag. For example, the command shown here sets the initial and maximum size to 64 MBs:

```
java -Xms256m -Xmx256m -Xmn64m ...
```

Configuration-wise, the permanent area is not considered part of the heap. By default, the initial size of the permanent area is 4 MBs. As your application loads and runs, the JVM will resize the permanent area as needed up to the maximum size for this area. Every time it resizes the permanent area, the JVM does a full garbage collection of the entire heap (and the permanent area). By default, the maximum size is 32 MBs. Use the `-XX:MaxPermSize` flag to increase the maximum size of the permanent area. When loading large numbers of classes in your WebLogic Server application, it is not uncommon to need to increase the maximum size of this area. The number of objects stored in the permanent area will grow quickly while the JVM loads classes, and it may force the JVM to resize the permanent area frequently. To prevent this resizing, set the initial size of the permanent area using the `-XX:PermSize` flag. For example, here we have set the initial size to 32 MBs and the maximum size to 64 MBs:

```
java -Xms512m -Xmx512m -Xmn128m -XX:PermSize=32m -XX:MaxPermSize=64m ...
```

WARNING When the permanent area of the heap is too small, the JVM will do a full garbage collection of the entire heap before resizing the permanent area. If you allow the JVM to control the size, these full garbage collections will happen relatively frequently because the JVM is ultra-conservative about grabbing too much space for the permanent area. Always set the `PermSize` big enough for your application to run comfortably.

By default, HotSpot uses a copying collector for the new generation area. This area is actually subdivided into three partitions. The first partition, known as *Eden*, is where all new objects get created. The other two semi-spaces are also called *survivor* spaces. When Eden fills up, the collector stops the application and copies all reachable objects into the current `from` survivor space. As the current `from` survivor space fills up, the collector will copy the reachable objects to the current `to` survivor space. At that point, the `from` and `to` survivor spaces switch roles so that the current `to` space becomes the new `from` space and vice versa. Objects that continue to live are copied between survivor spaces until they achieve tenure, at which point they are moved into the old generation area.

Use the `-XX:SurvivorRatio` flag to control the size of these subpartitions. Like the `NewRatio`, the `SurvivorRatio` specifies the ratio of the size of one of the survivor spaces to the Eden space. For example, the following command sets the new area size to 64 MBs, Eden to 32 MBs, and each of the two survivor spaces to 16 MBs:

```
java -Xms256m -Xmx256m -Xmn64m -XX:SurvivorRatio=2 ...
```

Figure 12.1 shows an overview of the HotSpot JVM heap layout and some of the parameters that we have been discussing.

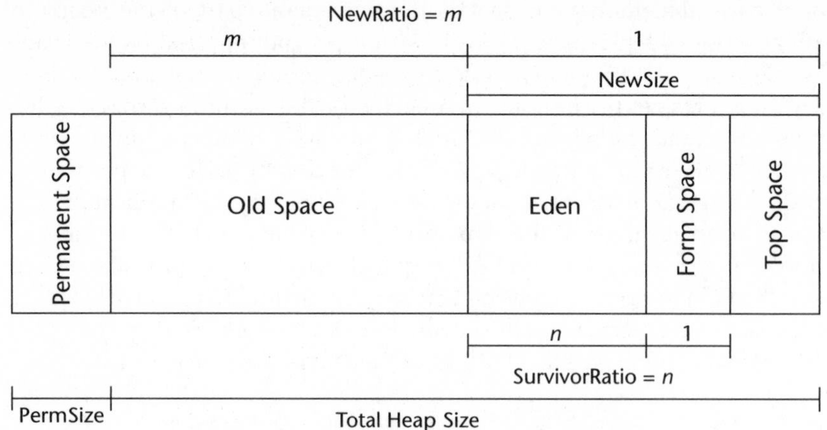

Figure 12.1 Understanding the HotSpot heap partitioning.

As we discuss previously, HotSpot defaults to using a copying collector for the new area and a mark-sweep-compact collector for the old area. Using a copying collector for the new area makes sense because the majority of objects created by an application are short-lived. In an ideal situation, all transient objects would be collected before making it out of the Eden space. If we were able to achieve this, and all objects that made it out of the Eden space were long-lived objects, then ideally we would immediately tenure them into the old space to avoid copying them back and forth in the survivor spaces.

Unfortunately, applications do not necessarily fit cleanly into this ideal model as they tend also to have a small number of intermediate-lived objects. It is typically better to keep these intermediate-lived objects in the new area because copying a small number of objects is generally less expensive than compacting the old heap when they have to be garbage collected in the old heap.

To control the copying of objects in the new area, use the `-XX:TargetSurvivorRatio` flag to control the desired survivor space occupancy after a collection. Don't be misled by the name; this value is a percentage. By default, the value is set to 50. When using large heaps in conjunction with a low `SurvivorRatio`, you should probably increase this value to somewhere in the neighborhood of 80 to 90 to better utilize the survivor space.

Use the `-XX:MaxTenuringThreshold` flag to control the upper threshold the copying collector uses before promoting an object. If you want to prevent all copying and automatically promote objects directly from Eden to the old area, set the value of `MaxTenuringThreshold` to 0. If you do this, you will in effect be skipping the use of the survivor spaces, so you will want to set the `SurvivorRatio` to a large number to maximize the size of the Eden area, as shown here:

```
java ... -XX:MaxTenuringThreshold=0 -XX:SurvivorRatio=50000 ...
```

Now that you understand the goals and controls you have for tuning the heap sizes, let's look at some of the information you can get from the JVM to help you make the right tuning decisions.

The -verbose:gc switch gives you basic information about what the garbage collector is doing. By turning this switch on, you will get information about when major and minor collections occur, what the memory size before and after the collection was, and how much time the collection took. Let's look at some sample output from this switch:

```
[Full GC 21924K->13258K(63936K), 0.3854772 secs]
[GC 26432K->13984K(63936K), 0.0168988 secs]
[GC 27168K->13763K(63936K), 0.0068799 secs]
[GC 26937K->14196K(63936K), 0.0139437 secs]
```

The first line that starts with Full GC is a major collection of the entire heap. The other three lines are minor collections, either of the new or the old area. The numbers before the arrow indicate the size of the heap before the collection, while the number after the arrow shows the size after the collection. The number in parentheses is the total size of the heap, and the time values indicate the amount of time the collection took.

By turning on the -XX:+PrintGCDetails switch, you can get a little more information about what is happening in the garbage collector. Output from this switch looks like this:

```
[Full GC [Tenured: 11904K->13228K(49152K), 0.4044939 secs]
       21931K->13228K(63936K), 0.4047285 secs]
[GC [DefNew: 13184K->473K(14784K), 0.0213737 secs]
       36349K->23638K(63936K), 0.0215022 secs]
```

As with the standard garbage collection output, the Full GC label indicates a full collection. Tenured indicates that the mark-sweep-compact collector has run on the old generation; the old heap size went from 11904K to 13228K; the total old area size is 49152K. The reason for this increase is that the new area is automatically purged of all objects during a full collection. The second set of numbers associated with the first entry represents the before, after, and total size of the entire heap. This full collection took 0.4047285 seconds. In the second entry, the GC label indicates a partial collection, and DefNew means that the collection took place in the new area; all of the statistics have similar meanings to the first except that they pertain to the new area rather than the old area.

By adding the -XX:+PrintGCTimeStamps switch, the JVM adds information about when these garbage collection cycles occur. The time is measured in seconds since the JVM started, shown in bold here:

```
21.8441: [GC 21.8443: [DefNew: 13183K->871K(14784K), 0.0203224 secs]
                      20535K->8222K(63936K), 0.0205780 secs]
```

Finally, you can add the -XX:+PrintHeapAtGC switch to get even more detailed information. This information will dump a snapshot of the heap as a whole.

To get more information on what is going on in the new area, you can print the object tenuring statistics by adding the -XX:+PrintTenuringDistribution switch, in addition to the -verbose:gc switch, to the JVM command line. The output that follows shows objects being promoted through the ages on their way to being tenured to the old generation.

```
java -Xms64m -Xmx64m -XX:NewRatio=3 -verbose:gc
     -XX:+PrintTenuringDistribution ...

[GC
Desired survivor size 819200 bytes, new threshold 31 (max 31)
- age   1:      285824 bytes,      285824 total
 34956K->22048K(63936K), 0.2182682 secs]
[GC
Desired survivor size 819200 bytes, new threshold 31 (max 31)
- age   1:      371520 bytes,      371520 total
- age   2:      263472 bytes,      634992 total
 35231K->22389K(63936K), 0.0413801 secs]
[GC
Desired survivor size 819200 bytes, new threshold 3 (max 31)
- age   1:      436480 bytes,      436480 total
- age   2:      203952 bytes,      640432 total
- age   3:      263232 bytes,      903664 total
 35573K->22652K(63936K), 0.0432329 secs]
```

Notice the desired survivor size of 819200 bytes. Why is that? Well, let's do the math. If the overall heap is 64 MBs and the `NewRatio` is 3, this means that the new area is one-fourth of the total heap, or 16 MBs. Because we are using the client JVM, the default value of the `SurvivorRatio` is 8. This means that each survivor space is one-eighth the size of the Eden space. Because there are two survivor spaces, that means that each survivor space is one-tenth of the overall new area size, or 1.6 MBs. Because the default `TargetSurivorRatio` is 50 percent, this causes the desired survivor size to be about 800 KBs.

You will also notice that the maximum threshold is always 31. Because of the `TargetSurvivorRatio` discussion previously, the garbage collector will always try to keep the survivor space at or below the target size. The garbage collector will try to age (copy) the objects up to the threshold of 31 times before promoting them into the old area. The garbage collector, however, will recalculate the actual threshold for promotion after each garbage collection. Remember, any full garbage collection cycle will immediately tenure all reachable objects, so always try to tune the garbage collector—especially the `PermSize`—to prevent full garbage collection cycles from occurring.

In the last entry, you will notice that the garbage collector changed the threshold from the default of 31 to 3. This happened because the garbage collector is attempting to keep the occupancy of the survivor space at its desired survivor size. By adding the size of the objects in all three age categories you will get 903661 bytes, which exceeds the desired survivor size; therefore, the garbage collector reset the threshold for the next garbage collection cycle.

Java 2 SDK 1.4.1 comes with several new garbage collectors that allow you to optimize the garbage collector based on your application requirements. Let's look at those now to understand the available collectors and what they can do for you.

Selecting the Garbage Collector

While the generational garbage collection makes the HotSpot JVM much more efficient, several problems remain. Both the copying collector and the mark-sweep-compact collector are stop-the-world collectors. Increasing the size of the heap that these collectors must manage means increasing the pause times, regardless of how much processing power the box has. The primary reason for this is that both collectors use a single thread to do their work and, therefore, cannot take advantage of multiprocessor machines. This severely limits their scalability on large Symmetric Multi-Processor (SMP) boxes.

Java 2 SDK 1.4.1 comes with three new garbage collectors: the parallel copying collector, the concurrent old area collector, and the parallel scavenger collector. The first two collectors are designed to minimize application pauses, while the last collector is designed to increase throughput for applications that can tolerate pauses.

The parallel copying collector works just like the copying collector except that it will use multiple threads, one per CPU by default, to do its work. To enable this collector, you can set the `-XX:+useParNewGC` switch. If the machine has only one CPU, the JVM will default to the copying collector because multiple CPUs are not available. You can force the JVM to use the parallel copying collector by increasing the degree of parallelism manually using the `-XX:ParallelGCThreads` option:

```
java ... -XX:+UseParNewGC -XX:+ParallelGCThreads=4 ...
```

The parallel copying collector can work in conjunction with either the concurrent old area collector or the traditional mark-sweep-compact collector.

When doing its work, the concurrent old area collector collects garbage in six steps, four that run concurrently with the application threads and two that stop-the-world. This makes for much smaller application pauses while doing an old generation garbage collection cycle. To use this new collector, simply set the `-XX:+UseConcMarkSweepGC` switch. If the concurrent collector is not able to keep up, the default mark-sweep-compact collector will step in. By default, the concurrent collector kicks in when the occupied percentage goes above 68 percent. You can control this threshold percentage using the `-XX:CMSInitiatingOccupancyFraction` flag, as shown here:

```
java ... -XX:+UseConcMarkSweepGC -XX:CMSInitiatingOccupancyFraction=40
...
```

By combining this and the parallel copying collector, you can significantly reduce the garbage collection pauses in your application on a multiprocessor machine.

To maximize the throughput for applications that can tolerate pauses, use the parallel scavenger collector by specifying the `-XX:+UseParallelGC` switch. Currently, this collector works only in conjunction with the old area's mark-sweep-compact collector. It works much like the parallel copying collector in that it uses multiple threads to accomplish its work; by default, it uses one thread per CPU. Just like the parallel copying collector, you can control the parallelism using the `-XX:ParallelGCThreads` flag. The parallel scavenging collector will perform much better when used in conjunction with the `-XX:+UseAdaptiveSizePolicy` switch. With this switch, the JVM automatically optimizes the size of the new area and the survivor ratio to maximize performance.

Choosing the Right HotSpot JVM Version

The Sun HotSpot JVM actually contains two different JVM implementations: a client JVM and a server JVM. By default, the HotSpot VM runs the client JVM. Setting either the `-hotspot` or `-client` switch tells the JVM to use its client configuration; setting `-server` tells the JVM to use its server configuration. Choosing the right version to use for your application depends on a number of factors:

Stability. The JVM and application must be stable, or performance gains are meaningless.

Hardware platform. The HotSpot JVM performance will vary depending on the type of hardware and operating system and on the size of the machine.

JVM version. JVM technology is constantly improving, so do not rely on past experience with previous JVM versions when making your selection for a new version of the JVM.

Experience benchmarking and tuning a large number of WebLogic Server applications on a variety of platforms and JVM versions yields some rules of thumb worth sharing. Of course, the usual caveat applies—you should perform your own stress testing and tuning exercise to choose the proper JVM for your application rather than relying on this or any other discussion of past results.

Benchmarking numerous applications across the Windows NT/2000 and Sun Solaris platforms using the older Sun 1.3.0 and 1.3.1 JVMs with HotSpot technology leads us to conclude that the client JVM generally performs better and provides a more stable environment on these specific platforms. On Windows platforms, the client JVM outperformed the server JVM on all but one of the applications we tested. On Solaris platforms running these older JVM implementations on SMP machines, the client JVM typically outperforms the server JVM when the machine contains up to four processors. Larger numbers of processors tend to favor the server JVM. Starting with the HotSpot JVM 1.3.1_03 release, however, it appears that the server JVM outperforms the client JVM on most WebLogic Server-based applications regardless of the amount of processors on the server.

As stated earlier, choosing the right JVM depends strongly on the specifics of your platform, version, and application. If no time is available to perform your own testing to make this decision, it is probably safest to use the client JVM on small systems and favor the server JVM on larger SMP boxes with more than four processors.

BEST PRACTICE **Choosing the right HotSpot JVM version depends strongly on the specifics of your platform, JVM version, and application requirements. Stress testing using both client and server JVMs in your environment is the best way to make the decision.**

Using BEA JRockit JVM

BEA is shipping a new JVM that it has optimized for the Intel platform. JRockit was designed from the ground up to be a server-side JVM. Instead of lazily compiling the Java byte code into native code as HotSpot does, it precompiles every class as it loads.

JRockit also provides more in-depth instrumentation to give you more insight into what is going on inside the JVM at run time. It does this through a stand-alone GUI console or through the WebLogic Console if you are using JRockit to run WebLogic Server. BEA's JRockit JVM supports four garbage collectors:

Generational copying collector. This collector uses a strategy very similar to the default generational collection strategy that HotSpot uses. Objects are allocated in the new area, known as the *nursery* in the JRockit documentation. This collector works best with small heap sizes on single-CPU machines.

Single-spaced concurrent collector. This collector uses the entire heap and does its work concurrently using a background thread. While this collector can virtually eliminate pauses, you are trading memory and throughput for pause-less collection because it will generally take the collector longer to find dead objects and the collector is constantly running during application processing. If this collector cannot keep up with the amount of garbage the application creates, it will stop the application threads while it finishes its collection cycle.

Generational concurrent collector. This collector uses a stop-the-world copying collector on the nursery area and a concurrent collector on the old area. Because this collector has more frequent pauses than the single-spaced concurrent collector, it should require less memory and provide more throughput for applications that can tolerate short pauses. Remember that an undersized nursery area can cause large numbers of temporary objects to be promoted to the old area. This will cause the concurrent collector to work harder and may cause it to fall behind to the point where it has to stop the world to complete its cycle.

Parallel collector. This collector stops the world but uses multiple threads to speed the collection process. While it will cause longer pauses than the rest, it generally provides better memory utilization and better throughput.

By default, JRockit uses the generational concurrent collector. To change the collector, use the `-Xgc:<gc_name>` flag, where the valid values for the four collectors are `gencopy`, `singlecon`, `gencon`, and `parallel`, respectively. You can set the initial and maximum heap sizes using the same `-Xms` and `-Xmx` flags as you do for the HotSpot JVM. To set the nursery size, use the `-Xns` flag:

```
java -jrockit -Xms512m -Xmx512m -Xgc:gencon -Xns128m ...
```

While JRockit recognizes the `-verbose:gc` switch, the information it prints will vary depending on which garbage collector you are using. JRockit also supports verbose output options of `memory` (same as `gc`), `load`, and `codegen`. Using the default `gencon` collector, the `-verbose:memory` output provides information on both new area (*young GC*) and old area collections, as shown here.

```
[memory ] young GC 10: promoted 31048 objects (1479096 bytes) in 22.684
ms
[memory ] starting old collection 0
[memory ] old collection 0 ended after 412.196 ms
```

Using the `-Xgcpause` switch will cause JRockit to print output each time the JVM has to pause other threads to complete garbage collection. The output looks like this:

```
[memory ] pause time for young collection was 22.683914 ms
[memory ] starting old collection 0
[memory ] pause time for oldcollection phase 1 was 86.980128 ms
[memory ] pause time for oldcollection phase 4 was 69.428148 ms
[memory ] pause time for oldcollection phase 5 was 0.116265 ms
[memory ] pause time for oldcollection phase 5 was 0.544331 ms
[memory ] pause time for oldcollection phase 5 was 0.196957 ms
[memory ] old collection 0 ended after 412.196 ms
```

As you can see, even the concurrent collector occasionally has to stop the application to do certain phases of its work. If you use the `-Xgcreport` switch, JRockit will print out a summary of the garbage collection activity before it exits.

We have touched on only the highlights of the JRockit JVM. For more information, please see the JRockit documentation at http://edocs.bea.com/wljrockit/docs81/index.html. JVM tuning is a complex and challenging topic, and we have barely scratched the surface. Nevertheless, it is time to continue moving up the layers in the architecture to the application server platform.

Application Server Tuning

In this section, we will discuss techniques and best practices for tuning the core aspects of your WebLogic Server environment. This discussion will include setting some important connection-related parameters, using the native I/O *muxer*, optimizing your execute thread count, and taking advantage of application-defined execute queues.

Configuring Connection-Related Parameters

During performance tests or on heavily loaded production systems, you may want to increase the length of the TCP listen queue, as we discussed in the "Operating System Tuning" section. While the operating system parameter we discussed controls the maximum length of the listen queue, WebLogic Server uses the `Accept Backlog` parameter to specify the queue size that the server should request from the operating system. The default value of 50 can be too small on heavily loaded systems. If valid client connection requests are being rejected, the listen queue may be too small.

WebLogic Server uses the `Login Timeout` parameter to help prevent certain types of denial-of-service attacks. This parameter sets a maximum amount of time for a non-SSL client to complete the process of establishing the connection and sending the first request. By default, WebLogic Server 8.1 sets the default values to 5,000 milliseconds, which may be too low for heavily loaded systems. Note that previous versions of WebLogic Server had a default setting of 1,000 milliseconds. If your clients are seeing their connections timed out by the server, then increasing the `Login Timeout` may help. WebLogic Server has a corresponding parameter for SSL connections called the `SSL Login Timeout` that defaults to 25,000 milliseconds. In certain high-volume SSL conditions, you may need to raise this limit as well.

Using the Native I/O Muxer

As we discussed in Chapter 11, WebLogic Server has several different socket multiplexing (muxer, for short) implementations: an all-Java muxer and a native I/O muxer. WebLogic Server 8.1 also has a new hidden muxer that is based on the new Java 2 Standard Edition 1.4 support for non-blocking I/O (NIO). By default, WebLogic Server uses the native I/O muxer whenever it can but will revert automatically to the Java muxer if the native I/O muxer fails to initialize properly—for example, if it cannot locate its shared library. In general, you should always use the native I/O muxer because it is far more scalable than the all-Java muxer.

The new NIO muxer should give equivalent scalability to the native I/O muxer, but with an all-Java implementation. Chapter 11 describes how to enable the new NIO muxer should you want to test it out. Be aware that as of this writing, the NIO muxer is not officially supported by BEA and does not currently work with SSL connections. We expect this to change, so please consult the BEA documentation for more information.

Tuning Execute Thread Counts

In this section, we discuss how to choose the right number of execute threads for your application. The next section will discuss using application-specific execute queues. As you will recall from our discussion in Chapter 11, the muxer reads a request from a socket and places it onto an execute queue. At that point, an execute thread will pick up the request, invoke the application code to process the request, and send the response back to the caller before going back to get another request from the queue. Your biggest task when tuning WebLogic Server is determining the right number of execute threads to use for your application. Therefore, we will concentrate here on choosing proper settings for performance.

WebLogic Server has the ability to tune the number of threads available for handling requests placed on an execute queue. When tuning the execute queue thread count there is no magic number that works best under all possible conditions. All applications behave differently and you should not try to generalize findings across different applications. The appropriate thread count will depend on the application workload and the physical environment in which the application is deployed. Ideally, the optimal thread count would be large enough to keep all of the server processors busy, but small enough not to cause excessive context switching or consume more system resources without enhancing the application's performance, scalability, and/or reliability.

Tuning the number of execute threads is an iterative process that will require some amount of testing. Here are some guidelines to get you started thinking about how to choose the right number of threads. Applications that perform no I/O spend all of their time executing CPU instructions; therefore, their performance and throughput are based solely on how efficiently their work can be divided among the available CPUs. Because these applications never block, the ideal partitioning strategy is to divide the application's work up over the same number of threads as there are available CPUs. The reason for this is simple. Because any CPU can run only one thread at a time, the system will spend more time processing if it never has to switch thread contexts for threads that never perform I/O operations. Of course, very few systems meet these criteria. All application-server-based applications spend some amount of time doing I/O to interact with files, sockets, and/or databases. The large majority of J2EE applications spend most of their time doing I/O.

As the amount of I/O work your application is doing increases, the amount of time your application threads spend waiting on I/O also increases. If all of the threads are blocked waiting on I/O at any point in time, the CPUs are sitting idle instead of doing useful work. The goal is to increase the number of threads to the point where you have the same number of runnable threads as you have available CPUs. Unfortunately, we have no magic formula by which you can calculate this number. You can use operating system tools and/or thread dumps at different points in time to get a better feel for what the application threads are doing. This, combined with iterative testing, is the best way that we have found to determine the optimum number of execute threads.

When doing these iterative tests, you want to simulate the actual production environment as closely as possible. Keep these best practices in mind when setting up your tests.

- Always tune with the version of the application that will go to production.
- Use a database that can simulate the production data sets, and ensure that all database indexes and constraints are present and enabled.
- Ensure that all layers of the application are in place, including firewalls, load balancers, Web servers, LDAP or security servers, application servers, and database servers.
- Use testing tools that can simulate a realistic workload comparable to production transaction-rate and concurrent-user expectations. While testing without think time may allow you to generate similar throughput with fewer users, the optimal number of threads will not necessarily be the same as it is for the more realistic case.
- Change only one variable at a time, and run multiple tests to verify that the results with a particular configuration are consistent. This will keep you from drawing incorrect conclusions.

Let's spend a few minutes talking about the overall process that you should use when running these sorts of tests. First, start with a reasonably tuned JVM, and use the guidelines presented previously and any experience with this application to select an initial number of execute threads. If you are trying to tune the application for production, we will assume that your previous testing has allowed you to identify and remove all application-related bottlenecks so that you can focus solely on tuning the application's environment.

Next, you should start with a series of shorter test runs to allow you to adjust the system's configuration. In these tests, you are trying to simulate the expected production load but allow the test to run at steady-state for 5 to 10 minutes. This is usually sufficient to get an idea of what the performance is like with sufficient garbage collection cycles so as not to skew the results. While running these short tests, you should monitor all system resources, including hardware status, software and process loads, network activity, application throughput, and execute queue length. The primary concerns are CPU utilization, throughput, and the execute queue length, but you will want to monitor everything to make sure that other bottlenecks do not exist. We will assume for the rest of this process that no application or system bottlenecks exist and that you can concentrate solely on tuning the application server's execute thread count.

You can monitor the length and throughput of the default execute queue with the performance monitoring tools available in the WebLogic Console, as illustrated in Figure 12.2. You should use the load-generation tool to measure the application throughput. Many load-generation tools can also gather system-specific resource metrics as well. We recommend using Unix tools like `iostat`, `vmstat`, `mpstat`, and `netstat` or the Windows `perfmon` tool to monitor low-level system resource usage because these tools are very lightweight and do not put significant load on the machines or the network.

Once you finish each of these short tests, you will need to combine and correlate the information. Study the test metrics to determine whether the application is CPU bound or the execute queue was backing up during the test. Always track changes to application throughput and response times very carefully because the ultimate goal is to increase throughput without exceeding your requirements for acceptable response times. Any changes that adversely affect throughput should be reverted to the previous settings before making the next change. If increasing the thread count causes performance to degrade or drives the CPUs to maximum utilization, then you have probably either exceeded the optimum thread count or exposed a bottleneck somewhere in the system. Table 12.1 provides some basic guidelines for how to adjust the number of execute threads.

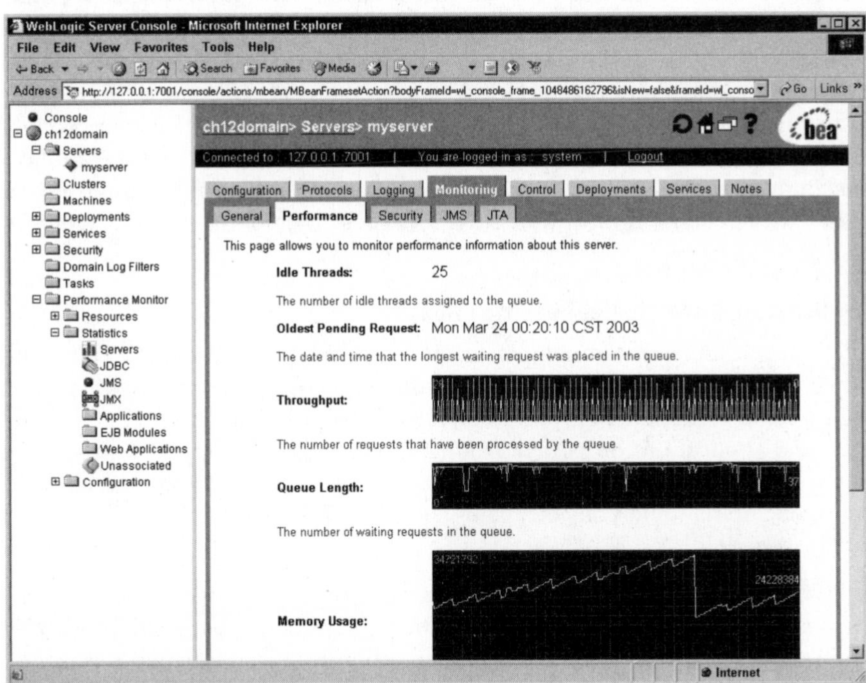

Figure 12.2 Administration console performance monitoring.

Table 12.1 Guidelines for Adjusting Execute Queue Thread Count

EXECUTE QUEUE IS BACKED UP?	APPLICATION IS CPU BOUND?	SOLUTION
Yes	No	Increase execute queue thread count.
Yes	Yes	Decrease thread count and explore JVM or application issues that may be causing high CPU utilization.
No	Yes	Decrease thread count and explore JVM or application issues that may be causing high CPU utilization.
No	No	Compare server throughput with previous tests. If the throughput increased, then increase the execute queue thread count. If the throughput decreased, then decrease the thread count.

Once you have found the optimum settings, you should go back and look at garbage collection to see if there is room for improvement in the garbage collector settings to improve the efficiency of the application. Before moving an application into production, we always recommend that you run a longer test to make sure that the application is stable under heavy load for 24 , 48 , or 72 hours. These tests can often reveal issues that might not show up in production for weeks or months, such as memory leaks.

Using Application-Specific Execute Queues

By default, all applications that you deploy on WebLogic Server use its default execute queue. While this is sufficient for many applications, there are situations where you might want to use WebLogic Server's ability to create application-specific execute queues and bind application components to them. By configuring application-specific queues you can allocate threads at a more granular level to isolate or throttle application components. You should consider using application-specific execute queues for the following scenarios:

Isolate mission critical applications. You can use application-specific queues to dedicate execute threads to critical application components that are deployed in the same WebLogic Server instance as other application components. For example, a stock-trading system might collocate the quotes and trading components in the same servers. By assigning the trading component to its own execute queue, you can dedicate a fixed number of threads to the trading component so that these requests are more isolated from the quote requests than they would be if both were using the same execute queue and thread pool.

Separate long-running requests from OLTP-style requests. Many applications have a mixture of both short- and longer-running requests. In many cases, these long-running requests may use large amounts of CPU and/or memory and affect the performance of core, time-sensitive OLTP-style requests. By assigning these longer-running requests to their own execute queue, you can throttle the number of these requests being processed concurrently.

Deploy message-driven beans. In WebLogic Server, message-driven beans use threads from the underlying execute queue. While you can control the size of each MDB's instance pool, the actual concurrency of the processing also depends on the execute queue being used and the number of threads available for use. As we discussed in Chapter 9, WebLogic Server will use up to about half of the execute threads from the default execute queue for MDB processing. By using application-defined execute queues, you avoid this limitation.

Create application-specific execute queues using the WebLogic Console. To assign a component to the queue, use the Web application or EJB deployment descriptor to set the `wl-dispatch-policy` to the name of the execute queue. Remember that this dispatch policy affects only requests that originate outside of the WebLogic Server to which the component is deployed. For more information, please refer to our discussion of execute queues in Chapter 11.

Performance Best Practices

In this section, we turn our attention to application design and configuration best practices that directly affect the performance of your WebLogic Server system. We'll start by reviewing a few design patterns that can improve performance, then present a series of Web Container and EJB Container best practices, and finish up with some best practices related to database access.

Designing for Performance

Good application performance starts with good application design. Overly complex or poorly designed applications will perform poorly regardless of the system-level tuning and best practices you employ to improve performance. Entire books have been dedicated to good application design, and we have only part of one chapter in this book, so we must limit our discussion to a few key principles and best practices. There are many books on J2EE design patterns and anti-patterns; two of our favorites are *Bitter Java* by Bruce A. Tate (Manning Publications, 2002) and *EJB Design Patterns: Advanced Patterns, Processes, and Idioms* by Floyd Marinescu (Wiley, 2002).

Design patterns are an important topic in the J2EE development community. Proper use of design patterns can provide significant benefits in the maintainability of application code through standardizing the approach to common design problems. Certain design patterns are also beneficial to performance because they reduce the overhead associated with transactions and inter-component messaging. Let's look at three of the more important patterns for J2EE applications. For a more extensive overview of well-known J2EE design patterns, take a look at *Core J2EE Patterns: Best Practices and Design Strategies* by Deepak Alur et al. (Prentice Hall, 2001).

Session Façade

The session façade pattern is a high-level wrapper for server-side components and was discussed at some length in Chapter 7. J2EE applications commonly implement this pattern by creating a stateless session bean that wraps business logic and the entity beans, database interactions, and Java objects required to perform the business logic. The *bigrez.com* application makes use of this pattern for key business services such as reservation creation and the rate and availability search processes.

Session façades improve application performance by exposing only high-level business operations and reducing the individual client invocations to components such as entity beans. This is especially important when accessing EJB components by remote interfaces, as the network and marshalling overhead for each remote call is substantial. Even with local interfaces, there is some overhead because the EJB container provides security, life-cycle management, and transaction control for each invocation. Chapter 7 presents an argument that local interfaces and client-controlled transactions reduce this overhead and make direct interaction with entity bean components more palatable, but the principle remains: reduce the number of invocations that require network, data marshalling, life-cycle, or transactional services to improve application performance. Session façades are one good way to follow this principle.

BEST PRACTICE Reduce the number of remote calls or other high-overhead invocations in your system to improve performance. Stateless session beans implementing the session façade pattern are one good way to reduce the number of these types of invocations.

Value Object

Another common and important mechanism available to reduce the need for remote invocations is the value object pattern. Creating a separate data object that contains all of the fields within an entity bean allows a single client invocation to retrieve all attribute data from an entity bean. These value objects also allow you to create and populate with information in the EJB client, which may be a stand-alone Java client, a servlet, or even another EJB. This works because the value objects are simply serializable Java objects rather than EJB components. Passing the entire object from an EJB client to a session bean or entity bean eliminates to invoke multiple *setter* methods from the client.

You can also use `HashMap` objects and other collections to pass information to the entity bean. The advantage of using these types of collection objects is that they are not tightly coupled to the entity bean interface. Entity bean attribute changes are easier to handle, and older clients can still work with the entity bean. This flexibility, though, comes at the cost of losing some compile-time checking of the client's use of the entity bean interface and therefore requires more run-time checking in the entity bean itself. Many times, it is simply better to use a value object that provides some parameter validation checks so that the entity bean does not have to handle validation.

The *bigrez.com* application uses value objects for key business data, such as reservation information. We did this for two reasons. First, this provides a single data structure to use when communicating with the reservation session bean. Second, because value objects are `Serializable`, their use allows us to store data in the `HttpSession`.

Command Pattern

The command pattern uses a single command object to encapsulate multiple steps or requests that are passed to the server for processing with a single invocation. Use this pattern by itself or in conjunction with the session façade pattern to further reduce individual component remote invocations. Systems that contain many business interfaces implemented as façades often use this pattern to create additional higher-level interfaces without creating additional session beans.

The command pattern resembles the business delegate pattern in that both patterns create a higher-level interface for multiple business services. The command pattern processes the logic within the command class on the server, while the business delegate pattern uses the client tier. In other words, while business delegates can simplify the interfaces to back-end systems by providing a higher-level interface, they generally execute on the client side of the application and create multiple invocations to back-end services. The command pattern may therefore be a better choice if performance is a key requirement for the design.

BEST PRACTICE Create objects that implement the command pattern to further reduce the number of remote calls or other high-overhead invocations in your system. When using remote clients, favor command objects over business delegates for better performance.

Understanding Web Container Best Practices

Many high-volume J2EE applications service hundreds, if not thousands, of page requests per second. Small improvements in performance within the Web Container can therefore lead to big improvements in overall system throughput and scalability. This section touches on a few important best practices related to servlets and JavaServer Pages (JSPs), the core components in most Web applications.

Session Management

As discussed in Chapter 1, many applications supplement the stateless HTTP protocol by storing session-specific data in the `HttpSession`. This session data will then be available during subsequent requests from the same browser session. In a reliable application, this session data must be available even if the server originally used to service the HTTP request fails or is shut down. WebLogic Server provides two options for session persistence:

In-memory replication. Session data is kept in memory on the primary server assigned to this session and replicated to a backup server in the cluster for failover.

JDBC-based persistence. Session data is stored in a special database table and read in to memory by the server processing an HTTP request.

In-memory replication is much faster that JDBC-based persistence and should be used when it meets your requirements. Recognize, however, that there is a cost associated with session persistence regardless of the persistence option chosen. When a Web application updates the `HttpSession` object, WebLogic Server must save these changes at the end of the HTTP request. The quantity of data the server needs to save depends on the structure of the data in the `HttpSession`. WebLogic Server uses the `HttpSession.setAttribute()` method to detect when changes to the session occur. At the end of each request, WebLogic Server saves each new or changed attribute value. This means that WebLogic Server will save the entire object graph bound into the attribute that changed. If your Web application updates only one or a few fields in a large object structure, you should consider breaking this large object structure up into smaller objects that are bound into different attributes in the session to reduce the amount of data the server has to save at the end of any particular request.

BEST PRACTICE **Avoid placing all session data in a single large object in the `HttpSession`. Use in-memory replication for session persistence unless you need JDBC-based persistence to meet your requirements.**

`HttpSession` objects also use system resources, so it is important to clean them up when you finish using them. WebLogic Server releases `HttpSession` objects in two ways:

Session time-outs. WebLogic Server will remove an `HttpSession` object after a period of inactivity, known as a *session time-out*. Session time-outs can be set using either the `session-descriptor` element's `TimeoutSecs` attribute in the `weblogic.xml` deployment descriptor or the `session-timeout` element in the `web.xml` descriptor. See the WebLogic Server documentation at http://edocs.bea.com/wls/docs81/webapp/sessions.html for more information.

Explicit invalidation. You can programmatically remove a session by calling the `invalidate()` method on the `HttpSession` object.

Too often, Web application programmers abuse the session object. You should carefully consider what you store in session objects. Make sure that you understand all of the other available options and the performance trade-offs associated with using sessions. The following list represents a set of best practices related to sessions.

- Avoid using the session to pass data between Web application components such as servlet controllers and JSP pages during the processing of a single HTTP request. You should use the `HttpServletRequest` object for passing data needed when forwarding or including other Web application components.
- Consider other alternatives when state can easily be maintained or derived. You can often store the state in local variables, the database, or client-side cookies.
- Keep your session objects as small as possible by always removing objects from the session that you no longer need with the session's `removeAttribute()` method.
- Understand your business requirements for session time-outs. Always make sure that you tune the session time-out interval to the smallest value consistent with your business requirements. This will prevent users from tying up valuable resources when they fail to exit the system when finished. WebLogic Server uses a default value of 3,600 seconds, or 1 hour. A value of 10 or 15 minutes is usually sufficient for most Web applications.

JavaServer Pages

Chapter 1 presented a number of the best practices related to JavaServer Pages. Here, we highlight two areas of particular importance to performance.

Using Sessions Efficiently

JavaServer Pages (JSPs) create `HttpSession` objects by default, as required by the JSP specification. If your pages are not using sessions, turning the default behavior off can enhance performance. Include the following JSP page directive to avoid creating unnecessary `HttpSession` objects:

```
<%@ page session="false"%>
```

Using Dynamic Content Caching

Chapter 1 presented the `wl:cache` custom tag and the `CacheFilter` servlet filter, two powerful techniques available for dynamic content caching in WebLogic Server. When determining what content to cache you should consider the following questions.

- How often is the content requested?
- How often does the content change?
- How expensive is it to create or calculate the content with each request?

Content items that change infrequently, such as headers or footers on a portal page, are excellent candidates. Additionally, repetitive database queries that are returning data that changes infrequently also offer the opportunity for performance gains from caching.

Be careful not to go overboard with caching, however, as it consumes memory on the server and there is currently no mechanism to limit the size of the response cache unless you are using *keys*. The `key` parameter in the `wl:cache` tag makes it very easy to cache response data for different key values. Be sure to set the `size` attribute to control the size of the cache when the number of possible key values is large enough to create a very large cache of responses.

BEST PRACTICE Use dynamic content caching when content is frequently displayed, is infrequently changed, and represents a fair amount of work to create with each request. Limit the size of the cache to avoid competing for heap space with other components.

As an example of appropriate caching, our *bigrez.com* application uses the `wl:cache` tag to cache the offers displayed in the left gutter of every page for a particular set of search criteria. Recalling the three questions presented previously, the offers are displayed every page hit, the offers associated with specific search criteria are relatively static, and the algorithm used to choose and prioritize offers based on the criteria is expensive. The offers display is therefore a perfect candidate for caching.

Servlets

Avoid using the `SingleThreadModel` for servlets. As discussed in Chapter 1, WebLogic Server creates a pool of servlet instances for each servlet that implements the `SingleThreadModel` interface. Its handling of the instance pool is efficient, but the pool does create some overhead for the container and should be avoided to achieve greater performance. If you do need to use the `SingleThreadModel`, you should set the pool size large enough to avoid the on-the-fly creation and removal of additional servlet instances.

Use the servlet's `init()` method to perform expensive operations that need to take place only once. Because the Web container calls the `HttpServlet.init()` method right after loading the servlet, it is an excellent place to invoke heavyweight operations that you want to perform only once.

In many cases, it is possible to speed up the writing of the output stream by using a `ServletOutputStream` object instead of a `PrintWriter`. `PrintWriter` performs character-set conversion; therefore, you should use it only when your requirements demand it. For cases where your servlet returns only ASCII or binary data, use a `ServletOutputStream` to get better performance.

Understanding EJB Container Best Practices

High-volume J2EE applications often use Enterprise JavaBean (EJB) components to provide transaction, security, and object-life-cycle services for key business processes and objects. The performance of EJB components can have a dramatic effect on overall system performance because they tend to perform much more processing per request than a Web component. This section highlights a number of best practices for improving the performance of your EJB components in a WebLogic Server environment.

JNDI Lookup Strategies

J2EE applications use the Java Naming and Directory Interface (JNDI) to locate many different types of resources. Excessive calls to JNDI to look up EJB home interfaces, `DataSource` references, and JMS connection factories and destinations can reduce system performance significantly. To minimize the overhead of these lookup operations, you should cache and reuse the objects. Several techniques are available for caching these objects; we will discuss two of them.

For many simple Web applications, you can simply look up the objects in the servlet's `init()` method and cache them in instance variables in the servlet. As long as the objects themselves are thread-safe, using instance variables in this way is also thread-safe because your servlet probably uses these objects to create other objects. For example, you use an EJB home object to create or look up references to EJBs and a `DataSource` to get a database connection from the JDBC connection pool.

A more elegant and useful approach requires a helper or factory class that you can use throughout your application to locate and cache these types of objects. You can create a separate locator class for each type of object, or create one general-purpose locator capable of finding and caching all types of objects. Our *bigrez.com* application uses a general-purpose helper class, called `Locator`, to find and cache all EJB home interfaces. This class not only provides home interfaces using a simple interface, `getHome()`, but also employs reflection to locate and return EJB bean instances with a single invocation:

```
RateHomeLocal ratehome =
    (RateHomeLocal)Locator.getHome("RateHomeLocal"); // get a home

PropertyLocal property =
    (PropertyLocal)Locator.getBean("PropertyLocal", 57); // get a bean
```

By having your application locate all home interfaces and bean instances through this class, you can maintain and age a single consolidated cache of home interfaces. See the downloadable source code for `Locator.java` and `CacheMan.java` for more information.

BEST PRACTICE Use caching to reduce the number of JNDI lookup operations for EJB home interfaces, `DataSource` **objects, and JMS connection factories and destinations. Favoring a centralized locator class will help you consolidate lookup and caching operations in a single place and is better than using per-bean or per-servlet caching.**

One caveat on caching worth noting is that the use of JNDI lookup caching can result in the client having a stale reference if the server on which the object resides shuts down. This is typically an issue only if the client using the object and the object are in separate processes. For example, stand-alone clients can avoid the problem of EJB home interface caching by deploying the EJBs to a WebLogic Server cluster. In a WebLogic Server cluster, each server in the cluster has a copy of the home object and the reference bound into JNDI is cluster-aware; that is, it knows about all of the copies of the objects in all of the servers. Should one server fail, the client-side stub can route calls around the failed server to another server with an equivalent component.

Optimizing Entity Beans

As the J2EE platform continues to mature, many companies are beginning to use entity beans as a mechanism to represent business objects in their applications. Unfortunately, entity beans have a reputation for poor performance, a reputation based largely on results from poorly designed applications using either bean-managed persistence (BMP) or earlier versions of container-managed persistence (CMP). Can you create a high-performance system that includes a heavy dose of entity beans? We believe you can, provided you understand the life cycle of an entity bean and use the right features in WebLogic Server to optimize and tune your entity beans according to how your application uses them.

First, make sure you take advantage of reference caching whenever possible. If your bean needs to look up references from JNDI and you are not using a single, centralized cache, you should do these lookups in the `setEntityContext()` method. Avoid looking up references in other methods, such as `ejbLoad()` and `ejbStore()`, because these methods are called more frequently than `setEntityContext()`. We still recommend that you use a centralized cache rather than a per-bean cache.

Second, you should always try to use CMP whenever possible. CMP gives the container more control and more visibility into the bean's attributes, relationships, and state; this allows WebLogic Server to optimize the container's behavior in ways that it simply cannot do with BMP beans. Container-managed relationships (CMR) are yet another reason to use EJB 2.0 CMP entity beans. Chapter 6 highlighted many of the important WebLogic Server EJB features related to CMP entity beans, including caching capabilities, finder optimizations, and preloading or lazy loading of attributes and relationships to improve performance. Although a detailed discussion of all CMP entity-bean optimizations available in WebLogic Server is beyond the scope of this chapter, a number of best practices stand out from the rest:

- As discussed in Chapter 6, always set `finders-load-bean` to `true` to ensure that bean data is retrieved during finder methods, thereby avoiding the *n + 1 query problem*.
- Avoid using finder methods that can return very large sets of data. While `finders-load-bean` can return the results in a single query, returning very large numbers of objects can fill up the bean cache, forcing other, more frequently used beans out of the cache.
- Use optimistic concurrency and set `cache-between-transactions` to `true` to take advantage of the automatic, cluster-aware caching built in to WebLogic Server, a feature that can improve performance dramatically.
- When an application reads an entity bean's data much more often than it modifies it, consider using *read-only* entity beans as a form of cache. While read-only beans have been largely superceded by the `cache-between-transactions` approach, the ability to set automatic time-outs and invalidate cached data programmatically provides a unique benefit for read-only beans.

- When implementing relationships in CMP beans, make use of relationship caching to fetch related beans automatically in a single finder query where it makes sense. If your application tends always to traverse the relationship when interacting with a particular bean type, relationship caching will eliminate lazy fetching of the related beans, a subtle but insidious performance issue not unlike the $n + 1$ query problem. Be aware that WebLogic Server does SQL *joins* to pull all of the data into the container in a single query. If your entity beans have many relationships with one another, relationship caching can lead to extremely complex join queries that can kill the performance of your database. Use relationship caching where it improves the efficiency of the application.
- Use field groups on beans having many attributes when common access patterns require only a subset of the bean attributes. Finders used to display lists of summary bean data are also good candidates for field groups. You should realize that partial loading of data can lead to data inconsistency in your entity bean because each field group might be loaded by a separate transaction. Whether this is a problem really depends on your application semantics.
- Avoid exclusive locking unless absolutely required by system requirements. Exclusive locking imposes a large burden on the EJB container in terms of locking overhead and the opportunity for queuing and blocking during bean access. Also, you should realize that WebLogic Server currently supports exclusive locking only within a single-server instance. Any concurrent calls for the same bean instance in different servers in the cluster will effectively be using database concurrency.

BEST PRACTICE Optimize entity beans in your application by favoring CMP persistence and leveraging all of the server optimizations available. WebLogic Server's `cache-between-transactions` **and optimistic concurrency are very powerful features that you should consider for the most active entity beans in your system.**

Finally, regardless of the persistence mechanism you have chosen for your entity beans, it is important to tune the size and behavior of the bean cache to reduce passivation overhead. Recalling the discussion in Chapter 6, there are two basic types of entity-bean cache, a *per-bean cache* and a *combined cache*:

- A per-bean cache ensures that a fixed number of cache entries are available for that bean at all times. It can be difficult to set these per-bean cache sizes properly unless you have good metrics for required cache sizes. If you go this route, start with the default value of 1000 and examine the entity-bean monitoring display in the WebLogic Administration Console to identify beans that are exceeding that limit on a routine basis for a possible increase in their per-bean cache size.

- A combined cache sets aside a single large cache for use by all entity beans configured to use it. Multiple combined caches can be configured to host different sets of beans, and you can set the size of the combined cache outside the EJB descriptor, making it somewhat easier to manage and modify. The downside of this option is the lack of separation between beans in the cache. There is no guarantee that any given bean will have a certain number of entries in the cache at all times. When the cache fills up the server may begin passivating beans that would be better left in the cache.

Recognize that the use of `cache-between-transactions` and read-only entity beans also has a dramatic effect on the bean cache size required for best performance. Under normal circumstances, with database concurrency and no caching, the bean cache need be sized only to store the maximum number of concurrent bean instances likely in the system. For example, there might be 10,000 customers, but if only 100–200 of them are accessed at any given instant a bean cache of 500 would certainly be sufficient to avoid passivation. If the customer entity bean was set to cache using `cache-between-transactions`, each time a new customer is used in the application the bean instance for that customer will be cached for future use. It is possible that over time all 10,000 customers will be loaded by the container, and only a bean cache exceeding that level would avoid passivation.

BEST PRACTICE **Choosing the right type of bean cache and setting proper cache sizes is a complex, iterative process best done during load testing by monitoring bean cache usage and passivation. Optimal cache sizes are generally much larger when using entity bean caching features.**

Using Appropriate Isolation Levels

Isolation is one of the four key properties of transactions: *atomicity*, *consistency*, *isolation*, and *durability* (ACID). This means that even if there are concurrent transactions occurring, the database must execute the transactions as if they are occurring one at a time. Isolation levels refer to the degree to which multiple interleaved transactions are isolated from one another. Databases use various mechanisms that control the reading and writing of transactional data to achieve transaction isolation. There are four conceptual isolation levels available for EJB components; which ones are available to your application depends on your JDBC driver and the database management system. These levels are as follows:

- TRANSACTION_SERIALIZABLE is the highest isolation level offering the best protection, but it is also the slowest because all requests are executed serially. Using this isolation level will cause methods to obtain exclusive write locks on data. This prevents other transactions from reading, updating, or inserting data until the transaction is complete.
- TRANSACTION_REPEATABLE_READ prevents transactions from changing data that is currently being read by another transaction.

- TRANSACTION_READ_COMMITTED prevents a write lock from being obtained on data that is currently being changed by another transaction, so reading uncommitted data is not possible.
- TRANSACTION_READ_UNCOMMITTED allows transactions to read uncommitted data and to be unaware when new records are added to a result set.

Higher isolation levels typically cause slower performance but provide higher degrees of safety with fewer potential data-inconsistency problems. Lower levels of isolation offer higher concurrency and better performance with a higher potential for data-inconsistency problems. Once isolation levels are understood they can be used to provide the proper level of concurrency for all deployed EJB components.

When choosing an isolation level, it is important to understand what levels your database management system supports and what the implications are for using them with your particular database. For example, Oracle uses the read committed isolation level internally. To support the serializable level, Oracle needs extra bookkeeping space and can throw errors when it is unable to serialize transactions. It is best to work with your DBA to choose an isolation level that is best for both your database and your application requirements.

BEST PRACTICE **Review isolation levels for deployed EJB components and reduce isolation levels where appropriate. Work with your DBA to choose the right isolation levels that work with your database.**

Taking Advantage of Pass-by-Reference

Enterprise JavaBeans are designed to provide *location transparency*: The caller may call the bean as if it coexists in the same JVM when it may actually be located on a completely different server. EJB components use Remote Method Invocation (RMI) to enable location transparency, but it comes with a cost. RMI uses serialization to pass method parameters and return values using a *pass-by-value* semantic—even if the caller and the bean are in the same JVM.

This marshalling and unmarshalling of data is expensive but necessary when the caller and EJB are in two different processes. It is also necessary if the caller and the EJB are in the same process but loaded using different classloaders. If both the caller and the EJB are in the same JVM and loaded with the same class-loader, it is possible to skip the marshalling and unmarshalling and pass the arguments and return values using *pass-by-reference* semantics. In many applications, the functional behavior of the application won't change by switching to pass-by-reference semantics; however, certain coding styles and practices can cause functional change. This is why the EJB specification requires the use of pass-by-value semantics for all EJB calls using the EJB's home and remote interface. EJB 2.0 adds support for local interfaces that support pass-by-reference semantics.

This pass-by-reference optimization is available only between components within an enterprise application. Separate applications running in the same JVM use separate class-loaders, so attempts to pass data by reference would invariably result in a

`ClassCastException`. WebLogic Server uses serialization in these cases. Don't forget that passing data by reference allows the called method to modify the contents of the passed object, in most cases, providing either a powerful feature or a debugging nightmare depending on how you use it.

BEST PRACTICE Deploy related components together in the same enterprise application to allow pass-by-reference semantics and maximize performance.

Historically, WebLogic Server has optimized calls made to EJB components within the same application by passing parameters and return values by *reference*, rather than by *value*, to improve performance. Because of J2EE licensing requirements imposed by Sun, WebLogic Server 8.1 changes the default behavior to always use pass-by-value semantics when using WebLogic Server 8.1 deployment descriptors. This change will likely cause WebLogic Server users a lot of pain and frustration. Therefore, we want to emphasize that in order to take advantage of this performance optimization, you now need to enable the optimization explicitly in the `weblogic-ejb-jar.xml` deployment descriptor for every EJB for which you want callers to be able to use pass-by-reference semantics with the EJB's remote interface. This example shows how to enable it:

```
<weblogic-enterprise-bean>
    <ejb-name>CustomerBean</ejb-name>
    <enable-call-by-reference>true</enable-call-by-reference>
</weblogic-enterprise-bean>
```

WARNING WebLogic Server 8.1 changes the default behavior for its `enable-call-by-reference` **optimization. If you are using WebLogic Server 8.1 deployment descriptors, the new default value is false, to make WebLogic Server J2EE compatible out of the box. This is new behavior and will cause the performance of existing applications to degrade when using WebLogic Server 8.1 unless you explicitly enable the optimization in your EJB deployment descriptors.**

Applying Database Access Best Practices

Efficient database access is critical to achieving high throughput and good scalability for your system. All of the other tuning and optimizations you perform, whether in the JVM, Web Container, EJB Container, or elsewhere, will be for naught if the database access in the application is slow. Worse yet, the techniques available for increasing database processing capability through hardware upgrades are generally more expensive than the simple clustering techniques available for increasing the processors available for the Web or EJB tiers of the application. You simply must start with efficient database access to achieve good overall performance.

This section will provide a number of best practices related to database access from within J2EE applications. This section is not intended to provide a complete treatment of database design or performance tuning. For more information about database performance tuning for Oracle, we recommend *Oracle 9i High-Performance Tuning with STATPACK* by Donald K. Burleson (McGraw-Hill Osborne Media, 2002). There are numerous books on database design, such as the classic *An Introduction to Database Systems, 7th Edition* by C. J. Date (Addison-Wesley, 2000) and *Case*Method: Entity-Relationship Modelling* by Richard Barker (Addison-Wesley, 1990).

Basic Database Principles

First, you need an efficient logical database design. Database designers tend to favor highly normalized designs requiring multi-way joins to fetch a typical business object and related data. A design that looks good in the data-modeling tool may become a real bottleneck in production. If performance is a key criterion for your system, it is important to push back in this area and work with your database designer to flatten or denormalize some critical tables.

Next, the physical database design must reflect the performance requirements of your application. Your DBA should be employing all of the optimization features available in the chosen database technology to achieve the best possible performance. Make sure to provide your DBA with a complete list of the queries your application uses, including all columns appearing in the `WHERE` and `ORDER BY` clauses, so that he or she can create the proper indexes on each table.

After creating and tuning your database, you still need to use efficient database-access coding techniques to ensure a high-performance application. Some basic rules of thumb include these:

- Always perform table access using a good, selective index. Work with your database administrator to view statistics on your queries and correct any inefficient database access.
- Avoid joining multiple tables unless your application logic requires it. This often means creating multiple versions of a query, one that avoids a join and fetches only limited data for each matching object and one that joins with related tables and fetches a fully-populated object.
- Avoid using queries that return extremely large result sets. This becomes even more important when using an `ORDER BY` clause that does not use the same index that the query's `WHERE` clause uses. When this happens, the database must order the rows manually—a very time-consuming process.
- Cache data when the access pattern is mostly read and the hit frequency is high.

Retrieve Columns Explicitly

Use explicit column lists in queries rather than selecting all columns from a table using the `SELECT *` syntax. Explicitly retrieving only the needed columns avoids internal

JDBC operations and reduces the amount of data transferred back to the application, improving query performance. Of course, the other benefit is that your code doesn't break if the table is altered to add new columns.

Cache Prepared Statements

Use prepared statements for database access if your application executes the same SQL statement repeatedly. The first time you execute a prepared statement the database must spend extra time parsing and compiling the statement before it can be executed. Most relational databases will then cache the statement and match new statements against the cached ones to avoid this performance penalty. Keep in mind that in order for the database to reuse a cached statement, the new statement must match the old statement exactly in all aspects except the values of bind variables.

WebLogic Server supplements this database-level caching with its own JDBC `PreparedStatement` cache built into its connection pooling support. Whenever your application calls `prepareStatement()` for a new statement, WebLogic Server will cache the `PreparedStatement` object returned by the JDBC connection for use during subsequent `prepareStatement()` requests made using this same JDBC connection. Cached statements are specific to a particular connection because that is the model that JDBC imposes; therefore, frequently used queries will likely have a cached statement per connection. Reusing JDBC `PreparedStatement` objects eliminates the need for parsing statements in the database, which reduces CPU usage on the database machine, improving performance for the current statement and leaving CPU cycles for other tasks. You configure a connection pool's prepared statement cache using the WebLogic Console.

Like most tuning operations, determining the proper size of the prepared statement cache is an iterative process. In general, the more prepared statements your application employs, the larger the cache should be. For example, if the application has 20 SQL statements, setting the pool's prepared statement cache size to 20 will allow WebLogic Server to cache all of the prepared statements since each pool connection has its own cache. One empirical, iterative approach for sizing the cache involves monitoring the SQL parse operations per second occurring in the database during a realistic load test. Continue increasing the size of the prepared statement cache until the number of parse operations per second stops decreasing, representing a point of diminishing returns.

Transaction Model

WebLogic Server supports both the local and distributed JTA transactions. Distributed transactions are transactions that span either multiple database connections or multiple resources. Distributed transactions require additional logging and extra network I/O, making them many times slower than local transactions. Whenever possible, use local transactions involving a single `Connection` object for the best performance.

As we discussed in Chapter 11, there is a three-way relationship between transaction models, JDBC `DataSource` settings, and the underlying JDBC driver. In most circumstances, you want to use a JTA-aware `DataSource`. To create a JTA-aware `DataSource`, you just need to make sure that the `Honors Global Transactions` checkbox is checked when you create the `DataSource` using the WebLogic Console.

In previous releases of WebLogic Server, you had to create a `TxDataSource` in order for the `DataSource` to be JTA-aware.

It is very common to have multiple EJB components involved in the same unit of work. The only way to accomplish this without using an XA-compliant driver is to have all participants share the same database connection. WebLogic Server will automatically and transparently make sure that all operations use the same connection when your application is using a JTA-aware `DataSource` with a non-XA JDBC driver. You will need to use an XA-compliant JDBC driver if your applications use transactions that span multiple resources, such as a database and JMS or two databases. If a particular transaction involves only a single resource, WebLogic Server's JTA transaction manager will optimize the transaction to use a single-phase commit instead of the more expensive two-phase commit.

BEST PRACTICE Use a JTA-aware DataSource to ensure proper transaction coordination when using EJB components or involving multiple resources in a transaction. When doing distributed transactions, you will need to use an XA-compliant JDBC driver.

Commitment Control Level

JDBC connections use a commit control level of `TRANSACTION_NONE` with the `autoCommit` attribute set to `true` by default. These are the correct settings when an application does not need to use transactions, such as when an application invokes a stored procedure or trigger that does run under transaction commitment control. These are unusual circumstances, though; in most cases, you should set `autoCommit` to `false` to increase performance by reducing the number of commit operations. When using non-JTA-aware `DataSource` objects, you should explicitly call `Connection.setAutoCommit(false)` before executing your queries and then call `Connection.commit()` at the end of the transaction, as shown here.

```
DataSource ds = (DataSource)ctx.lookup("java:comp/env/jdbc/TestDB");
conn = ds.getConnection();
conn.setAutoCommit(false);
...
conn.commit();
```

If you are using a JTA-aware `DataSource`, all connections will already have `autoCommit` set to `false`. Any attempt to invoke `setAutoCommit(true)` on the connection will throw a `SQLException`.

BEST PRACTICE Configure commit control properly on JDBC connections obtained from a non-JTA-aware `DataSource` by calling `setAutoCommit(false)` before executing any queries and `commit()` at the end of each transaction to improve performance and avoid committing after every statement.

Batch Updates

A *batch update* refers to a set of SQL statements submitted as a unit for processing. Sending multiple statements together can be much more efficient than sending each update separately. Always set `autoCommit` to `false` or obtain the connection from a JTA-aware `DataSource` when doing batch updates to avoid committing automatically when calling `executeBatch()`. The database will execute the SQL statements in the order they were added to the batch. The following code block illustrates this technique.

```
DataSource ds = (DataSource)ctx.lookup("java:comp/env/jdbc/TestDB");
Connection conn = ds.getConnection();
Statement stmt = conn.createStatement();
stmt.addBatch("INSERT INTO EMPLOYEE " +
              "VALUES (500, 'Jeff', 'Architect', 'Smith', 250000)");
stmt.addBatch("INSERT INTO EMPLOYEE " +
              "VALUES (501, 'John', 'Controller', 'Park', 300000)");
int[] updateNum = stmt.executeBatch();
```

Connection Pools

Establishing a JDBC connection with a database can be very slow and resource-intensive. If your application requires database connections that are repeatedly opened and closed, this can become a significant performance issue. WebLogic Server provides a connection pooling mechanism that allows users to access and share persistent database connections to avoid the overhead of constantly opening and closing new connections. When WebLogic Server starts, it creates each connection pool with an initial number of connections. These connections will be available to any application that uses a configured `DataSource` object associated with the connection pool. When an application closes the connection it got from the `DataSource`, the connection will return to the pool and be available for the next time the application needs a connection. Since the call to `DataSource.getConnection()` only checks a connection out from the pool and its call to `Connection.close()` does not actually close the connection, using the database connection pool adds very little overhead to the application.

You define and configure connection pools and DataSource objects using the WebLogic Console, as described in Chapter 11. During performance tuning you are interested in two configuration parameters in particular: `Initial Capacity` and `Maximum Capacity`. `Initial Capacity` specifies the initial number of physical database connections to create, as well as the minimum number the pool should try to maintain at all times. `Maximum Capacity` specifies the maximum number of physical database connections the pool is allowed to create.

In production systems, consider setting `Initial Capacity` equal to the `Maximum Capacity` so that you don't incur the hit for creating new connections on the fly when the server is busy. To ensure optimal performance, your connection pool should have enough connections to eliminate *waiters*. Waiters are nothing more than application threads that are forced to wait for a connection because all available connections are in use. By using the WebLogic Console to monitor the active JDBC connections during stress testing, you can properly size your connection pool to eliminate waiters.

BEST PRACTICE **Set** `Initial Capacity` **and** `Maximum Capacity` **to the same value in production systems to avoid creating new connections on-the-fly during load spikes. Find the proper size during stress testing by monitoring the pool for waiters.**

Release JDBC Resources

Always release JDBC resources when your application finishes using them. If the application does not release resources in a timely manner, application performance can degrade because other threads may need the resources but have to wait for them if all resources are currently held. JDBC `Connection`, `PreparedStatement`, `Statement`, and `ResultSet` objects should be explicitly closed when your application component finishes using them. Simply counting on the garbage collector to clean up after the objects is dangerous because there may be situations where these objects hold on to database resources outside the control of the JVM. WebLogic Server will try to clean up after sloppy application coding, but we advise you not to depend on this mechanism. We have seen numerous applications with memory leaks that turned out to be the result of not closing JDBC resources properly. The most common errors are not using a finally block to close them and not trying to close every resource in the finally block, even if you get an exception. Your JDBC code should always be structured similarly to that shown here.

```
Connection conn = null;
PreparedStatement ps = null;
ResultSet rs = null;
try {
... // Do JDBC work here
}
catch (SQLException sqle) {
... // Do error recovery here
}
finally {
    if (rs != null) {
        try { rs.close(); } catch (SQLException ignore) { }
    }
    if (ps != null) {
        try { ps.close(); } catch (SQLException ignore) { }
    }
    if (conn != null) {
        try { conn.close(); } catch (SQLException ignore) { }
    }
}
```

BEST PRACTICE **Always close JDBC resources as soon as you are done with them to reduce contention for connections and improve performance.**

Troubleshooting Performance Problems

Your application and environment are now tuned to perfection, users are happy, and the system is taking hundreds of hits per second without batting an eye, right? If not, then read on as we present a tried and true methodology for troubleshooting performance problems.

Successful troubleshooting requires a strong understanding of the system and its components, a good problem-resolution process, and knowledge of common performance problems and their solutions. Every system is different, and every performance problem is likely to be different, but there are a number of best practices worth outlining to help you through your own troubleshooting efforts.

Preparing for Troubleshooting

Troubleshooting performance problems can be a difficult and time-consuming process unless you prepare ahead of time. When the users are unhappy and the pressure is on, you must have the proper infrastructure, processes, and people in place to address the problem.

First, the application should have been thoroughly tested and profiled during performance testing. You need to know how the application performed in the test environment to know if the performance problem you are tackling is real or simply a normal slowdown under peak loads. Your test results also indicate the normal resource usage of the individual transaction under investigation for comparison with observed resource usage in production. Good testing is critical to efficient production troubleshooting.

Next, you must have all necessary performance monitoring mechanisms in place to provide information concerning system performance and activity. Recognize that many performance problems do not happen on demand, so you will need some form of logging to reconstruct system resource usage and activity during a period in question. Simple shell scripts that log selected output from system monitoring tools are often sufficient for this purpose.

Finally, you need a team and a process in place before the problem occurs. It is a good idea to form a multi-disciplinary *swat team* and make that team responsible for troubleshooting performance problems. Typically, we recommend using many of the same people who did the original performance testing because they already understand the behavior of the system under various loads. Create a well-documented process for responding to performance problems, including a database or other knowledge repository for storing information on previous incidents and remedies.

Once you've done everything you can to prepare for performance problems, all you can do is wait and see how the system performs. Should a problem arise, the team's first order of business is to identify the root cause of the performance problem, also known as the *bottleneck*.

Bottleneck Identification and Correction

A bottleneck is a resource within a system that limits overall throughput or adds substantially to response time. Finding and fixing bottlenecks in distributed systems can be very difficult and requires experienced multi-disciplinary teams. Bottlenecks can occur in the Web server, application code, application server, database, network, hardware, network devices, or operating system. Experience has shown that bottlenecks are more likely to occur in some areas than in others, the most common areas being these:

- Database connections and queries
- Application server code
- Application server and Web server hardware
- Network and TCP configuration

Remember that there is rarely a single bottleneck in a system. Fixing one bottleneck will improve performance but often highlights a different bottleneck. Bottlenecks should be identified one at a time, corrected, and the system tested again to ensure that another bottleneck does not appear before reaching the required performance levels.

In order to identify bottlenecks quickly and correctly you must understand your system. The team responsible for problem resolution must know all of the physical components of the system. For each physical component (server, network device, etc.), the team needs detailed knowledge of all the logical components (software) deployed there. Ideally, all of this information will be documented and available to the swat team members who are responsible for troubleshooting. The team can prepare for problems by identifying all the potential bottlenecks for each component and determining the proper way to monitor and troubleshoot these areas.

The following lists document some of the typical components and areas of concern related to each of them. The team must be aware of these potential bottlenecks and be prepared to monitor the related resource usage to identify the specific bottleneck responsible for a given performance problem quickly.

Common areas of concern for firewall devices include the following:

- Total connections.
- SSL connections—If you exceed more than 20 SSL handshakes per second per Web server you may need an SSL accelerator.
- CPU utilization—Make sure CPU utilization does not average above 80 percent.
- I/O—If the firewall is logging make sure it is not I/O bound.
- Throughput.

Common areas of concern for load balancers include these:

- Total connections.
- Connection balance.
- CPU utilization—Make sure average CPU utilization does not exceed 80 percent.
- Throughput.

Common areas of concern for Web servers include the following:

- CPU utilization—Make sure average CPU utilization does not exceed 80 percent.
- Memory—Make sure excessive paging is not taking place.
- Throughput—Monitor network throughput to make sure you do not have an overutilized network interface card.
- Connections—Make sure connections are balanced among the servers.
- SSL connections—Make sure that the number of SSL handshakes per second is not too much for the hardware and Web server software. Consider using SSL accelerators if it is too high.
- Disk I/O—Make sure the Web servers are not I/O bound, especially if they are serving a lot of static content.

Common areas of concern for application servers include the following:

- Memory—Make sure there is enough memory to prevent the JVM from paging.
- CPU—Make sure average CPU utilization does not exceed 80 percent.
- Database connection pools—Make sure application threads are not waiting for database connection excessively. Also, check to make sure the application is not leaking connections.
- Execute queue—Watch the queue depth to make sure it does not consistently exceed a predetermined depth.
- Execute queue wait—Make sure messages are not starved in the queue.

Common areas of concern for database servers include these:

- Memory—Make sure excessive paging and high I/O wait time are not occurring.
- CPU—Make sure average CPU utilization does not exceed 80 percent.
- Cache hit ratio—Make sure the cache is set high enough to prevent excessive disk I/O.
- Parse time—Make sure excessive parsing is not taking place.

For each area of concern, you may want to put system-monitoring tools in place that will take measurements of these variables and trigger an alert if they exceed normal levels. If system-monitoring tools are not available for a component, you will need to have scripts or other mechanisms in place that you can use to gather the required information.

BEST PRACTICE Identifying bottlenecks quickly in production systems requires a thorough knowledge of the hardware and software components of your system and the types of potential bottlenecks common in each of these areas. Ensure that system-monitoring tools capture appropriate information in all areas of concern to support troubleshooting efforts. Consider creating scripts or processes that monitor system resources and notify team members proactively if values exceed thresholds.

Problem Resolution

Troubleshooting performance problems should be accomplished using a documented, predefined problem resolution process similar to the high-level flowchart depicted in Figure 12.3. We will touch briefly on each step in the flow chart to give you a better feel for the process.

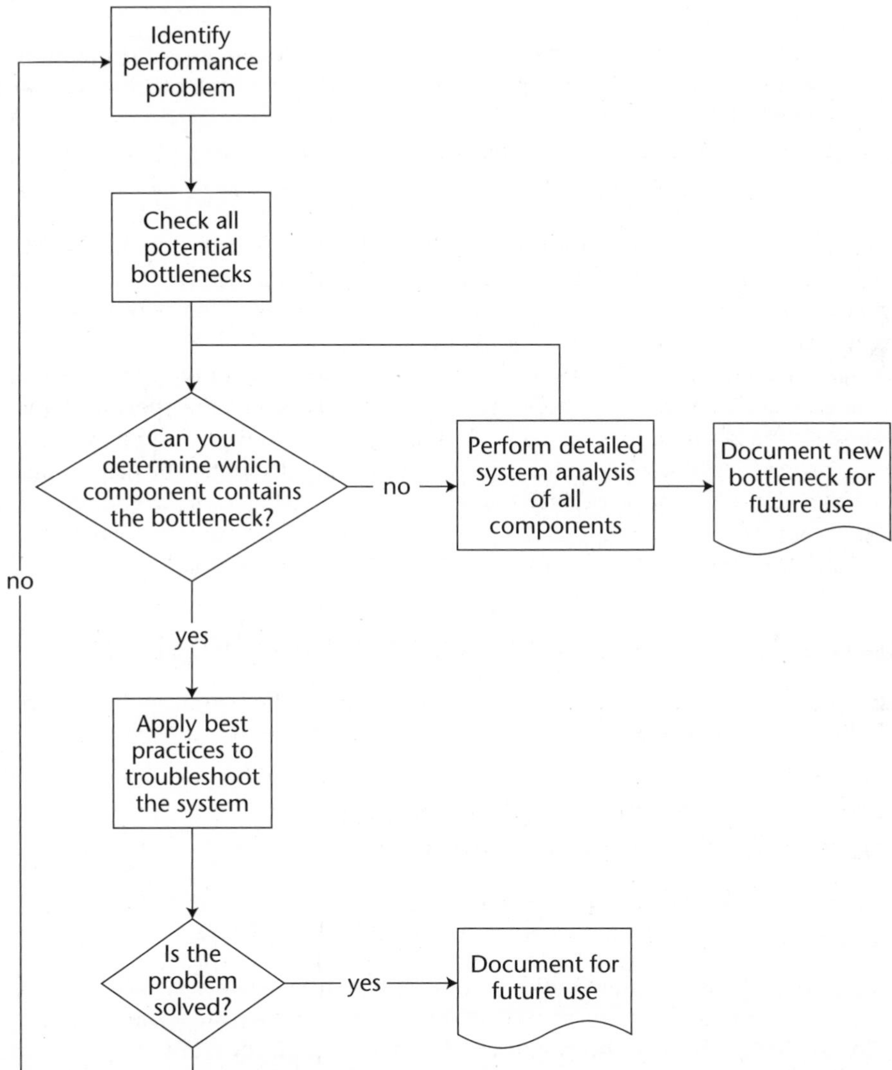

Figure 12.3 Problem resolution flow chart.

The first step in the process is to define the problem. There are two primary sources of problems requiring resolution: user reports and system-monitoring alerts. Translating information from these sources into a clear definition of the problem is not as easy as you might think. Reports such as "the system seemed slow yesterday" don't really help you define or isolate the problem. Provide users with a well-designed paper form or online application for reporting problems to ensure that all important information about the problem is captured while it is still fresh in their minds. Understanding how the user was interacting with the system may lead you directly to the root of the problem. If not, move on to the next step in the process.

The next step involves checking all potential bottlenecks, paying special attention to areas that have been problems in the past. Consult your system monitoring tools and logs to check for any suspicious resource usage or changes in normal processing levels.

If you are unable to identify the location of the bottleneck or root cause of the performance problem you will need to perform a more rigorous analysis of all components in the system, looking for more subtle evidence of the problem. Start by identifying the layer in the application most likely to be responsible for the problem and then drilling in to components in that layer looking for the culprit. If you discover a new bottleneck or area of concern, make sure to document the new bottleneck, adding it to the list of usual suspects for the next time.

Once you've identified the location of the bottleneck you can apply appropriate tuning options and best practices to solve the problem. Document the specific changes made to solve the problem for future use. If nothing seems to work, you may need to step back, revisit everything you've observed and concluded, and try the process again from the top. Consider the possibility that two or more bottlenecks are combining to cause the problem or that your analysis has led you to an incorrect conclusion about the location of the bottleneck. Persevere, and you will find it eventually.

Common Application Server Performance Problems

This section documents a variety of common problems and how you can identify and solve them in your environment.

Troubleshooting High CPU Utilization and Poor Application Server Throughput

The first step in resolving this problem is to identify the root cause of the high CPU utilization. Consider the following observations and recommendations:

- Most likely the problem will reside in the application itself, so a good starting point is to profile the application code to determine which areas of the application are using excessive processor resources. These heavyweight operations or subsystems are then optimized or removed to reduce CPU utilization.
- Profile the garbage collection activity of the application. This can be accomplished using application-profiling tools or starting your application with the `-verbose:gc` option set. If the application is spending more than 25 percent

of its time performing garbage collection, there may be an issue with the number of temporary objects that the application is creating. Reducing the number of temporary objects should reduce garbage collection and CPU utilization substantially.

- Refer to information in this chapter and other tuning resources available from BEA to make sure the application server is tuned properly.
- Add hardware to meet requirements.

Troubleshooting Low CPU Utilization and Poor Application Server Throughput

This problem can result from bottlenecks or inefficiencies upstream, downstream, or within the application server. Correct the problem by walking through a process similar to the following:

1. Verify that the application server itself is functioning normally using the `weblogic.Admin` command-line administration tool to request a `GETSTATE` and a series of `PING` operations. Chapter 11 walked through the use of this tool and the various command-line options and parameters available. Because the `GETSTATE` and `PING` operations flow through the normal execute queue in the application server, good response times are an indication that all is well within the server. Poor response times indicate potential problems requiring additional analysis.
2. If the `GETSTATE` operation reports a healthy state but the `PING` operations are slow, check to see if the execute queue is backed up by viewing the queue depth in the WebLogic Console.
3. A backed-up execute queue may indicate that the system is starved for execute threads. If all execute threads are active and CPU utilization is low, adding execute threads should improve throughput.
4. If the queue appears starved but adding execute threads does not improve performance, there may be resource contention. Because CPU utilization is low, the threads are probably spending much of their time waiting for some resource, quite often a database connection. Use the JDBC monitoring facilities in the console to check for high levels of waiters or long wait times. Adding connections to the JDBC connection pool may be all that is required to fix the problem.
5. If database connections are not the problem you should take periodic thread dumps of the JVM to determine if the threads are routinely waiting for a particular resource. Take a series of 4 thread dumps about 5 to 10 seconds apart, and compare them with one another to determine if individual threads are stuck or waiting on the same resource long enough to appear in multiple thread dumps. The problem threads may be waiting on a resource held by another thread or may be waiting to update the same table in the database. Once the resource contention is identified you can apply the proper remedies to fix the problem.

6. If the application server is not the bottleneck, the cause is most likely upstream of the server, perhaps in the network or Web server. Use the system monitoring tools you have in place to check all of the potential bottlenecks upstream of the application server and troubleshoot these components.

Troubleshooting Low Activity and CPU Utilization on All Physical Components with Slow Throughput

If CPU utilization stays low even when user load on the system is increasing, you should look at the following:

1. Is there any asynchronous messaging in the system? If the system employs asynchronous messaging, check the message queues to make sure they are not backing up. If the queues are backing up and there are no message-ordering requirements, try adding more dispatcher threads to increase throughput of the queue.
2. Check to see if the Web servers or application servers are thread starved. If they are, increase the number of server processes or server threads to increase parallelism.

Troubleshooting Slow Response Time from the Client and Low Database Usage

These symptoms are usually caused by a bottleneck upstream of the database, perhaps in the JDBC connection pooling. Monitor the active JDBC connections in the WebLogic Console and watch for excessive waiters and wait times; increase the pool size, if necessary. If the pool is not the problem, there must be some other resource used by the application that is introducing latency or causing threads to wait. Often, periodic thread dumps can reveal what the resource might be.

Troubleshooting Erratic Response Times and CPU Utilization on the Application Server

Throughput and CPU will always vary to some extent during normal operation, but large, visible swings indicate a problem. First look at the CPU utilization, and determine if there are any patterns in the CPU variations. Two patterns are common:

- CPU utilization peaks or patterns coincide with garbage collection. If your application is running on a multiple CPU machine with only one application server, you are most likely experiencing the effects of non-parallelized garbage collection in the application server. Depending on your JVM settings, garbage collection may be causing all other threads inside the JVM to block, preventing all other processing. In addition, many garbage collectors use a single thread to do their work so that all of the work is done by a single CPU, leaving the other processors idle until the collection is complete. Try using one of the parallel collectors or deploying multiple application servers on each machine to alleviate this problem and use server resources more efficiently. The threads in an application server not performing the garbage collection will be scheduled on processors left idle by the server performing collection, yielding a more constant throughput and more efficient CPU utilization. Also consider tuning the JVM options to optimize heap usage and improve garbage collection using techniques described earlier in this chapter.

- CPU peaks on one component coincide with valleys on an adjacent component. You should also observe a similar oscillating pattern in the application server throughput. This behavior results from a bottleneck that is either upstream or downstream from the application server. By analyzing the potential bottlenecks being monitored on the various upstream and downstream components you should be able to pinpoint the problem. Experience has shown that firewalls, database servers, and Web servers are most likely to cause this kind of oscillation in CPU and throughput. Also, make sure the file descriptor table is large enough on all Unix servers in the environment.

Troubleshooting Performance Degrading with High Disk I/O

If a high disk I/O rate is observed on the application server machine, the most likely culprit will be excessive logging. Make sure that WebLogic Server is set to the proper logging level, and check to see that the application is not making excessive `System.out.println()` or other logging method calls. `System.out.println()` statements make use of synchronized processing for the duration of the disk I/O and should not be used for logging purposes. Unexpected disk I/O on the server may also be a sign that your application is logging error messages. The application server logs should be viewed to determine if there is a problem with the application.

Java Stack Traces

This section discusses the reading and interpretation of Java stack traces in WebLogic Server. A *Java stack trace* displays a snapshot of the current state of all threads in a JVM (Java Virtual Machine) process. This trace represents a quick and precise way to determine bottlenecks, hung threads, and resource contention in your application.

Understanding Thread States

The snapshot produced by a Java stack trace will display threads in various states. Not all Java stack traces will use the same naming convention, but typically each thread will be in one of the following states: runnable, waiting on a condition variable, and waiting on a monitor lock.

Threads in the *runnable* state represent threads that are either currently running on a processor or are ready to run when a processor is available. At any given time, there can be only one thread actually executing on each processor in the machine; the rest of the runnable threads will be ready to run but waiting on a processor. You can identify threads in a runnable state by the `runnable` keyword in the stack trace, as shown here:

```
"ExecuteThread: '1' for queue: 'weblogic.socket.Muxer'" daemon prio=5
         tid=0x1068C2F0 nid=0xae runnable [10e8f000..10e8fd8c]
 at weblogic.socket.NTSocketMuxer.getIoCompletionResult(Native Method)
...
```

Threads waiting on a condition variable are sleeping, waiting to be notified by their manager that work is ready for processing. The stack trace indicates this with the `in Object.wait()` message:

```
"ExecuteThread: '4' for queue: 'weblogic.kernel.System'" daemon prio=5
         tid=0x007E3A00 nid=0x151 in Object.wait() [fb0f000..fb0fd8c]
 at java.lang.Object.wait(Native Method)
 - waiting on <0496C5C0> (a weblogic.kernel.ExecuteThread)
 at java.lang.Object.wait(Object.java:426)
 at weblogic.kernel.ExecuteThread.waitForRequest(ExecuteThread.java:149)
 - locked <0496C5C0> (a weblogic.kernel.ExecuteThread)
 at weblogic.kernel.ExecuteThread.run(ExecuteThread.java:175)
```

Applications use monitor locks, or *mutexes*, to synchronize access to critical sections of code that require single-threaded access. When you see a thread that has `waiting for monitor entry` in its stack trace, the thread is waiting to access synchronized code, such as the thread shown here:

```
"ExecuteThread: '24' for queue: 'weblogic.kernel.Default'" daemon
         prio=5 tid=0x1771A968 nid=0x76c waiting for monitor entry
                                                  [1896f000..1896fdc0]
 at mastering.weblogic.test.MutexServlet.doGet(MutexServlet.java:18)
 - waiting to lock <02C2E508> (a mastering.weblogic.test.MutexServlet)
 at javax.servlet.http.HttpServlet.service(HttpServlet.java:740)
 at javax.servlet.http.HttpServlet.service(HttpServlet.java:853)
...
```

Two different types of thread dumps can be produced in a typical environment: system-level process dumps, otherwise known as *core dumps*, and Java thread dumps.

Generating System-Level Process Dumps

System-level process dumps are generated by the JVM itself in response to a system error condition; typically, this happens because some native code is trying to access an illegal memory address. The content of this dump depends on whether the JVM can call the signal handler before the process itself core dumps. If the JVM can call the signal handler, then it will typically produce a text file in the current directory containing information about the process and the thread in which the low-level error occurred. If the JVM is unable to call the signal handler, a core dump file will be produced containing information about the JVM's native operating system process rather than the Java classes themselves. This type of dump is much less valuable and should be used only if no Java stack trace is available.

Generating Java Thread Dumps

Sending a special signal to the JVM generates a Java stack trace. On Unix platforms you send the `SIGQUIT` signal using the `kill` command. On most Unix platforms, the command `kill -QUIT <PID>`, where `<PID>` is the process identifier for the JVM process, will produce a Java thread dump that shows the call stack of every user-level thread in the JVM. On a Windows platform, you generate a thread dump by pressing the `Ctrl-Break` key sequence in the console window in which the Java program is executing. In addition, you can generate a stack trace either by invoking the static method `Thread.dumpStack()` or by invoking the `printStackTrace()` method on an instance of the `Throwable` class.

When analyzing or troubleshooting an application it is important to generate multiple thread dumps over a period of time to identify hung threads properly and better understand the application state. Start by generating 3 to 5 separate thread dumps approximately 15 to 30 seconds apart. If your servers communicate with each other using RMI it may be necessary to perform this operation on all servers in the cluster simultaneously to get a full picture. Depending on the number of servers in the cluster and the number of threads in the execute queue, this process may generate a large amount of output, but the output is invaluable in diagnosing thread-related problems. Later in this section we'll discuss how to read and interpret these thread dumps.

Reading Core Dumps

Sometimes it will be necessary to examine the core file to determine what has caused the JVM to core dump. When you are examining this core file, remember that Java itself uses a safe memory model and that any segmentation fault must have occurred in either the native code of the application or the native code of the JVM itself. On Unix systems a core file will be produced when a JVM fails. On Windows systems, a `drwtsn32.log` file will be produced when a segmentation fault occurs in a JVM.

There are several ways to examine these core files, usually through debuggers like gdb or dbx. On Solaris you can also use the `pstack` command, as shown here:

```
/usr/proc/bin/pstack ./core
```

When using dbx to examine the JVM core file, first move to the directory where the core file resides, then execute the `dbx` command with the binary executable as a parameter. Remember that the `java` command is usually a shell script and that you must specify the actual `java` binary in the command. Once you have started the debugger you can use the `dbx where` command to show the function call stack at the time of the failure, indicating the location of the segmentation fault:

```
dbx /usr/java/native/java ./core
(dbx) where
Segmentation fault in glink.JNU_ReleaseStringPlatformChars at 0xd074e66c
 0xd074e66c (JNU_ReleaseStringPlatformChars+0x5b564) 80830004
 lwz  r4,0x4(r3)
```

From this information you can often determine the location of the error and take the appropriate action. For example, if the segmentation fault is the result of a just-in-time (JIT) compiler problem and you are using the HotSpot compiler you can modify the behavior of the JIT to eliminate the problem. Create a file called `.hotspot_compiler` in the directory used to start the application, and indicate in this file the methods to exclude from JIT processing using entries similar to the following:

```
exclude java/lang/String indexOf
```

The specified methods will be excluded from the JIT compilation process, eliminating the core dump.

Reading Java Stack Traces

Java stack traces can be very useful during the problem-resolution process to identify the root cause for an application that seems to be hanging, deadlocked, frozen, extremely busy, or corrupting data. If your data is being corrupted, you are probably experiencing a race condition. Race conditions occur when more than one thread reads and writes to the same memory without proper synchronization. Race conditions are very hard to find by looking at stack traces because you will have to get your snapshot at the proper instant to see multiple threads accessing the same non-synchronized code.

Thread starvation or thread exhaustion can occur when threads are not making progress because they are waiting for an external resource that is either responding slowly or not at all. One particular case of this happens when WebLogic Server A makes an RMI call to WebLogic Server B and blocks waiting for a response. WebLogic Server B then calls via RMI back into WebLogic Server A before the original call returns from WebLogic Server B. If enough threads on both servers are awaiting responses from the other server, it is possible for all threads in both servers' execute queues to be exhausted. This exhaustion behavior will show itself initially as no idle threads available in the WebLogic Server execute queue when viewed in the administration console. You can confirm this problem by generating a stack trace and looking for threads blocked waiting for data in the `weblogic.rjvm.ResponseImpl.waitForData()` method. Look for entries like this:

```
"ExecuteThread: '2' for queue: 'weblogic.kernel.Default'" daemon prio=5
            tid=0x91e720 nid=0x26 in Object.wait() [d1e7e000..d1e7fc68]
 at java.lang.Object.wait(Native Method)
 - waiting on <06A9FBC0> (a weblogic.kernel.ExecuteThread)
 at java.lang.Object.wait(Object.java:426)
 at weblogic.rjvm.ResponseImpl.waitForData(ResponseImpl.java:76)
...
```

If a large number of threads are in this state you need to make appropriate design changes to eliminate RMI traffic between the servers or better throttle the number of threads allowed to call out and block in this way.

Deadlock occurs when individual threads are blocked waiting for the action of other threads. A *deadly embrace* deadlock occurs when one thread locks resource A and then tries to lock resource B, while a different thread locks resource B and then tries to lock resource A. This concept was discussed briefly in Chapter 6 in the context of exclusive locking for entity beans. Stack traces will show blocked threads within synchronized application code or within code that accesses objects using exclusive locking in one form or another. Remember that it is also possible for the application to be deadlocked across multiple JVMs with one server's threads in a deadly embrace with another server's threads.

A system that is inactive and has poor application performance may, in fact, be performing normally. The problem may instead be indicative of an upstream bottleneck, as described earlier in this chapter. A Java stack trace for a system in this state will display a high percentage of threads in the *default* or user-defined execute queue blocking until they receive some work, having a stack trace similar to the following one:

```
"ExecuteThread: '2' for queue: 'weblogic.kernel.Default'" daemon prio=5
           tid=0x00A8DB00 nid=0x28c in Object.wait()[d32f000..d32fdc0]
 at java.lang.Object.wait(Native Method)
 - waiting on <0392FBC0> (a weblogic.kernel.ExecuteThread)
 at java.lang.Object.wait(Object.java:426)
 at weblogic.kernel.ExecuteThread.waitForRequest
                                         (ExecuteThread.java:126)
 - locked <0392FBC0> (a weblogic.kernel.ExecuteThread)
 at weblogic.kernel.ExecuteThread.run(ExecuteThread.java:145)
```

The stack trace indicates that this thread is idle, or waiting for a request, rather than busy in application code or waiting on an external resource.

Understanding WebLogic Server Stack Traces

Stack traces of a WebLogic Server instance will also show a number of common elements based on the internal design of the WebLogic Server product. As you know from previous chapters, all client requests enter WebLogic Server through a special thread called the *listen thread*. There will usually be two listen threads visible in a stack trace, one for SSL and the other for nonsecure transport. Here is an example of the WebLogic Server listen thread waiting for a connection to arrive:

```
"ListenThread.Default" prio=5 tid=0x1068CEA0 nid=0xf5 runnable
                                        [1098f000..1098fd8c]
 at java.net.PlainSocketImpl.socketAccept(Native Method)
 at java.net.PlainSocketImpl.accept(PlainSocketImpl.java:353)
 - locked <05613F00> (a java.net.PlainSocketImpl)
 at java.net.ServerSocket.implAccept(ServerSocket.java:439)
 at java.net.ServerSocket.accept(ServerSocket.java:410)
...
```

Socket connections received by WebLogic Server are registered and maintained by the socket muxer. The socket muxer reads data from the socket and dispatches the request to the appropriate subsystem. Starting in WebLogic Server 8.1, the socket muxer has its own execute thread pool that it uses to read the requests off the socket by calling the `processSockets()` method, as shown here for the Windows version of the native socket muxer.

```
"ExecuteThread: '1' for queue: 'weblogic.socket.Muxer'" daemon prio=5
                 tid=0x0B3BADE0 nid=0xbd0 runnable [e19f000..e19fdc0]
 at weblogic.socket.NTSocketMuxer.getIoCompletionResult (Native Method)
 at weblogic.socket.NTSocketMuxer.processSockets (NTSocketMuxer.java:82)
 at weblogic.socket.SocketReaderRequest.execute
                                            (SocketReaderRequest.java:32)
 at weblogic.kernel.ExecuteThread.execute(ExecuteThread.java:178)
 at weblogic.kernel.ExecuteThread.run(ExecuteThread.java:151)
```

As you become more familiar with your application and better understand the internal implementation of WebLogic Server itself, your ability to interpret stack traces and troubleshoot problems will increase.

Chapter Review

This chapter covered many different areas related to WebLogic Server application performance, including basic principles and tuning options, design patterns and best practices, and specific performance best practices and troubleshooting tips. As you can tell from this wide-ranging discussion, there is a lot to know and consider when tuning or troubleshooting a complex J2EE system. Nothing beats experience when it comes to successful performance tuning, and experience is gained only by doing, so go do some performance tuning!

CHAPTER

13

Development Environment Best Practices

Congratulations! Your boss just gave you the go-ahead to build a new J2EE application using WebLogic Server. Months of meetings and proposals are behind you, and it's time to get started on the actual development. It's going to be a fairly large application, requiring a development team of 10 to 15 people. You have a reasonable budget for development hardware and software and the full confidence of management and the other team members. Now what?

It's not enough to know the technology inside and out. You must structure your development effort in a way that improves productivity and reduces the risk of failure. This chapter continues the discussion of development-related best practices with recommendations in the following key areas:

- Defining required development-environment hardware and software
- Installing WebLogic Server in the development environment
- Configuring the working directory structure
- Establishing a build process
- Choosing development tools
- Creating a unit-testing infrastructure

Obviously, there is a lot more to J2EE development than these six items. You need to choose a development methodology and team structure, create realistic plans with measurable deliverables, create useful design artifacts and specifications, and embrace all of the other development-phase best practices known in the industry. This book is not intended to cover best practices in these general areas, however. Good references for information on these topics include *Rapid Development: Taming Wild Software Schedules* by Steve McConnell (Microsoft Press, 1996) and the classic text, *Extreme Programming Explained: Embrace Change* by Kent Beck (Addison-Wesley, 1999).

Defining Required Hardware and Software

The specific hardware and software required for your development effort will depend on many details of your application and the chosen platform. The primary goals of the development environment are to do the following:

- Enable the isolated development, execution, unit testing, and debugging of the application on each developer's workstation
- Provide a centralized location for running, unit testing, and debugging a coordinated daily or weekly development build of the application
- Provide a centralized source-code management (SCM) repository and database for use by developers and the common build of the application
- Simulate the production hardware and software platform at a level sufficient to support development and debugging

Most J2EE applications will require at least two servers in the development environment to host the source-code management (SCM) server software, the development database, and the development build of the J2EE application. It is common to combine the SCM software and development build on the same server, yielding the following set of hardware and software requirements in the development environment:

- *Developer workstations* with WebLogic Server, development tools, database-client software, source-code management client, and build scripts and tools
- *Development server* with WebLogic Server, Web server software, database-client software, source-code management server and repository, and build scripts and tools
- *Database server* with RDBMS software and any required legacy-system integration software

Each server and workstation in this environment has a specific role in the development process.

Developers use the workstations to construct the individual components of the application and create local (workstation-based) builds for unit testing and debugging. In addition to all development tools and SCM client applications, the workstations also require a copy of WebLogic Server configured with the appropriate connection pools, JDBC `DataSource` resources, JMS destinations, and other supporting infrastructure required to run the application. Unless the development team is very small and can share a single development server for builds, you must provide local execution capability for developers on their own workstations.

BEST PRACTICE Provide local execution capability on developer workstations to avoid resource conflicts on the shared development server.

If it becomes impossible to provide local execution capability for some reason, you may be able to segregate the shared development server and provide an isolated environment to support each developer's execution and testing needs. The easiest way to segregate the server is to create separate domains for each developer with the servers defined in each domain configured to listen at a different port. The developers will still compete for server resources (CPU, memory) but will be able to run multiple copies of the application simultaneously. Again, this is not ideal. It is better to provide local execution capability on each workstation, if at all possible.

The development team uses the development server to host the shared source-code management (SCM) repository and as a central location for making and testing periodic builds of the application. We'll discuss the importance of periodic builds and regression testing in a later section. This server also provides an environment more similar to the production environment. A Web server is installed on the machine and is configured to proxy appropriate JSP and servlet requests back to WebLogic Server, for example, and the development server usually matches the vendor and operating system present in production. Often developer workstations are Windows-based machines while the development, test, and production servers are Unix-based systems.

BEST PRACTICE The development server should match the vendor and operating system of the test and production machines. Developer workstations may use a different platform, if desired.

The database server is used to host the common development database supporting both developer workstation builds and the central development build of the application. Gateway products and other legacy-system integration products also belong on this server, in our opinion. There is no strong reason to separate the database server and development server apart from the desire to mimic production as early in the process as possible. Production will undoubtedly include separate servers for the WebLogic Server cluster and the database, so it makes sense to provide this separation in development as well if the budget allows.

Sharing a common development database between multiple developers and the common development build sounds good on paper, but there is at least one significant problem with this simplistic approach that we need to solve: Changes to the database schema can break builds. For example, one developer may need to modify a database table to support the components he or she is changing and testing on his or her workstation. The database modification is very likely to break the build for all other developers and for the common development build, especially in a CMP entity bean application. Remember that the server checks the database schema for every bean during deployment, and nothing will deploy if there is a schema problem with any of the beans in the EJB archive!

The classic approach is to *serialize* the development process during database changes. Essentially, you make the database change, and the entire team waits for the developer to finish the changes, test them, and make the new versions of the components available in the current branch of the application. Everyone retrieves the new copy of the component from the SCM system and is able to build and run the application again. Although this approach might be appropriate for small teams or in some circumstances where it can be done very quickly, it simply becomes an untenable solution on a large project.

Fortunately, there is at least one reasonable solution that provides support for existing builds and for developers requiring database changes: create multiple copies of the development database on the development server, either as separate instances or separate schemas in a single instance. In its simplest form, this technique requires two complete copies of the database, called for our purposes DEVDB1 and DEVDB2. As shown in Figure 13.1, the common development build and the builds used by different developers connect to whichever copy of the database matches the components in that build.

In a two-database approach such as this, often a primary database is used for the periodic builds and an alternate database used for development of components requiring database changes. The database administrator usually toggles back and forth as each new set of changes is made, meaning that DEVDB1 is primary until the changes in DEVDB2 are made part of the common build, at which point DEVDB2 becomes primary and DEVDB1 is used for subsequent database changes. Clearly this technique can be extended to three or more databases, but two are usually sufficient.

You enable this database-switching behavior in the WebLogic Server application by creating multiple JDBC connection pools in the domains on the developer workstations and the development server. Ensure that all application components acquire database connections through a JDBC `DataSource` resource, then simply switch the connection pool associated with that `DataSource` as needed to reference the correct database.

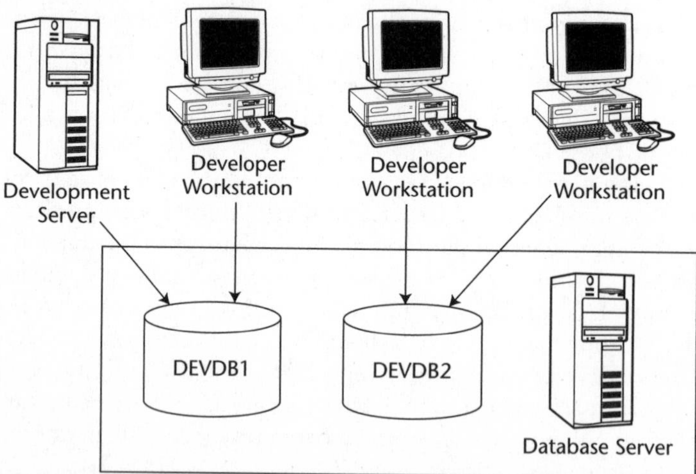

Figure 13.1 Multiple databases support different builds.

BEST PRACTICE Use multiple copies of the development database to support builds requiring different database definitions. Switch databases using domain configuration parameters.

You can refine this technique quite a bit if it makes sense in your environment. For example, tables that rarely change can be stored in only one database with synonyms or database links in the other database to provide visibility to the data from both versions. Developers might also have their own accounts in the database with synonyms to a shared set of all tables except the tables they need for development. Because these alternatives add complexity and represent additional work for the database administrator, it is usually best to keep things simple and have two completely separate databases with no synonyms or links between them.

Installing WebLogic Server Software

The installation program packaged with WebLogic Server provides a straightforward way to install WebLogic Server on all required machines in the development environment. Follow the instructions in the program, and choose the default parameters and a `Typical Installation` unless you have a strong reason to customize the process.

When the installation process is complete, each machine will have a copy of WebLogic Server, but it will not yet have an empty domain to use for your application. You must create a `Basic WebLogic Server Domain` on each machine in the development environment using the Domain Configuration Wizard program. This program is available from the Start menu in Windows or may be started using the `config` script in the `$WL_HOME/common/bin` directory. The wizard program allows you to set up an empty domain quickly, using the `Express Configuration` option, or to customize the created domain using the `Customized Configuration` option. See the online Domain Configuration Wizard documentation at http://edocs.bea.com/wls/docs81/adminguide/createdomain.html for detailed instructions.

NOTE The *bigrez.com* application uses an empty Basic WebLogic Server Domain called "bigrezdomain" located in the `/mastering/user_projects/` directory on each machine in the development environment. Server names, addresses, and ports use the default values, and the administrator username and password are `system` and `insecure`, respectively.

One final comment on hardware and software before we move on: Be sure to install WebLogic Server on the development servers in a manner consistent with your security and network rules. Never install WebLogic Server using the `root` account on a Unix machine, for example. Always create a `weblogic` or `bea` user account for this purpose and limit access to this account to certain developers or leads on the project. Create a `weblogic` group and make the `weblogic` user account a member of that group. Create additional developer accounts in the `weblogic` group and control their level of access to WebLogic Server files and directory structures using the standard permissions facilities of Unix.

BEST PRACTICE Install WebLogic Server using a `weblogic` user account, not `root`. Create separate developer accounts in the `weblogic` group to provide limited developer access to WebLogic services and files.

Configuring the Working Directory

Once you have hardware and software in place, it is time to configure the working directory used to organize application components. There is no single right way to organize application components in the working directory. The organization should reflect the specifics of the application, and it will often reflect the preferences of the development team. We'll simply present and explain the rationale behind a reasonable structure we recommend based on our experience building WebLogic Server applications.

Figure 13.2 presents a high-level picture of the recommended directory structure. Its major components include the following:

`/build`. A temporary directory structure containing compiled Java classes.

`/lib`. Directory containing third-party archive files used by application components.

`/src/java`. Root directory for Java source files.

`/src/web`. Root directory for Web application components.

`/src/scripts`. Directory containing SQL scripts and other scripts.

`/dd`. Directory containing deployment descriptors for the application.

With the exception of the temporary class files in the `build` directory, EJB archives, and any code-generated source and descriptor files, all components in this working directory structure should be controlled in the project source-code control system. The goal is to have every component and file required to build and deploy the application located in this work area to ensure proper control and promotion of the application during the development process.

Resist the temptation to place and edit Web application components directly in the `applications` area in the domain itself as a shortcut. Doing so complicates the source-code control process by involving directories not related by a common parent directory and makes the packaging and deployment process less self-contained. All creation and editing of components should occur in the working directory structure—the build and deployment process moves files to the proper location in the domain.

BEST PRACTICE Create and edit application components in the working directory structure. Don't edit Web application components or other files directly in the deployed application.

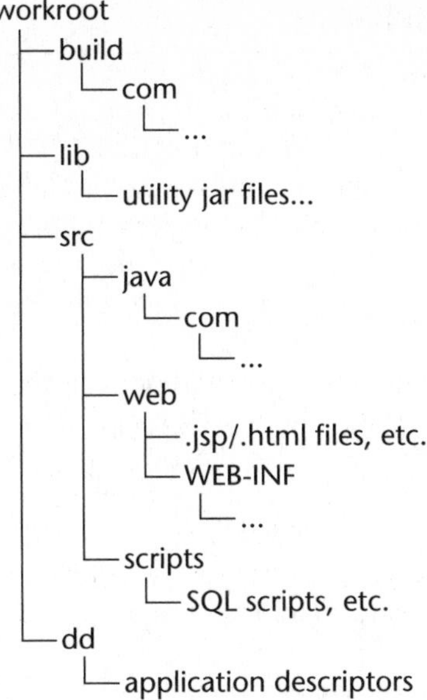

Figure 13.2 Recommended working directory structure.

The *bigrez.com* application includes two separate Web applications, as discussed in Chapters 4 and 5. The working directory structure for *bigrez.com* replaces the single `/src/web` directory in Figure 13.2 with separate `/src/web-user` and `/src/web-admin` directories, but it follows the recommended structure in all other ways.

You might wonder where EJB descriptor files such as `ejb-jar.xml` and the WebLogic Server-specific files `weblogic-ejb-jar.xml` and `weblogic-cmp-rdbms-jar.xml` are located in this directory structure. If these files are created and edited by hand, they should be placed in the `dd` directory. If the application requires multiple EJB archive files, and therefore requires multiple sets of descriptor files, consider using subdirectories under the `dd` directory for hand-created descriptor files. Obviously, these descriptors must be controlled in the source-code management system like any other source file in the system. If you are using a code-generation tool such as EJBGen, the EJB descriptor files can be recreated at any time using the bean input files and should not be placed in source-code control.

BEST PRACTICE **Avoid placing generated source files or descriptors in the source-code management system. When using EJBGen, only the bean source files are required to recreate all descriptors and interfaces, so only the bean files should be controlled and managed in the source-code management system.**

Managing Configuration Information

There is one problem with our goal to have everything required for the application located in the working directory structure: You cannot reliably control the JDBC, JMS, and other domain-level resources available to the application without manipulating the domain definition. WebLogic Server does provide some limited ability to configure JDBC resources in the application-level `weblogic-application.xml` descriptor file, a topic discussed in Chapter 8, but this technique does not currently simplify the problem enough to warrant its use.

You need a reliable way for developers to share configuration information to ensure that everyone has identical JDBC, JMS, security, and other resources configured on their machine. The classic approach in which a developer makes the configuration change on his or her machine and informs everyone else via email is not reliable or scalable. At least three mechanisms exist for sharing WebLogic Server configuration information among developers: controlling the `config.xml` file, script-based approaches, and new techniques for configuration template creation and replay.

Controlling the config.xml Configuration File

Recall that all services and resources configured in the domain are stored as XML information in the `config.xml` file, located in the domain's root directory, to make them available the next time the administration or stand-alone server starts. If, for example, some developer creates a new JMS destination through the administration console on his or her machine, that developer's version of the `config.xml` file will include elements not present in other developers' versions of the file. How does that developer propagate the new elements in `config.xml` to the other developers on the team?

The obvious solution is to place `config.xml` in source-code management, but there is a problem with this solution. WebLogic Server uses a hashing algorithm to encrypt passwords and other security information stored in the `config.xml` file, and the hashing algorithm depends on an encryption key that differs across domains. A `config.xml` file that works in one domain will fail in another domain because the other domain will not be able to decrypt the information. Because each developer has a separate domain, this clearly won't work.

We'd be unable to share the `config.xml` file through source-code management except for a little-known fact about the password attribute: You can hand-edit the value to be a clear-text version of the password, and the administration server will read it and encrypt it again using the proper key in your domain the first time it loads the file. Checking in the `config.xml` file with clear-text passwords allows the other members of the development team to check it out and reboot their servers to reflect your configuration changes.

Two security-related elements in the `config.xml` file also contain encrypted credential information and must be removed before checking in the file:

```
<EmbeddedLDAP
        Credential="{3DES}dU8ou74vb7..." Name="bigrezdomain"/>
...
```

```
<SecurityConfiguration
        Credential="{3DES}uPgUp1DsrQJ8URO..." Name="bigrezdomain"/>
```

Fortunately, these elements are not required for proper server operation in a simple development environment and may be deleted to create a clean, encryption-free version of `config.xml`. The next time the server is started these elements will be recreated automatically.

The primary advantage of this technique is its simplicity. It is easy for developers to update configurations; the work of creating a clear-text version of `config.xml` is performed once by the developer making the change, and no additional steps are required to make or import the changes to individual domains.

Disadvantages include the danger inherent in hand-editing the `config.xml` file and the fact that this technique provides no extension to the more-general problem of migrating configuration information between development, test, and production environments. We strongly recommend that you avoid using `config.xml` files to control and distribute configuration changes between developers.

BEST PRACTICE **Although it is possible to distribute and manage configuration information by placing the `config.xml` file in source-code control, this technique is not recommended.**

Using MBean and WLShell Scripts

All configuration information in WebLogic Server is accessible and configurable using MBeans. Scripts that access and manipulate these MBeans can therefore be used to control and distribute configuration information across the development team in much the same way a database-creation script is used to configure and manage a database schema.

weblogic.Admin Utility

The `weblogic.Admin` utility provides a command-line interface for issuing appropriate GET, SET, INVOKE, CREATE, and DELETE operations on MBeans in the WebLogic Server environment. MBeans are identified using either the `-mbean` parameter or a combination of `-type` and `-name` parameters:

```
-mbean domain:Name=xxx,Type=yyy,Server=zzz,parent=aaa
```

or:

```
-type yyy -name xxx
```

Commands can alter permanent configuration information by modifying the administration version of the MBean or modify current information on a particular server by manipulating the Configuration MBean associated with that running server.

See the online documentation for a detailed explanation of the different types of MBeans and their relationships. The important `weblogic.Admin` commands related to MBeans are the following:

CREATE. Create an Administration Mbean.

DELETE. Remove an MBean from the configuration.

GET. Retrieve property information from an Mbean.

INVOKE. Invoke a management method on an Mbean.

SET. Set a property value within an Mbean.

The syntax for these commands is shown here:

```
CREATE -name name -type mbean_type [-domain domain_name]
DELETE {-type mbean_type|-mbean mbean_name}
GET [-pretty] {-type mbean_type|-mbean mbean_name}
    [-property property1] [-property property2] ...
INVOKE {-type mbean_type|-mbean mbean_name}
    -method methodname [argument ...]
SET {-type mbean_type|-mbean mbean_name} -property property1
    property1_value [-property property2 property2_value] ...
```

WebLogic Server 8.1 also introduces a `BATCHUPDATE` command that executes a series of commands contained in a script. For example, the following command line invokes the `weblogic.Admin` utility and executes the commands contained in the `makepool.txt` file:

```
java weblogic.Admin -url http://localhost:7001
  -username system -password weblogic BATCHUPDATE -batchFile makepool.txt
```

The `makepool.txt` file contains the MBean commands required to create a JDBC connection pool, for example, and target it to a specific server in the domain, as shown here:

```
CREATE -name BigRezPool -type JDBCConnectionPool
SET -mbean mydomain:Name=BigRezPool,Type=JDBCConnectionPool
  -property DriverName oracle.jdbc.driver.OracleDriver
  -property URL jdbc:oracle:thin:@localhost:1521:DEV
  -property Properties "user=bigrez;protocol=thin"
  -property Password bigrezpw
  -property InitialCapacity 4
  -property MaxCapacity 10
INVOKE -mbean bigrezdomain:Name=BigRezPool,Type=JDBCConnectionPool
 -method addTarget bigrezdomain:Name=myserver,Type=Server
```

It is easy to see that a master script containing the appropriate MBean commands could be used to create and manage all JDBC, JMS, and security resources in the environment. This script would be easy to manage through the source-code management system and could become part of an update or build process on developer workstations. Separate master scripts might be maintained for test and production environments to provide an automated way to modify and promote configuration information in these environments.

Advantages of this simple `weblogic.Admin` scripting approach include the following:

- MBean scripts are easy to manipulate, edit, and share among developers.
- MBean commands can create and modify all configuration objects and services in a domain.
- Scripts are useful for promoting configuration information to test and production environments.

Disadvantages might include the complexity of the MBean naming syntax and the lack of conditional, looping, and branching logic in these simple scripts. These disadvantages are addressed by two alternate techniques that rely on the same underlying MBean infrastructure in WebLogic Server but provide a friendlier interface for accessing the MBeans.

wlconfig Ant Task

WebLogic Server 8.1 introduced a new Ant task, `wlconfig`, that provides a simplified technique for accessing and manipulating MBeans in the domain. The `wlconfig` task includes `get`, `set`, `create`, `delete`, and `query` functions and uses a simpler technique for naming and referencing MBeans in the domain. For example, creating the same JDBC connection pool using `wlconfig` requires the following elements in the Ant build file.

```
<wlconfig url="http://localhost:7001"
    username="system" password="weblogic">
  <query domain="bigrezdomain" type="Server"
      name="myserver" property="server.mbean"/>
  <create type="JDBCConnectionPool" name="BigRezPool">
    <set attribute="DriverName"
         value="oracle.jdbc.driver.OracleDriver"/>
    <set attribute="InitialCapacity" value="4"/>
    <set attribute="MaxCapacity" value="10"/>
    <set attribute="Properties" value="user=bigrez;protocol=thin"/>
    <set attribute="Password" value="bigrezpw"/>
    <set attribute="URL" value="jdbc:oracle:thin:@localhost:1521:DEV"/>
    <set attribute="Targets" value="${server.mbean}"/>
  </create>
  ...
</wlconfig>
```

Note that the `query` element defined a `server.mbean` property used later in a `set` element to target the connection pool to the desired server in the domain. Support for properties and the nesting of elements in other elements provide techniques for interrogating and traversing the hierarchy of MBeans in a build script.

Like `weblogic.Admin` scripts, `wlconfig` tasks placed in a master build file for the project represent a viable scripting technique for managing and sharing configuration information across developer workstations. Using the `wlconfig` task clearly provides better integration with build scripts in the development environment and represents an improvement over `weblogic.Admin` scripts in that role.

BEST PRACTICE **The `wlconfig` Ant task provides a powerful technique for scripting configuration information and integrating it in the overall development build process.**

Unfortunately, test and production environments are not typically managed using Ant so the `wlconfig` approach may not be suitable for migrating and promoting configuration information to those environments. Fortunately, there is one final scripting technique to discuss—a technique that appears to be both appropriate and powerful across all environments: the `WLShell` utility.

WLShell Utility

`WLShell` is a free shell interface for WebLogic Server written by Paco Gómez, an architect at BEA. It represents the hierarchy of MBeans in a domain as a directory structure and provides a Unix-like shell interface for traversing, listing, querying, and managing all MBeans in the hierarchy. For example, navigating to a JDBC connection pool and changing the maximum number of connections using `WLShell` requires the following commands:

```
wlsh> connect localhost:7001 system weblogic
wlsh> cd JDBCConnectionPool
wlsh> cd BigRezPool
wlsh> set MaxCapacity 20
```

MBeans can also be addressed directly using a syntax much like a fully qualified path to a file:

```
wlsh> set /JDBCConnectionPool/BigRezPool/MaxCapacity 20
```

Like the other scripting techniques, `WLShell` features the typical get, set, invoke, create, and delete commands for manipulating MBeans, but it provides many additional features as well. These features include the following:

- Powerful scripting language with loops, conditionals, variables, and many other features
- Shell environment featuring auto-completion and a command history
- Java explorer interface for viewing MBean hierarchy and contents
- Graphical monitoring tools to track any run-time MBean value or delta
- A config-to-script utility, `c2w`, capable of reading a `config.xml` file and creating the set of `WLShell` commands required to replicate the environment

As a simple example, the `WLShell` script required to create the `BigRezPool` JDBC resource looks like this:

```
connect localhost:7001 system weblogic
// create and target the pool
md /JDBCConnectionPool/BigRezPool
cd /JDBCConnectionPool/BigRezPool
set DriverName "oracle.jdbc.driver.OracleDriver"
set URL "jdbc:oracle:thin:@localhost:1521:DEV"
set Properties (java.util.Properties) "user=bigrez;protocol=thin"
set Password "bigrezpw"
set InitialCapacity 4
set MaxCapacity 10
invoke addTarget /Server/myserver
// save domain information to config.xml
invoke $savedom bigrezdomain
```

Space does not permit a detailed discussion of the many features of this tool. You are encouraged to download `WLShell` from its Web site, http://www.wlshell.com, and give it a try. While not a supported part of the WebLogic Platform as this time, it provides a much-needed command-line interface for administering WebLogic Server and appears to be a very solid application. `WLShell` works with WebLogic Server 6.1 and later.

Sharing and controlling configuration information would be straightforward using a master `WLShell` script for each environment. Like the previous alternatives, developers would modify the master script to reflect the changes made to their environment and then check in the modified script for use by the rest of the team.

One advantage of the full scripting language in `WLShell` is the ability to define resource-definition scripts with variables rather than hard-coded values and then combine these scripts with short scripts that define the parameters. In this way, it might be possible to share scripts between environments if the only differences involve configuration values, resource names, and other things that can be defined as variables. You could also write a script that interrogates the cluster for the names of all servers in the cluster and then loop through these names to perform some action on each server.

The bottom line is that `WLShell` scripts represent a very good technique for sharing and controlling configuration information in the development, test, and production environments. The tool itself is also very useful as a command-line management, administration, and monitoring utility.

BEST PRACTICE The `WLShell` utility provides a powerful Unix-like shell interface to WebLogic Server and a scripting language well suited for managing configuration information in development, test, and production environments.

Template Building/Replay Wizards

The three scripting techniques discussed in the previous section have one thing in common: They are all based on creating and managing resources by interacting with

MBeans in the domain. A new technique for managing domain and application configuration involves using the WebLogic Configuration Wizard that comes with WebLogic Server 8.1. The wizard allows you to create a new domain using templates, essentially "replaying" a prebuilt template to creating the new domain. This wizard also allows you to merge templates that contain application-specific configuration information into an existing domain.

The new WebLogic Configuration Template Builder allows you to create new custom domain templates that define resources, applications, security information, startup and shutdown scripts, and other domain-level information. This tool allows you to create new, preconfigured domains for your application's environment and use the WebLogic Configuration Wizard to replay them. This replay capability provides an easy way to bootstrap new domains that already contain the configuration information needed by your application.

You can also use the WebLogic Configuration Template Builder to create application-specific templates that contain only application components and their related resource information. These application-specific templates, known as configuration extensions, can be used to apply a set of changes to existing domains. This allows you to migrate applications and related resources as a unit or, when combined with an existing domain template, to create a new custom domain template.

Because this capability is new to WebLogic Server 8.1 SP1, it is too early to determine just how effective this will be as a mechanism for either sharing configuration information across developers or migrating configuration data from development, through test, and on to production environments. Given the fact that this appears to be BEA's direction for addressing these issues, it should have some distinct advantages over scripting techniques.

- The Configuration Template Builder and Configuration Wizard are easy-to-use GUI applications providing a step-by-step process for creating and replaying templates. A silent replay mode is available from the command line to support the build and promotion process.
- This technique is likely to understand and support the different products in the WebLogic Platform, meaning that it should handle configuration templating and replay for products like WebLogic Portal and WebLogic Integration, as well as WebLogic Server domains.

Your best bet is to try out the new template creation and replay capabilities and see how they work in your environment. We will now return to the development process itself and discuss one of the key aspects in any development effort, the establishment of a flexible and reliable build process.

Establishing a Build Process

The working directory structure contains everything required to build, package, and deploy the application to the local machine. The build process for a project refers to the scripts and tools used to perform these and other development and deployment steps in support of the overall development process. We recommend the use of the Apache build utility, Ant, to script and perform the build process in your WebLogic Server projects. There is a wealth of information available on Ant, including books, white papers, example build scripts, and the Ant project home page at http://ant.apache.org. Consistent with the intermediate to advanced nature of this book, we assume you have a basic knowledge of Ant and will concentrate on best practices related to its use in WebLogic Server development.

You should organize your `build.xml` build script based on the major steps required to build, package, and deploy the application. These steps or tasks generally fall into five categories: compilation and related activities, creating EJB archives, deploying locally, creating official deployment packages for promotion to test or production, and miscellaneous tasks used during development.

In each category you are likely to have multiple Ant *targets*, or high-level tasks, that perform a series of steps. In the `build.xml` file for *bigrez.com*, for example, the main Ant targets correspond to the categories in the manner indicated in Figure 13.3. We discussed many of these targets in detail in Chapters 5 and 8. Later in this chapter we'll describe the unit-testing process and discuss the purpose of the `dist-test` target shown in Figure 13.3 as a miscellaneous task. Additional targets in `build.xml` perform the compilation, packaging, and deployment steps for the Web services described in Chapter 15. These targets are not depicted in Figure 13.3.

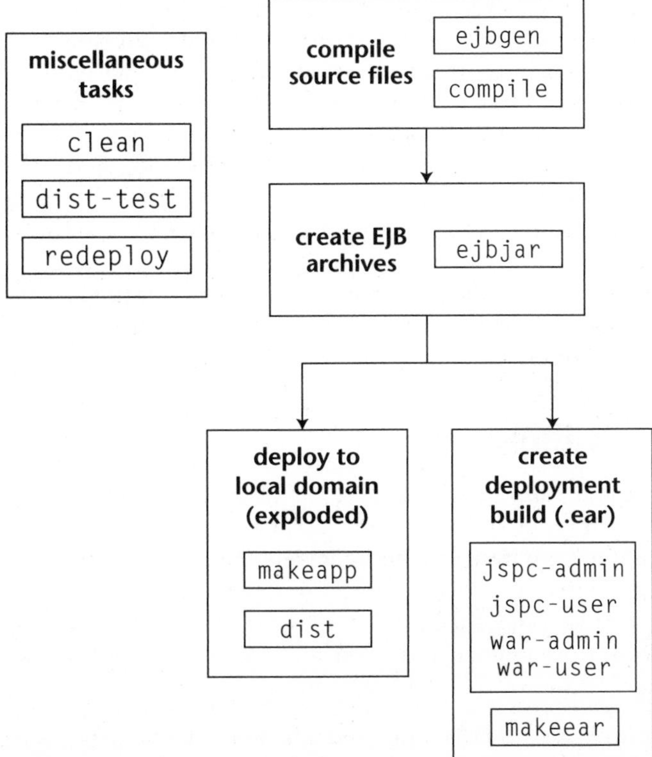

Figure 13.3 BigRez.com build targets.

There is no single correct way to name the targets in your build script. The Ant utility doesn't mandate a particular naming scheme, and you'll find many different configurations in the open-source development community. Pick a scheme that makes sense for your application. Be sure target names are an accurate reflection of the tasks performed by the target. Don't have the `compile` target move compiled class files to the exploded application in the domain, for example. That's the role of a `deploy` or `dist` task in most cases.

Many build files also include an `all` or `everything` target that explicitly invokes all of the targets in the build file in the correct order. If you link the main targets appropriately using `depends` attributes this should not be necessary.

BEST PRACTICE **Use the Apache Ant build utility to manage the build process for developer workstations and to create deployment archive files destined for test and production. Choose a consistent naming convention for your build targets, and keep each target focused on a single activity.**

Choosing Development Tools

At this point you have development hardware, software, WebLogic Server domains, a working directory structure, and a basic build process. Next comes the interesting and often difficult choice of development tool or integrated development environment (IDE) appropriate for your project. Let's face it: Every developer has his or her favorite tool, whether it's a full-blown IDE such as WebLogic Workshop or JBuilder, or a minimalist approach using emacs, TextPad, or some similar editor. There are pros and cons for each, and there is no right answer for all projects.

Rather than wading into the debate by advocating a particular choice, we'll identify and discuss some of the key features of these tools and IDEs and rate the relative importance of a particular feature in a WebLogic Server development effort. Use this discussion to decide which features are important to you, and then choose the development tool for your project accordingly.

Powerful Java-Aware Editing

The most important feature is the support for the core development process itself: Writing Java code one keystroke or mouse click at a time. Despite years of effort to create the perfect visual programming environment and alleviate the need for development at the source-code level, the reality is that programming is still based primarily on source files. The development tool must therefore provide a fast, efficient editing environment for the source-code components and other text files in the application. Typical requirements for a good editor include the following:

- Syntax highlighting for Java, XML, HTML, JSP, and any other languages present in your application
- Code completion, automatic indentation, and brace matching

- Javadoc creation and browsing
- Macros, keyboard shortcuts, class and code-block templates, and abbreviation support
- Code refactoring and usage searching

The environment should be fast and easy to use. The goal is to improve the productivity of the developers and the quality of their code. Make sure that the wealth of features present in the editor help the developers rather than slow them down. For example, nothing is more annoying to a fast typer than a slow code-completion feature than cannot be configured out of the way. The editor should allow features to be customized and configured by developers to accommodate the wide variance in skill and experience levels. Developers will spend 90 to 95 percent of their time writing and modifying code in the editor; make sure that time is spent as efficiently as possible.

BEST PRACTICE Ensure that the development tool's code editor meets the needs of the developers and provides a fast and efficient environment for source-code creation and editing.

GUI Interface and Environment

While not strictly a feature, the overall organization of the user interface and programming environment is perhaps the second most important aspect of a good IDE. When a developer begins using a new IDE he or she must rapidly learn the terminology, organization, and idiosyncrasies of the new environment. Good IDEs are picked up fast because they use standard terminology and organize activities in an intuitive way.

Many features and requirements fall into this category. Developers must be able to control the layout of the environment to make the best use of the limited screen real estate. They should be able to find the option or feature they want without hunting through dozens of menu options and dialogs. Wizards should provide real value and create useful code. Good cross-directory search-and-replace capabilities are a must, as are file-comparison and merging abilities.

Don't sacrifice the usability and quality of the overall environment to gain fancy features and capabilities, such as the advanced features discussed later in this chapter. It's not worth it. The developers need a well-organized, well-designed environment more than they need features like one-click application deployment or round-trip UML generation. Focus on the tasks performed tens or hundreds of times a day, and make sure the environment does them well. Don't sweat the tasks developers perform once or twice a day.

BEST PRACTICE Focus on the usability and quality of the overall development environment. Make sure that developers can learn the tool quickly and customize it to meet their needs. The wealth of features shouldn't get in the way of everyday work.

Integration with Source-Code Management System

One task performed many times each day is the interaction with the shared application components in the source-code management (SCM) system. Developers should be able to perform all of the standard SCM functions (check out, check in, add file, remove file, etc.) without leaving the IDE, preferably using keyboard shortcuts. Be sure that the IDE provides good integration to the SCM you've chosen for the project. Support for some SCM products is spotty.

Developers often need to compare and merge their local version of a source file with a version in the SCM system. Good IDE environments provide this level of integration.

Although it is possible to forgo integration with the SCM and use the tools and interfaces provided by the SCM product whenever these functions are required, this compromise will hurt developer productivity. Insist on good SCM integration in the IDE product.

BEST PRACTICE **Insist on good SCM integration in the IDE product. All commonly used features of the SCM system should be available without leaving the IDE, including file comparison and merging. Make sure the IDE works well with your chosen SCM product.**

Project and Build Processing Features

The final task you can be sure developers will perform many times each day is the execution of the build process. As recently as three or four years ago, the build process was usually performed by the IDE itself using scripts and configuration information placed in the *project* used by the IDE to organize the application components. Many IDEs still provide these IDE-specific build capabilities, but the industry has begun to standardize on using Ant for builds, and most IDE vendors now include support for Ant in their products.

Throughout this book we've advocated the use of Ant to create a cross-platform, generic build process that is not dependent on IDE build facilities. Choose an IDE that understands Ant `build.xml` files and can execute targets in build files using keyboard shortcuts or other simple operations in the environment. The output of the build process should be available in the environment, and the IDE should be able to parse the Ant output and automatically open the source file and locate the offending line of code corresponding to a compile error.

One final advantage of Ant is the ability to support multiple IDE products in the same development team. If IDE-specific features are used for building applications it may be difficult to keep all dependencies, steps, and outputs consistent across multiple IDE products. As long as every IDE integrates with Ant and uses the shared `build.xml` file, the build process will always be consistent.

BEST PRACTICE **Use Ant to implement the compile and build process for your application. Make sure the IDE has strong Ant integration, including the ability to edit and execute build targets and parse the Ant output to facilitate fixing compile errors.**

Debugging Features

The next feature present in most modern Java IDE products is an integrated debugger. Debuggers come in two flavors: *in-process* and *remote*. In-process debuggers allow developers to set breakpoints, watch variables, and step through application code running in the IDE. Assuming that your IDE supports the required JDK version, it is possible to run WebLogic Server inside the debugger and debug applications this way. Products like JBuilder SE that do not support remote debugging will support this type of server-side debugging.

Remote debuggers provide a mechanism to debug code running in a remote virtual machine. Remote debuggers allow developers to set breakpoints, watch variables, and step through application code running in a remote WebLogic Server instance. They can be very useful when an application problem is difficult to diagnose and an inspection of key variables during execution will shed light on the error. Products that support this type of remote debugging have historically been much more expensive that ones that don't. A new set of lower-priced or free IDEs is emerging that support remote debugging; these include WebLogic Workshop, IntelliJ IDEA, and Eclipse.

While developers should know their code well, a good debugger can save you significant amounts of time over the old *print statement* style of debugging. If you are leaning toward an IDE as your development tool for J2EE projects, we recommend that you make sure that the debugger integrates well with your application server and understands J2EE applications.

BEST PRACTICE When making a development tool decision, debugging support should be a consideration. Even though we believe that most developers will know their code well enough to avoid using a debugger every day, having a good debugger integrated with the IDE can save significant amounts of time when the need for more complex debugging arises.

Remote debugging a WebLogic Server application is actually very simple with modern IDE products. Three steps are required:

1. Compile the Java components with debugging information included in the class file.
2. Start WebLogic Server with debug options set in the Java command line used to start the server instance.
3. Configure the IDE to connect to the WebLogic Server instance using remote debugging and attach to the running instance.

Compiling the Java Components

To compile Java components with debugging information included in the class file, use the `-g` option on the `javac` command line or modify the `compile` target in the `build.xml` file to include the `debug` attribute in the `javac` task.

```
<target name="compile">
  <mkdir dir="${build}"/>
  <javac classpathref="dev.classpath" destdir="${build}"
         srcdir="${srcjava}" debug="on">
    <include name="com/**/*.java"/>
  </javac>
</target>
```

If you need the `ejbc`-generated class files to include debug information as well, include the `-g` argument in the invocation of `weblogic.appc` (if using that technique) or in the `weblogic` element in the `ejbjar` optional Ant task, as shown here:

```
<target name="ejbjar" depends="compile">
  <ejbjar srcdir="${build}"
    ...
    <weblogic destdir="${basedir}" rebuild="false" args="-g"/>
    ...
  </ejbjar>
  ...
</target>
```

The new `wlappc` Ant task also provides a `debug` attribute used to include debug information in the generated classes. Don't forget to delete all existing class files and rerun the `compile` and `ejbjar` tasks to create new versions of the class files with debugging information before deploying the application to WebLogic Server.

Starting WebLogic Server in Debug Mode

Next, WebLogic Server must be started with the Java Platform Debugging Architecture (JPDA) remote-debugging capability enabled. This capability is defined by the Java platform itself and allows any JPDA-compliant debugger to debug any Java application running in this mode. More information on JPDA is available at http://java.sun.com/products/jpda/ if you are interested in the details.

Starting WebLogic Server in debug mode requires a change to the start script used to boot the server. Enable debugging by including a `-Xdebug` option, and specify the technique used to connect to the running application from the debugger using a `-Xrunjdwp:<...>` option. The current Java implementation supports socket-based communication on both Windows and Sun platforms and a faster shared-memory-based communication on Windows only.

To enable debugging using sockets, modify the `JAVA_OPTIONS` variable in `startWebLogic` to add the following options (all on one line):

```
set JAVA_OPTIONS=-Xdebug -Xrunjdwp:transport=dt_socket,server=y,
address=5000,suspend=n %JAVA_OPTIONS%
```

On Windows platforms use the faster shared-memory communication when the debugger and the running application are located on the same machine:

```
set JAVA_OPTIONS=-Xdebug -Xrunjdwp:transport=dt_shmem,server=y,
address=javadebug,suspend=n %JAVA_OPTIONS%
```

The WebLogic Server instance will boot up and wait for a debugger to connect to the running application at the port specified or via shared memory. You may notice an increase in server boot time when running in debug mode and a significant slowing of the application when a debugger is attached to the server instance.

BEST PRACTICE Use the shared-memory communication technique for remote debugging when the debugger and running application are located on the same machine.

Configuring Remote Debugging

Finally, configure your IDE to connect to the running application at this location through the IDE-specific configuration screens. The IntelliJ IDEA product, for example, provides the dialog shown in Figure 13.4 in which the communication type, port, and other debug features are chosen.

Note that you want to *Attach* to the running application rather than *Launch* the application in the IDE virtual-machine environment. Be sure your IDE is configured appropriately.

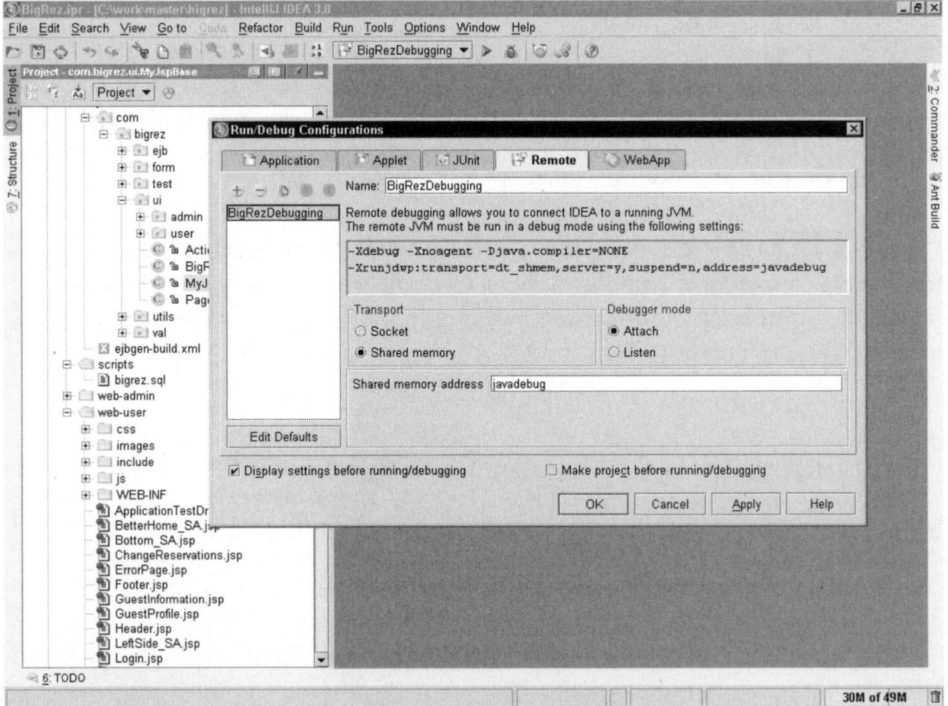

Figure 13.4 Configuring IntelliJ IDEA for remote debugging.

Now instruct the IDE to debug the application, and it will attach to the running server instance and be ready to go. You will be able to set breakpoints, step through code, and examine variables in the WebLogic Server instance. Use a separate browser window to access Web pages for debugging purposes or invoke appropriate unit tests that you may have created.

One problem to watch out for: If you set a breakpoint inside transactional code such as an EJB component or presentation-tier component with a user-defined transaction, the WebLogic Server transaction manager will time out the transaction after a fairly short period of time by default (30 seconds). You should increase the time-out value to at least 600 seconds to give yourself enough time to examine variables, step through EJB code, and perform other debugging tasks without having the operation time out and roll back.

BEST PRACTICE **Increase the Java Transaction API (JTA) time-out value in the domain to at least 600 seconds to provide enough time to step through transactional code and examine variables in the debugger without causing transaction time-outs.**

Setting breakpoints in JSP components can be problematic. We hope that you've chosen to use a model-view-controller architecture with servlets or Struts-based action classes encapsulating most presentation-tier business logic, so there should be little need to debug JSP pages. If you have this need, don't despair: Most IDEs deal with the problem of JSP-to-servlet conversion in one way or another and should provide you with a technique to set a breakpoint on a line in the JSP page and have the page stop at that point in the generated servlet.

In summary, remote debugging is fairly easy to configure and use with modern IDE products and will save you time when you need to debug your application. Our recommendation is to include the debugger in your overall development tool decision but realize that you probably won't use it every day, unlike some of the other features we have discussed so far.

BEST PRACTICE **You will need to provide at least some sort of remote debugging capability to your developers. Remember to emphasize well-written and well-instrumented code rather than simply allowing your developers to rely on debuggers to overcome bad code.**

Integration with Unit-Testing Packages

The eXtreme Programming (XP) movement has made *unit testing* a critical part of many development efforts, and it is helpful if the IDE supports the creation, management, and running of unit tests. Some IDEs have built-in test runners and include wizards for creating test cases, fixtures, and suites of tests. If unit testing is important in your development effort, examine the associated capabilities of your candidate IDE products.

Application-Server Deployment Features

Many IDE products boast of tight integration with application-server vendors and provide features in the IDE to package and deploy applications directly to a running server instance. We recommend that you avoid these features and rely on an Ant build script to perform all necessary packaging and deployment steps. Too many developers expect the IDE to do all of the work for them and lack the understanding and appreciation of the process that comes from building and deploying the applications manually.

Closely related to this feature is the EJB Wizard feature available in many IDE products. This feature typically provides a set of screens allowing the definition of EJB components, attributes, and configuration parameters. There is something to be said for a GUI-based technique for building EJB components when a developer is just starting out with EJB technology, but these wizards can become a crutch. One basic problem is that IDE products rarely keep pace with the new features in application servers, thereby limiting you to EJB capabilities available in the release supported by the wizard.

We advocated the use of EJBGen in Chapters 6 and 7 for the creation of EJB components and descriptor files, and we reiterate that recommendation here. The EJBGen utility combines many of the work-saving features of an EJB Wizard with the advantages of a file-based approach. It is also supported directly by BEA, ensuring that new WebLogic Server features are rapidly integrated into the code-generation process. We feel this approach is better than relying on wizards or other IDE-based techniques.

BEST PRACTICE Don't worry about application-server integration or EJB Wizards when selecting an IDE product. Application packaging and deployment are best accomplished through the Ant build scripts, and the EJBGen utility provides a better long-term solution for EJB creation than EJB Wizards.

Object Modeling Support

The fact that object-modeling support and related features has not been mentioned yet in this discussion should give you an idea where we feel these topics fall in the IDE-selection process: near the bottom. Good UML support and object-modeling features are important in the selection of a modeling tool, not the IDE, in our opinion.

Some IDE products include the ability to create application components from design models and reverse-engineer design models from application code. These features demo very well but have limited value in a realistic development effort. For example, in our experience the code-generation process works best for simple classes and interactions, but these simple components represent a very small part of the development effort on a typical J2EE project. And the reverse-engineering process acts more like an after-the-fact documentation tool than a true process enhancer. Design should come before construction! Don't fall into the *designed as implemented* trap by starting construction and allowing the design to fall out.

You may decide to build the entire development process around a fully integrated modeling and IDE product such as Borland Together or Rational XDE. We feel, however, that this decision should reflect your chosen development methodology and the importance you place on design artifacts rather than emphasizing developer productivity through the choice of IDE product. Developer productivity is our focus in this section, and that's why we feel UML support and related features are much less important than the topics covered earlier.

BEST PRACTICE Consider an integrated object-modeling and IDE product if your development methodology emphasizes design deliverables and reverse-engineering capabilities.

Web Services Support

A final consideration during IDE selection is the need for automatic generation of Web services for appropriate EJB components in your application. WebLogic Workshop provides a powerful environment for the creation of Web services, as do a number of newer IDE products. If your application requires Web services, this feature may be important in the IDE-selection process. Base your evaluation of its importance on your current project, upcoming projects, and your company's long-term direction. If Web services are not important in your near-term projects, we recommend placing less emphasis on this because the Web services support in the IDEs will likely have changed by the time you need these features.

With the selection and installation of a suitable IDE product, your development environment is complete. Be sure to document the configuration settings and installation specifics for everything in the environment to help the next person understand what you did and why. Conduct formal training sessions with new developers to explain the chosen directory structures and build process, and don't forget to allocate some time for training and ramp-up with the chosen IDE product.

Creating a Unit-Testing Infrastructure

Before discussing techniques for unit testing a J2EE application, we'll provide a brief review on unit testing. Unit testing is the process of testing an individual software component or program to identify, isolate, and remove software deficiencies as early as possible in the development process. The developer responsible for programming the component is also responsible for unit testing. This yields a *white box* approach to testing that leverages the developer's knowledge of the component's inner workings to create tests exercising all critical paths through the code. The primary goal of unit testing is to detect errors, not prove that the code is error-free.

Tests should be repeatable and self-contained to the extent possible. Although the developer creates and initially executes the unit tests as part of the component-development process, the same tests should be used as a form of regression testing whenever code changes may affect previously developed components.

The Importance of Unit Testing

The eXtreme Programming (XP) methodology advocates writing unit tests before writing the component itself as a means to clarify the expected behavior of the component and facilitate good design before coding begins. Although unit tests are valuable for XP and non-XP development efforts, by requiring unit tests before coding you are more likely to have complete unit tests at the end of the process. It is easy for developers to delay or eliminate the creation of unit tests when the schedule gets tight. Don't allow this to happen! Insist that unit tests be available and that the code successfully passes all unit tests before considering the work complete. The code review is a good time to review and sign off on these tests.

BEST PRACTICE Create unit tests for all business components in the system, and require all code to pass the tests before considering it complete. Use the code-review process to ensure compliance.

Why should you insist on a strong practice of unit testing in your development efforts? A few well-known advantages are these:

- Bugs found and fixed early in the development process are much cheaper, in terms of time and money, than bugs discovered later in system or user testing.
- A strong suite of unit tests makes design changes and other refactoring efforts less risky. You have the ability to regression-test everything affected by the change and ensure proper operation after a refactoring.
- Maintainability is improved because the unit tests provide future developers with solid definitions of expected behaviors and the ability to regression test the application after making changes.
- You'll sleep much better going into system and user-acceptance testing knowing that the candidate build has passed the entire suite of unit tests.

The problem isn't that developers and technical leads disagree with the *value* of unit testing—they just find it burdensome and time-consuming to write and organize the tests. In other words, the cost of writing a detailed unit test often seems to outweigh the apparent benefits. That's where a unit-testing framework comes in to play by reducing the tedious work of creating, managing, and running unit tests. With a good framework the value of unit testing will always outweigh the cost.

JUnit Testing Framework

The Java development community has rallied around the open-source JUnit testing framework as a solid foundation for unit testing Java applications. JUnit provides a number of important classes and facilities required for unit testing:

- The `junit.framework.TestCase` class provides support for pre-testing setup tasks, the unit tests themselves, asserting proper behaviors, and post-testing teardown tasks. All unit test cases are developed as subclasses of the `TestCase` class in JUnit.
- The `junit.framework.TestSuite` class represents a suite, or collection, of tests. A `TestSuite` may contain `TestCase` subclasses with unit tests, other `TestSuite` objects, or a combination of both. A typical hierarchical organization of `TestSuite` and `TestCase` objects is depicted in Figure 13.5.
- The `junit.swingui.TestRunner` utility provides a GUI-based environment for running and monitoring unit tests. A simple text-based approach is provided by the `junit.textui.TestRunner` class.

There are many additional framework components and extensions in JUnit, but this list represent the core classes and facilities used in the framework. Complete documentation and examples are available from the JUnit home page at http://www.junit.org.

Creating Tests for JUnit

JUnit is a powerful, flexible framework for unit testing, but it suffers from a number of weaknesses. The first is the tedious work required to create a `TestCase` subclass for each major component or subsystem in the application. Remember, the tests in the `TestCase` should test the component in a very thorough manner by invoking its methods with valid parameters, invalid parameters, and in any other way that exercises behaviors in the component. Creating a `TestCase` with this level of coverage may require many more tests than the number of methods in the tested component might imply.

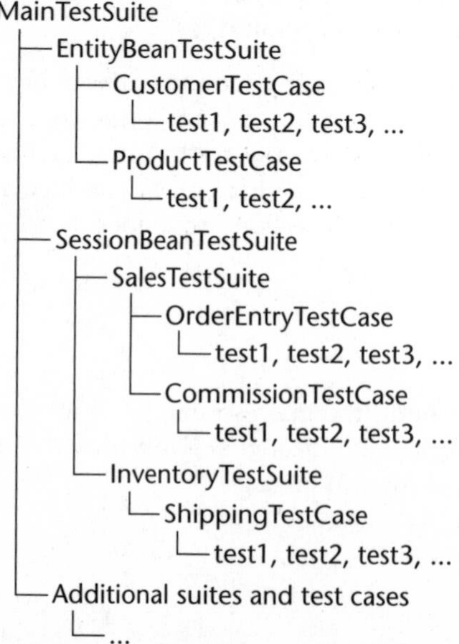

Figure 13.5 Typical hierarchy of JUnit TestSuites and TestCases.

The nature of good unit testing demands this type of complete, code-coverage testing of methods, parameters, and behaviors, and there is little that can be done to eliminate the work involved in writing these tests. Some IDE products provide a wizard or similar facility to create skeleton `TestCase` subclasses for a given Java component, but these simple skeletons would hardly be considered complete unit tests by our definition. The best approach in the absence of a perfect unit-test-creating tool is to mandate a certain level of test coverage, apply it consistently across the application components, and include the extra 15 to 20 percent effort required to create the tests in your development cost and time estimates. Don't cut corners and eliminate tests to meet the schedule.

BEST PRACTICE Mandate a consistent level of code coverage in your unit tests to maximize their value and bug-finding ability. Include realistic estimates of the required time and effort in your development estimates to avoid cutting corners to meet the schedule.

Using JUnit with J2EE Applications

The second weakness in the JUnit framework is the inability to test the full range of J2EE application components and architectures easily. J2EE is a distributed architecture, and JUnit is not. When a suite of tests is run in a JUnit `TestRunner` by a particular Java virtual machine, the tests must communicate with the tested components. The simplest form, direct invocation of component methods, is possible only when the tests and the tested components are collocated in the same Java virtual machine and loaded by the same classloader or by classloaders having a parent-child relationship, as in Figure 13.6.

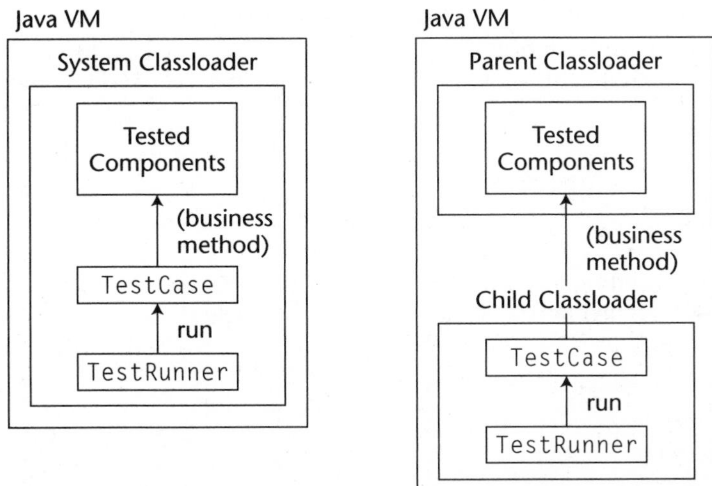

Figure 13.6 Direct invocation of tested components.

Once you introduce distributed components, such as EJBs, the test classes must communicate with the components through the standard local and remote interfaces like any other client. As shown in Figure 13.7, remote interfaces offer the ability to run the tests in a separate classloader from the tested components. The tests could be located in a separate Java virtual machine, as shown, or in the application server instance.

EJBs that have only local interfaces require that tests be located in the same classloader or a child classloader. In other words, if your EJB components rely on local interfaces, as most EJB 2.0 entity beans do, it will be impossible to test them without running the test cases *in* the application server. The tests must, in fact, be run in the enterprise application itself to have the proper visibility to EJB classes and supporting classes.

Our recommended solution is to deploy the `TestCase` and `TestSuite` classes to the application server as part of the overall enterprise application and run them from that location. The logical place is in one of the Web applications in the enterprise application. Classes in the Web application have full visibility to EJB components and all supporting value and helper classes, and they may invoke the EJB methods through local interfaces. This is exactly what we need to be able to write unit tests against the EJB components.

BEST PRACTICE Deploy unit tests to a Web application in the enterprise application. The tests will have full visibility to EJB and support classes in the application and may access EJB components using local interfaces.

Deploying and Executing JUnit Tests

Getting the test classes deployed in the Web application is actually very easy. Recall that Web applications automatically deploy any archive files found in their `WEB-INF/lib` directory. If you compile all of the `TestCase` and `TestSuite` classes and package them in a `.jar` file in this directory, they will be deployed the next time the Web application starts.

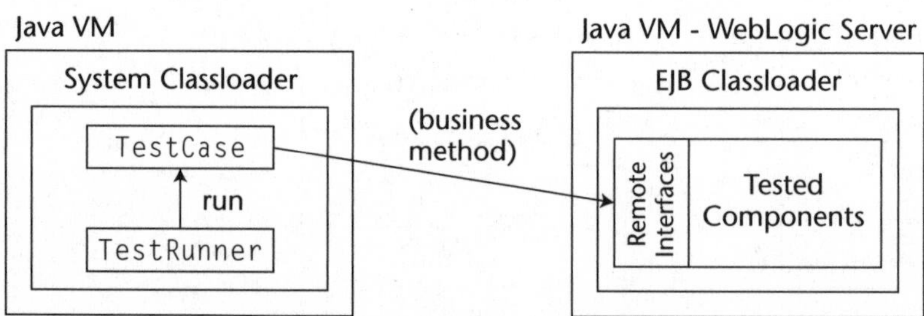

Figure 13.7 Invoking components using remote interfaces.

The *bigrez.com* build script includes a `dist-test` target that packages the unit tests and some administration-site support classes in a `junit-tests.jar` archive file and places the archive file in the `user` Web application in the exploded enterprise application:

```
<target name="dist-test" depends="compile">
  <!-- create jar file with all test and admin support classes -->
  <jar jarfile="${basedir}/junit-tests.jar">
    <fileset dir="${build}"
      includes="**/test/**/*.class, **/val/admin/*.class" />
  </jar>
  <!-- Copy testing jar file to user webapp WEB-INF/lib -->
  <property name="test.lib.dir" value="${webapp.user.dir}/WEB-INF/lib"/>
  <copy file="${basedir}/junit-tests.jar" todir="${test.lib.dir}" />
  <!-- Copy required support jars to webapp WEB-INF/lib -->
  <copy file="${basedir}/lib/junit.jar" todir="${test.lib.dir}" />
  <copy file="${basedir}/lib/httpunit.jar" todir="${test.lib.dir}" />
  <copy file="${basedir}/lib/Tidy.jar" todir="${test.lib.dir}" />
  <copy file="${basedir}/lib/js.jar" todir="${test.lib.dir}" />
</target>
```

Note that we've copied the main JUnit framework archive file (`junit.jar`) to the `WEB-INF/lib` directory, along with three archive files required for the HTTPUnit testing framework. We'll discuss the HTTPUnit framework later in this chapter. For now, simply recognize that placing the test cases and all required testing-framework archives in the `WEB-INF/lib` directory makes all of these classes available to the Web application after the next restart.

Executing the tests from within the Web application is straightforward; you simply run the tests from a presentation-tier component such as a JSP page or servlet. Although you cannot use the fancy GUI-based `junit.swing.TestRunner` to execute the tests in a Web application, the text-based version of `TestRunner` works fine when invoked from within a servlet or JSP page. Capturing and reporting the output requires a bit of code, but as Listing 13.1 shows, the JSP page that invokes the top-level `TestSuite` class for the *bigrez.com* application, `ApplicationTests`, is fairly simple.

BEST PRACTICE Run unit tests deployed in a Web application using a servlet or JSP page designed to capture the output of the text-based `TestRunner` **and present the results in the output page.**

```
<%@ page import="com.bigrez.test.ApplicationTests, junit.framework.*,
   junit.textui.*" %>

<HTML>
<HEAD><TITLE>Application Tests</TITLE></HEAD>
<BODY>
<H1>Test Results</H1>
```

Listing 13.1 RunApplicationTests.jsp executes JUnit tests. *(continued)*

```
<%
  ApplicationTests appTests = new ApplicationTests();
  OutputStream output = new ByteArrayOutputStream();
  TestRunner runner =
    new TestRunner(new ResultPrinter(new PrintStream(output)));
  runner.doRun(appTests.suite());
  out.println("<pre><font size=-1>"+output+"</font></pre>");
%>

</BODY>
</HTML>
```

Listing 13.1 *(continued)*

The output of this JSP is shown in Figure 13.8 for a series of successful tests. If a test fails the text version of `TestRunner` writes messages and exception traces to the `OutputStream` object that are then displayed on the page within the `<pre>...</pre>` tags.

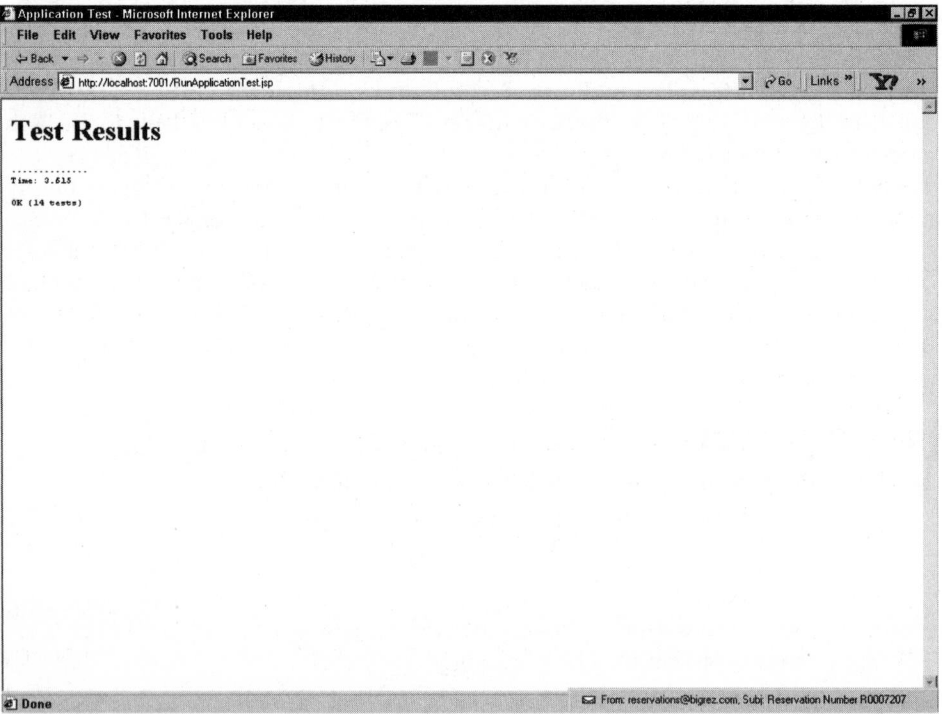

Figure 13.8 Successful run of bigrez.com application tests.

The simple `RunApplicationTests.jsp` page invokes the `doRun` method on the `TestRunner` and passes in the top-most suite in the testing hierarchy. Although this is useful as a starting point, what you really need is the ability to view all of the available `TestCase` and `TestSuite` classes in the archive and be able to invoke single tests or selected suites of tests according to your needs. We've got just the JSP for you—it's called `ApplicationTestDriver.jsp`. This page uses the recursive `suite()` methods defined in `TestSuite` classes to traverse and display the entire contents of the test hierarchy starting with the topmost class. As shown in Figure 13.9, the `ApplicationTestDriver.jsp` page displays the names of the classes as well as the individual `testXXX` methods in each `TestCase` class in the tree display.

Clicking on a test or suite name causes the page to refresh and runs the desired test or suite much like the simple `RunApplicationTests.jsp`. You can run the entire suite, one branch of the suite, or a single test case in one of the tests simply by clicking on the appropriate link in the tree display. The output of the desired test is captured and placed at the bottom of the page as before. The source code for `ApplicationTestDriver.jsp` is available in the downloadable examples.

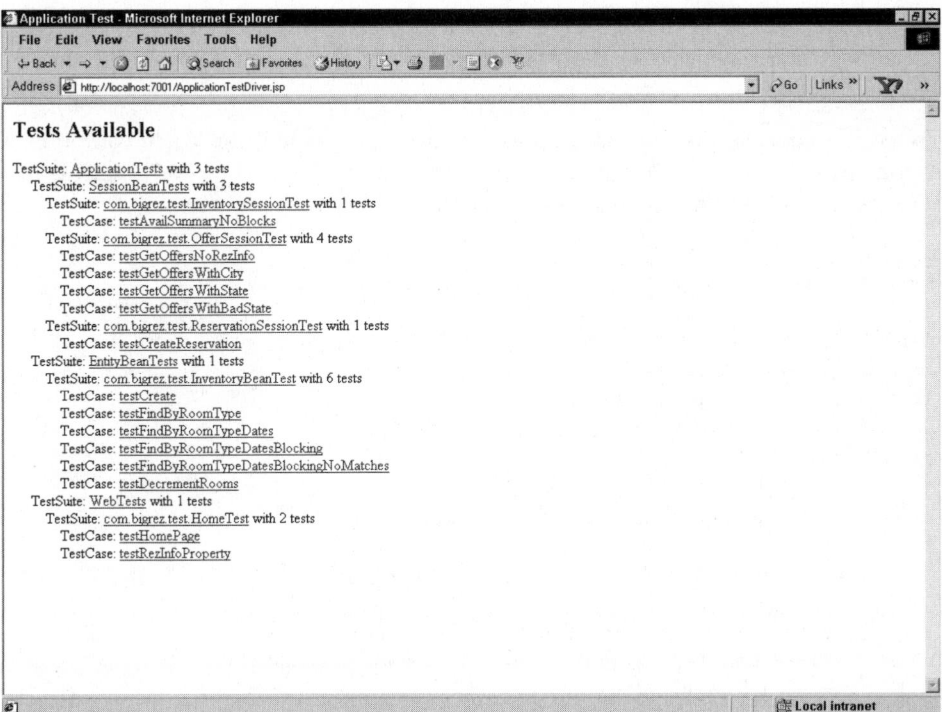

Figure 13.9 ApplicationTestDriver.jsp displays test hierarchy.

Organizing JUnit Tests

There are a variety of ways to organize the unit-testing classes for your application. One common scheme is a separate package structure in the working directory that mirrors the package structure of the tested components. If the tested component is located in `src/java/com/bigrez/util`, for example, the related `TestCase` subclass is located in the `src/`**`test`**`/com/bigrez/util` directory. The build script must be modified to compile the test classes to a separate build directory to keep them from being included in the deployment archives. This technique works, but we prefer a simpler technique: a separate `test` package in the same `src/java` file structure.

The *bigrez.com* application uses the special package `com.bigrez.test` for all unit tests and test suites. Placing the tests in a separate package from the tested components allows the build process to exclude the tests in the normal build, package, and deployment process. The *bigrez.com* tests are organized into three major sections:

- The *SessionBeanTests* suite contains tests associated with the stateless session beans in the application.
- The *EntityBeanTests* suite contains tests that exercise the CMP entity beans.
- The *WebTests* suite contains HTTPUnit tests used to test the behavior of JSP, servlet, and other presentation-tier components. HTTPUnit is covered in the next section.

In each major section, a `TestCase` subclass is created for each component (session bean, entity bean, and Web page) in the application. Listing 13.2 presents the `ReservationSessionTest` class as an example of a typical unit test.

```
package com.bigrez.test;

import com.bigrez.ejb.*;
import com.bigrez.utils.*;
import com.bigrez.val.user.*;
import junit.framework.*;
import java.util.*;

public class ReservationSessionTest extends TestCase
{
    private ReservationInfo createValidRezInfo()
    {
        ReservationInfo rezinfo = new ReservationInfo();
        rezinfo.setGuestProfileId(1); // known value
        rezinfo.setPropertyId(51); // known value
        rezinfo.setRoomTypeId(11); // known value
        Calendar today = Calendar.getInstance();
        Calendar tomorrow = Calendar.getInstance();
        tomorrow.add(Calendar.DAY_OF_MONTH,1);
        rezinfo.setArriveDate(today.getTime());
        rezinfo.setDepartDate(tomorrow.getTime());
```

Listing 13.2 ReservationSessionTest.java.

```
        rezinfo.setCardType("American Express");
        rezinfo.setCardNum("370000000000002");
        rezinfo.setCardExp("May 2005");
        ReservationRateInfo rateinfo =
            new ReservationRateInfo(today.getTime(),1,(float)99.0);
        ArrayList rezrates = new ArrayList();
        rezrates.add(rateinfo);
        rezinfo.setRezRates(rezrates);
        return rezinfo;
    }

    public void testCreateReservation()
    {
        ReservationLocal rez = null;
        try {
            ReservationInfo rezinfo = createValidRezInfo();
            ReservationSessionLocal bean = (ReservationSessionLocal)
              Locator.getSessionBean("ReservationSessionLocal");
            rez = bean.createReservation(rezinfo);
            assertTrue("Checking Property on rez = BigRez Inn",
              rez.getProperty().getDescription().equals("BigRez Inn"));
            assertTrue("Checking name on rez = Nyberg",
              rez.getGuestProfile().getLastName().equals("Nyberg"));
        }
        catch (Exception e) {
            fail(e.getMessage());
        }
    }

    public static Test suite()
    {
        TestSuite suite = new TestSuite(ReservationSessionTest.class);
        return suite;
    }
}
```

Listing 13.2 *(continued)*

We created only a handful of unit tests for *bigrez.com* to provide some examples. An application of its size would normally require at least 100 to 150 individual test methods to test all session beans and entity beans thoroughly. The Web components should also be unit tested during development. Techniques for performing this testing are the subject of the next section.

Testing Web Components with HTTPUnit

Before we discuss the HTTPUnit testing framework, we need to clarify the scope of this discussion. We're talking here about unit testing during the development process, not system or acceptance testing of the completed application. Many commercial and open-source tools are available for scripting and executing Web component tests once the site has stabilized and is ready for system testing. These tools tend to be complex and, in the case of commercial tools, expensive. You need a simple tool or framework to create basic Web component unit tests that can be used during development in the same way JUnit tests are used with business components.

One such framework is the open-source HTTPUnit framework written by Russell Gold. HTTPUnit allows you to write unit tests that execute Web pages in your application and then verify the response using a set of classes and facilities provided by the framework. The HTTPUnit framework simulates many browser behaviors including form submission, JavaScript, basic HTTP authentication, cookies, and automatic page redirection. Responses may be interrogated and tested for correctness as text, through an XML DOM, or with methods designed to find links, forms, and other elements on the page.

Listing 13.3 presents a very basic example demonstrating the use of HTTPUnit to test the home page in *bigrez.com*.

```
package com.bigrez.test;

import com.meterware.httpunit.*;
import java.io.IOException;
import java.net.MalformedURLException;
import org.xml.sax.*;
import org.w3c.dom.*;
import junit.framework.*;

public class HomeTest extends TestCase
{
    /** Test the content of the Home page */
    public void testHomePage() throws Exception
    {
        WebConversation conversation = new WebConversation();
        WebRequest request =
          new GetMethodWebRequest("http://localhost:7001/Home.page");
        WebResponse response = conversation.getResponse(request);
        String text = response.getText();
        assertTrue("Title present in response",
          contains(text,"<title>Welcome to BigRez.com!</title>"));
    }

    /** Test the behavior of the Property link on the Home page */
    public void testRezInfoProperty() throws Exception
    {
        WebConversation conversation = new WebConversation();
        WebRequest request =
          new GetMethodWebRequest("http://localhost:7001/Home.page");
        WebResponse response = conversation.getResponse(request);
```

Listing 13.3 HomeTest.java performs simple Web tests.

```
        WebLink propertyLink = response.getLinkWith("Choose Property");
        assertNotNull("Property link present", propertyLink);
        WebResponse response2 = propertyLink.click();
        String text = response2.getText();
        assertTrue("Form present in response",
            contains(text,"Please enter the state or city"));
    }

    public static Test suite()
    {
        return new TestSuite( HomeTest.class );
    }

    private boolean contains(String text, String want)
    {
        return (text.indexOf(want) != -1);
    }
}
```

Listing 13.3 *(continued)*

Note that the `HomeTest` class derives from the JUnit `TestCase` class, defines a `suite` method, and uses assertion methods just like a normal JUnit test class. It uses HTTPUnit classes such as `WebRequest`, `WebResponse`, and `WebLink` to invoke target pages and evaluate responses. See the HTTPUnit home page at http://www.httpunit.org for complete documentation and additional examples.

How useful is this type of testing in your overall development and unit-testing process? All unit testing is valuable, we believe, but the benefits must be weighed against the cost. In the case of standard unit tests, the benefits always outweigh the costs of creating and managing the test cases. The answer is not as clear with Web component unit tests. Writing HTTPUnit test classes and methods to test every link, form submission, and behavior in the Web site can be extremely tedious. Creating form data for submission requires a substantial number of method calls, and many pages respond properly only after many preliminary steps and pages required by the application. For example, the `ReservationThankYou` page in *bigrez.com* cannot be tested without walking through the entire reservation process.

We recommended that Web component unit testing be limited to a small number of tests, preferably one test for each page in the application. The resulting test suite can be used as a simple regression test when major changes are made to the application to ensure that all pages build properly (catching run-time JSP compile errors) and generate valid content. Testing critical navigation logic and presentation-tier functionality may also be worthwhile. Leave the complete testing of the Web site to the Quality Assurance team during system and user-acceptance testing.

BEST PRACTICE Create a limited number of HTTPUnit-based unit tests to verify the basic operation of Web components in the application. Use the resulting test suites for regression testing.

Chapter Review

This chapter presented a number of best practices to help you create and organize your development environment. The first section covered the necessary hardware and software in a typical development environment and discussed mechanisms for supporting multiple builds and databases in the same environment. Subsequent sections described the proper way to install WebLogic Server in the development environment, configure your working directory structure, establish an Ant-based build process, and choose the proper development tools for your project. The final section discussed unit-testing techniques and frameworks to help increase the quality and maintainability of your application code.

These recommendations should provide a strong starting point in the definition of your development environment and development process. Now all you have to do is build the system. Get to it!

CHAPTER

14

Production Environment Best Practices

In this chapter, we will discuss strategies and best practices for deploying WebLogic Server applications in a production environment. Our discussion will focus on three strategies:

Deployment. Determining the clustering approach, planning the production site configuration, and choosing the number and types of server machines.

Global traffic management. Utilizing local and global load balancers.

Production security. Securing your production environment and production WebLogic Server applications.

Designing, configuring, and running production systems represent complex topics, ones far too broad for us to cover in a single chapter. Unfortunately, it is difficult to refer you to other sources because there just aren't that many books written on the topic. Given the limited space available here, we have chosen these three areas of focus because these are the ones that customers frequently ask us about. We hope that this information proves useful to you in making these types of decisions.

Deployment Strategies

In Chapter 12, we discussed performance tuning and testing strategies. In this section, we will examine a number of deployment strategies you can use to meet your requirement for a secure, around-the-clock accessible, high-performance, reliable system in the presence of unpredictable usage and changing market conditions. We will focus primarily on two areas: selecting the number and size of machines for running the application server and designing your WebLogic Server clusters to meet your availability requirements.

When deploying highly available, high-performance systems, we recommend that you follow the guidelines shown here to allow your system to adapt to the ever-changing needs and complexities of enterprise computing:

- Choose solutions that are highly available and manageable.
- Choose systems that offer performance regardless of load and can scale to meet new requirements.
- Make sure that data is available and protected from corruption.
- Look at availability from the user's perspective. Understand that data is only one component of availability and all layers of your system must be available and resilient to failures. In most enterprise systems, achieving high availability will mandate providing redundancy at all layers of the system to avoid single points of failure.

By combining these guidelines with the system's business and technical requirements, you can deploy a system that meets your current and future requirements. In the sections that follow we will discuss best practices for selecting and designing a robust deployment environment using these guidelines. Before we jump into the strategies, let's think about how to evaluate the different strategies to come to some conclusion about what works best for your particular situation.

Evaluating Deployment Strategies

As with most architectural decisions, the selection of an appropriate production deployment environment involves trade-offs. Business and technical requirements must be understood in order to select the appropriate deployment environment. When trying to determine the appropriate deployment strategy, we recommend the following steps:

1. Map the business requirements into a technical architecture that allows the system to meet these requirements.
2. Using this technical architecture and the application's additional technical requirements, develop the criteria that your deployment architecture must meet.
3. Assemble a cross-functional team to explore the wide range of possible deployment architectures and narrow them down to a few that best meet the deployment architecture criteria.

4. Wherever possible, reuse existing deployment architectures, or pieces of them, to jump-start your selection criteria.
5. Use Proof of Concept evaluations to verify that the deployment architecture you've selected can meet the most difficult business and technical requirements.

First and foremost, the deployment architecture must meet the requirements of the business now and in the future. Once you understand the business requirements, you can map them to the technical architecture required to support the business. For example, you may have a business requirement to provide 99.5 percent availability where failing to live up to this will result in noncompliance of service-level agreements (SLAs) imposed on the system. This business requirement maps directly to a technical requirement for high availability that requires software, hardware, and network redundancy, as well as failover capabilities.

The application itself will have additional technical requirements defined by application user groups, operations, security, and any other group that interacts with or supports the system. By combining all of these requirements, you can develop criteria for the deployment architecture and apply weights to these criteria depending on the importance to your business. Common criteria include performance, manageability, scalability, flexibility, cost, security, administrative complexity, and maintenance. You can evaluate candidate deployment strategies developed in the next step against this weighted matrix of criteria to determine their appropriateness for your business and application.

Next, work with a group of interdisciplinary architects or technical personnel to select a few candidate deployment architectures that are likely to meet the business and technical requirements. Depending on the complexity of the requirements, scope of the deployment, and the group's experience with similar systems, you can evaluate each candidate either on paper or by doing a Proof of Concept (POC). One common practice is to select the best paper option and then use a POC to prove that the chosen architecture meets your requirements. It may sometimes be possible to combine this effort with preproduction functionality and performance testing of the application.

Your job is easier if an enterprise deployment environment is already in place and available for testing, requiring only a validation that the existing environment can meet the demands of the new system. Often this approach will not be appropriate because hardware, monitoring, and failover solutions are either not in place or have not yet been chosen. In this case, you should identify and develop an end-to-end slice (or portion) of the application that touches every layer of the system to use in testing the various candidate deployment architectures. This slice of the application should include the most challenging parts of the application and test the most challenging and/or strict operational requirements. You can then compare these results with the requirements selection matrix.

By performing POC tests and mapping the results against the requirements matrix, you can choose the best deployment architecture with a high level of certainty that it will meet all requirements. Unfortunately, it is not always possible to run your system in the *best* deployment environment. In many cases, you will have to make trade-offs. For example, you may have to deploy a more tightly coupled system than you would like in order to meet your users' performance requirements. Or you may not be able to use the best availability strategy due to cost considerations. These decisions and trade-offs are best made once you clearly understand the requirements of your business and you are able to differentiate these from other selection criteria.

BEST PRACTICE Evaluate deployment strategies by identifying and prioritizing business and technical requirements for the system, then mapping these requirements against candidate deployment strategies. Use Proof of Concept tests to validate new or unproven designs.

Now, let's look at a number of key strategies that you should consider when designing and selecting the best, or at least the *appropriate*, deployment architecture for your application.

Server Deployment Strategies

The first deployment strategies to consider are the size and type of server hardware to use in your environment, as well as the way to deploy your WebLogic Server applications on this hardware.

Determining the JVM to Processor Ratio

One of the most frequently asked questions is how many instances of WebLogic Server to run on a particular piece of hardware; the next is whether it is better to use a few larger SMP machines or more smaller machines. In an ideal world, applications would scale linearly as you add CPUs to the machine so that a single JVM would use all available CPUs and provide maximum performance. Unfortunately, in the real world, many factors can contribute to the nonlinear scalability of a Java application, including things such as I/O bottlenecks, garbage collection, cache-memory latency, and thread synchronization.

Garbage collection is of particular interest because it can have a dramatic effect on the application. Many older JVM implementations do not support parallel or concurrent garbage collection so the negative effect of garbage collection on performance grows considerably as we add CPUs on multiprocessor servers. For example, an application that spends 10 percent of its time performing single-threaded, stop-the-world garage collection will lose 75 percent of its throughput on a 32-processor machine, according to testing performed by Sun Microsystems (http://java.sun.com/docs/hotspot/gc/). Even on a smaller machine having only 5 CPUs this same application will lose approximately 20 percent of its throughput.

Most Java 2 SDK 1.4 JVMs have options to enable either parallel and/or concurrent garbage collection, though these are not typically the default settings. These can make significant improvements in the effects of garbage collection on JVM scalability across processors. Other factors, though, may still prevent you from achieving the level of scalability you need across a large number of processors.

Determining the ideal JVM-to-CPU ratio for a given application is an iterative process that is ideally done when stress testing the application for acceptance testing or capacity planning. On a multiprocessor machine, you should start by taking all CPUs offline except one and then tune the system until you achieve maximum throughput for that application on one CPU. This testing will provide the throughput information for one CPU to use as a baseline for determining linear scalability. From there, bring another CPU online and repeat the process. Continue this process until you cannot fully utilize the CPUs on the node or the linear scalability falls below an acceptable point. Remember, you will need to make sure that you have sufficient load to drive the number of CPUs available and that you watch for bottlenecks in other parts of the system. The goal is to determine the optimal number of CPUs for a single WebLogic Server instance. If you fail to achieve acceptable scalability during this testing, explore the possibility of running multiple instances of WebLogic Server on a machine.

Vertical Scaling

Scaling an application by simply adding more CPUs to a machine is often referred to as *vertical scaling*. Application server vendors have borrowed this term and have expanded it to include scaling an application by adding both processors and application server instances to a machine. A WebLogic Server instance consists of an application server running in its own Java Virtual Machine (JVM), so vertical scaling also implies multiple JVMs on the same machine. Vertical scaling can lead to better utilization of the server hardware and increased application throughput. You should balance this increase in utilization and throughput against the added configuration, maintenance, and monitoring overhead associated with running multiple server instances.

Running multiple instances of WebLogic Server on the same machine can also help minimize the effect of nonparallelized, stop-the-world garbage collection. Because multiple JVM instances will typically not all run garbage collection at exactly the same time, this means that you will almost always have at least one JVM available to schedule application-related work on other processors while another JVM does its stop-the-world garbage collection with a single thread. We recommend using the parallel and/or concurrent garbage collectors available with the new Sun HotSpot 1.4.1 and BEA JRockit JVMs.

BEST PRACTICE **Use parallel and/or generational garbage collectors to limit the scalability effect that garbage collection has on the application. Even then, you may want to explore the performance benefits of running multiple WebLogic Server instances on larger SMP machines. Before formalizing multiple instances per machine as your deployment strategy, make sure that you understand the effect this will have on configuration, maintenance, and monitoring so that you can make an informed decision.**

Horizontal Scaling

Scaling an application by simply adding more machines to your environment is often referred to as *Horizontal Scaling*. Typically, horizontal scaling is more specifically associated with the practice of employing multiple, relatively small server machines (generally four CPUs or fewer) in a production environment. In this scenario, each machine usually hosts a single instance of WebLogic Server and the application itself. Through the use of WebLogic Server clustering and/or external load balancers, this approach allows WebLogic Server-based applications to span several machines yet still present a single system view to the end users. You can use this strategy not only to increase scalability but also to improve the failover characteristics of your application. It also provides you with the flexibility of adding more machines on demand to handle increasing throughput requirements.

In many cases, you may want to combine horizontal and vertical scaling techniques to use multiple machines, each running multiple instances of WebLogic Server. This can make it easier to achieve both high CPU utilization and good failover and flexibility characteristics.

BEST PRACTICE Horizontal scaling gives you some failover and flexibility that you normally cannot get with only vertical scaling. Depending on your hardware, you might also want to consider combining the two techniques to increase CPU utilization. Whether this makes sense will depend on your hardware, application, and JVM.

Now, let's move on to look at single-site deployment strategies.

Single-Site Deployment Strategies

The next set of strategies relates to the deployment of scalable and highly available systems in a single site or data center. We will concentrate on clusters that reside in the application server layer of our system, but we will consider other layers where appropriate.

Two different scenarios will be discussed in the sections that follow. These scenarios reflect different sets of availability requirements:

- A simple WebLogic Cluster representing basic availability requirements
- A complex WebLogic Cluster representing more demanding availability requirements

Many other deployment strategies are possible, of course, each offering varying degrees of availability. It is important that you have a firm understanding of your requirements before choosing a strategy from among the many options available. You must also consider your cost structure and current enterprise standards.

For the purpose of this discussion we will make the following assumptions:

1. Local clusters are defined as a grouping of two or more servers residing in the same site or data center with WebLogic Server acting as the middleware.
2. Software, hardware, or a combination of software and hardware are utilized to achieve a high level of availability.
3. The minimum configuration involves at least two instances of WebLogic Server running in a cluster with each instance residing on a different server. This configuration allows protection against failure at the both the node level and the WebLogic Server instance level and is a good, basic configuration for discussing local clusters.

4. Load balancers are used to provide message distribution and failover of requests to the cluster of WebLogic Server instances. In all cases, you could configure Web servers as proxy servers to perform the same functionality.
5. Components resident in other layers of the system are redundant and provide high availability.
6. We will discuss only symmetric hardware configurations, which are also called *active-active* configurations. Asymmetric, or *active-passive*, configurations are also a viable solution. This type of deployment, though, is not typical at the application server level due to its higher cost caused by the use of passive servers.

Simple WebLogic Server Clusters

First, we will consider a Simple WebLogic Server cluster, which provides a basic level of high availability. Figure 14.1 shows a simple cluster that provides a simple, cost-effective, and highly available deployment architecture.

This type of configuration is commonly used under the following situations:

- A flexible and cost-effective solution is desirable.
- There are no disk-sharing requirements across the WebLogic Server cluster.
- Local data storage does not require high availability.
- The applications do not use, or participate in, XA transactions because the transaction logs will typically require high availability and failover.
- The applications do not use file-based JMS persistent messages because the JMS message stores will typically require high availability and failover.

Figure 14.1 depicts an active-active cluster running under normal conditions. Both instances of WebLogic Server are used during normal operation, with load balancing at the connection level provided by load-balancer hardware located between the clients and the WebLogic Server cluster.

Figure 14.2 shows the same cluster after a failure of either the WebLogic Server instance or the machine on which it is running.

The load balancer is now providing failover at the connection level, while WebLogic Server clustering software provides a single homogenous system view across both WebLogic Server instances. The key features that WebLogic Server clustering provides are these:

- Fail over and load balancing of JNDI, RMI, EJB (stateless session beans, stateful session beans with in-memory state replication, and entity beans), and JMS
- `HttpSession` replication
- Cluster-wide replication of the JNDI naming service
- Cluster membership discovery and cluster health monitoring

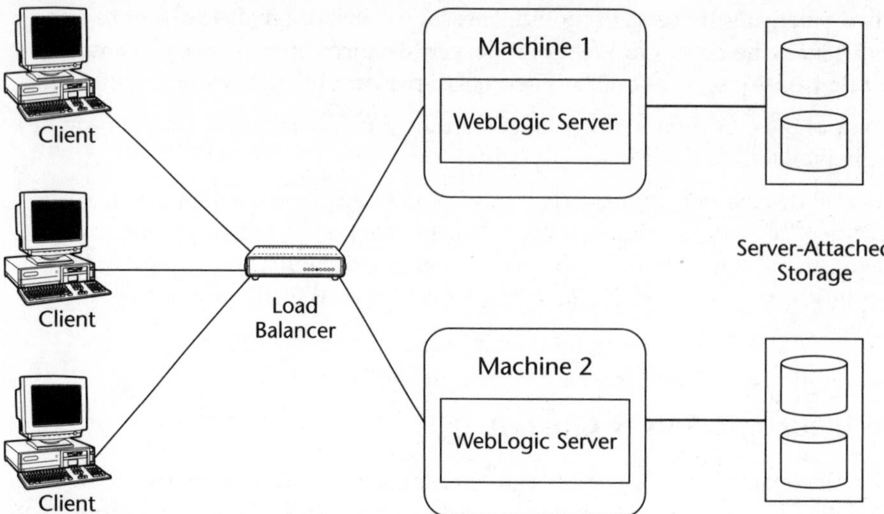

Figure 14.1 Simple cluster before failure.

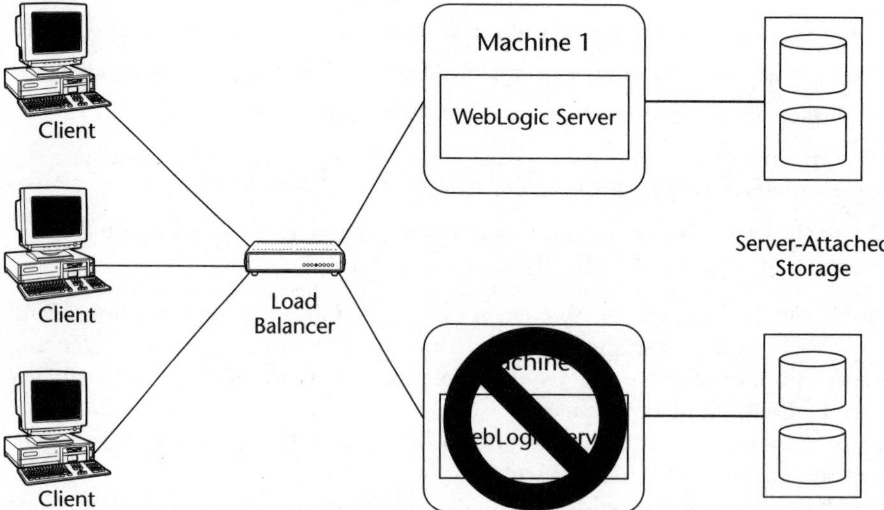

Figure 14.2 Simple cluster after failure.

When a failure takes place on either the WebLogic Server instance or the hosting node itself, the load balancer quickly notices that the WebLogic Server listen port is no longer responding to requests. The load balancer then removes that failed server from its list of healthy servers and begins routing all requests to a different, healthy WebLogic Server instance. This failure detection can be achieved in a more intelligent manner by having the load balancer periodically check the health of the WebLogic Server instance using the `weblogic.Admin PING` command. Once the WebLogic Server instance is back up and listening on the appropriate port, the load balancer will discover this fact and will once again start distributing requests to that WebLogic Server instance. Refer to Chapter 11 for more detailed information on WebLogic Server clustering.

This simple clustering configuration is a form of horizontal scaling, discussed earlier, in which additional nodes are added to the environment to increase processing capability. When horizontal scaling is used in conjunction with WebLogic Server clustering, it offers a cost-effective method to achieve both flexibility and availability. Servers can be added to the cluster dynamically; once the new WebLogic Server is added to the distribution list of the load balancer, traffic will begin routing to the new instance. If a server fails, the remaining servers will take over the load for the failed server until it can be restarted, thus allowing better utilization of hardware than an active-passive configuration.

TIP A simple WebLogic Server cluster is an appropriate strategy for a single-site installation, providing good scalability and fail-over characteristics.

Complex WebLogic Server Clusters

The second scenario we will consider has more demanding availability requirements, such as the following:

- The system must support global transactions between local and distributed resources such as JMS destinations and databases.
- JMS messages are persisted to the file system and must support failover and be highly available.
- Failover of both the node and any WebLogic Server instance-specific functionality, such as JMS destinations and JTA transaction recovery, must take place transparently.
- Distributed transactions must be recoverable and restarted in case of node or WebLogic Server failure.

Figure 14.3 presents one possible solution to these more demanding requirements. This solution would utilize the following components:

- WebLogic Server instances running in a standard WebLogic Server cluster.
- Redundant load balancers (not shown in the figure), which provide load balancing and failover of requests at the connection level.
- WebLogic JMS using multiple distributed destinations, providing high availability to both JMS producers and consumers.
- Veritas Cluster Server (VCS) or an equivalent product to provide transparent failover across nodes in the hardware cluster. VCS will manage and control both hardware and software resources, bringing resources online and taking them back offline when necessary.
- Storage area networks (SANs) to provide highly available shared disks for JMS queue storage.
- Veritas or another highly available file system for high performance and flexible volume management.

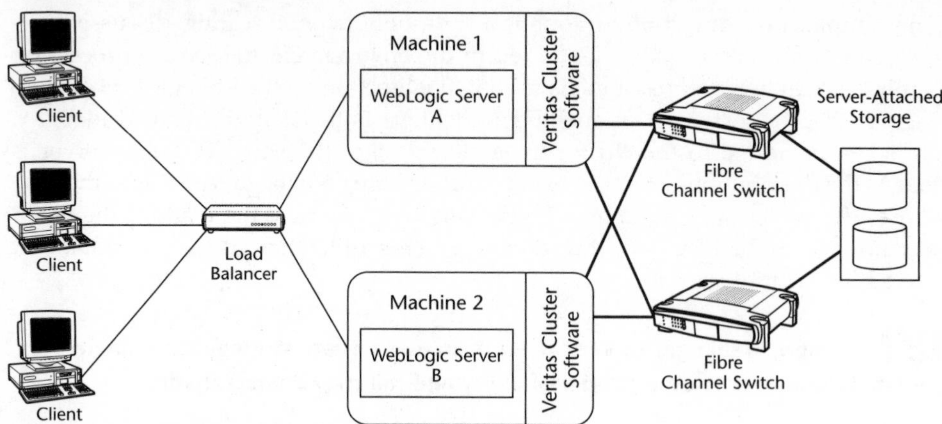

Figure 14.3 Complex cluster before failure.

Should one of the WebLogic Server instances fail, the VCS system will automatically migrate the instance to the other hardware, as depicted in Figure 14.4.

As noted previously, Veritas Cluster Servers are being used to monitor and control applications running in the configuration, and these clusters respond to a variety of hardware and software faults. Because VCS will be managing and controlling the WebLogic Server cluster you will need to produce various scripts and determine what type of health monitoring is required. This discussion will concentrate on scripts and monitoring of WebLogic Server only, although VCS is actually monitoring and controlling other resources such as IP addresses, disks, and network-interface cards. See the Veritas Cluster Server documentation for a complete description of these activities. Minimally, you will need to develop the following scripts:

Start scripts. Scripts that start the administrative server as well as all managed servers running in the WebLogic Server cluster.

Stop scripts. Scripts used to shut down WebLogic Server administrative and managed servers.

Forced stop scripts. Scripts that shut down WebLogic Server instances that are not responding to administrative shutdown commands.

Health monitoring scripts. Scripts used to determine the health of various subsystems in WebLogic Server.

VCS will use an *agent* to monitor and control the WebLogic Server resources. This agent will start the servers, stop the servers, and fail over the servers after a node failure. You will need to determine the appropriate response when a failure is detected in any monitored resources. We recommend a tiered availability approach concentrated on keeping the active server as available as possible and failing over the cluster only when it cannot be restarted. This approach relies primarily on WebLogic Server's clustering infrastructure and fails over only after a hard failure of a disk, node, or nonredundant device.

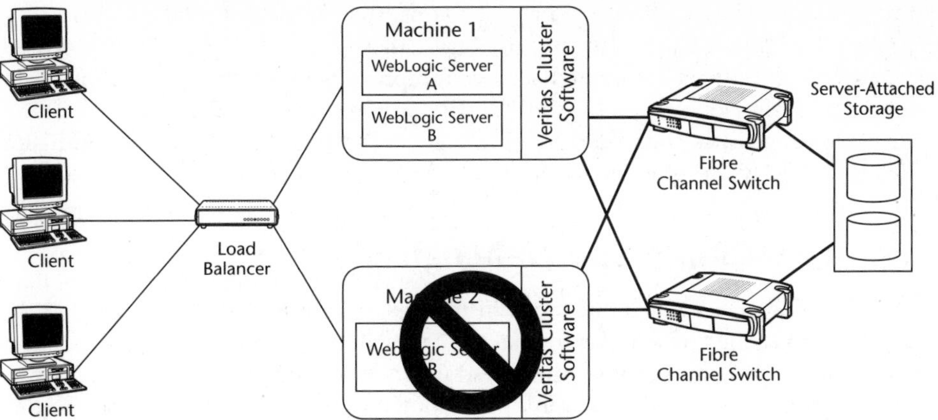

Figure 14.4 Complex cluster after failure.

You will also need to determine which failures should be handled automatically and which should only be reported so that manual action can be taken. In this scenario, the VCS agent will either perform the appropriate action itself or will propagate the information to a person through a page or send the alert itself to an enterprise monitoring console that will either take action itself or pass the alert to the appropriate personnel.

With our example scenario, no JTA or JMS migration is required during failover. The instances running on a failed VCS node will be migrated by VCS and then brought back online on the targeted node. The instance will come up and start processing just as it would when restarted locally. We should note that this is only one possible approach. We could just as easily have VCS migrate the JMS servers and JTA recovery service from the failed WebLogic Server instance to the other instance running on the other node.

BEST PRACTICE A complex WebLogic Server cluster will cost more than a simple cluster and require additional configuration and testing, but it is appropriate if your installation requires higher levels of availability.

Multiple Site Deployment Strategies

Multiple site deployment strategies are often discussed in the context of a continuous business paradigm, combining high-availability solutions with advanced disaster recovery techniques. The ultimate goal is to be able to manage both planned and unplanned outages with minimal disruption. These strategies allow continuous availability during failures as well as software and hardware migration without affecting availability. A complete discussion of this topic is beyond the scope of this chapter, so we will limit our discussion to key concepts and examine some configuration options.

Even though local clusters, in which all of the nodes and storage subsystems are in a single data center, offer good protection against smaller disasters such as single node failures or disk crashes, they do not protect against major disasters that could destroy or damage the entire facility. To protect against these kinds of failures you need to make sure that the cluster components are geographically dispersed. While most local clusters are designed around a shared disk-storage architecture where storage resources are physically connected to all nodes via SCSI or Fibre Channel, multi-site clusters usually rely on some type of replicated data architecture.

Designing Multiple-Site WebLogic Clusters

Including WebLogic Server applications in the design of a multi-site cluster is fairly straightforward as long as you ensure that the associated data is properly replicated to all data centers. It becomes more complicated when file-based JMS is used in a distributed transaction environment with multiple resources involved in a two-phase commit transaction (2PC) due to the exactly once nature of these services.

Additional design considerations covered in this section include the following:

- Active-passive or active-active cluster design
- `HttpSession` state management and replication
- Transaction collocation requirements
- Data replication

Cluster Design Options

It is possible to use both active-active and active-passive clusters with WebLogic Server applications. We recommend that you follow the same design that you used for your data-replication solution. For example, if the data replication between the two data centers is bidirectional, then an active-active design of your WebLogic Server applications may be desirable. If data replication is unidirectional, however, it may force you to stick with an active-passive design.

Session Replication

Managing and replicating `HttpSession` state is a major consideration for most WebLogic Server applications and has been discussed at length in earlier chapters. It tends to be less important in the design of the overall multiple site cluster, however, because the loss of `HttpSession` data in the event of a data-center loss is often acceptable to the business. If the loss of `HttpSession` data is not acceptable, the data can be stored in the database using WebLogic Server's JDBC-based session persistence mechanism, allowing the session data to be replicated like any other data in the database.

As with all disaster-recovery and high-availability planning, we recommend that you begin by first examining business requirements and then applying the proper deployment strategy that will meet the requirements. All data is not created equal, and it is likely that only a portion of application data is critical to the basic operation of the application.

As described in previous chapters, the most popular form of session persistence is in-memory replication. WebLogic Server uses a primary-secondary replication scheme in which the server first used to process a user's request is designated the primary server for that user and will create the primary copy of the `HttpSession` object. At the end of that first request and before the response is returned to the user, the primary server will create a secondary copy of the `HttpSession` data on a secondary server in the cluster. Typically, the primary server for a particular session receives all future requests for that session. If the primary server fails, the first request following the failure will be routed to another server in the cluster. This behavior puts several restrictions on your cluster design:

- You must ensure that subsequent user requests always come back to the same data center where the primary server is located.
- A typical WebLogic Server cluster does not span across data centers. The secondary session must therefore be created on a server in the same data center as the primary server. This also means that in the event of data center failure, data stored in the `HttpSession` object for that particular session would be lost.

It is possible to use in-memory replication across sites. The primary issue that you run into is not the replication itself so much as it is the multicast traffic needed for JNDI replications and cluster membership and monitoring. Because multicast is a requirement, this means that you really need complete control over the link between the sites because most Internet and ISP routers are not configured to forward multicast packets. Additionally, we have found that if your connection between the data centers has a tendency to lose packets or the latency is over a few hundred milliseconds, this can cause problems with WebLogic Server's clustering mechanisms.

BEST PRACTICE Prefer architectures that do not require using WebLogic Server clusters that span data centers. If you do need to support `HttpSession` **failover between data centers, consider using JDBC persistence and your existing data replication technology, which will work between clusters. If you need to use in-memory replication, you need to make sure that your connection supports multicast traffic, is not prone to packet loss, and has very low latency.**

Transaction Collocation Requirements

Your multiple site design should also consider that the application may use certain WebLogic Server services, such as JMS servers and JTA transaction recovery services, which are designed with the assumption that there is only one active instance of the service running in a cluster at any given time. You need to be able migrate the data associated with these services, data that is usually critical for the normal operation of the applications. Additionally, to take advantage of WebLogic Server transaction collocation optimization, it is also desired that all such operations from a specific user be directed to the same data center.

Data Replication

Finally, to provide data center failover capabilities, your design needs to ensure that all *critical* data is replicated to the secondary data center where the services will be restored in the event of primary data center failure. To determine the data-replication requirements, start with the following items:

- Domain configuration data stored in the domain root directory
- JTA transaction logs, usually located in the server directory—for example, for a server named `myserver`, the transaction logs reside in the `myserver` subdirectory underneath the domain's root directory
- JMS persistent messages, which can be stored in an RDBMS or the file systems, if applicable
- Data associated with the application business logic, usually stored in the RDBMS systems

You need to identify the items that must be available at the secondary data center to restart your application and recover all critical data, messages, and transactions.

Implementing Clusters That Span Multiple Sites

Implementing a multiple site WebLogic Server cluster requires reliable, high-speed networking technologies to support the cluster-wide communication used to monitor cluster members and replicate `HttpSession` contents, JNDI naming service information, and other application-level data. This is usually done in a campus cluster where great distances do not separate the cluster nodes.

A number of new technologies, including Dense Wave Length Division Multiplexing (DWDM) and long-haul Gigabit Interface Converters (GBICs), provide support for Fibre Channel communication at distances up to 100 kilometers. This has become attractive to many customers because it uses standard Fibre Channel components and relatively inexpensive modular storage. Additionally, the development of DWDM technology allows cluster architects to use dark fiber, high-speed communication links provided by common carriers, to extend the distances formally subject to the limits of regular Ethernet links.

Many of these cluster techniques require that the cluster components be on the same subnet, although it can have separately routed redundant links. If your company has this type of architecture, building a WebLogic Server cluster spanning multiple data centers is relatively easy, as it normally does not require any special configuration. Some of these clusters, though, can use more sophisticated data replication techniques, and the cluster architecture can span multiple subnets connected by WANs.

Figure 14.5 illustrates a possible configuration for a single WebLogic Server cluster that spans both sites.

As we mentioned previously, WebLogic Server clusters depend on multicast communication for cluster-wide JNDI change notifications and heartbeat messages. In order for this configuration to work, you must ensure that multicast messages are reliably transmitted to all server instances in the cluster. Configure all routers between the sites to propagate multicast messages. Recognize that most network administrators do not allow UDP packets across different subnets, so you may need to use one subnet for the entire cluster unless you control the network configuration. Low network latency is also critical for the cluster health; if your network latency is much more than 300 milliseconds, then you need to look at either other configurations or ways to reduce the latency. While the cluster may work with higher latencies, our experience has shown that higher latencies tend to be less reliable, especially during peak loads or failures. You must also configure the cluster's `Multicast TTL` value high enough to keep routers from dropping multicast packets before they reach their final destination, as discussed in Chapter 11.

Note that the local load balancers at each site are configured to route requests only to the servers in that site. Therefore, it is important to configure global load balancers to use a sticky routing algorithm so that requests associated with a particular user's session stick to the same site, except in the event of a site failure. This will keep the intersite traffic to a minimum but still allow global `HttpSession` failover. Also note that the local load balancers in this configuration can be replaced with a farm of Web servers configured to use one of the WebLogic Server proxy plug-ins. This approach, however, currently has one drawback.

With the hardware load balancer, the available servers to route to are preconfigured and the load balancer keeps track of which ones are up dynamically. This preconfiguration allows you to limit the visibility of the load balancer to the cluster members in the local data center. With the Web server plug-ins, the plug-in is preconfigured, but they normally update their cluster membership list with data returned by the WebLogic Server cluster. This causes a problem because now the plug-in will try to load balance requests across both data centers instead of just the local one, putting more load and stress on the network channel between the data centers. You can turn off the plug-in's dynamic configuration update feature by setting `DynamicServerList` to `OFF` in the plug-in configuration; however, this means that the plug-in cannot react to server failures as quickly or elegantly. We expect that BEA will address this limitation in an upcoming release, so please check your release notes for details.

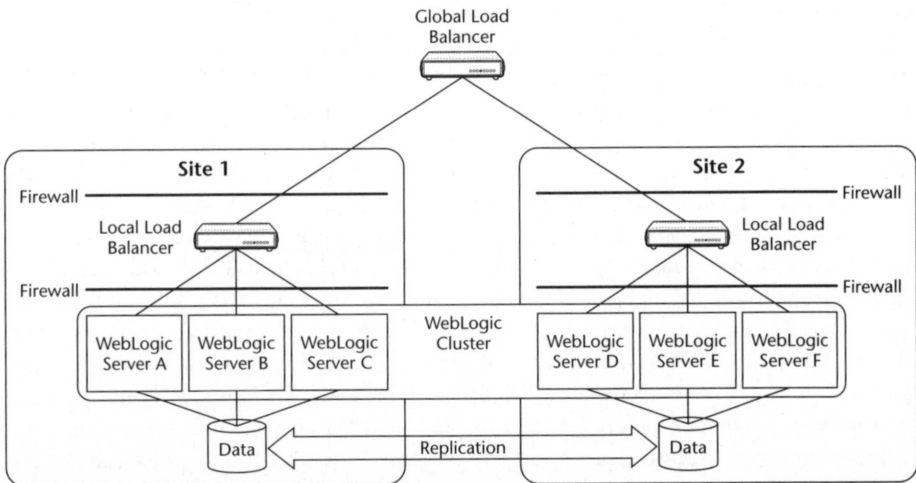

Figure 14.5 WebLogic cluster spanning multiple sites.

To support cross-site `HttpSession` failover properly, you will need to use replication groups to ensure that the `HttpSession` object's primary and secondary copies are in different data centers. Clearly, cross-site session replication adds some latency, but it does provide seamless failure of user sessions in the event of a site failure. All you then need to worry about is the proper replication of application data in the database, JTA transaction logs, and so on. For simplicity, we did not include JMS Servers in this design because the exactly once nature makes it more difficult and the appropriate architecture is very dependent on your application's use of JMS and your requirements.

This multiple-site cluster design using a single WebLogic Server domain may be a good choice if your primary and secondary sites have good network connectivity and you can properly route multicast packets between the sites. Again, we need to reemphasize the importance of high-speed, reliable, low-latency network connectivity between the sites for this architecture to work successfully. As the distance between the data centers grows, it becomes more difficult and more costly to achieve this type of connectivity. For continental clusters or other situations where you simply cannot meet the recommended guidelines for intersite connectivity, we strongly recommend that you consider using separate clusters in each data center, the topic of the next section.

BEST PRACTICE Consider using a cluster that spans multiple sites if your sites have good network connectivity and you need the seamless failover of session information. Remember that your network between the sites must support multicast traffic if you want to use this architecture.

Implementing One Cluster per Site

The previous section described a multiple-site WebLogic Server cluster that used high-speed networking to achieve a single cluster across multiple sites. A single cluster is not always possible or desirable, however, and this section will explore one alternative.

In this alternative design, each site is configured with an independent WebLogic Server cluster. By defining an individual cluster for each site, you immediately eliminate all of the WebLogic Server-specific intersite communication requirements. Of course, the application may have its own intersite communication requirements, which will almost certainly include data replication. If it meets your requirements, we believe this multiple cluster design provides a simpler, more flexible architecture while still taking advantage of WebLogic Server clustering features locally in each site. Figure 14.6 illustrates this alternative multiple-site, multiple-cluster design.

When a client first requests the URL for a Web application, the global load balancer will route the request to one of the data centers. The local load balancer will then route the request to one of the available servers in the WebLogic Server cluster at that location, and a user session will be created in a primary and secondary server in that cluster. The global and local load balancers remember where they sent the last request for a particular user session and will always attempt to route all subsequent requests from that user to the same data center and server. To accomplish this behavior, you will need to configure the global load balancer using a *static persist* policy and the local load balancer using a *sticky* load-balancing algorithm, topics discussed in detail later in this chapter.

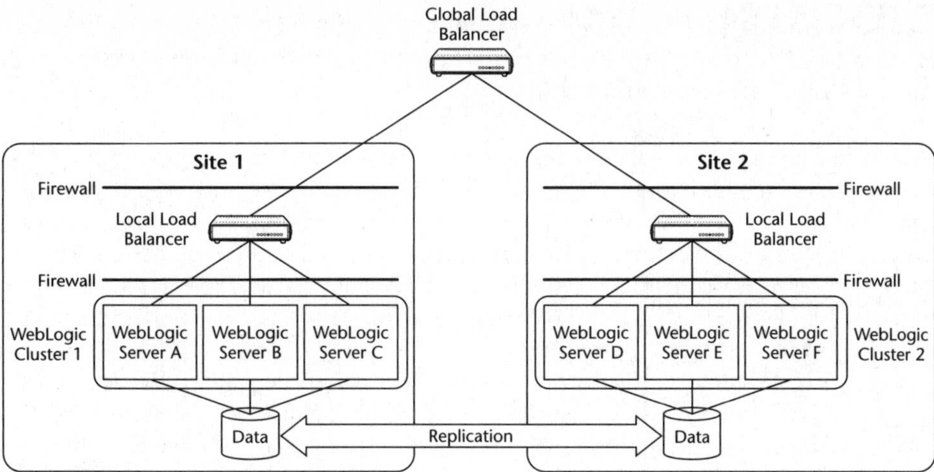

Figure 14.6 WebLogic cluster per site.

If the primary server fails, the global load balancer routes the request to the same data center, but the local load balancer will sense that the primary server has failed and route the request to a different server in the cluster. Note that the hardware load balancer does not know the identity of the secondary server containing the replicated session data for this request; it simply picks another server in the cluster and routes the request. There are then two possibilities:

- The request may have been routed to the server instance that was holding the secondary copy of this session. In that case, the secondary server is promoted to primary and a new server instance is chosen to hold the secondary copy of the session.
- The request may have been received by a server instance that has no knowledge of the required user session. The server will inspect the session ID to determine the locations for the primary and secondary copies of the user session. After sensing that the primary is unavailable, it will call out to the secondary server and request a copy of the session data. This new server then becomes the primary server for this session.

In both cases, the server chosen by the local load balancer has become the new primary server for subsequent requests. The load balancer will remember the new primary location and route all subsequent requests there.

This failover behavior at the local cluster level is available in this multiple-cluster configuration and in the previous single-cluster configuration. The difference is how well the design handles the failure of an entire data center. In the multiple-cluster case, the loss of all servers at one site causes a loss of `HttpSession` data because the data was not replicated at the other site, only on other servers at the same site. You can, however, use JDBC-based session persistence to allow session failover between data centers. Despite this limitation with in-memory replication, the advantages of independent operation and support for most data-replication techniques make this design a strong candidate architecture for multisite configurations.

BEST PRACTICE The multiple-site, multiple-cluster architecture is a very good candidate architecture for applications requiring high availability and good disaster-recovery characteristics.

As we mentioned earlier, applications that use persistent JMS messages and/or JTA distributed transactions complicate this model. For example, you may need to bring up the JMS server from a failed WebLogic Server instance on another instance, or even another site. While there are many different ways to use JMS and JTA distributed transactions, the common theme that is usually present is that you need to bring up the JMS server and/or JTA recovery service from the failed node to process messages and/or do recovery of the in-flight transactions.

For intrasite failures, typical strategies include either migrating the service to another WebLogic Server instance in the cluster or having another machine bring up the failed instance. For complete site failures, you typically need to have the ability to bring up the entire WebLogic Server cluster at the other site so that it can drain any messages in the JMS persistent stores and recover any in-flight transactions. This is relatively easy to set up provided that you do not need the failed cluster to interact with your users; configuring it to interact with your users is possible, just more difficult.

Unfortunately, space prevents us from going into detailed discussions of the different scenarios. It's time to move on to talk about load balancers and how they work with WebLogic Server.

Global and Local Traffic Management

Global and local load balancers figure prominently in many production environments. Their proper use is the subject of this section. We start with a quick look at some basic configurations that show how load balancers are used in production environments. Next, we discuss using local load balancers with WebLogic Server. We end by discussing the use of global load balancers to load balance and fail over between sites.

Using Load Balancers

As global enterprises have continued to open their systems to new customer channels, system designers have been forced to deal with unpredictable user demands while retaining high performance and high availability. These requirements have driven designers to the use of global and local traffic management devices, or load balancers, to better manage wide area network (WAN) and local area network (LAN) traffic.

Figure 14.7 illustrates a simple example of local traffic management using a set of redundant local load balancers to manage traffic to a cluster of servers.

Figure 14.8 extends this example to global traffic management by adding a global load balancer in front of two identical configurations of servers and local load balancers. Similar configurations were utilized in many of the design strategies discussed in the previous section.

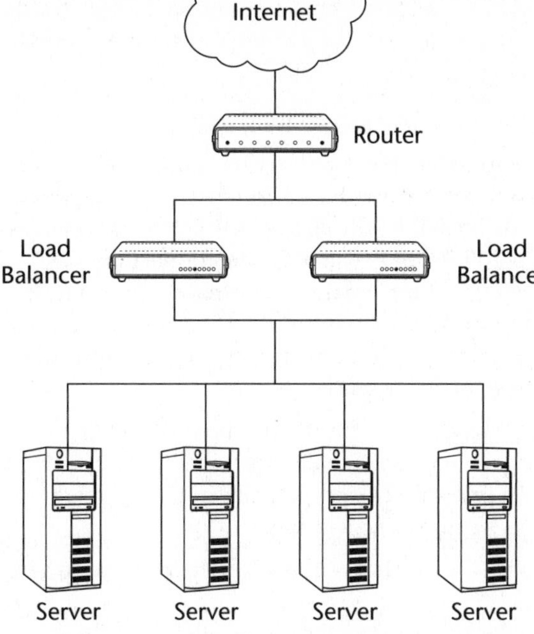

Figure 14.7 Local traffic management using local load balancers.

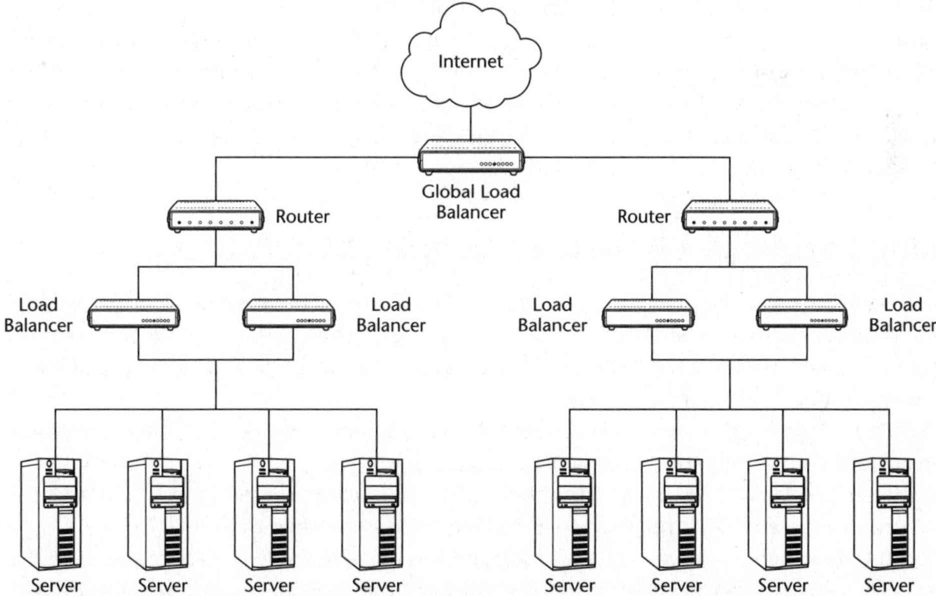

Figure 14.8 Global traffic management using global load balancers.

Many vendors offer these local and global traffic-management devices, including F5, Cisco, Rad Data Communications, and Nortel. Although they are commonly called load balancers, most of these devices offer features such as content switching, traffic management, and SSL acceleration in addition to load balancing. You should choose a product that provides at least the following features:

Intercept. The device must be able to intercept the incoming traffic.

Inspect. Once traffic is intercepted it must be inspected to determine its type and how it should be handled. Inspection is performed at different network layers depending on the requirements of the system. Simple inspection is performed at *Layer 4*, one of the seven layers in the ISO Open Systems Interconnection (OSI) Reference Model, and involves IP and port information. For many applications this type of inspection is sufficient to route or transform the message properly. More demanding systems may require inspection of HTTP headers or even the payloads in the packets to handle the traffic properly.

Transform. The load balancer may be required to transform the traffic in some manner, the simplest example being a change to the destination IP address and port. Advanced transformations can involve re-encryption of traffic, rewriting URL values, or even inserting cookies into HTTP headers.

Direct. The final step involves the actual directing of the traffic to the appropriate resources.

While performing all of these tasks, load balancers must also support multiple IP-based protocols, handle high levels of traffic, and perform very quickly with little overhead. Most load balancers support multiple distribution algorithms, such as round-robin, geography, round-trip time, random, ratio, least connections, application availability, and user-defined quality-of-service (QoS). The simpler algorithms often produce better results. Most commonly used algorithms include round robin or least connections for local area networks, and user-defined QoS, geography, and application availability for wide area networks and disaster recovery.

Using Local Load Balancers with WebLogic Server

Load balancers can be used to manage traffic to both clustered and nonclustered WebLogic Server instances. Any load-balancing algorithms can be used with these configurations, although there are limitations associated with certain protocols, SSL support, and stateful `HttpSession` data.

When using a hardware load balancer with HTTP requests, the load balancer sits in front of the Web application and is used to distribute the load across the members of the cluster and provide failover capability. Load balancers present one IP address for all clients and then distribute load to available WebLogic Servers in the cluster.

Load balancers are also used to provide session affinity, routing user requests to the WebLogic Server instance containing the primary copy of that user's session data, a technique known as *sticky* sessions. Once a user establishes a session on a primary server, that user will be pinned to the same WebLogic Server instance for the entire session. As described earlier in the chapter, a failure of the server hosting the primary copy of the user session data will be handled transparently by WebLogic Server using the secondary copy of the session data replicated to another server in the cluster.

If you are using `HttpSession` data with a WebLogic Server cluster, you must use a load balancer that supports a compatible passive or active persistence mechanism, unless you happen to be using JDBC-based session persistence. The proper configuration for this hardware load balancer depends on the type of persistence you choose:

- *Passive cookie persistence* refers to the ability of WebLogic Server to write a cookie containing session information through the load balancer to the client. The hardware load balancer must be configured to inspect the HTTP header and read the WebLogic Server cookie to route the request to the correct server instance properly.
- *Active cookie persistence* exists when the load balancer either creates its own session cookie or overwrites the existing session cookie. The load balancer then examines this cookie to route the request to the proper server instance during subsequent requests. Although active cookie persistence is generally compatible with WebLogic Server, a cluster will work properly only with load balancers that do not modify the WebLogic Server session cookie.

Hardware load balancers can also be used in front of a group of managed servers that are not clustered and do not replicate `HttpSession` data. Traffic will be distributed to the WebLogic Servers according to the load-balancing algorithm, and the load balancer will again provide the *sticky* session capability. Should a server instance fail, subsequent requests will be routed to another available managed server. Unless your applications are using JDBC-based session persistence, any session data will be lost. If the session is lost, the user will have to authenticate again and he or she will lose any state the server was maintaining.

Using Global Load Balancers with WebLogic Server

Unlike local load balancers used for distributing traffic among multiple servers, global load balancers are used to distribute traffic among different sites. Global load balancers can be used with or without clustering software and are often used in conjunction with local load balancers to eliminate single points of failure and route traffic away from poorly performing sites. Global load balancers are also vital for disaster recovery; most products provide policies to ensure that all traffic will be sent to a primary site unless that site is suffering an outage. During an outage, traffic can be manually or automatically routed to a secondary site.

Most global load balancers work by becoming the authoritative DNS server, which means that when a client requests a URL, the query returns the IP address of the global load balancer itself rather than the address of a local load balancer or server. When a client contacts that IP address, the global load balancer then provides the client with the IP address of the data center best suited to serve the request. Global load balancers usually sit outside the LAN and intercept requests before they hit the firewalls at the sites themselves, although configuration options exist for balancing in firewalls as well.

Most modern global load balancers provide numerous configuration options. For example, the 3-DNS Controller from F5 Networks provides both static and global load-balancing policies with various options. In the static mode, connections are distributed according to predefined rules, such as *global availability,* which chooses the server based on the order defined by the administrator, and *static persist,* which ensures that transactions requiring persistence are always routed to same server or data center. *Round-robin* and *return DNS* policies behave like a normal DNS server, whereas *random* and *ratio* modes can be used to do weight-based load balancing. The load balancer also collects various performance metrics that can be used to define dynamic load-balancing policies.

Production Security Strategies

In this section, we will review some of the key concepts and practices associated with locking down and securing your WebLogic Server installation above and beyond the WebLogic Server and J2EE security topics covered in Chapter 10. First, we will review the importance of understanding your application architecture and the potential security threats. We'll then proceed to discuss firewall and DMZ design, connection filtering, locking down Web applications, some miscellaneous security practices, and SSL acceleration approaches.

Understanding Application Data Flow

It's important to first understand the underlying data flow of your application architecture to better define the overall network layout and potential security threats. Once this review is complete you can begin defining and mapping application security requirements to the WebLogic Server security services and J2EE security features. As discussed in Chapter 10 and depicted in Figure 10.1, two general types of clients will be calling into the server: Web, or *thin*, clients and application, or *fat*, clients.

The first client type is the thin client, typically a browser or other Web Services client. Thin clients may call in to the application via the HTTP protocol using direct connections with the WebLogic Server or through a Web server running a WebLogic Server proxy plug-in component. Thin clients normally call Web application components and Web services in the server's servlet engine.

The second client type is the fat client, or application client. Fat clients may use the HTTP, T3, IIOP, or COM protocols to call directly into the server, invoking Web application components, Web services, EJB components, or JMS services in the server. Both thin- and fat-client calls can be routed through a single firewall or a set of firewalls for security. We will talk about suggested firewall layouts later in this section.

To define the specific security threats, also known as the *threat model*, you need to define both *what* you are protecting and *who* you are protecting it from. Once you have identified all of the client types and request paths for your application, you should then identify the data and operations on the server that they will be accessing and the required security for those resources. The security requirement could be as simple as requiring only SSL connections for all authentication or as complex as requiring an X.509 client certificate signed by a specific certificate authority for access. Consider each type of operation or data that will be used by clients and the ramifications if that resource were compromised in some way. Once you understand the security requirements for the server-side data and operations, the various clients, and the network types they will use, you have defined your threat model.

NOTE **One assumption we make in this discussion is the security of the underlying machine on which WebLogic Server runs. The physical security of the machine, the operating system, the user accounts on the machine, and other programs running on the machine, is critical to good security and should be thought through meticulously.**

Understanding Firewall Layouts

Firewalls provide a high level of security from untrusted traffic if used and configured properly. In this section, we will discuss the positives and negatives of some of the common firewall layouts used to separate corporate resources from the Internet and provide a layered security approach. The specific firewall used in this discussion could be any of the major firewall types. The most basic firewall is a stateless, packet-filtering firewall that performs network address translation (NAT). You can also use the more complex, stateful, packet-inspection firewalls if circumstances warrant their use. Regardless of type, by grouping our network layout in firewalls, we define specific, contiguous regions of a network that operate under a single, uniform security policy.

Another important point about using NAT firewalls is that you need to configure your WebLogic Server instances to be aware of the external addresses that the clients use to contact WebLogic Server. See Chapter 11 for a thorough discussion of this topic.

The simplest and most common firewall layout is a single perimeter firewall protecting the entire application from the untrusted zone, a configuration depicted in Figure 14.9. This untrusted zone might be the Internet, your company's extranet, or even anything outside your data center. This layout is typical of a small enterprise or division. The disadvantage of a single firewall is the lack of a layered approach to security—a single implementation flaw or configuration error in the firewall can lead to a complete loss of security.

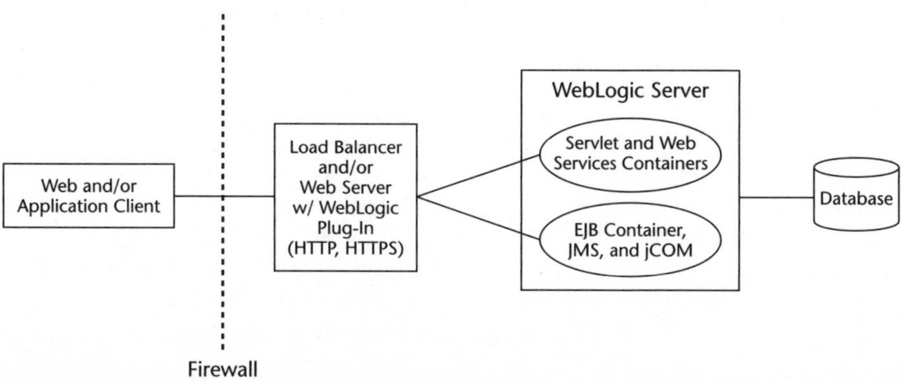

Figure 14.9 Single perimeter firewall layout.

Some corporate security policies can be very strict and may require several well-defined network regions, commonly referred to as *demilitarized zones* (DMZs), having their own security policies. The concept is simple: Putting servers or network appliances, with or without application code, in the DMZ limits your overall security exposure if the machines in that area were somehow compromised. A DMZ could include anything from only a router or hardware load balancer to the entire application; in the latter case, the application has a lower level of protection than other corporate resources not in the DMZ. Typically, the DMZ contains only a hardware load balancer and/or Web servers configured with a WebLogic Server Web server plug-in. Figure 14.10 shows a conceptual overview one of the most common configurations.

Of course, we have barely scratched the surface of what is possible with firewall configuration. Most companies have their own policies about how the network should be laid out. Therefore, we will move on to talk about connection filters.

Using a Connection Filter

One of the first rules of security is to refuse connections from unknown or untrusted sources, denying these sources any foothold in the environment. *Connection filters* are a powerful way to control the types of connections accepted by WebLogic Server instances, providing a programmatic control over every new connection with the server. There are two primary ways to configure a connection filter: use the built-in connection filter in WebLogic Server or write a custom implementation of the `ConnectionFilter` interface.

WebLogic Server's Built-In Connection Filter

The first and easiest way to filter connections uses WebLogic Server's built-in connection filter facility. You can enable and configure this facility using the `Security` folder's `Filter Configuration` tab in the WebLogic Console by defining rules that govern the types and sources of network connections to be accepted or denied. By default, there are no rules defined in the built-in connection filter, so all connections are accepted. Rules are very specific in format, and ordering is also very important. The first matching rule wins, even if another rule further down contradicts it. Because performance can also be a concern, place more general rules at the top of the list to allow most new connections to be identified quickly and allowed or denied.

Each rule is defined using the following syntax:

```
target localAddress localPort action [protocols]+
```

The `target` parameter defines the source IP address, including any subnet mask, to be filtered; the `localAddress` and `localPort` parameters define the WebLogic Server IP address and port for this rule, making it possible to filter connections on some network channels and not on others. You must set the `action` argument to either `allow` or `deny`, and the optional `protocols` parameters must be one or more of the following values: `http`, `https`, `t3`, `t3s`, `giop`, `giops`, `dcom`, or `ftp`.

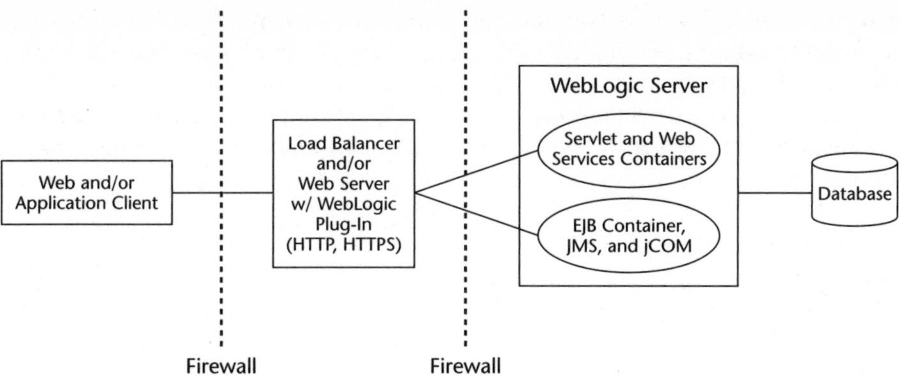

Figure 14.10 Typical DMZ firewall layout.

Let's look at a couple of examples. Imagine that you want to restrict access to any port on your WebLogic Server listening on 216.148.48.51 to anyone using an IP address that starts with 192.168 for both the HTTP and IIOP protocols. The following entry would accomplish this:

```
192.168.0.0/255.255.0.0 216.148.48.51 * deny http giop
```

You can also block access specifically to port 7001 on your site to anyone trying to access the site from any host in the baddomain.com domain. The following entry accomplishes this by denying access regardless of the protocol:

```
*.baddomain.com 216.148.48.51 7001 deny
```

Note that this rule requires a run-time DNS lookup to evaluate the rule properly for each network connection attempt, potentially creating a performance problem. Try to use IP addresses rather than domain names whenever possible.

This rule-based technique for configuring the connection filter provides significant flexibility. By combining `allow` and `deny` rules, you can configure the connection filter to refuse connections of certain types, perhaps `http` or `t3`, from all external IP addresses while allowing these connections from other servers in the cluster, Web servers, or hosts in the corporate LAN subnet.

Custom Connection Filters

The second way to filter connections involves writing a custom implementation of the `weblogic.security.net.ConnectionFilter` interface and configuring WebLogic Server to use this filter rather than the built-in connection filter. Your custom implementation class will receive a `ConnectionEvent` object via the `accept()` callback method whenever a new connection attempt takes place. This `ConnectionEvent` object contains information regarding the inbound connection, including the remote address and port, the local address and port, and the protocol. Your implementation of the `accept()` method should interrogate this object and determine whether to accept the connection, returning from the method without an exception if the connection should be accepted and raising a `FilterException` if the connection should be refused.

What follows is an example implementation of the `ConnectionFilter` interface that accepts all connections from the IP address 127.0.0.1 but refuses all other connection attempts:

```
class SimpleConnectionFilter implements ConnectionFilter
{
    public void accept(ConnectionEvent event)
        throws FilterException
    {
        String target =
            event.getRemoteAddress().getHostAddress();
        if (! "127.0.0.1".equals(target))
            throw FilterException("Connection refused!");
    }
}
```

Locking Down Web Applications

Several security considerations related to Web applications are not obvious and can lead to confusion if not understood. This section will supplement the general security information in Chapter 10 with some additional topics related to Web applications.

Access-Control Checks during Server-Side Forwards

A Web application deployed on WebLogic Server will restrict access to specific pages and resources based on the various security-constraint elements defined in its `web.xml` deployment descriptor. If the Web application sends an HTTP *redirect* to the client with a new resource URL, the client will send a new request to the server for the new URL. This second request will be required to pass any access-control checks using the same security-constraint elements in the deployment descriptor.

If the Web application does a server-side *forward* to a new resource URL, however, the client is never involved and no second request is made and checked against the security constraints. The same HTTP request is simply moved on to the next resource on the server side, evading a full access-control check. You can configure the Web application to perform a full access-control check for all server-side forwarding using the `check-auth-on-forward` element in the WebLogic-specific `weblogic.xml` deployment descriptor:

```
<weblogic-web-app>
  <container-descriptor>
    <check-auth-on-forward/>
  </container-descriptor>
  ...
</weblogic-web-app>
```

Session ID Cookies Safety

Web applications that run over both secure (HTTPS) and insecure (HTTP) sockets must be designed very carefully to avoid compromising the session ID stored in the cookie. Recalling previous discussions in Chapter 1 and elsewhere, the cookie is a token that is generated on the server and sent to the browser client for the purposes of identifying that browser session during subsequent HTTP requests. The browser will resend the cookie with every subsequent request it makes to that domain, and the server will identify the client by the uniquely generated session ID contained in the cookie. In other words, if the browser has authenticated itself, either via FORM or BASIC HTTP authentication, the session ID in the cookie serves as the only information the server needs for proof of the client's identity.

The problem is that if a user begins accessing a Web application over a plain-text, or insecure, socket, the cookie and the session ID in it are sent in plain text in the HTTP headers. This scenario is very common, and it could represent something like a catalog and shopping-cart area in an e-commerce site where it is perfectly acceptable to begin the session over plain text as no private information is being sent over the wire.

The real security problem occurs if the Web application later switches to a secure socket and allows the same cookie and session ID to be used during secure operation, the default behavior of a Web application. Continuing the e-commerce example, the site might switch to secure mode once a shopping cart is full and the user must log in or provide credit-card information to complete the transaction. This new user information and authentication context is still associated with the original session ID and cookie transmitted over plain text even though the secure protocol was used to perform the subsequent authentication or data-gathering steps. This is obviously a major concern because anyone who *sniffed*, or intercepted, the original session ID from the plain-text socket cookie can now impersonate the newly authenticated user with it, perhaps gaining access to user information or the data gathered during the secure communication. Note that the problem described here is nothing specific to WebLogic Server, but rather a problem in the way secure and insecure HTTP communication is used in typical Web applications.

The best solution to this insecure cookie problem involves designing your Web application to avoid it completely by splitting your Web application into two separate applications: an insecure portion and a secure portion. The first application would, for example, contain all of the catalog and shopping-cart functionality in your e-commerce site, establishing a user session and providing the session ID in a plain-text cookie. The second application would use a separate secure-only cookie and provide the secure authentication and data-gathering steps required for checkout. Data gathered during the insecure shopping-cart application would have to be supplied to the secure application via some mechanism other than the `HttPSession` because this would not be shared across the two applications. Alternatives include `POST` parameters referring to database-based storage or some other form of server-side storage.

To implement this solution you must first create two separate Web applications and scope the cookies to each Web application rather than allowing them to be global, domain-specific cookies. If the cookies are global, the default setting, the same session ID will be used across all Web applications in the server. You need to defeat this cookie sharing by declaring the cookie in the second, secure Web application to be a secure-only cookie using the following stanza in the `weblogic.xml` descriptor file for that application:

```
<session-param>
  <param-name>CookieSecure</param-name>
  <param-value>true</param-value>
</session-param>
```

You should also scope the Web application cookie by setting the `CookiePath` for the WebLogic Server session cookie to include the Web application context rather than the global "/" value alone. You can accomplish this using the following entry in the `session-descriptor` element of the `weblogic.xml` deployment descriptor:

```
<session-param>
  <param-name>CookiePath</param-name>
  <param-value>/mywebapp</param-value>
</session-param>
```

To further complicate matters, different browsers exhibit different cookie behavior when combining secure and insecure cookies for the same domain. Browsers store many cookies from various sites and will typically store these cookies in a table either in memory or on disk. Some browsers keep a single table for both secure and insecure cookies, and if a new secure-only cookie comes in from a domain, it overrides any previous cookie from that domain—for example, Netscape uses this strategy. Other browsers, like Internet Explorer, keep two tables, one secure and one plain text. This means that if a new secure-only cookie comes in from a domain, it is stored in addition to the previous plain-text cookie. This is troublesome because if that two-table browser moves back to a plain-text socket (HTTP) communication mode, the original plain-text cookie and session ID will be used and not the new secure one. This can result in an authentication failure if the server has already invalidated the insecure cookie, although it does prevent the secure cookie from being sent over an insecure socket connection.

Examining Other Security Considerations

This section offers additional recommendations and best practices for locking down various parts of a WebLogic Server installation. These include the following:

Use separate development and production systems. This eliminates any inconveniences associated with production-environment security during application development and early-stage testing. Areas such as the physical security of the machine, the operating system, the user accounts on the machine, and other programs running on the machine should all be as secure as you can make them. Having separate environments and a specific transfer audit will significantly reduce the risks of improper installation often associated with vulnerabilities.

Precompile all Java Server Pages (JSPs) on the production system. Some corporate security policies do not allow any source code on live systems. By using the `weblogic.jspc` or `weblogic.appc` utilities to precompile all JSPs, you not only improve the initial response time of the Web application but also have a cleaner security audit. To totally eliminate the need for JSP source files on your production system, you would need to register all of the JSP-generated servlets and their corresponding URL mapping in the `web.xml` deployment descriptor, just as you would any other servlet.

Use JSP comments rather than HTML comments. Also consider using only JSP comments in your JSP code, as the JSP comments are removed from the final class at compile time whereas HTML comments are sent to the client and may provide internal implementation details.

Use SSL/TLS whenever possible. While it is certainly true that the performance of SSL is not as good as a plain-text socket, the security benefit cannot be overlooked. SSL is a top-heavy protocol. The initial handshake, which uses asymmetric cryptography, is the real performance bottleneck. After the handshake is complete a shared secret exists, and better-performing symmetric cryptography is used. This is why it is important to understand SSL session resumption, a technique that allows an SSL client to remember specific SSL session information for reuse when connecting back to an SSL server. The client will then be able to present its SSL session information to the server and skip the expensive SSL handshake.

Use the best possible SSL strength. The default installation of WebLogic Server represents an exportable-strength SSL implementation. This means that the maximum SSL strength is 512-bit keys with 40-bit bulk encryption, levels not considered safe for many businesses. A stronger, domestic-strength WebLogic Server can be requested through your BEA sales representative.

Using two-way SSL can prevent man-in-the-middle attacks. If possible, distribute client certificates and set up the server to verify them. By telling the server which certificate authority to use, you know precisely what SSL clients are connecting to the server. This is commonly called a public key infrastructure (PKI). While some significant management concerns are associated with PKI, the authentication is very secure and could be worth the management and configuration investment.

Modify the time-out and maximum size values for the incoming protocol ports on the server to prevent denial-of-service attacks. The values for some of the main server protocols of T3, HTTP, COM, and IIOP can be adjusted via the server's `Protocols` tab in the WebLogic Console. The settings are located in the `Advanced Options` section of the `General`, `HTTP`, `jCOM`, and `IIOP` subtabs, respectively. The default time-outs are typically acceptable, but the default maximum message size should likely be lowered for each of the protocols, subject to the needs of your business applications.

Understand the user-password lockouts. The default user-password lockout values are probably fine, but looking them over is always a good idea. This configuration resides in the security realm's `User Lockout` tab in the WebLogic Console. If a user does become locked out, you can manually unlock the account before the lockout time is up using the server's Security Monitoring tab.

Use the underlying operating system file system security to protect the various applications and libraries of the WebLogic Server. While we have already recommended running with a secure and audited operating system on your production environment, you can also gain superior protection for the applications by using the file system security. Adjusting the ownership of the applications directory for access only by the user account that runs the server can be very helpful, and never install or run your WebLogic Server software as *root*. If you need to bind to a privileged port, make sure to configure the server to switch to a nonroot user using the machine's `General Configuration` tab in the WebLogic Console.

Use external system security facilities when possible. When connecting to a database from the WebLogic Server, you should enunciate a username and credential to use. By locking down the database to that specific user, you have reduced the threat against the database significantly. Using a firewall around the database will also limit the threat. The same recommendations hold true for any type of external system we might use from the WebLogic Server. Many back-end EIS systems have credentials applied via the Credential Mapper in the WebLogic Server security framework.

Audit the WebLogic Server log file often. By routinely monitoring the WebLogic Server system log and the security audit log, you will become familiar with normal operation and be able to identify abnormal use more readily. Without a baseline to compare against, the usefulness of the log files and audit trails is greatly reduced. You might also consider using the audit provider in the security framework as a nonrepudiation framework, useful in case an attack succeeds and legal proof of identity is required.

Have a security audit performed by an internal or external auditing group. This can help catch security flaws overlooked in the design, implementation, or deployment of an application. An audit can also qualify the current application deployment and help develop a longer-term security policy for your group or company.

BEA Systems has an email notification list for vulnerabilities found on the WebLogic Server platform. Email notifications contain information on the vulnerability as well as patching information. This is extremely valuable information for any WebLogic Server production system. It can be found online at http://dev2dev.bea.com/resourcelibrary/advisories.jsp.

Using SSL Hardware Acceleration

There are at least two good ways to increase your server's SSL performance:

- Use a load balancer with built-in SSL support.
- Run WebLogic Server on a machine having SSL hardware via the Java Cryptography Extension (JCE).

The first technique uses an external load balancer to handle the SSL. In this solution, the SSL socket is between the client and the load balancer, and all encryption and decryption take place on the load balancer's specialized hardware. The load balancer then uses the plain-text HTTP cookie in the decrypted socket to associate the session with a specific stand-alone server or a server in a cluster. This feature of load balancers is called *SSL persistence*, and many load balancers, such as Nortel and F5, incorporate it in their product offerings.

The second way to accelerate SSL with hardware is via the Java Cryptography Extension (JCE). The Java Cryptography Extension 1.2.2 is an optional package on JDK 1.2 and 1.3 and is part of JDK 1.4. WebLogic Server SSL packages use JCE for all cryptographic functions in the server. JCE is a pluggable framework for various cryptographic implementations. New providers for specific features can be added seamlessly and used without requiring modifications to application code. By configuring JCE with a hardware provider, WebLogic Server will be able to use accelerated cryptographic functions available on that platform. This pluggable JCE feature has been supported in WebLogic Server only since version 7.0 Service Pack 2. Prior to that, JCE providers were not configurable in any way.

One thing to remember is that to use specialized JCE hardware, the hardware, the device drivers, and the JCE classes all need to be installed and working correctly. Also note that for JDK 1.2 and 1.3, the additional JCE 1.2.2 classes and configuration files need to be downloaded and installed. See the WebLogic Server documentation at http://edocs.bea.com/wls/docs81/secmanage/ssl.html for more information about setting up JCE providers.

Chapter Review

This chapter focused on topics and techniques you need to consider when designing a production environment that must be scalable, secure, and highly available. We discussed a number of clustering and multiple-site design strategies, the use of hardware load balancers for global and local traffic management, techniques for employing full-featured clustering solutions with WebLogic, and best practices for securing your production environment and applications.

WebLogic Server provides a wealth of configuration options to support the most demanding requirements. The right combination of hardware, software, and networking strategies is certain to yield a production system that meets all business and technical requirements. It is up to you to identify and document these requirements and choose the proper strategy for achieving your goals.

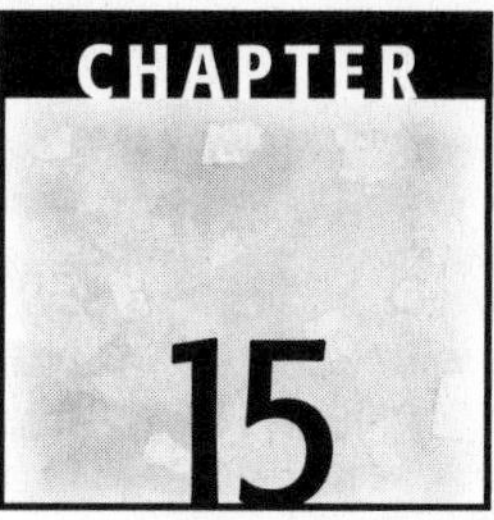

Developing and Deploying Web Services

In this chapter, we will discuss WebLogic Server's Web Services support and best practices for its use. We begin with a brief review of Web Services technology, then show you how to create simple Web Services using WebLogic Server. We then discuss more advanced Web Services capabilities built into WebLogic Server. Finally, we will use what you have learned to build the Web Services interface to *bigrez.com*.

Throughout the chapter, we refer to standalone examples that are available on the companion Web site at http://www.wiley.com/compbooks/masteringweblogic. We use code fragments in the text to demonstrate key points, but we encourage you to download and look through the complete examples as well.

Reviewing the Underlying Technology

Before we dive into building Web Services, let's review the underlying technology that makes Web Services work. This section will briefly touch on the core technologies and is not intended to provide a comprehensive introduction to Web Services technology. For a more complete introduction to Web Services, we recommend one of the fine books available on the subject, such as *Developing Java Web Services: Architecting and Developing Secure Web Services Using Java* by Ramesh Nagappan, Robert Skoczylas, and Rima Patel Sriganesh (John Wiley & Sons, 2003) and *Java Web Services* by David A. Chappell and Tyler Jewell (O'Reilly, 2002), or one of the online resources such as the Java Web Services tutorial at http://java.sun.com/webservices/docs/1.0/tutorial/.

SOAP

The Simple Object Access Protocol (SOAP) is the specification that defines the format of XML messages used to exchange information (see http://www.w3.org/TR/SOAP/). SOAP does not specify the underlying wire protocol used to send the message, though many people associate SOAP with its HTTP protocol binding. At the time of writing, various efforts were underway for defining SOAP bindings for other transport-level protocols such as TCP and Blocks Extensible Exchange Protocol (BEEP).

SOAP messages are sent using an XML format known as a SOAP envelope, with the following structure:

```
<env:Envelope xmlns:env="http://schemas.xmlsoap.org/soap/envelope/"
              xmlns:xsi="http://www.w3.org/2001/XMLSchema-instance"
              xmlns:soapenc="http://schemas.xmlsoap.org/soap/encoding/"
              xmlns:xsd="http://www.w3.org/2001/XMLSchema">
  <env:Header>...</env:Header>
  <env:Body>...</env:Body>
</env:Envelope>
```

The SOAP envelope is made up of two elements: the SOAP header and the SOAP body. While the SOAP header is an optional element, it is often used to transmit extra information about the context of the message. For example, the WS-Security specification (see http://www.oasis-open.org/committees/wss/) uses entries in the SOAP header to pass security information associated with the SOAP message. The SOAP body element contains the payload of the message.

SOAP defines two styles of operation: document and remote procedure call (RPC). The SOAP RPC style is typically associated with synchronous, request/response operations while SOAP document style is usually associated with asynchronous messaging-style operation. These categorizations are somewhat arbitrary because it is generally possible to build applications using either type of messaging paradigm with either style of operation. SOAP also defines two representations (also known as *uses*) that affect the content of the message: encoded use and literal use. The primary difference is that the literal use does not specify anything about the contents of the SOAP body (other than that its content is a valid XML document) while the encoded use defines how the different data types are encoded in the message. Technically this means that there are four distinct combinations of the interaction model and encoding, but SOAP document/literal (also called doc/literal) and SOAP rpc/encoded are the two most common mechanisms in use today—and they are only two required by the JAX-RPC 1.0 specification. WebLogic Server 8.1 supports SOAP 1.1 and 1.2, and it supports both doc/literal and rpc/encoded messages. For more information on SOAP, we refer you to one of the references listed at the beginning of the chapter.

WSDL

The Web Services Description Language (WSDL) is the specification that defines the XML-based, interface definition language used to describe Web Services (see http://www.w3.org/TR/wsdl). WSDL is intended to describe the Web Services interfaces to tools, rather than humans. One look at the WSDL description of even a simple

Web Service and you understand why. Although we will not attempt to dissect the entire WSDL 1.1 language here, we will cover the basic constructs so that you can understand how to read a WSDL document, should that be necessary.

The basic structure of a WSDL 1.1 document is shown below. WSDL documents describe Web services by starting with custom *type* definitions that are used to communicate information between the service provider and service requestor. Using these types, WSDL uses *messages* to represent the data passed to, or response returned from, a Web Service. The exchange of messages between the provider and requestor is called an *operation*. A *portType* is a collection of operation definitions. *Bindings* associate a portType with a specific protocol and message format. *Ports*, also known as service endpoints, associate physical network addresses with bindings. A *service* is just a collection of ports.

```
<definitions>
  <import>
    Other WSDL files to include
  </import>
  <documentation>
    Documentation about the web services
  </documentation>
  <types>
    Definitions of data types used by the web services
  </types>
  <message>
    Definitions of the messages sent to and/or received from
    the web services
  </message>
  <portType>
    Definitions of the operations supported by the web services
  </portType>
  <binding>
    Definitions of the web services' message formats and protocols
  </binding>
  <service>
    <port>
      Definition of the web service endpoint
    </port>
  </service>
</definition>
```

WebLogic Server 8.1 currently supports WSDL 1.1, as required by the JAX-RPC 1.0 specification.

UDDI

The Universal Description, Discovery, and Integration (UDDI) portion of the Web Services specification (see http://www.oasis-open.org/committees/uddi-spec/) defines a directory service for locating Web Services. Through the UDDI Business Registry (UBR), a public registry of Web Services information, businesses can register information about their organization, relationships with other organizations, and services that they provide. Instead of being a single, centralized registry, the UBR architecture is distributed and replicated so that many different registries may participate providing that they follow the rules laid out by the UDDI specification. Organizations can also choose to set up their own private UDDI registries that are not part of the UBR. While much of the initial hype of UDDI was around the idea of the UBR and dynamic discovery of services over the Internet, the dominant use of UDDI today appears to be focused on private registries in a single organization or across a limited set of trading partners.

UDDI also provides a programmer's API and set of associated data structures. These APIs define a set of SOAP services through which programs can query for information or publish information to a UDDI registry. As part of these SOAP services, UDDI defines a fairly complex set of data types that can be tedious to work with. Fortunately, most UDDI implementations provide a Java API for accessing these UDDI services that simplify the interaction with the UDDI registry; WebLogic Server provides such an API (see http://edocs.bea.com/wls/docs81/webserv/uddi.html). The Java API for XML Registries (JAXR) also defines a Java API for accessing a number of different types of registries, including UDDI (see http://java.sun.com/xml/jaxr/). In addition, many UDDI providers also supply some sort of tool that can be used to view and manage the UDDI registry without writing code; WebLogic Server provides the UDDI Directory Explorer for this purpose.

We will not spend any more time on UDDI because its use is fairly limited at the time of writing. WebLogic Server does provide a fully functional UDDI 2.0 implementation that you can use, as well as a UDDI browser that can be used to browse any UDDI directory.

JAX-RPC

The Java API for XML-Based RPC (JAX-RPC) specification (see http://java.sun.com/xml/jaxrpc/) defines a standard way for Java applications to develop Web Services clients and endpoints. Endpoints are just Web Services providers whose functionality is described using WSDL. JAX-RPC supports RPC and document style Web Services, as well as supporting SOAP attachments. It also defines message handlers that can be used to intercept calls on either the client or server side to augment or short-circuit the request or response. Finally, JAX-RPC provides both a strongly typed, static invocation interface and a loosely typed, dynamic invocation interface (DII) for constructing Web Services clients. WebLogic Server has full support for JAX-RPC 1.0, and all of the examples in this chapter will use the JAX-RPC interfaces. For more information on JAX-RPC, please see the online documentation at http://edocs.bea.com/wls/docs81/webserv/.

SAAJ

The SOAP with Attachments API for Java (SAAJ) 1.1 specification (see http://java.sun.com/xml/saaj/) defines a standard set of classes for creating and manipulating SOAP messages. These classes were previously defined by the Java API for XML Messaging (JAXM) specification but have been broken out into their own specification because of their more general applicability. As you might expect from the name, this specification contains the core classes needed for creating, attaching, and reading SOAP attachments from Java. For more information, please refer to the specification or the Javadocs for the `javax.xml.soap` package. WebLogic Server has full support for SAAJ 1.1, and several of the examples in this chapter will use the SAAJ APIs.

Creating Web Services with WebLogic Server

In this section, we show you how to build and deploy Web Services using WebLogic Server. Before we dive into the details, we briefly describe WebLogic Server's Web Services container architecture. Next, we discuss the general options and strategies for developing Web Services with WebLogic Server. Finally, we end this section with two detailed examples of building Web Services, one starting from Java and the other starting from WSDL.

WebLogic Server's Web Services Architecture

WebLogic Server provides a Web Services container that allows it to accept SOAP requests, dispatch these requests to the appropriate back-end components, and return SOAP responses. The Web services container architecture, shown in Figure 15.1, is based on the JAX-RPC 1.0 specification. SOAP requests are accepted and handled by the server's HTTP request processing mechanisms and dispatched to the appropriate application, as determined by the URL of the underlying HTTP request (see Chapter 11 for more information regarding this dispatching step). For all SOAP requests, a WebLogic Server-provided servlet known as the `WebServiceServlet` is the entry point into the application. It is responsible for preparing the request before dispatching it to the back-end Java component, receiving any response, and packaging it into a SOAP response.

The first step in handling the request is to invoke the `handleRequest()` method of any handlers that have been registered for the target Web Service operation. Assuming that the handlers do not short-circuit the processing, the incoming XML data is then converted into Java objects. WebLogic Server supports mapping between XML and Java for a large number of built-in data types. For data types that are not built in, this mapping is accomplished through the use of *serializers*.

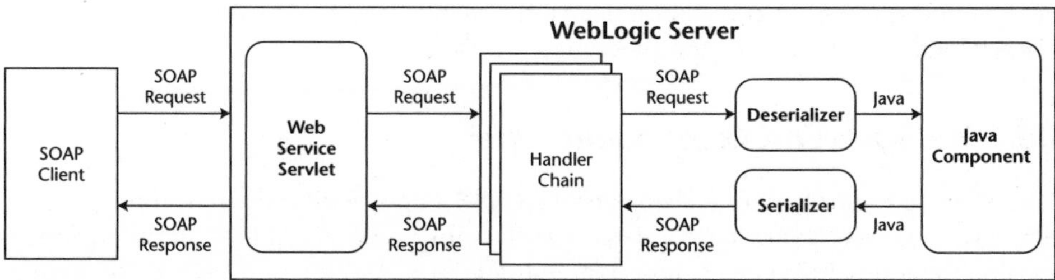

Figure 15.1 Web Services container architecture.

Serializers, and the accompanying Java classes to represent the data, can be automatically generated for most XML data using WebLogic Server's auto-typing capability. If you want more control, or if the data is too complex for the auto-typing feature, you can also write your own custom serializers and plug them into the Web Services container. For example, custom serializers can be used to map existing WSDL data structures into more convenient Java types for use in your business logic. This is shown in the customer serializer example where we map between a WSDL array of strings and a Java `ArrayList`.

Once the corresponding Java objects exist, the `WebServiceServlet` dispatches the request to the back-end component and waits for a response, if applicable. If a response is expected, the entire process is unwound by taking the response and converting the returned Java objects into XML. Again, this is accomplished either automatically for built-in data types or through the use of serializers. The `handleResponse()` method of any registered handlers is invoked in reverse order, and the resulting SOAP response is returned to the caller.

From a high level, this is really all there is to it. The WebLogic Server JAX-RPC client run time provides a mirror image of the server-side architecture. A Java client invocation is passed to serializers/deserializers, then to the handlers, and finally to the core run time that makes the actual invocation. Responses unwind through the same steps until they are returned to the Java client. Of course, we have skipped over a lot of the details that make writing a Web Services container hard. Fortunately, you don't need to worry about these details because WebLogic Server handles them for you. Now, let's look at the basic mechanisms you use to write your own Web Service.

Developing Web Services with WebLogic Server

When designing a Web Service, the most important thing is to define the right interface. What are the things to consider when designing the interface? The answer to this question will be discussed in various places throughout the rest of the chapter, but suffice it to say that it is something of an art. We will look at a few guidelines to use in defining Web Services interfaces in the "Adding Web Services to *bigrez.com*" section at the end of the chapter. For now, we will assume that the interface decisions have been made and now all you need to do is map that into a Web Service running in WebLogic Server.

In this section, we discuss the options at your disposal when building a Web Service. We begin with the types of back-end components that can be exposed as a Web Service, followed by the options for handling data type mapping. We follow this with the basic steps to build a Web Service, starting from either a Java interface or WSDL. This section ends with a discussion of building Web Services clients.

Choosing Back-End Component Types

When starting to implement a Web Service in WebLogic Server, the first thing to consider is what type of back-end component will be used. WebLogic Server 8.1 supports exposing the following types of components as Web Services:

- Stateless session Enterprise Java Beans
- Java objects
- JMS destinations

Determining the type of component to use is not always clear-cut. While we talk about some of the things to consider here, other factors will be discussed throughout the chapter that can affect this decision process.

WebLogic Server can expose the methods on a stateless session bean's remote interface as Web Service operations. Using an EJB gives your Web Service all of the traditional benefits of the EJB container including component-level security, transactions, persistence (when used in conjunction with entity beans), and concurrency control. Because each Web Service invocation is ultimately dispatched to the stateless session bean, you can depend on the semantic guarantees of EJB when writing the Web Service's business logic. The only real drawback in using a stateless session bean is the additional steps necessary to write an EJB versus a regular Java object. Because most Java IDEs support EJB development, we feel that the benefits of using an EJB generally outweigh any extra development effort.

You can expose the public methods on a regular Java class as Web Service operations in a similar manner to exposing the methods of a stateless session bean; however, you lose all of the advantages that the EJB container provides. Your Java class must meet several requirements, the most daunting of which is that your Java code must be thread-safe. The Web Services container creates a single instance of the Java class and dispatches all requests concurrently to that single instance. This does not necessarily impose any performance or scalability limitations. This is the same model used by servlet containers. It simply means that your code must be written with thread-safety in mind. Any synchronization points required to prevent data corruption can affect performance and scalability. The requirements for the Java class are as follows:

- Do not start any threads (this is not specific to Web Services and is a best practice for all server-side components).
- Provide a default, no-args constructor.
- Make public any operations that are to be exposed as Web Services.
- Write the code in a thread-safe manner.

WebLogic Server also allows you to expose a JMS destination directly as a Web Service. Each of these JMS Web Services allows the caller either to send a message to or receive a message from a JMS destination. This capability gives you some basic mechanisms by which you could build asynchronous Web Services. There are several issues to keep in mind, though, when you are considering this capability.

First, a Web Service that sends a message to a JMS destination must be an asynchronous, one-way operation. This means that the caller receives no indication of whether the server was able to process the message after it is delivered to the JMS destination. This is normal behavior for asynchronous processing. You need to write your application to handle error conditions in both the client and the back-end component processing the message. One way to do this is to write the message-driven bean that is processing the requests to always handle any exceptions and generate the appropriate error messages that will be sent back to the client.

Second, a Web Service call to receive a message does not provide a mechanism for the client to get a specific message. In normal JMS applications, you would use a message correlation ID, a temporary reply-to destination, or similar mechanism so that each client could be assured that it was receiving responses to requests that it sent. A Web Service client that receives a message from a JMS destination will get the first message in the destination. For applications where the only client is another application, the client might be expected to correlate the responses itself if it is sending multiple concurrent requests. Of course, for almost any application scenario that involves multiple processes making concurrent Web Service invocations, this limitation will be a significant issue. The current WebLogic Server Web Service implementation does not provide any support for the client to pass in any information to identify the specific message(s) in which they are interested. Therefore, any Web Services client that is dequeuing messages via a Web Service must be able to process any message in the JMS destination and not just ones associated with some previous request sent by that specific client.

Finally, many production sites will use distributed JMS destinations to allow the application's JMS destinations to be highly available. This works against us when a remote JMS client tries to dequeue a specific message from a distributed destination. The problem comes down to the fact that the caller will be associated with one of the physical member queues when making the dequeue request, but the member queue chosen by WebLogic JMS may not, in fact, be the one that contains the messages that the caller is trying to find. This means that the Web Service used to retrieve a JMS-based Web Service response must be associated with a physical destination in order to make sure that all of the responses are visible. While this is not a show-stopper, it does mean that you must use extra care in designing a Web Sservice-based application that retrieves JMS messages to guarantee the scalability, availability, and fault tolerance of the application.

As you will see in the "Adding Web Services to *bigrez.com*" section, we have chosen not to use JMS destinations directly as the back-end components in our *bigrez.com* site. We could have easily used them to accept incoming requests and used another mechanism to return the responses. See the "Adding Web Services to *bigrez.com*" section of this chapter for more information about why we have not used JMS destinations as Web services endpoints.

Handling Data Types

WebLogic Server provides mapping support between Java and XML for a large number of data types, including all of the built-in types defined by the JAX-RPC specification. For these data types, WebLogic Server automatically converts between Java and XML. For all other data types, custom serializer classes are used to perform the mapping. Using these non-built-in data types requires that you perform the following steps:

1. Write an XML schema representation of your data type.
2. Write the Java class that represents your data type.
3. Write the Java serializer class to handle the bi-directional conversion between XML and Java using the WebLogic XML Streaming API.
4. Update the `web-services.xml` with the data type information.

We will go through the details of these steps later in the chapter. You may never need to create serializers manually. WebLogic Server provides an auto-typing mechanism that will create serializers automatically via introspection of the Java classes that represent the data type. Through this auto-typing mechanism, WebLogic Server can perform the four steps listed here for virtually any Java object that can be represented using XML schema. This auto-typing feature is accessed through either the `servicegen` or `autotype` Ant tasks, which we will be using in our examples throughout the rest of this chapter.

Starting with Java

The most straightforward way to create a Web Service with WebLogic Server is to start by creating the Java component or EJB that implements the Web Service's functionality. Although the steps required to create the Web Service vary depending on the type, the main steps you go through to create your Web Service are as follows:

1. Write, compile, and package the Java code for the back-end components that provide the business logic for the Web Service.
2. For back-end components that use non-built-in data types, create the serialization classes required to convert the data between the Java and XML representations.
3. Create the `web-services.xml` deployment descriptor that describes the Web Service's deployment characteristics.
4. If the Web Service's clients will use the WebLogic Server Web Services client to access the Web Service, create the client jar file for the Web Service.
5. Package everything into a deployable ear file.

Fortunately, WebLogic Server provides a set of Ant tasks that can be used to automate steps 2 through 5. Typically, you will simply use the `servicegen` task that performs all of these steps. In some cases, it may be necessary to have more control over the process. For example, you may need to modify the deployment descriptor to modify the Web Service's functionality. In these types of scenarios, WebLogic Server provides four single-purpose Ant tasks that can be used to perform each step individually. The tasks are `autotype`, `source2wsdd`, `clientgen`, and `wspackage`, and each one performs one of the four steps (that is, steps 2 through 5, respectively) required to turn your back-end component into a deployable Web Service. Shortly, we will walk through an example that illustrates the use of `servicegen`. As we start building more complex examples, we will make use of the individual Ant tasks that make up the `servicegen` task.

Starting with WSDL

Occasionally, you need to create a Web Service that complies with a predefined interface written in WSDL. This requirement can arise for many reasons. It may be something as simple as wanting to upgrade or replace an existing application without breaking its interface contract. As we will see later in our *bigrez.com* example, it can also be the result of wanting to integrate with an application that implements asynchronous Web Services. To create a Web Service starting with WSDL, the main steps you go through are as follows:

1. For a WSDL description of a Web Service that uses non-built-in types, create the Java versions of those types and the serialization classes used to convert between Java and XML representations.
2. Create the back-end components that implement the operations defined by the WSDL description.
3. Create the `web-services.xml` deployment descriptor.
4. If the Web Service's clients will use the WebLogic Server Web Services client to access the Web Service, create the client jar file for the Web Service.
5. Package everything into a deployable ear file.

Again, WebLogic Server provides a set of Ant tasks that can be used to automate most of the process. The `autotype` task mentioned previously generates the Java versions of WSDL-defined types, the serialization classes, and an XML description of the types that will be used to create the type mapping information in the `web-services.xml` deployment descriptor. Once you have the type information, the `wsdl2service` task generates both a Java interface that represents the Java implementation of the Web Service operations defined by the WSDL and the `web-services.xml` deployment descriptor. If you want to include a downloadable client jar file, use the `clientgen` task to create the jar file from the WSDL. Once you have implemented the Java class that implements the generated interface, the `wspackage` task creates the deployable ear file. We will look at an example of how to do this shortly.

Writing Web Services Clients

When writing J2EE applications, you often need to access other back-end services (for example, a database or credit card authorization service) to access application data or functionality. With the introduction of Web Services, you may find that some of the back-end services you need to access are available only via a Web Service interface. You may also find that you need to write Java clients to access your WebLogic Server-hosted Web Services. Fortunately, WebLogic Server makes both of these jobs possible using its implementation of the JAX-RPC client run time.

With JAX-RPC, there are three different ways to write a client. *Static clients* are the simplest in that they provide a strongly typed Java interface to access the Web Service functionality. WebLogic Server provides the `clientgen` Ant task to generate the Web Service-specific classes needed to invoke a Web Service statically. Using either the WSDL or the WebLogic Server deployable Web Service ear file as input, `clientgen` creates a jar file containing the JAX-RPC Service implementation and the service-specific stub that a Java client will use to invoke the Web Service. The next method involves using *dynamic proxies* to invoke the Web Service. With dynamic proxies, no generated stub class is required, but you still get a strongly typed stub by generating a dynamic proxy that matches the interface of the service endpoint. JAX-RPC also provides a third mechanism for invoking Web Services that is similar to the Java Refection

APIs for invoking Java methods: *dynamic clients*. When writing dynamic clients, you don't need to use `clientgen` because no Web Service-specific classes are needed by the client.

WebLogic Server 8.1 provides three different JAX-RPC client run-time jar files that you can use to invoke Web Services hosted in any SOAP-compatible container; the one you need depends on your client, as shown here:

webserviceclient.jar. This jar file contains the WebLogic Server implementation of the JAX-RPC run time.

webserviceclient+ssl.jar. This jar file contains the WebLogic Server implementation of the JAX-RPC run time and SSL libraries.

webserviceclient+ssl_pj.jar. This jar file contains the WebLogic Server implementation of the JAX-RPC run time and SSL libraries for the CDC profile of J2ME.

One of the big advantages of using Web Services is that the client and Web Service implementation do not need to be using the same vendor's run times, or even the same programming language. We will provide examples of how to create and run both Java and Microsoft VisualBasic.NET clients later in this chapter.

Creating a Web Service Starting with Java

For the purposes of our initial discussions, we focus on simple Web Services that allow you to concentrate on the mechanics of building Web Services rather than the details of the business logic. Rest assured that the *bigrez.com* Web Services in the final section provides enough real-world complexity to understand the capabilities of WebLogic Server's Web Services support.

Suppose that we want to write a Web Service that supports searching for hotels by location. Let's start out by building a stand-alone Web Services application to do this. The complete example can be found in the Chapter 15 examples on the companion Web site (http://www.wiley.com/compbooks/masteringweblogic). Our Web Service will access the *bigrez.com* database directly rather than modifying the existing application to access it through our entity beans. The first step is to define the input and output data. We want to allow searching by city and/or state, or by zip code. The results will contain zero or more objects that contain information about each matching hotel. The Java objects that we use to represent the results are shown in Listings 15.1 and 15.2. Notice that each object is serializable and contains a default, no-args constructor and get and set methods for each attribute. This is required if you choose to use the `servicegen` (or `autotype`) Ant task to create your serializer classes automatically.

```
package mastering.weblogic.ch15.example1;

public class PropertyInfo implements java.io.Serializable
{
    private int id;
    private String description;
```

Listing 15.1 PropertyInfo.java. *(continued)*

```
    private String features;
    private String address1;
    private String address2;
    private String city;
    private String state;
    private String postalCode;
    private String phone;

    public PropertyInfo() { }
    public PropertyInfo(int id, String description, String features,
                        String address1, String address2, String city,
                        String state, String postalCode, String phone)
{
        this.id = id;
        this.description = description;
        this.features = features;
        this.address1 = address1;
        this.address2 = address2;
        this.city = city;
        this.state = state;
        this.postalCode = postalCode;
        this.phone = phone;
    }

    public int getId() { return id; }
    public void setId(int id) { this.id = id; }
    public String getDescription() { return description; }
    public void setDescription(String description)
        { this.description = description; }
    public String getFeatures() { return features; }
    public void setFeatures(String features)
        { this.features = features; }
    public String getAddress1() { return address1; }
    public void setAddress1(String address1)
        { this.address1 = address1; }
    public String getAddress2() { return address2; }
    public void setAddress2(String address2)
        { this.address2 = address2; }
    public String getCity() { return city; }
    public void setCity(String city) { this.city = city; }
    public String getState() { return state; }
    public void setState(String state) { this.state = state; }
    public String getPostalCode() { return postalCode; }
    public void setPostalCode(String postalCode)
        { this.postalCode = postalCode; }
    public String getPhone() { return phone; }
    public void setPhone(String phone) { this.phone = phone; }
}
```

Listing 15.1 *(continued)*

```
package mastering.weblogic.ch15.example1;

public class PropertySearchResults implements java.io.Serializable
{
    private String city;
    private String state;
    private String zip;
    private PropertyInfo[] properties;

    public PropertySearchResults() { }
    public PropertySearchResults(String city, String state,
                                 String zip, PropertyInfo[] properties)
    {
        this.city = city;
        this.state = state;
        this.zip = zip;
        this.properties = properties;
    }

    public String getCity() { return city; }
    public void setCity(String city) { this.city = city; }
    public String getState() { return state; }
    public void setState(String state) { this.state = state; }
    public String getZip() { return zip; }
    public void setZip(String zip) { this.zip = zip; }
    public PropertyInfo[] getProperties() { return properties; }
    public void setProperties(PropertyInfo[] properties)
        { this.properties = properties; }
}
```

Listing 15.2 PropertySearchResults.java.

Next, we will create a simple Java class to process the request. Our `PropertySearchServiceImpl` class, shown in Listing 15.3, exposes two public methods, `findByCityState()` and `findByZip()`, that will be turned into operations on our Web Service. The business logic is simplistic in that it looks for exact matches and ignores exceptions. Notice that we have been extra careful to make sure that the class is thread-safe—this is an important requirement for any regular Java class that you want to expose as a Web Service. If you would rather not worry about thread-safety, then you need to use an EJB instead.

```
package mastering.weblogic.ch15.example1;

import java.sql.Connection;
import java.sql.PreparedStatement;
import java.sql.ResultSet;
```

Listing 15.3 PropertySearch.java. *(continued)*

```
import java.sql.SQLException;
import javax.naming.InitialContext;
import javax.naming.NamingException;
import javax.sql.DataSource;

public class PropertySearchServiceImpl
{
    private static final String DS_JNDI_NAME = "BigRezDataSource";

    private static final String CITY_STATE_SQL =
        "SELECT id, description, features, address1, address2, city, " +
        "statecode, postalcode, phone FROM property WHERE city = ? " +
        "AND statecode = ?";
    private static final String ZIP_SQL =
        "SELECT id, description, features, address1, address2, city, " +
        "statecode, postalcode, phone FROM property WHERE " +
        "postalcode = ?";

    private DataSource dataSource;

    public PropertySearchServiceImpl()
    {
        getDataSource(); // try to pre-fetch the DataSource from JNDI
    }

    public PropertySearchResults findByCityState(String city,
                                                  String state)
    {
        PropertySearchResults results = new PropertySearchResults();
        results.setCity(city);
        results.setState(state);

        Connection conn = null;
        PreparedStatement ps = null;
        ResultSet rs = null;
        try {
            conn = getDataSource().getConnection();
            ps = conn.prepareStatement(CITY_STATE_SQL);
            ps.setString(1, city);
            ps.setString(2, state);
            rs = ps.executeQuery();
            results.setProperties(processResults(rs));
        }
        catch (Exception ignore) {
            ignore.printStackTrace();
            // Show how to handle expections later...
        }
        finally { closeDatabaseResources(conn, ps, rs); }
        return results;
```

Listing 15.3 *(continued)*

```
    }

    public PropertySearchResults findByZip(String zip)
    {
        PropertySearchResults results = new PropertySearchResults();
        results.setZip(zip);

        Connection conn = null;
        PreparedStatement ps = null;
        ResultSet rs = null;
        try {
            conn = getDataSource().getConnection();
            ps = conn.prepareStatement(ZIP_SQL);
            ps.setString(1, zip);
            rs = ps.executeQuery();
            results.setProperties(processResults(rs));
        }
        catch (Exception ignore) {
            ignore.printStackTrace();
            // Show how to handle exceptions later...
        }
        finally { closeDatabaseResources(conn, ps, rs); }
        return results;
    }

    private DataSource getDataSource()
    {
        // Instead of using locks, we accept the fact that multiple
        // threads might do the lookup concurrently. This is okay since
        // all threads will set dataSource to an equivalent value. The
        // first call should be from the constructor so dataSource
        // should already be set before multiple threads start invoking
        // this method.
        //
        if (dataSource == null) {
            try {
                InitialContext ctx = new InitialContext();
                dataSource = (DataSource)ctx.lookup(DS_JNDI_NAME);
            }
            catch (NamingException ignore) {  }
        }
        return dataSource;
    }

    private PropertyInfo[] processResults(ResultSet rs)
        throws SQLException
    {
        java.util.ArrayList list = new java.util.ArrayList();
        while (rs.next()) {
```

Listing 15.3 *(continued)*

```
            PropertyInfo property =
                new PropertyInfo(rs.getInt(1), rs.getString(2),
                                 rs.getString(3), rs.getString(4),
                                 rs.getString(5), rs.getString(6),
                                 rs.getString(7), rs.getString(8),
                                 rs.getString(9));
                list.add(property);
        }
        int len = list.size();
        PropertyInfo[] properties = new PropertyInfo[len];
        for (int i = 0; i < len; i++)
            properties[i] = (PropertyInfo)list.get(i);
        return properties;
    }

    private void closeDatabaseResources(Connection conn,
                                        PreparedStatement ps,
                                        ResultSet rs)
    {
        if (rs != null)
            try { rs.close(); } catch(SQLException ignore) { }
        if (ps != null)
            try { ps.close(); } catch(SQLException ignore) { }
        if (conn != null)
            try { conn.close(); } catch(SQLException ignore) { }
    }
}
```

Listing 15.3 *(continued)*

The only thing left to do is to build and deploy the Web Service. After compiling our three classes, we will use the WebLogic Server-provided `servicegen` Ant task to generate our ear file. Let's take a look at the `servicegen` task definition located in the `compile_example1` task in this chapter's `build.xml` file:

```
<property name="src" value="${basedir}/src"/>
<property name="build" value="${basedir}/build"/>
<property name="pkg_base" value="mastering.weblogic.ch15.example"/>
<property name="svc_name" value="PropertySearchService"/>

...

<servicegen classpathref="dev.class.path" destEar="ch15_example1.ear"
            contextURI="/ch15_example1">
  <service javaClassComponents="${pkg_base}1.${svc_name}Impl"
           targetNamespace="http://www.bigrez.com/ch15/example1/"
           serviceName="${svc_name}" serviceURI="/${svc_name}">
    <client useServerTypes="true" packageName="${pkg_base}1"/>
  </service>
</servicegen>
```

Using this task definition, servicegen will create a Web Service called Property-SearchService that will be accessible through the URI /ch15_example1/PropertySearchService on whatever server we deploy it. In addition to creating our Web Service, WebLogic Server provides a dynamically generated home page for the Web Service, the dynamically generated WSDL describing the Web Service, and a downloadable client jar file containing the stubs for statically invoking the Web Service from Java using the JAX-RPC programming model. The home page is accessible using the URL of the Web Service, which is a combination of the ContextURI and the ServiceURI in the servicegen task (for example, http://localhost:7001/ch15_examples/PropertySearchService). To access the WSDL, simply append the parameter WSDL to the home page URL (for example, http://localhost:7001/ch15_examples/PropertySearchService?WSDL). Before we move on, let's take a minute to look under the covers at exactly what servicegen did for us.

First, servicegen examined our public methods in our PropertySearch ServiceImpl class to determine the data types of the arguments and return types. Seeing that both methods use built-in types for arguments, servicegen had to be concerned only with the PropertySearchResults type being used by both operations as their return values. Because PropertySearchResults also contains an array of the nonbuilt-in type PropertyInfo, servicegen created the XML schema description of three types for us: PropertyInfo, PropertyInfo[], and Property SearchResults. In addition, servicegen also created a serializer and holder class for each of the three nonbuilt-in types. The serializer classes, with names like PropertyInfoCodec, handle the conversion of the data between Java and XML. *Holder classes* are the classes defined by JAX-RPC that you use to handle Web Services that use in-out and out parameters as arguments in order to return multiple results. Holder classes are not needed in our current example.

Next, servicegen generated our web-services.xml deployment descriptor (which is packaged as part of the Web application contained in the generated ear file). In many situations, you never have to worry about what is contained in the Web Services deployment descriptor, so we will not spend time looking at it just yet. Suffice it to say that it contains all of the information about the types, the operations, the Web Services, and their URIs for WebLogic Server to be able to deploy the Web Services and generate their WSDL dynamically.

Optionally, servicegen can generate a client jar file that contains the Web Service-specific classes needed to invoke the Web Service statically from a client using the JAX-RPC programming model. This jar file, in conjunction with one of the three JAX-RPC client run-time jar files we discussed previously, is all you need on the client. Of course, nothing says that you have to use these classes to invoke a Web Service. Numerous other tools and servers support Web services. These are provided for your convenience should you choose to use them. Shortly, we will use these jar files to write a simple client to test the Web Service we just wrote.

Finally, servicegen creates the Web application and enterprise application deployment descriptors and packages everything up into a deployable ear file. This step is really just a convenience for situations where your Web Service does not include a bunch of other auxiliary files that need to be packaged with it. As we will see later, many times the limitations of `servicegen` in packaging capabilities make it necessary to resort to the WebLogic Server-provided `wspackage` Ant task, or even assembling the pieces manually using the built-in `war` and `ear` tasks provided by Ant. Fortunately, we already know all we need to know about automating the creation of Web and enterprise applications, so this really isn't a problem.

Before we move on to discuss creating a Web service to match an existing WSDL description of it, let's test our Web service. Because our Web service is relatively simple, we can use the test pages that WebLogic Server generates for us, as shown in Figure 15.2. The home page is accessible through a URL of the form `http://<hostname>:<port>/<contextURI>/<serviceURI>`. Because we set the `contextURI` to `/ch15_example1` and the `ServiceURI` to `/PropertySearchService` in our `servicegen` task, the URL of our home page is http://localhost:7001/ch15_example1/PropertySearchService. If you forget the URL or are having trouble accessing your Web Service home page, you can find a link to it on the `Testing` tab for the Web application containing your Web Service (for example, `Deployments->Applications->ch15_example1->/ch15_example1` in the left-hand navigation bar) in the WebLogic Console.

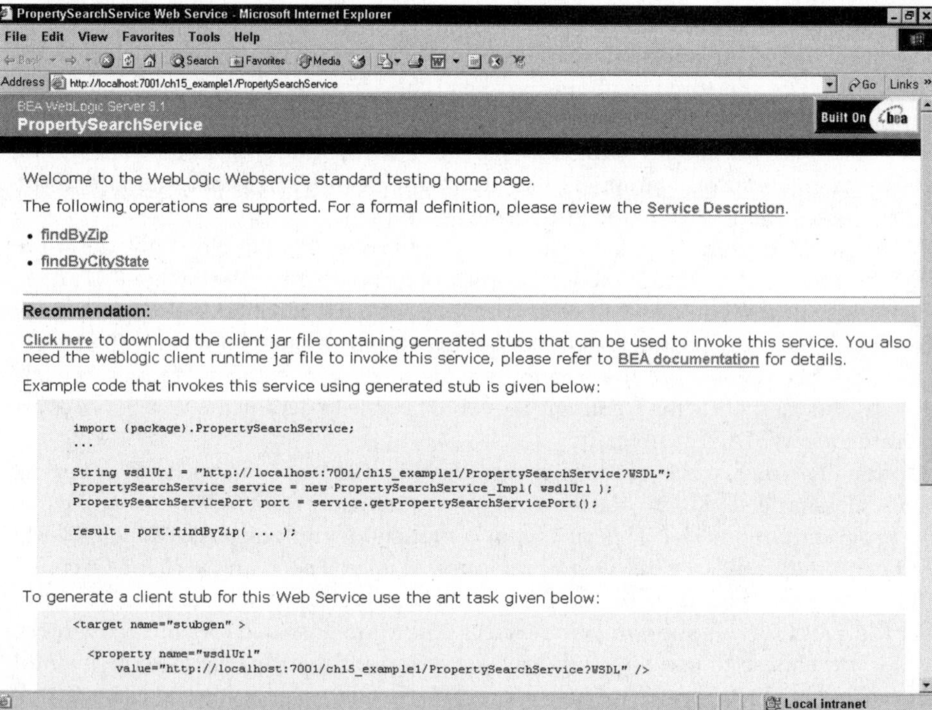

Figure 15.2 Viewing the Web Service home page.

From this page, selecting the `findByZip` link will take you to the input screen for our `findByZip()` operation. If we type in the zip code `55401` and invoke the Web Service, we will get back a results page similar to the one shown in Figure 15.3. As you can see, the test results page shows that the service found one hotel for zip code `55401`. Fortunately, most hotel Web sites don't search on zip codes by exact match. Now, let's look at writing a Web Service starting from WSDL.

Creating a Web Service Starting with WSDL

Suppose that we have an important potential partner organization that has applications already written to consume a property search Web Service from one of our competitors. As part of a big business deal to convince them to switch to our hotels, the CEO has agreed to modify our Web Service to match the WSDL of our competitor. In the interest of conserving space, we have chosen a WSDL document that is compatible with our Web Service implementation from the previous section. That way, we can spend our time looking at the mechanics rather than the details of the business logic. We'll begin with the `PropertySearchService.wsdl` file for this example, available in the downloadable code at http://www.wiley.com/compbooks/masteringweblogic.

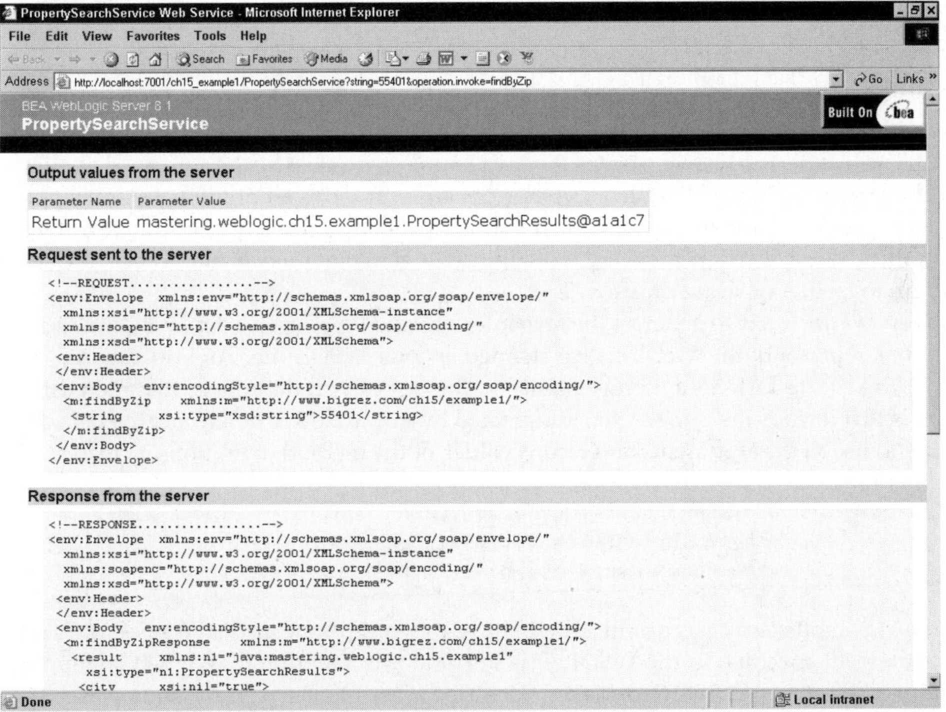

Figure 15.3 Testing Web Service operations.

WebLogic Server provides the wsdl2service Ant task that can take a WSDL document and produce the corresponding Java interface. Once we have the interface, all we have to do is implement it, package it, and deploy it. So, let's get started. Because our WSDL defines some non-built-in data types, the first thing we need to do is to generate the type information that wsdl2service requires. Fortunately, the autotype Ant task is specifically designed for this purpose. For each type defined in the WSDL document, autotype can generate the Java class representing that type, the serialization and holder classes, and the type definition and mapping information we need in the web-services.xml deployment descriptor.

Let's take a look at the autotype task definition that generates the type information:

```
<property name="src" value="${basedir}/src"/>
<property name="types" value="${basedir}/types"/>
<property name="pkg_base" value="mastering.weblogic.ch15.example"/>
<property name="pkg_base_dir" value="mastering/weblogic/ch15/example"/>
<property name="example2_wsdl"
          value="${src}/${pkg_base_dir}2/PropertySearchService.wsdl"/>

...

<autotype classpathref="dev.class.path" wsdl="${example2_wsdl}"
          targetNamespace="http://www.bigrez.com/ch15/example2/"
          packageName="${pkg_base}2" destDir="${types}"/>
```

We simply specify the WSDL file name (or URL), the target namespace for any types created, the package name to use for the generated Java types, and the output directory. The autotype task generates the Java source code classes, the compiled versions of those classes, and a file called types.xml that provides all of the type description and mapping information. Notice that we use a separate directory for the autotype output. The wspackage task that we will use to generate the ear file expects the serializers to be in a separate directory.

Now we are ready to generate the Java interface and Web Service deployment descriptor that represents the Web Service defined in our WSDL file. As you can see, the wsdl2service task definition is similar to the autotype definition; the main difference is that it reads the types.xml file created by autotype to determine the Java data types to use as the arguments and return values of the method definitions it creates:

```
<wsdl2service classpathref="dev.class.path" wsdl="${example2_wsdl}"
              typeMappingFile="${types}/types.xml"
              packageName="${pkg_base}2" destDir="${src}"/>
```

The Java interface class produced will have the same name as the Web Service's service element specified in the WSDL. It is important to mention that, when generating the web-services.xml deployment descriptor, wsdl2service assumes that you will be using a Java class to implement the service and that the name of that class will be of the form <packageName>.<serviceName>Impl. If either of these is not true, then you will need to edit the <components> section of the deployment descriptor accordingly. We hope that future versions of the wsdl2service will provide configurable attributes to control these assumptions, thus eliminating the need to edit the deployment descriptor should your implementation not match the assumptions.

We are now ready to implement our Web Service. Because we chose the WSDL to be compatible with our previous example, we simply took the code shown in Listing 15.3 and changed the package name to mastering.weblogic.ch15.example2. Once that is compiled, we can move on to the next step.

If desired, we can generate the client jar file using the clientgen task. As you might expect, clientgen simply inspects the WSDL and generates all of the Web service-specific classes that a JAX-RPC client would need to invoke the Web Service statically. For completeness, the clientgen task is shown here:

```
<clientgen classpathref="dev.class.path" wsdl="${example2_wsdl}"
           packageName="${pkg_base}2"
           clientJar="${src}/${pkg_base_dir}2/${svc_name}_client.jar"/>
```

Finally, we are ready to package the different elements of the Web Service implementation into a deployable ear file. WebLogic Server provides the wspackage task for this purpose. Let's look at our Ant script fragment dealing with packaging the Web Service:

```
<delete quiet="true">
  <fileset dir="${types}">
    <include name="**/*.java"/>
    <include name="types.xml"/>
  </fileset>
</delete>
<wspackage classpathref="dev.class.path" ddFile="${src}/web-
services.xml"
           contextURI="/ch15_example2" codecDir="${types}"
           filesToWar="${src}/${pkg_base_dir}2/${svc_name}_client.jar"
           webAppClasses="${pkg_base}2.${svc_name},
                          ${pkg_base}2.${svc_name}Impl"
           output="ch15_example2.ear"/>
```

First, we remove all of the Java source files and the types.xml from the types directory hierarchy. We do this because the wspackage task simply takes everything in the directory specified by the codecDir attribute and adds it to the Web application's WEB-INF/classes directory; this is why we chose to use a separate output directory for the autotype task. The wspackage task provides arguments that allow you to insert files almost anywhere you want in the enterprise and Web application hierarchy. For example, webAppClasses specifies other classes to place in the WEB-INF/classes directory while filesToWar specifies the files to place in the root directory of the Web application. The wspackage task should satisfy many of your Web Service application packaging needs; however, we will see in later examples that certain packaging requirements require assembling the application manually.

Once we deploy our packaged application, we can once again use the WebLogic Server-provided testing pages to verify that our Web Service is indeed functioning correctly. Now, let's spend a little time looking at how to write code that invokes a Web Service.

Creating Web Service Clients with WebLogic Server

In this section, we will briefly look at how to write a Web Service client. As we mentioned previously, JAX-RPC provides three different client-side programming models for invoking Web Services: the strongly typed, static-invocation model using generated stubs, dynamic proxies, and the loosely typed, dynamic-invocation model. In addition, WebLogic Server adds some client-side functionality that extends the JAX-RPC specification to allow the construction of more robust enterprise Web Service applications through asynchronous invocation and portable stubs. We will examine each of these mechanisms in the context of invoking a Web Service. We'll review each of the three models before presenting our recommendations for their use.

Rather than writing a client for a WebLogic Server-hosted Web Service, we are going to make use of a sample Web Service to calculate the distance between two zip codes. This Zip Distance Calculator Web Service is not intended for commercial purposes and is hosted by Imacination Software (http://www.imacination.com). The home page for this Web Service is available at http://webservices.imacination.com/distance/, and the WSDL URL is http://webservices.imacination.com/distance/Distance.jws?wsdl.

JAX-RPC defines four primary object types that clients use to invoke Web Services: `ServiceFactory`, `Service`, `Stub`, and `Call`. All of these objects are part of the `javax.xml.rpc` package. Which objects are used and whether the client application uses the objects directly or indirectly depend on which programming model the client uses. The list that follows summarizes the purpose each object serves in the JAX-RPC model:

ServiceFactory. This object is the factory through which clients can create an instance of the `Service` object without having to use the constructor of the `Service` implementation class.

Service. This object represents the Web Service and acts as a factory for the `Stub` and `Call` objects.

Stub. This object represents the service endpoint (also known as the port) on which any operations will be invoked.

Call. This object represents an invocation of an operation that is performed using the dynamic invocation model.

Using Generated Stubs

The JAX-RPC static invocation model uses generated classes that implement the `Service` and `Stub` objects and expose the operations of the Web Service endpoint as Java method calls. Using the `clientgen` Ant task, we generate our Zip Distance

Calculator Web Service client jar file using the WSDL as input. If you look inside the generated jar file, you will see the file structure shown in Figure 15.4 (the listing omits the Java source files that are also included by default).

WebLogic Server has generated everything we need to invoke the operations on the service endpoint. If the Web Service had defined nonbuilt-in types, `clientgen` would have generated the Java implementation, the serializer, and the holder classes, and it would have put the mapping information into the `DistanceServices.xml` file that is used by WebLogic Server's implementation of the client-side JAX-RPC run time. If we look at the `Distance` interface, we see six methods that correspond to the six operations defined in the WSDL. To invoke one of those methods, all we need to do is create the `Service` object, get the service endpoint, and invoke the operation, as shown:

```
private static final String WSDL_LOCATION =
    "http://webservices.imacination.com/distance/Distance.jws?wsdl";

...

DistanceService service = new DistanceService_Impl(WSDL_LOCATION);
Distance port = service.getDistance();
double distance = port.getDistance(zip1, zip2);
```

The complete program is available as part of Chapter 15's examples on the companion Web site (http://www.wiley.com/compbooks/masteringweblogic).

As a convenience and a performance booster, `clientgen` packages a copy of the WSDL in the client jar file. To take advantage of this, simply instantiate the new `DistanceService_Impl` instance using the no-args constructor. If you were to look at the generated Java code, you would see that this causes the instance to use the WSDL file included in the client jar file rather than making a separate call to the server to get the WSDL before it invokes the service.

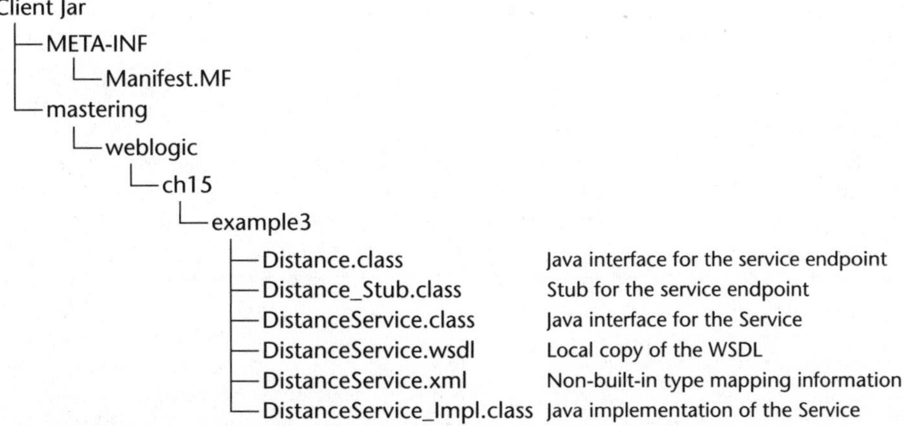

Figure 15.4 Client-specific jar file contents.

BEST PRACTICE **When using generated stubs, use the no-args constructor to create the service object to prevent an extra call to the server to retrieve the WSDL.**

Using Dynamic Proxies

Dynamic proxies are used to write a Web Service client that is independent of the underlying JAX-RPC run time while still providing a strongly typed interface for the service endpoint. To use this model, you will still need to have a Java interface that accurately represents the Web Service endpoint operations. You can either write this interface yourself using the JAX-RPC WSDL to Java mapping specification or use a tool to generate it for you. In our example, we use the `Distance` interface generated by `clientgen` in the previous section.

When writing a client that uses dynamic proxies, the first thing you need to do is create the `Service` object. Typically, you do this by using the `ServiceFactory` object. Because `javax.xml.rpc.ServiceFactory` is an abstract class, you must set a Java system property that specifies the name of your JAX-RPC run time's `ServiceFactory` implementation class. The name of this system property is `javax.xml.rpc.ServiceFactory`; the `ServiceFactory` class has a static attribute named `SERVICEFACTORY_PROPERTY` that contains this value. Once you have set this property, use the `newInstance()` and `createService()` methods to create the `Service` object. Now that you have the `Service` object, it is simply a matter of creating the dynamic proxy for the service endpoint by specifying the port name and the interface class that the dynamic proxy should implement. These code fragments from our next example illustrate the important steps in the process:

```
import java.net.URL;
import javax.xml.namespace.QName;
import javax.xml.rpc.Service;
import javax.xml.rpc.ServiceFactory;

...

private static final String WSDL_LOCATION =
    "http://webservices.imacination.com/distance/Distance.jws?wsdl";
private static final String TARGET_NAMESPACE =
    "http://webservices.imacination.com/distance/Distance.jws";
private static final String SERVICE_NAME = "DistanceService";
private static final String PORT_NAME = "Distance";

...

System.setProperty(ServiceFactory.SERVICEFACTORY_PROPERTY,
                   "weblogic.webservice.core.rpc.ServiceFactoryImpl");
ServiceFactory factory = ServiceFactory.newInstance();
QName serviceName = new QName(TARGET_NAMESPACE, SERVICE_NAME);
URL wsdlLocation = new URL(WSDL_LOCATION);
```

```
Service service = factory.createService(wsdlLocation, serviceName);

QName portName = new QName(TARGET_NAMESPACE, PORT_NAME);
Distance port = (Distance)service.getPort(portName, Distance.class);
double distance = port.getDistance(zip1, zip2);
```

When you have nonbuilt-in data types, you still need Java classes that represent the nonbuilt-in types and serializer classes that convert between their XML and Java representations. Because the `Service` object is dynamically created, you need to register all of the type mapping information using the `TypeMappingRegistry` object associated with the `Service` object.

All of this can theoretically be done in a JAX-RPC client run-time-independent way if you are willing to do all the necessary work. Unfortunately, standardization of the serialization framework is not covered by the JAX-RPC 1.0 specification. In addition, each run-time implementation tends to use a specific type of parser for processing the XML – WebLogic Server's run time uses a streaming parser. This means that your deserialization classes would need to be able to handle the type of parser used by the particular run-time implementation.

WARNING Because the JAX-RPC 1.0 specification does not standardize a serialization framework to convert between Java and XML, any dynamic proxy or dynamic invocation clients that invoke Web Services that require the use of nonbuilt-in Java data types will be dependent on the underlying JAX-RPC client run-time implementation.

Using Dynamic Invocation

Dynamic invocation takes the dynamic proxy model a step further by removing the need to have a predefined interface that represents the Web Service endpoint. With this model, the `Call` object replaces the strongly typed service endpoint. It is the client application programmer's responsibility to configure the `Call` object properly and to supply the correct arguments when invoking the operation. The code fragment that follows shows the important elements of our dynamic invocation client for the Zip Distance Calculator Web Service:

```
import java.net.URL;
import javax.xml.namespace.QName;
import javax.xml.rpc.Call;
import javax.xml.rpc.Service;
import javax.xml.rpc.ServiceFactory;

...

private static final String WSDL_LOCATION =
    "http://webservices.imacination.com/distance/Distance.jws?wsdl";
private static final String TARGET_NAMESPACE =
    "http://webservices.imacination.com/distance/Distance.jws";
```

```
private static final String SERVICE_NAME = "DistanceService";
private static final String PORT_NAME = "Distance";
private static final String OPERATION_NAME = "getDistance";

...

System.setProperty(ServiceFactory.SERVICEFACTORY_PROPERTY,
                   "weblogic.webservice.core.rpc.ServiceFactoryImpl");
ServiceFactory factory = ServiceFactory.newInstance();
QName serviceName = new QName(TARGET_NAMESPACE, SERVICE_NAME);
URL wsdlLocation = new URL(WSDL_LOCATION);
Service service = factory.createService(wsdlLocation, serviceName);

QName portName = new QName(TARGET_NAMESPACE, PORT_NAME);
QName operationName = new QName(TARGET_NAMESPACE, OPERATION_NAME);
Call call = service.createCall(portName, operationName);
Object[] opArgs = new Object[] {zip1, zip2};
Double distance = (Double)call.invoke(opArgs);
```

Like the dynamic proxy model, things get more complex when you have nonbuilt-in data types. Because the typical use of the dynamic invocation model is to invoke Web Services whose interfaces are not known at compile-time, any complex XML data types will need to be mapped to existing application classes and will require serialization classes capable of mapping the XML data to Java representations. As in the dynamic proxy case, you will need to register all of the type mapping information before invoking the Web Service operation. Because the serialization framework and XML parser interface to be used by it are not yet defined by the JAX-RPC 1.0 specification, any client that requires support for complex data types will not be independent of the JAX-RPC client run time.

BEST PRACTICE Use generated stubs whenever the Web Services your client is invoking are known at compile time and your client does not need to be independent of the JAX-RPC client run-time implementation. Use dynamic proxies whenever the Web Services your client is invoking are known at compile-time but you want your client to be able to use multiple JAX-RPC client run-time implementations. Use dynamic invocation only when your client needs to discover and invoke Web services dynamically at run time. Remember that the need to support complex XML data types will tie your client to a particular JAX-RPC 1.0 client run-time implementation; therefore, it is often simpler just to package up the JAX-RPC client run time with your application rather than trying to use dynamic proxies or the dynamic invocation model.

Using WebLogic Server's Asynchronous Invocation

The JAX-RPC client model supports both the synchronous request/response and one-way invocation models. WebLogic Server 8.1 extends the JAX-RPC model to support an asynchronous request/response model in a way that is completely independent of the server-side Web Services container. As a result, the WebLogic Server JAX-RPC client run time can be used asynchronously to invoke any request/response style Web Service operations.

To use this feature, the first thing that we need to do is generate the Web Service-specific client jar file using the `clientgen` Ant task with the `generateAsyncMethods` attribute set to `true`:

```
<clientgen classpathref="client.compile.class.path"
           wsdl="${example3_wsdl}" packageName="${pkg_base}3"
           generateAsyncMethods="true"
           clientJar="DistanceService_client.jar"/>
```

Once again, the complete source code is available on the companion site for your review. This flag causes `clientgen` to generate two extra methods per operation on the Web Service endpoint interface and stub; one to send the Web Service request to the server, the other to get the response. Let's look at an example.

In our Zip Distance Calculator Web Service, our generated stub client invokes the `getDistance` operation whose method declaration looks like this:

```
public double getDistance(String fromZip, String toZip)
    throws java.rmi.RemoteException;
```

When the `generateAsyncMethods` attribute is `true`, `clientgen` also produces the following two methods that we can use to invoke the `getDistance` operation asynchronously:

```
import weblogic.webservice.async.AsyncInfo;
import weblogic.webservice.async.FutureResult;

...

public FutureResult startGetDistance(String fromZip, String toZip,
                                     AsyncInfo asyncInfo)
    throws java.rmi.RemoteException;

public double endGetDistance(FutureResult _futureResult)
    throws java.rmi.RemoteException;
```

Now that we understand the effect of `generateAsyncMethods`, let's look at how to use these methods to invoke the `getDistance` operation asynchronously.

To invoke the `getDistance` operation asynchronously, simply use the `startGetDistance()` method shown previously. There are a couple of different ways to obtain the response. First, we can simply call the `endGetDistance()` method:

```
FutureResult result = port.startGetDistance(zip1, zip2, null);
double distance = port.endGetDistance(result);
```

This method will return the result, blocking if the result is not immediately available. While this is useful, many times we would prefer not to call `endGetDistance()` until we are sure that the result is available so that the call will not block. Fortunately, the `FutureResult` object has the `isCompleted()` method that allows us to determine if the call has returned and the results are available. The code fragment that follows shows a simplistic way of using this approach:

```
FutureResult result = port.startGetDistance(zip1, zip2, null);
while (!result.isCompleted()) {
    try { Thread.sleep(100); } catch (InterruptedException ignore) { }
}
double distance = port.endGetDistance(result);
```

The other approach is to register a listener that gets called back whenever the result is available. To do this, you need to create an `AsyncInfo` object on which you set a `ResultListener` that is to be called when the invocation returns:

```
import weblogic.webservice.async.AsyncInfo;
import weblogic.webservice.async.FutureResult;
import weblogic.webservice.async.InvokeCompletedEvent;
import weblogic.webservice.async.ResultListener;

...

AsyncInfo asyncInfo = new AsyncInfo();
asyncInfo.setResultListener(new ResultListener() {
    public void onCompletion(InvokeCompletedEvent event)
    {
        Distance port = (Distance)event.getSource();
        FutureResult result = event.getFutureResult();
        try {
            double distance = port.endGetDistance(result);
            System.out.println("The result is " + distance + " miles.");
        }
        catch (RemoteException re) {
            re.printStackTrace();
        }
    }
});
FutureResult result = port.startGetDistance(zip1, zip2, asyncInfo);
```

Once the call to the `getDistance` operation returns, the WebLogic Server JAX-RPC client run time will invoke the `onCompletion()` method on your `ResultListener`. Using the `InvokeCompletedEvent` object, you can retrieve the Web Service endpoint and `FutureResult` object, as shown previously.

It is important to understand that your callback object will be invoked from a different thread than the one that executed the code shown previously. You are responsible for passing information between the two threads. More importantly, the thread that started the call will continue to run regardless of when the callback occurs. For client applications, this is usually the desired behavior because the invoking thread may very well be the event thread of a client's graphical user interface (GUI). This behavior, however, can create unnecessary complexity for server-side applications that are waiting on the result in order to respond to a user request. Let's look at a quick example.

Imagine an application that uses an EJB that is responding to a user request by calling out to a Web Service to access some back-end data. Invoking the Web Service asynchronously allows the EJB to do other work while waiting for the result, but at some point the EJB will need to wait on the result before returning its response to the client. How do you as the EJB programmer prevent the EJB method from finishing before the result returns? How do you determine when the callback has been invoked? Remember, using thread-control primitives is strictly prohibited by the EJB specification and a bad practice even if the EJB container does not prevent their use. Having the `ResultListener` call back into the EJB will create a reentrant call to the EJB that is prohibited by the EJB specification for session beans and highly discouraged for entity beans. Of course, you could always poll the `ResultListener` object. Why would you do this when this is exactly the same thing that you can do with the `FutureResult.isCompleted()` method? Of course, the answer is you wouldn't. If your EJB finishes all of its other work, you would probably just call `endGetDistance()` to block and wait for the results.

BEST PRACTICE When calling a Web Service from within a synchronously invoked J2EE server-side component such as an EJB, prefer the explicit testing method of waiting for the results rather than using a `ResultListener` **to avoid the complexities of coordinating multiple threads.**

Using Portable Stubs

WebLogic Server's portable stubs feature is not about generating stubs that are independent of the JAX-RPC client run time. Portable stubs allow you to create Web Service clients that can run in any version of WebLogic Server without worrying about internal class name conflicts that might otherwise occur. For example, suppose that you want to use the new asynchronous client invocation capabilities in an application running on WebLogic Server 7.0, which doesn't support this new feature. As you can imagine, some of the JAX-RPC server-side run-time classes for 7.0 and client-side run-time classes for 8.1 share the same names but have different implementations. If you tried to package up the 8.1 `webserviceclient.jar` in your 7.0 application, you are pretty much guaranteed that it will fail because of the wrong class being loaded. Portable stubs help you solve this problem by renaming all of the WebLogic Server classes to make their names version-specific. We recommend using portable stubs with any server-side application that acts as a Web Service client.

To support the concept of portable stubs, WebLogic Server provides an alternate version of the JAX-RPC client run time. For WebLogic Server 8.1, the alternate version of the JAX-RPC run time is contained in the `wsclient81.jar` file and simply renames all of the classes in the `weblogic.*` packages to use `weblogic81.*` package names. This prevents the client-side run-time classes from conflicting with any server-side classes of the same name. Typically, you would package the `wsclient81.jar` file with your application, as you would for any other application-specific jar file, rather than adding it to your server's classpath.

In addition, WebLogic Server provides the `VersionMaker` utility that can take the Web Service-specific client jar file produced by `clientgen` and convert every class and reference from using the `weblogic.*` packages to the `weblogic81.*` package names. To use `VersionMaker`, you simply point it at the set of jar files that need to be converted and tell it the directory to which to write the modified classes, as shown here:

```
java weblogic.webservice.tools.versioning.VersionMaker output_directory
     DistanceService_client.jar
```

In general, we recommend that you always use portable stubs when building any server-side application that makes calls out to Web Services to reduce the coupling between your application and the specific version of WebLogic Server to which you deploy the application. The web services clients example on the companion Web site contains a working example that uses portable stubs.

BEST PRACTICE **Always use portable stubs for any server-side application that makes calls to Web Services to reduce the dependency of your application on a particular version of WebLogic Server. Always package the alternate JAX-RPC client run-time jar file as part of your application rather than placing it in the server's classpath.**

Moving Past the Basics

In the last section, we worked through examples demonstrating how to write a basic Web Service and different types of Web Service clients. Now, let's start to look at more advanced features of WebLogic Server that you can use to address more complex requirements. We do not attempt to provide exhaustive coverage of these features, but rather try to make you aware of their existence. For more information, please refer to the WebLogic Server Web Services documentation at http://edocs.bea.com/wls/docs81/webservices.html.

Using Document-Style Messaging

JAX-RPC 1.0 requires that WebLogic Server provides support for doc/literal (document-style with literal use) message formats. When building a Web Service endpoint or client starting from WSDL, the WebLogic Server-provided Ant tasks will automatically determine the format being used from the WSDL binding definitions. When building a Web Service starting with Java you need a way to specify that the Web Service will support the doc/literal message format. WebLogic Server determines the appropriate style for the Web Service by looking at the web-service element's style attribute in the web-services.xml deployment descriptor (see http://edocs.bea.com/wls/docs81/webserv/wsp.html for more information). Fortunately, you can use the style attribute of the service element in the servicegen Ant task to accomplish this automatically, as shown here:

```
<servicegen destEar="MyWebService.ear" contextURI="/web-services">
  <service javaClassComponents="MyWebServiceImpl"
           targetNamespace="http://www.xxx.com/"
           serviceName="MyWebService" serviceURI="/MyWebService"
           style="document"/>
</servicegen>
```

When using document-style Web Services, WebLogic Server requires that the Java component's method to which the Web Service call is mapped have only a single argument. Typically, you would use a Java type for this single argument that is capable of representing any XML document, like javax.xml.soap.SOAPElement or org.w3c.dom.Document. Of course, nothing prevents you from mapping to a strongly typed Java class either.

Customizing a Web Service Home Page

As we saw in the last section, WebLogic Server automatically generates a home page for your Web Service. This page is dynamically generated and therefore cannot be modified. While this is sufficient for many applications, you may want to provide your own custom home page for Web Services that are used by customers or business partners. To do this, simply add the appropriate files to the Web Service's Web application and designate the appropriate welcome file in the web.xml deployment descriptor, as shown here:

```
<!DOCTYPE web-app PUBLIC "-//Sun Microsystems, Inc.//DTD Web Application
2.3//EN"
                         "http://java.sun.com/dtd/web-app_2_3.dtd">
<web-app>
    <welcome-file-list>
        <welcome-file>PropertySearchService.html</welcome-file>
    </welcome-file-list>
</web-app>
```

Adding a custom home page to the Web Service does not disable the default page. To disable the default page, you must set the web-service element's exposeWSDL attribute in the web-services.xml deployment descriptor to false. Be aware that this disables not only the default home page but also access to the dynamically generated WSDL and to the HTTP-based testing facilities that the default home page uses. This seems reasonable because we expect that most Web services made available for external consumption will not want to allow any of these default features to be exposed.

BEST PRACTICE **When building a custom home page for your Web Service, set** `exposeWSDL` **to** `false` **in the** `web-services.xml` **deployment descriptor to disable the default home page. Be aware that if you want users to be able to access the WSDL for your Web Service, you will need to publish the WSDL statically.**

Publishing Static WSDL

By default, WebLogic Server dynamically generates WSDL for your Web Service based on the contents of the `web-services.xml` deployment descriptor. In some cases, you might want to publish your own static WSDL to provide additional information to users of your Web Service. Publishing your own static WSDL is almost as easy as adding your own custom home page. First, generate your WSDL and save it to a file; the WebLogic Server-provided `wsdlgen` Ant task is a convenient way of accomplishing this. Then, add the appropriate mime-mapping entry to your `web.xml` deployment descriptor:

```
<mime-mapping>
     <extension>wsdl</extension>
     <mime-type>text/xml</mime-type>
</mime-mapping>
```

As discussed earlier in the chapter, publishing your Web Service's WSDL statically does not automatically disable access to the dynamically generated WSDL. To prevent access to the dynamic WSDL, set `exposeWSDL` to `false` in the `web-services.xml` deployment descriptor.

WARNING **If you choose to publish a Web Service's WSDL statically, it is your responsibility to keep it up to date with the Web Service if any changes are made.**

The examples contains a working Web Service that uses a custom home page and publishes its WSDL statically. You can download the examples for this chapter from the companion Web site (http://www.wiley.com/compbooks/masteringweblogic).

Using Web Service Sessions

Web Services operations are stateless. When building enterprise applications, it is often necessary to maintain state between client invocations. While Web Services deployed in WebLogic Server have at their disposal all of the power of the J2EE container for persisting state to a back-end database or other EIS, there are situations where you might prefer a lighter-weight mechanism to maintain state across Web Service operations. WebLogic Server gives your Web Services a mechanism for accessing and using the `HttpSession`, including the ability to do session persistence.

To use Web Service sessions, your Web Service implementation class simply obtains the `WebServiceSession` from the current `WebServiceContext` and uses it as a Web application would use an `HttpSession`, as shown in Listing 15.4.

```
package mastering.weblogic.ch15.example5;

import java.util.ArrayList;
import weblogic.webservice.context.ContextNotFoundException;
import weblogic.webservice.context.WebServiceContext;
import weblogic.webservice.context.WebServiceSession;

public class CountingServiceImpl
{
    public int count()
    {
        WebServiceSession session;
        try {
            session = WebServiceContext.currentContext().getSession();
        }
        catch (ContextNotFoundException cnfe) {
            cnfe.printStackTrace();
            return -1;
        }
        Integer count = (Integer)session.getAttribute("count");
        if (count == null)
            count = new Integer(0);

        count = new Integer(count.intValue() + 1);
        session.setAttribute("count", count);
        return count.intValue();
    }
}
```

Listing 15.4 CountingServiceImpl.java.

In the client, you simply need to make sure that your client reads the `JSESSIONID` value from the response and attaches it to the next request. Fortunately, the WebLogic Server client run time does this automatically behind the scenes for you. The client simply reuses the same stub to submit subsequent requests, and the server is able to retrieve the `WebServiceSession` associated with that client session. Look at the `CountingClient` class in the examples to see how this works.

Using Custom Serializers

A JAX-RPC run time needs a mechanism to convert Web Service data between Java and XML for nonbuilt-in data types. While the JAX-RPC 1.0 specification provides an example serialization framework that is used in the reference implementation, it does not specify the interfaces that a framework must support for interoperability. Therefore, you should realize that any time you write custom serializers that plug into a JAX-RPC run-time serialization framework, you are writing vendor-specific code. We expect that future versions of the JAX-RPC specification will mandate that any JAX-RPC-compliant serialization framework must support a set of standard APIs and have well-defined behaviors.

WebLogic Server uses a serialization framework to handle the conversion of Web Service data between Java and XML. Use of any nonbuilt-in data type as an argument or return value of a Web Service operation requires a custom serializer class. As we have seen, WebLogic Server can automatically generate these serializer classes for most custom data types. In the event that you need to write your own serializer, WebLogic Server gives you the capability to do so. In this section, we look at the mechanics of writing a custom serializer that converts between a SOAP array of strings and a Java `ArrayList`—something that is not supported by the built-in auto-typing mechanism.

In the custom serializer example, we start with the very simple Web Service implementation class shown in Listing 15.5.

```
package mastering.weblogic.ch15.example6;

import java.util.ArrayList;

public class NumbersToStringsServiceImpl
{
    public ArrayList getResults(int numberOfStrings)
    {
        if (numberOfStrings < 0)
            return new ArrayList(0);
        ArrayList results = new ArrayList(numberOfStrings);
        for (int i = 0; i < numberOfStrings; i++)
            results.add(Integer.toString(i + 1));
        return results;
    }
}
```

Listing 15.5 NumbersToStringsServiceImpl.java.

Next, we need to write the serializer class. WebLogic Server provides an abstract class that your serializer class will need to extend: `weblogic.webservice.encoding.AbstractCodec`. The WebLogic Server JAX-RPC serialization framework uses the WebLogic XML Streaming API for manipulating the XML. If you are not familiar with this API and want more information, please refer to the BEA Web site at http://edocs.bea.com/wls/docs81/xml/xml_stream.html. Your serializer class needs to implement the following three methods:

```
public void serialize(Object obj, XMLName name, XMLOutputStream writer,
                      SerializationContext context)
throws SerializationException;
```

```
public Object deserialize(XMLName name, XMLInputStream reader,
                          DeserializationContext context)
throws DeserializationException;

public Object deserialize(XMLName name, Attribute attribute,
                          DeserializationContext context)
    throws DeserializationException;
```

WebLogic Server will invoke the `serialize()` method when it needs to convert a Java object into XML. The first `deserialize()` method is used when it needs to convert the XML on the input stream to an appropriate Java object. The second `deserialize()` method is important only when your data type is used as an attribute value in the XML. In the interest of space, we have chosen not to list the source code for the `ArrayListOfStringsCodec` serializer class. Please download the examples from the companion Web site before proceeding.

Let's take a look at the `serialize()` method. The first element we need to write has the attribute that defines the type and size of the array. This attribute refers to three different namespaces that should already be defined in the higher-level SOAP envelope; just in case, we create namespace attributes for each that match our namespace references in the attribute name and value. As a result, we need to create a `StartElement` using the element name passed in by WebLogic Server, the type attribute that identifies this element as an array of strings of the appropriate length, and the three namespace attributes:

```
...
ArrayList attrList = new ArrayList(1);
Attribute attr =
    ElementFactory.createAttribute("soapenc:arrayType",
                                   ("xsd:string[" + length + "]"));
attrList.add(attr);
Iterator attrIter = attrList.iterator();
AttributeIterator attrs =
    ElementFactory.createAttributeIterator(attrIter);

ArrayList nsList = new ArrayList(3);
Attribute soapenc =
    ElementFactory.createNamespaceAttribute("soapenc",
                                            SOAPENC_NAMESPACE_URI);
nsList.add(soapenc);
Attribute xsd =
    ElementFactory.createNamespaceAttribute("xsd",
                                            XSD_NAMESPACE_URI);
nsList.add(xsd);
Attribute xsi =
    ElementFactory.createNamespaceAttribute("xsi",
                                            XSI_NAMESPACE_URI);
nsList.add(xsi);
Iterator nsIter = nsList.iterator();
AttributeIterator nsAttrs =
        ElementFactory.createAttributeIterator(nsIter);
```

```
try {
    StartElement start =
        ElementFactory.createStartElement(name, attrs, nsAttrs);
    writer.add(start);
```

Next, each element we write will have a name of `xsd:string` and type attribute of `xsi:type=xsd:string`:

```
    XMLName xsdStringName = ElementFactory.createXMLName("xsd:string");
    attr = ElementFactory.createAttribute("xsi:type", "xsd:string");
    attrList.clear();
    attrList.add(attr);
    attrIter = attrList.iterator();
    attrs = ElementFactory.createAttributeIterator(attrIter);
```

Finally, we loop through each element in the `ArrayList` and create an entry for each value in the list and then end the document:

```
    for (int i = 0; i < length; i++) {
        String value = (String)list.get(i);
        writer.add(ElementFactory.createStartElement(xsdStringName,
                                                     attrs));
        writer.add(ElementFactory.createCharacterData(value));
        writer.add(ElementFactory.createEndElement(xsdStringName));
    }
    writer.add(ElementFactory.createEndElement(name));
}
catch (XMLStreamException xse) {
    throw new SerializationException("Stream error", xse);
}
```

The `deserialize()` method is even simpler. First, we get the `soapenc:arrayType` attribute from the enclosing element so that we can parse the value to determine the number of elements present in the array. We could have simply parsed the XML to determine this, but that would have made our example a little longer and not quite as easy to understand. Once we know the length, we find each entry's start element, get its enclosing contents, and add it to the `ArrayList`. Notice that we were careful to finish reading the entire XML element including the final end element. This is very important so that you leave the `XMLInputStream` in a consistent state for any other deserializers that may be invoked after yours.

WARNING When deserializing XML data in a custom serializer class, you must read the entire element off the stream before returning the Java object. Failure to do so can cause other deserialization that occurs after yours to fail because of improper cursor positioning.

Now, we are ready to assemble our Web Service. In this case, we need to create the `web-services.xml` by hand because we want to define the XML data type that corresponds to an array of strings and map that to our custom serializer. Rather than write the whole thing by hand, we cheated by changing the type signature in NumbersToStringsServiceImpl.java to use String[] instead of ArrayList and used the source2wsdd Ant task to generate a deployment descriptor that we could modify. Doing this, our deployment descriptor types section is equivalent to the XML shown here:

```
<types>
  <xsd:schema xmlns:xsd="http://www.w3.org/2001/XMLSchema"
              xmlns:stns="java:language_builtins.lang"
              elementFormDefault="qualified"
              attributeFormDefault="qualified"
              targetNamespace="java:language_builtins.lang">
    <xsd:import namespace="http://schemas.xmlsoap.org/soap/encoding/"/>
    <xsd:complexType name="ArrayOfString">
      <xsd:complexContent>
        <xsd:restriction base="soapenc:Array"
            xmlns:soapenc="http://schemas.xmlsoap.org/soap/encoding/">
          <xsd:attribute xmlns:wsdl="http://schemas.xmlsoap.org/wsdl/"
              ref="soapenc:arrayType" wsdl:arrayType="xsd:string[]">
          </xsd:attribute>
        </xsd:restriction>
      </xsd:complexContent>
    </xsd:complexType>
  </xsd:schema>
</types>
```

After hand-editing the type-mapping-entry to register our custom serializer, the type-mapping section looks like the one shown here:

```
<type-mapping>
  <type-mapping-entry xmlns:p1="java:language_builtins.lang"
      deserializer=
          "mastering.weblogic.ch15.example6.ArrayListOfStringsCodec"
      type="p1:ArrayOfString"
      serializer=
          "mastering.weblogic.ch15.example6.ArrayListOfStringsCodec"
      class-name="java.util.ArrayList">
  </type-mapping-entry>
</type-mapping>
```

This allows us to use an ArrayList in our server-side implementation class but be flexible in our client. If the client chooses to use the WebLogic Server JAX-RPC run time and our custom serializer, it can receive the array of strings that the service returns in an ArrayList. There is nothing preventing it from generating its client directly from the WSDL and receiving the string list using the standard data structure on its particular Web Services' run time.

Once we have the web-services.xml, we need to create a web.xml deployment descriptor for the Web Service's Web application and the application.xml for the Web Service's enterprise application. From there, we use Ant's built-in war and ear tasks to package everything into a deployable enterprise application. If we want, we can use `clientgen` to generate a client jar file. If we use `clientgen` with the `useServerTypes` attribute set to true, the generated stubs will use the `ArrayList`. Setting it to false causes the generated stubs to use `String[]`.

As this simple example demonstrates, custom serializers are one way to decrease the coupling between your WSDL and your Web Service implementation.

Using SOAP Handlers

Sometimes, you need to get access to the raw SOAP message either before it is sent or before the data is converted to Java. For example, you might need to compress messages before they are sent and decompress them before the JAX-RPC run time converts the XML data to Java objects. WebLogic Server's JAX-RPC run time supports the use of SOAP handlers on the client as well as the server. In this section, we will write a simple handler to write the SOAP request and response to a log file. This code can be found in the SOAP handler example on the companion Web site.

Handlers should extend the abstract class, `javax.xml.rpc.handlers.GenericHandler`, and implement only the functions required to provide the necessary functionality. The three primary methods of interest are `handleRequest()`, `handleResponse()`, and `handleFault()`. When a request is received by the JAX-RPC run time, the run time invokes the `handleRequest()` method of each handler in the handler chain in order. When the response is returned, each handler's `handleResponse()` method is invoked in reverse order. If the response is a `SOAPFault`, the `handleFault()` method call replaces the call to `handleResponse()`.

A handler can short-circuit the handler chain by returning `false`. If a handler returns `false` from a `handleRequest()` method, the rest of the handler chain and the back-end component is short-circuited, and the response handler chain starts with the `handleResponse()` or `handleFault()` method of the handler that short-circuited the call. If the `handleResponse()` or `handleFault()` method returns `false`, the rest of the handler chain is skipped and the current response message is returned to the client. For more information about handlers, please see the JAX-RPC specification at http://java.sun.com/xml/jaxrpc/.

Now, let's look at the important parts of our `LoggingHandler` class, which can be found in SOAP handler example on the companion Web site. The first thing to notice is the location of all of the XML-related classes we are importing:

```
import javax.xml.namespace.QName;
import javax.xml.rpc.JAXRPCException;
import javax.xml.rpc.handler.GenericHandler;
import javax.xml.rpc.handler.HandlerInfo;
import javax.xml.rpc.handler.MessageContext;
import javax.xml.rpc.handler.soap.SOAPMessageContext;
import javax.xml.soap.Name;
import javax.xml.soap.SOAPBody;
import javax.xml.soap.SOAPElement;
import javax.xml.soap.SOAPException;
import javax.xml.soap.SOAPMessage;
import javax.xml.soap.Text;
```

The javax.xml.rpc package contains the core JAX-RPC classes while the javax .xml.soap package contains the core classes needed to create and manipulate SOAP messages from Java, as defined by the SAAJ 1.1 specification.

In our `LoggingHandler`, we override the default implementations of the `init()` and `destroy()` methods defined in the `GenericHandler` class to trap the handler's life-cycle events. We use these to open and close the log file when the handler is created and destroyed, respectively:

```
public void init(HandlerInfo config)
{
    this.config = config;
    Map hConf = config.getHandlerConfig();
    String logDirectoryName =
        (String)hConf.get(LOG_DIRECTORY_ATTR_NAME);
    String logFilePrefix =
        (String)hConf.get(LOG_FILE_PREFIX_ATTR_NAME);
    if (logFilePrefix == null || logDirectoryName == null)
         throw new RuntimeException("handler not configured");

    try {
        File logDirectory = new File(logDirectoryName);
        if (!logDirectory.exists())
            throw new RuntimeException("directory does not exist: " +
                                       logDirectoryName);
        File logFile =
            File.createTempFile(logFilePrefix, ".log", logDirectory);
        log = new PrintWriter(new FileOutputStream(logFile));
    }
    catch (IOException ioe) {
        ioe.printStackTrace();
        throw new RuntimeException("IOException: " +
                                   ioe.getMessage());
    }
}

public void destroy()
{
    log.close();
}
```

The `getHeaders()` method is supposed to return the list of headers that this handler will process. Because we are simply writing out the entire SOAP envelope to the log file, we use a simple implementation that returns the list from the configuration information. `getHeaders()` is the only method in the `GenericHandler` class that does not have a default implementation.

```
public QName[] getHeaders()
{
    return config.getHeaders();
}
```

Finally, we implement the handleRequest(), handleResponse(), and handleFault() methods that do the real work. The handleRequest() method implementation is shown here:

```
public boolean handleRequest(MessageContext mc)
{
    try {
        SOAPMessageContext ctx = (SOAPMessageContext) mc;
        SOAPMessage request = ctx.getMessage();
        SOAPElement envelope = request.getSOAPPart().getEnvelope();
        writeRequestLog(envelope);
    }
    catch(SOAPException e) {
        e.printStackTrace();
        throw new JAXRPCException(e);
    }
    return true;
}
```

In the handleRequest() method, we have access to the entire context of the SOAP message. In our example, we simply get the SOAPMessage from the MessageContext and use it to retrieve the SOAPEnvelope. Once we have the SOAPEnvelope, the writeRequestLog() method walks through the SOAPEnvelope and prints out all of the XML information contained in the message. Because responses and faults have a similar structure to a SOAP request, handleResponse() and handleFault() are virtually identical to handleRequest().

Now that we have our handler, we need to understand how to use it. Handlers can be used on both the client and server JAX-RPC run times. To use a handler on the server, you need to declare a handler chain in the web-services.xml deployment descriptor and associate the handler chain with the appropriate operations. For handlers requiring no initialization parameters, you can use the handlerChain child element of the servicegen Ant task to declare the handlers and associate them with every operation in the Web Service. If you need to specify initialization parameters or want to use the handler chain selectively with only certain operations, then it will be necessary to edit the web-services.xml file directly. Take a look at the deployment descriptor for the LoggingHandler example to see exactly how this is accomplished.

Clients can also use handlers. To use a handler from the WebLogic Server JAX-RPC client run time, you will need to register your handler programmatically. The following code fragment shows the basics of how to register your handler:

```
QName portName = new QName("http://www.bigrez.com/ch15/example7",
                           "NumbersToStringsServicePort");
HandlerRegistry registry = service.getHandlerRegistry();
List handlerChain = registry.getHandlerChain(portName);

Map handlerConfig = new HashMap();
handlerConfig.put("logFilePrefix", LOG_FILE_PREFIX);
handlerConfig.put("logFileDirectory", LOG_FILE_DIRECTORY);
HandlerInfo handler =
```

```
        new HandlerInfo(LoggingHandler.class, handlerConfig, null);
    handlerChain.add(handler);
    registry.setHandlerChain(portName, handlerChain);
```

Using SOAP Attachments

SOAP attachments provide a way to attach any type of data to the SOAP message. Currently, this is the primary mechanism you would typically use to pass non-XML data along with the SOAP message. In the future, there may be other ways of including non-XML data in line in the SOAP message, but for now, SOAP attachments are the standard way to accomplish this. SAAJ provides a set of classes used to represent and manipulate SOAP attachments. Let's look at an example of how to use SOAP attachments.

In this example, we have written a simple file transfer Web Service that accepts the name of a server-side file and attaches the contents of the file to the SOAP response using a SOAP handler and the SAAJ APIs. The back-end service implementation doesn't do anything beyond making sure that the file being requested is valid and setting the MIME type of the file, as shown in Listing 15.6. For our simple example, we are using an XML document, so determining the correct MIME type is easy.

```
package mastering.weblogic.ch15.example8;

import java.io.FileNotFoundException;
import java.net.URL;

import javax.xml.namespace.QName;
import javax.xml.rpc.holders.StringHolder;
import javax.xml.rpc.soap.SOAPFaultException;

import weblogic.webservice.util.FaultUtil;

public class FileTransferServiceImpl
{
    public void getFile(StringHolder fileName, StringHolder mimeType)
        throws SOAPFaultException
    {
        String name = fileName.value;
        URL file = this.getClass().getClassLoader().getResource(name);
        if (file == null) {
            throw new SOAPFaultException(
                new QName("http://schemas.xmlsoap.org/soap/envelope/",
                          "Server"),
                "Unknown File", "file server",
                FaultUtil.newDetail(
                    new FileNotFoundException("file not found: " +
name)));
        }
```

Listing 15.6 FileTransferServiceImpl.java. *(continued)*

```
        int index = name.lastIndexOf(".");
        if (index == -1) {
            throw new SOAPFaultException(
                new QName("http://schemas.xmlsoap.org/soap/envelope/",
                          "Server"),
                "Unknown File Type", "file server",
                FaultUtil.newDetail(
                    new FileNotFoundException("invalid file name: " +
                                              name)));
        }
        String extension = name.substring(index + 1, name.length());
        if (extension.equalsIgnoreCase("xml")) {
            mimeType.value = "text/xml";
        else if (extension.equalsIgnoreCase("html")) {
            mimeType.value = "text/html";
        else if (extension.equalsIgnoreCase("txt")) {
            mimeType.value = "text/plain";
        }
        else {
            throw new SOAPFaultException(
                new QName("http://schemas.xmlsoap.org/soap/envelope/",
                          "Server"),
                "Unknown File Type", "file server",
                FaultUtil.newDetail(
                    new FileNotFoundException("invalid file type: " +
                                              extension)));
        }
    }
}
```

Listing 15.6 *(continued)*

This example introduces two new concepts. First, this Web Service example uses method parameters as a way to pass information back to the client (and, more importantly, the client- and server-side handlers). `fileName` is an in-out parameter used by the client to pass the name of the file to retrieve from the server. The primary reason for doing this is to make it easy to tell the handler the name of the file to attach to the response. In addition, `mimeType` is an out parameter that we use to tell the handler the MIME type of the file to attach. We could have just as easily put this logic in the server-side handler; however, using an out parameter allows us to pass the MIME type information back to the client (or client-side handler). Ultimately, we chose to use the out parameter to illustrate how to program a Web Service using both in-out and out parameters.

The second new concept is the explicit use of the `SOAPFaultException` as a mechanism to return error information to the caller. WebLogic Server automatically maps exceptions thrown in the server to SOAP faults as best it can. The richness of information included in SOAP faults, though, is generally greater than what the server can determine from an ordinary exception. Using the `SOAPFaultException` provides an explicit way to control the contents of the SOAP fault message sent back to the caller. For more details about the contents of SOAP faults and what the parameters mean, please see the SOAP specification at http://www.w3.org/TR/SOAP/ and the Javadocs for `javax.xml.rpc.soap.SOAPFaultException`.

BEST PRACTICE **Web Service implementations should use `SOAPFaultException` to pass back the context of the error explicitly to the Web Service container, ensuring that the content of the SOAP fault response includes detailed information regarding the nature of the problem.**

Let's look at the server-side handler that is attaching the contents of the file to the SOAP response. Rather than listing the entire contents of the `ServerFileTransferHandler.java` file, let's concentrate on those parts of the code that are specific to the attachment. As the following code fragment taken from `ServerFileTransferHandler` shows, creating the attachment and attaching it to the message is pretty simple once we have parsed the SOAP response to get the file's name and MIME type and read the contents of the file into a byte array:

```
AttachmentPart attachment = response.createAttachmentPart();
if ("text/xml".equals(mimeType)) {
    attachment.setContent(new String(fileBytes), mimeType);
}
else if ("text/html".equals(mimeType)) {
    attachment.setContent(new String(fileBytes), mimeType);
}
else if ("text/plain".equals(mimeType)) {
    attachment.setContent(new String(fileBytes), mimeType);
}
else {
    attachment.setContent(fileBytes, mimeType);
}
response.addAttachmentPart(attachment);
```

Because WebLogic Server expects the contents of `text/xml` attachments to be of type `String`, we do a simple test to see if the contents are XML, HTML, or plain text. If they are not, we try to set the content using the byte array directly. This obviously doesn't work for every case and is used to illustrate the point that the JAX-RPC run time may expect certain content formatting for objects of a particular MIME type. This expectation is controlled by the particular set of `DataContentHandlers` objects in use.

On the client, our example uses the `ClientFileTransferHandler` class to write the attachment's contents to the file system. Again, the `DataContentHandlers` determine the type of object returned by the `AttachmentPart.getContent()` method. SAAJ requires that the object returned be either a typed Java object that represents the type or an `InputStream` that can be used to read the raw bytes. The following code excerpt from `ClientFileTransferHandler.java` shows how we retrieve the attachment in order to read it:

```
iter = response.getAttachments();
AttachmentPart attachment = null;
if (iter.hasNext()) {
    attachment = (AttachmentPart)iter.next();
}
else {
    throw new SOAPException("Malformed message: " +
                            "attachment not found");
}
InputStream obj = (InputStream)attachment.getContent();
int len = attachment.getSize();
```

One thing we did not do was change the fileName return value. In our client handler, we are writing the file to a preconfigured directory on the file system that is passed into the handler during initialization. To enhance the handler's functionality, we could have written our handler so that it changes the response fileName to include the directory information defining where the handler has written the file on the client's file system. This would be a good exercise for you to get some hands-on experience with the SAAJ APIs to see what you can do with handlers.

Using JMS as the Transport

When using Web Services with WebLogic Server, SOAP messages are sent using the HTTP (or HTTPS) protocol; however, WebLogic Server also supports sending SOAP messages using JMS as the transport layer. Using JMS as the transport can be more efficient for processes that exchange large numbers of messages because the underlying RMI infrastructure used by JMS maintains a persistent socket connection between the sender and the receiver.

To build a Web Service that supports the JMS protocol (as well as HTTP), you simply need to set the web-service element's jmsUri attribute in the web-services.xml deployment descriptor. The format of the jmsUri attribute is <JMS ConnectionFactory JNDI Name>/<JMS Queue JNDI Name>. In the next example, we created a JMS connection factory with a JNDI name of Ch15_example9_ConnectionFactory and a queue with a JNDI name of Ch15_example9_Queue. The following code fragment from the web-services.xml deployment descriptor shows the web-services element; the highlighted section illustrates the change needed to support the JMS transport:

```
<web-service useSOAP12="false"
             targetNamespace="http://www.bigrez.com/ch15/example9/"
             name="NumbersToStringsService" style="rpc"
             uri="/NumbersToStringsService"

jmsUri="Ch15_example9_ConnectionFactory/Ch15_example9_Queue">
```

We need to create the necessary JMS objects before trying to deploy our Web service. In this example, you can use the create_jms target in the Chapter 15 examples build.xml file to create a JMS server, a queue that belongs to the JMS server, a JMS connection factory, and a JMS template (make sure your server is running first). The JMS template is required because the Web Services JMS transport uses temporary destinations to return the responses. WebLogic JMS requires a temporary template for any JMS server that supports temporary destinations. Therefore, the script sets the Temporary Template attribute of our JMS server to point at the Temporary Template template it created.

Once we have our client-specific jar file, we can write the client. The client looks almost exactly like any other client except that there is an additional port class that uses JMS as the transport, as shown here in the code fragment from the NumbersToStringsClient.java file:

```
NumbersToStringsService service =
    new NumbersToStringsService_Impl(WSDL_LOCATION);

NumbersToStringsServicePort port =
    service.getNumbersToStringsServicePort();
String[] result = port.getResults(numberOfStrings);
System.out.println("HTTP: getResults(" + numberOfStrings +
                   ") returned " + result.length + " strings.");
for (int i = 0; i < result.length; i++)
    System.out.println("\tString " + (i + 1) + " is: " + result[i]);

NumbersToStringsServicePort jmsPort =
    service.getNumbersToStringsServicePortJMS();
String[] jmsResult = jmsPort.getResults(numberOfStrings);
System.out.println("JMS: getResults(" + numberOfStrings +
                   ") returned " + jmsResult.length + " strings.");
for (int i = 0; i < jmsResult.length; i++)
System.out.println("\tString " + (i + 1) + " is: " + jmsResult[i]);
weblogic.webservice.binding.jms.ConnectionPool.getInstance().close();
```

To run the client, we need to use the WebLogic Server client run time. This can be accomplished using either the weblogic.jar or the new thin client that leverages the JDK's support for IIOP. By using the weblogic.jar, we use the traditional WebLogic RMI implementation, which defaults to the t3 protocol. To use the new thin client, we need to include wlclient.jar, which provides the basic RMI support, and the wljmsclient.jar, which provides the extra support needed for JMS. When using the new thin client with JMS as the transport, we need to add an extra call to tell the JAX-RPC client infrastructure to close the JMS connection; otherwise, the client program won't exit cleanly. This occurs because of a known issue in the Java IDL specification that requires the client to un-export all classes before the JVM is allowed to shut down. If you don't like the idea of using this method, you can simply replace the return call at the end of your main method with System.exit(0). We expect that BEA will work closely with Sun in an attempt to resolve this issue and remove the need to call this close() method explicitly in the future.

Using Web Services Security

Web Services Security is an emerging standard for securing Web Services. At the time of writing, work on the draft specification is being done by the Organization for the Advancement of Structured Information Standards (OASIS, see www.oasis-open.org/committees/wss/ for more information). WS Security is essentially focused on providing end-to-end message-level security (as opposed to just transport-level security, such as that offered by SSL). This translates into three different areas of focus:

- Message confidentiality through the use of encryption
- Message integrity through the use of digital signatures
- Identity propagation through the ability to pass security tokens as part of the message

At the time of writing, WebLogic Server 8.1 provides an implementation that follows an early draft of the WS Security specification. We expect that BEA will support the final specification once it becomes official. Until such a time, there is no guarantee that any vendor's Web Services security implementation will interoperate with any other vendor's implementation. For more up-to-date information, we suggest looking at the recommendation coming out of the Web Service Interoperability Organization (WS-I); see www.ws-i.org/ for more information.

WebLogic Server provides support for end-to-end Web Services security by providing transport- and message-level security as well as access control. In this section, we will first show you how to achieve transport-level security through the use of both one-way and two-way SSL. Then, we will show you how to use message-level security that provides for encrypting and/or digitally signing the SOAP message itself. We end this chapter by showing you how to protect your Web Services from unauthorized access. As in Chapter 10, we strongly recommend the use of domestic-strength certificates for transport- or message-level security. At the time of writing, you still have to contact BEA to obtain a domestic-strength license key.

Transport-Level Security

WebLogic Server provides transport-level security through the use of one-way or two-way SSL connections between the client and the server. We have already covered how to set up and configure a WebLogic Server for SSL in Chapter 10. We also looked at how to use SSL from a Java application client using either the RMI programming model or programmatic HTTP via the `URLConnection` object. This section is simply an extension of the Java application client discussion for Web Services clients using the WebLogic Server JAX-RPC client run time. If you need more information, please refer back to Chapter 10.

Setting up one-way SSL with the server is easy. As with other Java application clients, it is possible to use either the WebLogic Server's SSL or a third-party SSL implementation. Unfortunately, using a third-party implementation such as JSSE currently requires creating your own `SSLAdapter`, a task that we do not feel is reasonable and therefore will not cover. For more information on using third-party SSL implementations, see the WebLogic Server documentation at http://edocs.bea.com/wls/docs81/webserv/security.html.

To use the WebLogic Server SSL implementation, all you need to do is specify the certificates to trust, set a few additional command-line arguments, and use the `webserviceclient+ssl.jar` client run-time jar file in place of `webserviceclient.jar`. A complete working example is located on the companion Web site.

The Chapter 15 example build script defines the `create_keystores` task to automate the creation of the key stores, but you still need to configure the server to use the `ServerKeyStore.jks` and `ServerTrustStore.jks` key stores that the script creates in the `${SERVER_ROOT}/${DOMAIN}` directory, as defined by the `build.properties` file.

At the time of writing, the only way to set the trusted certificates is to add a few lines of code to the client:

```
import weblogic.webservice.client.BaseWLSSLAdapter;
import weblogic.webservice.client.SSLAdapterFactory;

...

SSLAdapterFactory factory = SSLAdapterFactory.getDefaultFactory();
BaseWLSSLAdapter adapter =
    (BaseWLSSLAdapter)factory.getDefaultAdapter();
adapter.setTrustedCertificatesFile("CertGenCA.pem");
```

Notice that the `setTrustedCertificatesFile()` method requires the use of a PEM-encoded file rather than a trust key store. We expect that this shortcoming may be addressed by the time you read this, so please check the WebLogic Server documentation at http://edocs.bea.com/wls/docs81/webserv/security.html for more up-to-date information.

You also need to set the Java system property `bea.home` to tell the WebLogic Server client run time where to find the BEA license file, which is currently required for using BEA's SSL implementation:

```
java -Dbea.home=c:\bea ...
```

To make your client use two-way SSL, add code to retrieve the client's certificate chain and private key and set them using the `BaseWLSSLAdapter.addIdentity()` method:

```
import java.security.KeyStore;
import java.security.PrivateKey;
import java.security.cert.Certificate;
import java.security.cert.X509Certificate;

import weblogic.webservice.client.BaseWLSSLAdapter;
import weblogic.webservice.client.SSLAdapterFactory;

...
```

```
KeyStore identityKeyStore = KeyStore.getInstance("jks");
identityKeyStore.load(new FileInputStream(clientKeyStoreFileName),
                      clientKeyStorePassword);
PrivateKey privateKey = (PrivateKey)
    identityKeyStore.getKey(privateKeyAlias,
                            privateKeyPassphrase.toCharArray());
Certificate [] certChain =
    identityKeyStore.getCertificateChain(args[3]);

X509Certificate[] x509CertChain =
    new X509Certificate[certChain.length];
for (int i = 0; i < certChain.length; i++)
    x509CertChain[i] = (X509Certificate)certChain[i];

SSLAdapterFactory factory = SSLAdapterFactory.getDefaultFactory();
BaseWLSSLAdapter adapter =
    (BaseWLSSLAdapter)factory.getDefaultAdapter();
adapter.setTrustedCertificatesFile("CertGenCA.pem");
adapter.addIdentity(x509CertChain, privateKey);

...
```

The only trick is to convert the certificate chain returned from the call to `getCertificateChain()` to the `X509Certificate[]` type that the `addIdentity()` method requires. At the time of writing, the version of the `addIdentity()` method we are using is mistakenly marked as deprecated. We expect this to be fixed by the time you read this book.

Don't forget to change the server's `Two Way Client Cert Behavior` attribute to either `Client Certs Requested But Not Enforced` or `Client Certs Requested And Enforced` to enable two-way SSL. We are not enforcing client certificates in the example to allow both the one-way and two-way SSL clients to run against the same server.

Message-Level Security

Through the use of digital certificates, a client can encrypt the SOAP message, digitally sign it, or do both. With that said, let's look at another example to see how to configure and use message-level security with WebLogic Server 8.1.

First, you need to create the client and server certificates and import the certificates, private keys, and trusted CA certificates into key stores that the client and server will use. We do not repeat the description of this process here because it is described in the *Setting Up SSL/TLS* section of Chapter 10.

If you are using digital signatures, configure the Identity Asserter so that WebLogic Server can validate the certificate used for signing the message. For our example, we use the built-in capabilities of the `DefaultIdentityAsserter` and `Default User Name Mapper` to map the CN attribute of the X.509 certificate that contains the machine's hostname to the user because the certificates created by `utils.CertGen` do not have a username or email address associated with them. Therefore, the first thing that you need to do is create a user with the same name as the hostname of your machine. After creating the appropriate user, you need to add support for X509 token types to `DefaultIdentityAsserter` and configure the `Default User Name Mapper` to extract the `CN` field of the certificate, as described in the *Identity Assertion* section of Chapter 10.

Once this configuration work is finished, we are ready to configure the Web service. The message-level security settings in the `web-services.xml` file are fairly complex, so we suggest that you start with `servicegen` to generate the initial deployment descriptor even if you ultimately have to edit the deployment descriptor by hand. Simply set the `signKeyName` and/or `encryptKeyName` attributes to the alias you used to import the server's private key into the key store and the `signKeyPass` and/or `encryptKeyPass` attributes to the server's private key passphrase for the features you want to use:

```
<servicegen classpathref="dev.class.path" destEar="ch15_example9.ear"
            contextURI="/ch15_example9">
  <service
javaClassComponents="${pkg_base}9.NumbersToStringsServiceImpl"
           targetNamespace="http://www.bigrez.com/ch15/example9/"
           serviceName="NumbersToStringsService"
           serviceURI="/NumbersToStringsService">
    <client useServerTypes="true" packageName="${pkg_base}9"/>
    <security signKeyName="server_key" signKeyPass="server_key_passwd"
              encryptKeyName="server_key"
              encryptKeyPass="server_key_passwd"/>
  </service>
</servicegen>
```

Optionally, use the `username` and `password` attributes to have the server attach an identity token to the SOAP responses.

If you look at the relevant section of a Web Service deployment descriptor created by `servicegen`, you will see that the private key passphrases and user password are all in clear text. WebLogic Server provides the `weblogic.webservice.encryptpass` utility that allows you to encrypt these passwords. Note that this `encryptpass` utility encrypts the passwords for decoding by a specific domain. This means that you will need to rerun the utility against the plain-text version for the domain to which you are deploying the Web Service.

Next, you need to make changes to the client code invoking the secure Web Service. Much of the client code is standard Java 2 security code, so we will not go through that here; see Chapter 10 for more information. If you look at the `compile_example11` task, you will see that we are generating the `NumbersToStringsClient.java` file from a template where we replace the username and password being used by the client. Let's look at the code fragments taken from `NumbersToStringsClient.java` shown here:

```
...
import java.security.PrivateKey;
import java.security.cert.X509Certificate;

import weblogic.webservice.context.WebServiceContext;
import weblogic.webservice.context.WebServiceSession;
import weblogic.webservice.core.handler.WSSEClientHandler;

...

X509Certificate clientcert =
    getCertificate(clientKeyAlias, clientKeyStoreFileName,
                   clientKeyStorePassword);
PrivateKey clientpk =
    getPrivateKey(clientKeyAlias, privateKeyPassphrase,
                  clientKeyStoreFileName, clientKeyStorePassword);

NumbersToStringsService service =
    new NumbersToStringsService_Impl(WSDL_LOCATION);
WebServiceContext context = service.context();
WebServiceSession session = context.getSession();
session.setAttribute(WSSEClientHandler.CERT_ATTRIBUTE, clientcert);
session.setAttribute(WSSEClientHandler.KEY_ATTRIBUTE, clientpk);

NumbersToStringsServicePort port =
    service.getNumbersToStringsServicePort();
String[] result = port.getResults(numberOfStrings);
```

The bolded sections illustrate new elements that are specific to WebLogic Server Web Service security. First, we import some Java 2 security classes and a few WebLogic Server-specific classes. Next, we retrieve the client certificate and private keys from the client's key store. Finally, we get the `WebServiceSession` object and set the security-related attributes before getting the port and invoking the operation.

Finally, to run the example we need to add the `wsse.jar` file to the client's classpath. If you look at the `run_example11` task, you will notice that we are setting another Java system property called `weblogic.webservice.verbose` to `true`. When you run the client with this property, the client will dump both the SOAP request and SOAP response to standard out. This feature is very useful when trying to debug Web Service requests.

TIP **When debugging a Web Service, set the Java system property `weblogic.webservice.verbose` to `true` to make the client print the SOAP messages to standard out.**

Access Control

WebLogic Server allows you to restrict access to your Web Service using the same mechanisms that you would employ for any other J2EE component. For example, restricting access to your EJB component that implements your Web Service prevents unauthorized uses from invoking it. For Web Services whose back-end components are regular Java objects, you must control access to the Web Service's URL using the standard Web application security mechanisms discussed in Chapters 4 and 10.

When using protected Web Service resources, the client needs to authenticate to WebLogic Server before accessing the Web Service. You do this either through simple username/password authentication or by using two-way SSL as an authentication mechanism; see the *Setting Up SSL/TLS* section of Chapter 10 for more information. To authenticate your Web Service client, set the `javax.xml.rpc.security.auth.username` and `javax.xml.rpc.security.auth.password` properties on the service endpoint stub:

```
port.setProperty("javax.xml.rpc.security.auth.username", "rpatrick");
port.setProperty("javax.xml.rpc.security.auth.password", "password");
```

`clientgen` also creates a specialized version of the `getXXXPort()` method that accepts a username and password as arguments to eliminate the need for setting the properties shown previously:

```
NumbersToStringsServiceImplPort port =
    service.getNumbersToStringsServiceImplPort("rpatrick", "password");
```

Two way SSL with Identity Assertion is another way for the user to get access to a protected Web Service.

If you are protecting the Web Service URL directly, your client must have access to the WSDL. There are two ways to accomplish this. The first method is to use the no-args version of the service's constructor. This causes the client run time to use the WSDL packaged with the client jar file created by `clientgen`:

```
NumbersToStringsServiceImpl_Impl service =
    new NumbersToStringsServiceImpl_Impl();
```

The catch with this option is that currently this WSDL always uses `http://localhost:7001/<contextURI>/<serviceURI>` as the location of the Web service. You may need to edit the location URLs in the WSDL in order for this method to work for real applications. The second method is to remap the WSDL location to something other than the default. Doing this requires you to publish static WSDL. See the downloadable code at http://www.wiley.com/compbooks/masteringweblogic for a working example that demonstrates the features described in this section.

The `servicegen` task allows you to require the use of HTTPS for all clients of a particular Web Service through its `protocol` attribute on the `service` element. Using this simply sets the `transport-guarantee` element in the `web.xml` to `CONFIDENTIAL`.

Adding Web Services to *bigrez.com*

We now have all of the knowledge we need to design the Web Service interface to *bigrez.com*. Because the Web Service interface is intended to support global reservation systems, we need to provide two Web Services: one to find a set of available hotel rooms matching the search criteria and one to book a reservation.

Our first design decision is whether these services should be synchronous or asynchronous. In general, we believe that application-to-application integration Web Services should be asynchronous to decouple the availability and scalability of the calling application from the Web Service. For booking reservations, this makes perfect sense. For querying our reservation system for matching hotels when a travel agent or user is waiting for an immediate response so that they can choose a hotel and book a reservation, we have chosen to make this Web Service synchronous to improve the response time that the user experiences. Let's look at the query service first.

BEST PRACTICE Use asynchronous Web Services for application-to-application integration. Synchronous Web Services are good for Web Services interacting with humans.

The next design decision we need to make is determining what operations are necessary to support the query service. Is one operation that takes the search criteria and returns all of the information about the hotel enough, or do we want to break this into two operations, one to return the list of matching hotels with limited information and one to get detailed information about a specific hotel? To answer this question, we need to look at how we expect the system to be used. Based on what our global reservation systems partners have told us, we expect that most people booking rooms will want to choose the hotel based on location and then check for availability and view more detailed information about a particular hotel. Therefore, to save the overhead associated with returning all of the availability and detailed information for each matching hotel, we will return only the minimum amount of information needed to identify a particular hotel in the first operation. We will include a second operation that returns availability and other detailed information for a particular hotel. These types of decisions can be key to building scalable Web Services.

BEST PRACTICE Proper Web Service design requires understanding how the services and the data that they return will be used. In general, Web Services should be coarse-grained, but care must be taken to avoid returning more information than is required by most clients.

For our asynchronous reservation Web Service, we need to determine what facility we are going to provide for the client to correlate the responses with the actual requests. Because, at the time of writing, there is no Web Services standard for accomplishing this, we need to create our own, keeping in mind that we do not want to compromise interoperability. Therefore, we want to include the correlation IDs as part of the main SOAP messages.

We could place the burden on the client for providing a correlation ID, but this would require us to augment that correlation ID with information about the client to prevent the possibility of multiple clients providing the same ID. Therefore, we take the responsibility of generating the correlation IDs. For this to work, we need to return the correlation ID to the client as the response to the call to book the reservation. This means that, in order for the reservation processing itself to be asynchronous but the returning of the correlation ID to be synchronous, we use a synchronous Web Service that generates a correlation ID, places the reservation request and correlation ID into a JMS message, writes the JMS message to a queue, and returns the correlation ID to the client. At that point, a message-driven bean picks up the reservation request, places the reservation, and creates a confirmation message for the client.

Once the reservation is made, we need to return the confirmation message to the client. There are multiple ways to accomplish this, some of which are the following:

Client polling. Having the client poll for the request makes our lives as programmers easier. We simply dump the responses onto a JMS queue or into a database and provide another synchronous Web Service that retrieves the response. We place the burden on the client for asking for the response. The problem is that this puts undue load on the server if the clients are frequently asking for a response before it is available. When the system is experiencing heavy load, the problem only gets worse because the system may have to process multiple poll requests before a particular response is ready.

Client-side callback Web Service. Having the client provide a Web service that we call to return the response when it is available reduces the load that a polling solution places on the server. This solution is much more scalable but requires that the client be capable of hosting a Web Service. While requiring end-user client applications to have a Web Service for callback purposes may not be reasonable, certainly large applications like a global reservation system will be able to provide such a facility.

We must make sure that our business logic for booking the reservation is decoupled from the process for returning the responses. This is critical because we cannot allow our reservation transaction processing to be slowed down, or caused to fail, by the availability or response time of callback Web Services we invoke to return the reservation confirmation message. Therefore, our reservation transaction writes the confirmation message to a JMS queue. We use another MDB to dequeue the message and invoke the callback Web Service to deliver the confirmation message.

BEST PRACTICE **Whenever possible, return asynchronous responses to callers via a callback Web Service provided by the caller. When using asynchronous processing, always decouple the sending of the response from the core business transaction.**

Now that we have settled on the high-level interactions, let's drill down to the next level and define the interfaces. We want to ensure that our interfaces have the right level of abstraction and are sufficiently decoupled from the implementation that even if we were to change the implementation technology, the interfaces would remain unchanged. As a result, let's start by defining the messages that are to be exchanged and any custom data types we need to represent those messages. One way to do that is to start with WSDL, which is how we chose to start our example. You could also accomplish the same thing by starting with a Java interface and data types. Regardless of how you choose to start, the important point is to make sure that you do not expose your business logic to the data structures used by the Web Service and vice versa. While not following this recommendation can simplify the job of providing a Web Service interface to your business logic, it effectively couples your business logic to the Web Service interface. Any changes to the Web Service interface require touching all of the business logic that uses the affected data structure. In our example, we take this one step further and decouple the WSDL operation names from the business methods we invoke.

BEST PRACTICE Resist the temptation to expose business methods and data types to your Web Service interface directly. Failure to do so can make it difficult and costly to evolve Web Service interfaces as the business requirements for your application change.

In our example, we used `wsdl2service` to generate a Java interface that the Web Service endpoint needs to implement. At this point, we need to decide what back-end component type to use to implement our Web Service. Using a regular Java object is attractive because `wsdl2service` generates a normal Java interface, as opposed to one appropriate for use by a stateless session bean. We also need the transactional semantics of an EJB to manipulate the entity bean references and relationships that our business methods return efficiently. Using a stateless session bean directly as our Web Service would require us to make manual modifications to the `web-services.xml` deployment descriptor generated by `wsdl2service`. Therefore, we decided to use a regular Java object that delegates interactions with the business components to a stateless session bean. While this adds an extra layer to the architecture, the Java class that implements the endpoint is so lightweight that it doesn't add any measurable amount of overhead. In addition, it simplifies the development and maintenance of our application because it allows us to use the WebLogic Server Ant tasks to automate Java type and deployment descriptor generation completely. Figure 15.5 shows the high-level architecture of our design.

Our `BigRezWebServiceImpl` class provides the three methods for finding properties, checking availability, and booking a reservation that our Web Service exposes and delegates these calls to the `BigRezWebServiceSessionBean` EJB. For the first two methods, our EJB simply calls directly to the back-end business logic EJBs and returns a response based on the business-logic response. In the `bookReservation()` method, our EJB creates a JMS `ObjectMessage` and places it onto the `GRSRequestQueue`. From there, our `JMSReservationRequestBean` MDB picks up the request, invokes the back-end business logic, and writes the confirmation response to the `GRSResponseQueue`—all as part of a JTA transaction. The fact that this whole process is part of a single transaction makes the application vulnerable to the poison message problem we discussed in Chapter 9.

Let's take a moment to make sure that we understand the problem before we describe the way we chose to address it. Because our Web Service is accepting messages that we are simply packaging up and placing in a queue, it is possible that the data provided may prevent the business logic from successfully booking the reservation. These failures can happen for multiple reasons but generally can be separated into two categories.

First, system-level failures, such as the database going down, prevent messages from being processed successfully. We call these system exceptions, and the normal way to deal with system exceptions is to re-enqueue the message by rolling back the transaction so that JMS redelivers the message later in hopes that the temporary system problems will be resolved in a timely manner. WebLogic JMS also allows us to specify an error queue to which the messages can be routed should redelivery continue to fail. This mechanism works well and meets all of our requirements for handling system exceptions.

Second, the processing of some messages may fail because of business rules, such as invalid credit card information or no availability for the chosen dates. We call these business exceptions, and the normal way to deal with business exceptions is to send an error message back to the caller to inform it that the request failed. A problem occurs, though, when the business logic requires the transaction to be rolled back, as would be the case when a partially completed reservation fails during credit card validation *after* the transaction has modified some data. Because the transaction is usually marked for rollback before the business logic returns control to the controller (that is, `JMSReservationRequestBean` in our example), it is not possible for us to write the error message to the response queue as a part of the transaction. We must allow the transaction to roll back.

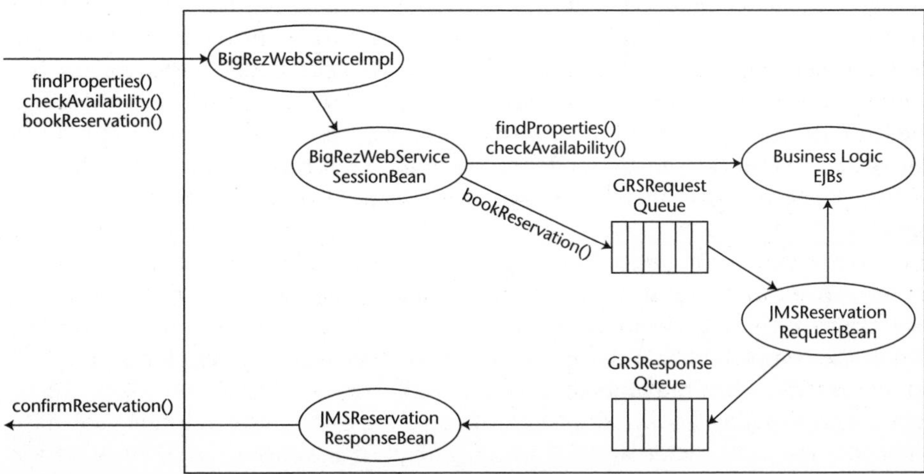

Figure 15.5 High-level bigrez.com Web Service architecture.

If we allow the transaction to roll back, the message containing the bad request is placed back on the input queue for redelivery. If we allow this, we place additional processing load on the system, plus we end up having both system and business exceptions on our error queue. Additionally, the client receives no response to its request while all of this redelivery and error-queue processing is taking place, causing the client to resend the bad request, thereby making the problem worse. How can we deal with this?

There are multiple ways to deal with this problem—some of them create other problems, but others require more work for the application programmer. We will consider only those approaches that do not create more problems. We considered two possibilities:

- Reordering the business logic to try to catch all business problems before updates are made
- Tracking the message IDs that failed for business reasons and writing the error response in a separate transaction

The problem with the first approach is that it is hard, if not impossible to achieve. Object orientation and encapsulation only make the problem worse because you would now need every component programmer to understand the global rules for making updates. Even if you could achieve this and do all of the checks up front, it is still possible for business errors to be encountered during the update phase of the transaction. Entity beans and caching only make this problem worse because the actual database updates may be delayed until the transaction commit phase, after the business logic has returned control to the container that started the transaction. Therefore, we have chosen the second approach.

To make the second approach work, we need to distinguish between system and business exceptions. Our business logic differentiates between these two types of errors by the exceptions it throws. We could have used any scheme that allowed us to differentiate between the two types of exceptions. We chose to throw a `EJBException` for system-level errors and a `BigRezBusinessException`, or a more specific subclass, for business-level errors. As you know, `EJBException` is a subclass of `RuntimeException`. The container automatically marks any active transaction for rollback when it encounters a `RuntimeException`. Our `BigRezBusinessException` is not a `RuntimeException`, so the container will not automatically mark the transaction for rollback; therefore, we need to do it explicitly in the application code.

For system exceptions, we allow the transaction to roll back so that JMS will redeliver the message later—after the transient problem that caused the exception is resolved, we hope. System problems that last for an extended period of time will cause messages to be delivered multiple times until the redelivery limit is reached. These messages are moved to the error queue. Because the normal mechanism to process messages from the error queue is to move them back to the input queue, you need to make sure that the component that normally does this stops when system-level problems occur and restarts when the problems are resolved.

For business exceptions, we need to add some logic for delivering the error messages to the response queue and for purging request messages for which we have already generated error messages from the system. To generate the error message, we use our controller MDB, the `JMSReservationRequestBean`, to catch any

BigRezBusinessException errors and generate the appropriate response message to send back to the caller. To get the message to the caller, we must write the message to the GRSResponseQueue in a separate transaction from the one used to dequeue the request. The easiest way to accomplish this is to create a JMSErrorResponse TrackingSessionBean that sets its transaction attributes to RequiresNew so that the calls to it are invoked in a separate transaction. By calling this JMSErrorResponse TrackingSessionBean, we write the error response to the GRSResponseQueue without having it removed when the original transaction rolls back.

Additionally, we need a mechanism to purge the original message from the system. Because the current transaction is going to roll back, the original message will be redelivered by JMS after the appropriate delay. We need to detect this redelivery and purge the message from the system rather than trying to process it again. To accomplish this, we maintain a history of messages that have already had their error responses written to the GRSResponseQueue but have yet to be removed from the GRSRequestQueue.

We use the JMSErrorResponseTrackingSessionBean to perform this tracking activity and help solve the redelivery problem. The first half of the solution requires writing some unique identifier for the request message to persistent storage when we write the error response to the GRSResponseQueue. For this, we simply write the JMS Message ID to a database table as part of the same transaction that sends the error response to the GRSResponseQueue. The second half of the solution is to detect when the current message has already been processed by the JMSErrorResponse TrackingSessionBean. This involves checking every message as soon as it is received to see if its JMS Message ID matches one in our database table. If it does, we use the current transaction to remove the message ID entry from our database table and commit the transaction, effectively removing the request message from the queue without processing it again. If the JMS Message ID is not in the tracking table, we dispatch the message to the business logic.

To return the response to the caller, we start with the WSDL that we and our global reservation system partners have agreed upon as the callback interface that they will provide for sending back confirmations and errors. Using the clientgen Ant task, we generate the client-specific jar file that contains the generated classes needed to use the JAX-RPC static invocation model. In the JMSReservationResponseBean, we invoke the Web Service using the JAX-RPC client directly from the onMessage() method. We use portable stubs for this to insulate our application from any version dependencies that the WebLogic Server Web Service run time might have.

Now, we are ready to look at how to build this application. While the build file is certainly more complex that the simple examples we have been looking at so far, there is nothing fundamentally different. If you refer to the ws-gen task, we start by using the auto-typing mechanism to generate the Java types, holders, and serializers for all of the WSDL custom types. Next, we use wsdl2service to generate the web-services.xml deployment descriptor and the Java interface class that the Web Service must implement. We also use the WSDL to generate the client-specific jar file to package with the Web Service. Before going on to do anything else, we must generate the Java types and the client jar file for the callback Web Service because our JMSReservationResponseBean uses these classes. While we are at it, we go ahead and generate the Java interface for the callback Web Service as well because we provide a simple implementation of it that we will use for testing. After this, we simply run EJBGen, compile, and package up the application for deployment.

Chapter Review

We have covered a lot of ground in this chapter. The chapter started off by talking about some of the basic technology behind Web Services. From there, we looked at the basic steps to create a Web Service using WebLogic Server and then proceeded to build a few simple examples. Next, we moved into a discussion of some of the more advanced features of WebLogic Server Web Service functionality. We finished the chapter off with adding some basic Web Services functionality to our *bigrez.com* example.

Index

B

F

L

M

O

P

R

S

T

W

X